THE
BIRTH
of the
WEST

THE
BIRTH
of the
WEST

Rome, Germany, France,
and the Creation of Europe
in the Tenth Century

PAUL COLLINS

PUBLICAFFAIRS
New York

Library of Congress Cataloging-in-Publication Data
Collins, Paul, 1940-
    The birth of the West : Rome, Germany, France, and the creation of Europe in the
tenth century / Paul Collins. — First edition.
        p.   cm.
    Includes bibliographical references and index.
    ISBN 978-1-61039-013-2 (hardcover : alk. paper) —
ISBN 978-1-61039-014-9 (e-book)
    1. Middle Ages.   2. Civilization, Medieval.   3. France—Civilization—1000-1328.
4. Holy Roman Empire—Civilization.   5. Europe—Civilization—Roman influences.
6. Europe—History—476-1492.   I. Title.
    D123.C65 2013
    940.1'44—dc23
                                                                2012037392

First Edition

10 9 8 7 6 5 4 3 2

For Marilyn,
with love and thanks for spending
almost as much time in the tenth century as I did!

CONTENTS

MAPS

THE EUROPEAN AND
MEDITERRANEAN WORLD
ABOUT 950-1000 A.D.

VIKING
ICELAND

ATLANTIC
OCEAN

VIKING
SCANDINAVIA

Baltic Sea

- - - - Approximate boundaries

POLAND

CATHOLIC EUROPE

HUNGARY

BULGARIA

Black Sea

Constantinople

MUSLIM BASE
(FRAXINETUM)

MUSLIM
AL-ANDALUS

Mediterranean

BYZANTINE EMPIRE

MUSLIM
SICILY

MUSLIM
NORTH AFRICA

Sea

MUSLIM
MIDDLE
EAST

0   500 MILES

0   500 KILOMETERS

MUSLIM
EGYPT

PROLOGUE

"From the Fury of the Northmen, Lord, Deliver Us"

T HE MONK MUST HAVE BEEN studying very late that night, struggling to read by the flickering light of a couple of candles. The text of Priscian of Caesarea's monumental *Institutiones Grammaticae* (Principles of Grammar) was in Latin but written in Irish script. Even at the best of times, reading a manuscript on Greek and Latin grammar would have been hard labor. But our monk was working late, eventually making some 9,400 interlinear and marginal comments on this 249-page work, 3,478 of his comments in Old Irish. He was most probably reading Priscian at Bangor monastery on the northeast coast of Ireland just after the year 850. Once the manuscript had been copied between 845 and 850 in the monastery's scriptorium, or copying room, it made its way into the monk's hands, where he inscribed the thousands of glosses in Old Irish. Somehow or other it later ended up at St. Gallen, Switzerland, where it is now a treasure in the *Stiftsbibliothek* (monastic library).[1]

The monk's glosses were intended to aid readers in getting a sense of the text. To today's scholars, they have become an important reference point for understanding the development of the Irish language. But they also tell us about the monk himself. Like many ninth-century Irish monks, he loved nature. He tells us so in a gloss about spending time reading the manuscript while sitting under a greenwood tree listening to a cuckoo as it flitted from bush to bush.

On this particular cold midwinter night, our monk heard something else: the howl of wind and a storm whipping up the sea and the surf crashing on a beach nearby. But rather than frightening him, this tempest gave him a sense of

1

security. It meant that for now at least Bangor monastery was safe from Vikings, who would certainly not be at sea on such a stormy night. In typical Irish fashion, he confided his sense of relief to the margin of the Priscian manuscript:

The bitter wind is high tonight
It lifts the white locks of the sea;
In such wild winter storm no fright
Of savage Viking troubles me.[2]

For seventy-five years, Irish coastal monasteries like Bangor had been raided by the Vikings, and our monk was writing just at the time when these raids were escalating in frequency, violence, and intensity. Monasteries were attractive targets for the warlike, pagan Vikings, who despised the monks; saw their assets, especially their often-precious church plate, as booty; and identified them and their neighbors as potential slaves. The raid on Bangor was just one incident in a more-than-two-hundred-year history that began in 775 with the burning of the holy shrine of the great missionary-monk Colmcille (Columba in Latin) on the island of Iona off southwestern Scotland. Eighty-six monks were butchered on the beach in another raid in 806. Our monk probably actually knew some of the community who in 825 were killed by Northmen seeking treasure and attempting to destroy the relics of Colmcille. "From the fury of the Northmen, Lord, deliver us" was a frequent prayer, and it was always uttered with sincerity. People felt very vulnerable.

Attacking suddenly and without provocation, the Vikings brought terror wherever they went. Ingvar, or Ivar "the Boneless," was one such Viking, and he waged a private war against England during our monk's lifetime. We don't know why Ingvar was called boneless; suggestions have ranged from unusual physical flexibility, to impotence (in the sense that he could not get an erection), to *osteogenesis imperfecta*, brittle bone disease. Some theorize that he was unable to walk and was carried about by four men on a shield. In any case, although born in Denmark, he learned the basics of being a Viking fighter as a young man in Ireland.

Ingvar led his "great heathen army" to commit wanton cruelty and violence. The *Anglo-Saxon Chronicle* says that early in Ingvar's invasion of England, "Saint Edmund the king [of East Anglia] fought against them, and the Danes won the victory [at Hoxne in November 869], and they slew the king and overran the entire kingdom, and destroyed all the monasteries to which they came."[3] Captured in the battle, Edmund refused to cooperate with the Danes. There are various accounts of his death, all of them horrible. Adam of Bremen says that Ingvar the Boneless "was the most cruel [Viking] of them all."[4] According to Abbo of Fleury's account from a century later, Ingvar "bound Edmund and insulted him ignominiously, and beat him with rods." He then tied the king to a tree and "beat him with whips . . . [and then] shot spears at him as if it was a game until he was entirely covered with their missiles like the bristles of a hedgehog." When Ingvar realized the king would not deny Christ, he had Edmund beheaded. His head was hidden in the woods, but people later found it protected between the paws of a large gray wolf.[5] In another story, Edmund was sacrificed to the Scandinavian god Odin by having his lungs ripped out of his ribcage and hung around his neck. It was precisely this kind of violence that terrified people. It also justified the epithet "most cruel" that Ingvar took with him to his grave.

Mind you, if our monk was honest with himself, there was really nothing new about these kinds of violent raids on monasteries. His fellow Irishmen did it all the time. But as foreigners and aliens, it was the Vikings who most terrified people, and so as he studied Priscian, our monk thanked the bitter storms for protecting his monastery for another night.

❧

The early tenth century dawned in violence and disorder. All effective government had broken down. People lived in fear and chaos. Vikings launched raids with impunity, Saracen Muslim pirates terrorized the Italian coastline seeking slaves, the Magyars (Hungarians) terrorized much of Germany and over the Alps into Italy, and the breakdown of central government meant that ordinary people across Western Europe, but particularly in France, often lived in terror of local nobles, who were really just thugs. So in the years I spent writing this book, there was one understandable question that I was constantly asked: why write about the "dark ages"? What is interesting about such violent times? I was often told that nothing that happened in the tenth century had any application to us, let alone any connection with us.

To tell the truth, at first I found it hard to answer the question. I was just personally interested in the tenth century because it was so different from our own time. I had no grand theories about it. But friends were persistent, and the question kept coming up. And then one day I noticed Oswald Spengler's *The*

Decline of the West on my bookshelf, and it suddenly dawned on me that I was actually writing about the birth of the West, the age when our culture first emerged. It was precisely from the chaos of the tenth century that the Western world in which we now live was born. The story of the tenth century is the story of the emergence of our civilization into the light of day. And the "our" here includes not only all the peoples of Europe, but also everyone of European extraction in the United States and Canada, Central and South America, Australia, New Zealand, South Africa, and many other countries. That is about a third of the world's present population. Remote as this era may seem, only about forty generations actually separate us from the erudite Bangor monk, as well as the appalling Ingvar.

Our civilization is the product of two sources: the Frankish-Germanic people of northwestern Europe and Rome or, more accurately, an idealized notion of what Roman civilization was like. Born into a society in chaos, this infant civilization struggled for order from the beginning, trying to establish some type of structured society with at least a basic notion of the rule of law. The subsequent course it followed reflects its origins. Power was widely diffused in medieval Europe. As a result, the new civilization didn't immediately embrace notions of "absolute" power and authority. (The notion of absolute monarchy didn't enter Western culture until the early sixteenth century.) Instead, power in medieval society was noncentralized, consensual, and consultative, even if the consent was limited to the more powerful. It was, in that sense at least, "protodemocratic."

Latin, or Western, Christianity was the heart and soul of this new culture. Catholicism totally permeated this society, and there was no distinction whatsoever between church and state in our sense. They were simply two sides of the same coin. Even in the chaos of the late-ninth–early-tenth centuries, the predominant idea was that Europe shared a common ecclesiastical-political ethos and that this was held together by a Catholicism that cut across linguistic and national boundaries. (Throughout the book I will use the terms "Catholicism" and "Latin" or "Western Christianity" interchangeably.) Nevertheless, there was always going to be a struggle between church and secular authority as to which was dominant. At first, royal or imperial authority was in the ascendant. In other words, the church was dependent on the state. Only in the last third of the eleventh century was this dominance seriously challenged by the papacy.

At the beginning of this lawless century, if people weren't dealing with the onslaughts of hordes of raiders, they were threatened by neighboring thugs who exploited the defenseless and decimated the wildlife of Europe in their hunting rampages. Life expectancy was short, especially for peasants and the lower orders. Pregnancy and childbirth were risky, and infant mortality rates high. It was a tough time to live.

Yet by the end of the century, order had been restored in Germany, owing almost entirely to the recently converted Saxons, who were the first to bring some political organization to the heartland of Europe. In fact, this book's subtitle might well have been "How the Germans Saved Civilization" by restoring a working central government. And elsewhere across Europe, the tide seemed to be turning. Poland and Hungary were converted to Latin Christianity and were emerging as separate states, Christian Spain was slowly expanding, Italy was prospering economically, the Vikings had been converted to Catholicism and their raids had ceased on the Continent, and even faraway Iceland had become Catholic. Stability wasn't shared uniformly, however: England and Ireland were still struggling, and France was a basket case, with local "noble" thugs dominating whole swaths of the countryside. But the church had introduced "the Peace of God," as it was called, to limit the ability of the powerful to ride roughshod over the powerless.

The birth of the West had come about because the German-Saxon rulers— Henry the Fowler, the three Ottos, and the Greek-born Empress Theophano (wife of the second Otto)—were able to bring order out of chaos and imagine and then realize a new and better way of governing society. Elsewhere, leaders such as Alfred the Great and his successors in England, Brian Boru in Ireland, and Sylvester II, the greatest genius ever to be pope, laid the foundations of the culture, politics, and good order in society that we have inherited. We owe these largely forgotten people much more than we know, for they got us through the birth pangs of our culture.

If there was one thing that everyone longed for in the tenth century, it was a well-ordered world. A young boy in a monastery training to join the small elite who could read and write quickly discovered in the first three chapters of the Book of Genesis that God had created an ordered universe. It was only when humans—personified in Adam and Eve—were deceived by the devil and disobeyed God that humankind was expelled from the structured world of Eden and chaos entered the cosmos. If our young student was really well schooled in the Greek and Roman classics, he would also have learned about the harmony of the universe and nature, which would have led him back to the carefully crafted world established by the Creator. But it wasn't only the educated who thought this way. The peasant tilling the land also longed for a world in which he was free of natural disasters, sickness, and pestilence. He valued the times when he could work in peace and feed his family without fear of invasion and destruction by rampaging raiders or neighboring "nobles."

This birth process also involved the role of Rome, not only the administrative-legal genius of the Roman Empire but also the actual tenth-century city. For people at the time, especially the Germans, Rome was the center of their spiritual universe, their Mecca, the place they longed to visit as pilgrims. They were prepared to go to great lengths to get there. Sure, Jerusalem played a similar role in their mental universe, but it was remote and the journey was dangerous because of Muslim occupation. Nevertheless, Rome was *the* city, the place where the founders of the church, Saints Peter and Paul, had been martyred and were buried. Spiritually, culturally, and psychologically, the tenth-century world was held together by a shared Catholic faith and the "idea" of Rome, the vague but pervasive recollection that Europe had once been a whole, a civilized empire spanning the known world. They looked back nostalgically to a golden age that was a model of culture and order. "All roads lead to Rome" is a cliché, but nonetheless it was certainly the case in the tenth century when the city was the symbolic center of Christianity. As soon as pilgrims came in sight of Rome, they sang *O Roma nobilis*:

> *O noble Rome, mistress of the world,*
> *Most excellent of cities . . .*
> *We sing a salutation to you forever.*
> *We bless you and salute you throughout the ages!*

It didn't matter that the real Rome was a depopulated, malaria-infested, economic backwater dominated by ruthless Mafia-like clans that didn't welcome foreigners, especially those who wanted to tell them how to run the place. In their arrogance, the Romans knew the pilgrims would keep coming, so they didn't bother to be too polite to them. And for a century and a half, they treated the papal office as their plaything. They appointed popes and sacked them, and when it suited them, they assassinated them, smothering or strangling them in prison.

એ

I discovered the tenth century more than a decade ago. I was writing a general history of the papacy, and it struck me that this was a particularly interesting, if violent time and that there was very little written about it. As I delved deeper, I realized that the prevailing image of the period was a misleading caricature. Hoping to change this, I will set out in this book a more factual account of the century, especially as we will be exploring how the main lineaments of what today we call "the West" emerged. Nowadays, we are particularly sensitive to environmental contexts, so we shall begin by examining the physical landscape of the tenth century, the actual world in which our historical drama was played out. We will then focus on the city of Rome, the psychological center of Europe. We will begin with probably the most hideous event in the long history of the papacy, the Cadaver Synod, when the dead body of Pope Formosus was dug up and put on trial for heresy. This split the local church, and a weakened papacy fell increasingly under the control of the powerful Roman clans, particularly the Theophylact family, with its impressive and dominant women Theodora and Marozia. Not all of the tenth-century popes were blackguards, but a number were, and the papacy in this period reached levels of viciousness and depravity that certainly exceeded the corruption and excesses of the Renaissance popes.

In a way, early-tenth-century Rome reflected on a broader scale what was happening across Europe. Western Europe had already witnessed the total collapse of the empire established a century before by Charlemagne. He had been crowned Holy Roman Emperor on Christmas Day 800 by Pope Leo III after uniting most of Western Europe under his sole rule. After Charlemagne's death in 814, his only surviving son, Louis the Pious, inherited the empire, but even during his life Louis divided the empire among his sons. After his death further disintegration occurred, and by the end of the ninth century ordered government had disintegrated. The whole of Western Europe broke up into smaller and smaller units, and emerging local powerbrokers were involved in semiconstant warfare with each other. This situation was particularly bad in France, which degenerated into a kind of feudal anarchy. Consequently, Western Europe had no defense against the Vikings, the Saracens, and, slightly later, the Magyars. England, Ireland, and Scotland, also weakened, were likewise subject to destabilizing raids by the Vikings. Even though most of Spain was under the dominance of the Muslim caliphate, the small Christian enclaves in the north were beginning the long *reconquista* that led ultimately to the formation of Catholic Spain in the late fifteenth century.

By 950 ordered government had reemerged among the Saxons of northeastern Germany. Recent converts to Catholicism, they were well governed by a series of able rulers, the most effective of whom was Otto I the Great (936–973), king of Germany, king of Italy from 951, and Holy Roman Emperor from 962 to 973. He and his successors were never absolute rulers, always ruling with the cooperation of the powerful German magnates (nobles), but they managed to establish a working administration and bring order to Germany and northern Italy. So successful were they that Otto I's grandson, Otto III, together with his mentor Gerbert of Aurillac, whom Otto appointed pope as Sylvester II, conceived a plan to restore the Roman Empire. Both died before anything could be achieved, but the idea of a reunited Europe had been planted. Otto's mother, the extraordinary Empress Theophano, born in the court in Constantinople, inspired Otto to include the Byzantine Empire in his plans for unity. Even though Otto and Sylvester were unsuccessful, the seed had been sown by the Germans, and what was to become the West was born.

Besides rulers and the powerful, we will also meet some of the ordinary people of the time, including some peasant families from the estate of the Saint Germain monastery near Paris; the greatest writer of the age, the acidulous and widely traveled Liutprand of Cremona, who spent much of his life as an unhappy bureaucrat and diplomat; some of the fascinating women of the century, such as dramatist-nun Hrosvitha of Gandersheim; as well as monks and priests and legendary figures such as the Irishman-on-the make Brian Boru. A careful reading of the sources shows that intelligent, perceptive people at the time sensed the glimmer of something new. Although this period was full of fascinating women and men who are our cultural and actual ancestors, their world has remained a *terra incognita*, an unknown historical landscape waiting to be discovered.

What I want to do is to explore this strange and alien landscape. This can induce a sense of disorientation, even of vertigo. But it is also an enriching experience that broadens our horizons as we meet people who valued order in society and established it despite the odds. And the order that they established actually provides the foundations upon which our current society is constructed.

Our tenth-century ancestors are not all that remote after all.

PART ONE

THE CITY
and the
WORLD

CHAPTER 1

The Physical Landscape of the Tenth Century

THE BIRTH OF THE WEST during the tenth century took place in a specific environment. I don't just mean a physical landscape—geography, demography, vegetation, forest cover—important as that is. I am also referring to other physical realities such as the weather, which in the tenth century was reasonably benign. But tenth-century people didn't see the natural world as an objective reality governed by its own laws and dynamics. Their approach was not scientific as is ours. For them, nature was controlled by other forces both benign and demonic. Above all, nature was controlled by God. So perhaps a very-tenth-century way of approaching the physical landscape of the time is through the strange story of a group of 'sky sailors' as told by Archbishop Agobard of Lyons.

The city of Lyons is situated on the confluence of the Rhône and the Saône rivers about 105 miles (170 kilometers) west of the Mont-Cénis Pass over the Alps from Italy. Always an important trade center, even in Roman times, in the ninth century Lyons was part of Burgundy, a region that stretched along the western side of the Alps north of the Mediterranean as far as present-day Switzerland. The whole region was then a province of the Frankish Empire.

People living in the city of Lyons would have been quite cosmopolitan, often seeing and meeting other people from Christian and Muslim Spain, elsewhere in Europe, and even the Middle East and North Africa. But those living in the surrounding villages, even if they met any foreigners, would not have had the slightest notion of who they were, let alone the geography of the outside world.

11

Peasant villagers were instinctively suspicious and often hostile toward out-siders. People in one particular village near Lyons were in an especially angry mood after a severe local hailstorm had flattened their crops and left their fruit lying rotting on the ground. Their village now faced starvation, and the villagers were convinced that the hailstorm had not been a mere accident of na-ture, but rather the work of forces hostile to them. So when four strangers—three men and a woman—traveling along the road from the Mount Cénis Pass to Lyons passed close to the village (we don't know its name), the locals be-came convinced that the strangers were lost sky sailors who had fallen from their sky ships or been abandoned by their compatriots.

Ordinary people believed that sky sailors came on the clouds from an imag-inary land they called Magonia to steal grain and fruit. The popular belief was that sky sailors employed weather-makers and sorcerers to cause thunderstorms so that they could steal the fallen fruit, load it in their sky ships, and sail back across the clouds to Magonia. Such popular beliefs were widely accepted, and odd as this story seems to us, it was typical of ordinary people's beliefs. People were convinced that bad weather and all natural disasters were caused by evil in-dividuals who had magical and supernatural powers, often derived from the devil and his minions. The Virgin Mary and the saints could provide protection from these ills, for only they could effectively intercede with God to protect people and their crops. Today this is superstition; to ninth- and tenth-century villagers it was reality.

Most likely the sky sailors were innocent travelers caught in the wrong place at the wrong time. They were heading along a well-used route from Italy across the Alps, the old Roman road from the Mont-Cénis Pass westward along the Arc and Isère River valleys to Chambéry and Lyons. They could have been stoned to death or maimed by the villagers who had seized them if not for the unexpected arrival of Archbishop Agobard.

Agobard was an unusual man. Having served as Lyons's archbishop from 816 to 841, he saw a great deal of this kind of behavior and did not approve. He was impatient with the kind of populist mixture of Christianity, paganism, and superstition that made up the religion of most people, and he was deter-mined to do something about it. His treatise *Concerning Hailstorms and Thun-der* confronted some of these popular beliefs head-on, characterizing them as foolishness, craziness, and stupidity. Agobard focused particularly on weather-makers or storm-makers, people who thought they could manipulate the weather through their incantations and magic. He confessed that even in his own archdiocese, "almost everyone . . . thinks that hail and thunder result from human decision. For as soon as they hear thunder and lightning they say, 'The air is raised up.' When asked how this happens, some reply with uncertainty, disturbed by their consciences, others confidently, as is typical of the ignorant, that the wind has been raised up by the incantations of men called 'tempest-raisers,' and therefore it is called a 'raised gale.'"[1] On the day in question, he probably had heard about the captured travelers and came immediately to the village to argue on the spot with the common folk who made such claims.

This doesn't mean that Agobard was a skeptical, protomodern empiricist who believed that nature worked according to its own laws. On the contrary, his approach was typical of the theology of the time: he ascribed all causality in nature directly to God rather than to magic or spirits. He argued that God had set up a well-ordered cosmos and that Christians ought to marvel at this, believing that everything that occurred in nature was the direct result of God's decisions. All natural causality belonged to God. Unlike most of his clerical contemporaries, Agobard had no patience with popular superstition. While some of his priests might have tried to persuade people not to deal with sorcerers, witches, weather-makers, or those who claimed magical powers, that didn't mean they doubted that ultimately the natural world was subject to manipulation by saints and devils for good or evil through the interaction of human and spiritual forces. Nevertheless, much to their astonishment, Agobard ordered the villagers, "made crazy by so much stupidity," to release the strangers immediately.[2] For the poor travelers caught up in this local hysteria, the archbishop's intervention must have been a welcome blessing, although they would have probably been as bewildered as the villagers at Agobard's decision.

The story of Agobard and the sky sailors takes us to the heart of tenth-century cosmology, to the way people viewed the world. Natural events were not natural in the sense that nature was an interacting, self-explanatory, independent system. Rather, it was something subject to divine, human, and demonic manipulation. Today we understand the dynamics of nature as independent, interconnected, and self-regulating and ultimately explained by science. For tenth-century people, the borders between the natural and human worlds were permeable. Magic, miracles, and a whole constellation of intermediaries, such as the Blessed Virgin and the saints as well as those in league with the devil, could influence what happened for good or ill through weather, sickness, pestilence, and all types of disasters.

At the level of the ordinary priest and people, the old pagan world and Christianity inextricably interpenetrated each other. Existing parallel with official church ministry was a vast world of what today we would call "popular religion," a realm of miracle-working saints, relics, pilgrimages, angels, devils, charms, spells, magic, a vast amalgam of orthodox Christianity and the still-lively paganism of the vast subclass of peasants and serfs. People believed that all of these forces could be manipulated for good or evil. While Agobard might have believed in a well-ordered world subject to God's decisions, for the vast majority of people reality was much more chaotic. And nothing appears more chaotic than the weather.

ↄ⸰

Medieval people were particularly vulnerable to weather. They depended on a subsistence economy, had limited storage facilities, and lacked the infrastructure to move food staples around quickly. Severe, destructive weather events could mean the difference between eating and starving, and severe winters, such as those of 873–874 or 939–940, caused high mortality among both humans and animals and resulted in widespread famine.

Global warming skeptics often incorrectly cite medieval weather for their arguments, maintaining that what we are experiencing now is not anthropogenic climate change but a fluctuation in the historical rise and fall of world and regional temperatures. The tenth century was right in the middle of the medieval warm period (MWP), which lasted from about 750 to after 1200, followed by the Little Ice Age (LIA) from the mid-fourteenth to the early nineteenth century. Skeptics contend that today we are simply in another warming period. However, the evidence indicates that "the Northern Hemisphere experienced from about 800 to 900 the warmest period in the last 2000 years, with the sole exception of the last few decades of our time."[3] This was followed by a slight cooling between 900 and 950, which was succeeded by a general warming until about 1100. Temperatures then slowly fell toward the advent of the LIA in about 1400. But weather is never constant, and the period 750–950 also saw at least eight, possibly nine, incidents of extremely severe winters.

Nevertheless, comparatively speaking, the climate in the ninth and tenth centuries was relatively benign. The average increase in temperature in the

MWP was probably not much more than 0.2° to 0.3° Celsius, enough to cause the retreat of sea ice in the North Atlantic and some melting of alpine glaciers. This led to a small rise in sea levels, particularly impacting low-lying coastlines around the North Sea. Greenland was settled by the Vikings in the 980s only because the North Atlantic sea ice had retreated sufficiently for them to reach Greenland from Iceland, despite unpredictable weather and fogs.

While there was considerable local variation, rising temperatures also quickly led to increased vegetation growth and a boost in food production. For instance, it was warm enough for vineyards to grow in southern England as early as the time of Alfred the Great (871–899). By 900 there is evidence of at least two vineyards in Britain, and the *Domesday Book* (a survey of the whole of England commissioned in 1085) makes forty-two references to vineyards across the southern part of the country.

Meanwhile, sea-level rise was transforming mainland Europe. Bruges, which nowadays is almost 8.5 miles (14 kilometers) inland, was in the late 800s a small port on an inlet off the North Sea. Today Bruges is called the Venice of the north, but in the second half of the ninth century Bruges was one of a number of small *praesidia*, fortified posts surrounded by moats about 3.5 acres (1.5 hectares) in area, set up to protect coastal Flanders from marauding Vikings. There is confusion about the origin of the name of the town: one popular etymology is that the word "Bruges" is derived from the Flemish word for "bridge," but it is more likely to have come from the Old Norse word *bryggja*, meaning a landing or mooring place, which also suggests proximity to the sea. The Vikings saw the place as a good spot to land raiders. That is why the town began as a fortress. The Bruges fort doubled as a port and quickly developed into a trading center.

At one stage in the early tenth century, the center of Bruges was only about half a mile (800 meters) from the sea. Belgian historian Adriaan Verhulst notes that "Bruges' link with the sea was, however, in a state of flux throughout the Middle Ages."[4] This resulted from rising and falling sea levels, which in turn depended on tiny climate fluctuations. Bruges was accessible to the North Sea until about 1050. Then the natural waterways began to silt up. Thanks to the MWP, the Flanders coastline regularly shifted as a result of sea-level changes, and low-lying land was often flooded. For example, the *Annals of Saint-Bertin* reports that during the winter of 838–839 there were severe floods and that on Saint Stephen's Day (December 26, 838) the whole of Frisia (present-day

Netherlands north of the Rhine) was inundated. "So great was the inundation
that the region became almost like the mounds of sand common in those parts
which they call the dunes. Every single thing the sea rolled over, men as well as
other living creatures and houses too, it destroyed. The number of people
drowned was very carefully counted: 2,437 deaths were reported."[5] This was a
large number for the time. The low-lying coastal plain of what today are Belgium and the Netherlands was not called the Low Countries for nothing! By
the fifteenth century, an increasingly cold climate led the North Atlantic ice to
freeze again and Bruges found itself more or less where it is today.

A region with a parallel history to Bruges is just across the North Sea in
Britain: the fenland of East Anglia, south of the Wash. A wetland wilderness for
centuries, the whole area in the tenth century was a swampy landscape dotted
with islands of higher ground, which provided safety for human settlement
and agriculture. Although there had been some reclamation in Roman times,
in the tenth century the land was waterlogged. The town of Norwich was almost reached by a kind of shallow fjord that stretched 23 miles (38 kilometers) inland from the North Sea. Anglo-Saxon Ely, which nowadays is 29 miles
(48 kilometers) inland south of the Wash and 15 miles (25 kilometers) north
of Cambridge, was a defensible island surrounded by water that held out for a
decade after 1066 against the Norman invasion.

෴

So what did tenth-century people see when they looked at their landscape? The
warmer weather encouraged vegetation growth, so they certainly saw forests,
but these were not as evenly spread across Europe as we might imagine. Real
wilderness in the modern environmental sense then constituted only about a
third of European forests. People also saw open farmland, most of which was
close to villages or towns, much of it dating back to Roman times. This cleared
land was in turn surrounded by forests, which "encircled the medieval world,
isolated it, and restricted it. [The forest] was a frontier, the no man's land par
excellence."[6]

Some of the most cleared, deforested areas that we see today in Europe
were then heavily wooded. Take, for instance, the Po River plain in northern
Italy. Flying over it on a rare clear day reveals a pale orange-brown industrial-
agricultural landscape still dotted with medieval towns and mixed with sprawl-
ing, ugly modern suburbs and industrial cities like Turin and Milan. There are

still small, scattered groups of trees, but nothing really resembling a forest until well up into the higher alpine valleys in the north, the foothills of the Apennines in the south, and the swamps of the Po delta on the Adriatic coast between Venice and Ravenna.

But at the beginning of the tenth century, especially along the river and its tributaries, the Po plain was largely covered by forests and woodlands of various species of oak (which can live for five hundred or more years), poplar, willow, and alder. There were also extensive stands of coniferous and birch forests, survivors from the Jurassic age, stretching right down to the plain from the high Apennines in the south and from the Alps in the north. The forests of the plain and those of the mountains intermingled, giving much of the area a Scandinavian-like appearance. The central Po plain itself was still dominated by water, with swamps fed by rivers flowing down from the mountains. There were about a dozen small walled cities, such as Pavia (then capital of northern Italy), Cremona, Piacenza, Parma, Ferrara, Mantua, Verona, Milan, and Ravenna, all of Roman origin. They were scattered across the landscape, surrounded by cleared farmland and domesticated woodland, and connected by degraded roads following the line of their once well-maintained imperial Roman predecessors. But forests and swamps dominated the Po landscape, with the human world almost an incidental presence surrounded by trees and water.

It had not always been this way. Throughout the classical period from the fifth century BC onward, much of the Mediterranean world was deforested by increasing population and the use of timber for shipbuilding and housing. After the collapse of the Western Roman Empire in the early fifth century until the tenth century, a sizable proportion of the forests recovered because the climate was warmer, which encouraged vegetation growth, and the population decreased after the Roman Empire collapsed. There were less people to destroy the forests.

By the early 900s, forests were the dominant form of European vegetation. Verhulst says that the European land surface was "for a large part . . . a natural landscape, consisting mainly of woods," although the extent of forest cover varied.[7] Central Europe, Germany, France, and Ireland in this period had very extensive forests and woodlands. But exactly how much of a specific landscape was covered by trees is hard to know. Historical geographer Michael Williams says cautiously that "there was a lot of forest and some of it was very extensive and dense."[8] Charles Higounet demonstrates that anywhere from about 15 to

80 percent of continental Europe and its offshore islands on the eve of the eleventh century was still in a natural state, mainly woodland, although it was broken up, regionally diverse, and fragmented into many large but separate stands. Chris Wickham reports that "there were vast differences between the sorts of forests and uncultivated lands found in northern and north-central Europe and those of the Mediterranean, differences emphasized by climate and geology alike."[9]

Higounet has mapped 159 separate forested areas on the Continent and England. There were large woodland areas east of the Rhine, as well as in the central and eastern parts of France up to the Alps. There was another extensive forest extending from the west bank of the Rhine between Bonn and Aachen onto the Eifel plateau, including the present-day Ardennes forest. Based on Higounet's work and other research, we can guess that about 65–70 percent of Germany and about 55–60 percent of France were forest covered. However, excluding Wales and the southwest, only 15–20 percent of England was. The *Domesday Book* records only about 15,500 square miles (40,000 square kilometers) of woodland. The reason seems to be that England had been cleared since the Bronze Age and the country was always widely, if lightly populated. Italy and Spain always had less forest cover than northern Europe, owing partly to the drier, hotter Mediterranean climate of the south and partly to greater population pressures until late Roman times. There had always been stable forests in the mountainous regions of the Italian peninsula, which lasted until industrial-scale forestry in the nineteenth and early twentieth centuries destroyed them. Natural forest landscapes in the tenth century amounted to possibly 30 percent of the Italian peninsula. The same can be said for Spain. Ireland, nowadays the least forested landscape in Europe, then had 80 percent forest cover, no doubt encouraged by warmer, wetter weather patterns rolling in from the Gulf Stream. Scotland was different, being 3 or 4 degrees farther north, with strong winds and little warmth. The mixed woodlands of Scotland were confined to low-lying areas, with the mountains as bare as they are today.

Several important questions about tenth-century forest coverage remain: were these forests wildernesses in the modern environmental sense largely untouched and hardly ever penetrated by people? How much forest was used to supply human needs? Were many forests cleared in this period to provide land for grazing and agriculture? Historians such as Wickham have shown that these issues are more complex than they at first may seem.

The English word "forest" is itself ambiguous. For us a forest can be a number of things: it can be a small group of trees in an otherwise open landscape; a wooded landscape used for various purposes, including grazing and gathering of natural foodstuffs such as honey; an artificial tree plantation; or an untamed wilderness region. The *New Shorter Oxford English Dictionary* gives all these meanings, but the clue to the original meaning of the word is found in the dictionary's first definition of forest as "a royal forest reserved for hunting." Originally, *forestae*, the Medieval Latin word for forests (derived from *foris*, meaning "out of doors" or "abroad"), were, strictly speaking, lands that kings and aristocrats reserved for personal hunting. It is this meaning that creates difficulty for those of us who don't think of forests in terms of hunting at all.

This is further complicated by other Medieval Latin words used for forest or woodland. The usual Latin word for woodland was *silva*; a less common word was *saltus*. Both words have connotations of woodland used for basic pastoral activities and imply a rather domesticated forest serving a range of human uses. The terms for woodland in the modern sense of wilderness are *locus desertus* and *solitudo* (which applied to 30 to 40 percent of the European landscape). *Foresta* first appears in the Latin of the mid-seventh century, and it came to signify "a property with specific rights attached . . . above all the right to hunt."[10] Thus, hunting, usage, and property rights were, from our perspective, confusingly intermingled.

Hunting animals was the absolute passion of the medieval upper class, and the only activity recognized as a real recreation. It served several social functions. It confirmed power, wealth, status, and prestige as the king or aristocrat went out with his retainers, horses, dogs, and, sometimes, trained falcons. It brought men of similar social background together and was good training for medieval warfare, keeping men and horses fit. It developed strategic thinking as the men hunted elusive and often dangerous quarries, such as wild boar, bears, wolves, and red deer. Late summer and, especially, autumn were the usual times for hunting, which was often dangerous. Accidents were common, especially among immature, testosterone-driven, risk-taking young men. The *Annals of Saint-Bertin* reports that in 864 the sixteen-year-old Charles of Aquitaine, the son of King (later Emperor) Charles the Bald

whom his father had recently received from Aquitaine and taken with him
to Compiègne, was returning one night from hunting in the forest of Cuise

[nowadays Cuise-la-Motte near Compiègne]. While he meant only to enjoy some horseplay with some other young men of his own age, by the devil's action he was struck in the head with a sword by a youth called Albuin. The blow penetrated almost as far as the brain, reaching from his left temple to his right cheekbone and jaw. . . . He suffered from epileptic fits for a long time, and then on 29 September [866] he died.[11]

Hunting accidents were also convenient ways of eliminating rivals and were sometimes used as plausible covers for assassinations.

Royalty and nobility weren't the only hunting aficionados. Local church synods constantly complained of priests and clerics hunting or using falcons for sport. The regularity of the condemnation indicated that the church's law against them hunting was often ignored. At the same time, the poor hunted and trapped small animals in the forests. If the upper classes and clergy hunted for sport, peasants and the poor did for survival. For the poor, hunting provided a supply of fresh meat and warm clothing and leather goods, which could be made out of animal fur and skin.

But the use of forests was not restricted to the hunting rights of royalty or nobility. Peasants had traditional rights to use royal or noble land to collect firewood and building materials, as well as food and other products, although the hunting of "big" game was reserved to the nobility. The term for forestland in the tenth century was "fisc." A fisc was a form of public land essentially owned by the king or ruler and held for general public use. So when hunting rights were enforced, this often led to conflict with peasants attempting to exercise their traditional use of the forest for food supplies. To complicate matters further, areas of fisc land were sometimes alienated, or taken out of public use, and granted by royal or ducal patrons to monasteries as endowments. This shifted control of the land from the fisc to the abbey and religious community, which may or may not have recognized the peasants' traditional rights to collect food and material from the forest. People's rights of possession and use "were extremely various, as well as looking extremely odd by Roman [law] standards," let alone by modern concepts of property.[12] The notion of full property rights inhering in a specific individual, family, or corporation is a much later idea. In some places, such as the Scottish Highlands, the notion of private property only came as late as the early nineteenth century. As a result of the underdeveloped notion of private ownership, substantial parts of all forests could be used by ordinary people, with the major restriction being hunting rights.

Fiscal land was not always covered with trees. Nevertheless, it certainly encompassed lands that were traditionally used by peasants for basic agriculture and for a silvo-pastoral economy that focused on collecting firewood and timber, hunting small animals, grazing cattle and, especially, breeding and pannage of pigs. They were the commonest domestic animal in Europe in the tenth century, and local forests could be used as pig runs where the animals could eat acorns and beechnuts. The usefulness of a forest was often measured by how many pigs it could fatten. Both cleared and forest landscapes could also provide basic pasture for sheep and cattle. All of this had quite destructive environmental consequences. Pigs are voracious and dig up the soil and tear out groundcover plants by the roots. This certainly contributed to the gradual decline of forests close to human settlement and certainly had serious impacts on native, nondomestic animals, which led to the decline and eventually extinction of a number of species.

What is clear is that, far from being untouched refuges, European forests were widely used from early on. As in all cultures, wood was a basic material used not only for building and tools, but also for heat. Woodland was also used for coppicing, the careful periodic cutting of timber to make poles, house and roof trusses and beams, fences and barrels, as well as firewood. Most buildings were constructed of timber, so timber production reached an almost industrial scale. For instance, in Rome in the late eighth and early ninth centuries the reroofing of churches and basilicas required an abundant supply of high-quality wood for long, strong beams, some more than 80 feet (25 meters) long.

Nowadays we associate clearance of woodland with agricultural production, and to some extent that was so in the tenth century. People certainly needed cereals to survive. But as Wickham says, these were "often insufficient and had to be backed up by silvo-pastoral resources." So forests that were close to towns, villages, and monasteries were frequently utilized. Wickham concludes that "only the largest blocks of woodland, or those furthest from areas of substantial settlement could remain with cores at their centre that were entirely unexploited."[13]

For tenth-century people, woodlands were thus a managed resource. In all probability, *solitudines* (wildernesses) were, except in northern Europe, rarer than we might suppose. They were largely dominated by oak (*Quercus robur*), beech (*Fagus*), lime (*Tilia*), and elm (*Ulmus*); remained largely untouched by human activity; and were filled with wild animals, especially brown bears and wolves, which were ruthlessly hunted. People generally feared and avoided *solitudines*. In spite of the influence of the church, the remnant folk memory of European paganism endowed the natural world with mystic, magical powers. Although we know little about Germanic religion, the tribes that invaded the Western Roman Empire after 408 saw the whole of the natural world as sacred. Certain trees, groves, and forests had spiritual and ritual significance. People felt that nonnatural, spiritual forces were enormously important in helping them deal with nature, especially the weather, crop success and failure, and human and animal health and illness. They felt they needed all the help they could get, whether Christian or pagan, to make the land and animals productive so that no one would starve. While there is evidence of an appreciation of the beauty of nature, people were completely unromantic about the natural world.

As Archbishop Agobard realized, the Christianity of his time was made up of an amalgam of Christian teaching and practice, with a lingering but powerfully influential substratum of pagan beliefs and practices. This included the gods of vegetation and fertility, the deities who influenced the home and farmyard, the fields, forests, springs, and mountains. So for most people, *solitudines* were particularly terrifying because of the spiritual and sacred forces believed to operate within them. Most people kept well away from these areas for practical reasons as well: they were often also the hiding places of thieves, outlaws, and psychopaths. Only hermits giving themselves over to radical commitment to God and brave hunters seeking wild animals ever penetrated the *solitudines*.

As the tenth century progressed and urban life developed, the cleared areas around towns began to increase. This was especially true in northern Italy. Italian environmental historian Vito Fumagelli comments, "Forests were eroded particularly in central northern Italy where the impetus for clearances came from the powerful towns well able to intervene in their surrounding territory."[14] At the same time, the swamps across the Po plain were being drained and the whole region was slowly being stripped of its original vegetation. Nowadays, the regional parks of the delta of the Po and Adige rivers are the only areas where we can see something of what the region once looked like. Fumagelli concludes nostalgically, "Hardly any examples of the great oaks have survived in Italy. . . . It is quite clear that . . . as early as the eighth century, as well as in the ninth, tenth and eleventh, there were clearances on a significant scale, as well as efforts to modify the environment by bringing new land into cultivation."[15] A key issue in these forest clearances for increasing cultivation was the growth in population, which had begun in the eighth century and escalated in the tenth and following centuries.

❧

At its previous peak, at the end of the second century AD, the total population of Europe, both inside and outside the Roman Empire, reached about 36 million (this figure is an approximation based on available evidence). At the time, the Roman Empire had expanded impressively in extent and numbers. But in the end the empire proved economically unsustainable, and a precipitous fall in population numbers followed. The barbarian invasions of the fifth century led to many deaths, and a deterioration in the climate and a decline in agricultural production led to an ongoing collapse in population.[16] Central authority crumbled, civil order broke down, and the barbarians pillaged what remained.

The nadir of European population came in the sixth and seventh centuries AD. By 600 the population had dropped to between 18 and 22 million. By the beginning of the eighth century, the population was increasing again, even if by fits and starts, limited by semiregular political crises, invasions, recurrent plague, and disease. Perhaps partly thanks to the MWP, numbers reached about 29 million by 800 and recovered to somewhere close to 36–39 million by the millennium.

The city of Rome itself is a good illustration of the contraction. At the height of the empire around AD 100, the population was 1 million or even more. By the time of the conquest of the city in October 312 by the emperor Constantine, it had already fallen to around 800,000—and it would keep falling. By the beginning of the sixth century, 100,000 people lived in Rome. By about 550, the number was down to around 30,000. Thereafter it fluctuated, rising to about 90,000 around 600, as a flood of refugees fled the Lombard invasion of northern Italy. But by the beginning of the tenth century, it had declined to a new low of between 25,000 and 35,000. At the same time, Constantinople's population was more than 800,000.

For the whole of Europe, any recovery in population was an uphill battle, given the common food shortages and recurrent plague from the mid-sixth to the mid-eighth centuries. The bubonic plague was described by Paul the Deacon in his *History of the Lombards* as the "groin pestilence." It was especially prevalent in the mid-sixth century in central-southern Europe. Historians have likened its spread in Italy to the period of the Black Death of 1348–1350.[17] Many felt that the end of the world was approaching. Paul the Deacon describes a depopulated northern Italian landscape hit by a catastrophe:

> Everywhere there was grief and everywhere tears. . . . You might see the world brought back to its ancient silence; no voice in the field, no whistling of shepherds; no lying in wait of wild beasts among the cattle; no harm to domestic fowls. The crops, outliving the time of harvest, awaited the reaper untouched; the vineyard with its fallen leaves and shining grapes remained undisturbed while winter came on. . . . There were no footsteps of passersby, no murderer was seen, yet the corpses of the dead were more than the eye could discern; pastoral places had been turned into a desert, and human habitations had become places of refuge for wild beasts.[18]

Meanwhile, much of central Italy was afflicted by food shortages and caught up in warfare between the Ostrogoths and Byzantines, to be quickly followed by the Lombard invasion of the Italian peninsula in the years 568–569. The latter years of the sixth century were a dark age indeed.

Intermittent plague continued across Europe for the next few hundred years, with England particularly affected during the second half of the seventh century. The *Annals of Saint-Bertin* reports that the winter of 855–856 in France and Germany was "extremely cold and dry. A serious pestilence carried off a sizeable part of the population."[19] In the following year, according to the *Annals of Xanten*, plague broke out again and "a great sickness prevailed among the people. This produced a terrible foulness, so that the limbs were separated from the body even before death came."[20] This is clearly a reference to septicemic plague, which results in necrosis (the death of organs, tissues, or limbs) and the onset of gangrene. The plague of the fourteen century was called the "black death" precisely because infected tissue turned black as gangrene took hold and putrefaction, accompanied by a repulsive smell, developed. Unless treated with antibiotics, primary septicemic plague is almost always fatal. It results from being bitten by infected fleas or handling infected animals such as rabbits, rodents, and, sometimes, cats.

The tenth century also saw intermittent plague, but the evidence is that it tended to be local rather than widespread. Certainly, the milder weather, which enabled increased agricultural production, would have contributed to a decline in the incidence of plague. As a result, people were stronger and more resistant to illness. The chronicler Flodoard of Reims records four outbreaks between 924 and 956. Two of these (in 927 and 934) seem to have been confined to the region around Reims. The others seem to have been more widespread. The first, in 924, affected the invading Magyars (Hungarians). Flodoard records that "the Magyars who were ravaging Gothia [the March of Gothia on the Mediterranean coast of France due south of Lyons] suffered a plague which caused dysentery and swelling of their heads, and very few survived."[21] A clearly much more widespread plague occurred in 956, which "spread out over Germany and all of Gaul, with many dying and falling seriously ill with weakness.[22] He specifically mentions the death of four bishops from this plague.

☙

From our perspective, the medievals were not environmental paragons. Hunting pushed many species close to extinction, and there was little distinction made between wild and domestic animals. Domestic pigs and wild boars lived alongside each other in the forest and interbred. Deer, beavers, Eurasian brown bears, aurochs (a wild ancestor of modern cattle), and European bison were still common, although the brown bear became extinct in England in the tenth century. The great auk, a flightless and therefore vulnerable seabird, was common along the coasts of Iceland, the Orkney and Shetland Islands, the western coasts of Scotland, and the Western Isles. It is now extinct. Wolves were very common and found throughout Western Europe until about five hundred years ago. Wolf packs scavenged in the streets of Paris in daylight as late as the fifteenth century. All of these species moved toward extinction from the late tenth century onward, largely owing to forest clearing, hunting, and deliberate destruction.

While agriculture developed and forest clearances began, people still saw wilderness as dark, nonhuman, alien, and intimidating, haunted by the spirits of the dead and home to fierce animals. Despite the fact that churchmen often wanted to destroy places in the natural world that were reminders of paganism, these practices persisted for many centuries among the European peasantry. Bishop Burchard of Worms in his *Decretorum* (Book of Decretals), in a chapter that focuses on incantation and divination, says, "Bishops and their assistants ought to fight zealously against the cult of trees consecrated to demons which the lower classes worship and hold in great veneration. These ought to be pulled up by the roots and burnt so that neither branches nor even twigs survive." He also warns about sacred stones and ruined places in the forest that were still centers of veneration in pagan cults.[23]

Despite remnant paganism, what really gained impetus in the latter part of the tenth century and then accelerated was a new attitude toward the natural world itself. It began with the spread of monasticism across Europe. The environmental modifications a simple hermit living alone in the forest could achieve were minimal. But once he was joined by a group of monks and a monastic community was established in a sparsely settled wilderness area, the impacts on the natural environment were more drastic. European monasticism valued physical labor, and forty or fifty monks clearing a forest, draining a marsh, planting crops, and grazing animals, let alone building large stone cloisters and churches, made a real impression on the landscape. Monasteries inevitably turned isolated areas into centers of settlement, culture, and human endeavor and impressed on these settlements the notion that nature revealed God's wondrous ordering of the world and his plan for salvation. People were also motivated by a desire to control nature, to escape from complete dependence on the vagaries of the weather, with prosperity or starvation depending on crop success or failure and the danger of attack by wild animals. Even though these new attitudes were beginning to emerge in the tenth century, the great monastic clearances really only came in the centuries following the millennium, especially with the founding of the Cistercians in 1098, reformed monks in the Benedictine tradition.

Christian Europe expanded from its heartland in northern France, the Benelux countries, and southwestern Germany northward and eastward in the ninth and tenth centuries. Under Emperor Charlemagne, Saxony and northern Germany were conquered and absorbed into the Carolingian empire and none too gently converted to Catholicism. It was then the turn of the western Slavs (the Poles and Bohemians) and the Magyars to be drawn into the ambit of Latin Christianity around the time of the millennium. Poland, Hungary, and what is now the Czech Republic and Slovakia emerged as bastions of Western culture, while the eastern Slavs in what is now Bulgaria, Ukraine, and western Russia entered the world of Byzantine Orthodox Christianity.

Hardly anyone, of course, talked about "Europe" in the tenth century. The word came into common usage only much later. People primarily defined their identity by the family and locality in which they were born and then through their membership in the church and their Catholic faith. If they ever broadly defined themselves at all, it was as belonging to *Christianitas*—Christendom.

࿇

The one determinant of life that has remained historically constant is the physical layout of the Continent itself. Four aspects of the geography of Europe play a central role in Western history: (1) the fertile, well-watered Great European Plain; (2) the Mediterranean; (3) the rivers of Europe; and (4) the mountain barriers of the Pyrenees, the Apennines, and the most important topographical feature of Europe, the Alps. Apart from these mountain ranges, the rest of Europe is either flat plains or low rolling hills. Spain is an exception; much of the peninsula is high plateau about 1,900 feet (600 meters) above sea level. With the exception of the higher mountains, Europe is fertile, with highly productive soil.

The Great European Plain extends almost 2,400 miles (4,000 kilometers) from the Atlantic Ocean and the Pyrenees in the southwest right across to the Ural Mountains in the east. The only interruptions to this are the Massif Central (a region of extinct volcanoes) in southeastern France; the low foothills of the Alps in northeastern France, southern Germany, and parts of Austria; the Harz Mountains in southern Saxony; and the Tatras and Carpathian Mountains of Eastern Europe. England and Ireland are either flat plain or low rolling hills, with the only significant mountain ranges being in Wales, northwestern England, and Scotland.

Europe has great rivers. The longest of these, the Volga, the Dnieper, and the Don, are in far eastern Europe and don't affect our story. The two that are influential are the Rhine, which is 820 miles (1,320 kilometers) long, and the Danube, which at 1,770 miles (2,860 kilometers) is the second longest river in Europe. Shorter rivers such as the Tagus in Spain; the Loire, the Seine, and the Rhône in France; the Elbe in Germany; the Oder on the German-Polish border; the Po in Italy; the Thames in England; and the Shannon in Ireland are important in this period particularly for providing highways for Viking penetrations inland. These rivers also provided secure water sources, as well as useful highways for the movement of goods.

The Mediterranean not only defined the southern border of Europe, but also confined and protected Christendom in the tenth century from the expansionist Muslims of the Middle East and North Africa. Spain is an exception here: it was the only part of continental Europe occupied by the Muslims, who conquered the southern two-thirds of the peninsula in the early eighth century.

As the most important topographical feature of the continent, the Alps extend about 650 miles (about 1,000 kilometers) on a generally northeast-southwest axis through Austria, southern Germany, Switzerland, northern Italy, and eastern France down to the Riviera, with the Alps Maritimes providing a kind of hook at the southwestern end as the range reaches the Mediterranean coast and follows it around to the beginning of the northern Apennines. At the widest point, the Alps are 100 miles (160 kilometers) wide. Several peaks rise above 9,840 feet (3,000 meters), and the highest is Mont Blanc at 15,780 feet (4,810 meters). The snow line is generally somewhere above 8,200 feet (2,500 meters). Between the snow line and the valleys lie the alpine pastures that have been used for centuries for summer grazing.

The importance of the Alps was enhanced in the ninth and tenth centuries because, unless a person was Italian, these mountains had to be crossed to get to Rome and Jerusalem, the most important pilgrimage centers of the Christian world. The sea route via the Mediterranean was usually closed owing to the Saracens. A group of particularly active Saracen pirates was based at Fraxinetum just above St. Tropez on the French Riviera; from there they threatened pilgrims in the Alps and the western coastline of Italy. Nevertheless, traffic back and forth across the alpine passes in this period was considerable. Even though most lower-class people rarely strayed farther than 60 miles (100 kilometers) from their birthplace, there was still a lot of "tourist traffic" of pilgrims across Europe to various shrines. For pilgrims, Rome was the most desired destination, but it took motivation and energy to get there. Only a tiny proportion attempted the more difficult journey to Jerusalem through both Byzantine- and Muslim-occupied areas. There was also considerable transalpine commercial traffic, with merchants moving luxury goods and staples around from fair to fair.

Although the alpine passes had been open since long before Roman times, the psychological and physical challenge for people crossing the Alps was considerable. They rise up steeply on both sides, and all of them are more than 6,500 feet (2,000 meters) high. The main passes cross high plateaus; getting up to these plateaus or descending from them is the hardest part. The most accessible passes are the Mont-Cénis between France and Italy (although on the French side part of the approach is through a very narrow ravine and the approach on the Italian side is particularly steep) and the Brenner (the lowest, easiest, and most easterly of the passes). During the tenth century, the central passes were also often used. Most of these are between Chur in Switzerland and either Bellinzona (then in Italy) and Chiavenna (Italy). The main passes in this region are the San Bernardino (Chur to Bellinzona—very steep on the northern side), the Septimer (from Chur to Bivio in Switzerland and on to Chiavenna—gentle on the Swiss side and steep on the Italian, but subject to sudden and unpredictable snowfalls), the Julier-Maloja, and the Splügen (a steep, difficult pass not often used). The Great Saint Bernard, one of the oldest known passes over the Alps, was also often used in this period.

Alpine travel was difficult. Much of it was conducted on foot up steep slopes or, if a person had some money, by mule or ass. Mules (a cross between a male donkey and a female horse) have a lot going for them. They are intelligent, sure-footed, calm animals, strong, adaptable, and with greater endurance than horses. They live longer and can travel up to 50 miles (80 kilometers) per day and are much cheaper to keep than horses. The horse had snob value—a bit like traveling business or first class—but usually only rulers, the wealthy, or important couriers used horses because they were expensive to buy and maintain. Their advantage was speed. Carts or coaches were rarely used for alpine travel because of the deplorable state of the infrastructure; the roads and bridges were often just the remnants of Roman originals or rutted, muddy tracks. Summer and fall were the best times to travel because there was less likelihood of extreme weather—although it could still get very hot in midsummer. Sensible people avoided alpine travel in winter.

Accommodation could be problematic. Much of it was provided free of charge by monasteries, which followed Saint Benedict's *Rule* that travelers and strangers always be welcomed. "Let all guests who arrive be received as Christ, because He will say: 'I was a stranger and you took me in' (Matthew 25:35). And let due honor be shown to all, especially to those 'of the household of the faith' (Galatians 6:10) and to wayfarers. . . . Let the greatest care be taken, especially in the reception of the poor and travelers, because Christ is received more specially in them; whereas regard for the wealthy itself procureth them respect."[24]

This put a great economic strain on most monastic communities, especially those on major pilgrimage routes. Benedict's strictures were not always

observed. Even though upper-class people were usually treated with better accommodation and food than the lower classes, what was provided depended on
the economic base of the monastery. "In times of need monasteries were especially besieged . . . [and] on the whole important visitors were probably less
burdensome than the daily mass feeding of the poor."[25] Things could get rau-
cous at night, especially after travelers had drunk deeply, so the guesthouse was
usually built some distance from the monks' dormitory.

If there was no monastery in a region, travelers had to depend on inns. The
quality of accommodation and services varied greatly. As a profession, hote-
liers had a bad reputation, and just like today there were upmarket and down-
market establishments. Many had names like The Crown or Lion or Black
Horse or Three Kings and were situated wherever there was a constant stream
of travelers and traders on the road. Accommodation was usually in dormitory-
like rooms, often with a number of people in each bed. Everyone slept naked.
Bed linen was not changed regularly, so these lodgings were often filthy, un-
comfortable, and dangerous. Skin diseases and fevers spread rapidly, and body
odors were omnipresent, although many would not have noticed them because
they had smelled them since birth. Latrines were basic, with no sewerage, and
except in monasteries baths were few and far between. Available food was restricted to bread, cheese, and, perhaps, some soup.

The traveler constantly faced threats from nature (storms, snow, floods,
landslides, and avalanches) and humankind (thieves, brigands, Saracens, and
invaders). Undertaking a journey, especially alone, was particularly hazardous,
so people tended to form groups for mutual protection. This was true particularly of traders who needed to protect their goods, normally carried by mules,
as they moved from fair to fair in places as far afield as Lyons, Venice, London,
Bremen, Frankfurt, or the Middle East. Much of the long-distance trade was in
luxury goods and had traditionally been carried on by Jews and Syrians, but by
the tenth century the Frisians and north Germans were also well represented.
Given the dilapidated transport infrastructure, most trade was interregional
rather than international.

We have a number of itineraries of journeys to and from Rome. One of the
most detailed records the exact route taken by Sigeric "the Serious," Archbishop
of Canterbury from 985 to 990, on his return from Rome to England in 990
after receiving his pallium.[26] Someone in the party noted the name of every
submansio (dwelling or abode) at which they stopped in the course of the jour-

ney to the French side of the English Channel, a journey of some 1,150 miles (1,850 kilometers), with eighty overnight stops. They headed north out of Rome probably in the high summer of 990 along the old Roman road, the Via Cassia, through Sutri, Viterbo, and Sienna. They then traveled through the mountains to Lucca, west-northwest of Florence. After briefly touching the coast north of Pisa, they left the Via Cassia and cut diagonally across the Apennines to the Via Emilia across the Po plain to Piacenza. It had taken thirty-eight days to travel about 260 miles (420 kilometers), about 6 miles (10 kilometers) per day, the slow pace owing to the mountainous terrain and possibly the heat of high summer.

Leaving Piacenza, they headed west-northwest for five days across the Po plain to Vercelli. Within two days they were in Ivrea and two days later in Aosta. There they began the ascent to the Great Saint Bernard Pass, climbing 8,100 feet (2,470 meters) to the main ridge of the Alps. The pass has been used since ancient times and is passable only in the five months of summer; even fall can be dangerous with early snowfalls. They crossed in one long, hard day from Saint Rhémy-en-Bosses (Italy) to Bourg-St. Pierre (Switzerland), a distance of 15 miles (25 kilometers) involving a climb of about 2,780 feet (850 meters). It made sense for the party to move quickly across the Great Saint Bernard. These isolated areas were dangerous; people were often robbed, and a monastery hospice for travelers would not be established for another sixty years. Also in these high, isolated areas, there was still a real danger of Saracen raids.

Within six days of crossing the Great Saint Bernard, the travelers were in Lausanne on the north shore of Lake Geneva. Four days later they crossed what is now the French border, arriving in Besançon. Now out of the mountains, they began to make much better time. Ten days later they were in Reims, and ten days after that were on the French coast at Sombre, now a tiny collection of rural houses and barns near the town of Wissant, just south of where the Channel Tunnel train line emerges into the French countryside midway between Calais and Boulogne. Since leaving Piacenza, they had traveled another 890 miles (1,430 kilometers) in forty-two days, an average of about 21 miles (34 kilometers) per day.

They would have taken ship for Dover from Wissant, which remained the regular departure point for Britain for centuries. It is just 21.7 miles (35 kilometers) across the English Channel from France to Britain. The ship on which Sigeric's party crossed the English Channel was probably either a merchantman or a vessel on a regular cross-Channel run. It would have been a wooden boat about 60 feet long (18 meters), with about a 13-foot (4-meter) beam and a light sail, and it would have been propelled by about twenty oarsmen. Such vessels were very seaworthy. Under favorable conditions the journey probably took twelve to fourteen hours.

After their conversion to Christianity, the Vikings remained the most experienced European travelers both by sea and land. "One of the most striking features [of transalpine travel] . . . is the large number of Icelanders, pilgrims and scholars, who made the journey."[27] Quite a number continued on pilgrimage to Jerusalem. One of the longest journeys we know about is that of Thorvald, a convert Icelander. After killing two men he blamed for composing a scurrilous ditty that made the rounds in Iceland suggesting he had had a homosexual relationship with a bishop, he concluded that "the Viking code of honor and Christianity's turn-the-other-cheek forgiveness were utterly incompatible."[28] So as a penance he set out in the early 990s to go on pilgrimage to Jerusalem. Jerusalem was seen as both the physical and spiritual center of the world, but very few pilgrims ever made it that far. Thorvald was an exception.

The other place everyone wanted to visit was the imaginary center of the tenth-century world: Rome. As we saw, Rome was the psychological center of the tenth-century European universe, and naturally everyone wanted to go there. For many the city would have been a disappointment because in fact it was an economic, social, and political backwater. So let's now explore what a tenth-century pilgrim might have found on arrival.

CHAPTER 2

Roman *"Harlots"*

From the Cadaver Synod to the Fall of Marozia

STANDING IN FULL VIEW of the crowd gathered in the great basilica, the young deacon fought the urge to vomit. Acute fear was part of it. The smell of the decomposing corpse was another factor, reminding him of the pungent odor of rotting food or of meat that had been left in the sun for days. Still, he had seen dead bodies before and had smelled the unburied, rotting carcasses of animals left lying around the city. Worst of all was having to stand beside the corpse of the kind, saintly Pope Formosus, who had nurtured his faith, who had been his bishop, and who had ordained him deacon in this very basilica. It was almost too much to bear.

The decaying body had been snatched from its tomb. It now sat in the papal chair in the apse behind the high altar, vested in a bishop's full regalia. Covering the undergarments was the coverall white alb reaching to the ankles. A stole, the symbol of priestly office, was around the corpse's neck, with the square dalmatic, a knee-length tunic that originally came from Dalmatia covering both alb and stole. Over the top of the vestments was the white chasuble, the large, poncholike coverall garment still worn by priests and bishops when celebrating the Eucharist. Around the neck of the corpse on the outside of the chasuble was the symbol of the pope's authority as bishop of Rome, the pallium, a band of white lamb's wool hung over the right shoulder with the ends hanging down the left side and reaching to the knees. The decaying flesh of the skull was covered with a camelaucium, a white cloth Phrygian-style conical cap shaped like a soldier's round helmet.

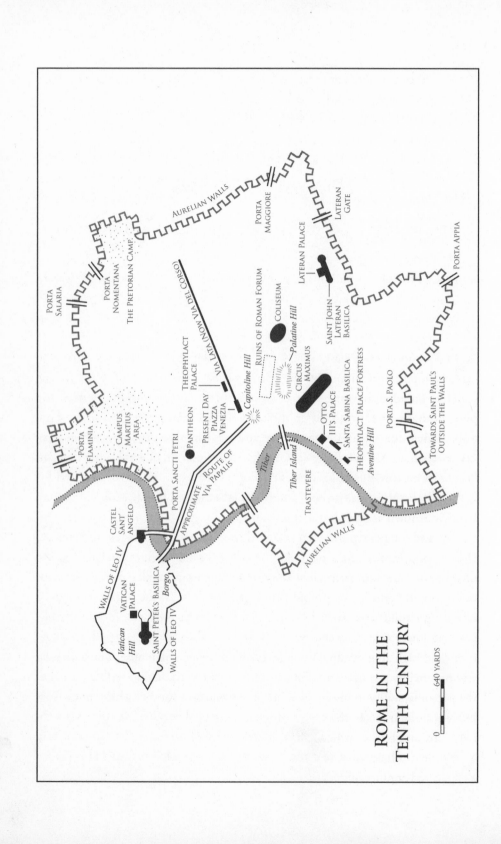

ROME IN THE
TENTH CENTURY

0   640 YARDS

WALLS OF LEO IV
VATICAN PALACE
Vatican Hill
SAINT PETER'S BASILICA
WALLS OF LEO IV
Borgo
CASTEL SANT' ANGELO
WALLS OF LEO IV

PORTA FLAMINIA
CAMPUS MARTIUS AREA
PORTA SANCTI PETRI
APPROXIMATE ROUTE OF VIA PAPALIS
PANTHEON
PRESENT DAY PIAZZA VENEZIA
THEOPHYLACT PALACE
VIA LATA (NOW VIA DEL CORSO)
Capitoline Hill

PORTA SALARIA
PORTA NOMENTANA
THE PRETORIAN CAMP
AURELIAN WALLS
PORTA MAGGIORE
LATERAN GATE
LATERAN PALACE
SAINT JOHN LATERAN BASILICA
PORTA APPIA

RUINS OF ROMAN FORUM
COLISEUM
Palatine Hill
CIRCUS MAXIMUS

Tiber
Tiber Island
TRASTEVERE
AURELIAN WALLS

OTTO III'S PALACE
SANTA SABINA BASILICA
THEOPHYLACT PALACE/FORTRESS
Aventine Hill
PORTA S. PAOLO
TOWARDS SAINT PAUL'S OUTSIDE THE WALLS

The deacon, whose name has been lost to history, was forced to stand beside the corpse following the orders of Pope Stephen VI. In a state of hysteria, the pope now shouted accusations of heresy and ambition at the corpse from an elevated wooden *pulpitum*, or lectern, erected immediately behind the high altar especially for the occasion. The deacon's role in this bizarre event was to answer Pope Stephen's crazed accusations as a kind of defense counsel on behalf of the corpse. And the deacon was aware that everything he said would be reported, word for word, to the fearsome Agiltrude of Benevento, who together with her unpredictable son, Lambert II, Duke of Spoleto and ruler of much of central Italy, occupied Rome throughout the period leading up to the synod and its aftermath.

Like all the priests and bishops present on that overcast, cold, winter day in mid-January 897 in the Basilica Salvatoris, the Basilica of the Most Holy Savior, in Rome, the deacon knew that the result of the trial was a foregone conclusion. He knew Agiltrude was lusting for revenge on the dead pope, who had favored an upstart German over her own son as emperor. He knew that torture, disfigurement, blinding, or even death would be his punishment if he were too effective an advocate on behalf of his dead client. Pope Formosus, the only pope of that name, would be condemned and all his acts and ordinations annulled, including the deacon's own. He also knew that having reached the rank of *scrinarius*, a clerk-writer who prepared official documents in the pope's chancery, his career in the papal curia was over while Stephen VI lived.

The Basilica Salvatoris is still the cathedral church of Rome today, though it is now known as San Giovanni in Laterano, Saint John Lateran. The original basilica and the neighboring palace had been given to the Christian community and the pope of the time, Miltiades (311–314), by Emperor Constantine after he brought three hundred years of intermittent persecution by the Roman state to an end and granted toleration to the church in the Edict of Milan (313). It was a large building about 377 feet (115 meters) in length, with a central nave and two lower side aisles with rows of high windows to let in light. The sanctuary and high altar occupied a large, elevated, semicircular apse. The high altar was covered by a square, marble baldachin, or canopy, supported by four thin marble pillars. The pope's *cathedra* (chair) was on a higher platform directly behind the altar facing the congregation, and the clergy of Rome sat on seats according to rank in a semicircle on either side of the *cathedra*.

By the ninth century, the building was in an advanced state of decay. It had a checkered engineering history and was probably jerry-built in the first place.

Archaeologist Rodolfo Lanciani claims that its adaptation into a church was poorly executed by Constantine's engineers, and it had been originally built from materials looted or left over from other ancient monuments.[1] Still, the whole altar and sanctuary area shimmered with gold, silver, and other precious offerings made by multitudes of rich and poor pilgrims over the centuries who had come to Rome to honor the tombs of the apostles Peter and Paul, who were buried in the city.

But on that midwinter day in 897, the basilica was the locus of the most macabre and demented incident in the long history of the papacy. Fate, or providence, had cast the deacon in a lead role in what historians have since branded the "Cadaver Synod," or, in the words of contemporaries, the *Synoda Horrenda*. The facts of what happened are well established. Pope Stephen VI (896–897), an ambitious, vicious, and mentally unstable man of aristocratic extraction, exhumed the recently deceased body of his predecessor Formosus (891–896), dressed the remains in full pontifical robes, and placed the cadaver in the bishop's chair to be tried for heresy. Next to the enthroned body of Formosus, the terrified deacon stood dressed in deacon's vestments: a white alb, covered with a stole worn over the left shoulder and across the body, and a coverall dalmatic. The judges at the synod, intimidated by the presence in Rome of Agiltrude, Lambert, and their troops, were bishops from neighboring dioceses with as many senior presbyters (parish priests) of the city as could be rounded up.

Formosus had been dead for almost ten months, having died on April 4, 896, at the ripe old age of eighty-one after a five-year papacy. By this stage his body would have been partly decomposed and the pungent stench would have permeated the large basilica and lingered for some time afterward. Embalming was not a common practice at the time, so, according to Roman custom, Formosus would have been placed in an aboveground sarcophagus decorated with sculpture. The word "sarcophagus" is derived from a Greek word meaning "flesh eater" because it was believed that stone, particularly limestone, decomposed corpses quickly.

Usually after nine to ten months, bodies are in an advanced state of decomposition, especially if exposed to the weather. However, protected by his tomb, Formosus's body must have been reasonably intact when exhumed. Summer in Rome is usually hot and dry. Given the dry conditions, the corpse would have quickly dehydrated. As a result, the skin would have turned hard, leathery, and black, creating a thick, protective shell around much of the body. But the underlying moist tissues would have produced a pungent smell, which would have been repulsive and sickening even in an age when people were used to the stench of death.

English poet Robert Browning (1812–1889) in *The Ring and the Book* immortalized the story of the Cadaver Synod for the Victorian era. Fascinated by medieval Italy and what for him were the superstitious and arcane rituals of Catholicism, and playing to typical mid-nineteenth-century English anti-Catholic prejudice, he describes the scene in vivid detail with Stephen, "in a beastly froth of rage," screaming for judgment against the corpse of Formosus propped up on the papal *cathedra*.[2] The seeming insanity of the pope was exacerbated by the presence of the vindictive Agiltrude and the unpredictable Lambert. No wonder our deacon was terrified.

The transcript of the synod was destroyed in the years that followed, so we don't know what the deacon said in the dead pope's defense, but essentially the charge against Formosus was that he had violated canon law and church teaching by transferring from one diocese to another when ancient custom forbade bishops doing so. This seems a trivial offense today when bishops often shift dioceses as they climb the ecclesiastical ladder, but the early Christians thought of a bishop as being "married" to his diocese and considered transfers as heresy and a kind of "divorce." The purpose of this rule was a good one: it aimed to stop ambitious clerics from getting promoted by using appointment to a minor diocese as a stepping-stone to a more powerful one. But by the end of the ninth century, this custom was more honored in the breach than in the observance, and many bishops moved from diocese to diocese. If a bishop were elected pope, he would simply move from his old diocese to become bishop of Rome. This is precisely what Formosus did. He had been bishop of Porto (the first-century Roman port, now near Leonardo da Vinci International Airport at Fiumicino) before being elected bishop of Rome and pope. The same applied to Pope Stephen himself; he had been bishop of Anagni, a lovely hill town to the southeast of Rome, before he was elected to Rome.

Stephen's purpose in trying Formosus was to protect himself. He had been personally ordained bishop of Anagni by Formosus. Now that he was pope, Stephen was determined to preserve his position by playing a kind of casuistic game in which he maintained that Formosus had intruded into the papacy because he had transferred from the diocese of Porto to that of Rome. Because it was still technically against canon law to do this, Formosus's election as bishop of Rome could be construed as invalid. Therefore, all his acts and ordinations were similarly invalid. Stephen's argument was that since he had been ordained bishop of Anagni by Formosus and if Formosus's ordinations were invalid, then Stephen had not really been ordained bishop of Anagni at all, so he still was free to become bishop of Rome validly. It was tortuous reasoning, but it worked for a time.

Lambert II and Agiltrude had a different score to settle with Formosus. They felt that he had betrayed them—and, indeed, Formosus had engaged in a very dangerous game. He had invited the German prince Arnulf of Carinthia, a distant descendant of Emperor Charlemagne, to Rome to protect the papacy from Lambert and his scheming mother. He then crowned Arnulf Holy Roman Emperor even though he had earlier crowned Lambert with the same title, playing the Bavarian potentate against an ambitious local thug. By January 897 Arnulf was dead, and now mother and son were in Rome to extract revenge, even if only from a corpse. And as long as they occupied Rome, Pope Stephen would do their bidding.

Understandably with Agiltrude and Lambert's troops threatening them inside the city, and perhaps inside the basilica itself, the terrified bishops and Roman presbyters (priests) swiftly agreed with Stephen, and judgment was quick. Within a day Formosus was found guilty of violating church law by transferring from the diocese of Porto to Rome. Robert Browning describes Stephen's response in *The Ring and the Book*:

> *Then, swallowed up in rage, Stephen exclaimed*
> *'So, guilty! So, remains I punish guilt!*
> *He is unpoped, and all he did I damn.*[3]

Formosus's papal acts were declared invalid and his ordinations to the deaconate, priesthood, and episcopate rendered null and void. A further ugly punishment was imposed: the dead body was stripped of its pontifical robes, the two blessing fingers of the right hand were cut off, and clothed only in his penitential hairshirt, which stuck to the decaying flesh, the dead pope's body was reinterred as a layman in unconsecrated ground in a cemetery reserved for the burial of pilgrims. The fate of our terrified deacon remains unknown, but it seems likely that he too was degraded, having been ordained by Formosus.

There are varying accounts of what occurred next. In one version, Pope Stephen stirred up the Roman mob to dig the corpse up once again to be thrown into the Tiber "that my Christian fish may sup," as Browning puts it.[4] Another version reports that after being thrown in the Tiber by the mob, Formosus's corpse later washed up on the bank downstream. It was recovered and hidden by a monk so that it could be reburied with honor after the demise of Stephen VI. Whatever actually happened, the Cadaver Synod marked the beginning of some of the worst internecine civil strife in the history of papal Rome.

Sometime in January 897, most likely a week or two after the synod, there was a minor earthquake. It caused the complete collapse of the already decrepit Basilica Salvatoris *ab altare ad portas*, "from the high altar to the massive entrance doors." During the earthquake, the weight of the roof forced the columns so far outward that, according to Lanciani, "the roof trusses came out of their sockets and the building collapsed."[5] Thieves and scavengers were soon combing the ruins for gold, silver, and precious ornaments and relics. The damage was so extensive that it is still difficult today to work out archaeologically the exact lines of the old building.

In an age when natural realities like earthquakes were interpreted as signs of God's moods and reactions, the collapse of the basilica was soon interpreted as a clear sign of divine disapproval of the decisions of the synod. Pope Stephen, however, was determined to enforce its decrees. If he had been hysterical during the synod, in the months following he let loose a ruthless and vindictive campaign to degrade every bishop, priest, and deacon ordained by Formosus, as well as anyone ordained by a bishop ordained by the dead pope. He demanded that they resign their orders and threatened with physical disfigurement anyone too slow in carrying out his will. It led to a complete breakdown in church order in Rome and central Italy.

Soon enough, Stephen overreached himself. His hysteria began to alienate people, and agitators from aristocratic elements in the city opposed to him began to stir up the ever-fickle Roman mob. It was reported that miracles were happening at the temporary grave of Formosus. This, compounded with the sudden collapse of the Lateran basilica, came to be seen as God's judgment on the violent pope. Needing to secure their base in the always-unstable politics of central Italy, Agiltrude, Lambert II, and their troops withdrew from Rome to their fortress in Spoleto. After their departure, riots broke out in the city. These soon coalesced into a full-scale rebellion, and Pope Stephen was seized by the mob. Deep resentment of any form of outside interference in the city's government, even if it came from nearby Spoleto, was always close to the surface in Rome. At that time the city and its immediate surroundings were dominated by a couple of powerful aristocratic clans, and no longer threatened by the upstarts from Spoleto, they made sure Stephen was deposed and, like Formosus, stripped of his papal garb. He was thrown into a dungeon, most probably in the Castel Sant' Angelo, where he was strangled in late July or early August 897.

What emerges from this episode is the extraordinarily *personal* nature of violence in the tenth century. People attacked each other individually, or clan attacked clan, and the duty of payback was widespread. These blood feuds could extend over several generations and often created a kind of endless low-level warfare between clans and groups. William Shakespeare shows something of this in the hatred and gang violence between the Montague and Capulet clans in *Romeo and Juliet*. The numbers involved were never large, but the violence was often extreme—and in Stephen's case, paid little mind to whether the target was still alive. Emotions ran very high, and personal self-control was minimal. People were extremely prickly about personal and family status and rank and were quick to avenge slights, real and imagined, even among the most civilized. There were many notable exceptions to this violence. Kings were expected to show forgiveness to those who threw themselves on their mercy. The Saxon monarchy was noted for its clemency and reconciliation with malefactors, even with those who had been disloyal to the royal house. But the kind of almost intimate, vindictive attacks launched against Formosus were nonetheless quite common.

Though all ages have produced psychotic behavior, Agiltrude and Pope Stephen's attitudes and actions at the Cadaver Synod manifested elements of personal revenge, blood feud, and madness in a most macabre way. They demonstrated the claustrophobic nature of Roman society at the time. This was a parochial, self-referential world in which the papacy increasingly became the plaything of local powerbrokers. It was symptomatic of the loss of any notion of a broader state authority and a retreat into the priority of the local.

ॐ

Rome's population in the tenth century was between 25,000 to 35,000 inhabitants. After Córdoba (100,000), it was the largest city in Western Europe. London at the time probably had less than 10,000. The area enclosed by the 12-mile (19-kilometer) circuit of the walls constructed by Emperor Aurelius in 270–275 was 3,390 acres (1,373 hectares). This was just under half the area of Constantinople, whose population was about 600,000. Clerics and their dependents had always made up a sizable proportion of Rome's population. By the year 1000, only one ancient aqueduct still seemed to be working, so people got water from the Tiber, wells, and streams. Rome's walls, however, had been well maintained and added to in the ninth century.

Although small in population, intramural Rome had a complex settlement pattern. The landscape was partly urban and partly rural, with housing widely dispersed within the walls. There were settlements around the Vatican, on the Forum, the Palatine Hill, the Campus Martius on a low-lying floodplain, Trastevere, and around the Lateran. These settlements were intersected by open areas, ancient ruins, orchards, vineyards, and disused space. The Campus Martius was the most closely settled area in the tenth century, even though it was subject to periodic flooding from the Tiber. From imperial times onward, the city had been divided into civil regions, which by the ninth century had become twelve (or fourteen) *rioni* (districts), each of which contributed to the urban militia. Pilgrims coming to the shrines of Peter and Paul brought wealth. People began to populate the hills again as economic life developed. Rome remained a lively city but beyond the regular pilgrim traffic was not a thriving economic center, although not as complete a backwater as some historians have claimed. The surrounding Patrimonium was also well populated, and many of the rural poor came into the city for work on building projects when needed.

Our knowledge of how people lived at the time is based on archaeological detective work carried out during the last forty years. Much of the medieval remains were lost during the Baroque and Mussolini periods, as new buildings were erected and archaeologists dug down to the classical remains beneath medieval buildings. Recently, however, two medieval houses have been excavated on the Forum of Nerva, close to the Victor Emmanuel Monument. The larger is a two-storied rectangular structure, 34 feet (10 meters) wide by 62 feet (19 meters) long, backing onto an ancient wall. The two stories were originally connected by an external wooden staircase. The houses were built from reused and differently sized *peperino* (building stones) from surrounding ruins, plugged with clay mortar. The downstairs living area, called a *stabulum* (stable or dwelling in Medieval Latin), had an earth floor and a hearth and was devoted to domestic tasks, storage areas, and housing for animals. The owners lived upstairs. There were open areas on both sides of the buildings for domestic animals, wells, and cesspits.

The main streets were the Via Lata between the present-day Piazza Venezia and Piazza Colonna, and the Via Papalis, which ran from the Ponte Sant'Angelo, the bridge across the Tiber from the Castel Sant'Angelo, through the Porta Sancti Petri (Gate of St. Peter) to the Campidoglio (the Capital), now just beside the Victor Emmanuel Monument and above the Piazza Venezia. No contemporary street exactly corresponds to the Via Papalis, although the Corso Vittorio Emanuele II approximates it to some extent. The dense population in this area supported the two main markets of the city. They were situated on either side of the Via Papalis, the Campo dei Fiori (flower market) on the Tiber side, and on the other side the Circo Agonale (Circus Agonalis), a racecourse constructed by the emperor Domitian (81–96) and now the beautiful Piazza Navona. Another occupied area was on the Caelian Hill near the Lateran basilica and Patriarchum. Given that this was the papal headquarters, it was populated largely by clerics who worked in the church bureaucracy and their wives and families. There were other settled areas, including Trastevere and the Vatican.

Richard Krautheimer comments, "Rome had become a rural town dependent on agricultural produce close at hand, within the Aurelian walls or just outside."[6] Most poor people lived in wooden buildings, which have left little or no trace. We know the Borgo near Saint Peter's was largely built of wood, which enabled a terrible fire in 847 to spread so quickly that it almost reached Saint Peter's. Other lower-class people resided in *insulae* (tenements), what we would call rundown, closely settled apartments. In Roman times they could be up to six or seven stories high, with shops at street level. Often jerry-built during speculative booms, the upper stories could be firetraps. A number of these ancient structures were still in use in the tenth century. Other Roman buildings, such as *horrea* (warehouses), were also often converted and reused as residences for the poorer citizens. Archaeologist Robert Coates-Stephens concludes that "early medieval housing in Rome consisted chiefly of the reoccupation and restructuring to varying degrees of both older houses and older public buildings."[7]

Who owned all this real estate? The simple answer is the church or, more precisely, the papacy. Land in Rome was leased through local churches for a small rent. Most of the leases remained current for three life spans, something like contemporary one-hundred-year leases granted on government-owned land in common law countries. Romans either leased the land from the church or subleased it from someone holding a lease. Since the rents were very low, it is hard to work out exactly what the local churches gained economically from this arrangement, but it must have been viable, and it certainly seems to have brought stability to the Roman economy.

Who lived in the city? Obviously, many residents were clerics and their families who either worked in the papal bureaucracy or served the almost two hundred churches in Rome. From about the sixth century onward, a man entered the ranks of the clergy through tonsure, a ceremonial cutting off of a portion of hair on the crown of the head by the bishop, symbolizing his leaving the world behind and making a commitment to the service of the church. Not all tonsured clergy went on to be ordained bishops, priests, and deacons. Some clerics were installed as subdeacons or in one of the four minor orders of porter, lector, exorcist, and acolyte, ranks that had appeared in the fourth century. Since the papacy was central to both the civil and ecclesiastical administration of Rome, it's reasonable to say that many Romans were employed by or depended on the church.

Young clerics generally entered the papal service as *cubicularii,* chamberlains or personal attendants of the pope. These were usually male youths from noble families, many of them already in minor orders, who lived in the papal household while gaining an education. Poorer boys could prepare for clerical careers through the *schola cantorum* (singing school), which trained young men for liturgical ceremonies. Others were educated in local monasteries. All these youths received a good education in grammar, rhetoric, dialectic, music, physics, arithmetic, morals, theology, and liturgy. The *cubicularii* illustrate the fact that, despite the pervasive presence of married clergy, the clerical world had for centuries been a somewhat closed milieu and that young men were initiated into this somewhat homoerotic world of all-male communities.

Entry into the clerical state or ordination to the priesthood, deaconate, and minor orders didn't require celibacy. Nevertheless, from the late fourth century onward in the Western Church, there was pressure from rigorist, strict, and austere Christians, often finding expression in local church councils and synods, to prevent priests, once ordained, from marrying or from remarrying if a spouse died. However, in reality the vast majority of men in major and minor orders continued to live married or de facto lives with their female partners; this included many of the Roman clergy. A number of popes in the first millennium were married, including Saint Peter. Ratherius of Verona commented that priests often arranged marriages for their daughters to other priests. He commented that if he expelled all priests who lived with women in his diocese or who married after ordination, there would be none left. As Gary Macy comments, "Not all bishops, priests and deacons separated from their wives or undertook a life of continence. . . . Clergy continued to marry and live normal, active married lives well into the twelfth century."[8]

❦

Within the structure of the papal government itself, the aristocratic Roman clans had considerable power. Many of the popes of the period were from the upper class and had risen through the ranks of the *cubicularii* and the administrative structures of the Lateran. Naturally, they reflected the interests and prejudices of their class. What is particularly striking is that the papacy had a professional civil service long before any other government in Western Europe.

How was all of this paid for? The *arcarius* was the pope's treasurer. He was assisted by the *sacellarius*, the principal paymaster, who often doubled as a diplomat, and the money was collected by the *actionarii*, the revenue collectors who answered to the *arcarius*. The papacy also received donations, especially from pilgrims. Papal finances were sufficiently organized for regular budgets to be drawn up from the time of Pope Zacharias (741–752) onward. Financial planning was not tackled by other European governments until at least the thirteenth century. What were the revenue sources? One source was Peter's Pence or Romescot, a contribution of one penny per household per year paid to the papal coffers. The custom began in Anglo-Saxon England in the late eighth century and may originally have been destined for the *Schola Saxorum*, the Anglo-Saxon pilgrim residence in the Borgo. In 1883 a terracotta vase containing 835 Anglo-Saxon coins from the first four decades of the tenth century together with a silver pin with the inscription *Domno Marino papa* was discovered hidden under the brick pavement of a room in a small medieval house in the ruins of the residence of the Vestal Virgins on the Roman Forum. Whether an official of Pope Marinus II (942–946) had stolen them or hidden them there for safekeeping remains a mystery.

A major source of papal revenue was the patrimony of the Roman church, the productive landholdings owned by the papacy in the good agricultural land around Rome. These landholdings were important because the biggest charge on the papal exchequer was providing Rome's food supply. As historian Thomas F. X. Noble says, the pope had become "Rome's grocer."[9] The papacy also provided charitable services to the poor and dispossessed. This strengthened the link between the papacy and Rome's citizens. But by the early tenth century, the papal grocer was having difficulties getting supplies. Historically, the popes, like the Roman emperors before them, had used landholdings in North Africa to meet Rome's grain needs, but these were lost in the Arab invasions of the late seventh century. Alternate food supplies from papal landholdings in Sicily and southern Italy were seized first by the Byzantines and then by the Saracens in the early ninth century. This contraction of food supplies might help explain Rome's decreasing population in this period.

So the popes had to fall back on their Italian holdings in the Patrimonium Petri (Patrimony of Saint Peter) to the north and south of the city. In the tenth century, the Patrimonium Petri stretched some 125 miles (200 kilometers) along the central Italian coast and inland into the surrounding hills and mountains for about 46 miles (74 kilometers). Here the pope was bishop and civil ruler. The papal agricultural holdings in the Patrimonium were consolidated in the late eighth century into large, centrally administered aggregates called *domus cultae*, some of which were very extensive. Essentially, they were model farms, and the whole area to the north and east of the city was occupied by these entities, as was the flat coastal area to the southeast toward Anzio and as far as Formia near Naples. Until the tenth century, these papal estates prevented the privatization of land in central Italy and meant that arable areas were held in common for the support of all. They formed the basis of what today we would call the "social justice" activities of the papacy and helped to maintain a certain level of equality among all the inhabitants of the Patrimonium. The peasants who were attached to and worked these estates were known as the *militia* or *familia Sancti Petri*. They were often used as a workforce in Rome and as a militia by the popes when they needed support to counterbalance the upper-class clans. As we will see, these papal estates were privatized throughout the tenth century so that by the millennium papal lands had been seized by already well-endowed, upstart landowners, leaving the Roman church with little support for its ministry to the poor and dispossessed.

While well organized, the papal government throughout the ninth and tenth centuries was under enormous pressure, both external and internal. The Cadaver Synod was a symptom of this, but the problems went back much further. Throughout the ninth century, the papacy had been under almost constant threat from Muslim Saracen pirates as well as upstart rulers like Lambert II from Spoleto. But at the same time it also had to deal with internal pressures from the aristocratic clans within the city of Rome itself. As we shall see, they virtually controlled the papacy for all of the tenth century and on into the eleventh. But to see all this in perspective, we will have to backtrack fifty years to tell the story of one of the worst of the Muslim raids on Rome.

☙

At first light on August 21, 846, a tiny group of people who eked out an existence at the mouth of the Tiber River woke to see an enormous fleet of ships gathering just offshore. They lived in shacks in the undefended rubble of the ancient town of Ostia, and their only defense was a timber fort erected five years earlier and already abandoned. From experience they knew immediately that this was a *razzia*, a plundering raid. Saracen pirates would soon arrive on shore, killing, raping, and seizing women and children as slaves. (The word "Saracen," the generic early medieval word for a Muslim Arab, is derived from the late Latin *Saracenus* and the Greek *sarakenos*, meaning "Arab.")

According to the *Liber pontificalis*, the series of official papal biographies, there were seventy-three ships. Most of the fleet was made up of smallish, lateen-rigged ships with white triangular sails suspended at a 45° angle, like Arab dhows of today. The ships were crammed with men and horses. The *Liber pontificalis* says that there were 11,000 men and about 500 horses, probably a considerable exaggeration.[10] The boats were very maneuverable in shallow water, just what was needed in the estuary of the Tiber. What the locals didn't know was that these Saracens were not just opportunistic pirates on a private raid; they were a Muslim strike force organized by the Aglabid administration in recently conquered Palermo, Sicily. Their purpose was twofold. They wanted to shock and upset the Christian world by desecrating the shrines of Saints Peter and Paul. They also hoped to rob, kill, and destroy as much of the center of Christendom as they could. The invaders established their base in Ostia's empty wooden fort.

Not that the papal government 22 miles (35 kilometers) away in Rome hadn't been forewarned. Eleven days previously, Adalbert of Corsica, Margrave of Tuscany had tipped off Pope Sergius II (844–847) that a large Saracen fleet had been observed heading in the direction of the Tiber mouth. He advised the pope, an elderly, gout-ridden, upper-class Roman, "to rescue the treasures of the churches of St. Peter the Apostle and St. Paul, and if possible bring these apostles' bodies inside Rome, so that the wretched breed of pagans could not rejoice over so great a source of succor to us."[11] But Sergius failed to protect the two major and several minor churches *fuori le mura*, "outside the city walls." The *Liber pontificalis* says Sergius was "rancorous, uncontrolled in speech and given to wrangling, unstable in deed and words, treating everything lightly. Then there was the pontiff's brother, one Benedict by name, very stupid and dull who because of the pontiff's infirmity had undeservedly usurped the care of church and state."[12]

Incompetence reigned supreme. Everyone knew the Saracens would head straight to Saint Peter's and the Vatican on the western side of the Tiber outside the city walls and to Saint Paul's Basilica about one mile directly south of the city on the Via Ostiense. But Sergius had not even bothered to remove to a safe place the treasure trove of portable gold and silver in these vulnerable churches that had accumulated over the centuries as offerings from pious pilgrims. The peasants and farmers of the Campagna, south of Rome, were asked to form a home guard to defend the coast, but they ignored the call-up and understandably focused on protecting themselves.

The only people with enough courage to make a stand were foreign students then resident in Rome. They were mainly from the Saxon, Frankish, and Frisian *scholae* (theological schools), and they lived mainly in the Borgo between the Castel Sant'Angelo and Saint Peter's. Their proximity to Saint Peter's placed them right in the firing line of the expected Saracen advance. So this ragtag student group, together with some Roman militia, marched downriver to Porto near the Tiber mouth. After a short siege and skirmishes with the Saracens, they briefly retook Porto. But they underestimated the size of the invading force. Knowing there would be a counterattack, the militia hotfooted it back to the safety of the city walls, leaving the gullible students behind. The *Liber pontificalis* continues:

> Next day then these [students] . . . were recklessly sitting down to a meal, the Saracens suddenly fell on them and surrounded and slaughtered them so that few survived. . . . [Then] taking their ships, [the Saracen] footmen and horsemen started hurrying to Rome. All day they journeyed with their ships [up the Tiber], and at twilight they came to the locations they had decided on; and there the horsemen swarmed from the ships, and made a surprise attack on Saint Peter the prince of the apostles' church with unspeakable iniquities.[13]

Horses were used to tow vessels upstream to be loaded with the expected loot. Most of the locals had already retired behind the safety of the city walls, which were strong enough to withstand the Saracen assault. Everything outside was vulnerable.

Saint Peter's was the first target that Saturday evening. It was close to the Tiber and undefended. The Saracens seem to have had good intelligence because they stripped the altar above Saint Peter's tomb of its accouterments, as well as any gold and silver they could find in the basilica, and most likely desecrated the actual tomb. Probable evidence of this was found eleven hundred years later during the 1940s excavation under Saint Peter's. While bones were found close to where the tomb in which Saint Peter was probably buried, there is debate as to whether they are the remains of the apostle. It may be that the Saracens succeeded in opening the grave and dispersing the remains of Peter and that all we have left are scattered bones. This is what the *Liber pontificalis* seems to refer to when it mentions the unspeakable iniquities that were perpetrated that evening in Saint Peter's by the invaders.[14] Certainly, there was horror across Europe that Saracens had penetrated Christendom's most precious shrine. The *Annals of Saint-Bertin* also suggests that the grave may have been despoiled when it mentions that "the very altar which had been placed above his tomb" was taken.[15]

The Saracens didn't get away scot-free, however. The next morning the Romans mounted a counterattack on the Campus Neronis, the present-day piazza of Saint Peter's, but we don't know what happened because right at this point the *Liber pontificalis* breaks off in midsentence. We also don't know if the Saracens raided the basilica of Saint Lawrence, but we do know that when "another enemy force reached the tomb of the Blessed Apostle Paul . . . they were crushed by the people of Campagna and all of them were slain."[16] Nevertheless, though the Saracens ultimately failed to penetrate the tomb of Paul, they seem to have done a lot of damage to the Pauline basilica. There is evidence in the sources that local nobles came to the assistance of the Romans, including Guido I, Margrave of Spoleto and grandfather of Lambert, who would later orchestrate the Cadaver Synod.

The Saracens then split into raiding parties. Some attacked churches and settlements outside the walls, while others ranged widely across the countryside attacking villages and farms. They penetrated as far inland as Frascati, Tivoli, and the Alban Hills. They killed many men and took women and children to sell as slaves from right across the region south and east of Rome. Lanciani says that "about three tons of gold and thirty of silver must have fallen into the hands of the Saracens—an almost fabulous booty, which well repaid them for the cost and trouble of their expedition."[17] Some of the loot was loaded on the ships in the Tiber, while the foot soldiers and mounted cavalrymen with the stolen ornaments and treasures from the apostles' tombs headed south along the Via Appia toward Gaeta on the coast. This heavy load slowed them down and made them vulnerable to attack. Guido I pursued one group to Civitavecchia, and the main body took up a defensive position near Gaeta, 100 miles (160 kilometers) south of Rome. In the end, the arrival of naval ships from Naples saved Gaeta from occupation, and summer storms and flooding prevented the Saracens from taking the great abbey of Monte Cassino. The main Saracen party gathered on the shore near the Garigliano River in the vicinity of Minturno, where they hamstrung their horses and sailed away.

If the Italian armies had proven unable to dispatch the Saracens, the weather took care of the rest. Soon after leaving Italy, they ran into a gale in the Straits of Messina. According to the gloating writer of the *Annals of Saint-Bertin*, "During the sea voyage they blasphemed with their foul mouths against God and Our lord Jesus Christ and his apostles. Suddenly there arose a terrible storm from which they could not escape, their ships were dashed against each other, and all were lost." Some Saracen corpses were washed up on the shore "still clutching treasures to their breasts." These were returned to Saint Peter's, but the rest of the stolen loot disappeared.[18]

As happens in this kind of raid, a group of Saracens in the hills about 18 miles (29 kilometers) west of Tivoli became cut off from the main force and were left behind. They took refuge on top of a 2,979-foot (908-meter) rocky outcrop. Isolated and abandoned, the trapped Saracens wisely decided to convert to Christianity as a condition of surrender. They were allowed to settle on their rock and formed the spectacular mountain village of Saracinesco. A few of their descendants still live there today in the largely abandoned but spectacular village. In 2005 Saracinesco's mayor's name was Giuseppe Dell'Ali, hauntingly reminiscent of the village's Muslim origin.

This 846 invasion typified the strategic situation of the ninth century. For more than a century, the Saracens had destabilized and terrified the people and leadership, as they constantly threatened the Mediterranean coast and hinterland of Italy with destructive raids. Papal attempts to contain the Saracen menace, however, never took on the lineaments of a crusade or religious war. The popes were only too conscious that "wicked Christians" were happy to cooperate with the heathen when it suited them. The Patrimonium sat close to the border between Christianity and Islam, and the popes' main aim was to safeguard the coast and papal territory. This remained a problem until 915 when the Saracen threat was largely eliminated.

ε∾

But the Saracens were only part of the problem for Rome and the papacy. Some threats were much closer to home in Rome itself and in the papal state, the Patrimonium Petri. Here the pope was bishop and civil ruler, and there was absolutely no concept of a separation of church and state. Nevertheless, the pope's control was not absolute. It was constantly threatened and constrained by the Mafialike clans or "gangster-baronies" that for two centuries dominated sections of Rome and the Patrimonium from their fortified mansions.[19] Scholar Alcuin of York (ca. 735–804) considered the Romans "ungovernable" and called them an *iniquus populus*, a "wicked, godless people."[20] The clans made the papacy their toy; they had no commitment to the papacy's role as the center of Latin Christianity. Their vision was entirely parochial.

Other threats to the papacy came from neighboring princelings such as Lambert II of Spoleto, whose father, Guido III (883–894), the husband of Agiltrude of Benevento, had seized much of the Patrimonium. The situation was further complicated by the larger strategic situation as what was left of Charlemagne's empire slowly disintegrated. The result was the collapse of any form of centralized government in the Italian peninsula. This convinced the popes that they had to do something about the defense of Rome.

The 846 Saracen sack of Catholicism's most sacred shrine had shocked people throughout Europe, and the new pope, Leo IV (847–855), decided to provide Rome with better protection. Emperor Lothar, Charlemagne's grandson, imposed a tax on his kingdom to assist the pope. So in 848 the papal government began a four-year-long program of fortification under the supervision of Greek engineer Agatho. He strengthened the city walls and built a U-shaped fortification right around Saint Peter's and the Borgo. The Tiber, rendered unnavigable by chains strung across it, formed the protective base of the two arms of the U. These new defenses became the 1.3-mile (2-kilometer) Leonine Wall, some of which still exists.

Yet even though the Vatican was now relatively safe, the papacy still had to deal with complex doctrinal and political issues with the rulers of Byzantium and the increasingly divided Western Frankish world. The only ninth-century pope strong enough to control the Roman clans who now dominated the top echelons of the papal administration was himself an upper-class Roman, Nicholas I (858–867). He saw himself as having authority over the whole church, not merely over central Italy. He looked outward to both Latin Christendom and the Eastern Orthodox Church. He was God's representative on earth, and as such he confronted the petty rulers of Italy, the Frankish kings, and independent hierarchs like Archbishop Hincmar of Reims.

But his successors were weaker and faced more unstable circumstances. There was continual civil unrest in Rome and in Italy. This came to a head under Nicholas's successor, Hadrian II (867–872), who at the time of his ascension was a seventy-five-year-old married Roman aristocrat. Well known for his charity and humility—he had already twice declined election to the papacy—he was popular with lower-class Romans. But he was indecisive, and his family suffered terrible violence as a result. Lambert I of Spoleto, son of Guido I, who had many sympathizers in Rome, suddenly invaded the city in 867, creating chaos that included robbery, rape, and murder. Then on March 10, 868, Hadrian's daughter was abducted and raped by her repulsed suitor Eleutherius; she was already betrothed to another man. Eleutherius then killed her as well as the pope's wife, Stephania. He was a brother or cousin of Anastasius Bibliothecarius (the papal librarian), who was accused of encouraging the crime. Eleutherius was eventually arrested and executed. However, Anastasius survived the charges and continued in the papal service. Ambitious and well connected in the Lateran administration, he survived this and other "significant lapses from papal grace under four successive bishops of Rome," including a brief stint as an antipope.[21] Besides his sheer talent and his bilingual abilities (he spoke fluent Greek), he was well connected to the pro-Frankish party in Rome, which helped to ensure his survival.

Among Hadrian's successors, John VIII (872–882) was a strong, able man who faced a decade of constant external difficulties and opposition from a powerful clique in the papal administration. Things came to a head on December 16, 882, when, according to the *Annals of Fulda*, John was murdered by relatives trying to seize the papal treasury. "John . . . was first poisoned by his relatives and then, as he was thought . . . to be likely to live longer than would suit their desires—for they wanted both his treasure and the ruling of the bish-opric—was struck with a hammer until his skull was bashed in, and died." He was the first pope to be assassinated, and his murder stirred up a horrified Roman mob. "The perpetrator of this evil deed," according to the *Annals of Fulda*, "terrified by the raging crowd around him, was seen to die on the spot, though he was not wounded or harmed by anyone."[22] However, as we shall see, there are suspicions that the clique of lay papal administrators, rather than John's relatives, might have been responsible for the murder.

John was succeeded by Marinus I (882–884), Hadrian III (884–885), and Stephen V (885–891). All experienced difficulties resulting from continued in-dependence among the Frankish bishops, intrigues within the city itself, at-tacks on Rome by several pretenders to the Italian crown, and threats from the Saracens who were still active in southern Italy. Then on October 6, 891, the long-lived Formosus was elected bishop of Rome. The process of that election remains mysterious. The traditional way of electing popes was that all bishops, including the bishop of Rome, were canonically elected by "clergy and peo-ple." In Rome the "clergy" were the bishops, priests, and deacons attached to the major basilicas (parishes in our sense), most of whom would have been ap-pointed by previous popes. The "people" were relatively easily led by the dom-inant aristocratic clans. In the case of the pro-Frankish Formosus, this probably meant that likeminded interests were dominant and that the clans, who usually tended to be pro-Byzantine, were not influential in the election. But the clans bided their time, and they exploited to the full the chaos that followed For-mosus's death.

Formosus had already had an extraordinary life. Able, intelligent, well edu-cated, and experienced, he was an ascetic who wore a hairshirt and led a virtu-ous life in a time of widespread priestly immorality. But he was driven by almost manic ambition. Probably born in Rome about 816, he was elected bishop of Porto in 864. Two years later Pope Nicholas I sent him as nuncio (ambassador) to Bulgaria. That country had been invaded by the Byzantines in 863, and the king, Boris I, was forced to sue for peace and accept Christianity. However, Boris's pagan subjects and nobles revolted against the new religion. He violently put down the revolt and sought the advice of Patriarch Photios of Constantinople about how to convert his country to Christianity. He also wanted to create an autocephalous church independent of Constantinople. For this he needed an independent patriarch or archbishop to head up the Bulgarian church. Photios refused to appoint one and sent missionaries instead to bring the kingdom under Byzantine church influence. Annoyed, Boris turned to Rome for help.

Much of the rivalry between Rome and Constantinople at this time focused on which church would control the fledgling Christian missionary churches in the Balkans. While sidestepping the issue of an independent church, Nicholas I took Boris seriously and sent Formosus as nuncio to Bulgaria. He got on very well with Boris, who then suggested that Formosus would be an ideal first patriarch of the Bulgarian church. Popes Nicholas I and Hadrian II refused because it was against canon law for a bishop to be transferred from diocese to diocese and Formosus had just been appointed bishop of Porto. The real reason was probably jealousy at Formosus's success engineered by rivals in Rome. As we saw, canon law about bishop's transfers was by that time largely ignored. Formosus was summoned back to Rome, Boris was peeved, and Bulgaria was lost to the Western Church. It is still an autocephalous Orthodox Church today.

Subsequently, Formosus carried out a number of other diplomatic missions for Popes Hadrian and John VIII, the most important of which involved negotiations in late September 875 with King Charles the Bald, the grandson of Charlemagne, inviting him to accept imperial coronation as emperor. Charles met Formosus at Pavia in northern Italy, and the papal coronation of Charles occurred in Rome on Christmas Day 875.

However, Formosus's political influence was waning in Rome. Many questioned the wisdom of the imperial coronation of Charles. Formosus was blamed when relations between the papacy and Charles soured. Suddenly in April 876, John VIII turned on him, realizing that Formosus had harbored ambitions to be pope himself and had schemed to thwart John's election. He was also closely associated with a clique of powerful laymen, among them corrupt papal officials such as Gregory the *Nomenclator* (head of protocol) and his son-in-law, the multiple adulterer, thief, and murderer George of the Aventine. George poisoned his brother to get access to his mistress and then married another woman, whom he subsequently publicly murdered in order to marry Gregory's daughter, the already twice-married Constantina. Gregory connived in the murder, and his patronage assured George of promotion in the papal service. Other members of the clique were Sergius, the *Magister militum* (military chief), who had abandoned his wife to live with his mistress and who had stolen money set aside for the support of the poor. This group had gained power under Hadrian II. John VIII was determined to break the power of this clique. Matters came to a head in late March–early April 876 when the pope accused them of misappropriation of papal finances and property. Being associated with such people could be very dangerous and the punishments vicious: being drowned or mutilated or having eyes or tongue gouged out. To forestall these grim possibilities, Formosus and the clique fled Rome to Spoleto in April 876 through the Porta S. Pancratii, leaving the gates open just as another ragtag group of Saracen thieves was close to the city.

John VIII was furious and called a synod, which degraded Formosus from the episcopate. By August 878 the situation had changed sufficiently for John to admit Formosus to lay communion after he professed his guilt and vowed to live in permanent exile. Motivated by revenge, it was this murderous clique, rather than relatives, that was most likely responsible for Pope John's assassination in 882. John was succeeded by Marinus I, who had been an assistant to Formosus in Bulgaria. He allowed his former boss to return to Rome and restored him to his old diocese of Porto. Formosus seems to have laid low during this and the following papacies of Hadrian III, who had George of the Aventine blinded, and Stephen V, who was forced to appeal to Guy III of Spoleto for protection from the Saracens and the chaos of central Italy.

ༀ

Three weeks after Stephen died on September 14, 891, Formosus was elected pope. That he was already bishop of Porto was not considered important at the time. Having worked so hard to achieve this position of power, Formosus set about using it with gusto. His register of letters shows him to have been an activist pope who did much to advance the church in England and Germany, and he maintained good relations with Constantinople.

His major problem was Italy, with its endless internecine strife. The papacy was now particularly threatened by its near neighbor, the Duchy of Spoleto. Duke Guido II, the brother of Lambert who had invaded Rome under Hadrian II, had seized power in central Italy south of the Po in 889 and proclaimed himself king of Italy. Then in February 891, he persuaded Pope Stephen V to adopt him as "his only son" and crown him "Holy Roman Emperor," the title first bestowed on Charlemagne in 800. The Spoleto dynasty was only distantly related to the direct descendants of Charlemagne by marriage, so they had no claim to the imperial title. In fact, they were the Italian branch of a far-flung kin group, originally from Burgundy, which was characterized by the recurrence of the names Guido (or Wido or Guy) and Lambert. They came to Italy in the early ninth century, and by the 840s had seized Spoleto and made themselves dukes. By now the title "emperor" meant little in practical terms, but it was attractive to upstarts like Guido. Their right to crown the emperor gave the popes a powerful bargaining chip and a chance to play off one ambitious thug against another, thus to some extent neutralizing them. But as Formosus would soon discover, he was involved with very dangerous characters. Guido was just the first of several Italian princelings over the next sixty years who persuaded various compliant or unwilling popes to grant them the imperial crown as they rose and fell through the vicious internecine strife characteristic of the period.[23]

Formosus became dangerously tangled in this web. Already emperor, Guido II had forced the pope to crown his son Lambert as coemperor. Then, suddenly in 894, Guido died. Abandoning Lambert and needing an outside protector to fend off Lambert and his unforgiving mother, Agiltrude of Benevento, the pope turned to the ambitious Bavarian duke Arnulf of Carinthia, who had a distant claim to the imperial title. Formosus begged Arnulf to rescue Italy and the *res Sancti Petri*, the property and territory of the papacy, from "bad Christians," specifically Lambert and Agiltrude. As Agiltrude saw it, Formosus had betrayed her, a very dangerous thing to do.

Arnulf, too, hoped to consolidate his power through imperial coronation and so responded to the pope's request readily. After a hard winter march across the Brenner Pass in 894, Arnulf was at first successful in Italy, but his army became infected with fever and he was forced to retreat to Bavaria. Goaded by Agiltrude, Lambert now demanded that Formosus recrown him as emperor. The pope unwillingly consented to a recoronation.

The following year Formosus again invited Arnulf to come to Italy to rescue the *res Sancti Petri* from Lambert. Arnulf set off again, in October 895, on an early winter crossing of the Brenner and reached Pavia in December. But he again ran into trouble in the winter of early 896 as he tried to cross the northern Apennines. The *Annals of Fulda* takes up the story: "Now the whole army was held up on the cliffs of the mountain-tops by violent storms and exceptional rainfall and flooding. [The army] wandered around and about and came through with difficulty. As a result of this there was a great sickness among the horses, more than usual because of the difficulty of the march, so much so indeed that almost the whole of the army had to transport its baggage in an un-accustomed fashion on oxen saddled like horses."[24]

The horse sickness was probably equine influenza, which is endemic in horses, is very infectious, and spreads rapidly. The wet weather may have triggered the outbreak. Most horses survive the disease but are usually left incapacitated for several weeks.

Meanwhile, Agiltrude was alert to Formosus's scheming. She quickly reoccupied Rome, so when Arnulf's troops eventually reached Rome's walls in February 896 after a forced march through central Italy, they found Rome closed against them and Formosus a virtual prisoner. An experienced soldier, Arnulf focused his attack on one of the city gates, the Porta S. Pancratii. According to the *Annals of Fulda*, the German troops captured the city in one day by storming the fortifications with stones and axes, digging under walls, and scrambling over the defenses with the aid of ladders. After pushing back the defenders by hurling stones from siege engines, they attacked the gates using swords and clubs. Eventually, the Porta S. Pancratii was forced open, giving the invaders access to what is the Trastevere region of Rome.[25] Chronicler Liutprand of Cremona, writing some fifty-five years later, says the Germans "found a beam fifty feet long and with it battered down the gates, storming that part of Rome called Leonine [now the Vatican area]. . . . Thereupon the other districts across the Tiber under compulsion of fear bowed their neck to Arnulf's dominion."[26] By evening Rome had surrendered, Agiltrude fled to Spoleto, and Formosus's plans were vindicated.

The next day, February 22, 896, Arnulf was escorted into the city across the Milvian Bridge by "the whole senate of the Romans," accompanied by hymns and acclamations.[27] He was warmly embraced as a liberator by Formosus on the steps of Saint Peter's and was then led into the basilica, anointed, and crowned emperor. Lambert was declared deposed. With seeming unity, the Romans hailed the Bavarian as Caesar Augustus. But unfortunately for Formosus, Arnulf's victory was to be short-lived.

After remaining in Rome for two weeks, Arnulf decided that his conquest was incomplete. He would finish the job by laying siege to Lambert and Agiltrude in their fortress in Spoleto, the ruins of which are now probably buried under the cathedral square and bishop's palace of the lovely hill town. Arnulf left Rome and besieged Spoleto, but in the midst of the attack Arnulf was suddenly struck down in terrible pain by "a severe illness in his head and broke off the plan unfinished and hurried back as fast as possible . . . to Bavaria."[28] This was probably a stroke, but the symptoms are too vague to give an accurate diagnosis. The same illness had crippled and killed both Arnulf's father and uncle. Arnulf would live in pain as a cripple for another three years before dying in Regensburg in 899. Formosus predeceased him; he died on April 4, 896, less than a month and a half after Arnulf's coronation.

With the departure of Arnulf, central Italy and the papacy descended again into chaos. Rome was divided by vicious feuds. Lambert briefly reemerged as the ruler of central Italy. Allied with factions in the city that hated Formosus and driven by Agiltrude seeking revenge, Lambert was determined to humiliate Formosus. In the new pope, Stephen VI, he had a pliant creature. Today it is hard to comprehend the level of passionate hatred for Formosus that motivated them, but feelings ran very high, the Christian virtue of forgiveness was in short supply, and vengeance was exacted ruthlessly. The result: the Cadaver Synod.

ဆ

Bad as the synod was, what followed was worse. For the next decade and a half, Rome and the papacy were wracked with division and strife. The clerical and lay elites were divided into pro- or anti-Formosus factions. Confusion was compounded by the attempts of the anti-Formosan party to continue the policy of Stephen VI denying the validity of the orders of bishops, priests, and deacons ordained by Formosus. This corrosive situation dragged on until the death of Sergius III in April 911. In the eight years after Formosus's death, there were eight popes and two antipopes, three of whom were certainly murdered, one probably murdered, and four deposed. Most were pro-Formosan. One of the antipopes was Sergius III, who was briefly elected in December 897 but was expelled from Rome by Lambert of Spoleto, even though he was a great hater of Formosus. Agiltrude had died, and Lambert now seemed to be attempting to bring some order to the papacy. But he was killed in a suspicious hunting accident ten months later in October 898.

The chaos continued until there came a split in pro-Formosan ranks. The just-elected Leo V (903–904) was overthrown in a palace coup and imprisoned in September 903 by Roman priest Christopher (pope from September 903 to January 904). When the upstart Christopher proved unpopular in Rome and was himself quickly overthrown, people began to turn again to Sergius, who had been abortively elected and then exiled in late 897. By January 904 he seemed to be offering stability to the Romans. He had spent seven years in bitter exile, some of that time at the court of Alberico I, Margrave of Camerino and Spoleto. Alberico, originally a Frankish freebooter and upstart, had seized Spoleto after murdering Duke Guido IV in 896, son of Lambert and grandson of Agiltrude, on one of Rome's Tiber bridges. In 900 Alberico united the territories of Camerino and Spoleto under his own rule.

With his patron now dominating the city, Sergius III was again elected pope, on January 29, 904. He dated his papacy from his first election in 897 and declared all intervening popes interlopers. But with two popes still alive, Sergius's legal position was on shaky ground. To secure his legitimacy, he most probably had his predecessors strangled in prison, "out of pity," some said. Another less likely story is that Sergius had Christopher reduced to a monk, and the saintly Leo V, whose election was not in doubt, murdered. Sergius, by birth a Roman aristocrat, was nasty, violent, and ambitious. Nevertheless, he had a pious, almost childlike devotion to the figure of Mary, the mother of Jesus, particularly to an eighth-century Byzantine icon in the small convent of Santa Maria in Tempuli. It was probably brought to Rome during the eighth-century iconoclast crisis in Byzantium. The legend is that Sergius attempted to remove the icon to Saint John Lateran. But unhappy there, the icon made its own way back at night to its convent home. So Sergius endowed the convent with estates and a lamp to be kept burning before the icon. He asked the community to sing daily one hundred *Kyrie eleisons* and *Christe eleisons* for his soul.

This more pious side of Sergius stands in contrast to his other behavior. Although it seems contradictory to us, religion was then identified more with external practices than with ethical integrity. He would likely have seen his behavior as perfectly consistent. Unlike most other clerics, he had freely participated in the Cadaver Synod. Because he had been ordained bishop by Formosus, Sergius claimed that his ordination was invalid because of Formosus's invalid orders, so he could now legitimately be elected bishop of Rome. He created enormous confusion by declaring all his predecessors since 897 intruding "wolves." He had a synod declare that not only were Formosus's ordinations of bishops and priests invalid, but also so were all orders conferred by all popes since 897. This created complete confusion, especially when he enforced this order with violence and bribery. Few had the courage to oppose him, and it was even forbidden to use the word *sacerdos* (priest) to refer to Formosus. The result: a large number of priests and bishops had to be reordained.

Alberico meanwhile retired to Spoleto. Ever the shrewd politician and looking for a counterbalance, Sergius turned to a man who was probably his distant cousin, Theophylact. Despite his Byzantine name, Theophylact was from Tusculum, nowadays Frascati, a charming town in the Alban Hills in a wine-growing region 13 miles (21 kilometers) southeast of Rome. Theophylact, which means "guarded by God," was then a common name. The name "Sergius" also has a Greek ring to it, so it is likely both men were of Greco-Italian extraction from southern Italy.

Theophylact and his wife, Theodora, quickly ingratiated themselves with Sergius. As we've seen, Rome was characterized by a long-term struggle for control of the city between the popes and the family-based clans, whose aspirations and interests were predominately local. The clans were descended from an armed *ordo*, or military class, established by the Byzantines during their occupation of Rome in the seventh century. They had become conscious of themselves as a group of *optimati* (aristocrats) and heirs of the ancient Roman senatorial class, civic-minded leaders representing the city. Important members of the clans held powerful posts in the ecclesiastical hierarchy, and this often led to demarcation disputes with the popes over unresolved issues of power and authority. They had close ties with each other through marriage. Each clan controlled particular *rioni* of the city from their fortified *palazzi*.

One significant subsidiary struggle was between those who wanted to maintain Rome's role as the international center of Catholicism and those who wanted to turn Rome and the Patrimonium into a local political entity whose vision did not extend beyond the petty affairs of central Italy. Nicholas I and Formosus were statesmen-popes with a sense of the wider world. Sergius, in contrast, reflected the clans' view that Rome should be turned into a city-state and the Patrimonium become "the local power base for a minor dynasty" representing "the atomism, the particularism, so characteristic of the times, the lack of any consciousness that went beyond the narrow sphere of personal and local interests."[29]

The Theophylacts were the first clan to gain complete control of the city, which they governed until 960. They occupied the Castel Sant'Angelo, the strongest fortress in the city. Originally the tomb of the Roman emperor Hadrian (117–138), by the sixth century it had become the key to controlling Rome militarily and remained so for a thousand years. Their townhouse was a fortified residence on the Via Lata (nowadays the Via del Corso), and they had another house on the strategic Aventine Hill above the Tiber. Theophylact was able and ambitious and rose quickly in the papal administration. Before Sergius's election he was appointed *Judex* (senior notary), and in 904 Sergius appointed him *Vestararius*, keeper of the papal treasury, one of the highest positions a layman could hold. It also gave him special responsibility for the government of Ravenna. Shortly afterward he became *Magister militum*, effectively the military commander of the Patrimonium.

His beautiful wife, the *Vestararissa* Theodora, was also very powerful. According to acidulous chronicler Liutprand of Cremona, she was a woman of extremely loose morals. He describes her as *scortum impudens*, a "shameless harlot," and as *meretrix satis impudentissima, veneris calore succensa*, "an utterly impudent street prostitute, consumed by the fire of lust."[30] He claims she had a continuing affair with Deacon John from Ravenna, later Pope John X. But the Neapolitan grammarian Eugenius Vulgarius thinks Theodora was a paragon of holiness and virtue. In a letter to her he comments, "For we hear many speak of the holiness of your way of life and we congratulate you with spiritual joy because through you God gives a shining light to the present age."[31] Both sources are problematic: Liutprand was writing half a century later in the interests of the German emperor Otto I, and Vulgarius was seeking a favor from Theodora, so naturally he praised her. Everyone concedes that Theodora was powerful in her own right, and she played a very active role in her husband's political affairs. She was an upper-class woman of the world who was certainly no saint. But she had a genuine devotion to Mary and was a reformer of religious life in Rome. With Theophylact, she restored the shrine of Santa Maria in Via Lata, which housed a miraculous icon that the couple believed cured their paralytic son, and they passed onto their children interest in the reform of religious life. They had four, possibly five children: Marozia, Theodora II, Sergia, Boniface, who died in infancy, and perhaps another son.

ఴ

It was into this dangerous world that their eldest daughter, Marozia, was born about 892. She is ranked by some, unfairly, as the most notorious woman in papal history. However, she is recognized by later historians as the most powerful woman ruler in Europe for several hundred years, and, like her mother, her role is hotly debated. Was she, as Liutprand maintains, a "shameful adulteress" to be compared to the biblical Herodias, the wife of Herod and mother of Salome, who asked for the head of John the Baptist on a dish? Or were mother and daughter victims of a campaign of defamation by Liutprand, who had an ax to grind for his imperial German employer? Both mother and daughter exercised real power, and this seemed to drive some men, particularly clerical men like Liutprand, to distraction. Liutprand, whom we will meet in detail later, is one of our main sources for the Theophylact period. If we believe him, the scandal-plagued story of Theodora and Marozia bears vivid resemblance to a modern erotic potboiler. He abhorred these women, and he was a particularly good hater.

According to Liutprand, soon after his election Sergius took Marozia as his mistress. She was about fourteen, and he was in his fifties. Probably the girl's parents colluded in this arrangement; they may have even proposed it. As an upper-class, pubescent girl, Marozia knew that it was her duty to advance the family fortunes through her sexual liaisons, and her relationship with Sergius would certainly have helped to consolidate the family's power. Clearly, the affair was well known in Rome. The *Liber pontificalis* says bluntly that the offspring of the affair was "*Johannes . . . ex patre Sergio papa*" (John, son of Pope Sergius).[32] While they cared for Marozia, the Theophylacts did so with a complete lack of sentimentality. Their pleasure in the birth arose from the fact that it brought their clan even closer to Sergius and enhanced their control over Rome and the Patrimonium. Theophylact was well aware that the pope could never marry his daughter, so she was still free to marry another powerful man, and he already had a good idea whom that should be. He had gained much through the pope's dalliance with Marozia. After John's birth Sergius probably took another mistress, but he remained close to the clan, and Theophylact soon became military dictator of Rome. Marozia was quickly married off to Alberico I of Camerino and Spoleto. As we saw, Alberico was an ambitious man, and Theophylact was determined to draw him into his clan's circle of influence. Marozia and Alberico I had three surviving children: Alberico II, Sergius, and a daughter, Bertha.

However, some historians, such as Peter Llewellyn, question whether relationships between Sergius and Marozia and John and Theodora even happened.[33] Their argument is that Liutprand was a scandal-monger writing years after the fact and was a committed apologist for Otto I and an enemy of the clans. By casting them as degenerates, he scored points for Otto in the propaganda war. The more contemporary and reliable chronicler Flodoard in his

Annals says that in 933 envoys of Reims's Archbishop Artoldus returned from Rome and reported, "Pope John [XI], the son of Mary, also called Marozia, was held in custody by his brother Alberico [II]," the son of Alberico I.[34] However, it was easy for a visitor to confuse a brother and *half*-brother, and Flodoard was relying on secondhand reports of archiepiscopal envoys. After weighing all the evidence, Ambrogio Piazzoni concludes that "the social surroundings and circumstances tend to confirm rather than exclude the birth of John from a relationship between a very young Marozia and a mature Sergius III."[35]

Meanwhile in Rome, Sergius's brutal aggression sparked a backlash. While there was no overt opposition, a pamphlet war began. Two of the most prominent pamphleteers were Auxilius and Eugenius Vulgarius. Auxilius was a pseudonym for a Frankish priest living in Naples. He had been ordained by Formosus, so he had a vested interest in maintaining the validity of the pope's ordinations. He was the author of three works on the theology of ordination of which the most important is *In defensionem sacrae ordinationis papae Formosi* (In Defense of the Ordinations of Pope Formosus) in two books.[36] He took the argument beyond legal issues to the whole question of the theological meaning of ordination. He argued that sacraments bestowed even by heretical or excommunicated bishops were valid and that men thus ordained did not require reordination as Sergius maintained. This debate dates back to Saint Cyprian, bishop of Carthage (d. 258), who maintained the rigorist view that sacraments bestowed by heretics were invalid. But the predominant theological opinion is that represented by Saint Augustine, which allows the validity of sacraments bestowed by heretics. Thus, Auxilius's position represents the traditional mainstream and Sergius's, a minority view.

Another pamphleteer was the Italian grammarian Eugenius Vulgarius, the author of *De causa Formosiana libellus* (The Little Book About the Case of Formosus).[37] After initially vacillating, Eugenius finally came out in support of Formosus, which he paid for by spending some time imprisoned in a monastery. The anonymous *Invectiva in Romam pro Formoso papa* (A Roman Denunciation on Behalf of Pope Formosus) also supports Formosus. Less theological than Auxilius, the unknown author correctly says that this was not the first time a pope who had been a bishop in one diocese had been elected in another. "The blessed Peter, prince of the apostles left Antioch and was translated to Rome," and just a decade earlier Pope Marinus I moved from Cerveteri to Rome. The *Invectiva* gives a series of other examples from the early church and highlights the central issue: the way the Romans focused on their own parochial interests and forgot the papacy's importance in the wider church. "The Apostolic See has been carried off by a council of nobles and the wisdom and virtue you possess will swiftly fall asleep. . . . O doubting and apostate Rome, carried away in dementia and madness, come back to God and you will be saved."[38]

None of this argumentation impressed Sergius, who, having eliminated the pro-Formosan group, pushed ahead with the rebuilding of the Lateran basilica. Lavishly redecorated, it remained standing until it was burned down almost completely in 1308 during the Avignon papacy. Supported by Theophylact, Sergius managed to maintain control of the papacy for seven years and died in his bed in April 911. While he had done much to restore the city itself, little record of his other activities survives, and papal historian Louis Duchesne describes him as "spiteful, brutal and a scoundrel."[39] All extant evidence supports this conclusion.

By this time, Theophylact and Theodora completely dominated Roman politics. It was theirs to determine who should be the next pope. After two short-lived, ineffectual papacies between June 911 and March 914, John, now archbishop of Ravenna, was elected in early April 914. Theophylact and Theodora had been observing this capable cleric for several years. First as a deacon and later as archbishop of Ravenna, he was often in Rome on diocesan business. Vituperative as ever, Liutprand asserts that Theodora was besotted with him and they became lovers not long after he first visited the city. "So inflamed was she by his handsome person that not only did she offer herself to him as his mistress, but forced him to comply with her desires again and again." Liutprand says that it was she who schemed to get him elected archbishop of Ravenna. But they were still physically separated, so, he writes, "Theodora, with a harlot's wanton naughtiness, fearing she would have few opportunities of going to bed with her sweetling if he were separated from her by the two hundred miles that lie between Ravenna and Rome, forced him to abandon his archbishopric at Ravenna, and take for himself—O monstrous crime!—the papacy of Rome."[40]

John was now sexually accessible.

Is the scuttlebutt right? Were they lovers? Certainly, there are problems with Liutprand's account, and the liaison seems, at first sight, to be unlikely. It might have been acceptable for Theophylact's daughter to be a papal mistress; after all she was advancing the affairs of the family by pleasing the pope, and although bishops were supposed to observe celibacy, this was often ignored. But it would not have been acceptable for Theophylact to allow his wife to have a semipublic affair with a mere deacon, no matter how talented. Nevertheless, this argument may underestimate the independence of a woman like Theodora and the ruthless, unsentimental ambition of Theophylact. Perhaps the affair began innocently enough, but a man like Theophylact is only cuckolded when he is ignorant of what is happening or is too weak to do anything about it. But the situation would be different if he saw an advantage in it for himself. He obviously viewed John as an able man who as pope could achieve things for Rome and the clan. Ambition trumped love and fidelity with Theophylact. Doubtless he could have stopped the affair dead in its tracks if doing so suited his purposes. Perhaps he even encouraged it, no doubt providing consolations for himself. Theophylact also realized that John, as an outsider, would be able to move Rome on from the endless divisions over Formosus that had plagued the city. Whatever the seedy details, Theophylact's confidence in John was well rewarded. The crisis over Formosus was left behind, and John was an excellent pope who ruled in partnership with the Theophylacts.

After John ascended to the papacy, his first major challenge was to deal with the continuing Saracen threat. For fifty years the Saracens had raided central Italy, threatening the church's rural estates and those of powerful clans like the Theophylacts. A Muslim assault on southern Italy in 902 brought the Saracen issue into sharp focus. Led by North African emir Ibrahim II, a ruthless, cruel fanatic described by both Christian and Arab contemporaries as an insatiable tyrant, a Saracen army invaded Calabria from Sicily. Calabria was Byzantine territory, but the whole area seems to have been undefended. Even when towns surrendered without a fight, Ibrahim was likely to slaughter everyone. Having swiftly taken much of Calabria, he suddenly died during the siege of Cosenza, most likely of dysentery. His army quickly disintegrated, and this Muslim threat evaporated almost as suddenly as it had appeared.

But Ibrahim's appalling violence emboldened many of the principalities of southern Italy to decide to eliminate the Saracens once and for all. While about a third of the landmass was Byzantine territory, there were several principalities, marquisates, and independent entities. At first some of these Christian ministates had welcomed the Saracens as counterweights against each other, but Ibrahim's brutality brought them to their senses. The Saracens were nothing but trouble, and they were particularly adept at creating divisions among the small states. Capua took the initiative and asked Constantinople for help. The Byzantines sent a contingent commanded by the *Strategos* (military governor) of Bari, as well as navy ships to blockade any escape by the Saracens. After protracted negotiations, Capua, Benevento, Amalfi, Salerno, and Gaeta formed an alliance, and Pope John X and Theophylact joined it. From previous popes John inherited a sense that the papacy was responsible for the protection of Italy. This "nationalistic" feeling first emerged in the eighth century, and it was to become a continuing theme in papal history. It became the role of the pope to draw the Italians into alliances against common enemies. So as soon as he was elected in early April 914, John X (914–928) joined the alliance and brought with him Marozia's husband, Alberico I of Camerino and Spoleto.

The most important Saracen enclave was in the territory of Gaeta. The Saracens had established themselves most probably in the ruins of the Roman town of Minturnae, close to present-day Minturno and the mouth of the Garigliano River on the Gulf of Gaeta between Rome and Naples. The Saracens often favored river sites like this one because they provided access to the sea. From here they raided the surrounding countryside, attacking the abbeys of Monte Cassino, Farfa, and San Vincenzo al Volturno, as well as the rural landholdings of Roman clans and the church. They also mounted raids right up to the walls of Rome itself. In June 915 groups of Saracens living outside the fort at Minturnae were rounded up, and then the stronghold itself was surrounded to the north, west, and south by Christian forces. The Byzantine navy patrolled the coast, a key factor in securing the blockade. The siege lasted three months before the desperate Arabs broke out in late August and made a run for the coast. But they were captured and massacred. Alberico and Theophylact returned to Rome with the pope in triumph. In a later letter to Herman I, Archbishop of Cologne, John boasted that on two occasions he had led troops into battle against the Muslims.[41]

❧

With the Saracen menace diminished, John X could turn his attention to wider matters. He completed the reconstruction of the Lateran basilica and improved the formation of the clergy. He exercised considerable influence in the wider church and did much to improve the reputation of the papacy. He was strongly supported by Theophylact and Theodora, but she died in the early 920s and Theophylact soon afterward. Alberico I, Marozia's husband, also died about

920. One theory is that he attempted to seize power but was lynched by the Roman mob and militia because he sought support from the Magyars (Hungarians), who were ravaging northern Italy and Tuscany.

Whatever actually happened, with her husband and parents dead, Marozia assumed the headship of the family with the titles *senatrix et patricia Romanorum*—"senator and patrician of the Romans." An extraordinary woman, her importance lies not in her paramours, but in the fact that she continued the tradition of the Theophylact clan in maintaining stability in Rome and the Patrimonium. Chris Wickham points out that she was "the only independent female ruler in her own right" for four centuries in the European West.[42] Of course, there were other powerful aristocratic women in both the West and Byzantium, but Marozia stands out. She understood that the sexual was political and was able to use this to her advantage in a patriarchal world. Obviously beautiful and alluring to men, she was also intelligent, strong-willed, and independent like her mother. Sadly, we have no contemporary image of her. Clearly unromantic, she realized that sexual relationships and arranged marriages were part of dynastic and political life. Perhaps it was this that utterly infuriated Liutprand; he was galled by the rule of an able woman and sought to destroy her reputation by caricaturing her as a whore. After the death of Alberico I, she didn't rush into a new match and remained single for about two years, living in the fortified Theophylact mansion on the Aventine overlooking the Tiber.

With Theophylact gone, John X obviously felt that he was now free to be his own man. Perhaps he even hoped to set up his own clan as rulers of Rome. But he made one crucial mistake: he underestimated Marozia and relied instead on his brother, Petrus. An opportunity for John came after the murder of Berengar I, the king of Italy, in March 924. The Magyars were threatening north-central Italy, and John and other Italian rulers were looking for a strongman who could bring stability to the peninsula. The person who emerged was Hugo of Arles, Duke of Provence. In this period Provence, Burgundy, and Italy were closely linked dynastically. Elected king of Italy in early 926, John met Hugo in Mantua, concluded a treaty with him, and crowned him. He clearly hoped to use Hugo as a counterweight to Marozia. Hugo moved to the northern Italian capital of Pavia, and Liutprand began his career as a choirboy there. He admired Hugo as "a man of no less learning than boldness, as strong in courage as he was in cunning . . . anxious in relieving the needs of the poor and solicitous for the welfare of the church. All these high qualities were marred by the way he yielded to the allurements of women."[43] Liutprand was gilding the lily: Hugo was not only promiscuous; he was also deceitful, mean, and cowardly.

Marozia and the urban oligarchy she represented were unhappy with the pope's alliance with Hugo. To weaken John, she began undermining his brother, Petrus, who had assumed the roles of consul of the Romans and had seized the marquisate of Spoleto. For about fifteen months, John and Petrus held out against Marozia. At one stage, they fled to Orte, where Petrus established himself in the local fortress. There he allied himself with the Magyars, who had invaded Italy again in 924. Together they raided the Campagna, Tuscany, and Sabina, an area where the Theophylact clan had considerable commercial interests.

The pope and Marozia were now in a struggle to the death, and she decided she needed a strong consort. So she married Guido III, Marquis of Tuscany, who also wanted to limit the power of Hugo. According to Liutprand, in June 928 the couple smuggled soldiers into Rome and "when the pope and his brother and a few friends were in the Lateran palace . . . [the soldiers] . . . rushed upon them and killed Petrus before his brother's eyes."[44] John was deposed and imprisoned. Marozia now moved into the Castel Sant'Angelo permanently, perhaps a sign that her power was not absolute in Rome. John's deposition was a tragedy because he was one of the ablest popes of the century. Guido died in 929.

Marozia was alone again. But she was an ambitious woman who was determined to expand her power beyond the narrow confines of the papal state. Perhaps she even had ambitions to bring the whole of non-Byzantine Italy under her control. She also had a trump card: her son John, who was the son of a pope. She hoped to make him pope and use him to enhance her own power. But he was still too young to be elected. She would have to bide her time.

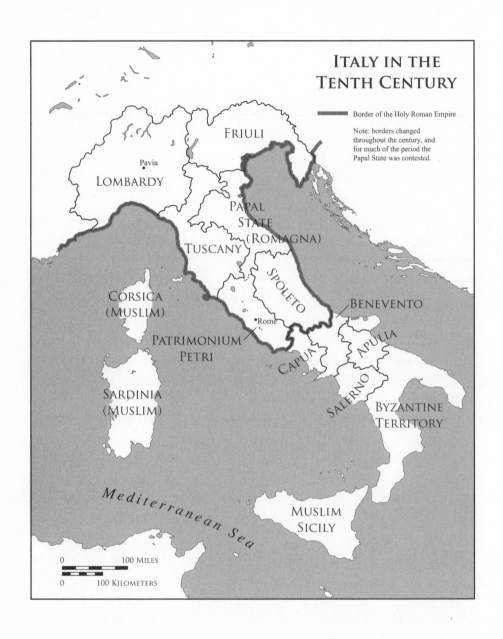

ITALY IN THE TENTH CENTURY

Border of the Holy Roman Empire

Note: borders changed throughout the century, and for much of the period the Papal State was contested.

FRIULI

Pavia

LOMBARDY

PAPAL STATE (ROMAGNA)

TUSCANY

SPOLETO

CORSICA (MUSLIM)

BENEVENTO

PATRIMONIUM PETRI

Rome

CAPUA

APULIA

SARDINIA (MUSLIM)

SALERNO

BYZANTINE TERRITORY

Mediterranean Sea

MUSLIM SICILY

0   100 MILES

0   100 KILOMETERS

CHAPTER 3

The Nadir of the Papacy

T HE PAPACY HAD BECOME a dangerous office to hold. John X learned this lesson firsthand after the murder of his brother, Petrus. Deposed and imprisoned in a dungeon in the Castel Sant'Angelo by Marozia in May 928, he was killed in mid-929. Flodoard says, "Some maintain that he was strangled," whereas Liutprand says he was suffocated with a pillow.[1] Marozia had solidified her hold on Rome for the moment. Her long-term goal was to get her son John, fathered by Sergius III, elected pope. But he was still only about twenty, and at a minimum, respectability demanded that he be at least twenty-five before election. So Marozia would have to fall back on stopgap popes—preferably not too healthy or long-lived, lest they delay the election of her boy.

Under her direction two popes were elected. Leo VI (May–December 928) seems to have achieved nothing during his short papacy. Stephen VII (929–931) was a pious man whose one distinction, according to an anonymous twelfth-century Byzantine writer, was that "he was the first pope who was shameless enough to shave himself and to order the rest of Italy to do likewise."[2] This was actually quite culturally important. Appearance and clothing indicated status, and Western clerics were expected to be clean-shaven and tonsured. By contrast, the fashion among Eastern Byzantine clergy was (and still is) long beards. The Eastern argument was that Christ had worn a beard and that it indicated a man's virility and dignity in contrast to women. Western churchmen maintained that Saint Peter had been beardless and that "it was essential that clerics should be distinct from the laity even in physical appearance."[3] So even in looks and style the Eastern and Western clergy were diverging.

Marozia's good timing was demonstrated when Stephen VII conveniently died in February 931. Her son John was still in his early twenties but had already been named cardinal priest of Santa Maria in Trastevere. It was his turn to be pope, and he was elected in March 931 as John XI (931–935). Marozia was now supreme—and her enemies knew it. A monk named Benedict of Monte Soratte complains, "Rome has been subjected to the power of a woman, as we read in the prophet, 'The women dominate Jerusalem.'"[4] But Benedict's clerical chauvinism missed Marozia's true aspiration: she intended to use her son to expand her own power beyond the Patrimonium Petri as she looked to create a more ordered and stable Italy.

John's first act as pope was consistent with Theophylact policy regarding the reform of monasticism. In March 931 he granted the reforming abbey of Cluny in Burgundy perpetual and complete exemption from secular and religious authorities, placing Cluny under the direct protection of the papacy. That same year a Byzantine ambassador arrived from Emperor Romanus I Lecapenus (920–944) seeking papal support for the appointment of his gormless sixteen-year-old son, Theophylact (no relation), as patriarch of Constantinople. This particular Theophylact had been castrated to assist his career in the church, but it didn't help to focus his mind on spiritual affairs because he was besotted with horses (he kept 2,000 of them) and he was more likely to supervise the birth of a foal than to shuffle his way through the liturgy. Rather than hay, he fed his horses a mixture of dates, figs, and pistachio nuts mixed with sweet wine. Marozia wanted to marry her daughter, Bertha, to a Byzantine prince, so she pressured John into supporting the appointment of Theophylact, much to the scandal of the Eastern Church. Two Western bishops were sent to Theophylact's episcopal ordination in February 933.

Despite her shrewdness and courage, Marozia felt she needed a husband to help maintain her position. In early 932, motivated more by her desire to be queen of Italy than love, she made overtures to her onetime enemy King Hugo, whose wife, Alda, had just died. Never one to refuse a beautiful woman and certainly attracted by the possibility of using marriage with the mother of the pope to enhance his ambition to become emperor and gain strategic control of Rome, Hugo quickly agreed to the match. There remained a canonical impediment: Hugo was Marozia's former husband Guido's half-brother. Marrying a brother's widow was against canon law. Hugo attempted to avoid this obstacle by declaring his two half-brothers bastards. But the still-living younger one,

Lambert, protested. With chilling efficiency Hugo captured, imprisoned, and blinded him, and Pope John swept the canonical technicality aside.

Hugo arrived at the gates of Rome in early fall 932. Leaving his Burgundian troops outside the walls, he entered the city with a small group of bodyguards. His marriage to Marozia was celebrated in the chapel of Saint Michael in the Castel Sant'Angelo, with the pope presiding at his own mother's wedding, a unique event in papal history. There was considerable opposition in Rome to the marriage, but Marozia and Hugo felt safe in the Castel. Forgotten amid all of the goings-on was John XI's half-brother, the tough, talented, and legitimate Alberico II, son of Marozia's first husband, Alberico I of Spoleto and Camerino. It was a serious mistake to have overlooked him.

Alberico II was born in the Theophylact palazzo on the Aventine Hill between 910 and 912. He had "a handsome visage like his father . . . but [was] much feared."[5] Being much feared was a handy psychological advantage in Rome. Nothing is known of him until Marozia's marriage. He was understandably an unwilling participant in his mother's nuptials, and as long as he lived, he was a threat to Hugo. While there were clear political advantages for Marozia in marrying Hugo, who commanded much of northern Italy, he was ruthless, chilling, and an insatiable womanizer. But politics outweighed romance, although it was obvious that as soon as Hugo was secure in Rome and had received the imperial crown from John XI, he would have incapacitated or killed Alberico. Marozia must have known this put her son in real danger. Either she was utterly ruthless or confident she could manage the situation. Perhaps both.

As he often did, Hugo overreached himself. Thinking himself safe from opposition, he assumed imperial pretensions and treated the Romans with contempt. Resentment quickly surfaced. Things came to a head in late 932 after the wedding but before Hugo's imperial coronation. At his mother's bidding, Alberico was acting as a page to Hugo. While washing the king's hands, he either accidently or deliberately spilled water on Hugo's clothing. Hugo punched him in the face as "chastisement for not pouring the water in a modest and respectful fashion."[6] For Alberico this was the last straw, and he fled the Castel. Having grown up in Rome, he had the right connections and knew exactly how to stir up the populace, especially when arrogant and pushy foreigners like Hugo were involved.

The Romans resented foreign upstarts who threw their weight around with the locals. Although it is unclear how Alberico was able to exploit this,

Liutprand's account of the arguments the young man would have used to win the clans and mob over to his side is probably close to the truth. Acting as a kind of tribune of the people, Alberico, according to Liutprand, told the crowd that if Hugo "hit me, his stepson, in the face when he had but just come here as our guest, what do you suppose he will do when he has taken root in the city?" Alberico made fun of the rustic, guttural speech of the Burgundians: "I say that 'Burgundian' is another form of 'Gurglian,' and that they are so-called either from their arrogant and guttural speech, or, more probably, from the way in which they use their gullets to indulge their greed."[7] It was clever to ridicule Hugo and cast his troops as rustic hicks. While the speech is clearly Liutprand's, it has a truthful ring about it.

Alberico was soon the leader of a revolutionary putsch. "The crowd began to sing out at the top of their voices as they donned their armour together, their voices ringing out everywhere."[8] The militia stormed the Castel Sant'Angelo between Christmas and New Year 932–933. They must have somehow caught Marozia and Hugo by surprise, for the virtually impregnable fortress was soon in Alberico's hands.

Cowardly to the end and lucky to escape with his life, Hugo abandoned his wife by scaling down the side of the Castel at night, taking refuge with his army camped outside the walls. Marozia and John XI were captured and "to avoid surprises" were placed "under strong guard."[9] Alberico incarcerated his mother and reduced Pope John, who was bitterly opposed to him, to impotence in the Lateran palace. Liutprand says Alberico kept the pope "like a slave in his dwelling."[10] John died in December 935, aged in his late twenties. Flodoard describes him as a *vir vacuus*, "a hollow man," and then adds that John was "lacking class and confined to ministry because his brother [Alberico] had seized all power." He further says that John and his "incestuous mother" were kept *sub claustra*, "under arrest."[11] During Alberico's twenty-two-year-long rule, four popes were elected under his direction. They were all his creatures.

℘

In 933 at the beginning of his rule, Alberico II was about twenty-one years old, intelligent, handsome, and commanding. He differed from his mother in that his political horizons were essentially central Italian. If he had a foreign policy at all, it looked more toward Byzantium than toward Western Europe. In fact, soon after Alberico's coup a second letter from Romanus I arrived trying to extract from the pope a guarantee that Rome would continue to recognize Theophylact as patriarch, and as an incentive Romanus dangled a marriage prospect before Alberico, which went nowhere.

Alberico ruled Rome with an iron fist. He held the title of *Vestararius*, which made him a senior official of the papal curia, a kind of prime minister, and also *primus senator nec non unicus dux Romanorum*, "first senator and the sole leader of the Romans." Even though Alberico's rise to power may have been accidental, it completed a process that Theophylact and Marozia had started. He separated the papacy from the state by limiting papal authority to spiritual matters. In the process, he turned the figure of the pope into a political pawn. In a sense, the rule of the Theophylact clan represents the dominance of local interests and a contraction of Rome's horizons to the Patrimonium Petri. This retreat to provincial concerns was typical of most of Europe at the time. What we would call international interests were secondary. However, there was still a larger strategic context into which Rome and the papacy crucially fitted.

By the end of the ninth century, the Carolingian empire had collapsed and disintegrated. Europe was left with a power vacuum that allowed opportunists to seize power in local regions. Italy was a prime example of this process: upstart rulers in Tuscany, Spoleto, Friuli (northeast Italy), and Ivrea (northwest Italy) swiftly seized the moment. These duchies were dominated by families who were originally non-Italian. Friuli was ruled by Berengar I (888–924), whose family came from the lower Rhine. Tuscany emerged in the ninth century to buttress the Mediterranean coast against the Saracens, and the ruling family originated in Bavaria. As we saw, Guido I (842–ca. 860), an ambitious upstart from eastern France, made himself duke of Spoleto. Alberico I, another Frankish adventurer, later seized power in the tiny enclave of Camerino. He then murdered Guido IV of Spoleto in 896 and united Camerino with Spoleto. Ivrea was ruled by Ansgario, who came from the same region in France as Guido I. Hugo was another foreigner, from Provence. These upstarts constantly vied with each other to be king of Italy and emperor, meaningless as these titles had become. Liutprand cynically comments that "the Italians always prefer to have two kings, so that they may keep one in check by threatening him with the other."[12]

Rome was willy-nilly involved in this game-playing even though Alberico's effective power had contracted to the Patrimonium. Even though Rome could feed itself, it lacked economic clout and was dependent on consumer goods produced elsewhere. Meanwhile, the southern half of the Italian peninsula was a different world, divided as it was into small principalities and Byzantine territory. Thus, the period saw an endless series of shifting alliances in which no one gained the upper hand and possession of the kingship of Italy was always tenuous.

Another strategic issue in Italy was the survival of a number of ancient and prosperous *civitates* (cities) from ancient Roman times, particularly on the Lombard plain. Control of Lombardy was the key to the kingdom of Italy, and the struggle for this region destabilized north Italy after 888. Here cities were always important, and a number of small but strategic ones prospered through the surplus agriculture produced by the fertile Po River basin and the rich lands in the river valleys flowing into the Po, no doubt assisted by the effects of warming temperatures. Cities such as Pavia, Cremona, Verona, Bergamo, Milan, and Ferrara developed booming agricultural markets, as well as industries such as metalworking. Safe behind their well-maintained ring walls, they could defend themselves against marauding hordes of Saracens and Magyars or local thugs on the make.

These cities had complex government structures. The most important person was usually the bishop, but he was often surrounded by a wealthy oligarchy. All free citizens took part in the *conventus*, the popular assembly. Thus, power was to some extent distributed among the population. Many of the bishops were non-Italian. One of the best known was Ratherius of Verona (888–974), a neurotic man originally from near Liège (Belgium), who seemed to fight with almost everybody but was much admired by Liutprand. The two had similar personalities.

Alberico modeled his government on Byzantine administrative forms and court customs. He appropriated the notion of the principality, a relatively small geographical area governed by a single ruler on a semihereditary basis. Other examples were Capua, Salerno, and Benevento. Alberico acted primarily as *princeps*, "first citizen" or "leader," the term Roman emperors used to refer to themselves. The protocol-minded Byzantine emperor Constantine VII Porphyrogenitus used this word when addressing Alberico. He parceled out tasks among the clans in order to keep them happy and in submission to his rule. But essentially he kept power in his own hands, and while the clans were associated with him, their dependence on him was made clear. Ferdinand Gregorovius says, "Reminiscences of antiquity were increasingly awakened in Alberico's Rome," and in a sense he was a classical tyrant.[13] His regime was a centralized, bureaucratic-style government in which the papacy became a department of state. Today we would call this "caesaropapism."

Initially, the Princeps established his court in the Theophylact, fortified palazzo on the Via Lata. He later gave part of this palazzo to his female cousins, Theodora III, Marozia II, and Stephania, as a convent. Alberico then moved to the family palazzo on the Aventine Hill, a strong defensive position with a splendid view over the Tiber toward Saint Peter's. The palazzo was close to Rome's most beautiful basilica, Santa Sabina. He later established a monastery in the grounds of this palazzo and built another residence on the site of the present Piazza Colonna. It was from these residences that he ruled the Patrimonium through a *camerlengo* (chamberlain), who acted as his agent in supervising the ecclesiastical and civil bureaucracy of the papacy. This is classical caesaropapism and was a real threat to the papacy as an international institution.

Crucially for the history that would follow, Alberico needed to maintain a strong central government. He had to fend off persistent threats from King Hugo, who was still trying to recover Rome and, presumably, his imprisoned wife, Marozia. To further solidify his position, Alberico also defended and expanded the Patrimonium beyond the relatively flat plains north and south of Rome, recovering what was former papal territory in the regions of Lazio and Umbria. He also had to deal with the Magyars, who appeared at Rome's Porta San Giovanni in June 941 and who for the next five years caused panic across the Alps and down the Italian peninsula.

The Magyars had a more psychological than a military impact, although they did penetrate as far south as Otranto. They first came to Italy in 899–900, and according to the *Annals of Fulda*, they "laid waste to the whole of Italy, so that after they had killed many bishops the Italians tried to fight against them and twenty thousand men fell in one battle on one day," a reference to the September 24, 899, Battle of the River Brenta near Padua.[14] Magyar attacks aimed principally at the extraction of bribes and semiregular raids into Italy continued, including a terrible one in 924 when Pavia was destroyed. They were finally defeated by Otto I at the Battle of Lechfeld, near Augsburg, in 955.

Essentially, Alberico proved a successful central Italian potentate who governed his enclave efficiently. But in order to achieve that, he neglected the other even more important role that Rome played as the center of Catholicism in the West.

ↄ

Alberico wasn't wholly innovative—after all, he inherited the administrative forms that the papacy had evolved. However, because of the conflation of the sacred and secular, he couldn't avoid being involved in ecclesiastical matters. So it was that an international institution was now controlled by a ruler whose interests were essentially parochial. Religion was subordinate to governance.

Not all the popes of the period were bad. However, all were creatures of Alberico elected to do his bidding and largely confined to liturgical functions. After the death of John XI, Alberico arranged the election of Leo VII (936–939). A devout monk, he happily continued to execute Alberico's policy of reforming monasticism. It was Leo who brought Abbot Odo of Cluny to Rome to reform the monasteries of the city. Odo also turned out to be a talented diplomat; he arranged a peace between Alberico and Hugo. No doubt his experience at Cluny in Burgundy assisted in negotiating with King Hugo, himself a Burgundian. Flodoard's *Annals* reports that Hugo's besieging army in 936 "was afflicted by a famine and by the loss of its horses. Hugo then made peace with Alberico . . . and broke off the siege."[15] This truce was sealed when Alberico married Hugo's eldest daughter, another Alda. Flodoard personally stayed with Pope Leo in the Patriarchum and describes him as a good, warm, wise man who also encouraged the reform of the German church by appointing Archbishop Frederick of Mainz as his vicar for Germany.

After Pope Leo's death, Alberico's control of Rome was tested by a number of plots. Leo's successor, Stephen VIII (939–942), may have been a pious, intelligent supporter of monastic reform, but he also seems to have participated in a conspiracy against Alberico. He was involved with a shadowy group that wanted to restore power to the clergy. From the garbled account of the monk Benedict, it seems that Marozia and her sister Theodora II were involved in the scheme. But after one of Theodora's daughters apparently betrayed the plot to Alberico, he had the male plotters flogged, beheaded, or imprisoned. Pope Stephen was horribly mutilated and died in October 942. Harsh as he was, Alberico could hardly kill his mother and aunt. In retribution for their plotting, he consigned them to the Via Lata convent, stripping them of all political influence. (There is some confusion about Marozia's role in the plot because some argue she had died in June 936, five years earlier.) At the same time, after Alberico's wife, Alda, died in 942, Hugo returned to besiege the city once again.

Stephen was succeeded by Marinus II (942–946), who, according to Benedict, "heard nothing except Alberico's orders."[16] He continued pursuing monastic reform and confirmed the appointment of Archbishop Frederick as papal *missus* (vicar) in Germany. According to Girolamo Arnaldi, "There was a revival of the papacy in the last years of Alberico's government."[17] This seems to have occurred during the more independent papacy of Agapitus II (946–955), who, unlike his predecessors, managed to administer the papacy with relative freedom.

Alberico's control over the popes didn't mean that they were completely severed from the rest of the church. The bureaucratic machinery of the papal chancery continued to work throughout this period. Correspondence with bishops and the broader church was maintained, and even though Rome was still a pilgrimage center, news of the new insularity in the city gradually spread across Europe. The result was a drop in pilgrim numbers, which was further exacerbated by harassment of travelers in the Alps by Saracens from Fraxinetum on the Mediterranean coast.

The struggle between Hugo and Alberico, which had now lasted fifteen years, continued. At this time Hugo was trying to marry off one of his bastard daughters to the grandson of the Byzantine emperor Romanus I. Alberico, not to be outdone, also sought an imperial Byzantine bride for himself, as well as an imperial prince for his sister, Bertha. He sent a relative, Benedict of Campagna, to Constantinople to negotiate. Playing a cunning diplomatic game to weaken both Hugo and Alberico, Romanus I seemed to consent to Alberico's requests, so much so that the Princeps began preparations to receive his Byzantine bride. He even gathered a bevy of beautiful local Sabine girls as bridesmaids, but, as the unsubtle Benedict says, "unfortunately she didn't appear in the bedchamber for the nuptials."[18] Alberico had been jilted. But there was a consolation: Hugo was suddenly confronted with a revolt led by Berengar II of Ivrea, supported by the German king, Otto I. In 945 Hugo finally abandoned the struggle to hold the Italian kingship and retreated to Provence, renouncing his claims to Rome in 946. Rome remained safe for the rest of Alberico's life.

Alberico had brought stability to the Patrimonium despite petty power struggles among local clans and the demands of the general populace. A key element of his authority was control over papal land. All land in the Patrimonium had been traditionally owned by the papacy, to be used for support of the community. Alberico defied this tradition by treating it as though it were his own personal property. This move was crucial to heading off the imminent threats that church land already faced.

The first threat was obvious: the Saracens. Farms in coastal districts were particularly vulnerable to raids, which could detrimentally affect Rome's food supplies. The Saracens were finally eliminated at Garigliano in 915, but serious damage had already been done to the organization of church holdings. The second threat was more subtle: it involved powerful laymen occupying and, in our terms effectively privatizing, church land. Peter Partner comments that "it was unlikely that a system to which the Roman nobility were . . . hostile would persist at a time when all over Italy the nobility were greedily seizing church lands."[19] The long-term result was that the Patrimonium was threatened with dismemberment. Aristocrats claimed that long occupation effectively gave them a prescriptive title. Strong popes like John VIII had tried to halt this illegal transfer of ownership but failed. John also failed to stop the building of defensive towers and small castles; in Italy this process was known as *incastellamento*. The idea was to use these structures to defend the land that had been seized; they infested the Patrimonium and Rome, and 140 of them later had to be either destroyed or demilitarized.

The alienation continued under Alberico. But the Princeps was shrewd. While allowing nobles to seize land, he managed to prevent them from using it to gain independent power. His weapon against the nobles was a strong centralized administration that managed to check "the growth of any real feudal devolution of government that the rest of Europe was experiencing."[20]

Alberico was a tissue of contradictions. Tough and ruthless politically, he was also genuinely devout. Like his grandparents, he worked to reform monasticism in the Patrimonium. Both male and female religious life in Rome had fallen on bad times. The Saracens had not only destroyed outlying monasteries, but had also laid waste to the agricultural estates that supported the religious communities of the city. The disastrous decline in the standards of religious life led to many monks privatizing community property and living on monastic estates as laymen with wives and children. The imperial abbey of Farfa in the Sabine hills, an influential establishment under Charlemagne, was temporally abandoned in 897 because of Saracen raids. The monastery was then burned by Christian looters and fell into ruin. Around 930 monastic life was reestablished, but in 936 two Farfa monks, Hildebrand and Campo, poisoned the monastery's abbot, Ratfredus. Campo, supported by Hugo's troops, was installed as abbot and lived the high life on the monastic estates, giving away land to his relatives. Reforming monks sent from Rome fled when threatened with murder. Farfa remained largely unreformed during Alberico's time, although he stormed the monastery in 947 and installed a new, reforming abbot, who was resisted by the community and poisoned in 953. Eventually, the monastery was reformed, and Farfa is still a Benedictine monastery today.

In Rome the numbers of monks were declining. The fall was most acute during the strife that followed the death of Pope Formosus, with the biggest drop in numbers occurring between 890 and 911. The dearth of monks was accompanied by a decline in spirituality and learning. Good leadership was lacking. The upper class no longer wanted its sons to join monastic communities because doing so no longer provided access to power and prestige.

To turn this around, Alberico and Leo VII had brought in Benedictine reformer Odo, whom Alberico made archimandrite (superior) of all monasteries in the Patrimonium. Though he visited Rome on only six brief occasions after 936, Odo managed to persuade most Roman monasteries to adopt the *Rule* of Saint Benedict. However, "the fact that this reform did not collapse after the death of Saint Odo must be ascribed to the zeal of Prince Alberico. . . . He used his prestige and considerable wealth to further the work of reform, and sought to reform derelict monasteries and to found new congregations."[21] Alberico donated part of his palazzo on the Aventine to a monastic community, which attracted recruits from well beyond Rome.

Alberico's example proved contagious. His work on behalf of the church inspired other upper-class Romans, and enthusiasm for monastic reform began to spread among the elite. Benedict of Campagna built a monastery in Trastevere, and two couples, Gratianus and Imilla, and Gregory and Domina Rosa, built a monastery on the site of the Circus Flaminius. A doctor, Petrus Medicinus, and his wife, Johanna, built S. Maria in Pallara on the Palatine Hill, and the nobleman Balduinus built S. Petrus in Horrea in honor of his deceased wife, Saxia. These monasteries needed the support of wealthy patrons to get them off the ground and once established required continuing assistance until they became self-supporting.

Altogether twelve new Latin monasteries and two Greek monasteries were founded in Rome between 936 and 1000; this was largely carried out by laypeople, with monastic advisers. It was not until two decades after Alberico's death that the papacy took the lead in monastic reform. The foundation of these monasteries somewhat reversed the alienation of monastic lands by laity. In fact, property went the other way, from the laity to the monks. One of the most interesting and successful new monasteries was SS. Bonifatius and Alexius on the Aventine, now the church of S. Alessio, completely disfigured in an eighteenth-century "restoration." Founded by a political refugee, Archbishop Sergius of Damascus, it was a joint Latin and Greek monastery governed by a single abbot, but with the monks living under different rules: the Greeks under that of Saint Basil and the Latins under Saint Benedict's. This monastery became a center of intellectual excellence and attracted good recruits from Western Europe and south Italy.[22]

This era also saw a revival of women's religious life. At the beginning of Alberico's reign, there were only three convents in Rome. One was Santa Maria in Tempuli. Its survival was probably due to the patronage of Sergius III. The abbess of the convent in Sergius's time was Efemia *venerabilis diacona*, "Venerable Deaconess" Efemia, and during the papacy of Benedict VII the abbess was Constantia, the daughter of Roman aristocrats. The convent church, rebuilt between 800 and 850, has survived to today. It is now deconsecrated and is owned by the Commune of Rome as a place for civil marriages.

The other convent we know about is that of Saint Cyriacus on the Via Lata. As we saw, this convent was founded and supported during Alberico's rule by his cousins Theodora III, Marozia II, and Stephania. Since we know both Marozia II and Theodora III were married and Stephania was governor of the town of Palestrina, we can be sure that they were not nuns. They probably intended the convent to be a place of forced retirement for their mother, Theodora II, sister of Marozia I, after the plot against Alberico.

Alberico's reform of monasticism was not entirely religious. It also had a defensive intention. To understand why, we need to recognize that the Patrimonium was, in fact, in military terms poorly defended. Archaeological remains show that early medieval fortresses outside Rome were relatively unimpressive. Alberico's intention was to defend the Patrimonium through the stability and disciplined organization that frontier monasteries brought. He used reformed monasteries as a way of bringing order to the lands in the forward defensive areas north and east of the city, making sure no strongman who opposed him could get a foothold. He also used monasteries as focuses of settlement and population, thus building up infrastructure and providing a local supply of able-bodied men to defend the Patrimonium. The monasteries of San Silvestro on Monte Soratte, Sant'Elia close to Nepi, where Alberico's brother Sergius was bishop, together with land held by city monasteries, formed a kind of protective arc north of Rome. To the east Subiaco Monastery, which controlled a series of defensive forts along the River Aniene, a tributary of the Tiber, was reformed. The one monastery where Alberico didn't succeed was Farfa. While the Apennines provided security on Alberico's eastern flank, in the flatter land and rolling hills to the northwest of Rome the Princeps used impregnable places such as Civita Castellana on a rocky outcrop above a ravine as a focus of protection. Nepi and Castel Sant'Elia on the same ravine also provided protection. The main route over the Apennines into Rome was the old imperial road, the Via Flaminia. It passed through these areas and was thus supervised and guarded. Alberico's defensive strategy was successful, and no invader was able to conquer Rome during his lifetime.

In 954 he suffered a serious malaria attack. As death approached, after a career of good decisions, he made one last, disastrous decision: he concentrated all power, ecclesiastical and civil, into the hands of one man, his bastard son, with the Roman name of Octavian the personal name of the emperor Augustus. On his deathbed, Alberico called the nobility and clergy together at the tomb of Saint Peter and made them swear that they would elect Octavian pope after the death of Agapitus II. They acquiesced. After Alberico died in August 954, Octavian assumed temporal control of Rome. He had to wait a year and four months to succeed to the papacy.

For all that he did to hold central Italy together during his rule, Alberico has been largely neglected. Even Italian historians give him short shrift, and an upper-middle-class street that runs from the Castel Sant'Angelo to near the Vatican, Via Alberico Secondo, remains his only memorial in Rome. Of the popes Alberico appointed, Agapitus was the ablest. He played an important role in Western European politics and helped organize the episcopal structure of the church in Denmark, then in the process of being converted to Catholicism, by confirming the extension of the jurisdiction of the diocese of Hamburg-Bremen over the Scandinavian countries. A fan of the German king Otto I, he sent a papal legate, Bishop Marinus, to Otto's court. He indicated that he was willing to crown Otto emperor, but Alberico refused to let any foreign ruler, no matter how powerful, enter the Patrimonium. This was a shrewd decision given that just six years later Otto I arrived in Rome to begin the reform of the papacy and an attempted suppression of clans, especially the Theophylacts. But the decision to combine ecclesiastical and political power in the hands of his immature son was to prove a disaster. He wrecked much of what his father, Alberico, and the earlier Theophylact rulers had achieved.

∾

Agapitus died in early December 955. In fulfillment of their promise to Alberico, the Roman powerbrokers quickly elected Octavian pope on December 16, 955. An election agreed upon in the previous pope's lifetime was canonically illegal, but this was swept aside. The name Octavian was considered too pagan, so he took the style John XII (955–964) but retained Octavian for secular affairs. Born about 937, he was about seventeen or eighteen at the time that he became pope. His mother is unknown. She might have been Alda, who is sometimes referred to as Alberico's *concubina* (this word was also sometimes used for a wife), or she might have been another concubine. Even if we take with some skepticism Liutprand's characterization of Octavian as an utter debauchee, he still stands out as among the most dissolute of all the popes. He was a testosterone-driven, late-adolescent lout whose lust was completely uncontrolled. Even worse than his promiscuity was his total failure to maintain his father's careful policies.

Under his rule, Rome quickly degenerated into factionalism and chaos. Individual clans controlled their own portions of the city and stalked the streets, murdering and raping with impunity. Even as pope, John himself acted as leader of a gang of youthful thugs who terrorized both citizens and pilgrims. Liutprand says that he turned the Lateran into "a harlot's brothel. . . . He took women pilgrims by force to his bed, wives, widows and virgins alike." There are accusations of the rapes of pilgrims within Saint Peter's basilica. There is something psychologically very dark about these reports, something approaching a deliberate sacrilege. In a sentence reminiscent of Leporello's "Catalogue Aria" in Mozart's *Don Giovanni*, Liutprand says John kept a bevy of women, some of whom "are fine ladies who . . . are as thin as reeds by dieting, others everyday buxom wenches. It is all the same to him." He was so blindly in love with one mistress that he gave her stolen church land and "the golden crosses and cups [chalices] that are the sacred possessions of Saint Peter himself."[23] He lacked any overall policy and governed largely on impulse, as demonstrated when he attacked Capua and Benevento in 958 hoping to extend the Patrimonium. His army was routed, and he himself fled in the disordered retreat.

Nevertheless, church administration continued to function, most probably owing to the clerks of the Lateran who kept up the flow of correspondence.

He presented palliums (symbols of office) to Archbishops Henry of Trier, Oskytel of York, and Dunstan of Canterbury. He showed interest in monasticism, supporting the Benedictine houses at Farfa and Subiaco.

By 959–960 the deplorable Berengar II, himself little more than a brigand, was emerging as a real threat to the Patrimonium. Many Romans felt that something would have to be done both to stop Berengar and to reform the papacy. The only hope seemed to be the distant Saxon king Otto I, whose star continued to rise in Germany. John was increasingly under pressure to call Otto in and offer him the imperial crown as Holy Roman Emperor. John initially resisted, but eventually in late 960 he sent Cardinal Deacon John and the *scriniarius* (secretary) Azzo to beg Otto to come to Italy and free the Roman church from the tyranny of Berengar. Conscious that he now "stood at the head of the Christian west [and] anxious to raise his dignity and prestige in the eyes of the Byzantine Empire," Otto prepared thoroughly for his first visit to Rome.[24] After securing the succession by having his namesake six-year-old son elected king and crowned, Otto gathered a large army and in early winter 961 he crossed the Alps into Lombardy. Berengar retreated in the face of the German forces. Otto restored order in northern Italy and then proceeded to Rome in late January 962 to receive the imperial crown.

Accompanying him was Liutprand of Cremona, who had fled Berengar's court and joined Otto's bureaucracy. His *Liber de Rebus Gestis Ottonis*, "The Chronicle of Otto's Doings," tells the story of Otto's Italian adventures. Here Liutprand is talking about events he personally experienced, although we always need to remember that he is for Otto and against the Roman clans, especially the Theophylacts.

On Candlemas Day (February 2, 962), Otto "was welcomed [in Saint Peter's] with marvellous ceremony and unexampled pomp, and was anointed as emperor by John the supreme bishop and universal pope."[25] The "welcome" certainly would have been tempered by mutual distrust and distaste on Otto's part because he had to submit to coronation by such a papal sleaze. He also faced sullen resentment from Rome's inhabitants that they had been forced to submit to a German "barbarian." During the coronation, Otto kept his knights close by in case of trouble, and according to Thietmar of Merseburg, he told his young sword-bearer, Count Ansfrid, "'Today, while I am praying at the threshold of the Apostles, you must continue to hold the sword above my head. For I am well aware that the Romans' loyalty to our predecessors was often suspect.'"[26] After the coronation Mass, the new emperor gave John lavish gifts and took the usual oaths to protect and defend the Roman church. In response, John and Roman oligarchs swore loyalty to Otto on the tomb of Saint Peter, promising to reject the traitor Berengar. But the realistic Otto took Roman oath-taking with a grain of salt. Even then to call a person a "Roman" was tantamount to an insult—it connoted that he was dishonest, untrustworthy, disloyal, and devious.

Several days later Otto issued the *Privilegium Ottonianum*, a charter document setting out the relationships between himself and the pope. According to the *Liber pontificalis*, it seems that before he left Rome, Otto attempted to have a heart-to-heart talk with John about passing "his whole life in vanity and adultery" and asked him to amend his life.[27] Otto was, after all, Europe's most experienced soldier and statesman, with the best possible advisers, and John was an ignorant youth surrounded by sycophants who changed sides at the drop of a hat. But it was all in vain; John's behavior remained impulsive and dictated by his immediate needs and the gratification of his lusts. This gave him an initial advantage over Otto, who sought advice and acted cautiously in the intricacies of Italian politics and was sometimes astonished by John's impulsive whims.

For instance, Otto was hardly out of Rome before the anti-German party in Rome persuaded John to switch his allegiance and offer the imperial crown to Berengar. But he was temporarily unavailable, with Otto in hot pursuit, so John then invited Berengar's son Adalbert to Rome from exile among the Saracens at Fraxinetum. At the same time, he commenced scheming with the Magyars. What John XII expected to gain from these suspect alliances is unclear. Without any coherent policy of his own, John was really just looking anywhere and everywhere for alliances that could be used as a counterbalance to Otto. John clearly suspected that the new emperor was about to attempt a reform of the papacy.

Otto sent Liutprand to Rome as an ambassador, and when he reported back John's machinations, Otto was remarkably tolerant. He commented that "[John] is only a boy, and will soon alter if good men set him an example. I hope that honorable reproof and generous persuasion will quickly cure him of these vices."[28] But the pursuit of Berengar prevented Otto returning to Rome to give John that honorable reproof. Otto's forces finally trapped Berengar and his wife, Willa, in the fortress of Montefeltre close to modern San Marino.

Forced to surrender, Berengar was exiled to Bamberg, where he died, and Willa was sent to a nunnery.

Otto was now free to deal with John, Adalbert, and the recalcitrant Romans. On November 1, 963, he returned to Rome. At his arrival, John and Adalbert fled to Tivoli with as much of the papal treasure as they could carry. With the pope gone, it was up to Otto to address the crisis. He summoned a synod of the Roman church in Saint Peter's to decide what should be done. The numbers in attendance were high: there were six bishops from outside Italy and thirty-nine from Italy, twelve cardinals (parish priests of Rome), and many local ecclesiastical and civil movers and shakers. This assembly set a theological and canonical precedent by judging and dismissing the pope and electing a new one. In contrast to his usual uninhibited style, Liutprand is careful in his account of the synod to identify people correctly and to quote what are probably their exact words. He was *the* expert on Italian and especially Roman affairs in Otto's court, and the synod saw the height of his influence on Italian politics during Otto I's reign.

Proceedings opened on November 6, 963, with Otto addressing the gathering and inviting John to attend. The case for the prosecution was outlined by a series of cardinals: Pope John had celebrated Mass without receiving Communion himself; he had ordained bishops and deacons for money; he was an adulterer; he had gone hunting; he had blinded "his spiritual father Benedict"; he had amputated the genitals and killed Cardinal Subdeacon John; and he had set houses on fire, appeared in public armed with weapons, drank wine "for love of the devil," and called on pagan gods for assistance when gambling. Regarding his adultery, he was accused of "carnal acquaintance" (which probably means rape) "with Rainerius' widow, Stephana, his father's concubine, the widow Anna and his own niece and that he had turned the [Lateran] . . . palace into a brothel and resort for harlots." Because the Romans "could not understand his native Saxon tongue," Otto asked Liutprand to address the synod in Latin on his behalf. Liutprand demanded that all present confirm the charges on oath, which they did. Otto then invited Pope John to return to Rome and answer the charges. John responded by sending a messenger who threatened all who attended the synod with excommunication if they elected another pope.[29]

Otto reconvened the synod with an increased number of Italian and foreign bishops present. After dismissing Pope John's threat of excommunication as "more fitting for a stupid boy than a bishop," the synod again demanded that John answer the charges in person. Otherwise, those present at synod "shall disregard your excommunication, and rather turn it upon yourself, as we have justly the power to do."[30] The messengers who took this response to John could not find him; he was apparently out hunting.

Otto reconvened the synod for a third and final time on December 4, 963. According to Liutprand, Otto justified his intervention in papal affairs before the assembled clerics, then called for the synod to make a decision. No doubt, like any good politician, he knew exactly what the decision would be in advance. The Roman clergy present called for John's removal as pope. "We therefore ask your imperial majesty that this monster, whom no virtue redeems from vice, shall be driven from the holy Roman church, and another be appointed in his place." With Pope John excommunicated, the emperor then invited synod members to nominate a candidate. They responded, "We elect as our shepherd Leo, the venerable chief notary of the holy Roman church [Protoscriniarius], a man of proved worth . . . and we hereby reprobate the apostate John because of his vicious life."[31] Two days after his election by consensus and acclamation, Leo VIII (963–965) was consecrated as pope.

Otto and Liutprand had succeeded in ousting one of history's worst popes. What they failed to reckon with was the fickle nature of the Romans. They also made the mistake of treating John as a purely spiritual leader and forgot his political role in the Patrimonium. In deposing Pope John, the synod had also de facto expelled Princeps Octavian, civil ruler of Rome. Though the synod had authority over the church's affairs, Princeps Octavian still had his backers among the Roman populace. Unwilling to tolerate Octavian's deposition, a month later, on January 3, 964, the Romans rose in revolt. This unrest was put down easily enough, but Otto could not remain in Rome forever, especially with Berengar's son Adalbert occupying Spoleto.

The emperor left Rome in late January to deal with Adalbert. Without him to stabilize the city, according to Liutprand, "the women with whom the so-called pope John was accustomed to carry on his voluptuous sports, being many in numbers and noble in rank, stirred-up the Romans to overthrow Leo . . . and bring John back again into Rome." This description is probably misogynistic bluster from Liutprand. It is more likely that the anti-German party in Rome that had previously supported Octavian mounted the rebellion. Whatever happened, Leo fled to safety with Otto's army, and John returned to Rome in February. He took savage revenge on those he captured who had given evidence against him, like Cardinal Deacon John and Protonotary Azo, "one of whom had his right hand cut off, and the other his tongue, two fingers and his nose."[32] John also convened a small synod of terrified clerics, who on February 26 reversed the decisions of Otto's synod and deposed Leo as a usurper.

Having finally defeated and exiled Adalbert, an outraged Otto prepared to march back to Rome. After a fruitless attempt at reconciliation, John decamped to the Campagna, where, according to the scuttlebutt, he died as a result of a stroke he suffered while having sex with a married woman. Another version of the story held that he was caught red-handed in bed by a cuckolded husband (in Liutprand's version he was caught by the devil), who bashed him so severely that he died within the week, on May 14, 964, having refused the last sacraments.[33] Before Otto could even get back to the city, the Romans, ignoring Leo VIII, whom they saw as tainted by Otto's support, elected Benedict V on May 22, 964. They then asked Otto, who was in Rieti, to accept Benedict as pope because he was a virtuous man and a reformer.

A furious Otto refused this request and besieged Rome. On June 23, 964, the city surrendered. Benedict, who refused to defend himself, was immediately deposed, stripped of his pontifical insignia, and exiled to Hamburg, where he died two years later. Interestingly, even the pro-Ottonian chronicler Thietmar of Merseberg is obliquely critical of the emperor's behavior in this instance. "The powerful and august emperor of the Romans," Thietmar says, "consented to the deposition of the lord Pope Benedict, his superior in Christ, who may be judged by no one but God. I hope that the accusations were unjust. He ordered him to be exiled to Hamburg."[34] Leo VIII died on March 1, 965.

A delay of seven months occurred while Bishop Marinus of Sutri and the mutilated Protonotary Azo were sent from Rome to Otto in Saxony asking that Benedict V be allowed to return to Rome as pope. Otto ignored this request by informing the delegates that he wanted John Episcopus (a surname), bishop of Narni, elected. Liutprand and Otger of Speyer accompanied the two delegates back to Rome, and John Episcopus (whose nickname was White Hen because of his light-colored hair) was unanimously elected as John XIII on October 1, 965.

Within two months the divided city was in revolt against Otto's new pope. This particular rebellion was prompted by John XIII's efforts to pull the clans into line. According to monk Benedict of Monte Soratte, some complained that

Otto's aim was to "destroy their [the clans] power and influence leading them into captivity," probably an accurate assessment.[35] John XIII was roughed up by the mob, imprisoned, and then exiled. But by November 966, the pro-German party was in the ascendency again in Rome and John XIII was welcomed back. He forgave his enemies. Not so Otto, who was enraged by the time he reached Rome at Christmas 966. Twelve of the leaders of the revolt were summarily hung, others were sent into exile, and the prefect of the city was hung up by his hair, then tarred and feathered, and finally sat backward on an ass to be ridiculed throughout the city.

If nothing else, this sad history illustrates the fact that the popes of this period were much more the local bishops of Rome than the heads of the universal church. All of these popes were the creatures of one or other political master or mistress. Certainly, correspondence from the papal chancery continued with the broader church—both East and West—but the horizons of these tenth-century popes had contracted to central Italy. In this they were typical of the rest of early-tenth-century Europe, where local issues far outweighed in importance broader preoccupations with the state and government. This emphasis on the parochial caused the Romans to continue to have difficult relationships with Otto and his successors, as we will explore later.

ᘓ

By bringing the story up to the 960s, we have got ahead of ourselves here. But Rome and more broadly northern and central Italy vividly illustrate the breakdown of any form of central government and the constant instability caused by a series of local upstarts seizing power for themselves, which was typical of the first part of the tenth century. The frustration experienced by Otto I in Italy originated in the clash between Italian and specifically Roman localism and the loss of any coherent conception of sovereignty over against the German vision of a larger integrated polity with a coherent government and clear lines of state authority. This is the core issue in the tenth century: how to recover some overall sense of central authority and to turn geographical expressions like "Germany," "France," and "Italy" into real states. Led by the Saxon monarchs, the Germans were the first to achieve this. What these last two chapters have also illustrated is how difficult it was going to be to reform the papacy, with its conflation of the spiritual government of the church and the political government of the papal state.

What we will do in Part Two is backtrack into the ninth century to see how the unity and effective government established by Charlemagne were lost. The causes of this breakdown were both external and internal. The external forces that destroyed the Carolingian empire were the Vikings, the Saracens, and the Magyars, whose incursions hastened the collapse of the ordered world set up by Charlemagne. But the core problem was internal. Lacking a tradition of primogeniture (inheritance of the kingdom by the eldest son), Charlemagne's ordered state quickly collapsed in what the contemporary chronicler Regino of Prüm correctly called "the dissention of kings."[36] It was not until these problems were eliminated that there was any possibility of a return to effective government either in church or state.

PART TWO

THE
WORLD
in
CHAOS

CHAPTER 4

Enemies of Christians

IN THE YEAR 885 the city of Paris was nothing more than a small, vulnerable *civitas* (town) of perhaps 3,000 people, built on an island in the River Seine, the Île-de-la-Cité. In the years to come, its population would swell, and Paris would grow into the world city we know today. But it almost didn't survive. The siege that began on November 25, 885, would challenge Paris's very existence.

A large Viking force had approached the island's defenses. The Viking leader, Siegfried, demanded that the local bishop, Joscelin (who was also abbot of Saint-Germain-des-Prés), allow the Viking ships passage to sail up the Seine to raid richer targets in the regions of Marne and northern Burgundy. Vikings were not a new presence to the Parisians. They had first appeared forty years earlier in 845. Since then, the French usually tried to buy them off with bribes, but this only encouraged them to come back again and again. They returned to Paris in 856–857, 861 (when they tried to burn the city), 865–866, and 869. By 885 the French were well acquainted with the Vikings' eagerness to prowl their rivers looking for booty. However, this attack was different because it was well organized.

Not that Paris was unprepared. Strong walls had protected the city since the early 880s. In 864 a low barrage bridge had been constructed across the Seine to prevent unfriendly boats getting upriver. The bridge forced the Vikings to portage their boats around the town, making them much more vulnerable to attack. Two such bridges—the Grand Pont and the Petit Pont—stood on the downriver side of the Île-de-la-Cité. Both had defensive towers protecting them, one of stone and one of wood.

Before the Viking attack on the city, Siegfried and the bishop held a parley. The Viking leader entered "the great hall of the famed shepherd" Joscelin. Acknowledging the bishop with a bow of the head, Siegfried asked him to "show mercy to yourself and to the flock given to you" by allowing his men to bypass Paris. He promised that "nothing in [Paris] shall we then touch." Joscelin refused. He had experience with Vikings: twenty-five years earlier they had taken him prisoner. He had been released only after payment of a large ransom. Joscelin told Siegfried bluntly that he had a duty to Emperor Charles "the Fat" (882–887) to guard the city, and he challenged the Viking leader to say what he would do if he were in the bishop's shoes. Siegfried replied honestly that he would prefer "my head were lopped off by a sword and thrown to the dogs" than surrender. However, without the grant of free passage to his warriors, "our siege engines, at daybreak, [will] hurl poisoned darts at you; with sunset you shall know hunger's curse." Siegfried threatened that the siege would "go on for years."[1] Well, perhaps not years, but it did last eleven months. Joscelin would be dead, probably from plague, before it was lifted.

We have inherited a rather romanticized account of the siege that comes to us from a naïve young monk, Abbo of Saint-Germain-des-Prés. Abbo's retelling of the history seeks God's hidden hand in all of the events that transpire. He tries to understand God's intention in cursing the city with Vikings. He also sees Paris's patron saints, Geneviève and Germain, as the true defenders of the town, which is ultimately saved through their intercession with God. As Abbo's translator, Nirmal Dass, correctly explains, "The medieval mind was steeped in teleology. . . . To search for strict [historical] accuracy is ultimately futile, for . . . action can acquire meaning only when it is lifted into the context of theology."[2]

Abbo, like many of his contemporaries, argues that the Vikings were a punishment from God. Neither rulers nor people had trusted God and had instead long tried to bribe their way out of the Viking threat. His narrative also tells the story of a brave people, their bishop's wise leadership, and a courageous young Count Odo (or Eudes) of Paris, who stood up to the heathens and outlasted them. There is something immature about the work, however. Abbo seems to strain to impress us with his knowledge of arcane Greek and Latin words and phrases and the poetic forms of classical literature, all of which he hopes may "find favor" with his reader.[3]

The Vikings had already been a menace for a century before the Paris siege. Since Charlemagne had never set up a fleet to patrol the sea and protect his territory, from the early ninth century on it was unsafe to cross the English Channel from the Continent to Britain. The Vikings also effectively controlled the North Sea, the Irish Sea, the Baltic Sea, and the North Atlantic routes to Iceland and Greenland. The Vikings found West Francia (France) a particularly appealing target, with its large, navigable rivers; fertile valleys; rich monasteries; and *civitates* (towns).

The *Annals of Saint-Bertin*, which covers the story of much of the ninth-century world, makes it clear that there was an absolute epidemic of Viking incursions. The sources also demonstrate that there was no effective central government to organize resistance. From 840 on there was a civil war between the sons of Louis the Pious and a weakening the Carolingian empire. The Vikings seized their chance and pounced on the undefended countryside.

The wave of attacks began in 841 and used the French river systems as highways. Vikings had already raided along the Rhine four times between 834 and 837. Now, as the civil war dragged on, their raids dramatically increased in frequency and intensity. Prime targets included the rich, populous port of Dorestad on the Lek River near Utrecht in the Rhine estuary, as well as Quentovic, which was about 6 miles (10 kilometers) inland from the northern French coast. In 841 "a fleet of Northmen made a surprise attack at dawn on the *emporium* [market town] called Quentovic, plundered it and laid it waste, capturing or massacring the inhabitants of both sexes. They left nothing in it except for those buildings they were paid to spare."[4] Quentovic, which no longer exists, was "perhaps the most important seaport of the . . . Frankish homelands."[5] Traveling along rivers such as the Seine, Vikings attacked Paris in 845, Xanten on the lower Rhine between 863 and 873, and even Pisa in Italy in 859. They often used their ships as bases from which to range across the countryside attacking monasteries and towns.

The Vikings deftly exploited local divisions. For instance, in May 843 Rainald, Duke of Nantes had been killed in an attack on his town on the Loire River by his neighbors Lambert from the lower Loire valley and Breton ruler Nominoe. In a counterattack two weeks later, Lambert was expelled from Nantes. What ensued was a complete regional breakdown of law and order. "So many and such great disasters followed, while brigands ravaged everything everywhere, that people in many areas throughout Gaul were reduced to eating earth mixed with a little bit of flour and made into a sort of bread." This was precisely the kind of situation that the Vikings were equipped to exploit quickly. In June 843 "Northmen pirates attacked Nantes, slew the bishop and many clergy and laypeople of both sexes, and sacked the *civitas*. Then they attacked the western parts of Aquitaine to devastate them too."[6]

At first the raids tended to be seasonal, allowing the Vikings to return to Scandinavia for the harvest. But then they began to spend winter on defensible islands like those in the Seine near Oissel on the outskirts of Rouen, or Jeufosse near Vernon, downstream from Paris. Other semipermanent settlements were established. Adrevald, a monk of Saint Benoît-sur-Loire near Orléans, reports that a group of Vikings wintered at "a base for their ships near the monastery of Fleury. They put up their huts . . . and there they kept their herds of prisoners in chains while they themselves rested. . . . They made unexpected forays from their base, sometimes in their ships, sometimes on horses and laid waste the whole province."[7] Another monk, Ermentarius of Noirmoutier, says that they "infested" the island of Noirmoutier, just south of the mouth of the Loire. He adds that "the number of ships increases, the innumerable crowd of Northmen swells and everywhere Christians are slaughtered and are the victims of burnings, destruction, robbery. . . . They seize whatever *civitas* they come to and no one resists them. They have seized Bordeaux, Périgueux, Limoges, Angoulême, and Toulouse. Angers, Tours and Orléans are ruined."

After the Vikings occupied the island, the monks of the monastery of Saint Filibert were forced to flee. Ermentarius says that he and his fellow monks headed upstream to Saumur with the relics of Saint Filibert. He also tells us that "a large fleet of Viking ships have sailed up the Seine. Evil haunts these parts: Rouen is attacked, plundered and burned, Paris, Beauvais and Meaux taken and the fort at Melun leveled, Chartres taken, Evreaux and Bayeux plundered and every other town besieged."[8]

The *Annals of Saint-Bertin* reports that 845 was "a very hard winter . . . [and] in March 120 ships of the Northmen sailed up the Seine to Paris, laying waste to everything on either side and meeting not the least bit of opposition. [King] Charles [the Bald] made efforts to offer some resistance, but realized that his men could not possibly win. So he made a deal with them by handing over to them 7000 lb [of silver] as a bribe, he restrained them from going further and persuaded them to go away."[9]

Even so, as the Viking group sailed "back down the Seine to the open sea they devastated all the coastal regions, plundering and burning." But, the *Annals* claims, they got their comeuppance: having sacked and burned a monastery, "they were struck down by divine judgment either with blindness or insanity, so severely that only a few escaped to tell the rest about the might of God."[10] In another incursion three days after Christmas 856, a group of Vikings again attacked Paris and burned parts of it. Others attacked Tours and surrounding regions. In 857 they came up the Seine, ravaging "everything unchecked," again attacking Paris, destroying churches, and only sparing others when a ransom was paid. They also attacked nearby Chartres, where Bishop Frotbald "fled on foot and tried to swim across the river Eure, but he was overwhelmed by the waters and drowned."[11]

The sheer terror the Vikings engendered is what motivated Frankish leaders to pay bribes to get them off their backs, at least temporarily. The reaction of the monk Paschasius Radbertus is typical of the defeatism and despair that infected many in France. Referring specifically to the Viking attack on Paris in 857, he says, "Who would have ever believed or thought possible that in our place and time we would be over-run by such fearful misfortunes? So today we are frightened as these pirate bands violate the borders of Paris and set on fire the churches of Christ on the banks of the Seine. . . . Who could have determined that such a glorious kingdom, so fortified, large, populous and strong would be humiliated and defiled by such a filthy race?"[12]

But capitulation made other people furious. Ermentarius of Noirmoutier comments that the Franks "ransom with tributes what they should defend with arms, and the kingdom of the Christians is laid waste."[13]

The year 865 was one of the worst. The Vikings "sailed up the Seine with fifty ships," while others on the Loire

made their way up the river with a favourable wind, divine judgement thus making it easy for them to launch a full-scale attack. They reached the monastery of Saint Benedict known as Fleury and burned it. On their way back they burned Orléans and the monasteries both in the *civitas* and round it, except for the church of the Holy Cross which, despite great efforts on the part of the Northmen, the flames proved unable to consume. So they sailed back down the river and after ravaging all the neighbouring districts they returned to their base.[14]

The same or another group "made their way on foot to Poitiers without meeting any resistance." They burned the town and returned to their ships unscathed. But they didn't get away scot-free. Robert, Count of Angers caught up with them and "slew more than 500 . . . without losing any of his own men."[15] Perhaps the Vikings were having a postraid party and were caught too drunk to defend themselves! Further north in October 865, they attacked the Abbey of St. Denis near Paris, "where they stayed for about twenty days, carrying off booty from the monastery to their ships each day, and after much plundering and without encountering resistance from anyone at all, they returned to their camp not far from the monastery."[16] They had already attacked the monastery in 858, taking Abbot Louis, a grandson of Charlemagne, captive and demanding and receiving a huge ransom for him.

One way of stopping the Vikings was to build wooden obstacles across the smaller rivers such as the Oise and the Marne. But these could be swept away by strong currents and needed to be kept in good repair. Unless a land fortress with guards was set up on both banks, the Vikings simply carried their boats around the obstacles. And the year 866 was even worse.

Northmen sailed up the Seine to the fort at Melun. Charles the Bald's squadrons advanced on both banks of the Seine, and the Northmen disembarked to attack what looked like the larger and stronger squadron. . . . The Northmen put them to flight even without a battle, and returned to their own people, their ships loaded with booty. Charles made peace with those Northmen at the price of 4000 lbs of silver, according to their scales. A levy was imposed throughout the realm to pay this tribute: 6 *denarii* were required from each free manse [a freeman's holding of about 50–120 acres], 3 *denarii* from each servile one [about the same size as a free manse], 1 *denarius* for each *accola* [a smaller holding than a manse], and 1 *denarius* also for every 2 *hospitia* [a very small landholding]; a tenth of the value of all goods owned by traders; and a payment was also required from priests, according to what resources each had. . . . Furthermore any slaves who had been carried off by the Northmen and escaped from them after the agreement was made were either handed back or ransomed at a price set by the Northmen; and if any one of the Northmen was killed, whatever price the Northmen demanded for him was paid.[17]

Clearly, Frankish resistance was intermittent, often depending on which aristocratic thug was occupied fighting another. Many would have been glad to see the Vikings attacking their enemies. Charles the Bald's government was far too weak to do anything, as shown by the draconian levies it imposed to pay off the Vikings. Capitulation had been the main response to the Vikings for several decades. But someone had to make a stand, and in Paris in 885 Bishop Joscelin's refusal to compromise with Siegfried signaled that, at least for some, enough was enough.

℘

With people from the surrounding region flooding into Paris in 885, there were probably about 3,000 to 4,000 people on the Île-de-la-Cité. Joscelin and Odo would have made a careful calculation of their ability to resist the Vikings given they had only 200 men-at-arms to hold the island, an area of about 22 acres (9 hectares). They were confident their defenses would hold.

They had ample warning of the Vikings' approach. The raiders had entered the Seine on July 25, 885, and it took them four months to cover the 145 miles (234 kilometers) of meandering river from Rouen to Paris. They were held up by a garrison near Pontoise for several weeks, but to take four months to get from Rouen to Paris was extraordinarily slow; they were traveling at a little more than 1 nautical mile per day, a snail's pace. Abbo says that when the Vikings arrived at the Île-de-la-Cité, they had 40,000 men and "seven hundred high-prowed ships and very many smaller ones," so many that the "deep waters" of the Seine vanished for "more than two leagues downriver" beneath the dense crowd of vessels.[18]

The numbers are clearly vastly exaggerated. Carroll Gillmor has shown that the smaller boats the Vikings used on rivers had 26 to 30 men as crew, with the ships around 60 feet (18 meters) long by 8.5 feet (2.6 meters) wide and with a draft of about 1.6 feet (0.5 meters). Even if there were 200 ships, then there would have been only about 5,200 warriors. But even this seems an overestimate if we consider what it would have taken for so many Vikings to live off the land as they traveled. A lot of time would have to have been taken up foraging. This might help to explain the slowness of the Vikings' progress upriver to Paris. These kinds of logistical questions indicate that the Vikings probably had about 85 ships with about 2,000 men, which was still a reasonably large force. Abbo's exaggeration was likely a means of emphasizing just how influential the intercession of Saints Geneviève and Germain was and how heroic Odo, Joscelin, and their small group of Christian defenders were.[19]

The Paris siege began the day after the parley with Bishop Joscelin. "Jumping into their boats," Abbo writes, "the Danes headed for the tower, and began to hurl stones at it and riddled it with arrows." The tower in question was the stone one on the right bank at what is now the Place du Châtelet. The Vikings attacked with catapulted stones and arrows aimed at the defenders. In the thick of the fighting was the nephew of Joscelin, Abbot Ebolus, who was hit "by a sharp-pointed arrow." There was nothing unusual about a fighting cleric; we've already seen Pope John X happily reporting that he had fought against the Saracens. In any case, it must have been only a flesh wound, for Ebolus was back fighting again the next day: "With a single spear he pierced seven Danes all at once, and in jest he said . . . to take them to the kitchen."[20]

The clear aim of the Vikings was to destroy the city's defensive stone tower, which was still being built. Nevertheless, Abbo reports that "its foundations stood firmly grounded" and during the first night a wooden tier was built on top to cover it.[21] He describes a couple of days of intense fighting in which the Vikings tried to undermine the tower or set alight any wooden structure within their reach. At one stage their fires resulted in intense smoke, which blew back on them, forcing them to retreat until, according to Abbo, they were ridiculed by their wives and shamed back into battle. Whether this is truth or exaggeration, Abbo's retelling paints the Vikings as cowards in stark contrast to the Christian heroes Count Odo and Abbot Ebolus.

After five days of fierce fighting, the Vikings seemed to have had enough. They dug in for an overwinter siege by building a defensive encampment near Saint-Dénis. Heavy rains came in midwinter, flooding the river, and Abbo reports, "At the still of the night the mid-section of the bridge broke; it was pulled apart by the raging frenzy of the current."[22] The next morning a Viking group got through to continue raiding upriver toward Le Mans and Chartres, while the main force remained behind to continue the siege. Even so, the Île-de-la-Cité held out and Abbo makes clear that the key to survival was Odo's and the soldiers' courage, Bishop Joscelin's leadership, and the relics of Saint Geneviève, which were paraded along the walls whenever things got really dangerous.

However, the siege was not over yet. Disease and hunger began to spread through Paris in April 866. Among the victims was Bishop Joscelin himself. The Vikings were not in much better shape. According to the *Annals of St. Vaast*, their daily attacks resulted in "many [Vikings] . . . killed and still more were disabled by wounds."[23] The Viking leader Siegfried abandoned the siege, but his second in command, Rollo, assumed leadership. Meanwhile, Count Odo had slipped through the Viking lines and petitioned Emperor Charles the Fat to come and help lift the siege. Returning to Paris, Odo had to fight his way back to the Île-de-la-Cité through a Viking trap. His horse was killed under him. Henry of Fulda, Charles the Fat's point man in resisting the Vikings, arrived in later winter 886, but his attempts to dislodge the Vikings made little difference as his army was exhausted after a midwinter march.

The Vikings made another attempt to take the Île-de-la-Cité after a spring flood but were repulsed by six hundred Parisian citizens. The Vikings "were crushed. They yielded, fled and were killed," says Abbo, as usual putting the best possible interpretation on events. Even those who sought sanctuary in churches were not spared, and "some three thousand Danes were slain," probably an exaggerated number.[24] But despite their serious setbacks, the Vikings maintained the siege until Emperor Charles himself arrived in October 886 with a large army, which initially scattered the Vikings. But when he settled down at Montmartre, groups of Vikings escaped upriver to ravage Burgundy. With no coherent system to deal with Vikings, Charles was again forced to pay them "protection money" amounting to 700 pounds of silver to lift the siege and leave Paris in spring 887. The Parisians were furious with the emperor, but their heroic resistance had put their city back on the political map. This was confirmed after Emperor Charles's deposition and death in 888 when Count Odo was appointed king in West Francia.

❧

The Paris siege was a climactic incident in a terrible onslaught that lasted from 789 until about 950. Not only was it the first long, drawn-out incident of resistance to the Vikings. It was also the first time Vikings settled down for a long siege. What is most significant is that they were not successful. Although it was a signal that Viking power was weakening, the reality was that raiding parties were eventually defeated more by nature than by Franks. A severe drought in 892 led to a small harvest, famine, and disease. With slim pickings the Vikings retired from West Francia to focus on attacking Britain.

Besides death and destruction, Viking influence on Europe had cultural consequences as well. Marriages between pagan Vikings and Christians hastened

conversion to the latter's Christian faith. Christianity was also penetrating the
Scandinavian homelands as Viking leaders entered into arrangements of con-
venience with Christian rulers. The process often combined aspects of both
Scandinavian religion and Christianity. Widukind of Corvey says, "The
Danes previously became Christians, but none the less they worship idols
with pagan rites."[25] Population pressures in Scandinavia and favorable climate conditions owing to the MWP led to Viking emigration and the establishment of colonies in the Shetland Islands, the Faroes, and, eventually,
Iceland, where they discovered that Irish hermit-monks had preceded them by
two hundred years. The monks traveled to the most isolated places, including
Iceland, seeking solitude.

Early Viking settlement in Iceland was characterized by blood feuds, but in
930 the settlers decided to form a kind of aristocratic-democratic parliament,
the *Althing*. It was this body that around the millennium formally decided to
adopt Catholicism. The recently converted Norwegian king, Olaf Trygvversön,
who had been baptized in England, sent a German missionary named Thang-
brand in 995, but he had little success with the Icelanders. Olaf was displeased
and conveyed this to them in no uncertain terms. Fearing the king, they debated in the *Althing* the wisdom of converting to Catholicism. In the year 1000
they decided to accept the new faith, which brought them into contact with
Latin culture and literacy and made them part of the broader Christian community. This, in turn, enhanced trade and established wider contacts.

Greenland was settled from Iceland in 986 because the North Atlantic sea
ice retreated sufficiently for Icelanders to reach the island, despite unpredictable
weather and fogs. The settlers, led by multiple murderer Eric the Red, discovered that the southwestern coast of Greenland provided just enough land to
begin subsistence agriculture. The retreat of the sea ice resulting from the MWP
also enabled the most daring Greenlanders to discover and briefly settle what
they called "Vinland" on the eastern Canadian coast. Recent archaeological evidence indicates that they landed and colonized the northeastern tip of New-
foundland at L'Anse aux Meadows for about three years. At first they traded red
cloth for pelts with the Native Americans (called *Skraelings* in Norse), but conflict broke out and the Vikings departed in about 1002, never to return. The
settlement in Greenland, however, was well established, and it was not until
the LIA in the mid-fifteenth century and renewed freezing of the North Atlantic that the settlement collapsed.

The Vikings also had enormous influence on Anglo-Saxon and Irish history, and we will return to them when discussing Britain and Ireland. But of all of the threats to Christian Europe at this time, the greater menace was the explosive spread of Islam.

☙

Islam, which in Arabic means "submission" to Allah (God), is a strictly monotheistic religion that began in seventh-century Arabia. Its prophet, Muhammad, whom Muslims consider to be the last and most important prophet, claimed that Islam's holy book, the Qur'an, was literally dictated to him by the archangel Gabriel in Arabic, Muhammad's native language. After the death of the Prophet in 632, Islam was spread by mullahs (Arabic-speaking preachers). Their task was made easier by the fact that Islam is an essentially simple religion without complex doctrines.

It was also spread by military campaigns, which proved spectacularly successful. Muslims already controlled much of Arabia before Muhammad's death, and the Arabs quickly overran the Christian Byzantine provinces of Palestine in 636, Syria in 640, Egypt in 642, and Cyprus in 649. Pressure on the Byzantine Empire was relentless, and contemporaries questioned whether it could survive the onslaught. Constantinople itself was besieged several times between 674 and 678. After destroying the Persian (Sassanid) Empire, the Muslim expansion pushed westward across Christian North Africa from Egypt, taking Carthage in 698 and reaching Tangier on the Strait of Gibraltar in 708. Spain was invaded in 711. The Islamic advance swept through the Iberian Peninsula and crossed the Pyrenees, taking Toulouse in 721. The armies were finally stopped by Frankish leader Charles, whose infantry defeated them at the Battle of Poitiers-Tours on October 25, 732. Charles was given the title *martellus* (the hammer), becoming Charles Martel. It had taken one hundred years for this burst of Islamic expansionism to run out of steam. Meanwhile, the *dar-al-Islam*, the "house of Islam," grew enormously.

Slowly, the armies of Europe began to push back at the edges. In 752 a Frankish counteroffensive began under Pippin III "the Short," gradually pushing the Muslims back over the Pyrenees. Pippin's son Charlemagne continued the campaign, and between 777 and 795 he drove the Arabs back to the Ebro River. This remained the border between Christian and Muslim Spain (al-Andalus, as it was called) for most of the tenth century. This counterattack and stabilization by Pippin and Charlemagne corresponded to a revival of Byzantine military fortunes under Emperor Leo III (717–741), when parts of Asia Minor were recovered.

Nevertheless, Islamic forces continued to probe and exploit the vulnerabilities of the Byzantine Empire, as well as defining the borders of Europe by control of North Africa and much of the Iberian Peninsula, thereby ensuring that Latin Christendom was confined to Europe and its offshore islands, Britain, Scotland, and Ireland. Throughout the ninth and tenth centuries, the *sà'ifa*, the Saracen summer campaign, became a semiconstant threat to the whole of the southern flank of Europe. Belgian historian Henri Pirenne argues that the Arab conquests cut Europe off from the Mediterranean world and stunted its economic growth.[26] What's more important was that Islamic control of the Mediterranean isolated Latin Christianity, confined it to Europe, and hastened its separation from the Eastern Church. This division was to become de facto complete in the eleventh century.

As of the early ninth century, Islam was into its second expansionist phase. Two new powers were emerging in North Africa: the al-Idrisi in Morocco and the Aglabid dynasty in present-day Algeria, Tunisia, and parts of Libya. The Aglabids took Malta in 870 and invaded Byzantine Sicily in 878. They encouraged the Saracen pirates, deploying them to further harass southern Italy. Throughout Rome and central Italy a sense of dread arose that the Arabs, as Barbara M. Kreutz says, were "closing in, moving to take over the whole of the central Mediterranean."[27] In response to these threats, a kind of "border Christianity" evolved in which negotiations with the Saracens became part of the political fabric of southern and central Italy.[28] As we saw, southern Italy was made up of a number of small Christian principalities and statelets, as well as a swath of Byzantine-held territory. Often as a way of outflanking their rivals, these statelets made common cause with the Saracens, inviting them in as mercenaries. This led to widespread destabilization in the region until the defeat of the Saracens at the Battle of Garigliano in 915.

Rome was particularly attractive to the Saracens, with its rich churches and shrines. As the center of Christianity, it also drew Muslim warriors imbued with a notion of *jihad*, "holy war," a sense that the fundamental aim of the pious Muslim was the expansion of Islam and the conversion of nonbelievers. Rome's economy declined as Saracen threats to the alpine passes led to a decrease in the number of pilgrims from northern Europe. Pope John VIII, who had unsuccessfully used both bribes and diplomacy to try to unite the southern Italian principalities against the Saracens, commented that they were "making themselves perfectly at home" in the Campagna and were often close to the walls of Rome with their slave raids, violence, and killing.[29] Citizens could no longer venture outside the walls to harvest their crops. At the same time, the Muslims continued to pressure Byzantine Sicily, finally conquering the whole island in 902. The consequence was that the Mediterranean effectively became an Islamic lake.

Saracen pirates were also active along the Provencal coastline. Liutprand claims twenty Saracens from al-Andalus driven off course in 888 landed on the French Riviera coast, slaughtered the local Christians, and established a base at Fraxinetum, nowadays La Garde Freinet, on a ridge in the wooded Massif des Maures (Massif of the Moors), 1,300 feet (400 meters) above St. Tropez. He says that the Saracens initially protected themselves with the sharp bramble bushes that grew there. They encouraged it "to grow even taller and thicker than before, so that if anyone stumbled against a branch it ran through him like a sharp sword."[30] Just as the Vikings benefited from strife in the Carolingian empire, so the Saracens took advantage of the breakdown of order in Provence. "Swayed by envy and mutual jealousy [the Provencals] began to cut one another's throats, plunder each other's substance and do every sort of conceivable mischief. . . . They called in the help of the aforesaid Saracens, men who were as perfidious as they were cunning and in company with them proceeded to crush their neighbours."[31] This was another example of border Christianity, which the Saracens exploited as they picked off one local warlord through alliance with another.

New recruits came to Fraxinetum from al-Andalus, and they were soon attacking monasteries in Provence. They pushed on into the alpine passes, where they threatened some of Europe's most important trade and communication routes. Flodoard reports that in 921, 936, 939, 940, and 951 pilgrims traveling to and from Rome were attacked. In 921 the Saracens caused a landslide that killed a group of *transmarini*—"people from across the sea," that is, English pilgrims, and later groups from both France and England were attacked on their way across the Alps.[32] J. E. Tyler says that the Saracens "spread along the axis of the Alps . . . [and] they seem to have been excellent mountaineers." They established seasonal bases near the routes across the mountains, threatened the Great Saint Bernard Pass, and in 940 penetrated the upper Rhône region, destroying St. Maurice and going as far north as St. Gall.[33] In 972 they captured Abbot Maiolus of Cluny as his party crossed the Great Saint Bernard. They were shrewd enough to extract 1,000 pounds of silver in ransom for him from Cluny, but not before he engaged in religious disputation with them. Various attempts were made to dislodge these Saracens, but it was not until Otto I decided to deal with them once and for all that William of Arles intervened to destroy the Fraxinetum base in 972 to forestall the arrival of the German emperor.

One of the most terrifying aspects of the Saracen raids was their practice of seizing prisoners to sell into slavery. The *Annals of Saint-Bertin* records a Saracen attack in 838 on Marseilles in which they "carried off all the nuns, of whom there was a large number living there, as well as all the males, both clergy and laymen, laid waste to the town and took away with them en masse the treasures of Christ's churches."[34] They then sold these nuns and priests into slavery. Besides those they captured from mainland Europe, the main sources of slaves for the Islamic world were sub-Saharan Africa, Slavs from Eastern Europe, Turks from Central Asia, and, to a lesser extent, Anglo-Saxons, whom they valued for their fair skin. The word "slave" is actually derived from "Slav" rather than from the Latin *servus*, meaning "servant."

Slavery was not common in Western Europe at the time; there were only a small number of slaves to be found there. The great majority was in the Byzantine and Islamic worlds. The Catholic Church disapproved of slavery, but Welsh and Irish slaves, many still adolescents, who had been captured by the Vikings, were nonetheless sold through ports like Hull, Bristol, Venice, and Barcelona to meet demand in the Islamic world. Jews were often blamed for maintaining the slave trade by being the middlemen. But Christians and, of course, Muslims were also involved. In the west Verdun, Lyons and Venice were the main slave-trading centers, with Córdoba and Cairo the principal markets in the Muslim world. Many male slaves destined for domestic service or the management of harems were castrated with the removal of their testes or penis, extremely painful operations done without painkillers.

As we saw, the Saracen threat in Italy was largely eliminated by the Italian victory at the battle on the Garigliano River near Minturno in 915. By the end of the tenth century, the Muslim world had dissolved into factions. Still, it remained united by Islam, a faith that stretched across North Africa, Spain, the Middle East, southern Russia, India, and western China. People of many races worshipped Allah, honored the Prophet, spoke and wrote Arabic, read the same scriptures, and shared interlocking economies.

Much has been made recently of Arab contribution to European knowledge—namely, that the Arabs preserved the philosophy of the Greco-Roman world at a time when unflattering comparisons could be made to the "primitiveness" and barbarism of Christian Europe. However, it is often forgotten in postmodernism's enthusiasm for multiculturalism and postcolonialism that almost all of this knowledge was nonetheless derived by the Arabs from Greek and Middle Eastern Christian sources in the first place or from India and China. The Arabs were a conduit for this knowledge rather than the originators of it. We shall look at this in more detail when we discuss Muslim Spain.

The question remains, however: How can we explain the sheer speed and overwhelming success of the Muslim onslaught? How did the Byzantine Empire lose three key provinces—Syria, Egypt, and Palestine—in a decade, to be followed by North Africa soon afterward? Part of the answer is that the Byzantines were caught flat-footed by the speed of events and by the fact that after Islam became supreme in Arabia, it was driven by an ideology of *jihad*, a determination to universalize itself and establish a Muslim world state. Islam assumes that everyone is "by nature" Muslim and that it is the duty of Muslims and Muslim states to spread Islam. Essentially, *jihad* is a kind of unrelenting and fervent missionary thrust that can be carried out either by persuasion or by the sword. There is a saying (hadith) ascribed to Muhammad comparing *jihad* to Christian monasticism: "The monasticism of the Muslim nation is the *jihad*." The Christian monasticism that Muhammad had seen was the intense commitment of desert hermits and the very strict religious communities.

Jihad highlights the essential difference between Byzantine and Muslim military attitudes at the time. For centuries, inspired by Christianity, the Byzantines had minimized aggressive war and had been primarily concerned with the defense of the empire's borders rather than conquest. So rather than taking the initiative and attacking the Muslims, the Byzantine emperors maintained a relatively defensive posture. They had inherited the Eastern Roman Empire and simply assumed that God had entrusted these Christian people to them to rule in peace. "The spirit of the [Byzantine] empire . . . had been by definition pacific. The proper Byzantines hated war; and one of the most urgent duties of their emperors was the preservation of peace, after the pattern of the Prince of Peace whom they claimed to represent."[35]

In fact, as philosopher Jacques Ellul points out, the notion of war as a means of spreading the faith actually finds it origin in Islam. "War is inherent in Islam. It is inscribed in its teaching. . . . It is coherent with its conception . . . that the whole world is destined to become 'Muslim' because, at heart, 'Islam is the only religion that conforms perfectly to nature.'"[36] Ellul argues that early Christianity was always suspicious of war given the teaching of Jesus that enemies must be forgiven and loved. But the Christians learned from the Muslims, and by the eleventh century Christianity was infected with notions of crusades and holy wars. Ellul also argues that Islam created a paramountcy of law over love in which law became the preeminent value. The jurist replaced the theologian. This flowed into a preoccupation with canon law and its subsequent dominance in Catholicism.

❧

The Magyars were the third external threat to the stability of Western Christendom. A Finno-Ugor people who first appeared on the eastern Frankish borders in 862, the Magyars came originally from the western slopes of the Ural Mountains near the Volga River. They then seem to have moved to southern Russia, north of the Black Sea. They were adept at fast-moving warfare on their small, wiry horses. The reasons for their westward movement in the late ninth century are unclear. Certainly, the Pechenegs, another seminomadic people allied to the Bulgarians, played a role when they attacked the Magyar homeland while the Magyar main force was absent invading the Slav kingdom of Great Moravia. "In order to prevent another surprise Pecheneg attack, Árpád [the Magyars' elected leader] made a westward move with his decimated people, to find a permanent home in the mid-Danubian Carpathian basin."[37]

Once settled in these central European grasslands, the Magyars seized the same opening as the Vikings and the Arabs did: they quickly realized that the internecine strife of Western Europe provided them with easy pickings. The Magyars were consummate tacticians. In battle they moved swiftly and were past masters at feigning retreats and then doing an about-face, encircling their enemies and mowing them down with a rain of bone-tipped arrows fired while still on horseback. In his *Taktika* the Byzantine emperor Leo VI the Wise (886–912) discusses Magyar strategy (he calls them "Turks") at length. He says that they were "very numerous and independent . . . [and] focus[ed] their attention only on conducting themselves bravely against their own enemies." They were governed by fear, he says, rather than love, and they "steadfastly [bore] labors and hardships. They [bore] up under heat and cold, as well as . . . lack of necessities, since they [were] a nomadic people." He describes them as "meddlesome . . . hostile and faithless. Possessed by an insatiable desire for riches, they scorn[ed] their oaths and [did] not observe agreements they [had] made." Leo maintains that they achieved their ends "not so much as by brute force as by deceit, surprise attacks and deprivation of necessities." After describing their weapons, Leo emphasizes that they were great horsemen and that "they devote[d] a great deal of attention and training to archery on horseback." They always traveled with "a huge herd of horses, ponies and mares." Leo describes their battle tactics in detail, concluding that "they prefer[red] battles fought at long range, ambushes, encircling their adversaries, simulated withdrawals and wheeling about and scattered formations." They were ruthless in pursuit of enemies on the run, never satisfied until they had brought about their "complete destruction." They lived off the land and were "greatly hurt by a shortage of pasturage because of the large number of horses they [brought]." Leo says that "since they [had] grown up riding on horseback, they [did] not last long on foot" and that they were consequently poor at hand-to-hand combat. They never directly attacked fortified places, but blockaded them. They even used smoke signals as a way of keeping contact between warrior bands. In Western Europe they mounted raids that reached as far as Otranto in southern Italy and Nîmes in southern France, and they caused terror equal to that of the Vikings. However, unlike the Vikings, they never settled in the regions they raided.[38]

They remained largely unchecked until they were defeated by Otto I at the Battle of Lechfeld just south of Augsburg in August 955. Notably, most of the Magyar losses were sustained after the battle as they retreated across flooded rivers with German forces harassing them. After Lechfeld the Magyar leadership was faced with the reality that Otto I had brought unity to the German lands, and Western Europe was no longer so easy a target. Taksony, a new prince-leader, emerged in 955, and under his leadership the Magyars appear to have reassessed their policy of raiding. Christian missionaries from Byzantium and Germany began to penetrate the Hungarian homelands. So the people who, according to Liutprand, answered the "wondrous Christian cry 'Kyrie eleison' 'Lord have mercy upon us' . . . [with] the foul and diabolical shout 'Huj huj'" were now in close contact with the faith they were soon to adopt.[39] (The word *huj* in modern Hungarian means something like "hip," as in "hip, hip, hooray.")

Taksony died in 971 and was succeeded by his son Géza, who after an agreement with Otto II was baptized by Wolfgang of Regensburg, who had been sent by the bishop of Passau. Géza, whose conversion seems more political than religious, imposed Christianity on the Hungarians. Chronicler Thietmar of Merseburg (who calls him Deuvix) says that when he became a Christian, "he turned his rage against his reluctant subjects, in order to strengthen this faith. . . . [Nevertheless,] he sacrificed both to the omnipotent God and to various false gods. When reproached by his priest for doing so, however, he maintained that the practice had brought him both wealth and great power, . . . [His wife, Beleknegini,] drank immoderately and rode a horse like a warrior. Once, in a fit of anger, she killed a man."[40]

They sound like a lovely couple!

Despite widespread opposition to the imposition of Christianity, Géza consolidated central power by establishing a capital at Esztergom and raising an army, even though his policy was one of peace with his neighbors. His son Vajk was later baptized as Istvan-Stephen. Born in the early 970s, Stephen succeeded as ruler in 997. Well educated, he had to struggle to establish himself as king. It was he who consolidated Christianity in Hungary.

We've already seen how the enemies of Christianity could exploit the internal European divisions that resulted from the collapse of the Carolingian empire. We will now look at how these divisions developed into the political chaos from which the German kings rescued Europe and reestablished ordered government.

CHAPTER 5

The Dissention of Kings

T HE LARGEST, BLOODIEST, and most destructive battle of the ninth century began at 6 in the morning on Saturday, June 25, 841, at Fontenoy-en-Puisaye, now a tiny village 22 miles (35 kilometers) south of Auxerre in France. Exactly how many men took part is uncertain. We know that probably between 25,000 and 30,000 were killed and many more injured, which indicates large armies and extreme violence. This battle was fought as part of what German historians call the *Brüderkrieg*, "brother war." Emperor Lothar fought on one side against his brother Louis the German and their half-brother Charles the Bald on the other. All were sons of Louis the Pious, and this was just one incident in the long civil war fought between them. The battle signaled the end of any possibility of restoring the unified empire stretching across France, Germany, the Benelux countries, Italy, and northern Spain that the three combatants' father, Louis the Pious, had inherited from his father, Charlemagne. After the Battle of Fontenoy, the possibility of an ordered state and good government vanished in Western Europe.

The battle didn't have to end in such bloodshed. According to Nithardus's reliable *Four Books of Histories*, Charles and Louis had spent the previous three days negotiating with Lothar, begging him "to remember that they were brothers . . . [and] asking him 'to leave the Church of God and the whole Christian people in peace.'" They offered him generous terms. Nithardus, a well-educated public official and soldier in the service of Charles the Bald, says that Lothar equivocated. Pretending to consider Charles and Louis's pleas, he was actually playing for time, awaiting the arrival of troops under Pippin II of Aquitaine.

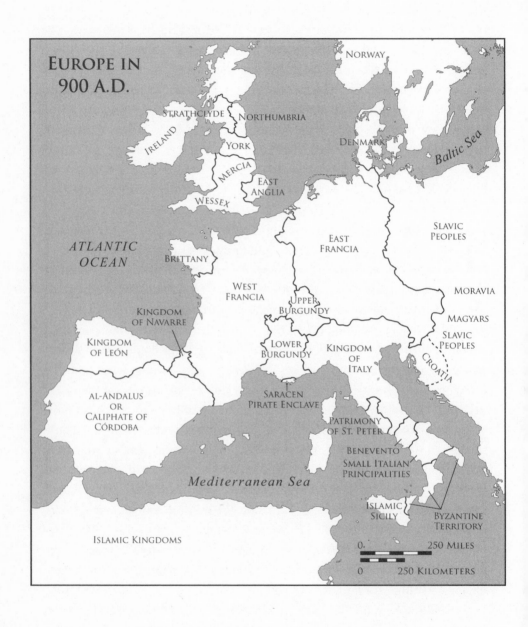

EUROPE IN
900 A.D.

NORWAY

STRATHCLYDE   NORTHUMBRIA

IRELAND   DENMARK   *Baltic Sea*

YORK

MERCIA   SLAVIC
EAST   PEOPLES
ANGLIA

WESSEX   EAST
                          FRANCIA
ATLANTIC
OCEAN   BRITTANY   MORAVIA

               WEST   MAGYARS
               FRANCIA   UPPER
KINGDOM   BURGUNDY   SLAVIC
OF NAVARRE   PEOPLES

KINGDOM   LOWER   KINGDOM   CROATIA
OF LEÓN   BURGUNDY   OF
                                     ITALY

AL-ANDALUS   SARACEN
OR   PIRATE ENCLAVE
CALIPHATE OF   PATRIMONY
CÓRDOBA   OF ST. PETER

                                     BENEVENTO
                          Mediterranean Sea SMALL ITALIAN
                                     PRINCIPALITIES

                                     ISLAMIC
                                     SICILY   BYZANTINE
                                                  TERRITORY
ISLAMIC KINGDOMS
                               0   250 MILES

                               0   250 KILOMETERS

Once Pippin arrived, Lothar broke off negotiations. So "Louis and Charles rose at dawn, occupied the peak of a mountain [it was actually a low hill] near Lothar's camp . . . and waited for Lothar's arrival and the striking of the second hour [6 a.m.]. . . . When both had come they fought a violent battle."[1]

The actual battlefield was a flat expanse surrounded by low hills. There seem to have been two interrelated fronts, as Charles and Louis attacked Lothar from separate low hills. Leading any of the armies at Fontenoy would have been difficult because tenth-century armies were not the highly organized and disciplined forces with clear lines of authority that we know today. The emperor or king would have been the overall leader, but his armies were made up of diverse units led by local warlords. Unused to cooperation with others, some of whom would have previously been their enemies, warlords would have found it difficult to submit to the king's instructions. The desire to achieve glory by exhibiting heroics would have been far stronger than any sense of discipline and obedience to the commander. Even though well trained and in good physical condition, the foot soldiers as well as the warlords would have been psyched up to enhance their reputation as warriors.

Tactics in this era were generally consistent from battle to battle. Action would begin with the terrifying war cries of foot soldiers. The core of the infantry was the *Heerbann*, a kind of trained militia. They usually opened the battle by moving forward in close formation protected by a strong shield wall. Their basic weapon was a long-handled throwing ax. Some wore light armor and used a stabbing sword. When the commander decided the time was right, he would order a mass charge of mounted knights, or any man who could afford a horse. Wearing body armor and carrying a spear as their primary offensive weapon and a shield for defense, the mounted troops usually rode sturdy Barb horses, a strong, wiry breed with a fiery temperament and good turn of speed, ideal for cavalry charges. Large massed cavalry charges would be followed by the kind of mounted hand-to-hand conflict between horsemen with swords that led to many of the injuries and deaths.

The Battle of Fontenoy proceeded indecisively for hours. It wasn't until about noon that finally a cavalry charge broke through Lothar's lines. This was followed by the bulk of the slaughter, in which many of the elite of the Frankish nobility were killed. According to the *Annals of Saint-Bertin* (which was sympathetic to Louis and Charles), "Many were slain on both sides; still more were wounded. Lothar suffered a shameful defeat and fled. The slaughter of fugitives continued . . . until Louis and Charles, aflame with generous feelings, ordered an end to the carnage."[2]

Nithardus, who fought in the battle, says, "The booty and slaughter were immense and truly astonishing." According to his telling, Charles and Louis "ceased fighting and plundering and returned to camp . . . to talk over what they ought to do next."[3] Next day they celebrated Mass, and the bishops who accompanied the armies asked for prayers and a three-day fast for the remission of the sins of both sides. While violent in combat, Frankish foot soldiers were otherwise generally well disciplined, sober, and religious, believing that God was on their side. They were supported by a well-organized commissariat. Accompanying this was a bevy of camp followers, including merchants who supported the army with supplies and brought women who prepared food and did other tasks and who acted as prostitutes when needed. The merchants always defended their supplies, and they were notorious for being drunken, lecherous, and foul-mouthed.

Fontenoy was unlike modern battles. It was not the impersonal, industrial-style modern warfare of World Wars I and II. It was man-to-man, one-on-one combat with long (5-foot, or 1.5-meter) and short (3-foot, or 1-meter) swords, spears, and lances (6 feet, or 2 meters), daggers (6 inches to 1 foot long), and crossbows and hand axes, all weapons that inflicted terrible wounds. Alain Mounier Kuhn has examined many medieval sources describing wounds and has found that more than half were to head, face, and neck. The most effective weapons were lances, swords, and bows and arrows. Body armor seems to have protected the torso, so most injuries were to the upper body, and Kuhn says that many injuries seem to have been sustained when soldiers were unable to defend themselves.[4] It was personal and brutal, kill or be killed. Part of the explanation for this kind of fighting was that people then were much more easily stirred up emotionally, violence was more generally accepted, and, as noted earlier, personal self-control was in short supply. Also, a warrior satisfied his lust for glory by killing, while at the same time believing that God was on his side. And given the nature of the weapons used (with the exception of longbows or crossbows), the only way the warrior could kill someone was up close and personal. Many also died soon afterward of the terrible slashing wounds inflicted, especially in light of ninth-century medicine. For many it would have been better to have been killed outright.

පෘ

So what was the cause of the *Brüderkrieg*, and why were these brothers engaged in such a vicious civil war?

The empire of Charlemagne looms large over the history of the ninth and tenth centuries. Charlemagne—or Carolus Magnus (Charles the Great)—inherited the kingdom of the Franks from his grandfather Charles Martel, the victor over the Muslims at Poitier-Tours, and his father, Pippin III "the Short." Charlemagne, a very tall, thin man, in contrast to his father Pippin, ruled from 768 to 814 and was crowned Holy Roman Emperor on Christmas Day 800 in Saint Peter's in Rome by Pope Leo III. He expanded the Frankish kingdom from the original heartlands in the Low Countries, southwestern Germany, and northern France to include the whole of present-day Germany, France, northern and central Italy, and northeastern Spain. Charlemagne established an efficient government and promoted education, church and monastic reform, and missions among the pagan people he had conquered.

However, Charlemagne's empire was always an artificial construct, held together largely by his powerful personality. None of his successors were able to wield it into a unified whole. Its breakup was gradual, the result not only of structural problems, but also of inexorable centrifugal forces. Disparate peoples with separate histories, laws, languages, and traditions were unwilling to be bound together into a single polity unless the ruler was strong enough to maintain unity. As Jacques Le Goff says, the Franks, despite their effort to assimilate the administrative inheritance of Rome, "had not acquired a sense of the state."[5] So after Charlemagne's death in 814 the empire began collapsing into its component parts.

The empire suffered from other stresses as well. Its northern and eastern borders were consistently under pressure from Vikings, Slavs, and Magyars, and the southern borders from the Saracens. And in the end, the empire simply ran out of rulers!

Frankish kings treated their kingdoms as private property, so they divided their kingdoms among all their sons. When two of Charlemagne's three sons predeceased him, his remaining son, Louis, inherited the entire empire. Charlemagne left Louis a state that extended from the Elbe River to northern Spain and from the North Sea to south of Rome. Actually Louis's French title, *le Débonnaire* (kindly or easygoing), is probably more accurate than what we call him in English (Louis the Pious) to describe his personality. With his brothers dead and other possible rivals such as his bastard half-brothers Drogo and Hugh under house arrest, Louis succeeded uncontested.

Louis moved quickly to secure the succession that would follow his own death. In 817 he issued the *Ordinatio Imperii*, the "Imperial Ordinance," dividing the empire among his three sons. The eldest, Lothar, was crowned as coemperor. Louis appointed his other two sons, Pippin and Louis, kings so that "after our decease they may hold sway with regal power under their elder brother."[6] Lothar received the traditional Frankish heartlands around Aachen, northern France, and the Low Countries. Pippin received Aquitaine, Gascony, and the March of Toulouse, essentially present-day southern France between the Loire and northern Spain. Louis the German received Bavaria, Carinthia (modern southern Austria), Saxony, and the eastern frontier region. In 822 Italy was added to Lothar's portion after the barbaric blinding and death of Louis's nephew Bernard, who had been king of Italy.

Although the empire was still conceived of as one and indivisible, it would be hard to find a better recipe for disaster than Louis's *Ordinatio Imperii*. The Frankish inheritance system had no conception of primogeniture: the right of the eldest son to inherit everything and thus keep the state intact. The centrifugal forces let loose by this arrangement put irresistible strain on the empire's already inadequate administrative structures. The result was that even in his own lifetime, Louis was constantly on the defensive trying to satisfy and, in a series of three civil wars, fight his own ambitious sons. Things became even more complex when Louis married a second time after his first wife, Ermengard, died in October 818. His second wife, Judith, produced a son named Charles in 823. He later became known as Charles the Bald. Louis had to find an additional kingdom for him. Resentments were simmering, and the *Brüderkrieg* was already becoming inevitable long before Louis's reign concluded.

In the spring of 830 a complex series of events involving the defense of Barcelona against the Muslims provoked a violent confrontation among Louis's sons and advisers arising from long-simmering resentments. First Pippin, then Louis the German, revolted against their father. Lothar, who was in Italy, rushed back to Aachen to protect his own interests. Louis the Pious was summarily overthrown in a palace coup and confined in a monastery. Lothar assumed power, but the sons' revolt was short-lived. Pippin and Louis the German, chaffing under their elder brother's authority, quickly turned against him and began plotting to restore their father's authority, which occurred in October 830. But the easygoing Louis was unwilling to punish his sons. Lothar was confined to Italy, and the others got off scot-free.

Things blew up again in midsummer 833. This time all three brothers conspired to overthrow their father. A brief civil war ensued in the summer of 834, ending in defeat for Lothar, who was relegated once again to Italy. Louis the German was confined to Bavaria. In late 837 at the instigation of Empress Judith, Louis gave Charles the Bald Frisia (the coastal area north of the Rhine) and the region between the Seine and the Loire. When Louis's second son, Pippin, died in 838, the emperor gave Charles the northern part of Aquitaine, infuriating his grandson, Pippin II, who was eventually captured and imprisoned.

That same year Louis the German and Lothar were plotting again, sparking a confrontation between Emperor Louis the Pious and his son Louis the German at Nijmegen in May 838. The *Annals of Saint-Bertin* reports that "there was a great argument, quite different from what ought to have happened. Louis [the German] lost whatever territory beyond and on this side of the Rhine he had wrongfully withdrawn from his father's authority . . . namely Alsace, Saxony, Thuringia, Austrasia [an area that includes eastern France, southwestern Germany, and the Benelux countries] and Alemannia [central-eastern France, French-speaking Switzerland, Alsace, and southern Germany]."[7] But an imperial decree was one thing; actually repossessing the territory was another. The emperor's primary aim was to get more territory for Judith's son, Charles the Bald. So in a move to isolate Louis the German, he proposed carving up the empire into two parts, one for Lothar, the other for his half-brother, Charles. Louis was to be squeezed out and confined to Bavaria. The emperor and Lothar sealed this agreement at Worms in May 839. But Louis the German still held much of Franconia (central southern Germany) and the area between Bavaria and the Rhine, and in spring 839 the emperor and Louis confronted each other across the Rhine near Mainz. After the imperial forces succeeded in crossing the river, Louis retreated to Bavaria. His father didn't pursue him, most likely because he was facing his final illness.

Louis the Pious died at age sixty-two on June 20, 840, in his hunting lodge "on an island in the Rhine downstream from Mainz, and within sight of the [imperial] palace of Ingelheim."[8] Louis had certainly been *débonnaire*, easygoing, kindly, and forgiving of his power-hungry sons. But this doesn't explain what Roger Collins correctly calls "the apparently suicidal behaviour of the Frankish empire" under him.[9] What were the causes of the empire's implosion?

Essentially, the Carolingian empire didn't correspond to political, social, economic, and linguistic reality on the ground and was thus irrelevant to most of its citizens. It was the ideological construct of a group of ecclesiastical advisers of Charlemagne who envisaged an empire modeled on Rome, but who failed to set up a strong administration able to withstand the political and strategic difficulties of Louis's reign, let alone the inherent differences that characterized the peoples who made up the empire. Localism increasingly dominated people's experience as central authority broke down. This opened the way for local strongmen to seize power at a local level. This trend only worsened after Louis's death.

But just before we proceed with the story of the break-up of Charlemagne's empire, let's take a look at the considerable influence that Jews had in this period, especially at the court of Louis the Pious. This is illustrated by a story of a "distressing scandal" that was "bewailed by all the children of the Catholic church" and that rocked the court of Louis the Pious and his second wife, Judith. In 839

> the rumor spread . . . that the Deacon Bodo, an Aleman by birth and deeply imbued from his earliest childhood in the Christian religion with the scholarship of the court clergy and with sacred and secular learning, a man who only the previous year had requested from the Emperor and the Empress to go on pilgrimage to Rome and had been granted this permission and been loaded with many gifts: this man seduced by the enemy of the human race had abandoned Christianity and converted to Judaism. . . . Thus he was circumcised, let his hair and beard grow and adopted . . . the name of Eleazer. He assumed a warrior's gear, [and] married a Jew's daughter . . . [and] entered the Spanish town of Zaragoza.[10]

In other words, the well-educated and well-connected court deacon Bodo from Alemannia, who was much favored by Louis and Judith and who had many friends and supporters at court, had not undertaken his planned trip to Rome at all. He had fled to Muslim Spain, where he abandoned Christianity, was circumcised, changed his name to Eleazer, declared himself a Jewish believer, and married a Jewish woman. He then actively tried to convert Christians in al-Andalus to Judaism and engaged in vigorous controversy with Christian scholars. Many people at the time were highly scandalized and angry at what they saw as a betrayal of Emperor Louis and the Catholic faith.

The story seems extraordinary because it apparently comes out of left field. But there is a context for it. Christian scholars were fascinated with Old Testament notions of kingship and the surprising fact that there really was a short period in the mid-ninth century when the influence of the study of Old Testament Judaism was so great that it almost converted other influential court intellectuals from Christianity to Judaism. There is a sense in which Bodo was just the tip of the iceberg. A key issue here was the influence of the Hebrew Scriptures (the Old Testament) on tenth-century notions of kingship and the reaction of conservative Christians to what was perceived as excessive Jewish influence on the ruling elite.

Under Charlemagne and Louis the Pious, Jews were protected by law and were granted a limited degree of self-government, and wealthy and influential Jews had ready access to the emperor. They were trusted, and many were quite successful in local business and had a dominant role in long-distance commerce. They were largely free to build synagogues and practiced their faith in the vernacular so that gentiles could understand their sermons. Jewish intellectual and social life developed in the Frankish world. Christians were not allowed to proselytize Jews without permission.

But this led to a reaction, and in this reaction we see the first appearance of medieval anti-Semitism. We have already met Bishop Agobard of Lyons. He was the author of several anti-Jewish tracts, the most comprehensive being *De iudaicis superstitionibus et erroribus* (Concerning the Superstitions and Errors of the Jews). He was well informed on Jewish life and practice, but it was his desire for a unified Christian world that led him to attack the Jews. He was very influenced by what he saw in his own diocese and was deeply concerned that Christians were not allowed to attempt to convert Jews; he saw this as a denial of the New Testament commands to go and convert all nations. As a kind of wedge issue, he demanded that the authorities attend to the problem of the baptism of gentile slaves. While he himself was not essentially anti-Semitic, the kind of tracts that he wrote provided the basis for the evolution of medieval and later anti-Semitism.

❧

In the immediate aftermath of Louis the Pious's death, the inevitable finally came to pass. The arrangements of 839 whereby the empire was to be divided among Lothar I, Charles the Bald, and Louis the German simply didn't work. None of Louis's sons were competent rulers in their own right. All, however, were very ambitious, and things could only get worse.

The impulsive Lothar was the first to make a move. He hurried to Aachen, assumed the imperial crown, and demanded oaths of fidelity from the most powerful magnates and bishops. Afraid to tackle Louis the German, who had consolidated his territories in southern Germany, Franconia, and Bavaria, Lothar turned on his younger half-brother, Charles the Bald. In so doing, he inadvertently created an alliance between Charles and Louis. The half-brothers went to war against Lothar and defeated him at the Battle of Fontenoy. After Lothar fled back to Aachen, low-level warfare continued. Lothar used terror tactics, including burning, rape, sacrilege, and thieving from church treasuries, to try to weaken his brothers. Meanwhile, the ever-opportunistic Vikings used the power vacuum to attack Rouen; they "plundered the town with pillage, fire and sword, slaughtered or took captive the monks and the rest of the population, and laid waste all the monasteries and other places along the banks of the Seine, or else took large payments and left them thoroughly terrified."[11]

As the civil war dragged on, Louis and Charles met at Strasbourg on February 14, 842, to strengthen their alliance and commit to each other through *sacramenta*, public oaths of commitment. What was most interesting about their meeting were the languages they used in the actual exchange of oaths and in the speeches they gave. Most of Louis's Germanic army would have spoken Old High German (*lingua teudusca*), while Charles's troops (a mixture of Frankish, old Roman, and Gallic stocks from central, southern, and western France) would have spoken a French Romance language (*lingua romana*), derived mainly from Vulgar Latin, which was the forerunner of French, Italian, and Spanish. The oaths are preserved in their original form in Nithardus's *Histories*. These are, in fact, the earliest examples we have of the languages used by ordinary people in this period. These two quite distinct languages were already beginning to emerge among ordinary people who could not read or speak the Latin that was the language of the church, officials, and public records. This language shift was symbolic of a deeper cleavage between what was to become Germany and France, with a kind of in-between region that was the realm of Lothar, Lotharingia, or Alsace-Lorraine as it was later called.

For the rest of 842 the three brothers engaged in inconclusive military maneuvering against one another. Lothar abandoned Aachen, taking with him "a silver plate of wonderful size and beauty. On it there shone a map of the whole world and it also showed the stars and . . . the planets."[12] It had belonged to Charlemagne, but Lothar had it cut up to bribe his deserting troops and induce them to stay loyal to him. Meanwhile, the Vikings and Saracens were making the most of the chaos, attacking and asset-stripping Quentovic on the northern French coast. Simultaneously, Moorish pirates sailed up the Rhône "to near Arles, ravaging everything on their route. . . . [They] got away again completely unscathed, their ships loaded with booty."[13]

In 841 Louis the German faced the *Stellinga* revolt in Saxony. The *Stellinga* were free peasants who had enjoyed considerable political influence before their forced conversion to Christianity under Charlemagne. This was a rare example of popular revolt, and Louis put it down by force in 845.

Despite his posturing and the fact that he bribed his soldiers to stay loyal to him, Lothar was unable to secure his military position, so he sued for peace. An initial meeting of the brothers occurred on June 15, 842, on an island in the Saône River just south of Mâcon. "There mutual forgiveness was sought and given for all the wrongs they had done to each other in the past, and each swore to his brothers an oath of peace and fraternity." A further meeting was planned "to make detailed arrangements for the division of the whole realm into equal parts."[14] Despite Louis the German and Charles the Bald's ongoing distrust of Lothar, the meeting eventually convened on October 19 in Koblenz to divide the realm. There *realpolitik* intervened, and the brothers decided they needed the consent of the powerful landowning warlords and magnates before making a division, so "they arranged a peace among themselves until they would be able to know which of these proposals their lords would be willing to accept."[15] While this was carried out, a series of truces were arranged until they reached a final agreement at Verdun in August 843.

No written copy of the Verdun treaty survives, but it essentially divided Charlemagne's empire into three more or less equal parts. The *Annals of Saint-Bertin* says that "Louis [the German] got everything east of the Rhine and on this side of [the river] he got the *civitates* and districts of Speyer, Worms and Mainz." Lothar got the lands

> between the Rhine and the Scheldt where it runs into the sea and . . . the
> counties which lie next to each other on the western side of the Meuse down
> as far as where the Saône runs into the Rhône, and down the Rhône to
> where it flows into the sea, likewise with the counties situated on both sides
> of it. . . . Charles himself was given everything else as far as Spain. Solemn
> oaths were sworn and everyone departed.[16]

Essentially, Lothar got a strip of land stretching from present-day Nether-lands in a southward direction between the Rhine and the Meuse and over the Alps into Italy. Louis and Charles received what were substantially to become Germany and France. Even though these nation-states were still centuries away, as early as the ninth century there was a linguistic and cultural coherence about them. Lothar seemingly received the lion's share of the spoils—including the imperial title and the major capitals of Aachen, Pavia, and Rome. However, he received contested territory and an inheritance that lacked cultural, linguistic, or geographical unity.

While all three ruled in their own right, the idea of an *imperium Chris-tianum*, a "Christian empire," under the collegial rule of the brothers survived. Nevertheless, their relationships constantly shifted, and trust and distrust of each other seemed to be in equal proportions. Lothar tried to subvert his broth-ers' realms by appealing to restive elements within them. He supported Pippin II of Aquitaine against Charles the Bald, and it was not until 848 that Pippin was defeated at Toulouse. Lothar also gave covert support to the *Stellinga* revolt in Saxony against Louis the German. In turn, Charles, and to a lesser extent Louis, lusted after Lothar's less cohesive and more easily divided kingdom.

After Verdun there was tentative peace among the brothers, but the three realms were still under external pressure. The years 844–845 brought a hard, cold winter and Vikings who "ravaged Charles' kingdom, [and] came by boat up the Seine as far as Paris," where they were bribed to depart in peace. "In Frisia . . . [the Vikings] fought three battles. In the first they were indeed de-feated but in the remaining two they were victorious and killed a great number of men. They also destroyed a castle in Saxony called Hamburg."[17]

Even nature seemed to conspire with the enemy. The cold winter brought "a terrible famine" in western Francia, and many thousands died.[18] In 846 there were summer floods. In May 849 Louis and Charles met and declared that they were "held by such strong bonds of fraternal affection" that they exchanged scepters and commended realm, wife, and children to each other if one of them died. But that "affection" was often strained.[19]

Nithardus's *Histories* describes the half-brothers as "both of medium height, handsome and graceful, and expert in every kind of exercise. Both were bold and generous as well as prudent and well-spoken. . . . Anything of value they possessed they gave to each other in great kindness."[20] This description is, of course, too good to be true; these are idealized kingly types rather than personal descriptions. Nithardus says, no doubt accurately, that they also often engaged in war games; it was good exercise and gave warriors a chance to develop and maintain their skills.

The reality, however, was that Louis the German was the senior party. He was seventeen years older than Charles, and on occasion it suited him to forget his fraternal affection and invade Charles's kingdom. For instance, in 858, according to the *Annals of Fulda*, restive elements in Charles's realm told Louis they "could no longer stand [his] tyranny. . . . Anything that was left to them, after the pagans from outside [the Vikings] had plundered, enslaved, killed and sold them off without even a show of resistance being made to them, the king [Charles] destroyed from within by his evil savagery." Produced in Louis's kingdom, the *Annals of Fulda* puts the best interpretation on his actions. The annalist says that everything Louis did was not done "out of a desire to extend his kingdom" but "out of concern for the people's well-being" in Charles's kingdom.[21] When Louis crossed the border, Charles offered only token resistance, and little actual fighting occurred. Eventually, Louis had to withdraw because of a revolt on his eastern frontier. Often the half-brothers seem to have been posturing and stumping rather than being serious about war against each other.

Meanwhile, Lothar, who was always the odd one out, abdicated, "worn down by illness and despairing of life." He became a monk at Prüm Abbey in the Ardennes forest but died six days later, on September 29, 855, at the age of sixty.[22]

In the usual Frankish fashion, Lothar had already arranged for his kingdom to be divided among his three sons, none of whom had legitimate male heirs. The eldest, Louis II, already ruled northern Italy, having been made coemperor in 850 by Pope Leo IV. The youngest son, Charles "the Child" (he was ten), received Burgundy. The second son, Lothar II, received the rest, essentially what are today the Benelux countries as well as the Rhineland and the French-German borderland. This further division led to a very complex situation because the male descendants of all three kings died young, the result of a combination of illness and misadventure. It also opened the way for the most powerful landholding magnates and the church to accumulate increasing local power and influence, thus further weakening the central governments of each realm. The Vikings continually threatened Charles's and Lothar II's territories, and the winter of 856–857 was severe, with "a serious pestilence" causing the death of "a sizeable part of the population."[23]

There was also a scandal precipitated by Lothar II's attempt to abandon his lawful marriage to Queen Theutberga. Lothar II had depended on the support of Theutberga's powerful family while establishing himself as king. By 857, no longer needing that support, Lothar was looking to get rid of her, and he accused her of sterility since she had not given him a male heir. What he really wanted was marry his mistress, Waldrada, with whom he had a son before his marriage to Theutberga. (Actually, even calling her his mistress is misleading—as we shall see, the definition of marriage in those times was not the same as our modern understanding.) When Theutberga refused to budge, Lothar accused her of incest involving anal intercourse with her brother Hugobert, a cleric, resulting in, Lothar claimed, an abortion. Though this is physiologically impossible, a fact that worldly wise contemporaries understood, others were confused, apparently including some bishops. Anal intercourse was considered a very serious sin, even between married partners. Theutberga denied the charges, and to support her claim, a champion of the Queen underwent an ordeal in boiling water. The theory behind this ordeal held that if the accused were innocent, her champion would not be injured. When her champion emerged unscathed, Theutberga was declared innocent and restored to her position. However, her troubles were not over; as the *Annals of Saint-Bertin* reports, "Instead of readmitting her to his bed, [Lothar] had her locked up."[24]

Lothar began divorce proceedings in 858. Exhausted by the situation, Theutberga apparently "confessed" that she had had an incestuous relationship with her brother to Lothar's archchaplain, Archbishop Gunther of Cologne. After Gunther publicly revealed what she had told him, she was dragged before a synod in Aachen in 860 to admit her "guilt," thus giving Lothar the excuse he had been searching for to abandon her. It also gave Theutberga an excuse to escape Lothar and enter a convent. Eventually, a synod at Aachen in April 862 granted Lothar his divorce, and he proceeded to marry Waldrada on Christmas Day 862.

But Theutberga had her revenge. She fled to the protection of Charles the Bald, then appealed to Pope Nicholas I, who deposed and excommunicated the blabber-mouthed Archbishop Gunther. Papal legates were sent to Metz (June 863) to examine the case, but they were suborned by Lothar and ultimately approved his marriage to Waldrada. Once Nicholas I learned that his legates had been bribed, he overturned their findings. A new legate threatened to excommunicate Lothar and reverse the Aachen synod's decision. During protracted and convoluted negotiations, Lothar, now desperate, introduced a new claim. He maintained that before his marriage to Theutberga, he and Waldrada had validly married. In August 865 Pope Nicholas ordered Lothar to take Theutberga back, excommunicating Waldrada. Once again exhausted, Theutberga retired again to her convent at Avenay. The new pope, Hadrian II (867–872), lifted Waldrada's excommunication, and she too retired to a convent. Lothar then set out for Rome to plead his case. But he died at Piacenza on August 8, 869, thus effectively solving the otherwise intractable problem.

The difficulty at the heart of this squabbling was that the definition of marriage was still nebulous, theologically speaking. Marriage was seen as a natural union between man and woman. The church got involved only in sorting out marriage breakdowns. Sacramental historian Joseph Martos says that "marriage was still a family matter similar to what it had been in the Roman Empire, and the clergy were not involved in wedding ceremonies except as guests."[25] Another problem arose in the difference among Roman and Frankish conceptions of what actually constituted marriage. In Rome the key issue was that spouses freely consented to be married to each other. The Frankish understanding was more fluid, involving family arrangements, a public ceremony, often with a priestly blessing, but "a spectrum of various types of marriage existed, creating confusion and thus ample room for manoeuvre for a figure such as Lothar."[26] It was not until the eleventh century that the church formally defined marriage as a sacrament. Martos also points out that before this occurred, the church had "no universal prohibition against divorce."[27]

As we have seen, there was considerable physiological confusion as well. During Lothar's divorce process, a group of bishops and laymen put a series of questions to theologian Archbishop Hincmar of Reims, the greatest Frankish bishop of the century. Referring specifically to the alleged incestuous relationship between Theutberga and her brother, they claimed that anal intercourse resulted in conception. They said that to hide her disgrace, "she had drunk a poison and aborted the off-spring."[28] In his long-winded, somewhat confused reply, Hincmar comments, "It is to be noted that scripture says that when a [virginal] woman receives semen through the male genital organ into the secret place of the womb . . . and [she] doesn't attract or receive the emission elsewhere or in another manner . . . what is conceived from the emitted semen is said by the same scripture to open the womb for the first birth." This, he says, can also "be learned by reading." He comments that it is unheard of for a

woman "to receive semen without intercourse," except in the case of the Blessed
Virgin Mary, "whose conception [of Jesus] did not result from nature, but
grace."[29] He suggests that Queen Theutberga's sterility might have resulted from
sorcery by Lothar's mistress, Waldrada. It is hard to see how anyone was the
wiser after reading Hincmar's reply!

Lothar II died in 869, and with no legitimate son to inherit his Lotharingian
realm, which was made up of the Low Countries, the Rhineland, and the
French-German borderland, was in peril. While his bastard son Hugh, then
aged about fourteen, gained some support from bishops and magnates, his un-
cles Charles the Bald and Louis the German moved quickly to subvert him.
Lotharingia was quickly divided between them in the Treaty of Meerssen (870).
The Rhineland and Alsace-Lorraine went to Louis and the Low Countries to
Charles.

Then on August 12, 874, Lothar II's brother Emperor Louis II died. At the
time of his death, he controlled northern Italy and the kingdom of Burgundy,
which then comprised French-speaking Switzerland and the Rhône region of
France. Pope John VIII (872–882) now took the initiative and invited Charles
the Bald to "be elected [emperor] for the honour and exaltation of the Holy
Roman Church and for the security of Christian people." The papal diplomat
who offered the crown to Charles was, of course, the then Bishop Formosus of
Porto. Accepting the invitation, Charles quickly crossed the Alps and was
crowned emperor by the pope in Rome on Christmas Day 875. Louis the German "was enraged at this and sent [his son Karlmann] with an army through
Bavaria to Italy. He himself . . . invaded Charles's kingdom. . . . But the army . . .
turned to plunder and seized or destroyed everything it found."[30] Charles hastened back to defend his realm, and by January 876 Louis had withdrawn.

Seven months later Louis the German himself was dead (August 876). Charles
the Bald took the opportunity of his half-brother's death to try to seize upper
Burgundy. But he was defeated at Andernach on the west bank of the Rhine just
upstream from Koblenz when an attempted surprise attack went badly wrong
on October 7, 876. Even the usually sympathetic *Annals of Saint-Bertin* criticizes
Charles and his army. Calling them "plunderers," it comments that "they now became the plunder of someone else. So total were the losses that those who did
manage to escape on horseback possessed, instead of spoils, only their own skins.
The rest were stripped of all they had by the local peasants; they had to cover
their private parts by wrapping themselves in grass and straw."[31]

Charles had already been seriously ill in 874 with dysentery, and in late 876 he had a bout of malaria. Two years after a miscarriage in March 875, Charles's second wife, Richildis, lost a second infant son at their favorite palace at Compiègne, north of Paris. The child had been born prematurely on the road at night after Richildis fled from their residence at Herstal following Charles's defeat at Andernach. For the first half of 877, Charles was extremely busy raising an enormous tribute to pay off the Vikings. He and Richildis then crossed the Alps to meet Pope John VIII in Pavia and to fulfill his oath to defend the Patrimonium, which was under attack from the Saracens from southern Italy. At the meeting Richildis was anointed empress. However, both pope and emperor hastily abandoned northern Italy after they heard that Louis the German's son Karlmann "was on his way [from Bavaria] to attack them with a huge body of troops." Then, compounding an already confused situation, Karlmann heard that "the emperor and Pope John were on their way to attack him with a huge body of troops, so he fled back" to Bavaria.[32]

On the return journey from Italy, Charles again became stricken with fever. He drank "a powder which his Jewish doctor Zedechias, whom he loved and trusted all too much, had given him to cure his sickness." The *Annals of Saint-Bertin* claims this was actually "a poison for which there was no antidote." He died on October 6, 877, "in a wretched little hut" on the Mont-Cénis Pass. Putrefaction quickly set in, and "because of the stench," his companions placed the body in a barrel lined with pitch, "but even this did nothing to get rid of the smell." So they buried him in a "little monastery" at Nantua.[33]

Charles had been an effective, extremely hard-working ruler, but much of his reign was subsumed by the Viking threat and family wrangling. He also had to confront separatist movements in the south and never really brought Aquitaine and southern France under his control. The focus of his power was the traditional Frankish heartlands in the north, but even there he had to struggle to maintain his authority with the magnates. In the latter part of his reign, he entrusted the government of the south to local aristocrats, which led them to claim increasing independence, prompting Hincmar of Reims to comment that Charles ruled more in name than in fact in the south.

What do we know about Charles as a person? What did he look like? Was he really bald? The nickname is certainly contemporary, so he may well have been bald, which would have amused his contemporaries. But it could have been an ironic nickname if he had been very hairy. We have nine extant portraits of him;

in those that are genuinely personal, he has a square jaw, an almost plump face, a prominent nose, and a long, thin moustache, but he is otherwise clean-shaven. Where we can see his head, he doesn't seem bald. He was energetic, persistent, and resourceful and could be pleasant or angry as circumstances demanded. He was two-faced like most "successful medieval kings: his friendly smile could win loyalty, his frown could terrify."[34] His ruthlessness was shown when he had his son Carloman, who had been forced into a monastery as a youth, blinded after he revolted in 870. Janet Nelson comments, "Contemporaries accepted that violence even within . . . the family might be a cruel necessity."[35]

Charles, unlike most of his contemporaries, was generally faithful to his wives, although his second, Richildis, may have first been his mistress. He was certainly fertile. His first wife, Ermentrude (d. 869), had eleven children and Richildis, three: altogether eight boys and six girls. His piety was conventional, with a devotion to Christ, the saints, and the liturgy. He used costume as a mark of rank effectively: the *Annals of Saint-Bertin* describes him at the Synod of Ponthion (876) dressed "in a gilded robe and clad in Frankish costume," surrounded by bishops "all clothed in their ecclesiastical vestments."[36]

Charles's death precipitated a crisis. Only one of his eight sons survived him, Louis "the Stammerer," who was forced to bribe powerful magnates to gain the crown. He died two years later in 879, aged thirty-three. He had three sons: Louis III, aged about fifteen; Carloman, fourteen; and a posthumously born son, Charles "the Simple." The young Louis III tried hard, but he had to deal with two aristocratic factions that forced a split in the realm, with Louis III ruling the north and Carloman II ruling Aquitaine and Burgundy. Louis III also had to confront the Vikings, and he had a victory over them at Saucourt near the mouth of the Somme in August 881. But he died prematurely in 882, and Carloman II followed him in winter 884 after a hunting accident. Charles the Simple was still a four-year-old when Carloman II died, too young to be king. The magnates looked elsewhere for one.

෴

Meanwhile, things were just as bad in Germanic East Francia. After the death of Louis the German on August 28, 876, the kingdom was divided among his three sons. Karlmann (or Carloman), the eldest, got Bavaria and Carinthia, the heartland of Louis's realm, as well as Italy in 877; the second son, Louis "the Younger," became king of the East Franks (the rest of Germany); and the youngest,

Charles "the Fat," became king of Alemannia (Swabia, Alsace-Lorraine, and Switzerland). By 882 two of the three had died without leaving legitimate heirs. Karlmann was incapacitated in late 878 and died in 880. Louis the Younger died two years later. We are not sure what caused Karlmann's incapacity: perhaps a stroke or epilepsy or even arteriosclerosis (hardening of the arteries). But as Eric Joseph Goldberg points out, "The real problem was Louis the German's longevity [he died in his early sixties], which forced his heirs to begin their royal careers unusually late in life. . . . A new Carolingian king usually needed at least a decade to overcome political opposition and military threats and thereby consolidate his rule."[37]

The only adult male heir to the whole of Louis the German's East Frankish realm and Italy was his youngest son, Charles III the Fat. With the death in 884 of Carloman II, the last effective Carolingian ruler in West Francia, the West Frankish magnates invited Charles to succeed in France as well. He was now personally king and emperor over three separate realms: Germania, Italia, and Gallia. However, now that he had an empire, he would have to work to keep it.

Charles the Fat's great test was the Viking siege of Paris. He had gone to Italy in 881 to receive the imperial crown after Pope John VIII had begged him to come to protect the Patrimonium Petri from "wicked Christians" and from Saracen "thieves swarming all across the country endlessly robbing and plundering."[38] While Charles happily took the imperial title, he did nothing to protect the pope. We have already seen how the young Count Odo escaped from Paris in late May 886 and probably through intermediaries begged Charles in Italy to come and raise the siege. Five months later Charles arrived with a large army, eventually bribing the Vikings to leave the Seine. After the heroism of the Parisians, this seemed like gross cowardice.

Although lambasted by some historians for weakness and incompetence, we know little about Charles's personality, whether he was "weak" or "strong." The epithet "the Fat" suggests laziness, although we are ignorant about his girth. It may not even have been contemporary; the nickname does not occur in sources earlier than the twelfth century. We do know that his health was bad and that he may have suffered from malaria picked up in Italy in 883. He also suffered from crippling headaches, which made it almost impossible for him to make decisions. In early 887 he "was afflicted by a severe illness in Alsace. Afterwards he recovered somewhat . . . and he had blood let to relieve pain in his head."[39] This probably means he was trepanned, a serious operation that consisted in drilling a hole in his skull to relieve the pressure presumed to be causing the headaches. Even though his symptoms are vague, he may have been suffering from epilepsy or strokes, "an affliction to which the east Frankish royal family seems to have been susceptible."[40] Clearly, he was a sick man.

He was also the victim of a smear campaign by one of the authors of the *Annals of Fulda*, probably from the circle of Archbishop Liutbert of Mainz, who had been sacked as archchancellor by Charles. Modern historians see Charles as a sick man who was beset by intractable problems but who was active in administration, cooperating with local elites and magnates. Simon MacLean shows that he was as effective as any early medieval monarch could be given that they always had to consult and please local powerbrokers, with their inevitable centrifugal tendencies. Charles's greatest weakness was his lack of an heir. He was married to Richgard of Swabia, later Saint Richgard. They had no children; she possibly lived a life of committed virginity, which obviously didn't encourage royal procreation. She spent her later life in a convent. Charles had a bastard son, Bernard, by an unknown mistress, and much of the latter part of his reign was taken up with attempts to get Bernard recognized as his successor.

In the end Charles's government simply collapsed. He was very ill during the winter of 886–887, and support for him gradually ebbed away. By early November 887 the crisis came to a head when Charles's nephew Arnulf of Carinthia, bastard son of Karlmann, appeared with a large army of Bavarians and Slavs near Frankfurt, where the emperor was meeting with civil and ecclesiastical powerbrokers to determine the succession. By mid-November Charles was totally deserted, and he was deposed as king and emperor. He died on January 13, 888, and, mourned only by monks, he was buried in the monastery church of Mittelzell on the island of Reichenau in Lake Constance. According to the *Annals of Fulda*, at the time of the burial "the heavens were seen to open by many beholders so that it could be clearly shown that he who had been spurned by men and stripped of earthly honour had been deemed worthy by God to be held as a servant of His heavenly country in happiness."[41] He was soon thought of as a saint.

Generally speaking, some historians see the death of Charles the Fat as the end of the Carolingian empire. But others argue that, although the empire split up, it continued in the sense that subsequent rulers always claimed some connection with the imperial family. And the Carolingian ideal of government lingered, to be revived by the German Otto I. Both views are essentially correct, but in the end it was the survival of the imperial ideal that was most important, for it inspired the establishment of the East Frankish *Reich*. It is sometimes assumed that the word *Reich* is derived from the Medieval Latin *regnum*, meaning "majesty" or "throne." This is incorrect. It is actually derived from Old High German and ultimately probably from Celtic. A clue to its original meaning is found in the contemporary German word *Reichtum*, meaning "wealth." Probably the best English word for *Reich* is "realm." Originally, there was an equivalent word in Old English, *rīce*, meaning "realm" or "rule" or even "rich." It has now disappeared from the English language except in the word "bishopric." The word "bishop" itself comes from the Old English word *biscop* and the suffix "ric" from the Old English *rīce*, meaning the rule or rank of a bishop or his jurisdiction.

ᏯᎥ

The coup d'état that ended Charles the Fat's reign temporary brought some stability to the East Frankish realm, where his authority had been focused. However, central government elsewhere quickly disintegrated. The *Annals of Fulda* says succinctly, "Many *reguli* [kinglets] sprang up in Europe."[42] Chronicler Regino of Prüm sees the deposition of Charles as a tragedy and comments that the empire imploded and that "each part spewed forth kinglets." He continues, "The kingdoms which had been subject to Charles, holding themselves bereft of lawful heirs, cut loose into separate realms. Now they looked for no prince of hereditary descent; each divided part elected a leader for itself *de suis visceribus*, from its own bowels. This caused great wars . . . [because] fortune armed them to destroy each other in the struggle for power."[43]

The result was civil strife, constant warfare, and the breakdown of central government. A kind of second "dark age" began with the breakdown and loss of overriding authority, which in turn led to the emergence of a form of warlord banditry by the magnates, the local strongmen-landholders who eventually evolved into the European aristocracy.

The perpetrator of the coup against Charles the Fat, Arnulf (887–899), should be familiar by now—we first met him in Italy when, on February 22, 896, he was crowned Holy Roman Emperor by Pope Formosus. At the time Formosus was using him as a pawn to undermine the power of Agiltrude and the House of Spoleto. Arnulf's interference in Italy ended with the apparent

stroke he suffered as he besieged Spoleto. He quickly lost Italy and was confronted with power struggles in his East Frankish homeland.

The successions that resulted from these power struggles make up a formidable list of names for the modern reader. After Arnulf died in 899, he was
succeeded by his son, Louis the Child, then aged six, who ruled until 911.
Meanwhile, in 888 Berengar of Friuli had become king of Italy, only to be
quickly replaced by Guido of Spoleto, who, when Arnulf refused to interfere,
Pope Stephen V was forced to crown Holy Roman Emperor in 891. Count
Odo, defender of Paris, was elected king in West Francia when the magnates
passed over the nine-year-old son of Louis the Stammerer. But Odo was a failure as king; he lost control of Aquitaine to Duke Ramnulf II, and constantly
harassed by the Vikings, he died on New Year's Day 898. Rudolf I seized Transjurane, or Upper Burgundy, which he held protected by the Swiss mountains.
It eventually became the kingdom of Burgundy. Lower Burgundy and Provence
went to Louis, son of Boso (d. 887), a former official of Charles the Bald, who
had struggled to establish a kingdom in the southern regions. Louis ruled successfully until he was tempted to invade Italy. After initial success he was captured by Berengar I, who, following the Italian-Byzantine custom, blinded him.
He fled back to Provence to reign there for twenty-five years as Louis the Blind
(890–928). In fact, it was Hugo, the Duke of Arles (or Provence) who ruled in
the king's name. This is the same Hugh whom we've already met as king of
Italy (924–945) and husband of Marozia.

These post-888 kinglets, all more or less related to the Carolingian dynasty,
really only ruled with the consent of their magnates. I use this catchall word
"magnates" to describe lay and ecclesiastical strongmen whose support and consent were increasingly needed for rulers to maintain their positions. So who
were these local strongmen, and how did they gain their power? To understand,
we need to see something of the late Carolingian political structure. The king
was at the heart of the structure. Being a Carolingian bestowed an almost supernatural legitimacy on the descendants of Charlemagne, and this lasted until
the total disintegration of the empire after 888. Thus endowed, the king led
armies into battle, formulated laws, judged cases, looked after the weak and
punished evildoers, protected the church from external threats and errors, and
operated a form of social security supporting the vulnerable and the poor.

But in order for the king's power to be effective, he needed local representatives with devolved power. In West Francia there had long been a tradition of

local government from Roman times. But this was swamped by Charlemagne, who imposed a centralized structure from above while at the same time ignoring the local aristocracy. The situation was different in East Francia. Here local communities maintained "a deep sense of their own individuality and memories of recent independence."[44] Louis the German's real power base was Bavaria, and Carolingian penetration in Saxony and Thuringia was superficial; Louis visited Saxony only a couple of times. Charlemagne's counts were powerful local officials in military, legal, and administrative affairs, and as centralized authority weakened during the civil wars under Louis the Pious and his descendants, counts gained more and more power. Soon they were handing this power on to their eldest sons, and a kind of hereditary nobility began to emerge.

One way of limiting counts' power was through the exemption of certain regions or people from their jurisdiction. Kings did this by granting immunity to bishoprics, abbeys, and churches from comital authority. Local bishops were also used to keep an eye on local affairs. But in the end these attempts to assert royal authority proved less and less effective and led to the collapse of centralized authority in the last two decades of the ninth century. It is very easy to see how a situation like this could easily evolve into what later historians called "feudalism."

So as the tenth century began, the "dissention of kings" had led Western Europe to a state of almost complete disintegration. It was out of this chaos that a separate and powerful German kingdom emerged—one that would form the basis for what we would recognize as modern European civilization. It is to the emergence of that German kingdom that we will now turn.

DIVISIONS OF
GERMANY IN 950
A.D.

DENMARK

0   200 MILES
0   200 KILOMETERS

ENGLAND

FRIESLAND

MARCH
OF THE
BILLUNGS

POMERANIA

PRUSSIANS

DUCHY OF
SAXONY

EAST
MARCH

POLAND

DUCHY OF
LOWER LORRAINE

THURINGIA MARCH OF
THURINGIA

DUCHY OF
FRANCONIA

DUCHY
OF BOHEMIA

DUCHY OF
UPPER
LORRAINE

MORAVIA

FRANCE

DUCHY
OF SWABIA

DUCHY
OF BAVARIA

HUNGARY

Lake Constance

BURGUNDY

MARCH OF
CARINTHIA

MARCH OF
VERONA

ITALY

Venice

CHAPTER 6

Salvation from
"That Very Savage People"

V ERDEN IS A SMALL north German town near the confluence of the
Weser and Aller rivers nineteen miles (30 kilometers) south of Bremen.
On a spring day in 782, it became the scene of a horrible massacre during
which more than 4,500 Saxon warriors were beheaded between dawn and dusk.
The perpetrator of this barbarism was Charlemagne. He waited until the Saxons surrendered their arms and then slaughtered them. At the time he was utterly frustrated by what the *Royal Frankish Annals* calls "the treaty-breaking
Saxons," and he was determined "to persist in this war until they were either defeated and forced to accept the Christian religion or be entirely exterminated."[1]

This was just the worst of a number of outrages committed by both sides in
a thirty-two-year-long war as the Franks tried to subdue Saxony. While for us
this was cold-blooded murder, the emperor saw himself acting like a biblical
king on behalf of God. He was much influenced by King David, who after the
defeat of the Moabites killed two out of every three men he captured, or like
Saul, who defeated the Amalekites and killed "man and woman, child and infant, ox and sheep, camel and donkey" (I Samuel 15:3). Charlemagne felt he
had biblical precedents. After Verden "the stubborn treachery of the Saxons
quieted down for a few years, mainly because they could not find convenient
opportunities for revolt."[2]

Until the 770s the Saxons were *gentes ultra Rhenum*, non-Christians from
beyond the Rhine, the northeastern edge of the Frankish realm. Yet it was from
this particular group of people, whose conversion to Catholicism was long and

135

violently resisted, that eventually ordered government and root-and-branch reform of the church itself emerged. After centuries of chaos and violence, it was
the recently converted Saxons who were to bring order to Europe.

Situated on the North German Plain, Saxony was a maze of forests and
marshland. Saxon society divided people into three rigidly structured *ordines*,
or castes. At the top were the *edhilingui*, the noble-warrior elite. Below them
were the *frilingi*, the free foot soldiers. Finally there were the *lazzi*, the original
indigenous inhabitants of the region, now semifree agricultural laborers. Intermarriage was forbidden between the castes. There was no king, and unwritten
Saxon practice prevented the rise of a monarch. The landscape was divided into
about one hundred districts making up three provinces: Westphalia, a central
region called Angria, and Eastphalia. A nobleman ruled each district, but the
nobles didn't have a monopoly on power because an annual general assembly
was held at Marklohe close to Verden. Here the nobles were joined by twelve
representatives of each caste from each district. The assembly made major political decisions, judged court cases, and elected a leader when war was declared.
Thus the two lower castes had considerable power, and, understandably, they
were unprepared to surrender it. The Saxon system was not entirely unique;
Iceland had semisimilar system. Also, the oddly democratic aspects of the Saxon
system were not unusual; other tribal societies in the past had representative
structures that gave voice to the whole society. So the Saxons fought hard
against a foreigner like Charlemagne who wanted to impose an alien religion
and nondemocratic system on them.

Even before Charlemagne invaded Saxony, for the previous decade there
had been intermittent attempts to convert the Saxons to Christianity, mainly by
their former fellow countrymen, the Anglo-Saxons, who had come to the Continent as missionaries from England. They targeted the *edhilingui*, the noble-
warrior class, and converted some. However, the other castes correctly perceived
the new faith as a threat to the Marklohe assembly and to their rights, and they
refused to renounce their ancestral religion.

Before Charlemagne, border skirmishes along the ill-defined Saxon frontier
were a common phenomenon. So between 772 and 804, in a series of campaigns that brought out the worst of Frankish brutality, Charlemagne forcefully integrated Saxony into his empire. This was followed by coerced
conversion to Christianity. As Charlemagne's biographer Einhard says, "No
war ever undertaken by the Frankish people was more prolonged, more full of

atrocities, or more demanding in effort." He says that the Saxons were "ferocious . . . [and] hostile to our religion" and that the war was fought "with immense hatred on both sides."[3] *The Life of Saint Sturm* says that "[Charlemagne] converted the majority of the people partly by conquest, partly by persuasion, partly even by bribes."[4]

The Marklohe assembly was abolished, and Carolingian structures were imposed on Saxony, including rule by converted Saxon nobles who became counts representing imperial overlordship. The *frilingi* and *lazzi* lost their political rights and traditional religion through the imposition of mass baptism. A draconian legal system, the *Capitulary for Saxony*, was formulated. It included capital punishment for anyone who "wished to remain a pagan" and avoid baptism, as well as for anyone who "out of contempt for Christianity . . . despised the holy Lenten fast and shall have eaten flesh." Even the pagan custom of cremation incurred capital punishment.[5] The Saxons were forced to pay a church tithe, even as the lack of missionaries prevented Christianity from being properly promoted. Alcuin of York (ca. 735–804), Charlemagne's religious and liturgical adviser, complained to his friend Meginfrid, Charlemagne's treasurer, that "if the light yoke and sweet burden of Christ were to be preached to the most obstinate people of the Saxons with as much determination as the payment of tithes has been exacted, or as the force of legal decree has been applied for faults of the most trifling sort imaginable, perhaps they would not be averse to their baptismal vows."[6]

Frankish rule left a seething sense of resentment that focused on Christianity as the symbol of these changes. The two lower castes rejected Christianity and clung tenaciously to paganism. In 841–842 these resentments exploded in the *Stellinga* uprising. *Stellinga* is a Saxon word that means "comrades" and carries the heroic connotation of brave warriors. Such revolts were rare in the medieval period. The Franks saw the uprising as particularly significant because they perceived it as a challenge to the new social order, with the *Stellinga* wanting to revert to their ancestral way of life.

But why wait forty years to revolt? What circumstances had changed? Until civil war broke out among Louis the Pious's sons, the Saxon nobility had kept a relatively tight rein on the lower castes. But this unity disintegrated in the year 841 when Louis the German fell out with Emperor Lothar. Louis, a clever, ruthless man who demanded loyalty and integrity from his officials, was related to some of the Saxon nobility through his wife, Queen Hemma. But the fraternal disagreement split the Saxon nobility. Those nobles whose lands were confined to Saxony supported Louis, whereas another group of powerful aristocrats opposed him and supported Lothar. This split provided a unique opportunity for the *frilingi* and *lazzi*. In early 841 the pro-Lothar and pro-Louis factions called up and armed their men. With the nobles divided, agitators soon arose to remind people of the Marklohe assembly and their traditional religion. The Saxon nobles lost control of their militias.

Strategically, the civil war went badly for Lothar; defeated at Fontenoy (June 841), he fled to Aachen. But he was far from surrender. Nithardus says that in July Lothar stirred up the *Stellinga* rebel militias, "promising them if they would side with him, that he would let them have the same law in the future which their ancestors had observed when they were still worshipping idols."[7] He also approached the Danes and Slavs from beyond the Elbe River. Thus, Lothar "dragged a regional popular revolt into the vortex of the Carolingian civil war."[8] The Saxon nobles who supported Lothar campaigned outside Saxony, isolating those who supported Louis in Saxony, thus exposing them to the *Stellinga* rebels. The *Annals of Xanten* says that "throughout all of Saxony the power of the underlings arose violently against their lords. They usurped the nickname *Stellinga* and perpetrated much madness. The nobility of Saxony suffered violent persecution and humiliation from the lower orders."[9]

Louis the German meanwhile counterattacked Lothar. By February 842 the strategic situation had shifted in favor of Louis, and Lothar's Saxon supporters abandoned him. By the end of June 842, in accordance with the Treaty of Verdun, Louis regained control of Carolingian lands east of the Rhine. With the civil war over, he could turn his entire attention to the revolt. "Louis marched throughout Saxony and by force and terror he completely crushed all who still resisted him: having captured all the ringleaders of that dreadful example of insubordination—men who had all but abandoned the Christian faith and had resisted Louis and his faithful men so fiercely—he punished 140 of them by beheading, hanged fourteen, maimed countless numbers by chopping off their limbs, and left no one able to carry on further opposition to him."[10]

But this was not the end of the business. A remnant of the rebels revolted again in November 842. "But when it came to battle they were put down in a great bloodbath."[11] In case they were still contemplating revolt, Mainz Archbishop Rabanus Maurus decreed that anyone participating in "secret oaths and conspiracies, rebellions and resistance" would be immediately excommunicated.[12] The policy seems to have worked because there were no more revolts in Saxony, and Christianity seems to have been eventually accepted. Louis the German never again set foot in Saxony.

Besides quelling the Saxons, Louis and his successors also had to negotiate control over the eastern frontier. I say "negotiate" because, as Timothy Reuter says, "to seal it off was not only impossible, it was not desirable."[13] Missionaries, traders, and others moved back and forth across the frontier, and the territory beyond the borders provided a handy place of refuge for the rebellious and those out of favor. So who lived beyond these fluid borders? The largest racial group was the Slavs, and the most troublesome were the Magyars. Some Slavs had already converted to Christianity. They had also split into a number of groups, and there was often tension and warfare between the Carolingians and Slavic groups, such as the Sorbs, Abodrites, and West Slavic Moravians, who organized a state, beginning in 833, that lasted seventy years. Once pacified, the Saxons became particularly important in defending the eastern borders. However, this frontier remained unstable even after the defeat of the Magyars in 955.

☙

As we saw, the abdication of Charles the Fat in December 887 led to a breakdown of late Carolingian political arrangements. West Francia (most of present-day France) disintegrated into a maze of feudal territories. This was a recipe for anarchy. The situation in East Francia (Germany) was different. Here the bastard son of Karlmann, Arnulf of Carinthia, succeeded and was recognized as overlord of the rest of the Frankish realms. A successful soldier, he defended the eastern border of the empire against the Moravians and had a significant victory over the Vikings at the River Dyle near Leuven in 891. But as we also saw, Arnulf's Italian adventure in mid-894 in response to Pope Formosus's request for aid was followed by the tragedy of his stroke as he besieged Spoleto. He returned crippled to Regensburg and died there on December 8, 899.

He was succeeded by his six-year-old son, Louis IV the Child, on February 4, 900. Even though Louis was accepted as legitimate king, the counts who had been appointed to administer local areas under Louis the German and Arnulf began to arrogate power to themselves, decreasingly recognizing centralized authority and thus effectively becoming magnates and rulers in their own right. The one man who confronted these centrifugal tendencies was

Hatto, Archbishop of Mainz. Of minor nobility from north of Lake Constance, Hatto was a strong supporter of Arnulf, who had appointed him archbishop in September 891. "A man of subtle mind," Hatto's vision was of a united German kingdom with a strong king.[14] This explains the animosity of the magnates toward him; they wanted to consolidate their power. Hatto had accompanied Arnulf to Italy and received his pallium from Formosus.

In the complex political situation created by Louis IV's minority, Hatto played a pivotal role as de facto regent. "There was a tacit agreement among the magnates to behave as if [Louis] . . . were a real king," but near the end of his reign "his kingship seemed to have lost its authority and cohesive force" owing to a defeat by the Magyars in a battle near Augsburg in 910.[15] Hatto gradually lost control of events, and despite acceptance of Louis, the centrifugal tendency of the magnates to dismember the kingdom was a real threat. But East Francia, in contrast to its western cousin, had one thing going for it: there were only a small number of dominant magnates and families with whom rulers had to deal. There were three dominant clans: the Liutpoldings, who had gained power in Bavaria after 899; the Liudolfings, who controlled Saxony; and the Hunfridings of Swabia. All three had de facto assumed responsibility for defending the eastern borders against the Magyars. Between 907 and 910 the Germans lost three battles against them, largely, it seems, by misjudging their own ability to win a pitched battle. As a result, the Magyars were free to raid the borderlands with impunity. But these losses also strengthened the independence of the magnates, particularly those from the three border clans. Building on long-established local loyalties, the magnates created their own territories, which quickly evolved into five great duchies: Franconia, Bavaria, Swabia, Saxony, and Thuringia. They even began to see themselves as ruling minor "kingdoms."

Only the Conradine clan of Franconia, whose territory centered on the Rhine and Main rivers near Frankfurt, unequivocally supported Hatto. Duke Conrad's sister Oda had married King Arnulf in 888, and she was Louis IV's mother. But there was a terrible feud between the Conradine clan and the Babenberg clan from northern Franconia, who had fallen foul of Arnulf. Both clans were trying to extend their influence along the Main River between Würzburg and Bamberg. At the battle of Fritzlar (906), the Conradines were victorious, but Duke Conrad and two Babenberg brothers were killed. There is a story that a third brother, Adalbert, surrendered to Hatto, who, despite the promise of a safe conduct, had him beheaded, thereby establishing a reputation for treachery.

With the death of seventeen-year-old Louis IV in 911, East Francia entered a new era in which a new order begins to arise out of chaos. It emerged from "that very savage people," the Saxons.

❦

The only direct descendant of Charlemagne available to take the East Frankish crown after the death of Louis was Charles the Simple, who ruled, at least nominally, in West Francia until 923. Unwilling to accept Charles as their ruler, the magnates and Hatto joined forces to elect Conrad the Younger as King Conrad I (911–918). The election of a non-Carolingian signified a decisive break from West Francia. Conrad was supported by the magnates until Hatto died in May 913. Hatto's reputation was subsequently trashed, first by Saxon chroniclers such as Widukind of Corvey (925–973), and then by later historians who characterized him as a scheming priest-politician. If Thietmar of Merseburg's *Chronicon* is correct, Hatto had been involved in a convoluted plot to assassinate Henry, Duke of Saxony, which Henry soon discovered. He "sent a representative to inform . . . [Hatto] that he had been found out and should quickly see to his own safety. . . . [Hatto] died soon afterwards, rather suddenly, and the good fortune with which the king [Conrad] had previously been blessed quickly shifted to Henry."[16]

Meanwhile, Conrad was unsuccessful in controlling the Magyars, who were now creating havoc. He soon alienated the other magnates, and with support ebbing away Conrad turned to the church for help. This achieved little. The newly emerging powerbrokers were the Saxon Liudolfing clan led by Duke Henry I "the Fowler" of Saxony, who negotiated an often-tense modus vivendi with Conrad. Originally from East Saxony, the Liudolfings were *duces orientalium Saxorum*, the military commanders of the East Saxon frontier. "Meanwhile, Conrad had long been restrained by illness [caused by a battle wound]," says Thietmar, "[but] he forgot all the hostility that Henry had directed at him," and before he died in December 918, Conrad nominated Henry as his successor, clearly recognizing the Saxon's ability to hold the kingdom together.[17] Widukind of Corvey says Conrad completely lacked *fortuna et mores*, which Reuter translates as "the authority and charisma of a new ruler."[18]

Following a brief interregnum, the east Frankish magnates gathered at Fritzlar in May 919 and elected Henry the Fowler as king. Perhaps rather than "fowler," Henry should be called "falconer" because he was very keen on hunting birds with trained falcons; one story holds that he was setting bird traps when a delegation came to offer him the crown. One wonders why he was not instead at Fritzlar playing politics given that he clearly wanted the crown. Nevertheless, he became the first "king of Germany."

King Henry (919–936) certainly had *fortuna et mores.* According to Thietmar, "The fame of the new king spread everywhere. . . . [People] recognized him as a man who knew how to treat his supporters wisely and to conquer his enemies by cunning and with force."[19] He was not dependent on clerical advisers as Conrad had been, and he refused to be anointed king by any bishop. Anointing implied that the king was *Vicarius Christi,* "Vicar of Christ," a holy, separate, sacred person. Perhaps Henry also rejected anointing because he disagreed with the notion that somehow the clergy made him a real king, or more likely he specifically rejected anointing by Archbishop Heriger of Mainz because he reminded Henry of Hatto. Henry wanted to be *primus inter pares* (first among equals) among the magnates, and he felt that anointing would have set him above them. Certainly, his rule was absolute only within Saxony; otherwise he had to work to influence the magnates to support him by friendship pacts, skillful maneuvering, compromise, reconciliation, vassalage (a relationship of allegiance and subordination), and, when necessary, threats and military action. In the case of Arnulf "the Bad" of Bavaria, it took two invasions to bring him to heel. Henry also successfully sought peace with West Francia. By 925 he had added Lotharingia and the Carolingian heartlands around Aachen to his kingdom and reached *amicitia,* a friendship pact, with Burgundy. An experienced, shrewd leader, he gradually established the kingdom of *Francia et Saxonia* and persuaded the magnates to recognize his overlordship.

However, Henry was faced with considerable disorganization on the eastern frontier in the regions between the Elbe and Oder rivers. This disorder gave the Magyars the chance to cause havoc. To deal with them, Henry had to establish order on the frontier by bringing the border Slavs to heel and then organizing and fortifying the defenses. He was bluntly reminded of the Magyar threat in his first year as king when a Saxon army was defeated.

But the worst years were 924–926, when the Magyars totally devastated Saxony, and Henry was holed up, probably from early in 926, in the massive fortress at Werla (40 acres [17 hectares] in area) at the foot of the Harz Mountains, the traditional place for assemblies of the Saxon nobility. By an amazing stroke of luck, his forces captured a Magyar from the royal Árpád house, although we have no idea who the captive was. This gave Henry room to maneuver. In exchange for the Magyar princeling and an annual payment, he exacted a promise from the Magyars not to raid the eastern borders for nine years. This gave him a chance to refortify the frontier and resurrect the Saxon tradition of *agrarii milites*, a peasant-warrior militia, which built and garrisoned the fortifications. At the same time he modernized the Saxon army.

After Henry refused to pay any more tribute in 932, the Magyars again invaded Saxony, leading to the decisive Saxon victory at the Battle of Riade in northern Thuringia on March 15, 933. According to Flodoard's *Annals*, "The Magyars divided their forces into three units. One of them went to Italy and another invaded the lands of [King] Henry across the Rhine. Henry set out against them, along with the Bavarians and Saxons and other peoples who were subject to him. He cut down all of them almost exterminating them. It is said that 36,000 were killed, not including those drowned in the river or those taken alive."[20] It was clearly a rout and ended the Magyar threat during Henry's reign. He was then able to secure the borders with his restructured army.

Henry had two wives: the first was the widow Hatheburg, who after the death of her first husband had briefly entered a convent. She brought a huge dowry to the marriage with Henry, and after the birth of their son, Thankmar, he repudiated her in 909, claiming divorce on the grounds that she had been a nun. He nevertheless managed to retain her dowry. He then married Matilda of Ringelheim, who bore him three boys and a girl. The eldest was Otto. Henry wisely decided to abandon the Carolingian practice of dividing the kingdom among all the sons and adopted the principle of primogeniture, although it was not yet widely accepted. So Otto inherited the entire kingdom. This *Hausordnung* (house rule) was confirmed by an assembly of magnates and important bishops at Erfurt in 935.

Henry had already procured a wife from England for the seventeen-year-old Otto: the nineteen-year-old Anglo-Saxon princess Eadgyth (Edith), granddaughter of King Alfred the Great and daughter of King Edward the Elder (899–924) of the West Saxons. They married in late 929. It made sense for Henry to seek an Anglo-Saxon wife for Otto. Not only had the Anglo-Saxons been Christian missionaries in Germany, but also Saxon and Anglo-Saxon culture and language, coming from the same root, were closely related and Otto and Eadgyth could understand each other. It also meant that the West Saxon monarchy, the oldest reigning dynasty at the time, recognized Henry's status as

a king, and this enhanced his reputation among the magnates. Edith became famous in Germany as a strong-minded, able, and charming woman who was
admired for her piety and generosity to convents and shrines.

Henry I died of a stroke on July 2, 936, in the palace he had built on a
rocky outcrop at Quedlinburg, a natural defensive position on the North German Plain just north of the Harz Mountains. His wife, Matilda, later built a
nunnery there to offer prayers for his soul.

                                    ⁊

Otto and Eadgyth went to Aachen for their coronation on August 7, 936. The
ceremony occurred in Charlemagne's *opus mirabile*, the still-standing, richly
decorated palace chapel, an octagon surrounded by a sixteen-sided polygon
and crowned by the first dome built north of the Alps. Otto had not only succeeded to the crown of the East Frankish kingdom, but by being crowned at
Aachen he also placed himself in succession to Charlemagne. Widukind of
Corvey says that the service began in the portico, where Otto was accepted by
"the dukes, leaders of the prefectures and the rest of the military leadership,"
who enthroned him and in a feudal gesture placed "their hands within his offering him their fealty and promising him help against his enemies." Otto then
entered the chapel proper, where Archbishop Hildebert of Mainz awaited him.
Leading him by the right hand, Hildebert addressed the assembled churchmen
and commoners: "'I present to you Lord Otto, chosen by God, designated by
the lord Henry and now acclaimed king by the princes. If this election pleases
you raise your right hand to heaven.' Everyone present raised their right hands
and acknowledged the new ruler."[21]

Dressed in a close-fitting Frankish tunic, Otto was then led to the altar, where
he was given the royal insignia: a sword, belt, and cloak with bracelets, staff, and
scepter. He was then anointed and crowned by Archbishops Hildebert and Wich-
frid of Cologne. Otto "was now *Christus Domini* . . . an anointed of the Lord; the
biblical admonition 'Do not disturb my anointed ones' applied to him . . . his
command was exempt from criticism."[22] Then Otto ascended a spiral staircase to
the upper gallery, where he was enthroned on Charlemagne's *cathedra regalis*, a
marble throne mounted on six steps, an exact replica of the throne of the biblical King Solomon (I Kings 10:19). (The *cathedra* is still there today.)

The service combined secular and sacred, with Otto explicitly placing
himself in the Frankish tradition of Charlemagne. He was now the anointed

king to whom the magnates owed fealty. This was reinforced at the post-coronation banquet when Otto, according to Widukind, "entered into his inheritance at a marble table decorated with kingly trappings and sat down with the bishops and all the people and was served by the dukes" Giselbert of Lotharingia, Eberhard of Franconia, Hermann of Swabia, and Arnulf of Bavaria. This ritual banquet was a clear statement of Otto's overlordship and his determination to bring the magnates to heel. Otto was beginning his reign from a position of strength. He was reported to have great dignity, and Widukind mentions his *oculi rutilantes*, his "fiery eyes that struck like a flash of lightning."[23] He was certainly a king with *fortuna et mores*—authority and charisma.

But not everyone was delighted with fiery-eyed Otto. His mother was absent, probably jealous of Eadgyth's influence. Otto's older half-brother, Thankmar, and his younger brothers, Henry and Bruno, the other sons of Matilda, felt particularly aggrieved because this new principle of primogeniture made the kingdom indivisible, even given the influence of the powerful families. Henry I had certainly looked after his other sons: he gave them lands and wealth. But they were still dissatisfied, and Flodoard reports that "there arose a conflict over the kingdom."[24] This grew so bad that young Henry was confined in Saxony during the celebrations in Aachen. After the coronation Otto returned to Saxony, specifically to Quedlinburg, where he turned the palace in which his father was buried into a convent that became a family shrine. He and Eadgyth had also founded a monastery at nearby Magdeburg on the Elbe River, and this became a favorite residence for them. He clearly envisaged Magdeburg as a basis for missionary activity east of the Elbe and consciously intended to shift the center of gravity of his world northeastward.

But troubles and grievances were brewing not only in the family but also in the broader political world. For Otto attempted to alter his relationship to the magnates by imposing royal prerogatives and rejecting promotions and deals to which they felt they were entitled. Externally, Widukind says, "the Saxons were troubled with many enemies, the Slavs from the east, Franks from the south, Lotharingians from the west and the Vikings together with the Slavs from the north." He might well have added Bavaria, where trouble began in mid-937. But Otto quickly got the Bavarians under control. A year later the Slavs, who seemed to prefer war to peace, revolted against the Saxons, "setting aside every misery out of love of freedom."[25] Two of Otto's most loyal generals fought this seemingly endless battle in the east—Duke Hermann Billung in the northeast and Count Gero in the southeast.

Almost simultaneously with the Bavarian troubles, Duke Eberhard III of Franconia, the son of Conrad I, revolted. The trouble started when Eberhard attacked Helmern castle on the border of Franconia and Saxony, killing many because its Saxon commandant, Bruning, refused to swear fealty to Eberhard, a non-Saxon. Otto's court fined Eberhard 100 pounds of silver, to be paid in horses, but, more importantly, humiliated him by forcing his men to carry dogs to the royal palace in Magdeburg, a old Germanic punishment that brought shame and loss of face.

Eberhard rebelled again and was joined by Thankmar, who resented Otto's support for Count Gero, maintaining that he should have been given command of the eastern territories. They seized Otto's younger brother Henry and imprisoned him in the Eresburg fortress (modern Obermarsburg). Thankmar was trapped in Eresburg in early 937 when, Widukind tells us, the local citizenry "who were loyal to the king, opened the gates" to Otto.[26] Thankmar retreated to the church of St. Peter and surrendered, as symbolized by his laying his golden necklace and sword on the altar. However, a common soldier named Meginzo attacked him from behind, killing him with a lance. For a soldier to kill a royal prince was considered a terrible crime. Although Otto is said to have avenged Thankmar's death, Meginzo was alive for two more years; he was later killed in battle.

Eberhard was briefly imprisoned. Then Otto's younger brother Henry seems to have betrayed Otto by entering an alliance with Eberhard aimed at overthrowing the king. In 939 Duke Giselbert of Lotharingia, Otto's brother-in-law, joined the rebellion. Otto now needed all the *fortuna et mores* he could muster, and with superior tactics he defeated the rebels at Birten on the Rhine. The victory was credited to Otto's possession of the holy lance, which was said to contain a nail from Jesus's cross and to have pierced Jesus's side. But then King Louis IV (936–954) of West Francia and Archbishop Frederick of Mainz entered the fray against Otto. So lance or no lance, he was in serious trouble. "Many abandoned Otto's camp," Widukind reports, "having lost hope in the rule of the Saxons."[27] Liutprand supports this assertion, saying that one opportunistic count tried to use the king's predicament to get him "to hand over to him the abbey of Lorsch with its rich lands." Otto responded by bluntly quoting the Gospel of Matthew: "Give not what is sacred to the dogs" (7:6).[28] Otto was also concerned because Queen Eadgyth was sheltering at Lorsch.

But Otto of the fiery eyes was not to be outdone. He defeated the rebels in 939 at Andernach on the Rhine near Koblenz; Eberhard was killed, and Giselbert of Lotharingia drowned in the Rhine trying to escape. The king had asserted his authority once more.

Things remained toxic within his family. Young Henry felt he had a better claim to be king. Liutprand of Cremona, who knew most of the protagonists, claims "perverse advisors" were responsible for leading Henry to adopt "an attitude of hostility." Widukind puts it down to Henry's *adolescens*—his "youth and impulsiveness." Thietmar's *Chronicon* says that Queen Mother Matilda "strove vigorously and long to secure the [royal] seat for her younger son."[29] This may have been because she was jealous of the influence Eadgyth had over Otto. While the situation was probably a combination of all three, including scheming magnates trying to destabilize Otto, Matilda was certainly stirring Henry. It led to him conniving in an aristocratic conspiracy to assassinate Otto during Easter 941 at Quedlinburg. Someone informed Otto. He carried on with the Easter celebrations, but under heavy guard. He then dealt with the plotters, who were imprisoned in the imperial palace at Ingelheim. Now forgiven twice, Henry was reconciled with Otto the following Christmas at Frankfurt. In 948 he married Judith of Bavaria, daughter of Arnulf the Bad, and became Henry I, Duke of Bavaria. He died in 955.

The person who constantly remained loyal to Otto was Queen Eadgyth. "Through the grace of divine mercy and through the continued intercession of his most holy wife . . . Otto escaped whatever open or secret dangers confronted him." Praying for her husband, giving alms, and pleading for those in trouble were part of her queenly role. But then "endowed with innumerable virtues . . . she was with her husband for nineteen years and died . . . on 26 January [946]. . . . The king received the painful news of Eadgyth's death while he was out hunting, in the hope of refreshing himself a little."[30] Thietmar speaks of Otto's "unspeakable sorrow," and Widukind talks of "the grief and tears of the whole Saxon people."[31]

Her final resting place was Magdeburg's lovely Gothic cathedral. Her tomb was opened in 2008 as part of restoration work, and archaeologists, who expected to find nothing, discovered a well-preserved, antique silk shroud covering skeletal remains. Her body had been moved three times, and she was entombed in her present grave in 1510. Were these the bones of Eadgyth? Two years' study in Mainz and Bristol universities proved that the bones were of a female aged between thirty and forty who had been a frequent horse rider and had eaten a high protein diet, including lots of fish. "All these results suggested a high status aristocratic lady." But the question remained: was this lady Eadgyth? Proof came from teeth in the upper jaw. A technique was used "that measures the strontium and oxygen isotopes that are mineralized in the [permanent] teeth as they are formed. The value of these isotopes depends on the local environment and its underlying geology that is then locked into the teeth. By combining oxygen and strontium results, it was possible to 'triangulate' the location of the first 14 years of this individual's life. The results unambiguously pinpointed the chalk regions of southern Britain."[32] This was undoubtedly Queen Eadgyth.

Otto also had a bastard son, William, born in 929, the year of his marriage. We don't know who William's mother was; she is simply described as a captive Slav woman. He was conceived before Otto's marriage to Eadgyth, which made the union opportune because Otto's youthful sexuality could be contained before it created real complications. William, after an at-times-strained relationship with his father, became archbishop of Mainz in 954.

By the early 940s Otto seemed secure on the throne. In 939 both Lotharingia and Franconia had lost their rulers. Otto didn't replace Eberhard, killed at Andernach, and he absorbed Eberhard's duchy of Franconia into the royal domain. Together with Saxony, he had now created a very large region under direct royal power. After interim arrangements, Otto appointed Conrad the Red (from the Conradine clan of Franconia) duke of Lotharingia in 944. He later married Liutgard, Otto's daughter. Otto's beloved son Liudulf, on whom he doted and designated as his successor in 946, married Ida, daughter of Duke Hermann I of Swabia, and when Hermann died in December 949, Liudulf became duke. This gave Otto access to the northern end of the central alpine passes to Italy because Swabia covered not just south-central Germany but also German-speaking Switzerland. Most transalpine journeys between Chur and Bellinzona went over the San Bernardino Pass, and those between Chur and Chiavenna went over the Lukmanier, Maloja, Septimer, and Splügen passes. All these passes were of strategic importance to Otto as he became increasingly involved in Italy.

℘

Having asserted his control, Otto had to maintain it. So how did the *Reich* work? To begin with, there was no fixed capital. Otto and his successors administered the kingdom through a kind of government-on-the-road. He traveled throughout the kingdom being "seen" by his subjects, as well as cementing relationships with important people, keeping them friendly and under control. The purpose of his travels was to give cohesiveness and a tangible sense of Otto's "real presence" at a time when communication was difficult and slow. People gathered to see the king, who gave gifts and honors and publicly celebrated church services. Otto constantly reminded his subjects personally that he was king, and his progress through the kingdom became an instrument of government. So Otto's court was almost constantly on the move between favored residences and focal centers of power and influence. Regional assemblies where the powerbrokers gathered with Otto were also essential to the government of the *Reich*. Usually, Otto would spend from a couple of days to a few weeks in any one place. His longest stay was six months in Pavia, capital of northern Italy.

We can trace much of his travel. It focused in three general regions. The primary one was southern Saxony, where Otto maintained more than thirty-five royal residences. Its core stretched south from Magdeburg and west of the Elbe River to the Harz Mountains. Magdeburg was Otto and Eadgyth's favorite residence, and it was their custom to spend Easter there. The second area was in the middle Rhineland around Frankfurt, Mainz, and Worms. The third was in the lower Rhineland, the original Frankish heartland around Aachen, Nijmegen, and Cologne.

But how could someone govern when always on the road? At least one basic question arises: where were the legal, property, and other royal records kept upon which decisions could be based? The answer seems to be that they were carried in written form in the wagon train. This was not Otto's invention. We know that Charlemagne, Louis the Pious, and Lothar I also used archives and libraries on wheels. Lacking quick retrieval systems, people in the past had much better memories than we do, so officials and bureaucrats would have also carried much remarkably accurate information in their heads.

This kind of travel required an enormous output of energy; kingship was no place for a laggard. Eadgyth sometimes accompanied Otto. Journeys were carefully planned, usually months ahead, and moved between royal fiscs (land-holdings) with palaces or residences, which were maintained throughout the kingdom, as well as monasteries and bishoprics. Royal perambulations moved within and between these regions along set routes. The distances traveled were considerable. Magdeburg to Frankfurt is approximately 230 miles (365 kilometers) and Frankfurt to Aachen about 140 miles (225 kilometers). On Otto's longer trips, for example from Magdeburg to Rome, he would have clocked up more than 700 miles (1,140 kilometers), including an alpine crossing. Saxon kings visited more remote regions (Bavaria, northern Saxony, Swabia, and Upper Lotharingia) less often. The royal entourage traveled along roads and bridges maintained and protected by labor employed by royal vassals, churches, or bishoprics. The size of the entourage was flexible; it could be anywhere between three hundred and one thousand people. Otto and his retinue rode horses; servants and others rode mules or walked. Itineraries were planned so that each night they arrived at a royal residence or a monastery or bishop's city. Here they received *fodrum, gistum et servitium regis*, "horse fodder, lodging, and kingly service." The king and his party were accommodated in the residence, and the rest camped around. All of this required careful logistics and each place visited had to support a large party with horses and pack animals.

On arrival anywhere, Otto "showed" himself as the anointed of God raised to a priestlike status. He was *Vicarius Christi*, and itineraries were designed to reveal him as a sacred person who symbolized the unity of the kingdom and actually held it together in his person. In this context church worship and royal liturgy merged into each other. Otto would be solemnly greeted at the entrances to monasteries or cities by abbots, bishops, and clerics. He would wear the crown, hold court, dispense justice, reward vassals, and punish enemies and criminals.

It helped that Otto was tall, with a commanding presence. He lacked a sense of humor and possessed a strong authoritarian streak; he was clearly a man who enjoyed and used power. He also worked very hard at ruling, was determined, persevering, and committed. He was both feared and admired, and this was where his fiery eyes came in handy. A fighter, he confronted enemies, but he was always willing to pursue policy by peaceful means and negotiation. He was also willing to forgive, a much-neglected Christian virtue. His piety was simple, and while no scholar, he encouraged learning. He followed the Germanic system that held that, while the state had a responsibility to protect society and punish criminals, it also aimed at what we would call "conflict resolution." Thus, even heinous and terrible crimes, especially those that could lead to blood feud, were resolved by *Wergeld,* a payment in money or kind as a substitution for punishment or bloody revenge that could last for generations.

ଏ୬

His position consolidated, Otto became increasingly involved in "foreign affairs," but not as understood today. Otto's relationship with non-German regions was driven by his ambition to restore the empire along Carolingian lines, to be king *in Francia ac Saxonia.* This was achieved more by *amicitia,* personal friendship ties and kinship or marital ties, than by "policy" in the modern sense. His aim was hegemonic—that is, to be the dominant ruler who exercised overall authority and influence—but he left local rulers sufficient power to control their own regions, thereby continuing policies initiated by Henry I. This involved relations with West Francia, Burgundy, Italy, and the peoples living on the eastern frontier.

West Francia had dissolved into its component parts, and the most that can be said is that its king had very limited authority. From 936 to 954 this was Louis IV *d'Outremer* (from overseas—he had lived thirteen years in England), a Carolingian who in 939 married Otto's sister Gerberga. Representing an alternative royal line opposed to Louis IV was Hugh the Great, Count of Paris, a nephew of Odo, hero of the defense of Paris against the Vikings and married to Otto's other sister, Hedwig. Thus, Otto had close kinship ties through his sisters to West Frankish affairs.

At first Otto supported Hugh, but after Hugh imprisoned Louis in 945, Otto intervened. After Louis was released, Queen Gerberga asked her brother for help. "Otto gathered a very large army from all of his kingdoms . . . [and] came into Francia. King Louis went out to meet them and was received by them in a friendly and honorable manner."[33] Together they besieged Laon, just northwest of Reims, a fortified *castrum* (walled town) on a 590-foot- (180-meter-) high chalky hill above the surrounding flat plain, which had been surrendered by Louis in exchange for freedom. The siege was unsuccessful. They did, however, recover Reims, a major achievement. After the war petered out, Otto returned to Germany. To settle affairs and assert his hegemony, Otto summoned a general synod at the imperial palace at Ingelheim near Mainz (June 948) attended by a legate of Pope Agapitus II, as well as Louis IV, and most of the bishops of Germany. The synod settled a dispute between two rival claimants to the archbishopric of Reims and ordered Hugh the Great to submit to Louis on pain of excommunication. The pope confirmed the decisions of the synod the following year. Essentially, Otto had restored the ecclesiastical and political status quo in West Francia by supporting Louis. This was a generally successful policy until the mid-960s.

By the late 940s Otto had gained control over the central alpine passes into Italy. In the early 950s Pope Agapitus invited him to Italy, but given the complexity of Italian affairs, it was not all plain sailing. As we saw, Hugo had resigned the "kingship" of Italy in 947 and retired to Provence. He was succeeded by his twenty-one-year-old son, Lothar, but real power was held by Berengar II of Ivrea, a magnate-thug who had spent time in exile at Otto's court. Lothar died in 950 (the rumor was he was poisoned by Berengar), leaving a widow, Adelheid, a sister of King Conrad of Burgundy (937–993) who had also grown up in Otto's court and who recognized his overlordship. Conrad was married to Matilda the daughter of Louis IV of West Francia. Thus, Adelheid was connected by marriage and family to several royal houses. She led the opposition to Berengar and was briefly imprisoned. Her biographer, Odilo of Cluny, probably exaggerates when he says she suffered "a variety of tortures. Her flowing hair was pulled out and she suffered frequent blows from the hands and feet of her tormentors. She was enclosed in a foul prison" from which, Odilo says, she eventually escaped.[34]

Adelheid appealed to Otto for help and may have even suggested that she marry him. Otto was no fan of Berengar and invaded Italy in 951 with a large army. Berengar retreated to his home region of Ivrea, just below the Alps. Otto married Adelheid and was crowned king of Italy in Pavia in September 951. Envoys of Otto approached Pope Agapitus II to explore the possibility of an imperial coronation. The pope, who as we saw admired Otto, would have crowned him, but Alberico II forced Agapitus to refuse; he didn't want foreign rulers interfering in Roman business. So the plan fell through, and Otto returned to Saxony. The scheming Berengar eventually accepted Otto's overlordship at Augsburg in the summer of 952.

But complicated, toxic family politics again surfaced. Adelheid quickly had a son, whom they named Otto, and the rumor spread that he was to be the heir. The king's beloved son Liudulf believed this; he only had to recall what had happened to Otto's own half-brother Thankmar after Henry I married a second time. Together with Otto's son-in-law, Conrad the Red of Lotharingia, who had supported Otto in Italy and felt insulted when his advice was ignored,

Liudulf hatched a plot to ambush the king at Mainz while on circuit in Franconia in 953. Otto soon discovered the plot and demanded that his son hand over the culprits. "[Liudulf] had neither the desire nor the capacity to do this because he did not wish to violate an oath he had sworn to his supporters."[35] They then took refuge in Mainz, which Otto besieged for several months. A complicated situation became ever worse when a revolt broke out in Bavaria against Otto's brother, Duke Henry. Regensburg was taken by the rebels, and Liudulf, who had escaped from Mainz, took refuge there. Otto demanded that his son and son-in-law hand over their coconspirators or become enemies of the realm. Conrad surrendered, but Otto now had to besiege his son in Regensburg. The siege was long and dreadful for the city's inhabitants, who refused to surrender. Meanwhile, the Magyars, always ready to take advantage of internal disturbances to grab booty, invaded Bavaria and Franconia. The rumor was that Liudulf had invited them to Germany.

Something of Otto's pain at his son's betrayal can be gleaned from a speech Widukind puts in his mouth:

> I could accept it if the anger of my son and his deceitful colleagues only tortured me and didn't stir up the whole Christian community. It would mean less to me that they invaded my cities like robbers and regions under my power if they had not soaked them in the blood of my relatives and most dear companions. Behold, here I sit without sons, while I endure the experience of my son as my worst enemy. . . . This might be tolerable if they had not brought in the enemies of God and humankind [the Magyars]. They have laid waste my kingdom, have captured and killed my people, destroyed our cities, burned churches, killed priests, the streets running with blood.[36]

However, the Magyars had the effect of uniting everyone, including many who were wavering, behind Otto. Liudulf lost support and eventually fell at his father's feet begging forgiveness as Otto was out hunting in the Thuringian forest. He forgave his son but responded firmly and deposed both Conrad and Liudulf from office as dukes; as a sign of reconciliation he allowed them to retain their estates. He handed control of Lotharingia to his youngest brother, Bruno, Archbishop of Cologne and the archdiocese of Mainz to his bastard son, William. But Otto now had to deal with the Magyars.

The eastern frontier had been a continuing source of instability since Henry I's time. Otto's two generals in the east, Hermann Billung and Count Gero, had carved out large marches (frontier territories) on the *Limes Saxoniae* (Saxon borders), from which they levied tribute, established bishoprics, and imposed Saxon custom and law, thus containing and converting the Slavs. While the Saxon military was dependent on heavily armed cavalry from Henry I's time onward, the fluid situation on the frontier also benefited from Henry's creation of *agrarii milites*, who could be called up at short notice. Henry had also built frontier fortifications, centers from which power could be projected outward. As a result, from the mid-950s overlordship was evolving into direct control. The Slavs resisted, and Widukind says that they told Otto in 955 that they "would pay [him] tribute as usual, but would keep the government of the region in their own hands."[37] So the Saxons had to keep increasing numbers of troops to be ready for action against possible Slav uprisings and incursions.

The Magyars were a different matter; they were raiders specializing in hit-and-run attacks. Hungary abutted the southeast Marches of Austria and Carinthia, so the Magyars usually invaded through there to Bavaria. By 950 the Germans were getting used to dealing with Magyar incursions and knew their military modus operandi. Also, Magyar military superiority was probably somewhat exaggerated, and by midcentury the Magyars were running out of steam. Now settled in the Carpathian Basin, their society was transmuting from that of nomad warriors to that of settled farmers. Their opportunistic August 955 invasion was probably something of a last fling. They besieged the fortified episcopal town of Augsburg, which was situated on important communication routes. The town held out, inspired by Bishop Ulrich, until Otto arrived with a quickly assembled army of Swabians and Franconians. Otto's arrival led directly to the decisive Battle of Lechfeld.

Despite its importance we know little for certain about the battle. The two armies first came into contact near the Lech River, a tributary of the Danube, in a flat, shallow valley just south of Augsburg. The mistake the Magyars seem to have made was overconfidence in their archers. They stood and fought, underestimating the heavily armed and well-disciplined German cavalry. In the end the engagements were indecisive, leading to a Magyar retreat. But Otto had created a series of in-depth fallback positions that, after August 10, caught the eastward-retreating Magyars at every river crossing. Incessant rain had swollen the rivers, and the Magyars were continually harassed as they attempted to cross flooded rivers. Eventually, the Magyar force disintegrated, and the Magyars never again threatened Western Europe. Otto attributed the victory primarily to his possession of the holy lance. The cult of relics was an omnipresent component of Otto's faith. Significantly, the Magyars converted to Christianity a little more than four decades later.

అ

Otto had now reached a kind of plateau. Most of cisalpine Europe was under his hegemony, and even though Italy still attracted him, he didn't rush to intervene. He had a friendly pope in Rome, Agapitus II, and his Roman nemesis, Alberico II, had died in 954. Agapitus approved the foundation of an archbishopric in Otto's favorite place, Magdeburg on the Elbe, as a basis for missions to the Slavs. Here in 937 Otto had built a palace and a monastery dedicated to Saint Maurice, a third-century Roman military officer who had died a Christian martyr. His beloved Queen Eadgyth was buried in the monastery chapel. In 955 he built a large church above her tomb and planned to make it a cathedral. However, his bastard son, William, Archbishop of Mainz opposed the plan, and it fell through. Discussions with Agapitus probably included subtle suggestions of an imperial coronation for Otto. But Agapitus died in 955, succeeded by Alberico's appalling bastard, Octavian–John XII.

Nothing happened on the Italian front until the ambitious Berengar II, who had asserted a kind of de facto independence from Otto, plundered the Patrimonium Petri and took Spoleto. As we saw, the egregious Pope John was eventually forced to beg Otto to come to Rome and protect the Patrimonium from the brigandlike Berengar. Otto responded with alacrity and was crowned Holy Roman Emperor in Saint Peter's on February 2, 962. But no sooner was he out of Rome than the pope was up to his old tricks. Liutprand paints Otto at this time as a patient older man waiting for the loutish John XII to wake up to himself. But eventually his patience ran out, and, utterly infuriated, he returned to Rome to deal with both the pope and the recalcitrant Romans once and for all. As we shall see, this was to prove easier said than done.

CHAPTER 7

Feudal France

FOR A CLASSIC EXAMPLE of the collapse of centralized government and degeneration into chaos, we need look no further than West Francia. In this chapter we will examine how Carolingian West Francia (most of present-day France), beginning with the death of Charles the Bald (877), collapsed into some fifty separate duchies, counties, ecclesiastical enclaves, marches, and royal domains. Central to this collapse was the figure of Count Odo of Paris.

We have already met Odo, for he was the hero of the 885–886 Viking siege of the Île-de-la-Cité. Abbo, writing his *Viking Attacks on Paris* after Odo became king, unsurprisingly stoops to flattery by citing him as "the most notable prince, the foremost of all the leaders of men that this kingdom has produced."[1] Even allowing for Abbo's exaggerations, Odo was clearly a daring, twenty-five-year-old who plunged into the middle of battle with reckless courage, especially in the first days of the siege when they were defending the island against the initial Viking onslaught. The "victorious Odo," Abbo tells us, "was . . . never routed in battle; he fortified those who were exhausted; revived their strength, and rushed about the tower striking down the enemy." In the best tradition of medieval sieges, he poured "oil and wax and pitch, which was all mixed-up together and made into a hot liquid on a furnace which burned the hair of the Danes; made their skulls split open. Indeed many of them died and the others went and sought out the river [Seine]." He also slew "many Danes" using a bow and arrow. In an arranged parley with the Viking leader, Siegfried, which turned out to be a trap, "a swarm of Danes scurried forward to capture [Odo] . . . [but] he struck at them first and with a mighty leap he bounded over the ditch below

157

the tower, shield and spear in hand." He was rescued when "his warriors rushed out that they might stand by their lord."[2] Regino of Prüm says he was "a vigorous man who when compared with others excelled them in beauty of form, height, strength of body and great wisdom."[3] While all this sounds like the kind of idealization usually accorded to rulers by chroniclers, it is nevertheless clear that Odo was a brave, good-looking soldier of some consequence.

His most spectacular feat was his escape from Paris in late May 886 to get help from influential lords and churchmen and to inform Emperor Charles the Fat, who was in Italy, of the dire situation in Paris. An even more remarkable feat was his return to the Île-de-la-Cité. He had arrived back in the Paris region with "three battalions" around the end of June 886. The Vikings tried to prevent him getting into Paris by setting a trap on the north bank of the Seine near the Île-de-la-Cité. Cornered, Odo charged "and galloped right through the throngs of the harsh foe" on a speedy horse and eventually reached the tower, the gates of which were held open for him. Some of the troops who had accompanied him fought a rear-guard action against the Danes to protect him.[4] Odo remained with the Parisians during the final awful months of the siege, which eventually fizzled out when the fatally ill Charles the Fat bribed the Vikings to withdraw.

What the siege did was to put Odo on the map as a man to be reckoned with when, in late 888, Charles the Fat, "stripped of his life and also his kingdom, [and] filled with great sadness," died. When offered the West Frankish crown, Odo happily, "took the title and authority of king . . . supported by all the Frankish people."[5] He was about twenty-six years of age.

So who was this new king of West Francia? Born about 860, Odo was the son of Robert the Strong, a relatively obscure upstart from East Francia, probably from the region between the Moselle and the Rhine rivers, who rose to prominence under Charles the Bald. He briefly broke with Charles and supported Louis the German in his 858 intervention in West Francia. But Robert quickly recovered Charles's favor and in 861 was made duke of Neustria (central western France north of the Loire), with the task of defending the region between the Seine and the Loire from the depredations of the Bretons, a Celtic people occupying present-day Brittany who had gained an independent duchy from Charles the Bald and had never accepted Frankish dominion. Robert eventually forced them to sue for peace. He then took on the Vikings, winning a great victory at the Battle of Brissarthe (near Angers) in autumn

866. But he was mortally wounded and died. He is described by the *Annals of Fulda* as "a second Maccabeus in our times, and if all his battles which he fought with the Bretons and Northmen were fully described they would be on the same level as the deeds of Maccabeus."[6] (Judas Maccabeus was a successful Jewish guerrilla leader who defeated the forces of King Antiochus IV Epiphanes [175–64 BC], who had tried to impose Hellenistic paganism on the Jews.)

Robert left two sons; the six-year-old Odo was the eldest. The boys' inheritance was seized by Charles the Bald and given to their guardian, Hugh, Abbot of Saint-Germain d'Auxerre, an ambitious, scheming warrior-monk. In 882, in his early twenties, Odo became count of Paris, and in 886 he inherited all his father's titles with the death of Abbot Hugh. During the siege of Paris, Odo succeeded his father as a successful warrior against the Vikings. But chaos would soon consume his world.

After the death of Charles the Fat, the Frankish world split apart and all pretense of central authority collapsed. In the absence of strong leadership, decisions had to be made at the local level. Local magnates came together to elect *reguli* (kinglets), as they were derisively called.[7] The "ideal" of the empire survived and, as we've seen, was even revived by the Saxon monarchs. In 888 the succession in East Francia, at least, was clear: Arnulf, the bastard grandson of Louis the German, was not only a key player in deposing Charles the Fat; he also actually had a legitimate claim to the throne based in his Carolingian ancestry.

However, the situation in West Francia was more complicated. Though there was still a direct Carolingian heir, it was Charles III the Simple, then a child of nine. Charles the Simple had already been passed over in 884 when his elder brother Carloman was accidently killed by a friend in a hunting accident. A child would scarcely be able to lead a strong defense against the Vikings, who still posed a real threat. So it was that the northern French magnates moved swiftly to elect Odo, a man with a proven track record, as interim king. Opposing this was Archbishop Fulk of Reims, who, anxious to become a political player, vigorously proposed a distant relative of his as candidate for king, Guido II of Spoleto, father-in-law of Agiltrude of Benevento. Guido rushed across the Alps and was crowned in early March 888 at Langres on the Marne by the local bishop. But Odo had beaten him to the punch; he had been crowned at Compiègne just days earlier, on February 29, 888. As Odo had a head start consolidating his rule and had a reputation as a local hero against the Vikings, Guido soon retreated to Italy rather than face the overwhelming odds of taking on the king of West Francia.

Odo nevertheless faced considerable odds of his own. Internally, he faced doubters among the magnates who saw him as a usurper displacing the child Charles, a legitimate Carolingian. Externally, he had to deal immediately with the Vikings. A victory over them in late June 888 at Montfaucon between Reims and Metz helped to strengthen his position. This success rallied some who were wavering in their support. But in 891 he was defeated by the Norsemen; he had already had to bribe them to depart from the Paris region in 889, and now his power was weakening.

He also suffered from the centrifugal forces released when Charles the Fat's empire collapsed. The new "kingdom" of Transjurane Burgundy emerged, which covered southwestern Switzerland and parts of eastern France. Odo also lost control of Aquitaine, which effectively meant the southern half of the country. With its complex politics, this region had been semi-independent for several decades and would consolidate during the tenth century. Provence had been independent since 879, and in Italy Berengar I seized power only to be immediately challenged by Guido II of Spoleto. Normandy and Brittany remained semi-independent. In France itself Odo's real authority was centered on the royal domains, a narrow north-south strip of land stretching from the Loire River and Orléans in the south to around Paris and north to Compiègne. But even here he was not unchallenged. In the north Odo had to deal with an opportunistic schemer, Baldwin of Flanders, who revolted in 892. And while Archbishop Fulk had apparently submitted after the Viking defeat at Montfaucon, he remained the leader of the pro-Carolingian party in West Francia.

As archbishop of Reims, Fulk had to be taken very seriously indeed. He was the ruler of a small ecclesiastical enclave. His predecessor, Archbishop Hincmar (845–882), had dominated both the ecclesiastical and political landscapes. The archbishop of Reims was the metropolitan archbishop of the West Frankish lands and, at least in theory, ruled the regional church in collaboration with his suffragan bishops. As church historian Friedrich Kempf says, "The metropolitan organization was, at least in the west, predominately collegial. The highest tribunal was the provincial synod, at which the metropolitan was not much more than the chairman."

But metropolitans could also act as official visitors in suffragan dioceses, and when a bishop died, the metropolitan controlled the "widowed diocese."[8]

Hincmar was a metropolitan par excellence, and as such he was often in conflict with the papacy. Fulk saw himself as another Hincmar, but he lacked both the charisma and authority of his predecessor. Nevertheless, he was no slouch, and by late 892 he was plotting to restore Charles III the Simple, who was now thirteen; according to Carolingian custom he would reach his majority at fifteen. But in Fulk's judgment, Charles had already reached the age when he could take and act on good advice. So while Odo was absent trying to assert his authority in Aquitaine, Fulk crowned Charles in the basilica of Saint Rémi in Reims on January 28, 893. Fulk immediately informed Pope Formosus and Arnulf in East Francia. Formosus sided with Charles and encouraged Arnulf to do likewise. But Arnulf cleverly inserted himself as arbiter in the dispute. But it all came to naught because Charles's supporters gradually deserted him, and by mid-897 he had to approach Odo begging forgiveness, which he received. When Odo suddenly died, aged about thirty-seven, at La Fère near Soissons on January 1, 898, from his deathbed he begged his supporters, including his brother Robert, to recognize Charles as king. Odo had barely been able to hold the kingdom together. After his death, Charles the Simple reigned over the near-total collapse of central government.

ↁ

Charles began his official reign in early 898. His initial position was strong—the all-important magnates of the south recognized him as a Carolingian descendant. However, Charles III the Simple (898–922) (*simplex* in the sense of uncomplicated and guileless, not simple-minded) faced a daunting task. Even though he was well educated, pious, and generous, he also came to the throne inexperienced and immature. A survivor, he managed to maintain his position as king by regularly appealing to his Carolingian ancestry, even if he lacked real power in many regions, being surrounded by forceful magnates in Neustria, Burgundy, Aquitaine, Flanders, the Auvergne, Toulouse, Flanders, and Poitou whose loyalty he needed to preserve the unity of the kingdom. The magnates also needed him to give them legitimacy.

His reign faced a critical challenge when, on June 17, 900, his supporter and adviser Archbishop Fulk was murdered, impaled with a lance wielded by an assassin named Winelmar acting on behalf of Count Baldwin II "the Bald" of Flanders. In a letter to the bishops of the region, Pope Benedict IV excommunicated both Baldwin and Winelmar. The clergy of Reims responded by regularly calling down an old Christian curse usually reserved for heretics on the two men: "May they be cursed in the town and cursed in the fields, cursed in their granaries, their mortal remains, the fruit of their bodies and that of their fields, their cattle, their flocks. May all be cursed who enter or exit their houses. . . . May they render up their bowels in the latrine like the perfidious Arius [a fourth-century heretic]."[9]

The threat posed by Baldwin was only one of Charles III's problems. He also had to deal with Odo's younger brother Robert. Having inherited the whole of Neustria between the Seine and the Loire, Robert now had control of what had previously been royal land. This restricted Charles's movements considerably; he rarely moved outside the royal domain around Paris.

Charles was also recognized, at least in theory, as king in Burgundy and Aquitaine. Generally speaking, up until about 910 Charles's authority was recognized and respected. He was peace loving and not a great military leader himself, so he left the defense of West Francia from the Vikings to more able military leaders, among them Robert of Neustria. When Frankish forces routed the Vikings besieging Chartres in 911 and putting them to flight, Charles gained some breathing space. This victory, as we will see, led eventually to the establishment of Normandy, which both contained the Viking threat and counterbalanced the power of Robert of Neustria.

Charles seemed to have scored another victory when he was asked by the local magnates to take control of Lotharingia in late 911 when the last Carolingian heir there, Louis IV "the Child," died. The province of Emperor Lothar II, who had died in 869, Lotharingia was known as *Francia Media*—"Middle Francia." Lacking both linguistic and ethnic coherence, it was an artificial political construct stretching from present-day northern Switzerland along both sides of the Rhine up to the county of Hainault in contemporary southern Belgium near the French border. It had been ceded to East Francia in 880, but the loyalty of the local magnates there had swung back and forth between east and west until the death of Louis IV. Then, led by Count "Long Neck" Reginar of Hainault, the Lotharingian magnates decided to throw in their lot with Charles the Simple, who had married a powerful and wealthy Lotharingian woman, Frideruna, with whom he had three daughters.

Conscious of himself as a descendant of Charlemagne, Charles fulfilled a long-held dream when he gained control of Lotharingia. He had always wanted to control the Carolingian heartland around Aachen. It also brought him wealth, land, and troops, compensating for what he had lost in Neustria. So he moved permanently into this Frankish heartland. He now saw himself as *rex Francorum*, "king of the Franks." As such he met the new king of East Francia, Henry I, who had also schemed to gain control of Lotharingia, on a barge in the Rhine near Bonn on November 7, 921. This was a kind of no-man's-land between the two kingdoms. Heinrich Fichtenau points out that rank was always central to these encounters, but on this occasion ceremony was kept to a minimum. There was recognition that both were *reges Francorum*, Charles of the west, Henry of the east, even though he was a Saxon. But in the written treaty Charles was mentioned before Henry, thereby reflecting "a certain superiority of the Carolingian king over the Saxon."[10]

But Lotharingia would become the noose around Charles's neck. After repudiating his first Lotharingian-born wife, who had provided him only with daughters, he married Eadgifu, a daughter of the Anglo-Saxon king Edward the Elder and sister of Eadgyth, who did provide him with a son, Louis, who was later nicknamed *d'Outremer*. West Francia was soon on the edge of revolt as the magnates, even those from Lotharingia, resented interference in their affairs by an obscure, lowborn favorite, Hagano, whose advice Charles constantly sought. Then Charles lost his wise counselor Archbishop Hervé of Reims, who died on July 2, 922. Archdeacon Seulfus, a creature of Robert of Neustria, was elected archbishop. Things got worse when Charles foolishly seized the abbey of Chelles near Paris from a daughter of Charles the Bald who was related by marriage to Robert and granted it to Hagano. The West Frankish magnates revolted and elected Robert king. He was quickly anointed by Walter, Archbishop of Sens, a family friend. Robert was recognized by Pope John X and Henry I of East Francia, who wanted to weaken Charles's hold on Lotharingia. In the ensuing civil war, Robert I was killed in battle with a lance at Soissons on June 15, 923, but his army was victorious.

Charles could still have recovered from this setback, but he was deceived by Heribert II, Count of Vermandois and Troyes, whose sister, Beatrice, was married to Robert I. Invited under oath by Heribert to a parley, Charles instead fell into a trap and was imprisoned at Péronne near Amiens. Heribert II was an ambitious, aggressive, and disloyal man determined to expand his county, and he wanted to use Charles as a pawn in that process. His imprisonment of Charles was considered to be a criminal kidnapping of an anointed royal person. Pope John X protested and threatened excommunication. Undaunted,

Heribert tried to capture Charles's children, both legitimate and illegitimate. Queen Eadgifu fled to England with their son, Louis. Charles died of mistreatment in prison in 929.

&

Robert's son Hugh was the natural choice for Charles's successor. His title, count of Paris, gave him control of the royal domain, and he already called himself "Duke of the Franks by the grace of God," referring to his control of Neustria. Thus, he dominated the whole region between the Seine and the Loire. He was later called "the Great." Shrewdly assessing that he would have more influence as the power behind the throne, Hugh refused the crown, and after complex negotiations the magnates turned to his brother-in-law Radulf (or Ralph or Raoul) of Burgundy.

Radulf was the son of Richard the Justiciar, first Duke of Burgundy (as distinguished from the Transjurane Kingdom of Burgundy). Richard the Justiciar and his brother Boso were, like their father, originally officials serving Louis the Pious and Charles the Bald. Their sister Richildis became Charles's concubine and then his second wife. Charles endowed the brothers with lands in Provence and southern Burgundy. Duke Richard remained a consistent ally of the Carolingian family and a fierce fighter against the Vikings. A tall man who was a warrior, his sobriquet "Justiciar," which implied a just ruler and was given to him later (the word only came into common usage in the twelfth century), is hard to understand. In fact, Richard had carved out his duchy with ruthlessness, seizing control over important monastic properties and dioceses. His aim was to subdue all the bishoprics in Burgundy so that he could appoint his own nominees. In a masterly strategic move, he gained control of the diocese of Autun by marrying his daughter to local Bishop Walo de Vergy's son. His actions in the diocese of Langres were far less subtle: in 894 he got his brother-in-law and supporter, the callous Count Manassès de Vergy of Autun and Chalon-sur-Saône, to tear out the eyes of Bishop Teutbold II and to imprison Walter, Archbishop of Sens. Both men had resisted Richard's ambitions. Richard and Manassès were subsequently excommunicated by Pope Formosus.

Richard died in 921. His son Radulf was married to Emma, the daughter of Robert I, so it was understandable that the magnates turned to Radulf after Robert's death in battle. Inevitably Radulf (923–936) was very dependent on Hugh the Great, who had refused the crown. Radulf quickly fell out with

Heribert II of Vermandois, who still held Charles the Simple prisoner and who had seized the important ecclesiastical enclave of Reims. He also demanded the strategically important town of Laon, which was often used as a residence for Carolingian kings. Radulf wanted Laon, a strong defensive position on a hill, as his base in northern Francia, so he refused to surrender it. Despite a heroic defense by Radulf's wife, Emma, of "the mount of Laon," as Flodoard's *Annals* calls it, Heribert seized the town for a period but was eventually displaced.[11] He then tried to use his prisoner Charles the Simple as a bargaining chip against Radulf by threatening to restore Charles to the throne. This threat became moot with Charles's death in 929.

Heribert had also used his control of Reims to impose his young son Hugh on the diocese as archbishop after the unexpected death of Archbishop Seulfus in 925. Showing complete contempt for ecclesiastical processes, "Count Heribert came to Reims and saw to it that both the vassals and clergy of this church respected his advice concerning the election of an archbishop." No doubt he reinforced his advice with threats. As a result, Reims "was committed to Count Heribert who managed it for his son Hugh, a small boy . . . not yet five years of age," which must be close to the record for the youngest bishop ever in church history.[12]

Control of Reims gave Heribert the ability to exploit the landholdings and wealth of the diocese. One of Heribert's hacks, Bishop Abbo of Soissons, went to Rome to persuade Pope John X to confirm the child's election. In trouble himself with Marozia, John X approved Hugh's election but nominated Abbo as interim administrator of the diocese. He was soon replaced by Bishop Odalricus of Aix-en-Provence, whose diocese had been overrun by the Saracens. But this was not the end of the child-bishop affair.

Strained relations and actual warfare between Heribert and Radulf continued as the king worked to extend royal power in northern Francia, although there were times when the two cooperated to contain Viking incursions. Radulf and Hugh the Great eventually recaptured Reims in 931. They immediately sacked the child archbishop Hugh and replaced him with a monk, Artoldus, from the local monastery of Saint Rémi.

Radulf had been very active throughout his reign with the thankless task of trying to control revolting magnates and warlords as well as defending the realm against the Vikings and Magyars. By 935 exhaustion had caught up with him, and "he lay seriously ill throughout the entire autumn."[13] He died on

January 14, 936. Immediately, Flodoard tells us, "Count Hugh [the Great] sent across the sea [to England] and summoned Louis, the son of Charles [the Simple], to take up the rule of the kingdom [of Francia]." Louis's mother, Eadgifu, had fled to England with him after the imprisonment of Charles the Simple. Louis's uncle, King Aethelstan, "sent him back to France along with bishops and others of his *fideles* [faithful followers] after oaths had been given by the legates of the Franks. Hugh and the rest of the nobles of the Franks set out to meet Louis when he left the ship, and they committed themselves to him on the beach at Boulogne-sur-Mer just as both sides had previously agreed." They then traveled to Laon, where Louis, now aged sixteen, was anointed and crowned by Archbishop Artoldus "in the presence of the *princeps* of the kingdom and more than twenty bishops."[14] It was an auspicious beginning for Louis IV (936–954).

But why did Hugh the Great invite Louis back as king? Why not seize the kingship himself? Louis was a Carolingian, a great-grandson of Charles the Bald. But then Heribert II of Vermandois was also a Carolingian, descended from a bastard grandson of Charlemagne, King Bernard of Italy. Some argued that Hugh the Great was suffering from a guilty conscience for his betrayal of Charles the Simple and that he was hoping to ease his conscience by restoring the legitimate Carolingian line. Pierre Riché remarks, "It is quite possible that Hugh's intentions were upright and sincere" and that no matter what happened, he still had the young king under his thumb, "retaining effective leadership in the kingdom for himself."[15]

After the coronation of Louis IV, Hugh the Great patched up his relationship with Heribert II of Vermandois, and in 940 Heribert again seized Reims. He reimposed his now nineteen-year-old son, Hugh, on the diocese as archbishop. According to Flodoard, the terrified Archbishop Artoldus "was persuaded to abdicate from the office and power of his see."[16] Pope Stephen VIII sent Hugh the pallium as a conciliatory gesture to try to shore up support for Louis IV, who had now been abandoned by Heribert and by Hugh the Great, both of whom were negotiating with Otto I. There was nothing new, of course, in magnates playing off the rulers of Western and Eastern Francia against each other. But the situation shifted again when Heribert II died unexpectedly on February 23, 943. The initiative shifted back to Louis IV, until in 945 he was betrayed and handed over to Hugh the Great, who imprisoned him.

Things swung back in Louis's favor when both Otto I and Pope Marinus II pressured Hugh to release him. Supported by Otto, Louis had a chance to consolidate his control of the area north of the Seine. He besieged Reims with a large army in 946, and Archbishop Hugh's allies advised him to surrender because "if the *urbs* [city] should be taken by storm they would not be able to intercede . . . to prevent his eyes from being torn out." Hugh surrendered, and Artoldus returned as archbishop. Archbishops Robert of Trier and Frederick of Mainz "received [Artoldus] and, with each one taking one of his hands, they restored him to the same episcopal throne."[17] He remained archbishop until his death in 961.

In mid-947 Archbishop Hugh, allied with Hugh the Great, again attacked Reims but withdrew after an eight-day siege. Negotiations and armed conflict over control of the diocese dragged on for another year until Pope Agapitus II, responding to a letter from Archbishop Artoldus, sent a legate to Otto I and asked him to call a general synod for the Frankish lands. As we saw in a previous chapter, this suited Otto's strategic plans, and the synod began deliberations at Ingelheim near Mainz on June 7, 948. The synod also aimed to reconcile King Louis with Hugh the Great. "These conflicts," Flodoard comments, "disturbed the entire kingdom of the Franks." The synod was attended by Otto I, Louis IV, papal legate Bishop Marinus, and thirty-one other bishops, including Artoldus. Archbishop Hugh refused to attend. Despite an attempt by a partisan of Archbishop Hugh to deceive the synod with a forged document, Artoldus was confirmed as archbishop of Reims, and "they excommunicated the aforesaid Hugh, the invader of the church of Reims, until he should do penance and make worthy satisfaction."[18] The other Hugh—Hugh the Great— "having invaded and ravaged the kingdom of King Louis should be struck down by the sword of excommunication unless he presents himself at the Synod and makes amends for his appalling impudence."[19]

But getting Hugh the Great under control was a challenging task. He was creating chaos in northern Francia. With a contingent of Vikings he besieged Soissons. "He killed many of the defenders and burned the . . . [cathedral]. . . . He also burned the canon's cloister and part of the *civitas* [town]." He "plundered the *villae* [agricultural estates] of the church of Reims. . . . Hugh's thieves killed many of the dependents, violated churches and raged so furiously that in the village of Cormicy they killed almost forty men around the church and plundered that temple of everything."

A synod at Trier, attended by papal legate Marinus and supported by Otto I, again excommunicated Hugh the Great "until he should come to his senses and make satisfaction. . . . If he should reject this he should go to Rome for his absolution."[20] Hugh tried to resist, but by early 950 with Otto now firmly supporting Louis, Hugh surrendered and made himself the "king's man." As part of the deal he surrendered Laon to Louis.

Sadly Louis's success was short-lived. Riding from Laon to Reims in early 954, he spotted a wolf ahead of him on the road. Unable to resist a hunt, he took off after the wolf but then fell off his horse at full gallop. He was badly injured, which was aggravated by an already-existing elephantiasis, a parasitic condition causing obstruction of the lymph and enlargement of a limb or the scrotum as a result. He had been suffering from this disease for several years and he died of his injuries soon afterward.

❦

From our perspective, West Francia in these years seems to verge on an incomprehensible and chaotic mess. A series of questions arises: what, really, was the role of the king? Were these men genuinely "kings" in any meaningful way or simply the first among equals for a brief period of time? How many magnates and warlords were there, and what power did they have? What were the guiding principles of government? In answering these questions, we need to see things from the perspective of tenth-century psychology and how people viewed government.

For us, it stands to reason that a king rules a kingdom, which is a geographical entity with delineated borders. If not, he must not be a real king. But during these times, kings were personal, rather than territorial, rulers. That is, their authority became real only when they were present. Furthermore the "kingdom" as a geographical entity was an abstraction that made no sense. People didn't use a word like "Francia" to describe the area within the borders of the kingdom. Rather, Francia was an ill-defined area traditionally occupied by the Franks around which the king moved, making his presence felt in a literal sense. Here, as Jean Dunbabin says, "the west Frankish king was powerful in some localities, he engaged in conflict elsewhere, he was important in yet other places; and the pattern changed with time."[21] While the notion of kingship as a sacred office remained, the king's direct authority was limited to the royal domains, and even there his authority was sometimes challenged. Elsewhere the extent of his authority varied from considerable to negligible to nonexistent. *Regnum* was the personal act of ruling. This was exercised in general terms by the king and locally by many others. Magnates and aristocrats "ruled," and like the king their authority depended on their presence. Of course, being local meant they were more "present" because they controlled smaller areas and could make their presence felt more effectively. From one perspective, West Francia was a kind of experiment in decentralized government. And the more local the control, the more focused and intense it was. Power and authority were increasingly devolved as the magnates saw themselves as partners in ruling and as the electors of kings.

From another perspective, West Francia progressively disintegrated as the power of the royal government diminished. In this kind of breakdown of authority, ambitious thugs with aristocratic ambitions inevitably seized their opportunity. With insecurity reigning everywhere, people looked increasingly to magnates and local warlords to shield them from rapine, brigandage, land grabbing, feuds, and atrocities by neighboring warlords on the lookout to extend their territories. In a prayer in his *History*, the monk Richer tells God that "people refuse to acknowledge the king's authority but are besotted with grabbing for themselves as much as they can from others."[22]

In the end West Francia simply disintegrated into its component parts. All that existed was a loose and constantly shifting confederation of dukedoms, counties, ecclesiastical and secular seigniories, and royal domains. There were wide differences in language, culture, ethnicity (Franks, Bretons, Normans, Gallo-Romans, Provencal, Spanish), law, economics, coinage, and even weights and measures. The cultural and linguistic differences between the Frankish north and the south, including the duchies of Aquitaine and Gascony, were considerable. Because this was a shifting and flexible situation, it is difficult to know precisely how many divisions there were within the generally accepted borders of West Francia at any given time. Around the year 1035, there were five duchies, one marquisate, at least forty-two counties (but probably more), two secular seigniories (lordships), eight ecclesiastical seigniories (enclaves ruled by bishops), plus the royal domains and two royal dependencies. There was much intermarriage between the rulers of the different divisions, which led to ever-more-complex sets of interrelationships and rivalries, which as often as not led to war rather than peace.

These family connections have provided a treasure trove for modern-day genealogists. In this context a certain amount of social fluidity was possible. An example is Baldwin I or Baldwin "Iron Arm" (ca. 830–879). He rose from complete obscurity to seize power in the thinly populated region of Flanders and to declare himself count. He gained real fame when he persuaded Judith, the daughter of Charles the Bald, to elope with him. Traveling to Rome, the couple then persuaded Pope Nicholas I to recognize their marriage. It was their son Baldwin II who had Archbishop Fulk of Reims murdered in 900. Another ambitious man on the make with genuine military prowess was Heribert II, who fought his way to control of the county of Vermandois and the surrounding regions. He then had to defend them. Fighting was the natural occupation of the upper class.

Essentially, authority was based on the ability to provide protection. Power bases tended to be either regional or local, dominated by dukes, counts, and other titled warlords with bands of *milites* (retainers) enforcing their will. *Castellani* (castles and fortifications) were increasingly built across the landscape. They were "sited to dominate the most important geographical point—road junction, river crossing, or valley—in a region which was vital to guarantee the holder control of the area, which meant frustrating any enemy attempt to penetrate the area."[23] Life for most people was confined to the immediate locality and to an economy based on community subsistence. Even though it was a primitive form of social arrangement, it did answer the actual needs of the times. Later historians have dubbed this "feudalism," although it shouldn't be seen as a generalized system as though it were the same everywhere. This arrangement was highly localized, and its twin poles were land use and armed protection. Wealth was dependent on possession of land, and armed protection provided by local warlords maintained that possession. Dunbabin pithily says, "What . . . [people] sought was a lesser Charlemagne in the neighbourhood."[24]

The result was that upper-class males faced the danger of injury or death from almost constant, low-level warfare. Warlords were often caught up in defending or extending their own territories or involved in wider regional struggles. This was particularly so south of the Loire, where aristocrats considered themselves outside all legal and royal control. Localized violence became a way of life. People who had become inured to the destructiveness of the Vikings now had to suffer the anarchy resulting from their own leaders' behavior.

ভ৲

Local power bases were the rule. We have seen such examples as Hugh the Great's in Neustria, Heribert II's in Vermandois, Richard the Justiciar's in Burgundy, and Counts Baldwin I and II's in Flanders. Another important duchy was Normandy. Its establishment was the most important act of Charles the Simple's reign because it altered the strategic balance in Europe. While it didn't end Norse incursions, Normandy created a buffer that to some extent protected inland West Francia from raids. After being defeated near Auxerre, a Viking force led by a certain Rollo (probably not the same Rollo who was at the siege of Paris in 885–886) was subsequently again caught flat-footed and vulnerable as he attempted to besiege Chartres in July 911 and was again driven off by now more confident Frankish troops. Seizing the opportunity, Charles the Simple began peace negotiations with Rollo.

We know nothing of Rollo's Scandinavian origins, although one possibility is that he was a Norwegian named Ganger Hrólf, or Rolf the Walker (Latinized as Rollo), because he was so big that no horse could bear his weight and therefore he had to walk everywhere. While documentation for the early history of Normandy is lacking, we do know that Charles and Rollo met in October 911 at St. Clair-sur-Epte, east of Rouen, to discuss establishing a region where the Vikings could permanently settle. According to the *Chronicle of Saint Denis*, written some two hundred years after the event, they were first offered the province of Flanders but "rejected it as being too marshy." Or, more likely, they knew they would have to deal with Count Baldwin. Eventually, Rollo accepted the region around Rouen and the lower Seine, the core of what became the county of Normandy.

Apparently a comedy of errors occurred when Rollo accepted Charles's offer but refused to kiss the king's foot. He "ordered one of his warriors to perform the act in his stead. This man seized the foot of the king and lifted it to his lips, kissing it without bending and so causing the king to tumble over backwards. At that there was a loud burst of laughter and a great commotion in the crowd of onlookers."

Charles recovered his dignity and could at least smile to himself when soon afterward "Rollo was baptized . . . by Franco, archbishop of Rouen. . . . The pagans, seeing that their chieftain had become a Christian, abandoned their idols, received the name of Christ, and with one accord desired to be baptized. Meanwhile, the Norman duke made ready for a splendid wedding and married [Gisela] the daughter of the king according to Christian rites."[25]

Gisela cannot have been much more than five at the time of the marriage. Rollo became a count subject to Charles. Most of the Frankish nobility had pulled out of the Normandy region, so the Vikings were unchallenged as they brought in their families for permanent settlement.

For Charles this was a wise move. It both contained the Viking threat somewhat and set up a counterweight to the power of Robert in Neustria. But it didn't entirely stop Norse raids. Flodoard's *Annals* records twenty-one separate attacks by Norsemen in West Francia between 919 and 948. And two other major and several minor Norse settlements had already emerged: the most important were those in Normandy and another in the Nantes/Loire region.

Vikings had been active along the Loire for seventy-five years. They first arrived there in 843, and making the most of a vicious feud between Rainald, Duke of Nantes and two Breton counts, they seized Nantes on the feast of Saint John the Baptist, June 24, 843. A terrible massacre followed. They "slew the bishop and many clergy and lay people of both sexes, and sacked the *civitas*." One version of the story is that Bishop Gohardus was killed while celebrating Mass. If later chronicles are right, this was a particularly barbaric attack mounted by the group of Vikings we have already seen settling on the island of Noirmoutier at the mouth of the Loire. By the early tenth century, the Vikings were settled in the county of Nantes, although "the city of Nantes remained for many years deserted, devastated and overgrown with briars and thorns."[26] The Viking's Princeps was one Ragenold, whose warriors ranged widely across Francia, sometimes in cooperation with the Norse from Rouen.

Celtic Brittany also suffered badly from Viking depredations, being attacked by both the Loire group and those from Normandy. But a revival of the Breton dukedom began in 936 when Alan II "Crooked Beard" returned from exile in England. Alan "was strong in body and very courageous and did not care to kill wild boars and bears in the forest with an iron weapon but with a wooden staff."[27] By 939 he had recaptured Nantes and expelled the Vikings from the lower Loire. This spelled the end of this Viking enclave, which had provided a model for Normandy. Nevertheless, Alan's Brittany remained vulnerable, and he was soon defeated in what Flodoard calls "a catastrophe" in 944 that led to "a massacre of the Bretons and pushing them out of their own land. Those Northmen who had invaded their lands had recently come from across the sea," that is, from England.[28] However, Alan survived this raid, and it was not until after his death in 952 that real trouble began for Brittany when Alan's son died young and his bastard sons fought each other for supremacy. Brittany languished as a weak principality for the next two hundred years. But it never lost its sense of identity as a Celtic enclave.

Early Norman history has scant source material because the Vikings were largely illiterate and keeping records was not part of their tradition. However, while they were not great chroniclers, the early Normans were a people in transition so that "by mid-century Normandy was not a Viking colony; it was a region of France, distinct, indeed, from other provinces (as they were distinct from one another) but unquestionably French."[29] So while it is difficult to be precise about the early years of Normandy, the facts seem to be that Rollo and his successors William I and Richard gradually expanded the duchy of Normandy by shrewd political and strategic deals, at the same time picking off vulnerable neighbors and bringing other Vikings in the region under control. Rollo seems to have acted as a Frankish count representing the king, even as he continued to rule by terror in the Viking tradition; criminal punishments were exceptionally brutal.

Widespread intermarriage occurred between Norse settlers from Denmark, northeast England, and Ireland and Frankish women. Pagan Norse traditions and Christianity coexisted, with many people having two names, a pagan Viking one and a Christian name. The monk-chronicler Adamar of Chabannes gives a more extreme example of having it both ways from the last days of Rollo's life. He says Rollo "had many prisoners beheaded in his presence in honor of those gods he had once worshipped. And as well he distributed an unlimited weight of gold to the churches in honor of the true God whose name he had accepted at baptism."[30]

About 927 Rollo seems to have handed over the rule of Normandy to his son William I "Long Sword" (927–942). In contrast to his semipagan father, William was a committed Christian and wanted to enter a monastery, but he eventually married the daughter of Heribert II, Liutgard. William certainly had to confront a great deal of resentment, even rebellion, from pagan elements in Norman society who resisted Christianity and the abandonment of traditional customs. He gradually got the situation under control and then invaded Brittany, presumably on the principle that there is nothing like a foreign war to unite people at home. In the latter part of his reign, he became involved in another nasty war with Arnulf I of Flanders (918–965) in which he "ravaged with raids and fire some *villae* belonging to Count Arnulf."[31] Arnulf's revenge was swift. He arranged the treacherous murder of William on a small island in the Somme River during a truce in late December 942.

William was succeeded by his ten-year-old son, Richard I (942–996). During Richard's long, peaceful reign, Christianity became firmly established in

Normandy and the population became "French" rather than Norse. Now the self-proclaimed "duke" of Normandy, Richard established a Carolingian-style administration, married Emma the daughter of Hugh the Great, and maintained peace with his neighbors largely based on fear of his military prowess. He also turned his attention to reform of the church, which included the restoration and strengthening of diocesan structures and the establishment of monasticism, including the magnificent UNESCO World Heritage site of Mont Saint Michel on the coast near Avaranches. By the time of Richard's death in 996, the duchy of Normandy was firmly established and was to become a major player in international affairs in the following century.

Another element in the West Francian mix was the southern duchy of Aquitaine. William I "the Pious" (875–918), Count of Auvergne controlled a large inheritance in southeastern Aquitaine, and Ranulf II (850–890), Count of Poitou controlled much of northwestern Aquitaine. Between them these two men dominated the region south of the Loire with the exception of Gascony and Catalonia. Their power depended on their ability to manage the aristocracy, most of whom were keen to carve out their own areas of influence. William was competent and pious; he was the founder of Cluny Abbey. His friend Ranulf II, in contrast, died early, possibly by poison, leaving no legitimate offspring. His titles were inherited by his bastard, Ebalus Manzer (902–934/5). The term *manzer* (or *mamzer*) in the rabbinical tradition refers to a person conceived in a forbidden sexual union, presumably in this case in a relationship between Ranulf and a married Jewish woman. After a decade as a refugee in the court of William the Pious and supported by Gerald of Aurillac, Manzer reconquered Poitiers and recovered his title as count of Poitou. His reign was not particularly distinguished, although he held the title of duke of Aquitaine from 928 until his death in 935.

William died in 918 and was succeeded by his nephew William II, who managed to lose all that his uncle had achieved. He died in 926. Confusion followed. Archibald R. Lewis comments that "the story of the first three quarters of the tenth century is one . . . of the failure of the territorial state in these regions, and a continuing decay of such machinery of government as survived. . . . By 975 what had emerged in southern France was not principalities, but a system which was so disorganized in a political sense that it approached anarchy."[32]

❧

The result of the limited competence of rulers like William II and Ebalus Manzer was that southern France became dominated by local warlords and thugs and grew into an epicenter of localized and often violent warfare. This was caused as much by the decentralized nature of the region as by the weakness of central government. The church tried to stem the extent of feudal warfare through "the peace of God." Beginning in the chaotic central-west of France in 989, the peace, later to become the "truce of God," spread rapidly over the next forty years, threatening warlords with excommunication if they seized church lands or infringed sanctuary when threatened people took refuge in a church. It was designed to use moral pressure to protect the clergy, church property, women, the poor and their animals and property, pilgrims, merchants, and all who didn't bear arms from marauding thugs. The biggest threat to those breaking the peace was the use of relics and the bodies of the saints to frighten warlords with curses from the afterlife if they engaged in warfare. Today we find this almost incomprehensible, but in the tenth century relics were thought to conjure up the very presence of the saint or holy person whose influence with God was thought to be very powerful. In some ways it was like pointing the bone except that the context was theological and its purpose was to prevent war and enforce social justice for the powerless. In other words, there was nothing like a dead saint or a visitation from a vengeful God or angel to tame an illiterate thug. Warlords gradually came to see the peace as a kind of treaty with God, the breaking of which would lead to divine chastisement. The movement soon took on a popular tinge as the church used crowds of ordinary people to persuade warlords to stop fighting.

The garrulous Burgundian monk Rodulfus Glaber describes how the peace of God worked around the year 1033. He says that the time leading up to "the millennium of the Lord's passion" (Jesus was thirty-three when he was crucified) were "years of famine and disaster . . . [and] violent rainstorms." These were followed by a time when "the happy face of the sky began to shine" and

> the bishops and abbots and other devout men of Aquitaine first summoned great councils of the whole people to which were borne the bodies of many saints and innumerable caskets of holy relics. The movement spread to Arles and Lyons, then across all Burgundy into the furthest corners of the French realm. Throughout the dioceses it was decreed that in fixed places the bishops and magnates of the country should convene councils for re-establishing

peace and consolidating the holy faith. When the people heard this, great, middling and poor, they came rejoicing and ready, one and all, to obey the commands of the clergy no less than if they had been given by a voice from heaven speaking to men on earth. For all were still cowed by the recent carnage, and feared least they might not obtain future abundance and plenty.

Glaber also reports that "the robber and a man who seized another's domains were to suffer the whole rigour of the law, either by a heavy fine or corporal punishment."[33]

There is a real sense in which this was really the first major popular movement in the European West. It began at a local episcopal gathering on June 1, 989, at the monastery at Charroux, near Poitiers in Aquitaine. Peace councils followed at Le Puy (990), Narbonne (990), Limoges (994), and Poitiers (1000). This movement coincides with the millennium, which was identified not only with God's judgment on the earth, but also with a peace described in a prophecy of Isaiah: "For the boots of the tramping warriors and all the garments rolled in blood shall be burned as fuel for the fire. . . . [God] will establish and uphold . . . justice and righteousness from this time onward and forever" (Isaiah 9: 5–7). Peace assemblies were held in the open fields, with increasingly large crowds gathering. Relics were brought in from surrounding sanctuaries, and the local nobility as well as abbots and bishops pledged to preserve the peace. Warlords swore oaths on the relics that they would preserve peace.

From central western France the movement spread northward to Orléans (1010) and then into the territory of King Robert II (996–1031) and eastward into Burgundy in 1025. Glaber tells us that Robert II "lived in peace with the rulers around his borders, especially the [German] Emperor Henry II." Henry and Robert met in 1023 on the Meuse River to strengthen the peace. Protocol demanded a midriver meeting on boats, but Henry II took the initiative and "arose at dawn, and taking with him only a small escort crossed the river to the king of the French; they embraced warmly and kissed, heard Mass celebrated by the bishops, and decided to take breakfast together."[34] They exchanged gifts and proclaimed a universal peace. By the middle of the eleventh century, the peace had spread to Italy and Spain.

The sustaining element in the movement was the popular assemblies. There was often a miraculous element in these assemblies. Glaber comments that "many sick people were cured at these gatherings. . . . Lest any doubt this, let it be recorded that as the bent legs and arms were straightened and returned to their normal state, skin was broken, flesh was torn and blood ran freely. . . . Such enthusiasm was generated that the bishops raised their crosiers to the heavens and all cried out . . . Peace! Peace! Peace!"[35]

While the rapid spread and the effectiveness of the peace of God has been widely acknowledged, there is considerable debate as to its ultimate effectiveness. It grew out of the assemblies of Frankish bishops, who had what we would now call something of a social justice tradition and a sense of obligation to protect the poor and vulnerable. The Carolingian monarchs Louis the Pious and Lothar also called triannual local assemblies that included the ordinary people and at which there was at least a semblance of consultation to balance the power of the magnates. As Carolingian power and central government declined, the church stepped into the breach, and diocesan church councils became the locus for demonstrations on behalf of the poor. This led to legislation that threatened the violent with excommunication and interdict if they broke the peace. Those who refused to keep the peace were excluded from Mass and Communion, refused forgiveness of sin, and denied church burial in consecrated ground, which effectively condemned them to hell. As Ronald C. Musto, the major historian of the Catholic peace tradition, says, "In an age when salvation was the goal of life, such measures were of incalculable power."[36] What is revolutionary about the peace of God movement is that it transformed the unarmed weak and poor from "victims" into active participants in society.

The energy that drove the peace movement could not last forever, and there were always warlords who ignored ecclesiastical threats. But the real threat to the movement came when the aristocracy institutionalized it into the truce of God, which simply limited warfare to specific days and seasons. The truce imposed a ban on violence on Sundays and holy days, which was gradually extended to holy seasons such as Christmas, Lent, Easter, and Advent.

But bellicose instincts soon found other outlets. At the very time that Pope Urban II (1088–1099) was legislating the truce of God into church law at the Council of Clermont in 1095, he was proclaiming the First Crusade, calling for the conquest of the Saracens and the recapturing of Jerusalem. In other words, warlike instincts were now being projected outward. Attaining peace was easier said than done.

✑

When last we left the West Frankish royal story, it was 954 and Louis IV *d'Outremer* had just died. Louis's wife, Queen Gerberga, the sister of Otto I, began negotiations with Duke Hugh the Great "asking for his counsel and aid. Hugh met with her receiving her honourably and consoling her" and promising that her thirteen-year-old son, Lothar IV, would succeed.[37] Lothar was crowned and anointed at Reims on November 12, 954, and immediately assumed office as king. Hugh must have been tempted to seize the office himself, but perhaps he still felt more influential as the power behind the throne. Also, his power "was perhaps less substantial than is commonly thought for his vassals increasingly looked to the betterment of their own fortunes rather than his," which suggests he was weaker than he seemed.[38] Hugh was appointed guardian of the royal estates but died suddenly in 956. Lothar's maternal uncle Bruno, Archbishop of Cologne, now ruler of Lotharingia and brother of Otto I, assumed the guardianship. Hugh the Great was succeeded by his young son Hugh Capet, who became count of Paris and duke of the Franks. Lothar was now fifteen and Hugh a bit older, possibly seventeen. The word "Capet" is most likely derived from the Latin *cappa*, meaning a "cape," which he may have worn as a lay abbot of the monasteries of Saint Martin at Tours and Saint Denis near Paris. While friendly with Lothar, Hugh Capet's power placed him in a complex relationship with the young king, who acted decisively to bring the northern warlords to heel. He forced Arnulf I of Flanders to return the royal enclave around Mentreuil and the Canche River, which Arnulf had seized. The king later took Arras and Douai from Flanders. He also intervened in Normandy in support of Richard I. Riché reports, "A certain equilibrium emerged between the magnates and the king in the north."[39]

Things were more difficult for Lothar in the east and south, especially when he attempted to retake Lotharingia from Otto II. Lothar ruled until 986, and near the end of his reign his authority decreased in favor of that of Hugh Capet. He was briefly succeeded by his son Louis V *"Le Fainéant"* (Lazybones), who was accidently killed during a hunting party on May 22, 987. He was the last of the Carolingians. There was now no one left with any claim to Carolingian legitimacy. The line had simply died out. In a way this was an advantage because it cleared the way for the emergence of men of real ability and talent to rule. This had already happened in East Francia (Germany) with the emergence of the Saxon monarchy and Otto I. West Francia (France) now had a chance to achieve something similar, but the sheer diversity of the region and the devolution of government to so many local units made it very difficult for any one person to consolidate sufficient power to rule the whole country. France would remain a "geographical expression" for several centuries. But at least in the north and in the region around Paris, the remnant of the Carolingian empire, an able man seized power. He was Hugh Capet, who was elected to succeed Louis V in July 987.

∾

We will turn now to Spain, where an ordered state certainly existed: the Saracen caliphate of al-Andalus, which covered much but not all of present-day Spain. Spain was also the southern frontier between the Muslim world and Christianity, the place where there were real and often tense and violent interactions between Islamic and Christian faith and culture. Approximately two-thirds of Spain came under Islamic dominance; one-third of the peninsula remained Christian. During the tenth century, the Christian enclaves were under great pressure, but eventually it was from these Christian remnants that the *reconquista*, the gradual "reconquest," of Spain by Catholicism emerged. This was not completed until the fifteenth century. So any attempt to discuss Western Europe in the tenth century that neglects Spain would not only be incomplete; it also would be unbalanced and in the end untrue. So it is to Spain that we will now turn to discover how the peninsula was conquered by the Muslims in the first place.

CHAPTER 8

Muslims and Christians in Spain

AFTER A CENTURY OF SWIFT Muslim military expansion across the Middle East and North Africa, it was greed that led the Moorish governor of al-Andalus, Abd al-Rahmān, into the defeat that signaled the end of an era. The defeat occurred on a Saturday in October 732 (probably October 25), on the old Roman road between Poitiers and Tours. The *Mozarabic Chronicle of 754* reports that Abd al-Rahmān had previously sacked Bordeaux and defeated Eudo, Duke of Aquitaine near the confluence of the Dordogne and Garonne rivers. The duke's army was "falling apart and fleeing" so that "only God knew how many died or vanished," most presumably drowned in the rivers.[1] Eudo escaped, but the Moors continued pursuing him northward while sacking forts and burning churches on the way, including Poitiers.

Their advance was slowed by the amount of booty they were carrying. However, spurred on by the promise of more, Abd al-Rahmān set his sights on Tours as his ultimate target. He knew that there was a pilgrimage church there, the shrine of Saint Martin, richly endowed with treasure. Also as a *ghazi*, a champion of the Islamic faith, it was incumbent on him to destroy the town, burn down the churches, and slaughter the Christians. But he could also take advantage of the spoils of war and add to his already large collection of booty.

Taking advantage of Abd al-Rahmān's protracted advance, Eudo had time to get a message through to the *major domus* (Mayor of the Palace) Charles, the de facto ruler of Merovingian Gaul, that the Muslims were leaving Poitiers for Tours. A consummate survivor of the ruthless and often deadly politics of the late Merovingian monarchy, Charles was also, according to the *Mozarabic*

181

Chronicle, "a man who from his warrior youth was an expert in military affairs."[2] He aimed to stop Abd al-Rahmān before he reached Tours.

The two armies first made contact about 13 miles (20 kilometers) north of Poitiers near the tiny hamlet of Moussais-la-Bataille. After a week of preliminary skirmishing, the main battle began. The *Mozarabic Chronicle* says that Charles adopted a careful strategy with his infantry in "a tight battle-line held together like a glacier in the cold zones."[3] Their discipline meant they were able to ward off repeated Moorish cavalry charges. The two armies disengaged as night fell. Early next morning the Franks scouted around the enemy's encampment ready for another engagement only to find the Moors had already retreated. They had fled because Abd al-Rahmān had been killed. They withdrew in tight formation back across the Pyrenees to Spain. It is hard to be precise as to how many men were involved at Poitiers, but there were probably about 40,000 Moors and about 25,000 Franks. Charles was given the epithet *Martellus* (the Hammer). The Franks recovered much of the stolen booty.

Was Charles Martel's victory the turning point in the defense of Christianity against the Muslim onslaught? Or was it just a Moorish raid gone wrong? Really, it was both. In any event, what it did do was to confine Moorish sovereignty in Spain and end a period of rapid expansion into France.

We have already seen the explosive expansion of Islam out of Arabia and across North Africa. After conquering North Africa, an army of about 12,000 mainly Berber soldiers crossed from North Africa to Gibraltar in early 711 under the command of Tāriq ibn Ziyard. The Christian Visigoths who had controlled Spain for two hundred fifty years had neither achieved stability nor eliminated civil strife during their rule. The resultant lack of unified resistance made Moorish victory easy. Tāriq and his successor, Mūsā ibn Nusayr, who led another army of 18,000 mainly Arab troops into Spain, quickly conquered most of the country.

Between 661 and 750 the Muslim world was ruled from Damascus by the Umayyad caliphate, but direct Umayyad control in western North Africa ebbed and flowed. So al-Andalus was ruled by a series of governors, some appointed from North Africa, others from faraway Damascus. The result was political instability. Berber revolts in North Africa in 731 and 739 stirred up their fellow countrymen in the occupying forces in al-Andalus, as did the violent and bloody Abbasid overthrow of the Umayyad caliphate in Damascus in 750. The Muslim occupiers, like the Visigoths before them, were riven with internecine strife.

The Moors never permanently occupied the whole peninsula. Nor was their control uniform: the Visigoths were not completely defeated in the north, and a Visigothic revolt between 718 and 722 led to the establishment of the kingdom of Asturias in the northwest corner of the peninsula. King Alfonso I "the Catholic" (739–757) drove the Moors out of Galicia and absorbed this far-western province into Asturias, which by 790 was a well-established northwestern state. Further expansion occurred under King Alfonso II "the Chaste" (791–842). He established his capital at Oviedo and revived Visigothic forms of government in church and state. The kingdom continued to expand with the absorption of Castille (from *castellum*, "castle") as a frontier buffer against the Moors, with further expansion and stabilization under Alfonso III "the Great" (866–910). His sons transferred the capital further south from Oviedo to León, and throughout the tenth century it was known as the Kingdom of León.

Whether under Muslim or Visigothic rule, relics and pilgrimage centers remained important in this period, and the kingdom of Asturias-León had the relics of Saint James the Apostle at Compostela. The legend was that Saint James preached briefly in Spain and then returned to die in Jerusalem. But in the early ninth century, Bishop Theodemir of Iria Flavia (now Padrón near Compostela) claimed to have found the body of Saint James in a field. A cult began in Compostela that soon became part of the ideology of the *reconquista*. Saint James was said to have appeared as a knight during a number of important battles and became known as *Matamoros*, the "Moor slayer."

Closely related geographically to Asturias was another group of people never conquered by the Moors, the Basques. A pre-Celtic people, the Basques are possibly the most ancient in Europe. In the eighth century they lived on the Bay Biscay where the coast turns westward, with their territory stretching eastward toward the mid-Pyrenees and south to the upper reaches of the Ebro River. Basque settlement also traversed the Pyrenees into Gascony, a word derived from Vasconia, the original Roman name for the Basque lands. Some Basque territory was absorbed by the kingdom of Asturias, but the Basques remained fiercely independent, as a number of intruders such as Charlemagne would find out at great cost.

Charles Martel and his son Pippin III "the Short" followed up the victory at Poitiers by driving the Moors out of most of southern France. When in 778 Charlemagne was invited into Spain by the dissident Moorish *wali* (governor) of Barcelona, the emperor-to-be was ensnared in a strategic quagmire, with infighting among his Muslim allies. His troubles increased when the Saxon revolt under Widukind forced him to retreat prematurely. He withdrew back across the Pyrenees, using the mountain pass at Roncevaux. Here the Frankish rear guard was trapped in mid-August 778 by anti-Frankish Basques.

The Basques staged an ambush. Hidden in forests above the 3,470-foot (1,050-meter) pass, they waited until nightfall, then attacked the baggage train and rear guard at the top of the pass. Charlemagne's biographer Einhard reports that they drove the Franks "down into the valley beneath," where they had no room to maneuver. "The Basques joined battle with them and killed them to the last man," with the Basques escaping in the darkness.[4] Among those killed was the Paladin (knight) Roland. By the twelfth century the story of Roland's last stand had taken on epic proportions and this relatively insignificant incident became the subject of the first great poem in Old French, *The Song of Roland*. A product of the crusading era, it blames the Moors for the slaughter rather than the Basques.

But Charlemagne didn't give up on Spain. To protect his southern flank, he reestablished the Kingdom of Aquitaine, including Gascony, in 781 and appointed his son Louis the Pious as king there. This opened the way for an exodus of Christian refugees from Spain, including Agobard, later bishop of Lyons. It also gave the Franks a base from which they could reoccupy the region south of the Pyrenees to the east of Asturias and north of the Ebro River, the frontier province that became the Spanish March. But it proved difficult to maintain as a unified whole, and from it the independent kingdom of Pamplona emerged in the mid-ninth century. The majority of the Basque population lived in Pamplona, which also embraced the small county of Aragon.

The Franks focused their efforts on the northeastern corner of Spain, which had a strong sense of connection with southeastern France. Soon after their initial invasion, the Moors had pushed up north into southeastern France as far as Avignon and the Rhône valley. The Frankish counterattack came soon after Poitiers, so that by 759 southeastern France returned to the Frankish crown. The Franks called the region Gothia, and it was ruled by the counts of Toulouse. By 801 the Franks penetrated south across the eastern Pyrenees and eventually took Barcelona. This area was to form the nucleus of what was to become Frankish Catalonia. Its borders remained fairly static until the eleventh century. The key ruler in the ninth century was Wifredus Pilosus I, or Wifred (or Guifred) "the Hairy" or "Shaggy" (870–897), who established a line of counts who remained loyal to the Carolingians even though they received very little in return for their loyalty. In the ninth century this was frontier territory, depopulated and neglected. Even though Wifred clearly began to put Catalonia on the map, he remains a "shadowy figure." The one thing we know for sure about him is that he founded the important monastery of Santa Maria de Ripoll in 888, which we will discuss in relationship to Gerbert of Aurillac.[5]

These small Christian entities in northern Spain are worthy of further exploration because they define the limits of the Moorish advance. As Stephen O'Shea says, "The momentum of Muslim victory may have been slowing anyway, but the Frankish wall of ice [at Poitiers] brought it to a full stop," giving the Franks an opportunity to counterattack.[6] They remind us that Spain was never totally under Muslim dominance, and "while none of these principalities of the Christian north were able to constitute a threat to al-Andalus," they did provide the basis for the *reconquista* that began early in the tenth century.[7]

 e/o

The initial Muslim invasion of Spain in 711 had been the product of a decision by the Muslim Berber leadership in North Africa, not the Umayyad caliph in Damascus. At first Arabs were in the minority in al-Andalus, but they gradually gained the upper hand over the North African Berbers. The Berbers rebelled against Damascus between 739 and 743. This forced the Umayyad caliph to send more Arab troops to Spain. These, in turn, created Arab factions based on tribal divisions between fundamentalist "Yemini" Arabs from southern Arabia and the more sophisticated Arabs from conquered Persian and Byzantine territories. The ensuing strife led the Moorish administration of Spain to collapse into disarray in the second half of the eighth century.

The one thing that held Moorish Spain together in this period was Islam. Yet it also brought into relief the underlying problem in Muslim-ruled Spain, as in all Muslim-dominated states: the relationship between religion and government. In traditional Islam there was no clear separation of what today we would call religion and the state. The key question of who should lead the community was left unanswered. At first the caliphs saw themselves as the successors of Muhammad. They claimed "to be *khalifat allāh* . . . vice regents of God. They assumed the protection and endowment of Muslim worship, the organization of mosques and the defence of the pilgrimage. They claimed authority in legal and doctrinal matters and the right to defend the Muslim community against heresy."[8]

However, this initial assumption of authority by the caliphs soon evolved "from a religious to a monarchical identity"; in other words, their authority became more focused on the secular than on the religious. This, in turn, led to the emergence of "Muslim scholars and holy men . . . Qur'ān reciters, scholars and ascetics [who] became in daily practice the custodians and teachers of Islam."[9] These men provided leadership in the religious community, but the bigger questions still remained: who would lead the broader political community? Who would govern the state and administer ordinary politics? Should the political leader be an elected prophetic-religious figure selected according to spiritual criteria from the scholars and holy men? Or should it be a hereditary political figure like the caliph? The champions of religious leadership were the Shiites. Their emphasis was on finding a theocratic and righteous caliph, an *Imām*, designated by Allah who had some claim to descent from Muhammad. Contemporary Iran is an example of this. Sunni Islam held that the community had to sort out this question of leadership for itself, the result usually being a hereditary-aristocratic, or nowadays dictatorial, form of civil government.

What emerged from the chaos of eighth-century Spain was a hereditary-style leadership centered in Córdoba that ruled until 1031. The first hereditary emir of Córdoba was Abd al-Rahmān I (not to be confused with the Abd al-Rahmān who was defeated at Poitiers-Tours), who seized power in 756. A refugee from the overthrow of the Umayyad caliphate in Syria by the Abbasids, he had come to al-Andalus from Damascus via five years of hair-raising adventures pursued by bounty-hunting assassins. In Spain, he found support among Umayyad loyalists. Having seized Córdoba, he made it his capital. Umayyad refugees flocked in from Syria. It took Abd al-Rahmān twenty years to bring the Berber and Arab factions under control, but he created the foundations upon which the greatness of al-Andalus was built. Near the end of his life, he seems to have gone mad. He died in 788. His successor, Al-Hākim I (796–822), was a libertine, poet, and bloody despot who faced several economically motivated rebellions, which he put down brutally. The most common forms of execution were beheading and crucifixion on the city walls, a common exemplary punishment for crimes under *sharia* (Islamic law). Al-Hākim's son Abd al-Rahmān II (822–852) brought some stability to the state, but his successors saw that stability dissipated. "Strong separatist tendencies found among the Muslim elites in the provinces" caused the collapse of centralized authority.[10] This fraught situation was exacerbated by the *muwullads*, native converts from Christianity to Islam, who demanded equality with Arabs and Berbers.

The geography of the peninsula also encouraged political fragmentation. To hold the northern and northeastern frontier against the Christian statelets, the Muslim rulers set up military marches, frontier regions that acted as buffers between Muslim- and Christian-held areas. The military leaders in these rough-and-ready regions often showed complete disregard for Córdoba's authority. Richard Fletcher speaks of "the limitations of central power over a segmentary society dominated by feud in a region of peculiarly intractable terrain."[11] So the actual power of Abd al-Rahmān II's successors fluctuated; sometimes it was restricted to the valley of the Guadalquivir River and to the cities of Córdoba and Seville. This was the situation that Abd al-Rahmān III (912–961) inherited.

୧୬

Many details about society in Spain after the Muslim invasion remain somewhat obscure to us. Population figures from the past are notoriously difficult to pin down, but Josiah C. Russell estimates that Spain and Portugal had about 7 million people in the year 1000.[12] Fletcher thinks that by the late tenth century a large proportion (about 75 percent) of the population of al-Andalus was Muslim.[13] Jews numbered about 60,000. They cooperated happily with Muslims, whose policies were a relief after the anti-Semitism they had endured under the Visigoths.

Sources indicate that society as a whole was generally peaceful, although Catholics and Jews were constantly reminded of their second-class status. They were *dhimmi*, "protected ones," or "people of the book." *Dhimmi* were granted a special residential status to live in Muslim-dominated countries in return for paying *jizya*, a poll and land tax. Generally, there was no outright persecution of Christians until the time of the vicious dictator al-Mansūr (976–1002).

There were certainly many conversions from Christianity to Islam during this time. The reasons were straightforward enough: switching religions permitted escape from the *jizya* and enhanced economic and social opportunities and mobility. Many saw little difference between Christianity and Islam, especially given that Visigothic Christians had originally been Arian, which, like

Islam, is more simplistically monotheistic than mainstream Catholicism and Christianity, which believe in a Trinitarian God. Many converts were people on the make, senior bureaucrats and magnates maintaining their local power. Those who remained Catholics were called "Mozarabs." This term originated in the northern Catholic enclaves because people there saw their coreligionists gradually becoming bilingual and more like Arabs in dress and diet. The Mozarabs spoke Vulgar Latin, later to evolve into Spanish. But their Catholicism became static and fossilized. They had little or no opportunity to debate with Muslims because the slightest criticism of Islam could land a person in serious trouble.

So despite living in a lively, urban culture, the Mozarabs became a self-enclosed group. This, in turn, led to a kind of deluded desire for martyrdom. Stories of the Mozarab martyrs are preserved in Archbishop Eulogius of Toledo's *Memorialis Sanctorum*; he refers to them as the "Martyrs of Córdoba." While Eulogius, who was eventually martyred himself, exaggerates their heroism, the text has an authentic feel regarding the details of their lives. Most of the martyrs were either monks or priests, or the products of mixed marriages between Muslims and Catholics. Eulogius suggests that by 851 some Mozarabs had reached the end of their tether. Even though Christianity has never approved of *jactatio*, literally a person "boasting" about faith before persecutors and begging for martyrdom, it seems that many Mozarabs unconsciously felt the time for *jactatio* had come. In the mid-ninth century the rate of conversion to Islam was growing and the emigration of Catholics northward was increasing. This motivated the more zealous of those who remained behind to proclaim their faith and denounce Islam.

The martyrdom movement exploded spontaneously after a former Córdoba civil official and later Catholic monk named Isaac attacked Islam and cursed Muhammad before a somewhat dumbfounded Córdoba *qâdî* (judge). With the approval of Abd al-Rahmān II, Isaac was beheaded on June 3, 851 and his headless body publicly displayed upside down in the city. Two days later a young Christian soldier named Sanctius followed Isaac's example, quickly followed by six more Catholics. A spokesman for the six told the *qâdî*, "We maintain the same profession, O judge, which our most holy confreres Isaac and Sanctius professed. Hand down your sentence, pile on your cruelty, let your anger explode in vengeance for your prophet. We confess Christ to be truly God and your prophet to be the predecessor of the anti-Christ and the author of false teaching."[14] All were beheaded as blasphemers. A more cautious priest, Perfectus, was nonetheless trapped by Muslim schemers into denouncing Muhammad; he too was beheaded. Then, five weeks later, three more people came forward and cursed Islam and suffered the consequences. There was no more *jactatio* for three months, and then another group, including several women, confronted the authorities. As Eulogius tells their stories, we get an insight into the conditions under which many Mozarabs lived.

Take laywomen Flora and Maria, for instance. Flora was born in Córdoba. Her Muslim father died when she was very young, and she was secretly educated as a Christian by her Catholic mother. But Flora had a Muslim elder brother with considerable clout. The pressure of being a secret Christian led Flora to flee home. The Muslim brother realized he had been deceived, and to get her back, he put pressure on the Catholic community in Córdoba. To protect her coreligionists, Flora returned; he turned her over to the authorities. She could not be accused of being an apostate as she had been a Catholic since birth. Still, she received a severe flogging and was placed under her brother's control. She again fled.

While praying in a church, Flora met Maria. Her father was a Catholic who had married a Muslim woman who then secretly converted to Christianity. To protect the wife, the family moved to another village. After Maria's mother died, her father decided to take on a life of penance. Maria was settled in a convent where her abbess, Artemia, had once been married. Two of Artemia's sons had been executed three decades earlier, probably because they were apostates; presumably her husband was a Muslim, but her sons had subsequently become Christians. Maria's brother, Walabonsus, was a deacon, and he was in the first group of eleven martyrs who surrendered to the authorities. Flora and Maria decided that they too had to denounce Islam. They reported themselves to the *qâdî*. Technically, Flora was also an apostate because her father was a Muslim. She was given a chance to renounce Christianity and save her life. She held firm and was executed with Maria in July 851.[15]

Within a period of five years, some forty-three Catholics surrendered themselves to the authorities. These comprised twelve monks, nine priests, four deacons, three nuns, seven laymen, and eight laywomen. These, of course, were not the only executions. Many others suffered either because their religious convictions had somehow offended Muslim sensibilities or because they had converted to Islam and then reverted to Christianity.

Adolescent martyr Saint Pelagius falls into a different category. He was a northern Christian handed over as a hostage to Abd al-Rahmān III in exchange for a captured bishop. Abd al-Rahmān became sexually infatuated with Pelagius and wanted him to convert to Islam. There is nothing unusual in this; many rulers of al-Andalus had male as well as female harems. It seems that the light-skinned, blue-eyed, blond European women and men were considered attractive, for many slave-concubines were imported from the Christian north. German nun-dramatist Hrosvitha of Gandersheim later told Pelagius's story with an emphasis on his physical beauty and on the fact that Abd al-Rahmān was completely besotted with him. Pelagius rejected his advances and was executed. For Hrosvitha the key issue in the story was not so much Abd al-Rahmān's lust-besotted overtures as Pelagius's heroic witness to Christ and his refusal to convert to Islam to save himself. Christians used this story for propaganda purposes, portraying Muslims as homosexually obsessed, but as Mark D. Jordan points out the story is ambivalent because it was Mozarab monks who instituted Pelagius's feast day, sang the praises of his attractive body, and seemed "as much bothered by his beauty as was the caliph."[16]

All these stories demonstrate that al-Andalus was far from a nirvana of tolerance.

☙

Despite being susceptible to infatuation, Abd al-Rahmān III was undoubtedly the greatest ruler of al-Andalus. He became emir in 912, inheriting a chaotic situation and a contracted realm from his depressed grandfather, Abd Allāh (888–912). Abd al-Rahmān's mother was a Christian slave-concubine from the north named Munza. His grandmother was also a hostage Christian princess from Navarre. As Fletcher says, he was "three-quarters . . . Hispano-Basque, and only one-quarter Arab," and he dyed his red hair black to match that of his Arab subjects.[17]

At first Abd al-Rahmān's authority extended no farther than Córdoba and its immediate surroundings. His army and administration were small and unimpressive; previous emirs had faced strong separatist tendencies among the provincial elites. A restless man, Abd al-Rahmān determined to reverse this situation. He immediately began expanding his power in the south. He enlarged his army by buying young Slav slaves who were then drafted into a standing, professional army that was completely loyal to him. Mercenaries, local levies, and zealous volunteers who signed up for a period of *jihad* against unbelievers further expanded the army. By mid-century it numbered about 60,000 troops. He then used this army in the *sa'ifa*, the summer raids against the northern Christian states, more as a way of asserting his role, as the hadith (sayings ascribed to Muhammad) says, as "the one who fights for the faith of Allah" than of actually gaining territory.

Over the course of Abd al-Rahmān's campaigns against the Christians, he achieved some victories. One Moorish chronicler says that after a battle in July 920 at Valdejunquera, southwest of Pamplona, there were so many heads of the Christian dead to take back to Córdoba to set up around the city walls that the mule trains could not carry them. These raids were also used to capture slaves and to extract ransom. But victory was not a one-way street. Christian forces almost captured Abd al-Rahmān himself in 939 near Valladolid, seizing his standard, tent, and personal copy of the Qur'an. Besides military might, Abd al-Rahmān's power relied on expansion of the agricultural economy, no doubt partly due to the MWP and improvements in trading networks. The slave trade grew as Frankish, Anglo-Saxon, Irish, and Slavonic slaves were traded into the Middle East via al-Andalus. After a string of successful expansions of his power, on January 16, 929, at Friday prayers, Abd al-Rahmān proclaimed himself *khalifa*, "caliph," meaning successor of the Prophet, and *amir al-mu'minin*, "prince of believers."

The caliph's palace increasingly became the center of the state. In 936 Abd al-Rahmān began building an enormous new marble palace complex on three levels, decorated by jasper and precious metals, 8 miles (13 kilometers) west of Córdoba in the foothills of the Sierra Morena; the complex was called *Madinat al-Zahra*, "beautiful town." It was surrounded by a greenbelt of gardens irrigated from the surrounding mountains, a menagerie, pools, fountains, and administrative buildings. Here Abd al-Rahmān and his successors held court following ceremonial practices that paralleled those of the Abbasids in Baghdad. In Moorish culture the palace was meant to be a place of splendor, mystery, political intrigue, amorous trysts, and adventures. Access to its core was restricted to the family, favorites, and household slaves. Courtiers, civil servants, and ambassadors of foreign powers penetrated only the public areas. Commoners saw the exterior, which was meant to dazzle them. Sadly, the palace was destroyed by fire in 1010 in a civil war; the site was later neglected. Excavations and restoration began in 1910, and today the site is an archaeological curiosity.

Abd al-Rahmān III was very aware of the emerging kingdom of Otto I, and in the early 950s he sent an ambassador to Frankfurt, ostensibly to congratulate Otto on his victories. Otto was deliberately slow to respond; he claimed Abd al-Rahmān had shown insufficient respect for Christianity. However, in 953 he sent Benedictine monk John of Gorze to Córdoba with a letter and valuable gifts.

John, who comes across in histories of the period as excessively sanctimonious, faced a difficult assignment. Though he traveled to Spain with a group of merchants who knew the country, he ran into trouble immediately on arrival in Córdoba. The letter from Otto that he carried focused on a problem we've already seen: attacks on Christian pilgrims transiting the Alps and piracy on the Mediterranean coast from the Saracen freebooters based at Fraxinetum. However, these Saracens were informally aligned with the Moorish rulers of al-Andalus. There is little doubt that these pirates had good contacts in al-Andalus, and Abd al-Rahmān may have been concerned Otto would intervene militarily against them. He was also concerned that Otto's letter might be insulting to Islam. So he refused even to meet John or read the contents of the letter. In response John refused to tell the caliph verbally of the letter's contents. This led to an impasse, and John was placed under virtual house arrest.

The Jewish official Hasdāi ibn Shaprut and later another John, the Mozarab bishop of Córdoba, tried to negotiate the issue. According to the *Life of John of Gorze*, Bishop John pointed out that the ambassador's refusal to negotiate placed the local Christian community in some danger. He asked the monk-ambassador to "consider the conditions under which we [Mozarabs] exist. . . . The Apostle (Paul) forbids us to resist legitimate power. There is only one consolation in this calamity, that they do not forbid us our law. . . . In the circumstances, therefore, it seems wise to comply with all things which do not hinder our faith." To which, according to the *Life*, the sanctimonious John, showing no sympathy whatsoever for the circumstances under which Mozarabs lived, replied, "You who appear to be a bishop, are the last person who should speak thus. . . . It is a thousand times better for a Christian to suffer the cruel torment of hunger than to eat the food of the gentiles [in this context, non-Christians] at the cost of his soul."[18]

To resolve the situation, Abd al-Rahmān sent Recemund, a Christian official who would later be appointed bishop of Elvira by the caliph, directly to Otto's court. There he met and was befriended by Liutprand of Cremona, who dedicated his *Antapodosis* to him. Recemund returned in 956 with a more diplomatic letter from Otto. John of Gorze was released and received at court, where, true to form, he insisted on wearing his Benedictine habit.

This was not the only diplomatic exchange with Christians. Otto II sent another ambassador in 974. There was also contact between Córdoba and Constantinople on various occasions. Abd al-Rahmān II's ambassador, al-Ghazzāl, amused Emperor Theophilus (829–842) when he claimed that he could not concentrate on conversation when Empress Theodora was present because he was completely distracted by her beauty. Perhaps he was also disconcerted because he was unused to dealing with upper-class women without veils—although there is some doubt about whether women were required to wear veils under Abd al-Rahmān.

Besides having to deal with both the Christian East and West, Abd al-Rahmān faced a major issue in foreign affairs as the Abbasid regime in Baghdad fell apart. The Abbasids had been in trouble since the mid-ninth century, and despite a revival from 870 to 900, they entered a period of terminal decline in the first decade of the tenth century. As a result, several regional Muslim regimes emerged, including the Fatimid regime in North Africa. The Fatimids (they claimed descent from Fātimah, a daughter of Muhammad and wife of Ali) were Ishmailis, a sectarian subdivision of Shia Islam. Ishmailis claimed to have discovered hidden, mystical meanings in the Qur'an and looked forward to the arrival of the *mahdī*, the "rightly guided one," a kind of Islamic redeemer-messiah. They were led by Imam Ubayd Allah, a refugee from Syria who actually claimed to be the *mahdī*. He began a movement in Ifriqiya (Tunisia and eastern Algeria), eventually seizing power and assuming the title of caliph in 909. Abd al-Rahmān probably assumed the same title in reaction. While Ubayd Allah's ultimate aim was to take Egypt, he also expanded his territory westward in North Africa, seizing control of western Mediterranean trade. This threatened the caravan routes from sub-Saharan Africa, which brought gold and slaves to al-Andalus. It raised alarm bells in Córdoba, and in response Andalusi troops occupied Ceuta (on the northwestern tip of Africa) and Tangier and supported separatist movements among the Berbers. The threat lessened when the Fatimids took Egypt and established their new capital in Cairo in 973, which relieved the pressure on al-Andalus.

Abd al-Rahmān III died in 961 and was succeeded by his scholar-son, al-Hākim II (961–976), who built up a magnificent library in Córdoba. A peaceful, enlightened, and tolerant man, he governed largely through intermediaries. Exclusively homosexual, he maintained a large male harem. Though homosexuality was not expressly forbidden (at least to the elite) at this time, for al-Hākim it did complicate the question of an heir. The solution was to introduce him to a Basque-Christian slave-concubine and singer named Subh, who, some said, called herself "Jafar" and dressed in boy's clothes to seduce him. She became the mother of the heir apparent, Hishām.

Al-Hākim's case notwithstanding, homosexuality was never officially condoned, and in al-Andalus the influential Malikite legal tradition stipulated that penetrative homosexual intercourse would be punished by stoning, just like adultery. Still, among the elite, homosexuality remained common, especially among upper-class men. Michael Gerli says, "Both pederasty and love between adult males" were common among the al-Andalus male elite and the figure of the "'beardless youth' was seen as representing the divine in human form. Although homosexual practices were never officially condoned, prohibitions against them were rarely enforced, and usually there was not even a pretense of doing so."[19] This homoerotic culture expressed itself especially through poetry. Ibn Hazam's (994–1046) *The Dove's Neck-Ring About Love and Lovers* is a kind of practical psychology of infatuation and falling in love, which the author sees as an enjoyable sickness from which we don't want to recover. Most of his examples describe heterosexual love, particularly infatuation with lovely slave girls. But there are also examples of homosexual love in the poems, which he sees as no different from heterosexual relationships.

European Christian chroniclers report that they were taken aback, even shocked, by such tolerance of open homosexuality. The reaction of Catholics against Andalusian homosexuality is understandable given that it was based on slavery and many of the slaves were young Christians. The prevention of slave raids, the ransom of Christian slaves, and the later founding of religious orders specifically dedicated to ransoming people from Muslim slavery became a priority for the Hispano-Christian states.

By the end of the tenth century, the caliphate was declining. Hugh Kennedy comments, "In this rather closed, even claustrophobic, political society where access to the ruler was tightly controlled, it was easy for a few individuals to wield enormous power quite unrelated to their origins or to their wider political support."[20] Al-Hākim's short-lived successors held the title of caliph, but they didn't rule. Power was increasingly in the hands of the upstart vizier al-

Mansūr bi-Allah (Victorious by the grace of Allah) or, as he was known in the West, Almanzor. He had worked his way through the bureaucratic system, becoming chief administrator for Subh, the leading wife of homosexual al-Hākim II. He was soon her lover.

After al-Hakim died in 976, al-Mansūr became one of the regents for the eleven-year-old Hishām II after al-Mansūr had strangled an older claimant to the throne in front of his family. By 981 al-Mansūr had eliminated the other regents. Now supreme, he kept Hishām distracted by his harem and ruled for the next twenty-one years using Berber and slave mercenaries. To support the army, he imposed taxes on the peasantry, which led to the decline of the al-Andalus agricultural base. His most spectacular undertaking was the construction of a new palace and administrative complex east of Córdoba near the Guadalquivir River, *al-Madina al Zahira*, "the glittering city," built to rival the caliph's palace, *Madinat al-Zahra*, to the west of Córdoba. Today little of al-Mansūr's palace survives.

Like any good dictator, he created a cult of personality and used foreign invasions and wars as ways of distracting the populace from economic problems at home. As the focus of the Fatimid Empire shifted eastward toward Cairo, al-Mansūr occupied western Morocco north of the Atlas Mountains to ensure his ability to recruit Berber mercenaries for his army and to secure the sub-Saharan slave and gold caravans. But it was his almost constant *jihad* against the Christian north that brought him most success. While he posed as an orthodox Muslim to impress conservative religious authorities, he was no religious fanatic. The aims of the northern raids were, according to Fletcher, "to extract tribute, plunder, livestock, slaves, treasure: not to strike a blow for Islam against Christendom."[21]

The problem was that al-Mansūr needed money and lots of it. He somehow had to finance his army, his building program, tax cuts, presents, and bribes. To that end, he attacked monasteries and churches to seize their riches and resources rather than to destroy Christianity itself. His most spectacular attack occurred in 997 when he advanced through the mountains of Galicia to sack the shrine of Santiago de Compostela, seizing the bells of the church to install them in the magnificent mosque of Córdoba, which he expanded.

Al-Mansūr died in August 1002, signaling the coming end of al-Andalus. The citizens of Córdoba complained that their slave supplier was gone. The Catholics simply thanked God that he had been seized by the devil and buried in hell. He was succeeded by his son, who carried on his policies until dying of a heart attack in 1008. Then came the reign of an undistinguished half-brother whose lack of ability led to al-Andalus sliding further into anarchy.

Al-Mansūr's dictatorship had corrupted both culture and the state. By sidelining the legitimate authority of the caliphate, he fatally weakened the office. It is thus no accident that the caliphate was swept away by civil war in 1031. This gave the Christian enclaves in the north a chance to recover so that they were able to achieve a kind of equilibrium with Islam. The momentum of the *reconquista* increased in the eleventh and twelfth centuries, with Christian volunteers arriving in Spain to do penance by fighting the Moors. By 1249 the reconquest of Portugal was complete, and by 1252 all of Spain was under Christian control except the Emirate of Granada, which was finally taken in 1482 by Catholic monarchs Isabella I of Castile and Ferdinand II of Aragon.

ↄ

The great cultural achievements of Abd al-Rahmān III were underpinned by Islam. Originally, Hispanic Islam was rather primitive and fundamentalist, but gradually scholars came from the East with more orthodox versions of the faith. This became important as the influx of converts from Christianity increased; they needed instruction to integrate into the Muslim community. By the early ninth century, the predominant Islamic school influencing al-Andalus was Malikite, the oldest and most traditional, literal school of interpretation of the Qur'an and the hadith. In the Malikite school the *faqihs* (legal scholars) followed the interpretation of the religious teacher Mālik ibn Anas, who died in Medina in 795. The Malikites were conservative and traditional, in contrast to more open approaches being taken in other parts of the Muslim world. The Malikite interpretation held that the Qur'an had been literally written by Allah and that therefore it was universally binding on all people for all time. This view formed the basis of jurisprudence from the time of Emir al-Hākim I (796–822). The rulers of al-Andalus appointed *qādīs* from the Malikite school, and these judges reciprocated by supporting the regime. Spanish Islam lived on the margins of the Muslim world far from the centers of learning, so perhaps believers unconsciously felt the need for a more orthodox approach.

Malikite conservatism also makes sense within a historical perspective. Early Islam, like early Christianity, faced a fundamental theological conundrum: Was Islam's primary revelation, the Qur'an, a perfect book? Was it created and writ-

ten by Allah himself and therefore coeternal with him and beyond human context and interpretation? Or was it an Allah-inspired document written by a
human being in a specific cultural context that revealed divine truth that could
be interpreted in the light of historical context and experience? (This is the
Christian understanding of revelation.) The Malikite interpretation held that
the Qur'an is beyond human interpretation because it has always coexisted with
Allah, who personally wrote it in Arabic and revealed it to Muhammad through
the archangel Gabriel. Therefore, all that believers can do is to develop a legal
structure (*sharia*) that enforces the teachings of the Qur'an. In this view, legal-
ism replaces theology. Today this is the Sunni position.

In contrast, the more speculative Mu'tazilah school of theology held a position somewhat closer to mainstream Christianity's notion of revelation: the
Qur'an must have been created, that is, written by a person in a specific historical situation; it is not coeternal with Allah and is therefore subject to rational human understanding and interpretation. Reason is central to faith, and
both must be held together. Theology thus becomes a way of mediating and in-
terpreting the nexus between belief and culture. This school flourished in the
golden age of Baghdad in the Abbasid period. But by the end of the tenth century, the Mu'tazilah (the word means "dissenter" or "heretic") school and its
emphasis on the primacy of reason were marginalized in Islam.

The Mu'tazilah school was never welcome in al-Andalus. Certainly, there
were sectarian movements in al-Andalus, but their influence was marginal. Enlightened caliphs like al-Hākim II were more interested in books, mathematics,
science, and medicine than in theology, so the religious establishment was never
challenged. Under al-Mansūr, Malikite orthodoxy was enforced. His personal
piety was more show than reality, but he enforced orthodoxy to ensure conservative support for the costs involved in his constant wars. He destroyed books
that upset the orthodox faithful from al-Hākim II's great library, and he crucified a Mu'tazilah scholar whose views were considered heterodox. Al-Andalus
was far from an open, tolerant society even for Muslims.

Yet despite the constrictive orthodoxy imposed by Malikite Islam, the artistic and intellectual achievements of Andalusian culture were impressive, even if
derivative and dependent upon Middle Eastern culture for inspiration. Its finest
achievement was Córdoba itself. Hrosvitha called it "a fair ornament . . . a city
well-cultured . . . illustrious because of its charms . . . renowned for all resources, especially abounding in the seven streams of knowledge," even though

she had never visited the city.[22] Throughout the tenth century, it was the largest city in Western Europe, with a population about 100,000. Influenced by the architecture of Damascus, its wealth and beauty were seen in its buildings, especially the great mosque, the spiritual and intellectual focal point of the city. A Roman temple and Visigothic cathedral preceded the mosque on the site. Construction began in 784 under Abd al-Rahmān I. Abd al-Rahmān III, al-Hākim II, and al-Mansūr enlarged it. In 1236 with the *reconquista* it reverted to Christian worship and remains the cathedral of Córdoba. It retains its essential shape, with a "forest" of 856 (originally 1,293) mainly reused Roman columns supporting strikingly proportioned orange and red arches, which hold up the roof. Much of the original Moorish decoration has been preserved. Now a UNESCO World Heritage site, it is still one of the most beautiful buildings in Europe.

A kind of "green revolution," as Fletcher calls it, took place in al-Andalus. Watered by irrigation techniques, new imported crops, including rice and other fruit and vegetables, entered the regional diet and swept across al-Andalus in the ninth and tenth centuries.[23] Mohamed Abū'l-Quasim Ibn Hawqal visited Córdoba around 950 and reported that the city had "no equal in the Maghrib, and hardly in Egypt, Syria or Mesopotamia, for the size of its population, its extent, the space occupied by its markets, the cleanliness of its streets, the architecture of its mosques, the number of its baths and caravanserais."[24] Sadly, in the eleventh century Córdoba contracted in both size and splendor owing to the collapse of the caliphate and civil war.

It was in the sciences and cosmology that al-Andalus most excelled. This knowledge flowed into Islamic culture when the original Hellenistic-Christian centers of learning in Syria and Egypt were overrun and seized by the Muslims. Thus, Islam inherited the tradition of Plato, Aristotle, and Greek philosophy and science. Islamic dominance also spread eastward to Persia and India, where the Arabs encountered the mathematical and scientific knowledge that these cultures had developed. Certainly, to absorb so much new knowledge required real "intellectual athleticism."[25] So even though Arabic knowledge remained largely derivative, the Arabs cleverly developed what they had inherited, especially in terms of practical applications in, among other subjects, medicine (anatomy, pharmacy), mathematics (algebra and trigonometry), navigation (the compass and astrolabe), and philosophy. Arabic genius consisted in being able to combine these disciplines into an overarching scheme of knowledge, as well as translate them from language to language.

Al-Andalus itself produced some of Islam's greatest mathematicians, geographers, and astronomers. Madrid-born Maslamah al-Majriti (ca. 950–1008) was a mathematician (he produced a book on commercial arithmetic for businessmen) and an astronomer (he translated Ptolemy's *Planisphere* into Arabic) who redefined the position of the stars. He was also a chemist and virtually invented surveying and triangulation. He was deeply interested in the use of the astrolabe and composed a simple guide to its construction. Another slightly later figure was Abū Ishāq Ibrāhīm al-Zarqālī (1029–1087), who began his career as a metalworker and instrument maker but is remembered most as a great astronomer. Many Arabic scholars traveled widely and understood several languages, so they became disseminators of Hellenistic and Eastern knowledge.

Geographer Mohamed Abū'l-Quasim Ibn Hawqal (920–990) was a typical scholar. Born at Nisibis in northern Iraq, his influential book *The Shape of the World* was based on accurate observation and wide travel. Noted for its acute observation and scientific approach, the book contained a map of the world with the Nile River at its heart, indicative of the contemporary Arabic worldview. Ibn Hawqal began traveling when he was twenty-three and continued for the next forty years. He visited North Africa, Spain, Algeria, the southern Sahara (he may have got as far as Ghana), Egypt, Armenia, Azerbaijan, Iraq, Persia, Afghanistan, and Central Asia. There is a suspicion that he may have been acting as a spy for the Fatimids as they established their power base in Egypt. This suspicion is reinforced by the fact that he observed how militarily vulnerable the caliphs in al-Andalus actually were, wedged between the Christian north and the Fatimids to their east. He was also something of a geographical economist, and his text focused on basic agricultural products and manufactured goods rather than on luxury items.[26] He retired to Sicily and disappeared from history.

Since there was no distinction between the state and the faith, the caliphs, like their Catholic contemporaries, controlled both aspects of life. The ruler of al-Andalus employed religious scholars as both educators and civil administrators so that a highly trained religious scholar could include among his many tasks the role of chief of police. The court attracted scholars, writers, poets, philologists, philosophers, scientists, and mathematicians from all over the Muslim world. As Bernard F. Reilly says, "Trained in poetry to some extent, the religious scholar was equipped to function as a courtier as well."[27] Poets were particularly valued, and al-Andalus produced some of the finest poetry in Arabic. New genres were developed in which poets experimented with rhyme and meter, expanded their themes, and investigated old themes, especially love and the description of nature, in new and vivid ways. Possibly some of these poems were meant to be sung. There was a strong emphasis on belles lettres, and one way for the upwardly mobile, well-informed person to gain literary sophistication was to study an *adab*, a kind of encyclopedia of worldly wisdom, a miscellany of prose, poetry, proverbs, practical advice, and even general knowledge. Scholar and poet Ibn 'Abd Rabbih (860–940) produced *The Unique Necklace* to fulfill precisely this niche.

The library built up by al-Hākim II was astonishing in its breadth and depth and was far larger than any comparable library in Christian Europe. Perhaps the most important practical manuscript was the gift of Byzantine emperor Constantine VII Porphyrogenitus in 949 to Abd al-Rahmān III of a Greek copy of *De materia medica* by first century AD surgeon Pendanius Dioscorides, which was recognized for 1,500 years as the authoritative work on pharmacology and the medicinal qualities of plants. In a collaborative effort, it was translated into Arabic by a Greek monk named Nicholas and a Sicilian Arab who knew Greek. It had already been translated into Latin and was available in several European monastic libraries.[28] One who drew on Dioscorides's work was Córdoba-born surgeon Abū Qasim ibn Abbas al-Zahrawi (936–1013). His illustrated, multivolume medical and surgical encyclopedia, *Katib Al-Tasrif,* (Method of Medicine) covers the whole range of medicine and remained influential for centuries.

Cooperating in the translation of *De materia medica* was a Jewish Talmudic scholar, adviser, and personal physician to Abd al-Rahmān III, Hasdāi ibn Shaprut (ca. 915–975). A leading figure in the Jewish renaissance and a fine example of the cosmopolitanism of al-Andalus under Abd al-Rahmān III, he supported Jewish learning across the Muslim world, contributing to the Talmudic academies of Mesopotamia. He succeeded in making contact with the "Thirteenth Tribe," the Jewish Khazar kingdom in the north Caucasus and the southern Ukraine. At home he was a patron of Jewish-Andalusi figures such as poet, grammarian, and commentator Dunash ben Labrat (ca. 920–990) and Menachem ben Saruk (ca. 920–970), a poet and author of a Hebrew dictionary that was vigorously criticized by Labrat. Shaprut used his medical skill to help the massively overweight King Sancho I "the Fat" (956–966), so obese no horse could carry him, to lose weight.

❦

Nowadays there is a tendency among many to romanticize al-Andalus and to contrast it with tenth-century Christian Europe. The culture, tolerance, and government of Muslim Spain are often contrasted nowadays with the state of Europe at the same time, and a caricature has emerged in some contemporary popular historical writing and in TV history shows that contrasts al-Andalus with the Christian north, which is characterized as lost in barbarism and superstition. David Levering Lewis, for instance, says there were "two Europes." One—al-Andalus—was "secure in its defenses, religiously tolerant, and maturing in cultural and scientific sophistication; the other [Christian Europe] an area of unceasing warfare in which superstition passed for religion and the flame of knowledge sputtered weakly."[29]

Lewis argues that the Muslim defeat at Poitiers was a tragedy; if Islam had dominated Europe, the continent would have ended up a much better place. He describes the other, Catholic Europe as "economically retarded, balkanized and fratricidal . . . that . . . made virtues out of hereditary aristocracy, persecutory religious intolerance, cultural particularism, and perpetual war." This stands in contrast to a "Muslim *regnum* unobstructed by borders . . . one devoid of a priestly caste, animated by the dogma of equality of the faithful, and respectful of all religious faiths."[30] Both of these characterizations are caricatures. The reality of both cultures was much more complex. This kind of approach to history derives in part from the biases of a postcolonial multiculturalism and a kind of "clash of civilizations" theory that regularly compares Christianity unfavorably with Islamic regimes.

The truth is that historical reality doesn't bear out that particular reading. At the heart of Lewis's argument is *convivencia*—tolerant living together—in contrast to the kind of forced conversion that Charlemagne, for instance, imposed on the Saxons. The problem is that al-Andalus simply wasn't the kind of tolerant paradise that Lewis imagines, especially for Christians. It was a highly stratified society with a strict demarcation of roles, including for a period the wearing of identifying badges for Jews and Christians. Mozarabic Catholics were cowed, second-class citizens in what had originally been their own country.

This is not to deny the high culture of Muslim Spain. It is simply to try to achieve some balance. As Fletcher says after a lifetime studying Spain, al-Andalus "was not a tolerant and enlightened society even in its most cultivated epoch." He argues that "the critically important function of Moorish Spain was to act as a channel for the transmission of knowledge from east to west in one of the most sensitive periods in Europe's rise to dominance."[31] He is correct, for much of this scientific knowledge was passed on to Western Europe via al-Andalus. But it was a one-way traffic. Islam, isolated and convinced of its own superiority, felt it had nothing to learn from Christian Europe. We will return to this knowledge transmission when we consider Gerbert of Aurillac. All of this suggests the need for a more nuanced appreciation of al-Andalus. In the end the greatness of Moorish Spain was something of a mixed blessing.

If al-Andalus was on the geographical edge of the Muslim world, England was in a similar position, cut off to some extent by the English Channel from Christian Europe. But it was far from the barbarized, superstition-ridden society that Lewis caricatures as Christian at the time. Despite having to deal with almost constant Viking incursion for almost two hundred years (the mid-ninth through the early eleventh centuries), the country had nevertheless achieved a degree of political and cultural unity under the West Saxon monarchs, whom, as we saw, were recognized by the Saxon king Henry the Fowler as the most ancient royal line in Europe. So leaving behind the gilded world of Islamic al-Andalus, we will cross the English Channel to meet the much-more-robust Anglo-Saxons, who were to play an equal, if not far more important, role in the history of Europe.

CHAPTER 9

Anglo-Saxon England

T HE YEAR WAS 866. In the words of the *Anglo-Saxon Chronicle,* "This year . . . came a great heathen army into England, and fixed their winter-quarters in East-Anglia, where they were soon horsed; and the inhabitants made peace with them."[1] Thus began an organized Viking invasion of eastern England that was to determine the shape of things on the island for the next century and a half.

The "great heathen army" of probably 3,000 to 4,000 men, mainly from Denmark, was led by the sons of Viking pirate Ragnar Lodbrok (Hairy Breeches), who may well have also led the raid on Paris in 845 before being bought off by Charles the Bald. Lodbrok became a legendary figure in Viking folklore before he died in England, probably around 865. The exact connection between his death and the invasion of the great heathen army led by his sons Ingvar the Boneless (whom we met in the Prologue) and Healfdene is not clear. The legend is that Lodbrok was captured on a raid in England by King Aelle of Northumbria, who threw him into a snake pit, where he was protected from being bitten by his hairy breeches until his tormentors pulled them off. Apparently, his sons led the army into England in revenge.

Whatever the motive, they arrived in East Anglia in 865. Edmund (841–869), King of East Anglia paid off the Danes by supplying them with horses. They spent winter at Thetford and then moved north to the *emporium* (trading center) of York. It turned out that this was not just a random raid but a planned invasion. England, like France, was a rich country, and the Vikings

ENGLAND IN THE
TENTH CENTURY

Region of Danelaw

KINGDOM OF PICTS & SCOTS

NORTHUMBRIA

STRATHCLYDE

IRELAND

KINGDOM
OF YORK
(939)

•York

WEST MERCIA
(ANNEXED BY
WESSEX IN EARLY
TENTH CENTURY)

DANISH
MERCIA
(924)

EAST
ANGLIA
(924)

WALES

Approximate route
of Watling Street
(former Roman road)

London

KINGDOM OF WESSEX
(899)

•Winchester

0   100 MILES

0   100 KILOMETERS

were again taking advantage of local squabbles over succession between provincial rulers to raid and further destabilize the country.

Recurrent civil war in Northumbria between Kings Aelle and Osbert had left York (then called Eoforwic) undefended. All Saints Day, Friday, November 1, 866, was the fateful day that the Danes captured the city. All Saints was a special feast day in York. All of the leading citizens would have been at Mass in the cathedral, so it was all too easy for the invaders to round up the local power-brokers, killing some and holding others for ransom. After their easy victory in York, some of the Danes seem to have continued on, wintering farther north on the Tyne River. The majority, however, continued to occupy York.

Seemingly undaunted by the Viking incursion, the Northumbrians continued their civil war. Once King Aelle had defeated Osbert, he tried to recapture York the following year, on Palm Sunday, March 21, 867. He was defeated and killed by the Vikings, and, according to the *Anglo-Saxon Chronicle*, "an immense slaughter was made of the Northumbrians there, some inside, some outside [York]."[2] This was not the usual type of Viking hit-and-run raid—the warriors claimed the territory outright and would hold it for the long haul. For the next eighty-nine years, Eoforwic became Jórvik and remained a Viking city. Under the Vikings the schools, churches, and libraries (the library at York was one of the best in Europe) of Northumbria stagnated. The Viking presence did nothing for the stability of the region or for the whole country. However, the Vikings did encourage trade, and Jórvik became something of a link between the Viking town of Dublin to the west and Europe and the Scandinavian homelands to the east.

This was not the first Viking incursion into Anglo-Saxon England. The Norsemen had first appeared at the great monastery of Lindisfarne just south of Tweedmouth in 793. The attack seems to have come as a complete surprise to both the monks and the Northumbrian authorities. Nevertheless, England, unlike continental Europe, had escaped most of the worst of the Viking raids during the late ninth century. The great heathen army was the first organized attack. For eight years that army created havoc, and eventually the Danish invaders established themselves in several separate places in England.

The England that the Danes found was an island politically divided. With much of the old Roman road infrastructure still usable, the invaders were able to move swiftly around, attacking vulnerable points. Though several small, often belligerent Anglo-Saxon kingdoms dominated the landscape, they found it difficult to band together and expel the raiders. Most people simply fled rather than face Viking ferocity and destructiveness.

Northumbria was the oldest kingdom and the one immediately impacted by the invaders. It quickly fell under Viking control. Aside from Northumbria, the kingdom of Mercia, which had originally covered most of southern England had gradually lost territory to the West Saxon kingdom of Wessex, which was then emerging as the most organized and powerful. East Anglia, where the heathen army first landed, was small and in a vulnerable position on the coast bordering the North Sea.

After taking York in 866, the great army invaded Mercia and took Nottingham, where it was besieged by a joint Mercian–West Saxon force, a rare show of unity among Anglo-Saxon kingdoms. The Danes were forced to retreat to York, but they still controlled a quarter of England. In 871 they invaded Wessex. Only at that point did they face resistance from a well-organized kingdom with good leadership and government. Wessex had emerged in the early sixth century as a tiny kingdom. Over centuries it slowly expanded so that by 825 the West Saxon king Egbert (802–839) controlled much of southern England, including Kent, Sussex, and Surrey, regions originally occupied by the South and East Saxons. Egbert also seems to have conquered the Cornish. In 830 Egbert even controlled the Kingdom of Mercia, though only briefly. Egbert's descendants continued to rule Wessex, sustaining their position through shrewd maintenance of family wealth accompanied by generous patronage of the church, monasteries, and powerful laymen. Their position was sufficiently consolidated for King Ethelwulf (839–858) to leave England for two years (855–856) to go on pilgrimage to Rome and to visit Charles the Bald's court as it moved across central northern France.

Succession matters were handled far more neatly in Wessex than in other English kingdoms during this time. Ethelwulf's four sons by his first wife, Osburga, succeeded him by agreement to ensure that Wessex could be protected from the rule of minor children when the kingdom was threatened by the Vikings. It was a successful arrangement: Ethelbald (855–860), who married Judith, his father's second wife and a daughter of Charles the Bald, whom we've already seen eloping with Baldwin II of Flanders, was followed by Ethelbert (860–866), Ethelred (866–871), and Alfred (871–899). All four carefully managed royal property and, in contrast to the descendants of Charlemagne, tried to keep competition within the central kin group to a minimum.

The Vikings had been probing the south coast of England since about 836, and constant defensive warfare against them was draining West Saxon resources. These attacks intensified from the early 850s onward, and given that some of the groups that raided England had also been active in France, the arrival of the heathen army came as no surprise to Wessex, which had already lost many men fighting the Vikings. It is even possible that the brief reigns of the three "Ethels" (a prefix meaning "landed" or "noble") can be explained by war injuries sustained defending Wessex.

In 871 the decisive battle was joined at last. The *Anglo-Saxon Chronicle* recounts that that year the heathen army, strengthened by the arrival of a "great summer army," invaded Wessex. "In the course of the year nine general engagements were fought against the host [i.e., the Vikings] in the kingdom to the south of the Thames, besides innumerable forays . . . which were never counted."[3] King Ethelred died in the middle of the campaign, and the twenty-one-year-old Alfred became king in April 871.

By the end of the year both sides were exhausted. The Danes took up winter quarters in London. Though the armies of Wessex had successfully fended them off, their invasion of Wessex was in fact a distraction. Their real interest was in establishing themselves in Northumbria, after which they again invaded Mercia, seizing the royal center of Repton in the Trent Valley near Derby in 873. The Mercian king escaped but died in exile.

At Repton the Viking army split: Healfdene returned to consolidate York, and a new leader named Guthrum continued intermittent warfare against Wessex. Alfred managed to hold the Vikings at bay until midwinter 878, when they defeated the West Saxons at Chippenham on the borders of Wiltshire and Somerset. Then, according to the *Anglo-Saxon Chronicle*, the Vikings "rode over Wessex and occupied it, and drove a great part of the inhabitants overseas [into slavery], and of the rest the greater part they reduced to submission, except Alfred the king; and he with a small company moved under difficulties through woods and into inaccessible places in marshes" on the plain of Sedgemoor just east of Taunton.[4] He had probably hunted here as a youth. A legend later arose that he was so preoccupied with plotting how to counterattack against the Vikings that he accidentally burned a peasant woman's cakes. Whatever happened, he clearly came up with a plan, assembling a mobile army from Somerset, Wiltshire, and Hampshire. Using guerrilla tactics, he began to wear down Guthrum's Danes. The West Saxons were very loyal to the royal house because Alfred's family had continuously provided good government to Wessex.

In May 878 Alfred seems to have decided that he was strong enough to tackle Guthrum in a pitched battle at Edington in Wiltshire. Alfred's biographer Asser recounts, "Fighting fiercely with a compact shield wall against the entire Viking army he persevered resolutely for a long time; at length he gained the victory through God's will. He destroyed the Vikings with great slaughter. . . . He seized everything that he found outside the stronghold—men (whom he killed immediately), horses and cattle. He besieged the fortress for fourteen days and eventually the Vikings surrendered."[5]

It was a decisive victory, and the arrangement that followed showed Alfred as a generous victor. The Danes were allowed to continue to settle east of a borderline that ran roughly from London to Chester along the old Roman road called Watling Street. Guthrum agreed to be baptized with Alfred as his godfather and to become king of East Anglia.

The following decade, the 880s, was a period of relative peace in England. Quick as ever to seize upon a destabilized kingdom, the Vikings turned their attention once again to a weakened Francia under Charles the Fat. Wessex was left in peace for a decade. It gave Alfred breathing space to prepare for their inevitable return.

જી

Many historians see Alfred as the greatest English monarch because of his defense of the island against a foreign enemy. We also know a great deal about him. Patrick Wormald asserts, "Alfred is three-dimensional, as no other early English ruler is."[6] Wormald's judgment is borne out by Alfred's whole life and extraordinary achievements in a whole range of areas. He tackled a complex of problems of which the first and most obvious was military. Something had to be done to stop the Vikings. They were mobile not just on the sea but also on land. They could adeptly take advantage of both the rivers and the Roman road system, which they demonstrated when they virtually occupied Wessex in the 870s. But Alfred used the 880s to improve Wessex defenses. The first thing he did was to build a navy. The *Anglo-Saxon Chronicle* reports, "King Alfred ordered warships to be built to meet the Danish ships. They were almost twice as long as the [Danish]. . . . Some had sixty oars, some more; they were both swifter, steadier, and with more freeboard than the others; they were built neither after the Frisian design nor after the Danish; but as it seemed to himself that they could be most serviceable."[7]

Alfred's ships seem to have been effective, though some would be caught by retreating tides and therefore wind up beached and useless. He also borrowed Charles the Bald's defensive method of constructing low wooden bridges across rivers to prevent Viking fleets penetrating inland or to trap them up-river once they got there.

However, Alfred's greatest achievement was administrative. He organized the burghal system, a network of small-to-larger fortified towns, or *burhs* (from which our word "borough" comes). Alfred strengthened old Roman towns such as Exeter with intact walls or Winchester (where Alfred had his palace), whose walls he restored. For other towns such as Wallingford on the Thames or Wilton, he had new earthen walls constructed and topped by timber palisades. The defenses were manned through a centralized organization based on local assessments of the number of men required to defend each *burh*. For instance, Winchester had 2,400 men; Oxford, 1,400; Bath, 1,000; Hastings, 500; and tiny Lydford, 140. These men were a kind of peasant militia rather than a standing army. They assembled to defend their town when invasion threatened. The burghal system became the first successful organized and ongoing defense against the Vikings in Europe whereby everyone was within proximity of a safe place.

Alfred also reorganized the regular army of about 5,000 men through a system of conscription so that there were always enough workers at home to supply food to both the army and the general population. This mobile force could react quickly to immediate Viking dangers. The small numbers of troops indicate that the number of Viking invaders could not have been many more and was probably less.

By the beginning of 890 the Vikings controlled Northumbria (the kingdom of York) and East Anglia. About half of Mercia was also under "Danelaw," an area where Danish, rather than Anglo-Saxon, law, custom, and language prevailed. After Alfred retook London in 886, the remnant kingdom of Mercia began cooperating with Wessex, and the *Anglo-Saxon Chronicle* says that "all the English people submitted to him [Alfred], except those who were in captivity to the Danes."[8]

In 892–893 the Vikings returned to England after more than a decade exploiting the weakened and confused situation in Francia under Charles the Fat.

Eighty Viking ships departed from Noirmoutier on the mouth of the Loire; they landed in Kent. Simultaneously, some 250 ships sailed from Boulogne and landed near Folkestone. But Alfred had used the peaceful interlude well; he eventually defeated the Viking forces on land with "very great slaughter."⁹ Meanwhile, a Danish fleet under King Sigfrid of York was unsuccessful in attacking Exeter and eventually retreated to Dublin. This became typical: when the Vikings went on the attack, they were unsuccessful. Alfred's defenses and organization held against the invaders, though Wessex and Alfred himself were consequently placed under terrible pressure.

However, by 896 Viking forces were disintegrating. "Then the following summer . . . [896] the host dispersed, some to East Anglia, some to Northumbria, and those without stock got themselves ships there and sailed south oversea to the Seine." But what the Vikings had failed to do, plague, pestilence, and animal disease did. "The English people," the *Anglo-Saxon Chronicle* continues, "were much more severely crushed during those three years by murrain and plague [and] most of all by the fact that many of the king's servants in the land passed away during those three years."¹⁰ Essentially, the Vikings had not been defeated and Wessex, with terrible losses, was still on the defensive. And then in 899 Alfred died.

In many ways Alfred's heritage was extraordinary. It is a tribute to him that such a sophisticated system as the *burhs* of Wessex was organized successfully. It also had the important secondary purpose of making these towns market centers and places where royal mints could be situated. Alfred had inherited the West Saxon system of shires presided over by an ealdorman (from which our word "alderman" comes), usually someone of noble birth or high rank appointed by the king. Even before Alfred's time, Wessex was expanding, and this continued under his rule. With this expansion, shire division spread and to some extent is coterminus with present-day counties in southern England. Shires were further divided into hundreds—that is, ten groups of ten households with each household holding a hide, a measure of land of about 60 to 120 acres (25 to 50 hectares). Yet no matter how well organized, government in the ninth and tenth centuries was never an easy task. Patriotism in the sense of loyalty to the king and to what we call the "nation" was not an instinctive feeling; many of Alfred's contemporaries were only too happy to make common cause with the Vikings when it suited them, no matter how bad the Vikings were perceived to be.

But Alfred was not just a fighter. He was an educator, writer, religious reformer, and legal pioneer. His reign ushered in a period of fundamental change whose effects were felt long term in English history. He was deeply concerned that Wessex had degenerated into ignorance and superstition, so he established a program to teach reading and writing. He began with himself; he learned to read and write both Old English and Latin in his thirties so that he eventually translated Augustine's *Soliloquies*, Boethius's *Consolation of Philosophy*, and Pope Gregory I's *Pastoral Rule* into Old English. He began but didn't complete a translation of the Psalms. He demanded that officials learn to read and write, and he set up a program for universal literacy; we don't know how this worked. He also gathered a group of local and overseas scholars around him as Charlemagne did. Religion and culture in Wessex were in poor shape, and Alfred's "court school" aimed at bringing the latest in both fields to improve the kingdom. The *Anglo-Saxon Chronicle* seems to have begun in Wessex in the late ninth century, most likely in Alfred's reign. It was written in Old English and presented a view of history very much from a West Saxon point of view.

Alfred also established a law code that drew on Mosaic law, church law, and the legal traditions of the Anglo-Saxons. Not only was he interested in the practical application of the law to issues such as oaths, treachery, and blood feuds; he also wanted to present himself as a lawgiver in the tradition of Moses, Solomon, and King David. He was conscious of himself as the leader of the new chosen people, the English people. Under Alfred England was moving in the opposite direction from the Continent. While Alfred was consolidating England into a coherent kingdom based in Wessex, with effective overall government, contemporary East and West Francia were falling apart, degenerating into their component parts with the breakdown of all centralized authority. It was a study in contrasts.

What was Alfred like as a person? Much of what we know comes from Welshman Bishop Asser of Sherborne's *Life of King Alfred*. Asser, from a monastery in the tiny kingdom of Dyfed in far southwestern Wales, was summoned by Alfred to work in his court. What Asser ended up writing does not resemble a biography in the modern sense; like all such biographies in those times it idealizes the king. Richard Abels says, "The *Vita Aelfredi* was meant to be an encomium, a celebration of Alfred's greatness for the edification of its multiple audiences: the monks . . . the royal court, the king's sons, and, first and foremost, Alfred himself to whom the work was dedicated."[11] Influenced by Einhard's *Life of Charlemagne*, Asser says Alfred was born at the royal estate at Wantage near Oxford. As a child he visited Rome twice, once in 853 when he was aged four; Pope Leo IV "anointed [him] as king, ordaining him properly, received him as an adoptive son and confirmed him." He visited the city two years later with his widowed father.[12] He married Ealhswith, a woman related through her mother to the royal house of Mercia. Asser tells us nothing of Alfred's physical appearance, and unlike his granddaughter Eadgyth some of whose physical remains are preserved, a chance to study Alfred's bones was lost more than two centuries ago. Buried in Winchester, his grave was moved twice and came to a final resting place in 1110 with other family members in Hyde Abbey just outside the walls of the town. The monastery was destroyed by Henry VIII in 1539, but the royal graves were preserved. But in 1788 the local council bought the site for a bridewell, or jail. The prisoners clearing the site discovered the graves, broke them open, stole the lead linings in the coffins, and scattered the bones.

Even though the bones can't be recovered, Asser certainly tells us a lot about Alfred's illnesses—and he was a sick man. Oddly, the first symptoms appeared at his wedding reception in Mercia before he became king. Asser reports, "He was struck without warning in the presence of the entire gathering by a sudden severe pain that was quite unknown to all physicians." This illness continued "from his twentieth year up to his fortieth and beyond." From his youth, Asser tells us, Alfred suffered from piles, or hemorrhoids, which he saw as a "gift" from God that helped him suppress his youthful libido. He spent much time in prayer "when he realized he was unable to abstain from carnal desire," and he asked God to "strengthen his resolve in the love of His service by means of some illness which he would be able to tolerate."[13] Asser says that the perianal problem disappeared when he was hit by the acute pain at his wedding reception.

Alfred's symptoms have been carefully studied by both medical doctors and historians, and "the evidence available points to inflammatory bowel disease."[14] That is, he probably had Crohn's disease, a persistent inflammatory condition involving the end of the small intestine or the beginning of the large intestine or both. The cause is unknown. But it did mean that he spent most of his life in considerable abdominal pain, fever, tiredness, and painful stools, making his achievements even more remarkable.

Alfred is the only English monarch who is referred to as "the Great," and coinage from the end of his reign indicated that he saw himself—and, in fact, effectively was—"king of the English." He had a clear vision of a better, more peaceful, and well-governed England, and he had the statesmanlike ability to make his vision a reality, at least in the part of England over which he ruled. Given that England was to become so important in the development of "the West," Alfred's role in the process of Western beginnings was a key one. He also set the pattern that later medieval rulers of England were to emulate. Alfred died aged fifty "six nights before All Hallows Day" (November 1, 899) after having "ruled the kingdom for twenty-eight and a half years."[15]

⁊

But the succession was anything but straightforward. The designated heir was Alfred's eldest son, Edward the Elder (899–924), who was about nineteen. But there was another claimant, the *Ætheling* (prince) Æthelwold, nephew of Alfred and cousin of Edward. Taking direct action, Æthelwold seized Wimborne Minster in Dorset in the Wessex heartland. It was the burial place of his father and close to two Roman roads. He had been passed over when Alfred became king because he was a minor child at the time. When Alfred died, he was again ignored. He was probably hoping that Edward would divide the kingdom between the two of them. Æthelwold's actions were typically early medieval: challenges, boasts, threats, and claims to titles were used more often than set-piece battles.

But Edward was having none of it. "Then the king and his levies rode until he encamped at Badbury Rings," a stone-age fort just west of Wimborne that dominated the surrounding landscape.[16] Edward thus prevented Æthelwold from seizing land farther west. The tactic worked because Æthelwold fled at night for Northumbria and joined the Vikings. He took an abducted *wif* (consecrated nun) with him; she was possibly a member of the royal family whom he hoped to use as a hostage or bargaining chip.

Æthelwold quickly established himself as a leader, even as a "king" in Viking Northumbria. He was clearly successful because by 902 he was able to land in Essex "from overseas with all the ships he could muster." He was accompanied by Viking adventurers and mercenaries who were chaffing at the bit to begin raiding again. Æthelwold then persuaded the East Anglians to join him. The *Anglo-Saxon Chronicle* says that "they harried across the whole of Mercia until they came to Cricklade and there crossed the Thames [into Wessex]: they seized all that they could both in Braydon Forest and in the surrounding countryside and then went east homewards."[17] Æthelwold failed to take the *burh* of Cricklade, so he and his fighters were reduced to raiding around Braydon in Wiltshire. Instead of tackling them head-on, Edward, trusting in the defenses built by his father, outflanked them and ravaged East Anglia "as far north as the fens."[18]

Æthelwold's East Anglians rushed back to defend their homeland. Edward, trying to avoid a set-piece battle in foreign territory, retreated, but the men of Kent refused and fought Æthelwold and his allies at Holme, an unknown location at East Anglia on December 13, 902. "On the Danish side were slain their king Eohric and prince Æthelwold, who had incited him to this rebellion . . . and many others besides these. . . . On each side there was great slaughter made, and although the Danes had possession of the place of slaughter they suffered greater losses."[19]

King Edward was now free from the threat of Æthelwold. This gave him the chance to take the initiative, especially now that his sister Æthelflaed, "the lady of the Mercians" as she was called, was now ruler of Mercia after her husband Ethelred, ealdorman of Mercia, had been killed in battle in 911.

Already in 909 Edward had launched an attack on the Danelaw out of Mercia supported by Ethelred and Æthelflaed. A Danish counterattack from York into Mercia was decisively defeated by Edward's forces at Tettenhall in early August 910. The power of the Viking kingdom of York was broken, and Edward and Æthelflaed began a reconquest of the Danelaw, essentially the old Anglo-Saxon kingdom of Mercia south of the Humber. This reconquest gained momentum especially after 917 when the Mercians stormed Derby, led by Æthelflaed herself, and the Danish kingdom of East Anglia was taken after the Danes were defeated at the Battle of Tempsford by Edward. By late 918 King Edward had conquered the whole of England south of the Humber.

After the death of his sister, he annexed Mercia in what amounted to a coup d'état. Just before she died, the Danes of York had submitted to Æthelflaed, but her death prevented this being pursued, and the kingdom of York was seized by Regnald, a Viking from Dublin who recognized Edward's overlordship, as did the king of the Scots, the ruler of Bernicia (southeast Scotland and northeast England), and the neighboring kingdom of Strathclyde. The Welsh princes also acknowledged him.

Edward was now the "king of England." He had achieved this because he had inherited a standing army from Alfred that could remain in the field for as long as was needed, with a back-up structure to maintain security and food supplies in the Wessex homeland. But just as important was the fact that the Vikings were disunited and had settled down with homes to defend. They had lost their edge.

When Edward died on July 7, 924, he was succeeded by his son Æthelstan (924–939), called "a towering figure in the landscape of the tenth century" by historian Simon Keynes.[20] If Edward had established "England," his son turned it into a lasting reality. He so influenced his time that we can truly speak of an "age of Æthelstan." His mother was Ecgwynn, Edward's first wife, although some claimed she was a concubine of low birth. Æthelstan had grown up under his aunt's tutelage in Mercia, where he was proclaimed king at twenty-five. His half-brother Ælflaed was proclaimed king in Wessex, but died two weeks later. While there was residual resistance to Æthelstan among some in Winchester, he was crowned at Kingston-on-Thames in summer 924 as "king of the Anglo-Saxons." His aim was to become not just king of England, but *rex Anglorum*, "king of the English."[21]

He achieved this through war and shrewd political maneuvering. He married his sister to Sihtric "the Squinty," a Dublin Viking who was king of York. Sihtric quickly became a Catholic and just as quickly reverted to Viking religion, abandoning his wife in the process. Sihtric died in 927 and was succeeded by his brother Guthfrith. Æthelstan drove Guthfrith out of York and according to the *Anglo-Saxon Chronicle* "annexed the kingdom of Northumbria; he brought into submission all the kings in this island. . . . They established a covenant of peace with pledges and oaths at a place called Eamont Bridge [in Cumbria] on 12 July [927]. They forbad all idolatrous practices and then separated in concord."[22]

Æthelstan was now both king of England and *rex totius Britanniae*, "king of the whole of Britain." However, the Welsh and Scots had their own ideas; there was opposition to an overall Anglo-Saxon king of Britain from the start. In fact, many Celts would still have preferred the Anglo-Saxons to be permanently driven out of Britain. In 937 Constantine mac Áeda, King of Alba (i.e., most of Scotland) decided that the time had come to puncture Æthelstan's pretensions. He and Owein I, King of Strathclyde (southwest Scotland, Cumbria, and northern Wales) joined the Norse Dublin king Olaf III Guthfrithsson and invaded England.

Æthelstan headed north, assembling an Anglo-Saxon army. The opposing forces met in summer 937 in the bloodiest battle of the century. It was fought at Brunanburh, an unknown location, but most likely Bromborough on the Wirral peninsula near the mouth of the Mersey River and the city of Liverpool. The Vikings preferred a river estuary as a battle site for a quick retreat to the sea. The *Anglo-Saxon Chronicle* waxes lyrical about Æthelstan's victory in the fiercely fought battle:

> *In this year king Æthelstan, lord of warriors,*
> *Ring-giver of men, with his brother prince Edmund,*
> *Won undying glory with the edges of swords,*
> *In warfare near Brunanburh.*
> *With their hammered blades the sons of Edward*
> *Clove the shield-wall and hacked the linden bucklers,*
> *As was instinctive in them . . .*
> *The foremen [Scots nobility] were laid low . . .*
> *And the host from the ships [Vikings] fell doomed. The field*
> *Grew dark with the blood of men.*[23]

The Celts and Vikings were defeated, but how badly remains debated. Certainly, many died including Owein of Strathclyde, but the *Anglo-Saxon Chronicle* tells us only the victors' side of the story. Nevertheless, this important battle consolidated Anglo-Saxon England. The Vikings were stopped in their tracks, and the Celts were confined to Scotland and Wales. In a sense it was the day on which "Angleland" began to become England.

Æthelstan was exceptionally able, and Keynes argues that he established "a monarchy invigorated by success, developing the pretensions commensurate with its actual achievements and clothing itself in the trappings of a new political order."[24] His court was an educated and cultured one and his government efficient. He was especially devoted to lawmaking to regulate the common good and to establish peace and prosperity. The kingdom was still quite divided, and localizing tendencies still predominated in most places. So it was always a struggle to control an unruly people who resented West Saxon dominance. Personally, Æthelstan was a devout Catholic, and, although a bachelor, he cared for a complex family of eight half-sisters and three half-brothers, the product of Edward the Elder's three wives. Æthelstan died on

October 27, 939, and was succeeded by his brother Edmund I (939–946) the "Magnificent."

ৎৎ

Edmund's reign continued the consolidation of England, although early on he lost the North. In 940 Olaf Guthfrithsson retook York and Northumbria without opposition and then pushed on into the East Midlands. Watling Street again became the border, but after Olaf was killed in Northumbria in 941, Edmund retook much of the East Midlands and then in 944 marched north and seized York, expelling the Viking leadership and bringing "all Northumbria under his sway."[25] York's importance was as a major trading center, and economic interests dictated the loyalties of the locals. Most of Northumbria remained a law unto itself. The Dublin Vikings usually gained access to York and the North through Strathclyde, and Edmund was determined to stop this. So in 945 he invaded Strathclyde, killed King Donald mac Donald (937–945), and handed over the entire region to Malcolm, King of Scots on the condition that he would stop the Dublin Vikings using Cumbria as a throughway to York.

Edmund was stabbed to death on May 26, 946, by an outlaw named Leofa. It was the feast of Saint Augustine of Canterbury, and Edmund was attending a banquet at his royal lodge at Pucklechurch, north of Bath. He had already drunk heavily when he spotted Leofa, a man he had previously outlawed, present at the banquet. Furious, Edmund attacked Leofa and threw him to the ground but was himself fatally stabbed in the struggle. Edmund was twenty-five.

His successor was his brother Edred (946–955), who continued Edmund's policies and thereby maintained continuity in government. However, from 948 to 954 the Danish kingdom of York became independent once again when the northerners invited Eric "Bloodax," son of King Harold "Fairhair" of Norway, to become king. According to one account, Eric earned the epithet "Bloodax" by murdering two of his brothers in a Norwegian power struggle. Another story claims the word is ironic and he was hopelessly henpecked and in thrall to his wife Gunnhild, who is represented in the sagas as an evil witch. Eric was defeated by Edred's forces and was betrayed and killed at Stainmore in Cumbria in 954. He was the last Viking king of York, which, with Northumbria, now permanently became part of England. Scotland also acknowledged Edred's overlordship.

A pious and good man, Edred "loved the blessed Father Dunstan" and made him chief adviser and administrator. Abbot Dunstan (909–988) of Glaston-bury, later archbishop of Canterbury, will reappear in the next two reigns. In royal charters Edred was variously referred to as king of the Anglo-Saxons, Northumbrians, pagans, and Britons. His successes came despite the fact that he was sick and nauseous for most of his reign with a serious digestive ailment, probably achalasia, a congenital narrowing of the esophagus or the inability of the lower end of the gullet to relax, causing regurgitation of food. This leads to a severe loss of weight; in the end, the victim often dies of pneumonia. The *Life of Saint Dunstan* says that Edred sucked the juices out of food, chewed on what was left, and then spat it out. He may well have been incapacitated for the last years of his reign. According to the *Life of Saint Dunstan*, "Being anxious about his life by reason of his long sickness," Edred began to distribute his goods "with a willing and free disposition," but before the distribution was completed, he died on November 23, 955, aged about 30.[26]

King Edwy, or Eadwig, the "All-Fair" (955–959), a handsome son of King Edmund and born about 940, succeeded his uncle on October 1, 959. Trou-ble started immediately. The *Life of Saint Dunstan* says that he was "a youth in-deed in age and endowed with little wisdom in government"—in other words, a petulant adolescent aged about sixteen. He became infatuated with "a woman [Æthelgifu], foolish, though she was of noble birth, with her daugh-ter [Ælgifu], a girl of ripe age . . . [and] he acted wantonly with them, with dis-graceful caresses, without any decency on the part of either." When Edwy failed to attend a banquet after his coronation owing to an assignation with the two, Dunstan and the bishop of Lichfield were sent to summon him. They found newly crowned Edwy in flagrante delicto, with the crown "carelessly thrown down on the floor, far from his head, and he himself repeatedly wal-lowing between the two of them in evil fashion, as if in a vile sty." Not a man to mince matters, Dunstan literally dragged the king "from his licentious re-clining by the women, replaced the crown and brought him with him to the royal assembly."[27] Needless to say, this didn't go down well with either Edwy or the women.

While there is no doubt the king had affairs with both women, it is hard to be certain how much of the story can be accepted at face value. The *Life of Saint Dunstan* was written well after the event, and Dunstan and Edwy were bitter enemies. Dunstan was exiled to Flanders as a result of his confrontations with the king. In behavior reminiscent of his contemporary Pope John XII, Edwy became increasingly irresponsible, relying on adolescent friends who were as feckless as he was. He plundered monasteries, seized their lands, and continued to sleep with many women. It is clear that, as Keynes says, his misrule "led to a social and political upheaval in the heart of [his] kingdom, which can hardly reflect well on the quality of his rule."[28] Eventually, Mercia and Northumbria renounced Edwy and acknowledged his younger brother Edgar as king.

In late 956 Edwy attempted to marry the younger woman, Ælgifu. But enemies in the church hierarchy declared the marriage to be within the forbidden degrees of consanguinity; she was probably his third cousin once removed. Church practice at the time prohibited marriage within the fourth degree of consanguinity. Still only about eighteen, Edwy died in mysterious circumstances on October 1, 959. He "was succeeded by Edgar his brother who ruled over Wessex, Mercia and Northumbria; he was then sixteen years old."[29]

Edgar (959–975) was born in 943. His mother died within a year of his birth, and his father was killed three years later by Leofa. Edgar was crowned at Kingston-on-Thames and inherited a united kingdom. He established an efficient administration, and his peaceful reign reinforced social stability. His practical legal reforms reached right down to the local level. They were also harsh, with physical mutilations decreed for many crimes. Communal punishment was also applied. For example, in 969 Edgar "ordered the whole isle of Thanet [at the far eastern end of Kent] to be harried [ravaged]" because some islanders had robbed merchants who had landed there.[30] He was also conscious of his role as a Christian king appointed by God. To demonstrate this, he had himself anointed and crowned a second time at Bath at Pentecost 973. This coronation had imperial overtones resembling those of Otto I. Edgar was sometimes referred to as "the emperor of all Albion." After his coronation, Edgar led his army north to Chester, where he received the submission of the kings of the Scots and the Welsh and other local rulers.

Like Edwy, Edgar was sexually voracious. While he married Ethelflaeda "White Duck" in 960, his affairs were legendary. Once he tried to seduce the beautiful daughter of an Andover nobleman, but to protect her, her parents substituted a naïve maidservant, who left his bed early the next morning to start her housework. Furious when he realized he had been duped, Edgar made the maidservant the mistress of the whole household. Even nuns and novices were not safe.

"Women in these troubled centuries were pitifully vulnerable to both rape and seduction. Monastery walls increased their security, but no woman seems to have been safe from the pressures of powerful suitors."[31] We can see this in the story of Wulfhilda, a young novice nun at Wilton whose aunt Wenfleda, abbess of Wherwell, connived with Edgar by inviting Wulfhilda to visit her at Wherwell, where the king planned to seduce her. When she realized what was happening, Wulfhilda escaped through the convent drains and returned to Wilton. Edgar pursued her there, but she escaped again, claiming sanctuary at the chapel altar. She was professed at Wilton, and Edgar later made her abbess of Barking. She died about the year 1000 and is now a saint. Perhaps she was saved by another Wilton novice, Wulftrude, whom Edgar seduced. He then abducted her and kept her as a sexual slave. She bore him a child, the future Saint Edith. After her daughter's birth, Wulftrude returned to Wilton convent and resumed the life of a nun while caring for her daughter. Edgar seems to have actually loved them, eventually making Wulftrude abbess of Wilton. After his wife, Ethelflaeda's, death in 963, he made several attempts to persuade Wulftrude to be his wife, but she was now totally committed to her convent.

In 962 he was pursuing another beautiful woman, Ælfthryth. He sent his foster brother and friend Æthelwold to check her out, but the young man himself became infatuated with Ælfthryth, and they secretly married and settled in Devon. Edgar soon realized what was happening, invited both of them to court, and then "accidentally" killed Æthelwold with a javelin during a hunt in Harewood Forest. He then married the widowed Ælfthryth in 964.

Despite his voracious sexuality, Edgar supported the renewal of monasticism. He brought Dunstan back to England and made him archbishop of Canterbury in 960. Dunstan reformed established religious houses according to the strict Benedictine rule and established new ones. This revival was part of a broader European revival of monasticism that we will see later. Given the close intersection of church and state, a renewal of monastic life inevitably would have important overflow consequences for the state. This close interaction was really a form of caesaropapism, a system in which the state effectively controlled the church.

The key figure in this reform was Dunstan. Exiled by Edwy in 956, he took refuge at Saint Peter's monastery in Ghent, where he came in contact with Continental monastic reform. He brought these reform principles back to England,

and, supported by Edgar and the important bishops Æthelwold of Winchester and Oswald of Worcester, the reform movement began. By the end of the century, there were thirty-four new or refounded monasteries in southern England and six convents for women. A book to regularize monastic life and customs, the *Regularis Concordia*, was issued about 970 by a royal council at Winchester.

Edgar died on July 8, 975; he was thirty-two. The *Anglo-Saxon Chronicle* boasts, "No fleet however proud, no host however strong, was able to win booty for itself in England while that noble king occupied the royal throne."[32] Actually, that's not strictly true. In fact, Edgar was lucky: the Vikings stayed home throughout his reign, and his government was administered by men of considerable competence both at national and regional levels. Yes, he was competent himself, but also lucky, unlike his predecessors and certainly unlike his unfortunate successors.

ↄ

Edgar's early death precipitated a crisis of succession. There were two claimants to the throne. One was Edward, certainly the son of Edgar and probably of Ethelflaeda, who was about thirteen; the other was Ethelred, Edgar's second son by Ælfthryth, who was about eight or nine. Both had groups of supporters. The final decision was made in the Witan, the advisory assembly of counselors, bishops, and important men who had to approve the succession of a new king. What is significant is that there was never any discussion of dividing the kingdom. There was clear agreement that England was a united country, and even though primogeniture was not the Anglo-Saxon custom and all a king's sons were thought to be worthy of the throne, there was still no move in the Witan to divide the country between the two claimants. The Ethelred faction represented ealdormen and landholders who were upset by Edgar's practice of granting land to the monasteries, which increasingly made abbots the most important local landowners in an economy that was posited on landholding. But the group supporting Edward outmaneuvered Ethelred's and was led by the highly competent Archbishop Dunstan. So Edward was appointed. Edward II (975–979) is popularly known as "Saint Edward the Martyr," a much later, totally inappropriate appellation. He seems to have been a petulant, even violent adolescent. The anonymous author of the *Life of Saint Oswald*, archbishop of York (961–972), says that "he not only struck fear but even terror in all, both by his words and by actual whip lashings, especially to those of his own household."[33] People were reminded of the equally adolescent Edwy fifteen years previously. Historian Sir Frank Stenton comments, "[Edward] offended many important persons by his intolerable violence of speech and behavior. Long after he had passed into veneration as a saint it was remembered that his outbursts of rage had alarmed all who knew him, and especially the members of his own household."[34]

With a violent adolescent on the throne, trouble was not long in coming. Already there were premonitions in nature. According to the *Anglo-Saxon Chronicle*, "In the autumn of [975] there appeared that star known as the 'comet.' The next year a great famine and many disturbances throughout England."[35] For the medieval mind these premonitions indicated trouble ahead. The comet in question was Halley's Comet; it was also sighted and recorded in Constantinople and in China. With the country seething over Edgar's monastic reforms, especially his alienation of land to support monasteries, there was widespread resentment among many landholders. With Dunstan and the reforming bishops trying to hold the line, an antimonastic faction gained strength. "On account of his [Edward's] youth, God's adversaries broke God's laws. Ealdorman Ælfhere and many others . . . destroyed monasteries, dispersed monks and put to flight God's servants. . . . Widows were robbed many a time and oft, and many injustices and evil crimes flourished. . . . Things went from bad to worse."[36]

A plot to assassinate the king was hatched. The schemers included the Ætheling Ethelred, Ealdorman Ælfhere, and, most likely, Ethelred's mother, Ælfthryth. After careful planning, the assassins struck at Corfe just south of Taunton in Somerset on March 18, 978. The aim was to catch Edward without protection. The king, who was staying in the area, was invited to Corfe Castle to greet his half-brother and stepmother. The unsuspecting sixteen-year-old arrived unescorted. He was pulled from his horse by armed thanes and was quickly dispatched. "And very quickly afterwards," Ethelred II was consecrated and crowned at Kingston.[37] No one was ever punished for the crime.

Ethelred "the Unready's" long reign (978–1016) was the beginning of the end for Anglo-Saxon England. A formerly prosperous, well-governed, and ordered nation was brought to its knees under a single king. Even though Ethelred was little more than a child when Edward was murdered, there is a sense in which his whole life was stymied by this event. Yet somehow throughout his disastrous reign, people remained loyal to him. In March 979 in an act of repentance, Ealdorman Ælfhere reburied the body of Edward at Shaftsbury nunnery "with great ceremony."[38]

In 980 the Viking raids began again, with seven ships raiding Southampton. This was just the overture to a larger campaign. For the first decade of Ethelred's reign, the Danes engaged in increasing numbers of hit-and-run raids, exploiting a weakened but still wealthy kingdom. With the navy laid up to save money, the raiders were never challenged. The ealdormen entrusted with defending the coastline were both too old and too lazy to tackle the invaders. By the mid-980s it was clear that the now-Christian Danes under their national leadership intended to exploit a weakened England and eventually to make it part of a Scandinavian empire. The Danish state had been consolidated by a series of able leaders—Harald Bluetooth, who introduced Christianity to Denmark, Olaf Trygvverson, Sven, and Cnut (or Canute). Everything that Alfred the Great had built was now threatened.

While it is true that Ethelred had lost most of his best counselors (Dunstan died in 988) and his most experienced warriors by the beginning of the 990s, the blame for the failure of the English must be laid at the feet of Ethelred himself. Both government and defense systems failed, and according to Keynes, Ethelred "lacked the strength, judgment and resolve to give adequate leadership to his people in a time of grave national crisis; who soon found out that he could rely on little but the treachery of his military commanders; and who throughout his reign tasted nothing but the ignominy of defeat."[39]

The first serious Viking invasion came in 991 when Olaf Trygvverson, leading a fleet of ninety-three ships, raided the Thames estuary and around the coast to Ipswich. They were trapped on a tidal island in the Blackwater River near Maldon by Ealdorman Brihtnoth and the Essex *fyrd* (militia). What we know about the battle has come to us via the fragmentary Anglo-Saxon epic poem *The Battle of Maldon*. According to the poem, the giant Ealdorman Brihtnoth (in fact he was a bit over six feet) chivalrously allowed the Danes to leave the island so that the battle could be fought honorably on dry land. It led to a complete massacre of the English. After Brihtnoth had been killed, the Essex men fought on, encouraged by "an old retainer" whose speech is very moving:

> *The spirit must be the firmer, the heart the bolder,*
> *Courage must be the greater, as our strength diminishes.*
> *Here lies our leader all cut to pieces,*

The great man in the dirt. He will have cause to mourn forever
Who thinks of turning away from this battlegame now.
I am advanced in years; I do not intend to leave,
But I beside my lord,
Beside that well-beloved man, intend to die.[40]

The brave men of Maldon were really betrayed by Ethelred and his adviser Archbishop Sigeric "the Serious" (whom we've already met going to Rome for his pallium), who almost immediately began paying ransom rather than making a strong stand against Olaf Trygvversön. They arranged a treaty that amounted to a capitulation and agreed to pay 22,000 pounds of silver *Danegeld* (annual tribute). This set a pattern: they paid 16,000 pounds in 994, 24,000 pounds in 1002, and 36,000 pounds in 1007.[41] The amounts involved reflect the wealth of the English and the greed of the Danes.

The next two decades tell a tragic story of an incompetent, cowardly, but vindictive king; a bungling government; and ealdormen happy to play a double game by cooperating with the Danes when it suited them. The *Anglo-Saxon Chronicle* reflects the sheer frustration of ordinary English people in 999 as they tried to deal with military and administrative incompetence:

In this year the [Danish] host again came round into the Thames, and so up the Medway to Rochester. They were opposed by the Kentish levies, and a sharp encounter took place: but alas! All too quickly they turned and fled, because they did not get the support they should have had, and the Danes had possession of the place of slaughter, and got horse and rode far and wide as they pleased, destroying and laying waste almost the whole of Kent. Then the king and his counselors decided to advance against them with both naval and land levies. But when the ships were ready there was delay from day to day which was very galling for the unhappy sailors manning the vessels . . . so in the end these naval and land preparations were a complete failure and succeeded only in adding to the distress of the people, wasting money, and encouraging their enemy.[42]

Straight talk indeed!

Another invasion came in 994, led by Sven and Olaf Trygvversön. The Danes came again in 997 and remained until 1000. They returned in 1001, and a peace was arranged in 1002 when 24,000 pounds was paid in *Danegeld*. But there seemed to be no end to Ethelred's monumental stupidity. On November 11, 1002, he secretly ordered a kind of ethnic cleansing of Danes, many of whom had been in England for decades and who had been very loyal to the English crown. The king "gave orders for all the Danish people who were in England to be slain on Saint Brice's day [November 13] because the king had been told that they wished to deprive him of his life by treachery . . . and then seize the kingdom."[43] A particularly nasty massacre took place in Oxford when the loyal Danes took sanctuary in a monastery chapel, which was then burned to the ground, killing most of them. Probably thousands of innocent Danes were killed. This must have been a horrendous introduction to Ethelred's second wife, Emma the daughter of Duke Richard I of Normandy, who married Ethelred in the spring of 1002. Emma (a name that sounded foreign) was forced to change her name to Ælfgifu, which, embarrassingly, was also the name of Ethelred's first wife. Emma was to live a long life and have a wide influence on events and people leading up to the Norman Conquest of 1066.

Danish revenge under King Sven, whose sister Gunnhild had been killed on Saint Brice's day, was swift. He led armies into the defenseless country in 1003, 1004, 1006, and 1007, shrewdly omitting 1005 when there was a famine. In 1007 the English had to pay 36,000 pounds of silver. In 1009 it was the turn of the Dane Thorkell "the Tall" to arrive with a large army to devastate the countryside. Eventually, 48,000 pounds of silver was paid as ransom. Sven returned in 1010 with a huge army. All attempts to stop the Danes were useless, and according to the *Anglo-Saxon Chronicle*, Ethelred sued for peace

> on condition that they should cease their harrying. They had by this time overrun (I) East Anglia, (II) Essex, (III) Middlesex, (IV) Oxfordshire, (V) Cambridgeshire, (VI) Hertfordshire, (VII) Buckinghamshire (VIII), Bedfordshire, (IX), half of Huntingdonshire, and (X) a great part of Northamptonshire, and to the south of the Thames all Kent and Sussex and the district around Hastings, and Surrey, and Berkshire, and Hampshire, and a great part of Wiltshire. All of these misfortunes befell us by reason of bad policy in that tribute was not offered them in time.[44]

London was one of the few places that held out.

In 1013 London surrendered, and Sven controlled most of England. Ethelred went into exile in Normandy with Queen Emma. Then in February 1014 Sven died, and his son Cnut was elected king by the Danes, although they seem to have been destabilized by Sven's death. This gave the English a chance, and the Witan recalled Ethelred from Normandy, but, coward to the last, he sent his young son Edward to test the waters in England. Once he was sure it was safe, Ethelred returned and was welcomed. Cnut had withdrawn to northern England, and challenged by Ethelred's army, he withdrew to Denmark. Ethelred's son Edmund Ironside quickly emerged as a real leader of the English. But he had to deal with the gormless Ethelred until he died on April 23, 1016, and the endlessly traitorous and deceptive Eadric of Mercia. Cnut returned in late summer of 1015 and by the summer of 1016 controlled most of England, with only London and Wessex holding out for Edmund Ironside.

Finally on October 18, 1016, Edmund (betrayed at the last minute by Eadric of Mercia) and Cnut's armies met at Ashingdon in Essex, "and there a fierce battle was fought. . . . Cnut was victorious and won all England by his victory. Among the slain . . . [were] all the flower of England."[45] But Edmund lived up to his epithet "Ironside." He simply kept fighting until he and Cnut negotiated a treaty in which Wessex was returned to Edmund. But the treaty proved useless because Edmund suddenly died on November 30, 1016. He was buried at Glastonbury beside King Edgar.

King Cnut now controlled the whole of England. The great achievements of the Wessex kings, particularly Alfred the Great, seemingly lay in ruins. If nothing else, England proved how difficult it was going to be to reestablish good government and to resist both external and internal enemies who were determined to destroy the common good for the sake of personal pillage. If the Saxon monarch Otto I had both *fortuna et mores*, his Anglo-Saxon cousins might have had *mores*, but they certainly lacked *fortuna*. But at least a model had been set.

Another country that was constantly troubled by the Vikings throughout the tenth century was Ireland. But even Ireland, whose whole history was characterized by resistance to any form of centralization, actually embraced the concept of a unified state under a remarkable leader, Brian Boru. But national unity, as we shall see, was to be something of a flash in the pan.

CHAPTER 10

The Celtic Lands

Ireland, Scotland, and Wales

AT THE BEGINNING of the book, we met a monk studying Latin and Greek grammar at Bangor. Like many Irish monks, he was also a student. As Thomas Cahill correctly points out, it was the Irish after all who had "saved civilization" in Europe in the seventh and early eighth centuries.[1] Irish monks preserved Latin and Greek learning well before the great days of Muslim al-Andalus, and these same monks, from the seventh century onward, spread that learning and culture across Continental Europe and England via their missionary work. They truly were wandering educators and teachers. They provided the continuity between the ancient Greco-Roman world and the medieval world. Without them Western civilization would not have survived. In many ways they did this against the odds. Their country was traditionally tribally divided, with seemingly endless internecine warfare, and throughout the ninth and tenth centuries they were under tremendous pressure from Viking incursions. Yet despite all this, the Irish monastic educational and cultural tradition survived.

As our Bangor monk illustrates, there was a continuing interest in books and grammar, and many wandering Irish scholars crisscrossed Europe teaching literature. For example, the mid-ninth-century Irish scholar Sedulius Scottus (the Latin *Scottus* confusingly means "Irishman") was a kind of scholar-in-residence to the bishop of Liège. Clearly a man who enjoyed life, he says, "I read and teach and say my prayers, and snoring sleep."[2] No slouch, however,

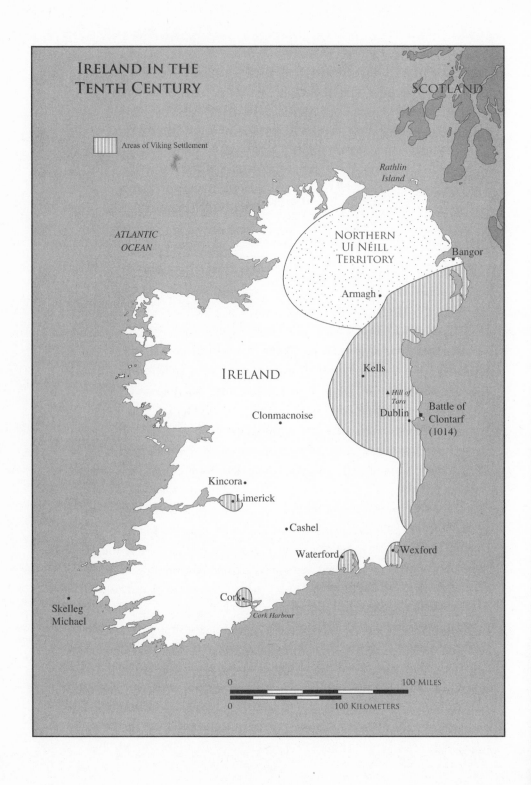

IRELAND IN THE
TENTH CENTURY

SCOTLAND

Areas of Viking Settlement

ATLANTIC
OCEAN

Rathlin
Island

NORTHERN
UÍ NÉILL
TERRITORY

Bangor

Armagh

IRELAND

Kells

Clonmacnoise

▲ Hill of
Tara
Dublin

Battle of
Clontarf
(1014)

Kincora
Limerick

•Cashel

Waterford

Wexford

Cork

Skelleg
Michael

Cork Harbour

0   100 MILES

0   100 KILOMETERS

Sedulius produced biblical commentaries, texts on grammar, collections of rare Latin and Greek works, a book of behavior for Christian princes, and translations of biblical works from Greek. We know he feared the Vikings and may well have fled Ireland to escape them, although it is hard to see how he would have been safe from them in Liège.

But by far the most important scholar-philosopher of the ninth century was John Scottus Erigena (John "Irish-born"). Born about 810 somewhere in Ireland, he spent most of his life abroad. He first appears at Reims and was commissioned by Archbishop Hincmar to write a refutation of the monk Gottschalk's work on predestination. Gottschalk argued for a "double predestination," meaning that some people are destined by God to salvation and others to damnation (we will return to Gottschalk later). John had some sympathy with Gottschalk's views, so his response, *De praedestinatione* (On Predestination), was perceived by contemporaries as somewhat ambiguous. However, he survived the criticism to become a friend of Charles the Bald, who appointed him master of the school of Laon. There is a great story told that one night after the king and scholar had drunk deeply, Charles, trying to be smart, asked, "*Quid distat inter sottum et Scottum?*"—"What's the difference between a sot and an Irishman?" Quick as a flash, John replied, "The width of a table." Sadly, a German scholar has demonstrated that this Latin construction is uncharacteristic of John, but I take it at face value as an example of Irish humor.[3]

John was a profoundly original Neoplatonist philosopher for whom God was ultimately unknowable unless he revealed himself through revelation and creation. John had leanings toward mysticism and translated the important mystical works of the Syrian monk and/or bishop Dionysius the Pseudo-Areopagite (ca. 500) from Greek into Latin. John's last years are completely shrouded in mystery, and we have no idea where he died. After him Irish scholarship went into decline.

The ninth century also saw the production of the last great works of Irish manuscript illumination, particularly the *Book of Kells*. This book's provenance and precise date are much debated, but it is probably from the late eighth or early ninth century. One theory holds that it was produced at Iona off the Scottish coast and was brought to Kells, north of Dublin, for safekeeping after Viking raids and a massacre of monks at Iona in 806.

After the ninth century artistic emphasis shifted to stone, which was more permanent in the face of Viking destructiveness. The tenth century was the great period of the creation of high crosses, such as those at Clonmacnoise, Kells, and Monasterboice. Muiredach's cross at Monasterboice has vivid scenes from both the Old and New Testaments carved into separate panels on both sides, while the two cats at the base of the western face give the cross an almost domestic feel. Monasteries were also increasingly built in stone, accompanied by the round towers that nowadays are still so characteristic of Ireland. However, as people found who took refuge in monastic towers during raids, these unfortunately served as excellent chimneys when set on fire, leaving little hope of survival for those inside, along with their treasures and books.

As artistic and intellectual life declined, politics and government retained the complexity and chaos of a tribal society. This was a preurban society, and until the Vikings came, the only real hubs of population and economic activity were the great monastic centers. The overall population of Ireland at this time was perhaps 300,000. But by the ninth century, the monasteries were in decline after the golden age of the sixth and seventh centuries.

Politically, a complex hierarchy of kings ruled over the territory. The *Lebor na gCert*, "The Book of Rights," divides Ireland into seven overkingdoms and more than one hundred petty kingdoms. It also defines the relationships between these kingship levels and the tributes or taxes required of each. Kings didn't own all land, which was shared out between aristocratic and free commoner families. Just as among the Franks, the underlying notion of a "Christian king" was formed within the context of Old Testament notions of kingship.

There were four levels of kings. The local king ruled a *túath*, a small kingdom. Overkings ruled their own *túath* and were overlords of several other *túatha*. Above them were those who ruled the seven kingdoms. Even before the arrival of the Vikings, these petty and regional kings were in decline as dominant dynasties gradually seized their lands and assets. The overlord of Ireland was the high king, *ard rí*, the king of Tara. For centuries the Uí Néill clan from Ulster and the midlands controlled the Tara kingship, which was basically an honorary and ceremonial role. In the southwest the Eóganachta clan controlled the Rock of Cashel, from which as king-bishops they dominated much of their region. This whole arrangement was a recipe for chaos. When the Vikings arrived at the beginning of the ninth century, there was no organized resistance, except at the local level.

In the period leading up to the Viking incursions, the role of the church was changing. The latest research shows that originally the Irish church was not highly organized, although it was more or less based on a diocesan model as generally existed on the Continent. However, by the eighth century church government, such as it was, had shifted from a form of episcopal control to that of monastic control. In other words, monasteries had become central to Irish Catholicism. The greatest monasteries with large populations and land-holdings began to form *paruchiae*, the Old Latin word for a "diocese," with abbots partially replacing bishops.[4] While retaining their educational role, monasteries in the ninth century had become increasingly secularized owing to their social and economic clout. Patrick J. Corish points out, "They became associated with the established major dynasties, and in consequence became centers of secular power. . . . Monastic armies fought with kings and against kings." Nevertheless, in a society haunted by a fear of death and judgment, monasteries still "offered the protection of their saintly founder, and the Lives composed to glorify him show how paganism had diluted Christianity, for in them the saint appears as a figure of power, strong to bless, no doubt, but especially strong to curse."[5]

Kingly families ruthlessly raided and sacked monasteries when it suited them. Some monasteries had their own militias made up of local peasants, whom they used to fight other monasteries. The *Annals of Ulster* gives as an example "the battle between the community of Cluain Moccu Nóis [Clonmacnoise] and the community of Dermag [Durrow] in which fell . . . two hundred men of the community of Dermag."[6] So much for "Love your neighbor"!

ॐ

For those like the early Irish who believed in portents, the signs of impending disaster were plain to see. There had been droughts, famines, and cattle disease, and then in 774 "Eógan son of Colmán died of the bloody flux [dysentery], and many others died of that same illness."[7] The *Annals of Ulster* records that after the dysentery epidemic, "the moon became red like blood on the twelfth of the Kalends of March [788]" and in 789 an unseasonal "deep snowfall on the third of the Kalends of May" occurred. The *Annals* records that in 784 "devastation of all the islands of Britain by heathen" occurred. In 795 it was Ireland's turn.[8] The *Ostmen*, the men from the east, had arrived. They came first from Norway and Viking settlements in Scotland. The incursions followed the same pattern as those in Francia and England. The initial raiding period lasted until about 836 and was confined to monasteries on the coastline and up to 20 miles (32 kilometers) inland. Monasteries were seen as rich pickings: they had land, stock, supplies, and people to be sold into slavery. Their valuable artistic and religious objects were secondary targets.

In the early ninth century the pattern changed: large fleets arrived during summer, and the invaders began using navigable rivers such as the Shannon, Liffey, Erne, and Boyne to penetrate inland. After 836 Clonmacnoise, one of Ireland's largest monasteries, 145 miles (230 kilometers) up the Shannon, was attacked six times by the Vikings. (To keep things in perspective, it was attacked eleven times in internecine Irish strife in the same period.) Glendalough, southwest of Dublin, and Clonmore, near Carlow, were first attacked on Christmas night 835. Both monasteries were burned, and many were killed or enslaved.

By then, just as in Francia and England, the Vikings had started spending winter in well-defended *longphuirt* (the plural of *longphort*, an enclosure that protected both ships and men). The first of these was Dublin, where in 837 there were some sixty Viking ships on the Liffey in *duibh linn* (the dark pool). A permanent settlement was established in 841. The *Annals* reports, "There was a naval camp at Duibh Linn from which the Laigin [Leinster clans] and the Uí Néill were plundered, both states and churches."[9] One of the early Norse leaders was Turgeis, who seems to have briefly ruled most of the eastern Vikings (he was killed in 845) and may have set himself up as a pagan high priest at Armagh. Another story has his pagan *spea*-wife (a prophetess with supernatural powers), Ottar, giving oracles from the high altar at Clonmacnoise. Dublin grew quickly into a trading post and a center for the slave trade. Another early *longphort* was at Annagassan on the northern coast.

Much of our knowledge of the Dublin settlement would have been lost forever were it not for the priest-historian Father Francis Xavier Martin, widely known as "FX." In the late 1970s the Dublin Corporation wanted to build new offices on the site of dilapidated Victorian buildings at Wood Quay on the south bank of the Liffey in central Dublin. Early archaeological excavations on the site revealed the remains of the original Viking *longphort*. But archaeology was not a priority of the Dublin Corporation; it wanted to build its offices despite the international public outcry over the decision to destroy the most important Viking remains in Europe. FX and the Save Wood Quay campaign slowed down the destruction through successive court cases and public demonstrations. While a particularly ugly modern building now occupies the site, it wasn't built until extensive archaeological work had been carried out.

What is striking about early Viking settlement in Ireland was that it was never extensive, unlike in England, where almost half the country was occupied. One reason is that at first smaller numbers of invaders were involved, and once they settled, they became vulnerable to attack. The other reason is that eventually the Irish did achieve some unity and made stands against the intruders. In 848 the Vikings suffered four major defeats. The *Annals of Ulster* reports that "the high king, Máel Sechnaill, won a battle against the heathen at Forach [near Skreen, County Meath] in which 700 fell." Two other battles are recorded that year in which 500 and 200 Vikings, respectively, were killed, and then "Tigernach [an Uí Néill king in the midlands] inflicted a rout on the heathens in the oakwood of Disert Do-Choma [an unknown location] and 1200 fell there."[10]

The first Viking settlers were now also under threat from subsequent waves of their Viking kinsmen. In 849 "a naval expedition of seven score ships of adherents of the king of the foreigners came to exact obedience from the foreigners who were in Ireland before them, and afterwards they caused confusion in the whole country." The *Annals of Ulster* refers to the new Vikings as "dark heathens," seemingly not referring to their complexion but to the fact that they were probably Danes, possibly from England. "The dark heathens came to Ath Cliath [Dublin], made a great slaughter of the fair-haired foreigners [Norwegians] and plundered the naval encampment, both people and property. The dark heathens made a raid at Linn Duachaill [Annagassan] and a great number of [Norwegians] were slaughtered."[11]

Beginning in the 850s Dublin became the central focus of Viking activity in Ireland. At one stage it was controlled by Ingvar the Boneless, whom we have already met. Dublin Vikings were also active in Northumbria and Scotland. They brought slaves and seized goods to Dublin, which became something of an emporium. The Vikings were certainly the tenth century's capitalists and small businessmen.

The Dublin settlement was in decline by the early 870s as many Vikings were moving to Francia and England for raiding. And the Irish were beginning to win more battles against them. "Aed, son of Niall [a northern Uí Néill king], plundered all the strongholds of the foreigners . . . in the territory of the north . . . and took away their heads, their flocks and their herds. . . . A victory was gained over them at Loch Fegail [Lough Foyle] and twelve score heads were taken thereby."[12]

From 902 to 917 the Dublin settlement itself was under Irish control. When the Vikings left, they "abandoned a good number of their ships and escaped half-dead after they had been wounded and broken."[13] Intermarriage had already occurred between Viking and Irish, and the period 876 to 914 was relatively free of Viking raids.

This breathing space gave the Irish a chance to do what they did best—fight each other! Then in 914 the Danes mounted a second "invasion" of Ireland because Anglo-Saxon England was better defended after the reforms of Alfred the Great, and Francia was less attractive because of a series of bad seasons. In 914 a large fleet arrived from northern Francia at Waterford, which now became a permanent Viking settlement, as did Wexford (921) and Limerick (922). After defeating the Irish in 917, the Vikings reestablished their presence in Dublin, which was now developed into an actual town rather than a mere settlement. The Vikings again became a real menace raiding across the countryside from their coastal enclaves.

"The whole of Mumhain [Munster] became filled with immense floods and countless sea-vomitings of ships . . . so that there was not a harbor, nor a landing port, nor a Dún [fortress], nor a fastness in all Mumhain without fleets of Danes and pirates. . . . And assuredly the evil which Erinn had hitherto suffered was nothing compared to the evil inflicted by these parties."[14] While composed at the beginning of the twelfth century and probably exaggerated for the sake of a good story, this account from *The War of the Gaedhil with the Gaill* does give some sense of the depredations of the second wave of Vikings. But the second-wave Vikings soon caught the Irish "disease"—internecine warfare among themselves—just as the Irish became increasingly adept in dealing with them. Gradually, the Vikings became an integral part of Irish politics, joining in the ever-shifting alliances and coalitions that battled for control of Ireland.

Meanwhile, the Dublin Vikings became increasingly caught up in mercantile interests across the Irish Sea in the Isle of Man, the Hebrides, Iceland, and northern England, especially in Jórvik and Northumbria. But this brought vulnerabilities. King Æthelstan's victory at the Battle of Brunanburh in 937 put a stop to Viking ambitions to control northern England. Gradually, through intermarriage, the Dublin rulers became at least nominally Catholic as they slowly lost their Viking identity. They had already suffered from a smallpox and dysentery outbreak in Dublin in 951, and the *Annals of Ulster* says that in

965 there was "great and intolerable famine in Ireland, so that the father was wont to sell his son and daughter for food."[15] Then in 980 the Dublin Norse suffered a serious defeat. "The battle of Temair [Tara] was won by Máel Sechnaill [an Uí Néill] against the foreigners of Ath Cliath [Dublin] . . . and a very great slaughter was inflicted on the foreigners therein, and foreign power ejected from Ireland."[16] Well, not quite ejection, but at least the Dublin Viking kingdom now paid tribute to the Irish kings. The defeated Dublin ruler, Amlaíb Cuarán (945–980), ended his life in 981 as a pilgrim on Iona, the first Irish monastery attacked by his forebears.

༚

By the last part of the tenth century, there was a new man rising in the land. He was the most famous of all Irish kings: Uí Briain, or as he is known today, Brian Boru. Brian is popularly seen as an almost mythic figure in Irish history, a nationalist who expelled the Vikings. However, historians such as Michael Richter more realistically see him "as a talented, ambitious and ruthless politician who battled against the Vikings among others, but whose real aim was to become high king."[17] In other words, he was a man on the make.

To understand his rise, we must backtrack. In the early 930s a clan known as the Dál Cais arose to prominence in eastern County Clare north of the Shannon estuary. They were obscure upstarts who invented a noble lineage for themselves, an easy enough thing to do in tenth-century Ireland. Under the leadership of Cennétig mac Lorcáin, they began to make their presence felt in northern Munster. Cennétig had possibly eleven children, most of them sons, four of whom were killed in the internecine wars that brought the clan to prominence. Orlaith, the one daughter we know about, was the second wife of the Uí Néill high king Donnchad Donn. He had her killed after accusing her of adultery with her stepson. For decades Cennétig's sons battled over control of the Munster region, whose power was centered on the throne of Cashel ruled over by a king-bishop.

Meanwhile, another important power shift was occurring. The ruling groups of the Uí Néill clan were left without an agreed successor to the high kingship, which in turn led to a savage internecine war. It raged for three decades between the northern and southern Uí Néill clans, with complex and shifting alliances, including the involvement of the Dublin Vikings. This war weakened "the dynasty and gave it few opportunities to assert its old dominance."[18]

It also created an opportunity for the Dál Cais to seize the kingship of Cashel, which Brian Boru was not slow to do.

Brian was born in the region of Lough Derg on the Shannon, possibly at Killaloe or at the now-excavated fortress site at Beal Boru a mile north of Killaloe town. If not born there, Brian probably spent time in his youth in this ring fort of about 4 acres (1.6 hectares). The fort controlled a ford across the largely Viking-dominated lower Shannon. Part of the Boru legend was that he spent time as a kind of guerrilla leader in the forests of Clare fighting the Limerick Vikings, but this is now viewed as later Dál Cais propaganda. Certainly, he was a seasoned fighter by the time he assumed the kingship of Cashel in 976. He defeated the Limerick Vikings and killed Ivar, the local Viking leader, and his two sons after they had retreated to the Scattery Island, a monastic settlement a mile off Kilrush in the Shannon estuary. Brian then defeated and killed his brother's murderer, Máel Maud, one of his rivals for the kingship of Cashel. He spent the next four years consolidating his hold on Munster.

Brian was organized and strategic. His conquest of Ireland can be divided into three stages. In the first stage, between 985 and 997, through a complex combination of military force and tactical maneuvering, he eventually gained control of Munster and Leinster, essentially the whole of southern Ireland. This was recognized at a summit meeting in 997 with the Uí Néill high king Máel Sechnaill (979–1002) at Clonfert in central Ireland. Máel was a very able man who led the forces trying to contain Brian's expansionism. Brian followed this up with an attack on Dublin, forcing Viking leader Sitric "Silkenbeard" to become a subking under his authority and to marry his daughter, the second stage of his conquest of the whole of Ireland.

He was now ready for the third stage, an attack on the northern half of Ireland. Again, after a series of strategic victories and retreats, by 1007 he more or less controlled the north, but it was not until 1011 that this victory was consolidated. Máel Sechnaill acknowledged him as *ard rí* in 1002, and he was crowned in Cashel. But despite all his successes Brian's power was limited by the kings and kinglets who still ruled across provincial Ireland. However, "the claim of the Uí Néill to the monopoly of the kingship of Tara had been broken effectively for the first time and, from then on, it was clear that the contest for the high kingship was open."[19] Open, that is, until the Norman invasion in 1169.

Brian was now high king of Ireland, and the *Book of Armagh* calls him "*Imperator Scottorum*" (Emperor of the Irish).[20] Clearly, he had great personal ability and military prowess. He was also lucky; he had *fortuna et mores*. His rivals, particularly the Uí Néill, were hopelessly divided. Also, the traditional power structure in Gaelic Ireland was collapsing, which largely explains the violence of the time as men on the make struggled to establish themselves and eliminate rivals. As high king Brian was an able administrator who encouraged education and sent young men to the Continent for further education. He also upgraded roads and bridges so that his army could move quickly across the country. He used the traditional system of tribute as a form of taxation, which he made sure he received from local kings. His insistent demands led to his nickname "Brian of the Tributes."

Resentment at Brian simmered below the surface. A story from the mid-twelfth-century *War of the Gaedhil with the Gaill*, whether true or not, illustrates this. Mael Mordha, the king of Leinster, together with the Dublin Vikings, had been defeated by Brian at the Battle of Glen Mamma near Dublin in 999. Mael fled the battlefield and hid in a yew tree, from which he was dragged down by Brian's son. In 1013 Brian demanded three ships' masts as tribute from Leinster. Mael personally assisted in carrying some of the masts to Brian's palace at Kincora (Killaloe). In the process he lost a button from a fine tunic that Brian had given him, and when he arrived at Brian's palace, Mael asked his sister Gormflaith, who was also Brian's wife (or mistress?), to sew the button on again. She threw the tunic into the fire and viciously upbraided Mael because he had disgraced himself by his subservience to Brian. This led to a major domestic quarrel, which also involved Brian's son, who reminded Mael about the "yew tree" incident. Mael stormed out, later bashing one of Brian's messengers on the head.[21]

There was trouble in the north in 1012. Mael seized this opportunity to declare war on Brian. This split the south, with some kings supporting Mael and others remaining loyal to Brian, now in his early seventies, some of whose troops were Viking mercenaries. The Dublin Vikings, however, joined Mael, and their leader, Sitric, appealed for help from the Norse earl Sigrud of the Orkneys and Brodin, Viking leader on the Isle of Man. Brian marched through Leinster and blockaded Dublin in spring 1014. A Viking attempt to break the siege led to the Battle of Clontarf on Good Friday, April 23, 1014.

As Brian prepared to attack the city, the foreign Vikings, in a masterly maneuver, placed themselves between Brian's forces and Dublin at Clontarf, nowadays a somewhat upmarket Dublin suburb on the north side of the Liffey estuary. At dawn, both armies in a shield-wall formation, engaged. The *Annals of Ulster* reports, "A valiant battle was fought between them, the like of which was never before encountered. Then the foreigners [Vikings] and the Laigin [Leinster men] first broke in defeat, and they were completely wiped out. There fell on the side of the foreign troop in this battle Mael Mordha . . . king of [Leinster]. . . . Six thousand were killed or drowned."[22]

This is out of the 7,000–8,000 troops who participated. Brian himself was treacherously killed while praying in his tent by the Viking pirate Brodin from the Isle of Man. He was later captured and appallingly killed (he was tied to a tree with his own intestines) by Ulf (or Wolf) the Quarrelsome, who was possibly a stepson of Brian. Only two of Brian's sons survived Clontarf.

Though the battle of Clontarf is popularly thought to have driven the Vikings out of Ireland, the fact is that Viking power had already been broken. Rather, Clontarf was, as Donnchadh Ó Corráin says, "part of the internal struggle for sovereignty and was essentially the revolt of the Leinstermen against the dominance of Brian, a revolt in which their Norse allies played an important but secondary role."[23] The battle's most important effect was to break the power of the Dál Cais clan and the Munster kings, just as the Dál Cais had broken the power of the Uí Néill.

The death of Brian Boru ended any hope of consolidation under strong, centralized leadership. Instead, it opened the way for a century and a half of strife and petty rivalry that made Ireland easy pickings for the Anglo-Normans who arrived in 1169. The English stayed until Monday, January 16, 1922, when Dublin Castle was formally handed over by the British to Michael Collins representing the Irish Provisional Government. He was seven-and-a-half minutes late for the appointment, and when reproached by a pompous British officer for tardiness, he quipped, "After seven-and-a-half centuries you're welcome to seven-and-a-half minutes."

❧

For the Romans, Caledonia, or Scotland, was beyond the borders of the known world. But for seven years beginning in AD 77 under the command of the very able governor of Britain, Sextus Calpurnius Agricola, some 5,000 troops of the Ninth Legion fought their way across what we now call Scotland. In 83 the Ninth faced some 30,000 *Caledonii*, seminaked men with red hair and body tattoos wearing brightly colored tartan trousers, at a place the Romans called

Mons Graupius, most likely Bennachie, a breast-shaped mountain about 20 miles (32 kilometers) east of Aberdeen. The result was a rout. Possibly 10,000 Caledonians died, with only 360 Roman casualties. However, though Romans won the battle, they nevertheless lost the war.

Political expediency saw Agricola recalled. The Romans withdrew south to Hadrian's Wall, which ran 72 miles (117 kilometers) across Britain from Newcastle-on-Tyne to Carlisle. In 159 the Romans sallied forth again into Caledonian territory to build the Antonine Wall from the Forth to the Clyde. This defensive line was soon abandoned, and the Romans permanently withdrew to Hadrian's Wall until they abandoned Britain altogether in 410 as the Western Empire collapsed. The Romans called the Caledonians *Picti*, probably meaning "painted men" from the tattoos, and the name stuck.

Roman Britain had become largely Christian in the fourth century. After the Romans left, the British Christian communities that remained began sending missionaries to the Celtic peoples, the most famous of all being Saint Patrick in Ireland. Christianity also spread northward—we know there was a Christian community at Whithorn on the Scottish Galloway coast by the mid-fifth century. According to Bede's *Ecclesiastical History*, a British bishop named Ninian built his monastery and *candida casa* (white house) there. The west coast of Scotland had close contact with Ireland, and Christianity soon spread across the northern Irish Sea, with the monk Columcille, or Columba in Latin, founding the monastery of Iona off the Isle of Mull. Columba later went on *peregrinatio*, a kind of voluntary exile, wandering through Scotland and contacting the Picts of northeastern Scotland around Inverness and Aberdeen. He met the Pictish king Bridei (555–584), who may have already have been a nominal Christian and whose death is recorded in the *Annals of Ulster*.[24] Another missionary was the Christian Scot Kentigern or Mungo, who became a monk and was active around present-day Glasgow.

By the early ninth century Scotland was an amalgam of tribal peoples, most of them Christian, still living in an Iron Age economy. Picts lived in the Highlands and the area northeast of the Firth of Forth, and the Christian Gaelic (Irish) kingdom of Dalriada was in Argyll and the isles and was linked to County Antrim in northeast Ireland. There were also groups of Celtic Britons in the borderlands of the north. One British group occupied Cumbria and Westmorland, whose king Urien Rheged (ca. 530–590) was a Christian, and another made up the kingdom of Strathclyde, which centered on the rock of

Dumbarton on the Firth of Clyde near Glasgow. In the seventh century the Anglo-Saxons pushed as far north as the Firth of Forth. They brought Christianity with them. However, by the time of King Edgar (957–975), the Tweed River had become the permanent border between the Anglo-Saxons and the Scots.

In 794 the Vikings arrived and attacked Iona, killing and enslaving monks and stealing treasures. They returned in 802 and again in 806, when "sixty-eight [monks were] killed by the heathen."[25] From then until the end of the tenth century, the Norsemen became a major disruptive element in Scottish history. They occupied Caithness (Scotland north of Loch Shin), the Inner and Outer Hebrides, the western edges of Strathclyde, western Dalriada (thus cutting it off from Ireland), the Isle of Man, and the Orkney and Shetland Islands. Scotland "found itself cut off from the mainstream of English influences on its southern flank, just as its Irish contacts had been violently severed in the west."[26] Norse settlement began a process that pushed the northern and western Picts and the western Irish (Scotti) southward and eastward, and the two groups gradually merged. Their common Christianity assisted this. They formed the kingdom of "Scotia" or "Alba." We don't know the details of how this happened, but the first person to emerge from this amalgamated kingdom in the mid-ninth century with some clear lineaments was Cináed mac Ailpin (King Kenneth I). It seems he was originally a Gael king from Dalriada who through marriage inherited the leadership of the Picts and enhanced a process already under way to merge and unite the Pictish and Gael peoples.

This process seems to have reached completion under King Constantine II mac Áeda (900–943). Again the details of his reign are hard to pin down, although we know that he tried to arrange peace with the Vikings by marrying his daughter to Olaf III of Dublin. Olaf was trying to clear a corridor across northern England to facilitate access to Jórvik, and Constantine's alliance with him dragged him into the Battle of Brunanburh (937) when both of them and Owein I of Strathclyde were decisively defeated by King Æthelstan. Constantine abdicated in 943 in favor of Malcolm I and became a monk at Saint Andrew's, dying in 952.

In the latter part of the tenth century, the kingdom fell apart, with three factions fighting each other. It was Malcolm II (1005–1034) who murdered his way to the throne in 1005 by eliminating all rivals. But then Malcolm had to deal with a feud-ridden kingdom. He knew that it was useless fighting the Vikings, who were now part of the fabric of Scotland, and that his real enemies were the Anglo-Saxons to the south. He marched south in 1006 to Durham, where he was stopped by the Anglo-Saxon earl Uhtred. Malcolm returned ten years later allied with Owein "the Bold" of Strathclyde. They defeated Uhtred, who was summoned south by King Cnut and assassinated, which led to a blood feud that lasted for several generations. When Owein died, Strathclyde came under the control of Malcolm's grandson, Duncan.

Malcolm was murdered in 1034 in a hunting lodge at Glamis, and Duncan I (1034–1040), Malcolm's grandson, ascended the throne. Caught up in seemingly endless feuding, Duncan was defeated and killed at the Battle of Pitgaveny near Elgin by Macbeth. Both Duncan's sons survived the battle. Macbeth of Moray (1040–1057), a grandson of Kenneth II who also had a strong claim on the throne, succeeded Duncan. Shakespeare's *Macbeth* is historically inaccurate because the real Macbeth was no manic-depressive haunted by guilt over the supposed murder of Duncan. Nicknamed "Red King," Macbeth was not a tyrant but an able, generous ruler who supported the church and the poor. He visited Rome on pilgrimage in 1050. But in the latter part of his reign, he made the mistake of interfering in English affairs and according to the *Annals of Ulster* was defeated in 1054 in "a battle between the men of Scotland and the English in which fell 3000 of the Scots and 1500 of the English."[27] Eventually in 1057 he was defeated by Malcolm III, son of Duncan I, at the Battle of Lumphanan, west of Aberdeen, and died of his wounds.

Historian Alfred P. Smyth reports, "The Scots had [now] established the most stable and successful monarchy in Britain prior to the Norman invasion."[28] That was quite an achievement and certainly stands in contrast to the internecine strife of Ireland at the beginning of the eleventh century. Like England under Alfred, Scotland had emerged from tribal chaos to become a coherent state, and the country was able to maintain a tradition of good government for over a century and a half until an ill-fated invasion of England by William I "the Lion" in 1174 saw Scotland defeated and placed virtually directly under English rule.

℘

One of the loveliest long walks (177 miles [284 kilometers]) in the United Kingdom is along Offa's dyke from Prestatyn on the north Wales coast along the present-day Anglo-Welsh border to Chepstow on the estuary of the Severn River near the Severn Bridge. So who was Offa, and what was his dyke? King

Alfred's biographer Bishop Asser says that "a certain vigorous king called Offa, who terrified all the neighbouring kings and provinces around him, had a great dyke built between Wales and Mercia from sea to sea."[29] In fact, the dyke was actually shorter, stretching some 63 miles (103 kilometers). Offa was the Anglo-Saxon king of Mercia (757–796) with a major headache: the Welsh.

Wales, Cornwall, and Cumbria were the Celtic holdouts in Britain after the Anglo-Saxon invasions of the fourth to the sixth centuries. By the eighth century Wales was made up of two major kingdoms: Gwynedd in the northwest and Powys along the eastern frontier with England. There were nine other smaller kingdoms in the west and the south. A common Welsh language was in use by the eighth century. Wales was Christian, probably dating back to fourth century Roman times in Britain. While there was a strong Pelagian, or ascetic-moralistic, emphasis in Welsh spirituality (theologian Pelagius [ca. 350–ca. 425] was, after all, a British Celt), there was also an awareness of the beauty of the world, as this late-ninth-century prayer-poem the "*Juvencus Englynion*" demonstrates:

> The world cannot express in song bright and melodious, even though
> The grass and the trees should sing, all thy glories, O true Lord.
> The Father has wrought such a multitude of wonders in this world
> That it is difficult to find an equal number. Letters cannot contain it,
> Letters cannot express it . . .
> He who made the wonder of the world, will save us, has saved us . . .
> Purely, humbly, in skilful verse, I should love to give praise to the Trinity.[30]

But back to Offa's dyke. There was always tension along the divide between the pre-Roman Celtic Welsh and the Germanic Anglo-Saxons. In the mid-seventh century the kingdom of Powys was strong enough to defeat Mercia, but Offa responded vigorously by building the dyke. It consisted of a ditch and rampart aligned to give a clear view into Wales. The ditch was about 88 feet wide (27 meters) and 25 feet (8 meters) from the bottom to the top of the bank. An amazing feat of construction, it controlled the movement of people and goods, but its defensive value was questionable.

By the ninth century England was undergoing massive changes as different Anglo-Saxon kingdoms were absorbed into Wessex. England's internal problems meant the Welsh could focus on their own affairs. King Rhodri Mawr

(844–878) of Gwynedd inherited Powys through his mother, Nest, daughter of the king of Powys. He gained Deheubarth (southwest Wales) through his marriage, and he defeated the Vikings on the island of Anglesey in 856. He resisted King Alfred's claim of overlordship of Wales, but some of the minor kings saw recognition of Alfred as a way of limiting Rhodri's power and protecting themselves against the Vikings. Welshmen like Bishop Asser appeared at Alfred's court, and in 893 Gwynedd accepted Alfred's authority.

The tenth century brought a reversal of Gwynedd's fortunes. A new king, Hywel Dda "the Good" (920–950), a grandson of Rhodri, inherited Deheubarth. He gained the small kingdom of Dyford through his marriage. In 942 the king of Gwynedd, Idwal Foel "the Bald" (916–942) was killed in a battle with the English and Hywel seized his kingdom. He was now king of the whole of Wales except for the southeast. He maintained peace with England and visited Winchester. An intelligent man who spoke English and Latin as well as Welsh, he made a pilgrimage to Rome in 928. Inspired by Alfred and by his observations while traveling, Hywel decided to consolidate and codify the laws of Wales. He achieved this by consultatively bringing together people from across the country. His law code was much concerned with the regulation of relationship between kin groups. Significantly, there is no record that his kingdom was attacked by the Vikings during his reign. Given what we have already seen, that was quite an achievement.

After his death the kingdom was split into three: Deheubarth, Gwynedd, and Powys. This opened the way for the Dublin Vikings, and the last half of the tenth century saw much Viking activity. Anglesey was one of their main targets, as was St David's on the southwest coast. But just like Ireland, in the end it was not the Vikings but the English who were to affect Wales most. But that is another story.

౿౨

Until now our story has been largely one of the disintegration of whatever state structures were left after the breakup of the Carolingian Empire or of places such as Italy, England, Ireland, or Scotland that had never experienced or not experienced for a long time the benefits of a unified polity and government until kings like Alfred the Great and his Anglo-Saxon successors. But despite the work of these great kings, the predominant emphasis in the late ninth and early tenth centuries was on localism, with centrifugal forces dominant. So the tenth century began with Europe broken up into its component parts at the most basic and localized level.

In Part Three of our story we will come into contact with the counterforces that were moving toward stabilization and unification and the building of larger communities of people who shared a language and some sense of cultural identity. Certainly throughout this period, most people still retained their strong sense of local identity, their consciousness of belonging to the place where they had been born and where most of them lived out their lives. This identification with place was especially strong among the peasants and lower orders. Membership in the church, in an overarching community that was *Christianitas* (Christendom) or Catholicism, would have given people a sense of context, especially among the literate and better educated.

But a third level of belonging was beginning to emerge as the tenth century progressed. This was a sense of belonging to a larger community with common ties of place and culture that transcended localism, a sense of being German or English. This new consciousness was coterminus with the development of better government administered by monarchs such as Henry the Fowler and Otto I. The Saxon government succeeded because it was well led, but also because it developed a small but competent bureaucracy.

We will begin our exploration of this new world by meeting one of Otto I's most competent administrators and without doubt the greatest Latinist and writer of the tenth century—Liutprand of Cremona.

PART THREE

THE
SECOND
SPRING

CHAPTER 11

Liutprand of Cremona

Cynic, Diplomat, and Stylist

IT WAS MIDAFTERNOON on Thursday, June 4, 968, and Liutprand, Bishop of Cremona, an abrasive man at the best of times, was frustrated and furious. He had arrived on a heavily overcast morning outside the massive walls of Constantinople as ambassador of Emperor Otto I. But his party was denied entry. Fully aware that he had been deliberately snubbed and self-important as always, he immediately presumed that the upstart Byzantine emperor Nikephoros II Phokas had given orders to keep him waiting in the heavy, driving rain. Without shelter he was soon soaked to the skin. This treatment didn't improve Liutprand's opinion of the Byzantines. Already a keen, cynical observer of the world, his jaundiced ruminations on Byzantine life, mores, and leading personalities were to have wide influence in Western Europe for several centuries to come, reinforcing a generally negative assessment of the Eastern Empire.

Even in a downpour, most other Europeans would have stood awestruck at the sheer size of Constantinople, with its population of more than 600,000. Visitors to Constantinople were astounded by the moat and walls, large sections of which are still standing in the Istanbul suburbs. Running four miles (6.5 kilometers) from the Sea of Marmara or Propontis in the south, the walls crossed the peninsula to the Golden Horn in the north, a narrow inlet from the Bosporus. The area enclosed was 6,400 acres (2,600 hectares). Constructed of white brick, stone, and marble, the walls shone even in the overcast light of that June morning. The white stonework was interspersed with strips of red brick in the walls, the arches over the battlement windows, and the tips of the battlements. Built by Emperor Theodosius II, the walls were completed in 423 and extensively rebuilt after a severe earthquake in 447. At intervals along them there were rectangular or octagonal towers with narrow battlement windows that allowed raking fire to be poured on attackers who may have penetrated the outer defenses. On passing through one of the ten nonmilitary gates, a tenth-century tourist would have found that the walls were not one, but a complex of several defense systems, all designed to force a besieging army to think twice before attempting to penetrate the city.

Liutprand was no tourist, however. He had been an ambassador to the Byzantine capital before and knew the ropes. Immediately on arrival at Constantinople, he had gone straight to the *Pyli Charisiou*, the "Gate of Charisius." He expected immediate entry as befitted his important rank. But his party was stopped in its tracks by the military guards. No reason was given. Liutprand was an observant man, part of whose task as an ambassador was to report back to Otto I on the state of things in the Byzantine capital. So he no doubt noted that the Byzantine guards were tall, well-armed, respectful, disciplined men who were probably from the *Scholae* regiment, the oldest of the four principal regiments making up the *Tagmata*, the core of the Byzantine army.

The soldier who first stopped the party was a *skutatos*, a low-level light infantryman armed with a sword and spear and dressed in a round steel helmet tapering to a peak and hip-length lamellar armor made of small connected metal plates held together by leather lacing over a red, gold-braided tunic reaching to above the knees. His leg coverings were similar to modern-day pants, with knee-high boots. He referred Liutprand, who spoke good Greek, to an officer. This man, dressed in a knee-length light blue tunic, orange cloak, and darker blue stockings and black shoes, respectfully but firmly shunted Liutprand and his party back out of the sheltered gate area into the open outside the walls. There they were left to cool their heels beside a large necropolis and forest park in what Liutprand calls "heavy rain," as much less important people came and went.[1]

Liutprand assumed the guards were consulting the emperor himself. In fact, they were taking instructions from the officials of Leo Phokas, who was brother of the emperor, *curopilates* (chancellor of the court), and *logothetes tou dromou*, "minister or secretary of the postal department," which included supervision of the postal service, imperial communications, the police, and foreign diplomats inside the empire. He was what today we would call an interior minister or a homeland security secretary.

To Liutprand's utter frustration, he was impotent to do anything about the slow-moving officials. There was no doubt that the imperial officials knew he was coming and whom he represented. They probably even had guessed at his purpose. The Byzantine intelligence system was then the best in the world, and spies would have noted his departure from Rome in late March or early April 968 as well as his arrival in Brindisi in southern Italy, where he first entered Byzantine territory. From there he had crossed the Adriatic Sea on a Byzantine ship to Korypho (Corfu) and then via a roundabout journey to Salonika to avoid central Greece, which was then occupied by the Bulgarians. A diplomatic party would have been carefully watched, and its expected arrival time would have been reported to the capital. Imperial messengers with relays of fresh horses could travel a lot faster than Liutprand's mounted party of probably four people with a couple of pack mules in tow, trudging along the Via Egnatia across southeastern Europe. Now, as Liutprand commented, the Byzantines were showing a "studied insult" by treating him "ignominiously and harshly." This treatment was directed, of course, at his imperial master, Otto I, on whose business the bishop of Cremona had come to Constantinople. Liutprand and his party would also have stood out because they were riding horses, which only the wealthy or those on official business could afford. As a traveling bishop-ambassador, he also no doubt had a comfortable saddle with back support.

Standing in the rain outside the Charisius Gate, Liutprand had a chance to observe closely the complex defenses of Constantinople. An attacking force would first face a rock-lined, water-filled moat, a little more than 60 feet (18 meters) wide and 20 feet (6 meters) deep. Aqueducts, which were hidden underground, passed through the moat to supply the city with water during a siege. Beyond the moat was a wall about 6 feet (2 meters) high and behind it a flat, open area called the *parateichion*, designed to expose attackers who had crossed the moat and wall to a withering crossfire. Behind this the outer wall stood about 26 feet (8 meters) above the *parateichion*. The towers in the outer wall were on average a little more than 32 feet (10 meters) high and jutted out beyond the wall itself about 16 feet (5 meters). Behind this wall was another higher flat area called the *peribolos*, which was about 65 feet (20 meters) wide. It served as a staging area for troops defending the outer wall, and if this defense line were penetrated, it served as an open area in which attackers were exposed to crossfire from defenders in the towers in the inner wall. This was the strongest line of defense, much of it still standing and marking the borders of the old city of Istanbul. These walls were breached only twice in a thousand years, once by the thugs of the Fourth Crusade in 1204 and then by the Ottoman Turks in 1453, the final act in the destruction of the Byzantine Empire.

Eventually, Liutprand and his party finally made it out of the rain and through the Charisius Gate. He says that "at five o'clock Nikephoros ordered us to be admitted on foot, for he did not think us worthy to use the horses."[2] Liutprand hurried to his accommodation to change into dry clothes. But another disappointment awaited him. The marble-lined government guesthouse lacked its own water supply, and was "large and open, but it neither kept out cold nor afforded shelter from the heat. Armed soldiers were set to guard us and prevent my people from going out and any others from coming in. This dwelling . . . was so far from the emperor's residence [about 2 miles (3 kilometers)] that we were quite out of breath when we walked there—we did not ride."[3] Even the wine was bad: "To add to our troubles, the Greek wine we found undrinkable because of the mixture in it of pitch, resin and plaster [gypsum]."[4] Their landlord was anything but welcoming. Liutprand calls him a "warden." "If you were to seek another like him, you certainly would not find him on earth; you might perhaps in hell. . . . In our hundred and twenty days not one passed without bringing to us groaning and lamentation."[5]

❧

We have met Liutprand several times already. John Julius Norwich calls him "one of the most valuable—and certainly the most colorful—of our sources of tenth century history in both the Eastern and Western Empires."[6] Highly educated, he was the finest Latinist of the century. His history of his time, *Antapodosis* (Tit for Tat or Retribution) is a chronicle of intrigue, scandal, and revenge in which nothing is private or hidden. It purports to recount the contemporary history of Italy, but it "became a way to get even with his main Italian antagonists."[7] In fact, our first encounter with him was as a source for the scandal-plagued saga of the Theophylact clan, whom he abhorred.

He was encouraged to write *Antapodosis* by Abd al-Rahmān III's ambassador Recemund on a visit to Otto's court. The two became friends, and Liutprand dedicated the book to him. "I began it [in 958] at Frankfurt . . . and I am pushing on with it today [960] in the island of Paxos," where he was stranded while on an apparently aborted second journey to Constantinople.[8] Liutprand's other works are *A Chronicle of Otto's Reign*, *The Embassy to Constantinople*, and a recently discovered sermon. His output is an apologia for Otto I; papal historian Horace Mann calls him Otto's "parasite."[9] While the accuracy and objectivity of Liutprand's writings must be weighed carefully, he does provide us with a real insight into the attitudes of the age. In *Antapodosis* he delights in recording the gross, manipulative lasciviousness of upper-class Italian life, where fact and rumor about prominent "personalities" are mixed into a fascinating and salacious narrative that makes modern celebrity magazines and tabloid newspapers seem completely tame.

The word "personality" is the clue here. Liutprand has left us sketches of *personae*, masks of how people presented themselves and were perceived by others, rather than explorations of their intimate selves. While we feel that we can "get to know" Liutprand from his writings, most of what we actually encounter is a carefully constructed persona. His most recent translator, Paolo Squatriti, speaks of "his acute awareness of how written words could become the best means of self-presentation, or even self-invention."[10] Liutprand is an interesting precursor for our own times, when manufactured image and constructed celebrity are the hallmarks of sophistication. Although psychoanalysis of people from a thousand years ago is a hazardous process, I think we can say that Liutprand was a highly intelligent person who felt surrounded by powerful upstarts, foolish courtiers, and hangers-on. He gave vent to his resentment in acerbic prose that palpitates with a sense of immediacy and liveliness. While *Antapodosis* is not autobiography, a form of expression uncommon in his time, the book still quivers with anger, a perverse sense of humor, and a preoccupation with sex. With no laws of defamation to limit him, Liutprand's writing has an aggressive edge, and he paints memorable prose portraits and tableaux that leave nothing to the imagination. He pursues his quarries, no matter how powerful, exposing their foul intentions, violence, vulgarity, gratuitous cruelty, sadism, and obscenity.

Liutprand was ruled by an ethic of revenge toward those he felt hurt, slighted, or annoyed him. He believed in retributive justice, and he held that what was not sorted out in this life certainly would be at the last judgment. His theology reflects a harsh, tough political world in which no quarter is given or expected. Liutprand scholar Jon N. Sutherland calls him a "moralist" in that he explains the world in terms of retribution and revenge. I prefer to call him a "muckraker" who ruthlessly exposes the Machiavellian politics and personal depravity of his time. Sutherland characterizes him as a "complex man" who tended "toward paranoia."[11]

Liutprand is particularly harsh on powerful women. Time and again he portrays them as dominated by sexual manipulation and lust for power. He asserts that women are less able than men to resist their sexual urges and that they used their gender ruthlessly to exploit foolish men, who were often gulled by them. Sutherland says that his attitude to women indicates "the existence of some abnormality in his view of life. . . . Not only do Liutprand's attitudes toward women confirm the suspicions suggested by his petulant outbursts and self-praise, but they also provide the best opportunity to explore his capacity for extravagant invective and his tendency toward fantasy."[12] Although clerical misogyny was widespread, Liutprand seems to have taken woman-hating to a new level.

There may be another purpose behind his misogyny. Casting the powerful Theophylact women as whores allows Liutprand to cast doubt on their legitimacy. This renders the clan vulnerable to Otto's claims of overlordship. This argument is strengthened by the fact that he simultaneously exalts the beauty and virtue of the womanhood of his German patrons. For instance, he extols Empress Adelheid as "charming both by the beauty of her person and the excellence of her character," while claiming that Ermengarde, second wife of Adelbert of Ivrea, held power because "she carried on carnal commerce with everyone, prince and commoner alike."[13] Liutprand was concerned about the consequences of rampant sexuality in both sexes. It upset due order in society, and he worried that infidelity could lead to social disorder. He valued order highly, having grown up in a time of chaos. Already an experienced politician and diplomat, he was also a shrewd judge of politics, throwing in his lot with the Saxon monarchy once he perceived that the Saxons were the coming powerbrokers.

છ૭

Liutprand was born in Pavia in late 921 or early 922. He grew up in a loving, supportive, and wealthy family of court functionaries and diplomats. Given the insecurity of the time, family and clan were all important, and Liutprand reflects this. A person's immediate relatives were the most trusted people, and family loyalty was basic. Liutprand's father died when he was young, but his stepfather cared for him. He speaks of the kindness of "the fathers and sons of my family" and of the need "to render hearty thanks" for them.[14] At the time Pavia, on the Ticino River just above its confluence with the Po, was the capital of northern Italy. On the main pilgrim route from northern Europe to Rome, Pavia became the capital in Lombard times and retained this status. It

had a royal palace, several beautiful churches, and a school at which prominent Irish monk, teacher, astronomer, and poet Dúngal taught in the 820s.
Pavia's economy was thriving; it had a silver mint whose coins were recognized
throughout Italy. Liutprand was essentially an urban man; he loved his native
city, which he considered far superior to Rome.

Pavia experienced a difficult period in the early tenth century as Berengar I,
King of Italy (888–924) struggled to maintain his position against Guido I and
Lambert II of Spoleto. The situation was complicated by periodic raids by the
Magyars, who first arrived in Italy in 898. Even though they never stayed long
because they had to find pasturage for their horses in the summer months, the
Magyars brought terror to Italy. Around 920 Berengar made a deal with them
against his Italian rivals. Deal-making with Magyars was completely unacceptable to other Italian magnates, who revolted against Berengar and defeated him
at the Battle of Fiorenzuola d'Arda (July 17, 923). Giuseppe Sergi says this was
"one of the bloodiest battles in the history of the kingdom [of Italy] . . . [and]
the huge number of deaths on both sides decimated Italy's aristocracy."[15]

This opened the door for the Magyars to wreak havoc across the Po plain,
which they did in 924. They besieged Pavia and burned it on the morning of
March 12, 924. Liutprand was about four at the time, and his family had already fled the city. He speaks of "the mad rage of the Hungarians" and the citizens who, "owing to their past sins, could not resist them in battle nor were
they able to appease [them] by gifts." The Magyars built earthworks around
the walls, which allowed them to throw firebrands into the city. The result was
that many wooden buildings caught fire and the March winds drove the fire
onward. Citizens who tried to escape were killed by the Magyars with "impious
glee." Describing the scene Liutprand bursts into poetry:

> *The gold that we in chests had stored away,*
> *Lest any strangers on it hands should lay,*
> *Runs through the sewers, mixed with mud and mire.*
> *Our fair Pavia falls consumed by fire!*
> *Bright silver bowls to molten metal turn;*
> *The very corpses in the graveyard burn.*[16]

Flodoard says the Magyars destroyed "vast resources" and that "forty-four
churches were set afire and Bishop John, along with the bishop of Vercelli who

was staying with him, were killed by the fire and smoke." Only two hundred survivors remained.[17] The Magyars didn't occupy the city but left it in ruins and continued raiding in Italy. The citizens who had fled returned, and Pavia recovered quickly.

Hugo of Arles (924–945) was elected king of Italy in 924 after the defeat of Berengar I, and he rebuilt Pavia as his capital (he would later become the husband of Marozia). For the first decade of his reign, he had to struggle to maintain his position against continuing Magyar invasions. About 931 Liutprand became a chorister in Hugo's court. Never one for false modesty, Liutprand says he "had won the favour of King Hugo by my sweet voice. He was passionately fond of singing, and in that respect none of the boys who were my contemporaries could surpass me."[18] Well schooled in Latin literature, Liutprand became a cleric and deacon. Despite Hugo's insatiable predilection for beautiful women, Liutprand held the king in high regard, probably because he maintained a scholarly court and was keen on music. J. J. Norwich comments that "Liutprand's characteristic combination of prudishness and prurience may well stem from an adolescence spent among the courtesans who came flocking to Pavia from all over Italy and beyond."[19]

But by 945 Hugo's star was waning, and he was defeated by Margrave Berengar of Ivrea, grandson of Berengar I. Always a coward, Hugo decamped to his native Provence and died there in his bed. Meanwhile, Liutprand's politically astute family made sure he was gradually withdrawn from Hugo's court and introduced to Berengar II (950–966). "My parents were so allured by Berengar's reputation and his fame for courtesy and generosity that they put me into his service, and at very great expense got me appointed as his private secretary responsible for all state dispatches."[20] This is an exaggeration; he was probably a minor functionary. He was no admirer of Berengar, but he kept that to himself. He later described him in *Antapodosis* as a "caitiff under whose tyranny all Italy is now groaning."[21]

Nevertheless, Liutprand was appointed Berengar's ambassador to Constantinople in 949. The Byzantines had reconquered much of southern Italy from the Saracens and were experiencing an economic revival, and they wanted to improve relationships with the West. Liutprand's father and stepfather had already acted as ambassadors to Constantinople. Now it was Liutprand's turn. The immediate circumstances were that Emperor Constantine VII Porphyrogenitus (913–959), who cultivated the art of diplomacy, had sent friendly em-

bassies to Berengar II and Otto I. Otto quickly appointed an ambassador, Liutefred of Mainz, and, not to be outdone, Berengar, "stuffed full of cunning,"
looked for a way of sending an ambassador on the cheap. So he put the hard
word on Liutprand's stepfather to pay for the twenty-nine-year-old to go.
The stepfather consented only so that Liutprand could learn Greek. "My stepfather . . . fired by hope, contributed to all the expenses of the journey and
sent me off, the bearer of handsome gifts, to Constantinople."[22] Leaving Pavia
on August 2, 949, he sailed down the Po to Venice. Joining up with the Byzantine ambassador to Otto and Otto's ambassador, Liutefred, Liutprand sailed
from Venice on August 25, 949, and after a fourteen-day journey arrived to a
warm reception in Constantinople.

Unlike his gimlet-eyed reflections of subsequent trips, Liutprand reports that
he was astonished at what he saw during his first visit to Constantinople. His descriptions show how impressed he was with the palace and particularly the throne
room. Here there was a tree "made of bronze gilded over, whose branches were
filled with birds, also made of gilded bronze, which uttered different cries, each
according to its varying species." The imperial throne at first "seemed a low structure," but it was attached to a device that lifted it "high into the air" to preclude
direct conversation with the emperor. It was guarded by lions made of either
bronze or wood, "who beat the ground with their tails and gave a dreadful roar
with open mouth and quivering tongue." After making the customary triple
prostration, Liutprand looked up to find that "[Constantine VII] whom just before I had seen sitting on a moderately elevated seat had now changed his raiment
and was sitting on the level of the ceiling."[23] While there is something childish
about such tricks, the technology that drove them was sophisticated. "Behind
the often frivolous artifacts, historians of technology recognize the beginning of
a rich and continuous tradition leading . . . to the precision mechanisms of modern science and industry."[24] Court ceremonial was a form of theatre designed to
exalt the emperor, highlight "the harmonious movement of the universe" in the
emperor's favor, and "appear magnificent and beautiful and to impress the
subjects"—and visiting ambassadors.[25] Liutprand says that "[Constantine] did
not address me personally . . . but by the intermediary of a secretary he enquired
about Berengar's doings and asked after his health."[26] Following these pleas-
antries, Liutprand was dismissed with a nod from the secretary.

It was the custom of ambassadors to bring gifts, but all that Berengar sent
was a letter "full of lies." So Liutprand produced a set of gifts provided by his

stepfather "as coming from Berengar," and he tried to talk his way around "my humble present with fine words." He presented Constantine with a set of weapons, shields, cauldrons, and "what was more precious to the emperor than anything, four *carzimasia*; that being the Greek word for four young eunuchs who have had both their testicles and penises removed."[27] It is hard to see how Constantine would have seen these eunuchs as "more precious" than the other gifts, given he had a palace full of eunuchs and slaves. But the gifts managed to get Liutprand an invitation to an imperial banquet at which an extraordinary acrobatic act was performed. After the banquet Constantine bestowed a "handsome present" on Liutprand.[28]

On Palm Sunday 950 he was again invited to the palace, this time to the annual payment of imperial officials and courtiers. This occurred in the large hall of the Nineteen Tables. Here Constantine stood behind a big table covered with bags of gold and precious silk garments. Officials were summoned in order of rank to receive their salary from the emperor's hands. The ceremony emphasized the personal connection between Constantine and his assistants and their dependence upon him. They were paid annually in gold, many receiving more than they could personally carry. Constantine sent his chancellor to ask Liutprand how he was enjoying the ceremony. Always the opportunist, Liutprand replied, "It would please me . . . if it did me any good." Quoting the gospel story of the rich man in hell and Lazarus, the poor man in heaven, he more or less directly asked the Emperor for a handout. "The emperor smiled in some confusion, and mentioned me to come to him. He then presented me with a large cloak and a pound of gold coins; a gift he willingly made and I even more willingly received."[29]

A pound of gold coins was not a lot; in *Antapodosis* he says this was the equivalent of what third-class knights, chamberlains, and treasury and admiralty officials received annually. At this point the story suddenly breaks off; *Antapodosis* was left unfinished.

Liutprand seems to have stayed about seven months in Constantinople, possibly until after Easter 950, to learn Greek. Thereafter he used Greek words and phrases in his writing, obviously showing off his linguistic erudition to a society where few people could read or speak another language. He had also established good relationships in Constantinople with some of the ruling elite, and on his return to Italy he was recognized as an expert on Byzantium.

But Liutprand was not happy working for Berengar II, and he was not the only one. "[Berengar's] conduct would have almost driven me to despair if I had not found many others as companions in misfortune."[30] The problem was probably associated, in part, with Berengar's conflict with the northern Italian cities and the bishops who were their effective rulers, often conjointly with citizens' assemblies. Because of their defenses, the cities were able to resist the Magyar incursions, and they gained influence at the expense of the rural land-based aristocracy, who suffered from the Magyar raids. As a result, Geoffrey Barraclough says, "the bishop and the body of citizens together sought and obtained privileges which made the city independent of the count and of the county." Rulers like Hugo and Berengar never really controlled these urban centers, and it placed "ultimate power in the hands of the Lombard bishops. They could not, perhaps, make a king; but no king could maintain his position for long without their support or against their opposition."[31] It was precisely these bishops who encouraged Otto I to come to Italy to get rid of Berengar II. Always politically astute, Liutprand would have quickly perceived the direction in which politics was moving. The Saxon star was in the ascendant, and this would have motivated his move to Otto's court.

No doubt his unhappiness deepened when Berengar was crowned king of Italy in 950. This, combined with the king's meanness in not financially supporting Liutprand's diplomatic mission, was probably the last straw for Liutprand. When Otto I invaded Italy in 951, Liutprand immediately knew that Berengar's rule was finished and that the place to be was the German court. Liutprand crossed the Alps sometime in the early 950s to join an already growing crowd of Italians at Otto's court. Now a servant of Otto, Liutprand made sure that Berengar II and his wife, Willa, became villains in *Antapodosis*.

Symptomatic of Liutprand's vengeance-driven style is a story he tells about Queen Willa. Liutprand says that Willa had in her service "a priestling named Dominic, a fellow of short stature and swarthy complexion, boorish, hairy, intractable, rough, shaggy, wild, uncouth, fond of mad strife, with a wanton tail-like appendage, and no regard for right." Willa had entrusted her daughters Gisla and Gerberga to Dominic for their literary education. In reality, according to Liutprand, Willa lusted after "the hairy, unwashed priest" and used his intimacy with the girls to give him "costly robes and delicate food" and, ultimately, to seduce him. Their affair was "not only known to the chamberlains and other officials of the court, but was the common talk of all the tradesmen of the town," everyone apparently except Berengar! One night "this hairy creature" was on his way to Willa's bed when he disturbed a dog. It started barking and bit him several times,

waking up the whole household. When asked what he was doing, Willa got in
first and told everyone, "The villain was after my maids." Taking his cue from his
mistress, Dominic confessed that this was true. After this Willa "began to plot
against his life, but could not get her plan executed. . . . [She] had recourse to
soothsayers and sorcerers hoping that their charms would help her." Berengar
heard the gossip and asked what was happening. "Whether success was due to
[the sorcerers'] incantations or to Berengar's weakness I do not know," Liutprand
confesses, but "at any rate her husband gave way and of his own accord put his
head into the conjugal halter. . . . The lady herself received more than ever of
Berengar's affection." Poor Dominic was castrated, and Liutprand reports that
"his tool, they discovered, was worthy of Priapus himself," which, Liutprand says,
explained Willa's attraction.[32]

ɞ

Having escaped Berengar, Liutprand entered the clerical *familia* of the far more
promising Otto I in Frankfurt. Here he worked as chaplain, administrator, and
diplomat, bringing a special expertise in northern Italian and Byzantine affairs
thanks to his personal knowledge of the main actors. No doubt he bad-
mouthed Berengar, who, he claims, was "not a king but rather despot of Italy
and . . . Willa, who because of her boundless tyranny is rightly called a second
Jezebel and because of her insatiate greed for plunder a Lamia vampire." (In
classical literature Lamia was a savage, child-stealing woman.) Even though
there were other Italians in the German court, Liutprand felt lonely in Germany. Essentially, he was the product of Italian city culture where there were intellectual stimulation and social interaction. Now he was working at a court
that was constantly on the move through the countryside dealing with the politics of land-based magnates.

The petulance revealed in his attacks on Berengar and Willa and in other
parts of *Antapodosis* may also betray a response to the ridicule that he might
have experienced in Otto's court when he first arrived. Perhaps people doubted
his ability, and there were questions about his foreign origin and his loyalty to
the Saxon monarchy. But his importance as an adviser increased as Otto turned
his attention to Italian affairs and in late 960 sought the imperial crown from
the pope.

Otto's excuse to invade Italy was provided by Berengar II. He had already
been defeated by Otto in 951 and was permitted to continue as "king of Italy,"

but he governed as a German vassal, though his despotic rule eventually alienated the northern Italian bishops and local rulers. When he invaded papal territory, it was the last straw. John XII (955–964) appealed to Otto, offering him the imperial crown to rid Italy of Berengar II. Liutprand reports in *Liber de rebus gestis Ottonis* (A Chronicle of Otto's Reign), an apologia for Otto's Italian policies, that "the most pious king was moved by their tearful complaints and considered not himself but the cause of Jesus Christ. Therefore . . . [he] collected his forces and marched in haste to Italy," crossing the Brenner Pass in the early spring of 961.[33] He entered Pavia unopposed. Berengar had retreated to his redoubt in the mountains of Friuli.

Liutprand either accompanied Otto's army across the Brenner or followed soon afterward. When Otto was reconfirmed as king of Italy in Milan, he looked to the major bishoprics of the Po plain to support him. In need of trusted supporters in these dioceses, he had Liutprand appointed bishop in Cremona on January 14, 962, both as a reward and as a means to provide a stipend to support him. As we saw, Otto was crowned emperor in Rome in February 962. He captured Berengar and Willa soon afterward. They were sent into exile, which for Willa meant a nunnery. If Liutprand were to be believed, she would have found the celibate life rather constricting given her voracious sexual appetite!

It was around the time that Liutprand was appointed bishop that he seems to have abandoned work on *Antapodosis*. No doubt his diocesan work and fast-moving political events distracted him, and the eventual murder of Berengar satisfied his lust for revenge. Also as Squatriti points out, *Antapodosis*, like most medieval works, was different from a modern book, which is written and published as a finished product. Medieval writers could and did change and adapt their handwritten works, which were not published in the modern sense, so a book was really finished only when the writer died or finally abandoned it.[34]

❧

So why was Liutprand treated so badly when he arrived in Constantinople on his second trip in June 968? He learned the first reason two days after his arrival. On Pentecost eve he was summonsed to meet the tall, shrewd *logothete*, Leo Phokas. He made it clear to Liutprand that the Byzantines were furious that Otto I had assumed the title *basileus*—"emperor" in Greek—at his coronation in Saint Peter's. This caused consternation in Constantinople, where they were convinced that there was only one *basileus* and that the German "barbarian" was a mere upstart.

However, such Byzantine sensibilities had apparently not really occurred to Otto, although surely Liutprand would have realized that the Byzantines alone considered themselves the sole successors of the Roman emperors. Seemingly oblivious of this, Otto's only concern was to gain respectability as a "new" emperor by getting a Byzantine princess as his son's wife. He also wanted to make peace with the Byzantines in southern Italy.

There had already been negotiations about diplomatic marriages between East and West as far back as 765, and these continued throughout the ninth century. Most of the earlier marriage proposals had come from Constantinople rather than from the West, and already two marriages had been arranged. So Otto was optimistic, and after allowing things to settle down following his coronation, he sent Liutprand to Constantinople to try to persuade Emperor Nikephoros II Phokas (963–969) to consent to a diplomatic marriage between Otto's son and an imperial daughter. The other key issue in the negotiations was the need for a settlement in southern Italy to defend the region against the Saracens. But the Byzantines were in high dudgeon. Liutprand says that he and Phokas had "a fierce argument over [Otto's] imperial title. He called you not 'emperor,' which is *basileus* in his tongue, but *Rex*, which is 'king' in ours. I told him that the thing meant was the same though the word was different, and then he said that I had come not to make peace but to stir up strife." Of course, Phokas was right; the words don't mean the same thing. So feigning diplomatic outrage, Phokas "got up in a rage" and refused to receive Otto's letter directly "but through an interpreter."[35]

The second reason for Byzantine anger was more immediate and strategic. Otto had occupied Rome and attempted to break the power of the clans. These were allied to Constantinople, and it suited the Byzantines to maintain their power by keeping Italy divided into enclaves and preventing any powerful enough state to arise that threatened their control in southern Italy. Then, late in 967, Otto had added insult to injury by reasserting Charlemagne's claims to overlordship of Rome and Byzantine-controlled southern Italy. He formed an alliance with Pandulf I "Ironhead," Prince of Capua and Benevento, a local ruler on the make against the Byzantines, and invaded Byzantine territory. An ignominious defeat at Bari had forced Otto to make a hasty retreat. Liutprand wisely doesn't mention this in the *Relatio* (The Embassy to Constantinople).

Given that Liutprand was dispatched to Constantinople very soon after, probably in early April 968, it is no wonder that he was unwelcome.

Given this situation, a third reason emerges as a possibility: Liutprand could have been acting as a spy, at least as far as the Byzantines were concerned. The treatment at the diplomatic residence is then explained by Byzantine suspicions about his intentions and the need to keep an eye on him. Karl Leyser suggests that Liutprand's real mission may have been to make contact with anti-Nikephoros dissidents "under the guise of conducting official negotiations which . . . he and Otto I knew could not succeed."[36] Certainly, the contrariness of the Byzantine police who guarded the diplomatic palazzo in which Liutprand stayed, as well as the behavior of his landlord, indicated that they were suspicious and edgy. Liutprand reports, "The poor of Latin-speech [probably stranded Venetian or Italian traders] who came to me for alms, they seized or slew or put in prison," again indicating the jumpiness of the Byzantines.[37] He also speaks of "my Greek friends," perhaps a reference to elements opposed to the Nikephoros government. These suspicions are reinforced by a secret meeting he had in a church that contained a relic of the true cross. Liutprand says, "Amid the noisy crowd [in the church] some persons approached me unnoticed by my guards and cheered my sad heart with words of furtive conversation."[38] This approach could have been entirely innocent, but it might have been a clandestine meeting with those who opposed the regime.

Whatever his real purpose, Liutprand was received by Nikephoros II Phokas on Pentecost Sunday, June 7, 968. As the *Relatio* constantly emphasizes, Nikephoros was a usurper who had seized the throne in a kind of *coup de mariage*. He had basically muscled his way into power when his short-lived predecessor, Romanus II (959–963), died suddenly and mysteriously at the age of twenty-three. The rumor was that Romanus's wife, Empress Theophano, had poisoned him. It was untrue, but given Theophano's background, it was understandable why people believed it. She was the daughter of a Greek hotelkeeper. Strikingly beautiful, ambitious, and ruthless, she struck down anyone who got in her way. She had two young sons by Romanus, the six-year-old Basil and the three-year-old Constantine. The sudden death of her husband placed her in a dangerous position.

The most powerful men in the empire were two well-placed brothers, both able generals, Nikephoros and Leo Phokas. They were successful militarily because they led from the front and transformed the approach of the Byzantine army. For centuries the Byzantines had adopted a defensive stance, even against the Islamic onslaught. Nikephoros went on the attack and was consequently nicknamed "the White Death of the Saracens." Highly successful on the Eastern front, he also reconquered Crete, which for one hundred fifty years had been a base for Muslim piracy. Nikephoros changed Byzantine attitudes, and Romilly Jenkins comments that his army "reminds us of the Cromwellians in ruthlessness, discipline and commitment."[39] But while successful and adored by his troops, Nikephoros was never popular among ordinary people, especially in Constantinople.

Nikephoros was ambitious. On learning that Romanus had died on March 15, 963, he rushed back to Constantinople from a series of stunning victories in Syria, overthrew the unpopular chief minister, Joseph Bringas, and declared himself emperor. Despite being a confirmed bachelor, he suddenly became besotted with Theophano and persuaded her to marry him. It was most unlikely that she would have been attracted to him. He was older than fifty, an ascetic who wore a hairshirt as a penance; inclined toward the monastic life; and, as Liutprand delights in telling us, very ugly. As J. J. Norwich elegantly puts it, "We cannot seriously imagine this exquisite and pleasure-loving young Empress, immediately after a happy if short-lived marriage with the outstandingly attractive Romanus, feeling anything but repugnance for a sanctimonious puritan more than twice her age."[40] But she had to protect herself and her boys, so marriage to Nikephoros was probably the safest bet. Nikephoros had been emperor for five years when he met Liutprand on that Pentecost Sunday in 968, and his own downfall was only a year and a half away. By then he had managed to alienate both the civil service and the church, and while he had expanded the borders of the empire, these victories had created an enormous tax burden, which fell largely on ordinary citizens. He was increasingly isolated.

At his meeting with Nikephoros, Liutprand was treated respectfully but was bluntly told that his monarch, Otto, was not an emperor but a mere king. Liutprand says he defended his Otto stoutly, but in fact he was probably a lot more meek and mild than he makes out. Laying it on with a trowel in the *Relatio*, Liutprand compares Otto's comeliness, resplendence, power, mercy, and virtue to Nikephoros's ugliness.

He is a monstrosity of a man, a dwarf, fat-headed and with tiny mole's eyes; disfigured by a short, broad thick beard half going gray; disgraced by a neck scarcely an inch long; pig-like by reason of the big close bristles on his head; in color an Ethiopian and, as the poet [Juvenal] says "you would not like to meet him in the dark"; a big belly, a lean posterior, very long in the hip considering his short stature, short legs, fair-sized heels and feet; dressed in a robe made of fine linen, but old, foul smelling and discolored by age; shod with Sicyonian slippers; bold of tongue, a fox by nature; in perjury and falsehood a Ulysses.[41]

Elsewhere he says Nikephoros "has long hair and wears a tunic with long sleeves and a bonnet [i.e., female headgear]; he is lying, crafty, merciless, foxy, proud, falsely humble, miserly and greedy; he eats garlic, onions and leeks, and he drinks bath water."[42]

Scarcely a flattering portrait!

The emperor had no children of his own and sired none with Theophano, but she had four children by Romanus, the two princes already mentioned and two other *porphyrogenetoi*, princesses born in the purple-hung porphyry chamber of the palace, the traditional birthing place of either sons or daughters of a reigning emperor or a designated heir to the throne. Purple was the imperial color and was worn only by the emperor. But Nikephoros had no intention whatsoever of allowing any of his four stepchildren to be used in Western diplomacy. So when, on Otto's behalf, Liutprand asked for "the daughter of the Emperor Romanus and the Empress Theophano"—here he was probably referring to the princess Anna—to be given in marriage to Otto junior, Nikephoros bluntly refused.[43] The best he would offer was a non-*porphyrogenite* princess, although in negotiation with Leo Phokas, Liutprand was told the Byzantines would provide a purple-born wife if Otto I were willing to hand over Ravenna, Rome, Capua, and Benevento. While Benevento and Capua might have been negotiable, central and northern Italy were not. Negotiations collapsed.

Having failed in his mission, Liutprand prepared for his return to Italy. But the Byzantines were not going to let him go easily, especially given their concerns about his possibly being a spy. They took further umbrage when an embassy arrived on the feast of the Assumption of the Virgin (August 15) from Pope John XIII (965–972) with a letter that addressed Nikephoros as "Emperor of the Greeks." This was considered a deliberate insult for diminishing his position, but more likely it was an unintended lapse of protocol. Regardless, it complicated Liutprand's position considerably.

Now concerned for his own safety and, it seems, ill with some kind of sickness, Liutprand was again summoned to the palace, on September 17, and was interviewed by patrician eunuch Christopher and three other officials. Liutprand says Christopher "gave me a courteous reception." He told Liutprand:

> "The pallor of your face, the emaciation of your whole body, the unusual length of your hair and beard, all reveal the immense pain that is in your heart because the date of your return to your master has been delayed. But be not angry with the sacred emperor, we pray, nor with us. The cause of your delay is this. The pope of Rome . . . has sent a letter to our most sacred emperor . . . calling him 'emperor of the Greeks,' and not 'emperor of the Romans.' [Certainly] this has been done at your master's instigation."[44]

Liutprand maintains that he stoutly defended both pope and emperor, but Christopher and his assistants kept talking. "'Listen,' they said, ' . . . the silly blockhead of a pope does not know that the sacred Constantine transferred to this city the imperial scepter, the senate . . . and left in Rome nothing but vile slaves, fishermen, confectioners, poulterers, bastards, plebeians, underlings. [The pope] never would have written this letter if your king had not suggested it; and how dangerous for both of them it will be, unless they come to their senses.'"[45]

Liutprand tried to explain, but the Byzantines were determined to be insulted. He then tried confrontation, but that didn't work either. After a "vigorous exchange," they more or less agreed to differ. Christopher then "bade me farewell and sent me off with many sweet and loving kisses."[46] But not before they confiscated some purple garments Liutprand had bought, and while they provided horses for him and his retinue, they refused to provide pack mules for the baggage. So "to my great and natural annoyance, I had to give my *diosostes* [guide] a present worth fifty gold pieces as an extra fee."[47] Eventually, after one hundred twenty frustrating days, Liutprand was permitted to leave Constantinople on October 2, 968. He was delayed in Corfu by an earthquake and eclipse of the sun until January 869. He reached Cremona a month later.

Liutprand's second visit to Constantinople made him very sour about everything Byzantine. The most he could do to annoy the Byzantines was leave some graffiti carved on the wall of his hated dwelling as well as on a wooden table. "Trust not the Greeks; they live to betray; nor heed their promises, what'er they say."[48] His view that Greeks could not be trusted became common throughout Western Europe. The tragedy of this attitude was that it deepened the alienation between East and West and led to the final separation between the Orthodox and Catholic churches during the next century. It was not so much the refusal of a royal Byzantine bride—as we shall see, in the very next reign a Byzantine bride was negotiated for Otto II—that helped the split between Eastern and Western Christianity, as was the fact that Liutprand as an influential writer, especially among the elite, reinforced the stereotypical caricature in the West of stubborn, untrustworthy, and arrogant Easterners.

Being as cantankerous as he was, Liutprand no doubt rejoiced when a year later he heard the news that Emperor Nikephoros II Phokas, had been assassinated. In an extraordinarily convoluted and incestuous affair, Nikephoros was murdered in his own bedroom in a plot hatched by Theophano and her new lover, Phokas's old friend and colleague who had once saved his life, the dashing, handsome general John Tzimisces (969–976). The empress participated in the murder, making sure that the assassins gained entrance to the palace and to Nikephoros's bedroom. So it was that during a severe storm on the dark, midwinter night of December 10, 969, after six years on the throne, Nikephoros was tortured and violently murdered by a group led by John Tzimisces. Liutprand would have smiled at this news.

❧

In Cremona once again, Liutprand slipped back into the life he had led since his episcopal appointment before going to Constantinople. Prior to sending him on this embassy, Otto had used him as an Italian official, advising, translating, and assisting government. The emperor visited Italy on a semiregular basis, and it was then that Liutprand came to the fore. For his first five years as bishop Liutprand divided his time between Cremona and Rome. In Cremona he devoted his time to diocesan affairs and to the writing of *Liber de rebus gestis Ottonis*. As we saw, much of his time in Rome was taken up with the deplorable John XII. He acted as a translator for Otto and as a major functionary in deposing the pope. In April 967 Liutprand attended the Synod of Ravenna summoned by Otto and John XIII. The synod discussed the designation of Magdeburg as a metropolitan archdiocese and as a center for the Christian missions in the Slavic regions, deposed the archbishop of Salzburg and appointed a successor, and restored Ravenna and other territories to the Patrimonium Petri. After visiting Rome again in early 968, Liutprand left for Constantinople on his ill-fated mission.

When he returned in February 969, he resumed his previous administrative regime and seems to have begun to rise in imperial favor, perhaps a sign that the emperor was pleased with his diplomatic activities even though he returned without a prospective imperial bride. Liutprand probably spent several months in Cremona writing the *Relatio*. By May 969 he was in Rome again, and later that year he was commissioned by Otto to restore the suppressed diocese of Alba, southeast of Turin. He was also made count of Ferrara. "During the last years of his life Liutprand must have commanded considerable respect in imperial circles; certainly his star was on the rise."[49] However, he was never an intimate of Otto, who considered him a diplomat and literary defender of the Saxon regime.

His considerable experience of Byzantine affairs led to his inclusion in another mission to the Byzantine court led by Archbishop Gero of Cologne in late 971, again seeking a bride for the emperor's son, Otto II. This mission was successful, but it was Liutprand's last journey. He seems to have died sometime in early 972. It would be ironic if he were buried in Constantinople, a city he could not stand, although the evidence is that he made it back to Italy but died before returning to Cremona. There was certainly another bishop in Cremona in March 973.

In a sense Liutprand could be seen as an almost sub-Christian figure dominated by an ethic of revenge. By that I mean that Liutprand, while nominally a Christian, had never really integrated the basic Christian virtue of forgiveness and the concept of a merciful God into his worldview. His God is vengeful and unloving. Liutprand found himself in a world he couldn't control dominated by scum like Berengar II and Willa and swept along by events he couldn't manipulate or avoid, which gives his writing "immediacy unknown in Carolingian historiography." Claudio Leonardi says that if "a Christian God exists in his writings, His actions are mechanical."[50]

But this is not the whole story. Liutprand also displays close familiarity with the text of the Bible. The 1984 discovery of one of his sermons in the episcopal library of Freising has revealed him in a much more genuinely Christian light and gives us a different insight into his spirituality. Almost certainly written by Liutprand himself, the "Homily of Liutsios the Italian Deacon" is not a "homily" in our sense of the word; it is a sermon in the traditional sense, filled with doctrinal instruction. It shows that Liutprand was sincerely distressed by the many evils he saw, especially in the church. There were some particularly good preachers in his time; Liutprand was one of the best. The text consists of a dialogue between Liutprand and a Jew. It was probably not preached in church because it has overtones of the lecture hall rather than the cathedral. Liutprand's theology tends to be darkly Augustinian; it emphasizes the fall of humankind, sin, and the need for redemption and grace. The most striking thing about it is that it reflects none of the anti-Semitism of Agobard of Lyons. In Liutprand's world, Jews were tolerated and in many circles favored. The imagined Jew in the sermon is no caricature, but a learned scholar with a real knowledge of the scriptures. While Liutprand refers to the Jewish scholar as the "foolish one," he occasionally concedes a point: "O Jew, I grant you asked a most useful question."[51] Throughout the sermon the Jew is the more polite gentleman and Liutprand the "boots and all" Christian.

The first part revolves around whether the Christian belief in the Trinity actually implies having three gods. Liutprand responds that in the Hebrew Scriptures God often reveals himself in threes: three men visit Abraham; three angels appear to Moses. From this he argues that Abraham and Moses were Trinitarian believers. This kind of allegorical argument is foreign to us but made sense in an age more attuned to symbol and metaphor in the biblical text. The discussion then moves to the role of Christ, and the Jew asks "how the uncorrupted, immortal Son of God could cling to a corrupted and mortal humanity without himself being corrupted?" Liutprand replies that King Solomon, "whose multifarious wisdom you cannot deny, foresaw the Incarnation . . . when he wrote, 'Wisdom has built herself a house (Proverbs 9:1).' By that [Solomon] means the Son of God prepared himself an appropriate dwelling in the virgin, which was holy, uncorrupted and worthy of him, and whence he took on that enfleshed form which his Father had placed little lower than the angels, and under whose feet the Father had subjected everything."[52]

The text is packed with indirect biblical references that reflect Liutprand's intimate knowledge of scripture. Having made his argument, he turns directly to his Catholic listeners. He warns that divine judgment awaits everyone: "If it pleases you that we preach about the pious and forgiving God, let it also frighten you that we profess faith in a true and just Judge."[53] Liutprand then unexpectedly makes concern for the poor *the* test of genuine Christianity. The poor are the *familares*, the intimate friends of Christ. Emphasizing that God could have made anyone poor or blind, he cites the gospel story of the rich man and Lazarus the pauper at his gate (Luke 16:19–31). He is even critical of bishops who live high on the hog when the poor have nothing: "For he who denies to the poor that of which he has plenty will be forced in the severe examination of judgment to declare why he illicitly stole."[54]

Although a sophisticate, Liutprand was a man of his times in his interest in relics. This is illustrated by the rather deplorable story of Liutprand grabbing the body of Saint Hymerius. His colleague the bishop of Amelia in Umbria had lost favor at the imperial court. He asked Liutprand to intercede for him. Liutprand agreed to help, but only if the bishop helped him steal the body of Hymerius, who had died about 560, from Amelia's cathedral. The two bishops pilfered the body at night after Liutprand bribed the guards. When Liutprand brought the body to Cremona, the locals were ecstatic with their new patron and intercessor with God. Hymerius's body is still in Cremona; we don't know what happened to the bishop of Amelia.

∾

Liutprand is an example of a new breed in the tenth century, the scholar-bureaucrat. Both aspects of his life are equally important. As a writer he influenced the educated elite to see the reestablishment of the Holy Roman Empire by Otto I as a positive step toward good government and as the building up of a broad vision of a genuinely "European" community. While deeply attached to his home city of Pavia, he was able to conceive of the politics of Italy as a whole. As a bureaucrat and adviser to Otto on the complexities of Italy, he worked to make that vision of a unified Italy a reality. There is also a real sense in which Liutprand is the tenth century's first really "international" man. Few other Europeans had visited Constantinople three times, and few spoke Greek with Liutprand's fluency. Even if many of his views were rather jaundiced, he still brought a real awareness to politics of a world bigger than the narrow horizons of most of his contemporaries. While he was certainly lucky in having a monarch like Otto I, whose own vision was also a broad pan-Germanic one in his effort to restore the Carolingian world, Liutprand brought an awareness of the other half of Christianity represented by Byzantium. We will now turn to the larger political context in which Liutprand lived out the latter part of his life as a bureaucrat and adviser to Otto I.

CHAPTER 12

"That Greek Woman"

Theophano, Otto II, and Her Mother-in-Law

WHEN LAST WE BROKE OFF recounting the course of the papacy, it was the year 964 and Pope John XII had just perished in his late twenties either in bed with or after having had sex with a married woman. The role of the cuckolded husband in his demise remains unclear. The most significant event of his shameful papacy was the coronation of Otto I as Holy Roman Emperor. After John XII's death, however, confusion again reigned.

Emperor Otto I's chosen pope, Leo VIII, was expelled by the Romans. They proceeded to elect another pope, Benedict V on May 22, 964. A furious Otto returned to Rome in late June. He immediately dismissed Benedict V, exiled him to faraway Hamburg, and reimposed Leo VIII. Perhaps conveniently, Leo VIII died just ten months later, clearing the decks for an undisputed election. Even so, after John XIII (965–972) was elected seven months later, a brief revolt against him by clan leaders in Rome resulted in Otto returning to Rome from Germany at Christmas 965 and punishing the ringleaders severely.

Otto had grown tired of Roman recalcitrance. He was now determined to deal decisively with the papacy and Italian affairs. To achieve this, he remained in Italy for six years from late 965 to 972. Several days after he had been crowned emperor, he had issued the *Privilegium Ottonianum* (the Ottonian Privilege or Pact), a charter written on purple parchment in gold Carolingian lettering determining relationships between papacy and emperor. It gave the much-expanded Papal State to the pope as a "donation" and promised

269

imperial protection. It also laid down the imperial rights granted to the emperor over Rome. While the charter guaranteed free papal elections, it required a new pope to inform the emperor of his election before his consecration and take an oath of loyalty recognizing the emperor as feudal overlord of the Papal State.

What was unusual about Otto's new position was not the *Privilegium* itself, which only spelled out the same oaths popes had been making since Charlemagne, or the coronation as emperor, which added nothing to Otto's actual power. What was new was the restoration of the title "Holy Roman Emperor." This was the title first held by Charlemagne, and his coronation as emperor gave Otto a dignity that raised him above all other European rulers and exalted imperial rule to make it seem an essential part of the divine order for the world. Church historian Friedrich Kempf says the title endowed Otto with "a mysterious glamour supported by a genuine symbolic force. . . . He appeared . . . [to be] entrusted in a special manner with the protection of the pope."[1] It bestowed on the emperor a responsibility for and a degree of control over the papacy. Implicit also in Otto's coronation was the Germans' view of their empire as a continuation of the ancient Roman Empire (Otto called himself *Imperator Augustus*), a fact not lost on the Byzantines. From the German perspective, the main role of the pope was to confirm by coronation the succession of German monarchs. But the popes and Romans still saw things very differently. They believed that imperial coronation was theirs alone to bestow on the person *they* chose. So the scene was set for a very contentious relationship.

In a sense the coronation of Otto was the *actual* birth of the West. While in itself a relatively unimportant incident, the coronation was actually a symbol of something more fundamental: the recognition of an authority abroad that transcended the local and the parochial and that actually had the power to project that authority in Germany, Italy, the Eastern frontier, and, to a much lesser extent, West Francia. Later, in the eleventh century, the empire was also to step in to reform the papacy, itself a potential international player. A reformed papacy then challenged the German emperors to launch what later became the greatest constitutional conflict of the Middle Ages.

Italy seems to have been an irresistibly attractive prize for the Germans. It was not only the warmer climate and brighter light, the economic prosperity and the developed resources, particularly in northern Italy, that attracted them. It was also the influence the emperors could exercise over the papacy, which indirectly gave them even more power over the church in Germany. Pavia-trained courtier-bureaucrats like Liutprand also brought a level of sophistication to Otto's administration that had previously been lacking.

So after he was satisfied that he had got the situation in northern and central Italy and the Patrimonium Petri under control, Otto turned his attention to reclaiming southern Italy, much of it a Byzantine sphere of influence. He resurrected papal claims to the region and formed an alliance with Pandulf I Ironhead (961–980), Prince of Capua and Benevento who was trying to extend his territory. To curry favor with Otto, Pandulf had protected Pope John XIII in 965 when he had been driven out of Rome, and was rewarded by Otto with Spoleto and Camerino. Thietmar of Merseburg's *Chronicon* says that Otto also "wanted to acquire a wife for his son from the emperor at Constantinople." According to Thietmar, he sent ambassadors, but they were ambushed "by the Greeks with their customary slyness" in Calabria. "Taking the loss of his envoys very seriously," Otto sent a reprisal party into southern Italy, who returned "happy and loaded down with spoils."[2] Thietmar gives no more details, and Liutprand doesn't mention the incident, so perhaps some hotheaded southern Italians attacked the ambassadorial party, thereby indicating the level of Byzantine resentment to German interference in southern Italy.

In early 968 Otto and Pandulf again invaded Byzantine territory and headed for the strategic town of Bari, a major port and administrative center that was virtually impregnable and surrounded on two sides by water. Otto was unable to take it. Humiliated, this appears to have prompted Otto to dispatch Liutprand to Constantinople on his unpleasant trip of early April 968. The diplomatic mission was ostensibly to arrange a royal marriage, but also to negotiate a peace in southern Italy in light of his failure at Bari. As Barbara Kreutz says, this was really "an ingenious (if misguided) attempt to snatch victory from defeat."[3] It is thus understandable why Liutprand was unwelcome in Constantinople and why his interlocutors were so annoyed that Otto had subverted one of "their men," Pandulf Ironhead.

As we saw, Liutprand's mission failed dismally and negotiations collapsed. In the winter of 968–969 Otto returned to campaigning in southern Italy, but then he had to head north to deal with other issues. The Byzantines took advantage of his absence. Though Pandulf was left in charge, the Byzantines swiftly took him prisoner and brought him to Constantinople. Acting in concert with the Neapolitans, the Byzantines then began the dismemberment of

Pandulf's principality. Otto quickly returned with a new army and attacked the Byzantines and their Neapolitan allies, who were punished by having all their animals seized. The two sides seemed to be settling in for a long war of attrition when circumstances suddenly changed in Constantinople.

Emperor Nikephoros II Phokas (963–969) was murdered, and John I Tzimisces (969–978) succeeded him. Tzimisces was anxious to build good relations with the West because, rather than concerning himself with defending all of southern Italy, his priorities were defeating the Saracens and the Bulgarians. He could not afford to maintain another front in Italy. So Pandulf was released from Constantinople, peace was restored in central-southern Italy, and Tzimisces floated overtures concerning the possibility of a marriage alliance. Otto responded positively—having already been in Italy for four years, he realized that the Byzantines with their fortified *kastra* (castles) were impregnable. So another diplomatic party was sent to Constantinople in early 971, this time led by Archbishop Gero of Cologne, accompanied by two other bishops. Liutprand was almost certainly one of them, but where his mission had been impossible, Gero's was successful because attitudes in Constantinople had changed and they were ready to negotiate.

Gero's brief seems to have been to negotiate for Princess Anna, daughter of Romanus II, but he had authority to negotiate other options if Anna were unavailable. When that proved to be the case, Tzimisces offered his niece Theophano. He also offered Otto continuing control of Capua and Benevento as a kind of bride's dowry. Gero accepted the offer. For Otto this at last brought peace and stability in southern Italy.

෩

Who was Theophano? She was related to Tzimisces but not *porphyrogenita*, born in the birthing chamber of the palace. Born in Constantinople before 960, she was the daughter of court aristocrats Constantine Skleros and Sophia Phokas and a niece of Nikephoros II Phokas.[4] At the time of her marriage, she would have been at least twelve, the minimum marriageable age for a girl, and probably a year or two older. Widukind of Corvey calls her a *puella*, a pubescent girl at the right age for marriage.[5] In her marriage charter, a copy of which—possibly Theophano's own—is held in the Lower Saxony State Archives at Wolfenbüttel, she is referred to as *neptis clarissima*, "most distinguished niece" of the emperor. Despite his wife's relationship to the assassinated Phokas, Theophano's father supported Tzimisces, so Theophano was brought up close to the center of power. An intelligent girl, she would have had some basic schooling in Byzantine culture, imperial ideology, church affairs, and politics. Certainly, she was highly intelligent and adaptable and able to fit into Saxon social patterns. Once it became clear that diplomacy required her to marry Otto II, she would have taken a crash course in Latin and the deportment and manners required in her new circumstances.

So, aged about fourteen, Theophano set out with Archbishop Gero's party for Rome. In his *Chronicon*, Thietmar says that she was "accompanied by a splendid entourage and magnificent gifts."[6] She was going have to use all her wits and learn fast under pressure in her new life, not least having to master vulgar and literary Latin, as well as something of her husband's subjects' various vernaculars. A Greek-Latin Psalter (psalm book) was produced in Trier specifically to help her learn Latin.[7] She would have also needed to know some Old High German. Her Latin would have helped with Italian. Although derived from Vulgar Latin, Italian was emerging in the tenth century as a distinct language with several dialects. The *Magdeburg Annals* suggest that Theophano gained "a clever command of language," that is, considerable fluency in both literary and vernacular speech.[8] From all accounts, she was an extraordinary young woman who showed stamina and intelligence.

Bringing with her a chaplain, advisers, ladies-in-waiting, and servants who looked after her wardrobe, clothes, jewels, and the rich dowry she brought, Theophano and her group arrived by boat at Otranto in Byzantine Italy, from whence they made their way overland 325 miles (520 kilometers) to the border of the Principality of Benevento, where they were met by Bishop Dietrich of Metz on behalf of Otto I. He accompanied them to Rome, where Theophano met her husband-to-be for the first time.

Otto II was nicknamed *Rufus*, "the Red," because of his red hair and fair complexion. He had been quickly crowned coemperor in December 967 when a Byzantine marriage was first proposed, although he was never given any power or responsibility. The son of Otto I's second wife, Adelheid, the sixteen-year-old was intelligent, well educated, and small of stature. In spite of his small size, Thietmar says he had "outstanding physical strength," which "initially tended toward recklessness"; he "rejected more mature counsel, but after enduring much criticism [he] learned to restrain himself with praiseworthy virtue."[9] In other words, he matured. Theophano assisted that growing-up process, and they became corulers together. This fitted Ottonian custom: the empress not only ruled the royal household; she also assisted in ruling the kingdom.

The marriage of Theophano and Otto II was a truly grand ceremony. It was celebrated before the *Confessio* in front of the high altar of Saint Peter's Basilica on April 14, 972, immediately after she had been crowned empress by Pope John XIII. Among the wedding guests was the century's greatest genius and a former tutor of Otto II, Gerbert of Aurillac. Many were impressed with Theophano's beauty, but sadly no genuine image of her has survived. In the marriage charter drawn up between the partners, Otto II conferred upon her lands and estates in Germany, Italy, and the Low Countries. However, once the fact that she was not *porphyrogenita* was revealed there was a lot of criticism. Some advisers, Liutprand probably among them, counseled Otto I that he had been deceived by the Byzantines. Thietmar says, "There were some who tried to dissuade the emperor [Otto I] from this alliance and recommended sending the bride home."[10] But Otto, although at the height of his power, was old and tired and had been away from his Saxon homeland for almost six years in Italy. He was committed to assuring the succession. Theophano was an impressive young woman, and she had hardly arrived empty-handed. Not only had she brought treasure; she had also brought the friendship of John I Tzimisces and the release of many prisoners, including Otto I's old friend and vassal Pandulf Ironhead, whom he delegated to administer central Italy for him. So Otto decided that Theophano should stay.

Responding to Saxons disgruntled by his long absence from his homeland, Otto I and the newlyweds headed for Germany soon after the marriage. Theophano matured quickly under pressure, much of which sprang from her domineering mother-in-law, Empress Adelheid. Adelheid clearly saw herself as in charge of Theophano's formation as her son's spouse. Together with her daughter, the formidable Abbess Mathilda of Quedlinburg, Adelheid initiated Theophano into her duties as empress-in-waiting. A powerful woman in her own right, Adelheid maintained connections to several royal houses, so it was in her interest to keep Theophano under her thumb. But the young woman was by no means a pushover and there seems to have been tension between them. This was certainly part of the cause for nasty criticism of Theophano after her death. In contrast to Adelheid, Theophano's sister-in-law, Abbess Mathilda, became her adviser, emotional support, and close friend.

While Otto and Theophano had been brought together in an arranged marriage, the couple clearly fell in love, and during Otto's life Theophano wielded real power and influence. She was *consors regni* (consort of the king) and *coimperatrix augusta* (distinguished coempress)—a new title in the West that may have originated in Byzantium. Her position is vividly illustrated in a magnificent ivory dated about 981 in the Musée de Cluny in Paris showing a towering, full-frontal Christ crowning Otto and Theophano. Both wear similar imperial insignia—in fact, the figure of Theophano is slightly taller, as Otto stands on a higher footstool, crushing a conquered enemy. We also know that she often intervened with her husband to push causes that were dear to her. Favors or benefits were granted by royal *diplomata* (formal documents produced by the royal chancery), and we know she intervened seventy-six times during Otto II's life. As Karl Leyser comments, "From the wording of the texts it is often clear that the *petitio* or *rogatio*, the request for the grant, stemmed from her."[11]

This was a time when strong and talented women had an opportunity to exercise real power. Under Roman law, which applied in Italy and was adopted by the Ottonians, women could own and accumulate property that was totally separate from that of their husbands. They could also control their husband's property after his death. We have already seen Marozia's dominance of Rome, and likewise both of Otto I's wives, Eadgyth and Adelheid, played powerful roles in the political life of the kingdom. Nevertheless, the first task of the empress was to provide offspring as soon as possible, and Theophano obliged. She bore five children, three daughters and then twins, one of them a son, another Otto, heir to the throne. Otto III and his sister were born in mid-980 while the court was on the road between Aachen and Nijmegen in the Reichwald, a forest close to Kessel and some 9 miles (15 kilometers) from the palace at Nijmegen. It was probably a difficult birth because the girl lived only for two months. Theophano made sure that all of her children were well educated, and she inspired her son with a vision of a Europe united with Byzantium that was remarkable for the tenth century.

Just thirteen months after his son's marriage, Otto I died, aged sixty, on May 7, 973, at his favorite palace, the *villa regia* at Memleben, north of Weimar. He was buried in Magdeburg Cathedral, and his tomb is still there in the sanctuary. Otto II, already elected and crowned, became sole emperor and Theophano reigning empress.

This was an important moment. Imperial authority had been handed on peacefully both in Germany and in Italy. Son had succeeded father without challenge both as German king and as Holy Roman Emperor. The two titles were fused, and as James Viscount Bryce in his late-nineteenth-century history of the empire argues:

> It was natural that the great mass of Otto [I]'s subjects, to whom the imperial title, dimly associated with Rome and the pope, sounded grander than the regal [the kingship of Germany] . . . were confounded. . . . The sovereign and his ecclesiastical advisers, with clearer views of the new dignity and of the relation of the offices to one another, found it impossible to separate them in practice, and were glad to merge the lesser into the greater. For as lord of the world, Otto was Emperor north as well as south of the Alps.[12]

In other words, a pattern had been set, and the empire was to last until 1807, when it was finally abolished by Napoleon I. Ottonian rule was based on a combination of realities: military strength, efficient administration, the ability of the ruler, and the consent of the powerful magnates. Under Otto I the eastern borders of the empire had expanded as the Slavic peoples and principalities were converted to Christianity and brought under the suzerainty of the dynasty and the diocesan structure of the church. This was not a conquest in the sense of occupation; it was more like a confederation as people agreed to take part in the empire. Thus, the Ottonian monarchs always had to check that powerful people throughout the land remained loyal. As they moved around their empire, they had, like jugglers, to keep a number of balls in the air. With no set capital, they were always on the move. The "capital" was wherever the emperor and court happened to be. Otto II followed this pattern, and Theophano always accompanied him. This shows the ability of Theophano perhaps more than anything else. She not only adjusted to administrative processes totally foreign to her; she also mastered them.

While Otto treated her as an equal, it was not all plain sailing with her mother-in-law, Adelheid. If Abbot Odilo of Cluny (ca. 962–1049) is to be believed, Adelheid was a saint. She reputedly worked many miracles after her death and was canonized by Pope Urban II (1088–1099). In an encomium that is reminiscent of the Reverend Mr. Collins speaking of Lady Catherine De Burgh in Jane Austen's *Pride and Prejudice*, Odilo describes Adelheid's "nobility of spirit," which, he claims, exceeds "the capacity of any mortal." In contrast, Odilo refers to Theophano as *illam Grecam*, "that Greek woman," and *illa imperatrix Greca*, "that Greek empress."[13] The monk-chronicler Alpert of Metz asserts that Theophano was unpleasant and talkative. No doubt those used to hectoring others found it difficult to have to listen to a woman. Clearly, Theophano and Adelheid had a tense relationship, which at one stage involved a full-scale family row. The tension was based on several factors: the relationship of mother and daughter-in-law, two powerful personalities sorting out their respective spheres, cultural differences between Greek and Frank, and the different expectations that each woman had of the other.

ตะ

Following the death of his father, Otto II, aged almost eighteen, faced problems in both Germany and Italy. Some of these were of his own making, resulting from his immaturity and impulsiveness. The problems in Germany were the most immediate, and they kept him busy for almost five years. To begin with, he had to deal with Henry *der Zänker* (955–976 and 985–995), Henry the "Quarreler" or "Wrangler," Duke of Bavaria, a nephew of Otto I and Otto II's cousin. The cause of the conflict is hard to pin down, but Henry seems to have felt somehow dishonored by Otto II. Gerd Althoff says that to ignore "the claims by magnates to honor could easily be seen as a slight or insult, *offensio*. If they did not react . . . their followers lost confidence in them which meant a loss of real power; and their rivals and opponents lost respect for them which threatened their position still further."[14]

Henry was also ambitious to expand Bavaria, and he was soon outright threatening to dethrone Otto. Magnates were always ready to exploit any royal weakness to enhance their power, and they quickly moved to exploit Otto's immaturity and inexperience. Henry organized several uprisings on the eastern frontier in alliance with Mieszko of Poland and Boleslav II of Bohemia. But Otto was not only able to maintain his position; he also managed to outmaneuver and depose Henry, who forfeited his duchy for nine years and was imprisoned in Utrecht. Carinthia (southern Austria) was cut off from Bavaria. Other minor revolts occurred, which Otto was able to control, and he was eventually able to quell disputes on the western frontier with his colleague King Lothar (954–986). As Timothy Reuter comments, these uprisings demonstrate

"the underlying stability of the empire," which now had an effective and working government.[15] Stability had returned to the German lands.

Meanwhile, the inevitable family row broke out. Adelheid's influence at
court had declined since her husband's death. She certainly didn't accept this
gracefully. Odilo says that the rift was caused by "wicked men" who deceived
Otto II "by their flattery," which led to a waning of "his affection for his
mother." So Adelheid, in a huff, decamped to her Burgundian homeland,
where, according to Odilo, "she was accorded a kind and honorable reception
by her brother, King Conrad" and his wife, Mathilda.[16] No doubt Adelheid's
tension with Theophano exacerbated the situation. Theophano was probably
glad to see the back of her obstreperous mother-in-law, but the whole situation was embarrassing for the imperial couple. So, according to Odilo, "moved
by deep regret," Otto sent intermediaries that "he might regain his mother's
favor, lost through his own misdeeds." Mother and son met in Pavia in December 980. Odilo says that when they met, "they fell prostrate upon the
ground crying and lamenting. . . . The son expressed his humble regret, the
mother, gracious forgiveness."[17] It certainly seems to have been cathartic, because from then on Theophano and Adelheid worked together reasonably co-
operatively, especially after the birth of the third Otto, son and heir. It was also
at this time that Otto II's chancery began to refer to him as *imperator Romanorum augustus*, "august emperor of the Romans." Again, the Roman reference was not lost on the Byzantines.

After things settled down in Germany, Otto crossed the Alps to Italy in 980
to deal with affairs in Rome after Benedict VII (974–983) appealed for his protection. As usual, the pope's problems resulted from the seedy politics of the
Roman clans. The Theophylacts had been replaced as rulers of Rome by a
closely related family, the Crescentii. The dynasty came to power when Giovanni Crescentii married Marozia's niece, Theodora III. As Otto I had already
discovered, the key problem in Rome was the tension between the local and the
international, between the Roman factions that saw the papacy as their plaything and imperial interests that recognized the pan-European significance of
the papacy. Caught in the middle of this complex web, the more responsible
popes struggled to maintain some spiritual independence. Benedict VII was
one such pope. He had come to the papacy after his predecessor, Benedict VI
(973–974), had been strangled in the Castel Sant'Angelo by a priest acting on
behalf of the usurper antipope, Boniface VII.

The murder is a perfect example of the tension already described. Benedict VI had been the nominee of Otto I. The increasingly influential Crescentii family, now led by Giovanni and Theodora's son, Crescentius I, nicknamed Crescentius *de Theodora* (out of Theodora), had a candidate of their own, Deacon Franco. Benedict was elected, and while Otto I lived, Benedict was safe. But Otto died in May 973 and with Otto II caught up in German affairs, the Crescentii began undermining Benedict. A month after the death of Otto I, a revolt broke out, probably supported by Byzantines anxious to destabilize German influence in Rome, and despite the intervention of Count Sicco, the imperial representative, Benedict was strangled a month later in July 974.

His replacement, styled Boniface VII, was thoroughly in the pocket of the Crescentii. But the mob quickly turned on Boniface, who fled with the papal treasury to Byzantine southern Italy. A fresh election was held, and the imperial candidate Benedict VII, a kinsman of Alberico II and therefore acceptable to the clans, was elected. Still, Boniface remained a threat, and in 980 he staged a coup in Rome that drove Benedict VII out. It was at this point that Benedict appealed to Otto II.

On Easter Sunday 981 Otto and Theophano entered Rome. To escape Otto's reach, Boniface fled all the way to Constantinople. But Otto's plans were larger than simply expelling a renegade pope. Together Benedict and Otto, in cooperation with Maiolus, Abbot of Cluny, began a program to reform monasticism in Rome, Italy, Germany, and France. Benedict encouraged missionary activity in the Slavic lands, setting up the bishopric of Prague. He forbad simony, the sale of holy orders, and his reform work in league with the imperial couple enhanced the prestige of the papacy after blackguards like antipope Boniface.

Now living in Rome, Otto, probably encouraged by Theophano, succumbed to the temptation to invade southern Italy. Theophano was personally devoted to Byzantine emperor John Tzimisces, who had died on January 10, 976, possibly poisoned by his corrupt chamberlain; he might also have died of an infection like typhoid. Described by J. J. Norwich as "one of the very greatest of Byzantine emperors," Tzimisces was nevertheless a usurper.[18] He was succeeded by Basil II "the Bulgar Slayer" (976–1025), the legitimate heir to the throne. Theophano was no fan of Basil, and she would have encouraged Otto's ambitions to extend imperial control to the whole of Italy. He found a reason to invade the south after aggression by Sicilian Saracens led by Emir Abu al-Qasim, who wanted to wage jihad against the Germans. Otto II should have been warned by his father's ignominious defeat in southern Italy some fourteen years earlier. But living in Rome seems to have persuaded Otto that he was a *Roman* emperor, and the conquest of southern Italy was appealing.

Emperor Basil II was caught up in wars on several fronts and could not reinforce southern Italy, so after getting the Lombard principalities of central-southern Italy under control by January 982, Otto invaded Byzantine Apulia. He had initial success capturing Taranto in March and defeating a Saracen army on July 13, 982. But the Byzantines were in temporary alliance with the Saracens to resist the Germans, and things came to a head at a battle fought against the Saracens at Stilo near Cape Colonna just south of Crotone on the east coast of Calabria. At first Otto's army was successful, and the Saracens took flight after al-Qasim was killed. But they rallied and counterattacked, killing up to 4,000 Germans, including many of the Ottonian military elite. Otto escaped by the skin of his teeth in a boat.

It was the worst German military disaster since the Magyar invasions at the beginning of the century. Fortunately, Theophano and her children were holed up farther north in Rossano and were safe. Although the Saracens were forced to retreat to Sicily, they remained political players in southern Italy, causing trouble for both the Byzantines and the independent principalities. News of the defeat encouraged revolts among the Slavs on the eastern frontier, and much of the successful missionary work of Otto I was swiftly undone. Otto II had overreached, and now he faced basic questions about his policy, his military tactics, and even his ability to govern.

Otto returned to northern Italy. In May 983 at an imperial diet at Verona, Otto's three-year-old son was declared co-king with his father to assure the continuance of the dynasty. The diet also essentially united Germany and Italy into a single empire. For some time Otto had been referring to himself as *Romanorum imperator augustus*, and the decision to unite what had been two separate kingdoms into one realm was no doubt influenced by Theophano's conception of an empire drawn from Byzantine models. The child Otto then left for coronation in Aachen, arriving in late May 983. Otto II and Theophano meanwhile returned to Rome to negotiate the election of a successor to Pope Benedict VII, who had died in July. The emperor first offered the papacy to the saintly Abbot Maiolus of Cluny, but he refused. Otto then appointed his archchancellor for Italy, Peter, Bishop of Pavia, as pope. He became John XIV (983–984). There seemed to have been no election.

But Otto had picked up a virulent strain of malaria, no doubt in southern Italy. Medical intervention probably made his situation worse. Tenth-century treatment followed the treatment laid down by the Greco-Roman physician Galen, who prescribed bleeding, purging, or a combination of both to expel the "humors" supposedly causing the disease. The result of this treatment was that malarial anemia was intensified and death quickly followed. Otto was no exception; following bleeding and purgation, his condition quickly deteriorated, and "after making his confession, in Latin, before the pope and the other bishops and priests, he obtained the absolution he desired," and he died in Theophano's arms on December 7, 983.[19] He was buried in Saint Peter's Basilica. He was just twenty-eight. According to Thietmar, "The Empress, Lady Theophano . . . oppressed by her horrible and recent loss and by the absence of her only son, came to the Empress Adelheid in Pavia. Adelheid received her with deep emotion and soothed her with affectionate comfort."[20] Theophano's good friend Abbess Mathilda of Quedlinburg was also in Pavia to support her.

ભ્

There was little time for grief. The three-year-old Otto III had been anointed and crowned king of Germany and Italy on Christmas Day 983 in Aachen by Archbishops Johannes of Ravenna and Willigis of Mainz (symbolizing the union of Italy and Germany) before the news of his father's death reached the city. When news did get through to southern Germany, "the joyous occasion [came] to an end. The hearts of many were moved with unspeakable pain."[21] Otto II's first cousin, Henry the Quarreler, was immediately released from prison by Bishop Folkmar of Utrecht; as a personal prisoner of the emperor, the law required that he be released when Otto II died. Immediately taking advantage of the situation, he claimed a role in managing the affairs of the child king. As the child's closest male relative in Germany, he demanded that Otto III be handed over to him. People took his claim to propinquity at face value, and there was little or no opposition to this move.

Henry also exploited the sense among the magnates that a warrior needed to be in charge rather than a woman. As Reuter comments, "There was no book of rules which laid down how successions were to be settled," with arrangements being made on each occasion according to the way events played out.[22] But the blustering Wrangler completely underestimated Theophano's political skill. Supported by Adelheid, she would eventually regain possession of her son and assert her own authority. Henry had grabbed the child in Cologne from Archbishop Warin, who was Otto's temporary custodian, and took him back to Saxony. It quickly became clear that Henry wanted to usurp the throne even though he initially put himself forward as regent. It was imperative that Theophano return to Germany as quickly as possible. But she also needed to build coalitions against Henry. In Pavia she met the great scholar Gerbert of Aurillac, whom she persuaded to act as a kind of ecclesiastical ambassador with the southwestern German bishops. She eventually crossed the Alps and reached Germany in late May 984.

While he still dominated the scene, Henry now proceeded to make a number of strategic errors, not least of which was his failure to show *clementia* (mercy and forgiveness) to two Saxon nobles who requested it. In other words, he demonstrated a lack of magnanimity, one of the most important marks of a true king in the medieval mind. This did him a lot of political damage.

He celebrated Holy Week at Magdeburg and Easter at Quedlinburg as though he already were the monarch, but it soon became obvious that support for him among senior nobles and ecclesiastics was ebbing away. Henry realized that he would have to pursue his claim with military force, but he was cautious. He knew that doing so could lead to civil war, and he was wise enough to perceive that he could attain more by negotiation, including restoration as duke of Bavaria, than by fighting. So he entered into protracted negotiations with Theophano and her advisers, including Adelheid and Mathilda, at Rohr in Thuringia. None of the sources give any information about the actual negotiations, but they do emphasize in a very tenth-century way that "a marvelous and memorable sign appeared to the astonishment of all who were present and saw it." The *Annals of Quedlinburg* for 984 reports that "a star of brilliant light shone down upon the partisan struggle from the midst of heaven, in an unheard of fashion in the middle of the day, as if it wanted to grant God's help to the captive king."[23] The result of the month-long negotiations was that Otto was surrendered to his mother and a final settlement was reached.

This was "published" before the court at Frankfurt in 985. In typical tenth-century style, Henry ritually acted out in public the agreement arrived at in private. The *Annals of Quedlinburg* describes what happened:

When the royal child Otto III came to Frankfurt, he [Henry] also came and humbled himself according to custom. . . . Humble in demeanor and action, hands clasped, he did not blush to swear his faith under the eyes of the assembled people and in the presence of the imperial ladies who cared for the kingdom, the child's grandmother [Adelheid], mother [Theophano] and aunt [Abbess Mathilda]. To them he yielded the royal child whom he had taken captive when he was orphaned and whose kingdom he had torn away by force. In true faith he promised furthermore to serve him, asking nothing but his life and begging only for mercy.

The women responded by receiving Henry, pardoning him, and raising him again "to the ducal dignity . . . as the law of kingship demanded."[24]

This was true royal magnanimity, Saxon style. It was the antithesis of the behavior of the Italian clans and the Byzantine ruling class of the time, who, if they had got hold of a young child rival, would have immediately killed or maimed him. Not only did Henry refrain from incapacitating the child by blinding him and thus rendering him incapable of kingship; he also actually handed him over safe and sound once it became clear that his own aspirations were not going to be fulfilled.

This whole incident shows that an ability to compromise and work through conflict resolution to reconciliation was very much part of the Saxon way of doing things. It is worth noting that the Saxons had been converted to Christianity only in the eighth century, so we are talking here about third- or fourth-generation Christians. But they had clearly absorbed the gospel value of forgiveness and reconciliation. It also shows the way in which ritual was used as a form of communication. As Althoff says, "Rituals, demonstrative acts and symbolic deeds, were all theatrical devices to publicize claims, objectives, or new circumstances." The ability to reach reconciliation through forgiveness required "mature techniques of amicable conflict resolution," and they reflect very well on the German elite of the tenth century.[25]

☙

This ability of the Ottonian ruling class to negotiate proved to be of lasting importance for the regency of Theophano. She never held absolute power. Even if final decisions were hers, all diplomas were still issued in the name of Otto III. Adelheid also shared in the regency; she seems to have seen herself as administering Italy, although her exact role didn't become clear until after Theophano's death. Meanwhile, Theophano was far from being beloved by all, for some resented her foreign background and decisive style. She was supported and advised by the court chaplain, Bishop Hildebold of Worms, and the chancellor, Archbishop Willigis of Mainz; these clerics had much influence on the regency. Her power also depended on the goodwill of the magnates. The empire was what Althoff calls a "personal-alliance state," a polity in which order is maintained through relational commitments.[26] That the decade-long regency was peaceful and free of conflict was owing in large part to Theophano's ability.

In his *Chronicon*, Thietmar cautiously admires Theophano's capacity: "Although of the fragile sex, her modesty, conviction and manner of life were outstanding, which is rare in Greece. Preserving her son's rulership with manly watchfulness, she was always benevolent to the just, but terrified and conquered rebels." Thietmar, as a cleric, was delighted that two of her daughters became nuns. "From the fruit of her womb, she offered daughters to God as a tithe, the first called Adelheid, at Quedlinburg, the second, called Sophia, at Gandersheim."[27] Needless to say, both women became powerful abbesses of their respective convents.

Theophano did not face an untroubled regency. There were difficulties on both the eastern and western frontiers of the empire. The relationship with the West Franks hinged on control of Lotharingia, the territory wedged between the empire and northern France. Even though it was now a permanent part of the empire, King Lothar IV (954–986) of West Francia attempted to seize Lotharingia from Otto II, but was unsuccessful. Lothar tried again in the difficult period following Otto's death, encouraged by Henry the Quarreler. But Lothar's own death in 986 put paid to these incursions. After his impulsive young brother and successor, Louis V, was killed in a hunting accident in mid-987 without an heir, Hugh Capet was elected king of the West Franks on June 1, 987, and brought peace to Lotharingia.

Before Hugh's election, Theophano had spent a lot of energy trying to maintain peace as well as possession of Lotharingia. She used her relationships with other noblewomen to achieve these aims through mediation. For instance, in 985 we have evidence of a *colloquium dominarum*, a meeting of royal ladies at Metz to bring peace between disputing royal houses. Besides Theophano, others present might have been Queen Emma (wife of Lothar IV and daughter of Adelheid and thus a sister-in-law of Theophano), Duchess Beatrice of Upper Lotharingia (Hugh Capet's sister), Adelheid (Hugh Capet's wife), Queen Mathilda of Burgundy, Gerberga (sister of Henry the Quarreler and abbess of Gandersheim), Abbess Mathilda of Quedlinburg, and Gisela (wife of Henry the Quarreler)—a virtual "who's who" of tenth-century royal women. There is evidence of at least three other such meetings, and Theophano was present or represented at all of them. The women were not always successful, but what is significant is the pivotal role they played in peacemaking through negotiation.

Theophano inherited an even more unstable situation in the East. The Liutzi, one of the Slavic tribes living east of the Elbe River, had revolted after receiving the news of Otto II's defeat at the Battle of Stilo (982) in southern Italy. They destroyed the bishoprics of Brandenburg and Havelburg, which had been set up as centers for the promotion of Christianity among the pagan Slavs. They then crossed the Elbe into Saxon territory. The situation remained unstable after Otto II died and was further exacerbated by the scheming of Henry the Quarreler. Two Christian Slavic leaders, Mieszko I of Poland and Boleslav II of Bohemia, supported Henry's claims, even though they were mutual rivals. After Theophano made peace with Henry, she had to decide how to resolve the instability of the northeastern frontier.

She decided to divide the two leaders and then conquer them. Theophano oversaw the formation of a coalition with Mieszko I. Then, in a two-pronged strategy, in 985–986 the Saxons attacked the Liutzi from the west while the Poles attacked them from the rear. The tribes were forced to retreat. But Saxon control over the no-man's-land between the Elbe and the Oder rivers remained largely nominal until the conversion of these Slavic peoples to Christianity in the late eleventh century. This was the first campaign in which Otto III personally participated even though he was only six. Having recognized his overlordship during Easter celebrations in Quedlinburg, Mieszko presented Otto III with a camel.[28] However, the ongoing instability of the eastern frontier and the land beyond it was exacerbated by the fact that "Saxon margraves and bishops [were] active even without the king and without his mandate [and] were apparently motivated by a longing for revenge and a greed for booty or tribute."[29]

Theophano made only one visit to Italy during her regency in the years 989–990. Its primary purpose was to visit Otto II's grave in Saint Peter's on the anniversary of his death and to have prayers and Masses said for him. Thietmar's *Chronicon* says she was concerned about Otto II's salvation, especially after a dream in which the martyr Saint Lawrence appeared to her "with his right arm mangled." Saint Lawrence told her, "That which you are now contemplating in me was done by your lord, who was seduced by the words of a man whose words caused discord among the great multitude of Christ's elect." The "man" was Archbishop Giselher, who had been bishop of Merseburg and who had persuaded Otto II to suppress (a technical legal term meaning to abolish) his diocese so that he could be transferred to Magdeburg. An unnecessary suppression, it was a particularly "hot" issue for the chronicler Thietmar, who came from Merseburg and who resented the suppression of his home diocese. According to him, the dream frightened Theophano sufficiently to get prayers said for "the eternal salvation" of Otto II and to attempt the reerection of the diocese. However, this didn't occur until 1004. Both publicly and anonymously, Theophano maintained a policy of generosity to the poor, hoping that in so doing, she could release her husband *ab incendio*, from the fire of Purgatory.

While in Italy, free of Saxon custom, she acted far more unilaterally in her own name. She signed her name in masculine form: *Theophanius gratia divina imperator augustus,* "Theophanius, by divine grace august emperor." In Rome she kept in contact with the Greek community and with Greek spirituality. She met with the famous Saint Sabas, who helped her with advice and whom she visited on his deathbed. She seems also to have been influential in bringing Byzantine iconography to the West, particularly images of the Crucifixion and the Virgin Mary. Historian Krijnie Ciggaar says, "Scholars are now convinced that Theophano's arrival in the West made an important contribution to the development of the cult and iconography of the Virgin there."[30]

Despite her piety, it was while she was in Italy that she became increasingly influenced by Johannes Philagathos, Archbishop of Piacenza. Originally an ethnic Greek from Rossano in southern Italy, Philagathos introduced a new frisson of scandal into Theophano's life. She first noticed this ambitious, self-assured man when he was working as her notary. He became a tutor in Greek to young Otto III and then chancellor (financial comptroller) of Italy. The *Annals of Quedlinburg* says that he became more and more "fox-like" and that "he used his cunning to deceive . . . [Theophano] to such an extent that . . . she most clemently bestowed her favor upon him."[31] Odilo of Cluny, who, as we saw, was a great supporter of Empress Mother Adelheid, obliquely suggests that there was more to Theophano and John's friendship than good advice. What may well have been little more than scuttlebutt was later reported by the obnoxious monk Pietro Damiani as fact. He claimed straight out that Theophano had an affair with Philagathos. He describes Philagathos as "a sly and underhand man who . . . burned with ambition for glory and high estate and . . . [had] a shameful affair with the empress of that period."[32] Damiani hated both Greeks and highborn women, so the two fitted his caricature perfectly. The extremity of his views makes him an unreliable witness, especially in sexual matters. Philagathos, as we shall see, was to come to a sad and violent end as an antipope.

Nevertheless, Theophano succeeded in ruling for ten years without great crises and conflicts. As Althoff remarks, "That is surely accomplishment enough, when one considers how rarely such a statement can be made of rulers in this era."[33] Not long before she died, there seems to have been another serious falling out with Empress Adelheid, who lived semipermanently in Pavia. Odilo suggests that there was ongoing tension between Theophano and Adelheid that blew up into a full-scale row just before Theophano died. Odilo says that Theophano "following the advice of a certain Greek [obviously Philagathos] as well as that of other flatterers . . . actually threatened [Adelheid] . . . as she announced: 'If I survive the entire year, Adelheid will reign nowhere in the entire world, her dominion will not even fill the palm of one's hand.'" Odilo, almost gleefully, then adds, "Through the judgment of God that ill-considered statement came true. In less than four weeks the Greek empress departed from this world, leaving august Adelheid alive and well."[34] Clearly for Odilo, Adelheid could do no wrong; the Reverend Mr. Collins was alive and well.

Theophano died, still a young woman aged between thirty-one and thirty-three, on June 15, 991, in her favorite palace at Nijmegen. We don't know the cause of her death. Her son was ten years old, still too young to be emperor in his own right. Adelheid stepped in temporarily as regent. Theophano was buried in the now-much-restored Romanesque church of Saint Pantaleon in Cologne. She had brought the relics of Pantaleon, a doctor and martyr (d. ca. 305), with her from Constantinople, and Pantaleon may have been her personal patron. Today Theophano is buried in a small chapel in a splendid sarcophagus. The church is now administered by the priests of Opus Dei.

It is significant that she died in Nijmegen; she liked the place. Out of 107 different stopping places where Theophano stayed in her royal peregrinations as an Ottonian empress, she stayed 8 times at the *palatium* in Nijmegen, 3 of them during her time as regent. Two of these 8 stays were for two of the most important moments in her life: the birth of her son, Otto, and her death. However, we should not romanticize her staying at Nijmegen; the place was also important to her because she owned large tracts of land in the region, which had come to her as part of her marriage dowry.

Odilo was not alone in disliking Theophano. Many of her contemporaries disliked her probably because they resented a foreigner, especially a foreign *woman*, being in a position to exercise real power. Being Greek didn't help either, as the Greeks were often despised by Westerners like Liutprand of Cremona. Caricatures of their *fallacia* (deceitfulness), *invidia* (jealousy and prejudice), and *arrogantia* (pride) were widespread. After her death Theophano was quickly condemned to hell. A German nun is reported to have had a vision of her *in maximo tormento*, "in great torment." The nun told monk Otloh of Saint Emmeran about her vision in which the empress accepted that she deserved eternal damnation because of her addiction to "luxury," a common accusation against upper-class women in the period. In the vision Theophano asked the nun to pray for her so that she could be released from torment. Somehow this sounds more like Purgatory than hell if the nun's prayers can release her. Otloh preserves the story in his *Liber visionum*, "Book of Visions."

Clerical authors particularly criticized Theophano's introduction of what they deemed to be "luxury" into Western society. Essentially, they were criticizing her because she brought some refinement with her from Constantinople, including bathing daily and being the first to bring the fork to Western Europe. The Byzantines used a two-pronged instrument to carry food from the plate to the mouth. The common Western practice was to take food by well-washed hands and put it in the mouth. If the food was greasy, hands were often washed during the meal and always at the end of it. Failure to wash hands was considered the height of bad manners. The fork seems to have had a brief period of use in the eleventh century, but, except in Italy, it fell into disuse again until early modern times. Some argue that it was actually the Byzantine wife of the Venetian doge, Domenico Selvo, who introduced the fork to the West, but the earlier influence of Theophano as empress on table manners would have been much greater than that of a mere *dogaressa*.

In many ways Theophano still remains an enigmatic figure despite much recent research on her. Without doubt she was an extraordinary woman whose ability to adapt to social, religious, cultural, and linguistic conditions so different to those in which she had been born and nurtured almost indicates a touch of genius. The tragedy is that she didn't live longer; she may well have influenced her son Otto III in a more practical direction as he tried to realize his dream of a united Christendom. But what the story of the regency of Theophano exemplified was that the state that Otto I had established was strong enough to survive the problems inevitably involved in government by a regency for an underage king—Otto III was three when he came to the throne. In other words, this was already a mature polity whose structures were able to negotiate and reconcile not only a royal kidnapping by Henry the Wrangler, but also twelve years of regency. Clearly, the Saxons had already established a stable state that was to survive for the whole of the Middle Ages.

We will now pause in our account of the political developments of the second half of the tenth century to see what life was like for ordinary people.

PART FOUR

LIVING
in the
TENTH
CENTURY

CHAPTER 13

Monks and Nuns

So FAR OUR STORY has focused on attempts to establish some level of stability in the tenth-century state in Western Europe. In Germany this attempt was successful, whereas in West Francia (present-day France) it was totally unsuccessful. In England a coherent state had been established by Alfred the Great and his Anglo-Saxon successors, but it was later torn down by further Viking depredations and the incompetence of Ethelred the Unready. We have also seen a strong and successful missionary movement in Eastern Europe and into the Scandinavian countries so that by the end of the eleventh century these peoples were all converted to Catholicism or to Orthodox Christianity. Conversion brought in its wake a level of state stability; as an overarching force for cultural coherence, the church broke down the localism and petty antagonism that encouraged people to focus entirely on the local.

But underlying all of these efforts to develop a common Christian culture, and to spread the Christian faith by missionary endeavor, was monastic life. In fact, the new world that was tentatively emerging in the second half of the tenth century was underpinned by monasticism. *Stabilitas* (stability) was one of the ideals Saint Benedict put before his monks as an ideal foundation for their religious and community life. But as well as the development of the spiritual life, monasticism emphasized education, culture, and the preseveration of learning through libraries and teaching. As we saw right at the beginning of the book, it was the Irish monks who "saved civilization" and learning in the West, a project that continued through the Carolingian period and on into the tenth century. The ability to reform itself was one of monasticism's great strengths, and one of the great reforms of Western monasticism emanated from the monastery of Cluny in southern Burgundy and spread across Western Europe in the tenth and eleventh centuries. In this chapter we will examine monastic life for both men and women and see how it provided a foundation for the other important shifts in tenth-century life. As a way of entering the monastic story, I want to look at the life of a well-known monk who was not happy in religious life.

He was the Saxon Gottschalk (ca. 804–ca. 869), who claimed that he had been forced into monastic life after being offered as an oblate child aged somewhere between seven and ten, along with his inheritance, to Fulda abbey by his father the Saxon count Bernus. This oblation bound Gottschalk permanently to Fulda; his later lifelong monastic vows were seen by the church and monastic tradition as a confirmation of the commitment his father had made on his behalf as a child. To us this seems unjust, even abusive; however, in those times it was not unusual.

Many children were brought by their parents to monasteries and nunneries and promised to monastic life in a liturgical ceremony. Essentially, the parents were making vows their children would have to live out as adults—including lifelong celibacy, poverty, community life, and obedience. Until the twelfth century when monastic leaders abolished the practice, *oblatio puerorum* (the offering of young boys) was the principal form of monastic recruitment. Some historians, such as John Boswell, have argued that poor parents, unable to support their children, handed them over to the kindness of the monks as a form of humane abandonment, what Mayke de Jong calls "a kind of religiously disguised family planning." However, the fact is that most children given to monasteries were, like Gottschalk, from noble families who were well able to support them. Child oblation, as de Jong says, is one of those issues that illustrate the deep gulf between our world and the tenth century.[1]

Medieval parents committed their children to religious life as a gift to God. "Unreservedly offered by their parents, oblate children were to be holocausts to God, in due course turning the parental obligation into a gift of self through a life of obedience."[2] The influence of the Old Testament was paramount in many aspects of the spiritual life of the tenth century, so parents offered their children as the Bible proscribed. The archetypical example was from the First Book of Samuel (1:24–28) when Samuel's mother dedicates him to God's service in the temple. She says, "As soon as the child [Samuel] is weaned, I will bring him that he may appear in the presence of the Lord and remain there forever." Specific formulae were used when children were handed over to the monastery: "I wish to hand over my son to Almighty God, to serve Him in this monastery, since the Lord prescribed in the law of the children of Israel that they should dedicate their offspring to God."[3] Parents saw their children entering into another kinship group that would nurture and care for them as they would themselves. Almost always a monastic education would far surpass anything the natural parents could offer in terms of "material care, personal protection and training in specialized skills meant to provide a child with new opportunities."[4]

As a result of his oblation, Gottschalk received an excellent formation at Fulda. His *scholasticus* (master) was Rabanus Maurus (ca. 776–856), who had studied under the scholar Alcuin of York. Rabanus says that "some [oblates] professed *in infantia* [in childhood] . . . are dedicated to the study of sacred literature from the cradle . . . until they have enough education to be promoted to holy orders."[5] After learning to read and write, Gottschalk would have learned Latin and studied the Bible, patristics (the early church theologians), and the basics of classical literature. After personally taking his monastic vows at Fulda, he was sent to the premier school of the ninth century, the monastery of Reichenau, with its great library, on an island in Lake Constance.

It was here that Gottschalk met his lifelong friend Walafrid Strabo "the Squinter" (ca. 808/9–849), a poet and theologian, later abbot of Reichenau. We have already met Walafrid—he was a friend of Deacon Bodo who converted to Judaism and fled to al-Andalus. Walafrid and Gottschalk's friendship was not unusual in this period; there was much emphasis on male friendship, especially in monastic circles, and men were more open than we are today about feelings and emotions. They were also much given to passionate, effusive expressions of affection. For instance, in the group of monks who studied with Alcuin, the deacon who was effectively Charlemagne's education minister or education secretary, Alcuin's language in letters and poems to male students, friends, and monks was, to say the least, intense and erotic, especially when the beloved was absent. He often uses pet names like "Daphnis" and "Dodo" for his students, and he tells an older friend he wants to lick his breast and to wash the beloved's "chest with his tears."[6] The poems exchanged between Gottschalk and Walafrid fit into this context. Walafrid had written to Gottschalk when he was in faraway

Friuli (Italy) asking him to send a poem. This is Gottschalk's response to Walafrid's request:

> *O my young lad, you would have me sing—*
> *Why? O Why?*
> *What song, my boy, do you seek to wring*
> *From such as I?*
> *Singing is sweet, but not from me*
> *Who am exiled deep in the distant sea—*
> *Why will you make me sing?*
> *O my little son, it were better far*
> *I weep my wrongs—*
> *Tears from a broken heart, they are*
> *More than songs.*
> *And O belovèd, it cannot be*
> *You seek such singing as this from me—*
> *Why will you make me sing?*
>
> *You must know, little brother, that I desire*
> *Your sympathy;*
> *Child, let not the help of you tire—*
> *Pity me!*
> *A generous heart and soul brought low,*
> *Yours and mine—I would have it so—*
> *Why will you make me sing?*[7]

The Latin of this poem is extraordinarily concise, with the use of diminutives like *pusiloe* (tiny one), *filiole* (little son), *puerile* (little boy), and *fratercule* (little brother) conveying a sense of fond affection and evoking, Boswell says, "a wealth of associations, secular and religious, erotic and spiritual, paternal and lover-like."[8] Helen Waddell says Gottschalk's "verse [was] the most musical written in Europe for centuries," and this lyricism gives expression to the Socratic emphasis on noble and passionate friendship.[9] The Carolingian Franks placed a high value on friendship, and Walafrid's response is the equally beautiful poem *Ad amicum* (To My Friend). In his garden at night at Reichenau (he wrote a book on gardening, *De cultura hortorum*),

Walafrid looks at the moon and the stars and remembers how the sky binds together

> *Two that have loved, and now divided far,*
> *Bound by love's bond, in heart together are.*[10]

This was the kind of tenderness Gottschalk needed. Waddell calls him "a scarred and tormented figure" who was driven by "the dark flame of his black and passionate sincerity."[11]

Walafrid accidently drowned in 849.

It is a very twenty-first century question to ask if these relationships were genital as well as passionate. The evidence in the sources certainly points to a distinctly homosocial subculture in some monastic and clerical circles, although such relationships in the ninth and tenth centuries were not usually thought of as sinful. Where homosexual acting out occurred, it was generally tolerated because such relationships didn't result in progeny or threaten the preservation of church property or the ritual taboos associated with women and menstruation. However, it remains impossible to say for certain.

When Gottschalk returned to Fulda, he was clearly unhappy, and he claimed that he had been forced to take vows and tonsured against his will by Rabanus, who was now abbot. He wanted a dispensation to leave monastic life and demanded the return of his inheritance. Rabanus, a conservative stickler for prerogative, refused point-blank on the grounds that such laxity would lead to social chaos. This was, after all, the period leading up to the civil war between Louis the Pious and his sons, and West Francia was already experiencing the very social chaos Rabanus feared most.

Gottschalk countered that monasticism was a form of slavery, which was unacceptable to free Saxons like himself. Rabanus considered such views to be heretical. In his *De oblatione puerorum*, "On Child Oblation," Rabanus conceded that monks were slaves, but specifically slaves of God. To oppose that notion was "to fight against the Lord" and to hold opinions that were contrary to Catholic faith.[12] At a synod in June 829 in Mainz, Gottschalk, supported by his family, was granted his freedom on condition that he would not claim back his inheritance. A synod at Worms soon afterward presided over by Louis the Pious confirmed the decision, and Gottschalk became something of a wandering scholar. He visited the monasteries of Corbie near Amiens and Hautvilliers (much later the home of Dom Pérignon of champagne fame) and the city of Reims, where he lived for some time with Archbishop Ebbo.

For reasons that are not clear, Gottschalk again entered a monastery, this time at Orbais in the diocese of Soissons. He didn't stay long because he was under imperial suspicion owing to his closeness to Archbishop Ebbo, who had supported Lothar in his revolt against his father, Louis the Pious. Gottschalk was hastily ordained priest in 835 without the permission of his bishop, Rothad of Soissons. He set off again, this time as a missionary, which allowed him to bypass the monastic rule of *stabilitas loci* (stability of place) that is, once someone committed to a monastery, he was there for life. Becoming a missionary was Gottschalk's escape route. Through Walafrid Strabo he obtained an introduction to the scholarly and saintly Frankish duke Eberhard of Friuli, who had married Gisela, the daughter of Louis the Pious and sister of Charles the Bald. From 829 to 838 Walafrid was in Aachen as a tutor to Charles and chaplain to Louis's Empress Judith. Eberhard had a great library and corresponded with theologians.

We don't know much about Gottschalk's time in Italy. He might have visited Rome and even Bulgaria. We know that he spent time in northern Dalmatia (present-day Croatia) as a missionary. Friuli was a frontier march bordering Dalmatia, a region occupied by the Croats, who were just in the process of becoming Christian. Croatia was ruled by the strongly pro-Frankish Duke Borma (d. 821). There has been speculation that "Duke Borma was none other than Bernus, Gottschalk's father," which helps to explain the monk's interest in the region and his missionary visit there in 846–848.[13]

In Friuli trouble caught up with him again. The *Annals of Saint-Bertin* claims that Gottschalk, "puffed up by his learning, had given himself over to false teachings. He had gone to Italy under the guise of pious motives, and had been thrown out from there in disgrace. Then he had assailed Dalmatia, Pannonia and Noricum, constructing by the perfidious things he said and wrote teachings quite contrary to our salvation, especially on the subject of predestination."[14]

His theology of predestination explains the rest of his tragic life.

Gottschalk had studied Saint Augustine closely on grace, freedom, and predestination. Simply put, Augustine holds that human nature has become so completely corrupted by sin and evil that we are unable to attain salvation. Therefore, we are completely dependent upon God's gratuity. For reasons inaccessible to the human mind, God offers final perseverance and salvation to those whom He has freely chosen. While still maintaining a doctrine of free will (although it is hard to see how), Augustine says everything depends on God. Salvation doesn't depend on anything we do; it is all up to God. This is a dangerous position because the implication is that if God chooses some for salvation, then he must abandon others to damnation, what is called "positive predestination." Augustine doesn't go this far, although he gets close to it in *The City of God*. This was one area of theology into which most medieval theologians were unprepared to follow Augustine.

Gottschalk, however, went the whole way. He believed in predestination, and he came to the conviction that salvation is an arbitrary gift given to some by God and denied to others, no matter how good they are. His ideas began to take hold. This made sense among people who were already haunted by fears of damnation. But Gottschalk's ideas were causing concern among bishops. In the end, the long arm of Rabanus, now archbishop of Mainz, caught up with Gottschalk in faraway Dalmatia. Rabanus sent letters to Count Eberhard and to the bishop of Verona attacking Gottschalk's ideas on predestination. Gottschalk impulsively returned to Fulda, where Abbot Hatto was a friend. Though Gottschalk may have initially won his freedom from oblation, Rabanus was now one of the most powerful men in the empire and Gottschalk a poverty-stricken wandering monk with heretical ideas. The Irishman John Scottus Erigena, by far the most brilliant mind of the ninth century, was unhappily enlisted to refute the heretic.

At an October 1, 848, imperial diet presided over by Louis the German and attended by Rabanus, Gottschalk "was exposed and convicted. After that he was compelled to return to the metropolitan *civitas* of his diocese, namely Reims, where that venerable man Hincmar was [archbishop]." What the *Annals of Saint-Bertin* doesn't mention is that Gottschalk was publicly flogged. From Reims he returned to Orbais to await a summons from Hincmar, who wanted to squash his ideas once and for all. In March 849 a synod was held at Quierzy, northwest of Soissons. Condemned again, Gottschalk received "the sentence his perfidy deserved. That most energetic practitioner of the Christian faith, King Charles [the Bald] . . . ordered Gottschalk to be brought before them. He was duly led forward there, publicly flogged and compelled to burn the books containing his teachings."[15] He was deposed from the priesthood and imprisoned in Hautvilliers abbey.

Gottschalk's ideas continued to circulate, and he was not without defenders. Doubts about the justice of his condemnations began to circulate, but for over a decade Hincmar held out against widespread criticism by bishops of his treatment of Gottschalk. Even Pope Nicholas I (858–867) intervened and in 863 commanded that Gottschalk and Hincmar appear before two papal legates at the Council of Metz. A sheepish Hincmar told Nicholas that he received his letter too late to attend and that if the pope wanted to judge Gottschalk, he could, or if he wanted him released, Hincmar would not object. But nothing happened, and by now Gottschalk seemed to have descended into insanity. He died in October 868, begging for the sacraments, which had been denied him for twenty years. The intransigent Hincmar would give him Communion only if he signed a recantation. He refused and died without the Eucharist. Eugen Ewig says that Gottschalk was "a fascinating personality of great brilliance. . . . He was a man of the most profound inner fervour . . . [and] gave expression to this in poetry that will never die."[16] Most of Gottschalk's works were completely lost until the Benedictine monk Dom Germain Morin discovered his writings in 1931 in the Bongars-Bibliothek at Bern University. They were published in 1945.

℘

The story of Gottschalk illustrates the power of monasticism in the social structure of the tenth century. The theory behind this system held that the monk and the nun were tasked with living on earth the kind of life that the saints lived in heaven. Clearly, many monks like Rabanus Maurus were deeply involved in the world, but the essence of the monastic ideal remained contemplative. And while not all monks were educated, monasteries did preserve learning and education. Monasticism stood outside the shifting boundaries of kingdoms and transcended the petty politics of localism. Monasteries were beacons of stability and learning in a landscape characterized by the collapse of any coherent form of government.

Monasticism was an integral part of Charlemagne's reform of government, and he had employed ascetic monk Benedict of Aniane (ca. 750–821) to systematize monasticism and impose the Benedictine rule on all monasteries in the empire. This reform was one of the great emperor's lasting contributions to the centuries that followed, and monasticism became the bedrock upon which the culture of the tenth and following centuries was built. The monastic *fa-*

milia gave people a chance to escape the oppressive societal structures that hedged in most common people. Not all monks were priests; a reasonably large minority were not ordained and were just ordinary "brothers" but not clerics. Belonging to a monastery or convent also placed monks and nuns in the small elite who could read and write. It pretty much guaranteed bed and board and the support of the community during sickness. Often monastic infirmarians had a better knowledge of herbal medicine and treatments than doctors. Monastic life provided a basic social security net and acted as a social leveler. In a hierarchical society the monastery was one place where everyone was equal and social status, at least in theory, meant little. Nevertheless, given the diverse backgrounds of monks, it was inevitable that there were often tensions in monasteries, as the story of Gottschalk illustrates.

Though most monks were recruited through childhood oblation, some came as adults after living a secular life. Most of the best monastic leaders came from the latter group, whereas monastic scholars and historians came from the former group, reflecting, no doubt, the difference in formation: the oblates were formed from childhood within a narrow monastic experience but were nevertheless well educated, while the mature recruits reflected their adult formation and experience in a broader world. Men sometimes entered monasteries to die. Emperor Lothar, for example, became a monk at Prüm Abbey six days before his death in September 855. The idea was that when a sinful man most needed help at the end of his life, he found it as a monk.

In terms of numbers, there were large monasteries such as Fulda, Gorze, and Corbie, which at one stage had some three hundred monks; middle-sized establishments with seventy to one hundred monks; and small monasteries usually with about twelve monks. The monks usually owned all of the land surrounding the monastery. In the tenth century these holdings were reasonably small, enough to support the monks and the monastery's tenant farmers.

Monasteries in Western Europe were all Benedictine, following the sixth century *Rule* of Saint Benedict (ca. 480–550). According to Benedict's *Rule*, monks took vows of obedience (which included poverty and chastity), stability (although the period is full of monks on the move), and conversion of heart. We have an architectural plan of an ideal monastery, probably designed for St. Gallen and most likely drawn up at Reichenau. As a kind of heaven on earth, the plan envisages a mathematically balanced "villa" attuned to the harmony of the spheres, with all the necessities of life covered. The plan shows accommodation

for ninety-five monks and twelve novices, including a large stone church with
a cloister courtyard attached. There is a dormitory built above a warming room
(pervasive cold was a real problem in winter even in the MWP), with a refec-
tory, kitchens, cellars, infirmary, herb garden, school, bathrooms, privy, accommodation for visiting monks, and a detached guesthouse to shelter the
sleeping monks from any loud, late-night rousing by travelers. The *Rule* decreed that the poor and travelers had to be received as though they were Christ
and given accommodation and food. The plan shows a trade section with work-
shops for craftsmen, servants' quarters, a farm, and an orchard. Heat and light
were provided by fires and candles.

If the social role of the monastery was clear enough, what was its religious
purpose? First, monks and nuns were not committed to religious life just for
their own salvation; their lives also had broader social, political, and religious
purposes. They saw themselves fighting spiritual battles, just as soldiers conducted military campaigns. This is the hardest thing for the secularized mind
to understand. For tenth-century people the spiritual world was as real, if not
more real, than the natural, political, and social worlds. For them the safety
and protection of entire societies depended upon the prayers, discipline, and
good works of frontline troops like monks and nuns to ward off the forces of
evil and the devil. As the statutes of a major monastery in Winchester put it,
"The abbot is girded with spiritual weapons supported by a phalanx of monks
endowed with the heavenly gift of expelling the airy wiles of demons from the
king and the clergy, assisted by the strength of Christ."[17]

Monks also offered their lives in penance for the sins of others. The church's
penitential system still imposed quite heavy penances (usually forms of fasting)
even for common sins. Given that all people sinned, their lives could be tied up
for long periods performing endless penances. But they weren't because it was
widely accepted that others did their penance for them. Even extreme rigorist
Pietro Damiani says, "When priests impose a penance on certain sinners they
sometime impose a sum of money for the annual measure of fasting so that those
who dread long fasts may redeem their bad deeds by alms."[18] In this sense the
monk's life was a lived penance for others. They did this through the *opus Dei*, the
"work of God," which consists of Mass and the chanting of the office seven times
each day, as well as through study, hard physical work, and, above all, obedience.
Originally, Benedict intended that the vast majority of monks be laymen, but by
the tenth century the majority were priests because while "prayers of all religious

were good, the best were those offered in the Mass by priest monks."[19] This was particularly the case when Masses were offered for the dead.

This explains why kings and magnates constantly established monasteries and why there was such interest in the ongoing reform of monastic life. Ordinary monks and nuns would have found religious life taxing, and there was always the temptation to grant dispensations from the most rigorous forms of monasticism. We have already seen the corrupt state of monasteries in Rome and the Patrimonium Petri such as Farfa. So it was that by the beginning of the tenth century there was a need for *semper reformanda*, "constant reform," a regular call to return to the pristine Benedictine ideal. In Lotharingia monasteries such as Gorze near Metz, Trier, and Einsiedeln (in Switzerland) became centers of reform; in West Francia it was Fleury and, above all, Cluny that fulfilled this role. In England the great monastic reformer was St. Dunstan. Geoffrey Barraclough comments that "it would be difficult to exaggerate the importance of these reform movements in changing the tone of society." He points out, "Revived monasticism broke down regional differences and encouraged a uniform civilization" and "a common sense of identity." The reforms also encouraged literary and artistic life.[20] These reform movements became increasingly widespread and thus dispersed the ideas and the culture that gradually became foundational in the evolution of the West.

☙

Without a doubt the most important of these reforms emanated from the abbey of Cluny in southern Burgundy. Part of the problem that monasteries faced was that they were often founded by lay magnates anxious to engage a group of monks to pray and offer Mass for them and their clans, especially after death. A further problem was that those who conferred the land and the endowment to the monastery inevitably felt they owned it. Lay proprietorship became one of the curses of church and monastic life. Often the worst offenders were the descendants of the original donor. They felt they could interfere in the life of the monastery, appoint inappropriate lay or absentee abbots, many of them actual family members, all in order to regain control of the community's assets and land, thus weakening the monks' commitment to the *Rule*. As a result of the collapse in social order in the late ninth century, the standards of monastic life and observance fell considerably. Many monasteries were destroyed, and lay control was widespread.

Cluny turned this around. Founded in 910 in a wide valley surrounded by wooded hills, the abbey was located in a favorite hunting forest of William I (875–918) the Pious, Duke of Aquitaine and Count of Auvergne. Influenced by his wife, Angilberga, William gave the land to Abbot Berno of Baume (now the village of Baume-les-Messieurs), a reformer in the tradition of Benedict of Aniane. Berno gathered a community of twelve monks, and on September 11, 910, Duke William issued a charter establishing Cluny abbey "with the court and the demesne manor and the church . . . together with all the things pertaining to it, villas, chapels, serfs of both sexes, vines, fields, meadows, woods, waters, incomes and revenues . . . all without reserve." According to the original *Charter of Cluny*, William felt that God had "made it possible for rich men, by using well their temporal possessions able to merit eternal rewards." So he wanted to return "some portion [to God] for the good of my soul." The monastery was dedicated to Saints Peter and Paul so that "there the monks shall congregate and live according to the rule of Saint Benedict, and that they shall possess and make use of these same things for all time." After Berno's death "those same monks shall have the power and permission to elect any one of their order . . . as abbot." The *Charter* placed the monastery directly under the protection of the papacy.

To protect the monks further, William decreed that "no one of the secular princes, no count, no bishop, not even the pontiff of the aforesaid Roman see, shall invade the property of these servants of God, or alienate it, or diminish it, or exchange it, or give it as a benefice to anyone, or set up any prelate over them against their will."[21] In other words, Cluny was to be free from all ecclesiastical and civil authority and was to answer to Rome alone, which was a long way away and, as we've seen, was then quite weak. Pope John X acknowledged Cluny's papal protection in 928, and in March 931 John XI confirmed "the liberty, goods and privileges" of the abbey. These privileges were confirmed by successive popes, and Gregory V (996–999) in 999 granted Cluny far-reaching exemption from episcopal control. The abbot alone had the power to invite bishops to Cluny to celebrate Mass or ordain monks to orders.[22]

From the start, Cluny benefited from strong, effective leadership. Berno established strict observance of the *Rule*, and when he died in 927, he was succeeded as abbot by his disciple Odo. The abbot's right to designate his successor became customary at Cluny, assuring continuity (even though it ignored the guarantee in William's charter that the monks could elect their own abbot). A member of the community from its inception, Odo served as abbot from 927 to 942. A flexible man who was generous to the poor and outcasts, he set a high standard, insisting on silence, chastity, simplicity, and commitment to perpetual prayer and chanting of the office. At Cluny liturgical exercises took priority over hard labor as the essence of the monastic life.

Success at Cluny allowed Odo to take his reforms to the larger monastic community. Invited by Alberico II to reform local monasteries, Odo visited Rome on six occasions after 936 and using Saint Paul's *fuori le mura* as his base, he became superior of all monasteries in the Patrimonium. While his visits were too short to achieve much, he persuaded most Roman monasteries to adhere to Cluny's strict interpretation of the *Rule*. The reform also spread quickly throughout the monasteries of Burgundy and southern France. Many attached themselves to Cluny, and the movement began to resemble something like a modern religious order, with subordinate communities established in the Cluniac tradition under the supervision of a prior who was responsible to the abbot of Cluny. Today throughout southern Burgundy there are churches, many of them built in the Cluniac style by Lombard builders from northern Italy, and monastic estates that were part of the abbey as it expanded. The estates were important in that Cluny paid careful attention to economic management and independence from lay and episcopal financial interference.

Cluny's leadership remained one of its great strengths throughout the years. Successive abbots were not only saintly reformers, but also effective organizers who were often invited to other monasteries to aid their reform efforts. Because of his humility and lack of self-aggrandizement, Odo was also called in to help settle political disputes, such as that between King Hugh and Alberico II in Rome. Odo also found supporters in the court of King Rudolf II (912–937) of Burgundy, and in 929 he was asked to reform the monastery of Romainmôtier (now in Switzerland) by the great-aunt of Princess Adelheid (later empress), daughter of Rudolf II. Odo established a lifelong link with Empress Adelheid, and one of Cluny's later abbots, Odilo, eventually wrote her somewhat-fawning biography. Other important monasteries such as Fleury-sur-Loire, Limoges, and St Julien at Tours were reformed under Odo's guidance. He was succeeded by Aymardus in 942, but he resigned owing to blindness in 948 in favor of Maiolus, formerly archdeacon of Mâcon.

Maiolus was a well-educated diplomat influential in the Burgundian kingdom. His long abbatial rule from 948 to 992 (some date his election to 965 when Aymardus died) and continuing contact with Empress Adelheid gave Cluny ongoing influence in the highest Ottonian circles. He was often called upon by Otto I, Otto II, and Adelheid to resolve disputes, both political and ecclesiastical. While a number of abbeys in France and Italy were entrusted to Cluny to be directly reformed, much of Cluny's best work under Maiolus was achieved by example rather than direct jurisdiction. In 972 Maiolus was captured by Saracen raiders as his party crossed the Great Saint Bernard Pass in the Alps. He was ransomed and was followed as abbot by Odilo, Adelheid's admiring biographer.

A short, humble man of iron will, Odilo served as abbot from 994 to 1048. He was deeply committed to the care of the poor, and during the dreadful famine of 1033 following five years of crop failures, he melted down and sold Cluny's treasures to help feed the starving. He was also one of the prime movers in the movement known as the "Peace of God," which was designed to limit feudal warfare. Prayer for the dead was one of the prime justifications for monasticism, and Cluny took this responsibility seriously. Odilo introduced a special day of commemoration for departed members of the community, benefactors, and all the Christian dead. "The cosmic totalizing scale of this project is quite striking."[23] Catholics still celebrate this on All Souls Day on November 2. The struggle against the pervasive influence of demons in both human life and the natural world was also part of the Cluny project.

Odilo also deeply influenced medieval religiosity through his emphasis on the incarnation and humanity of Jesus and the role of Mary, thus beginning the modulation of spirituality into a new key: from an emphasis on Christ's association with what Friedrich Heer calls "a God of power" to an emphasis on a more subjective, personal relationship with Christ in love and trust.[24] At the invitation of Otto III, Odilo took up again Odo's work in reforming the monasteries of the Patrimonium, including Farfa, which followed Cluniac usages while preserving its own government. Farfa is still a working monastery.

It was Odilo who welded the Cluniac houses into a formally organized system. He did so for both economic and spiritual reasons. Economically, his purpose was, as Friedrich Kempf says, "to avoid the fragmentation of property which began in France and Italy at the end of the tenth century," which would have had implications for the independence of the Cluniac system. Spiritually, the system incorporated into the order geographically diverse monasteries, keeping them "under discipline by the Abbot [of Cluny] by means of visitation and other measures."[25] Marcel Pacaut says that Odilo introduced a model of government at Cluny that was essentially an "adaptation to a feudal society."[26]

Ω

What was it like to be a monk at Cluny under Odilo? A typical monk—let's call him Brother Eblus—entered as a mature man. He was already a priest, so he was literate and educated and he knew Latin. When he arrived at Cluny, he would have entered the novitiate, where he would receive his basic training as a monk. The novitiate was, in a literal sense, the monastic boot camp. In the novitiate he would have met a few other mature men like himself, as well as youngsters who had entered as child oblates (like Gottschalk) and who had had all of their basic education in the monastery as children. These youngsters were permitted to enter the novitiate from the monastic school after they turned fifteen. We would consider this far too young today, but with a shorter life expectancy and an assumption that a person entered adulthood at fifteen, this was not considered too young to become a monk. After all, in the tenth century girls were considered sexually mature at pubescence (when they were twelve or thirteen). Eblus would have spent the novitiate learning by heart the complex customs of the Cluniac order, including the sign language used during the *maguum silentium*, the great overnight silence and the other periods when monks could not speak to each other. He would have also been introduced to the Cluniac interpretation of Benedict's *Rule* and the intricate complexities of the liturgical offices.

After twelve months—perhaps a shorter time because he was already a priest—the abbot and community would have voted on his acceptance and he would have taken vows during the community Mass of *stabilitas loci, conversio morum* ("conversion of life," which included poverty and chastity), and obedience to the *Rule*. From now on Brother Eblus would dress as a monk. "Let clothing be given to the brethren according to the circumstances of the place and the nature of the climate in which they live," Benedict's *Rule* (ch. 55) wisely advised. Eblus would have worn underwear consisting of loose linen drawers or shorts that were held up by a drawstring at the waist. Over the basics he wore a long woolen robe held in at the waist with a belt and over that a scapular worn over the shoulders and reaching to the ground. Both were black. He would also have had socks, shoes, winter boots, sheepskin gloves, and a sheepskin pelisse and hood for winter. His clothes were washed weekly. He would also have had writing tablets, stylus, wooden comb, a knife to cut food, and needles and thread. Like all the monks, Eblus was clean-shaven, with a wide tonsure. He also had two square meals a day, even if they were vegetarian. He was assured of good medical help and care in the infirmary if he was sick. All in all for a tenth-century son of free peasants, it was a secure life.

Eblus had felt called to the monastery because it was meant to be a prefiguration of heaven on earth. The Cluniac monk lived to chant constantly the praises of God, as did the angels in heaven. The monastery was now his family, a "perfect" family in the sense that it was carefully organized according to the *Rule*. It was also a hierarchical family, ruled by the abbot assisted by the prior, who organized the day-to-day running of the monastery. But then Eblus was born into a hierarchical culture; for him the earthly hierarchy mirrored on earth the angelic hierarchy in heaven.

Life was strict, and even the slightest infractions of the rule were publicly exposed at the daily chapter meeting. Penances even for small faults and forgetfulness could be severe, such as being beaten with a rod. For major infractions such as fighting, absence without leave, talking to a woman, drunkenness, swearing, and quarreling, the punishment was more prolonged and severe and involved exclusion from the community, humiliation, floggings, and imprisonment. This was not a life for the fainthearted. Privacy was at a minimum. Eblus slept in his own bed in a common dormitory. By the time he entered Cluny, the old ninth-century, Carolingian emphasis on male friendship was being replaced by a much more puritanical attitude and an unspoken fear of homosexuality. Personal interactions between the monks were much more circumscribed than in the past. The lack of personal space would have been intolerable for us today, but privacy as we know it did not exist in those times. Besides, given the insecurity of the time, most people simply felt safer closer together.

The thing Eblus would have appreciated most was that the formal liturgical life at Cluny replaced the commitment to hard physical work that had characterized traditional Benedictine life. Eblus now spent much of his time in chapel chanting set cycles of psalms, scripture readings, and prayers, which were divided into nine sections, or "hours," as they were called. It was a demanding regimen. The monks rose long before dawn in summer or at 2 a.m. in winter (with a compensating midday siesta) for vigils (psalms, reading, and prayers for the dead), followed by a brief sleep, after which they rose again for matins and lauds (antiphons, psalms, scripture readings, and prayers) at dawn. A period of meditation was followed by prime, terce, sext, and none all made up of antiphons, psalms, and prayers; these were sung with intervals of three hours. A private and then a community Mass were fitted in between the hours. Vespers was sung at sunset and compline after nightfall. Each day Eblus chanted 138 psalms. There were also processions, additional prayers, and litanies added on feast days. Most of Eblus's waking hours would have been taken up with these liturgical obligations. The sacristan at Cluny was responsible for rousing the monks, and given that he had no clock, he had to read the time from the heavens or from stars (if he could see them) for the night offices. It must have been a nerve-wracking job.

For the rest of his life this would be the daily round for Eblus. Any spare time could be devoted to study, private prayer, and copying of manuscripts. He might occasionally have had a break from his regular life if he were called on to travel for the business of the monastery or for some other reason associated with the church. In fact his life was probably less onerous than it seems on paper; monks certainly got around Europe for all types of reasons. While average life expectancy for ordinary people was in the late thirties, it was probably a good bit higher for monks who lived a regular life with a stable food supply and good basic health care. They were also were generally safe from the constant fighting that injured and killed so many men. Not all the monks were "choir monks" like Eblus. Some of them would have been exempt from some of the hours in order to do the practical work of the monastery, such as preparing meals, cleaning, keeping contact with the peasants working the monastery land, and buying materials the monastery needed or selling its surplus products. This would have involved much more contact with the outside world.

Cluny was the main source of the energy for church reform in the eleventh century. But there were other sources. Saint Romuald of Ravenna (ca. 950–1027) entered the Cluniac reformed abbey of Sant'Apollinare in Classe near Ravenna as a penance after his father had killed a kinsman in a duel. Unsatisfied with the observance at Sant'Apollinare, he retreated to the Po marshes, where he lived a life of rigid asceticism as a hermit. The troubled and depressed young Emperor Otto III visited him there seeking advice. Romuald's study of the desert fathers, the early Christian hermits of Egypt and Syria, convinced him that solitude and strict asceticism were the ideal form of monastic life.

Leaving the Po marshes, he lived a wandering life in Italy for some thirty years founding monasteries and hermitages. The two most important were Fonte Avellana in 1012 and Camaldoli in 1023, both in the forested mountains above Arezzo. Both are still operative monasteries.

One of his disciples was Pietro Damiani (1007–1072), who lived a life of extreme austerity after entering the Romuald-founded monastery of Fonte Avellana in 1035. He became famous for preaching against worldliness among the clergy and monks. In keeping with other vociferous ascetics of the time, he also targeted the prevailing homosocial tolerance among the clergy in his *Liber Gomorrhianus* (Book of Gomorrah). Even when we allow that strong, dramatic language was common in his time, there is something hysterical about Damiani's moral panic, with his book suggesting an epidemic of homosexual sex among monks and clergy, particularly between younger monks and their spiritual "fathers" or guides. He divides "this form of criminal wickedness" into four categories: "some sin with themselves alone; some commit mutual masturbation . . . some femoral fornication [i.e., one man rubbing his penis between another's upper thighs] . . . and others the complete act against nature [i.e., rectal intercourse]." He goes so far as to say that "it seems to me to be more tolerable to fall into shameful lust with an animal than with a male."[27] Such language is abhorrent to us because we see sexuality as related to love and intimacy, whereas Damiani and his contemporaries thought solely of sexuality in terms of reproduction. So for him "sodomy," as he calls it, was unadulterated eroticism without the possibility of reproduction and as such was against the order of nature as set up by God.

Damiani notwithstanding, it was monastic reform that provided the basis and impetus for the broad cultural, spiritual, and ecclesiastical reforms emerging in Western Europe in the second half of the tenth century. Prominent monks, as we saw, were becoming important figures in political as well as ecclesiastical life. The monastery of Cluny was to last until the French Revolution, when the extensive buildings were seized by the French revolutionary state and sold off to a man on the make in Mâcon who used the magnificent monastery as a quarry.

∾

It is a relief to leave the somewhat perverse world of Damiani and his moral panic and enter the much more humane world of the nuns. Probably the best known of this era is Hrosvitha of Gandersheim, the first woman dramatist in Europe. All that we know about her comes from her own works. An aristocratic Saxon born about 935, she entered the nunnery at Gandersheim in Lower Saxony either as a child or in her early twenties. Hrosvitha was part of an intellectual renaissance that flowered during the reigns of the three Ottos. Another famous writer was Liutprand of Cremona, and the greatest scholar and polymath of the age, Gerbert of Aurillac (Pope Sylvester II), was also a product of this period. This renaissance was also evident in art, architecture, and manuscript illustration. It was underpinned by a coherent political theory and an ordered imperial government. Living in the midst of this renaissance, Hrosvitha studied Virgil, Terence, Ovid, and the Latin classics as well as early Christian writers, philosophers such as Boethius, music, biblical studies, and mathematics. She says she was broadly educated "through the instructive guidance of our learned and kindly teacher Richardis, and of others who taught in her stead; and then through the . . . royal [Abbess] Gerberga . . . who rightly instructed me in those various authors from whom she herself studied under the guidance of learned teachers."[28]

Abbess Gerberga, who ruled Gandersheim from 949 to 1001, was the niece of Otto I and cousin of Otto II. Established in 852 by Henry the Fowler's grandfather, Gandersheim was a royal convent. It maintained a close tie to the Ottonians until 947 when Otto I granted the abbess complete freedom with the right to hold her own court, to have troops to protect the abbey, to mint her own money, and to sit in the imperial diet. Gerberga was the first to use these privileges to the full.

Technically, Hrosvitha was a secular canoness. That is, she was *not* a cloistered nun in the Benedictine tradition. Thus, Hrosvitha was bound to celibacy and obedience, but not to poverty. She could own personal property and had her own apartment and servants. The relationship of canonesses to fully vowed nuns is a complex one. Historian of women's religious life Jo Ann Kay McNamara says, "Modern historians have great difficulty distinguishing between 'canonesses' and 'sanctimonials' [that is, vowed nuns, or what we understand by nuns today] when the sources do not address the subject, and the religious often seem to have avoided definition."[29] It made sense for these highborn, free women to keep definitions of their role flexible so that they were not tied down by lifelong vows to religious constraints. Canonesses claimed that they were not nuns, which allowed them to provide charitable services outside the convent.

They didn't take permanent vows of celibacy, so technically they retained their right to marry.

Hrosvitha used her education to the fullest. She was a playwright, historian, and poet who wrote six plays in imitation of Roman playwright Publius Terentius Afer (Terence), whose own plays were produced between 166 and 160 BC. Hrosvitha also wrote eight poems on saints' lives in dactylic hexameter, the verse of classical poetry; two narrative poems, one on Otto I *Carmen de gestis Ottonis imperatoris* (Poem on the Deeds of Emperor Otto) and the other on the history of her convent; and a short poem, all in Latin. She spent her whole life at Gandersheim and probably lived to just beyond the millennium. Her writings were lost until the late fifteenth century when they were rediscovered in Regensburg, where there is evidence that they inspired other nun-playwrights in the eleventh and twelfth centuries. One of her poems features the life of Saint Pelagius, the young male Catholic hostage in Muslim Spain with whom Abd al-Rahmān III wished to have sex. Hrosvitha, who probably derived her information from an actual witness of the event, emphasizes that the actual sin lies in sexual intercourse between a baptized Christian and an unbaptized Muslim, rather than in the act as such. Hrosvitha has Pelagius telling the caliph:

> *"Nor should a Christian, anointed with holy oil*
> *Accept a kiss from a servant of a filthy demon."*[30]

Hrosvitha's plays, although in the style of Terence, offer a chaste alternative to Terence's sexual explicitness. She says, "I, the strong voice of Gandersheim, have not hesitated to imitate in my writings a poet whose works are so widely read, my object being to glorify . . . the laudable chastity of Christian virgins in that self-same form of composition which [Terence] used to describe the shameless acts of licentious women." She admits that she has "blushed" when she has had to depict "the dreadful frenzy of those possessed by unlawful love and the insidious sweetness of passion—things which should not even be named among us."[31] But that doesn't stop her. In two of her plays her prostitute heroines repent and undertake severe asceticism as Hrosvitha celebrates female strength. In the other plays she takes up the theme of female vulnerability overcoming male power as she praises the courage of women as they stand against the power of the pagan Roman emperor. In fact, what she is doing is presenting women as agents, offering an alternative vision to that of misogynist clerics like Liutprand, Rather of Verona, and Atto of Vercelli, who reduced women to temptresses of gullible men and polluted beings unable to touch anything sacred. Hrosvitha had influence at court, and Otto II commissioned her to compose a verse epic in honor of his father; and her unfailing support, Abbess Gerberga, asked her to write a history of Gandersheim.

But the secular canonesses were not the only nuns. There were also vowed nuns living an enclosed life according to the Benedictine rule, bound to singing the office like the monks and to embracing stability and poverty. Originally, a woman simply took a vow before the abbess and donned a veil. But this became more elaborate as nuns were increasingly seen as brides of Christ. By the tenth century a ritual had evolved that included a male guardian "giving away" the prospective nun during Mass. The nun's veil and the ring, the symbols of her espousal, were blessed oftentimes by the abbess. This was sometimes referred to as "castimony," meaning "chaste matrimony," making vowed chastity an analogue to matrimony. This was not seen as an erotic fantasy but as a legal bond. "If Benedictine reformers tended to think of nuns as pure and unsullied brides of Christ, canonesses were apt to interpret castimony as a more practical matter of housekeeping and hospitality. Their devotions were incessant . . . though carried-on in the hustle and bustle of a busy world."[32]

The number of convents also increased as upper-class women with property vulnerable to predatory males established communities to protect themselves and other women. By the tenth century abbesses were powerful not just in their own right, but also by virtue of seeing themselves and being seen by many others as ordained. Historian of women's ordination Gary Macy has conclusively shown that abbesses were not just "installed"; they were actually ordained into their role. He quotes a number of ordination ceremonies for abbesses and shows that these women exercised genuinely priestly roles, including the hearing of confessions and the giving of blessings both within their communities and, sometimes, in the territories attached to them. Abbesses were at least seen as the equivalent of ordained deaconesses in the early church. Macy is unequivocal in his conclusions: "First and most important: women were ordained in the early Middle Ages. According to the understanding of ordination held by themselves and their contemporaries, they were just as truly ordained as any bishop, priest or deacon. . . . Further, the ministries to which these women belonged encompassed ritual actions that came to be reserved only to the male diaconate and presbyterate."[33]

This makes sense in the context of the royal Saxon women who entered the convent. These were women used to exercising authority, and they certainly saw themselves as the equivalents of bishops and far superior to local priests. An example is Mathilda, Abbess of Quedlinburg. She was the daughter of Otto I and granddaughter of Matilda of Ringelheim, wife of Henry the Fowler who built the convent to offer prayers for Henry's soul. Just a little more than 30 miles (50 kilometers) from Magdeburg, Quedlinburg is situated in a region northeast of the Harz Mountains and west of the Elbe, the home range of the Ottonians. The Ottonians returned here for all their family affairs and for the celebrations of Christmas and Easter. Otto I and his first wife, Eadgyth, were buried in Magdeburg cathedral, and Queen Matilda, wife of Henry, was buried beside him in Quedlinburg in 968. The royal nunnery here was built for secular canonesses on a hill surrounded by the flat and fertile North German Plain.

Abbess Mathilda was a formidable woman. The youngest daughter of Otto I and a close friend of Theophano, she was made abbess at the age of eleven in April 966 and later proved herself a woman of great ability. Exercising bishoplike authority, she acted as a very able regent in Germany when her brother Otto II went to Italy in 980. In the best tradition of Ottonian women, she successfully accomplished her aims by prayer and persuasion rather than by violence. She played a key role in getting the child emperor Otto III returned to his mother, Theophano, after he had been kidnapped by Henry the Wrangler. In essence, her achievement was to establish a small convent-state that remained independent for eight hundred years until it was disbanded by Napoleon in 1802.

Close to Quedlinburg is Gernrode, another convent of secular canonesses, this one established by Margrave Gero, upon whom Otto I so often depended to protect the eastern frontiers of the empire and to integrate and convert the Slavs. Gernrode was originally a fortress, named after Gero, in a forest clearing. After his only son's death, Gero went on a pilgrimage to Rome and returned with a relic of Saint Cyriakus, a Christian martyred in the persecution of the early-fourth-century Roman emperor Diocletian. A convent was established dedicated to the saint and flourished for the next couple of hundred years. The church still survives intact, one of the best examples in Germany of Ottonian architecture. Begun in 959, it was completed before 1014.

Most convents were small, with perhaps ten to twelve nuns, and with the largest having less than one hundred. There seems to have been a distinct decrease in the number of religious women in the ninth and tenth centuries, and the numbers didn't increase again until well into the eleventh century. With the exception of the larger royal convents in Germany, most were poor with small endowments, which meant that feeding the sisters could be a major task. What little knowledge we have of their diet indicates that it was unbalanced, lacking protein and vitamins but not lacking calories. For instance, at the nunnery of Notre-Dame de Soissons each nun was given a daily ration of 1,440 grams of bread, 1.38 liters of wine, 70 grams of cheese, 133 grams of dry vegetables, 16 grams of salt, and 0.6 grams of honey. This adds up to 4,727 calories, which is double what a modern woman would need.[34]

ↁ

Monasteries and convents clearly stood out as havens of stability, culture, and intellectual life amid the general chaos of life in the later ninth and early tenth centuries. Even though they were meant to prefigure the ordered and hierarchical life of heaven, in fact these institutions modeled real possibilities for life here on earth. An order like Cluny showed that a kind of monastic "empire" could be established and administered that was both larger and more efficient than anything else in France at that time. More than that, monasteries and convents provided educated people who could assist monarchs to develop more ordered and efficient government structures and create the kind of cultural and intellectual life needed to underpin the renewal of secular society. Monastic and convent life provided the ordered context in which the West was born.

CHAPTER 14

*Ordinary Life in
the Tenth Century*

So FAR WE'VE TALKED about popes, emperors, monks, and nuns, all of whose activities are documented in historical sources. But what about those whose stories aren't preserved? What was life like at the base of the social pyramid? How did ordinary people survive, and what were their preoccupations?

With a bit of detective work we can reconstruct something of what their life was like. We've seen the chaos and violence that people of this time were all too frequently subjected to—yet despite external disorder, tenth-century society was, in a sense, highly ordered. It was hierarchical, and everyone had a clearly defined place, symbolized through custom, ceremony, and costume.

Tenth-century society was roughly divided into *ordines*, "orders," or socially arranged groups. Everyone was ranked according to his place in the social *ordo*—kings, bishops, clergy, nobility, peasants, serfs, slaves. These distinctions were reinforced by costume, social gestures, and even economics. Both religious life and secular life were highly ritualized. From cradle to grave there was a ceremony, prayer, and blessing for every social event and transition. In a world where reading and writing were the preserve of clerics, monks, nuns, and scholars, rituals and rules of external conduct became increasingly important as rites of passage sealing a person's place in the social pecking order and reinforcing social differences. *Ordo* maintained society and community.

Nevertheless, there was a small but very real possibility of social mobility. The church, for instance, sometimes provided a bright peasant boy with the opportunity to climb the ecclesiastical pile right to the top. An example is Gerbert of Aurillac, born the son of peasants, who died in 1002 as Pope Sylvester II. But while *ordo* was valued, this was not a tidy world. It was diverse, complex, and sometimes quite unpredictable. Tying down exactly how institutions—such as the church—worked in practice is difficult to do. The main outlines can be easily ascertained, but there were exceptions, and even though people knew their place, this was a more restless, surprising, and flexible society than at first appears. Order was enforced not so much by direct compulsion as by social pressure; each person knew *quid agendum sibi esset*, "what she had to do" to live in her apportioned place. Outward social conformity was far more influential than the development of an interior conscientious commitment to right behavior. Acting out of personal conscientious conviction against society's mores was deemed eccentric, even demonic.

Let's start at the bottom rung of society and meet the peasants Bodo; his wife, Ermentrude; their boys, Wido and Gerbert; and their girl, Hildegard. Their names are recorded in a polyptych, an estate book or inventory, compiled sometime between 809 and 839 by Abbot Irminon of the monastery of Saint-Germain-des-Prés near Paris.[1] While incomplete and difficult to interpret, it is the most detailed polyptych we have, listing almost 8,000 people on 1,378 farms. (This was a monastic estate, but the same categories applied to land controlled by a secular lord or magnate.) Divided into various parcels of land, the abbey comprised a huge 91,500 acres (37,000 hectares) around Paris, of which about 56,800 acres (23,000 hectares) were arable.

Bodo's family lived on a fisc, or separate abbey estate, called Villaris, now parkland overlooking the Seine in the western Paris suburb of Saint Cloud. The fisc was divided into the demesne, which was land directly farmed by the abbey under the supervision of a steward, and manses, various sized plots occupied by tenants. While living on abbey land, the tenants had a permanent hold on their manses, which they could use to support themselves. We know that Bodo occupied "a little farm of arable and meadow land, with a few vines."[2]

The *Estate Book* also describes twenty-eight other fiscs owned by the abbey, including one called Villeneuve–Saint Georges, now a suburb close to Orly Airport. Here we meet Arctardus, a *colonus*, a freeman who held a *pecunium*, a right in perpetuity to farm the land he occupied because he had improved and worked it by his own labor, and his wife, Eligildis, a *colona*, a freewoman, and their six children, Ageteus, Tendo, Simeon, Adalsida, Deodata, and Electardus. On the same fisc the *Estate Book* also mentions Aclebertus; his wife, Frotlindis; a serf; their child, Aclebrug; and another serf, Teutfridus, who lived with his mother.

Essentially, there were three levels or categories of people, although in practice there was very little difference among them. Bodo and Arctardus were *coloni*. Aclebertus was a tenant farmer, and his wife was *serva*, a serf. Teutfridus was also a serf. Bodo and Arctardus were *liberi*, freemen whose small parcels of land could be inherited. But they paid taxes and fees to the abbot and were obliged to work for him. The second group of the *libri* comprised the rent-paying peasantry like Aclebertus. They leased their plots from the landowner, lord, or abbot. As well as rent in kind, they worked for stipulated periods on the owner's land. About 85 percent of lower-class people were free—that is, they were not slaves or serfs. This contradicts the modern caricature of the Middle Ages as containing an elite of nobles and clergy, a tiny group of freemen, and a vast subclass of serfs. It is difficult, however, to ascertain what freedom meant in practice because there was very little difference between the lifestyles of the free and those of the serfs and the whole issue is lost, as Robert Fossier says, in "obscurity and confusion."[3]

There was also another group who served the monastery or, on secular estates, the households of lords. In this group were most of the unmarried women, older girls, and many of the unmarried male *servi* (serfs). Analyzing the *Estate Book*, David Herlihy concludes, "This suggests that the household system was two-tiered. The richer households . . . were taking the older children . . . especially girls and returning them at marriage age to their families."[4] It was the children of the least advantaged who were most often transferred out of their homes, thus helping the poor live within the limits of their resources.

Serfs, or bondmen as they were known in Anglo-Saxon England, were subordinate people dependent on a lord or an abbot and lacking some of the rights of the free. Some serfs were former domestic slaves who had gained manumission; others were freemen who had fallen into serfdom because they were seeking protection or were unable to meet their obligations. Others were domestic servants. Most were tenant farmers who owed days of labor to their lord. They also faced restrictions on their personal lives, such as having to get permission to marry or being subject to financial exactions such as draconian inheritance taxes that kept them poor. "They were not beasts—they were baptised, could possess moveable property and have skills," but, as Fossier says, it is "clear that 'servitude' was a pillar of the [economic structure]."⁵

The *Estate Book* describes the fisc of Villeneuve in detail. It deals first with the demesne, abbey land supervised by a steward or mayor who tax-farmed it for the landholder. Stewards were often hated. The demesne comprised

> 172 *bunnaria* [about 145 acres] which can take 800 *modios* [a cubic capacity approximating a small wagonload] of grain for sowing. There are 91 *aripennos* [about 76 acres] of vineyard from which about 1000 *modii* [the cubic capacity of an average-sized wagonload] can be collected; of meadow, 166 *aripennos* [about 140 acres], from which 166 carts of hay may be gathered. There are three mills from which 450 *modios* of grain have come as rent. . . . There is woodland 4 leagues in circumference [about 12 miles], where 500 hogs can be fed.⁶

Clearly, the monks kept good land for themselves. There was also "a church, well constructed, with all its furniture."⁷ This church would have provided Mass and the sacraments for the local peasants and was probably served by one of the monk-priests.

The freeman Arctardus and his family were reasonably prosperous, with a holding of "5 *bunnaria* of arable land and 2 *antsingas* [about 5.75 acres], 4 *aripennos* of vineyard [3.35 acres] and 4 and a half *aripennos* [about 3.7 acres] of meadow," a total of about 14.8 acres. But they had to pay abbey taxes, which varied from year to year: one year it was four silver *solidi* for protection; the next year it was two *solidi* "as tax on their animals"; the third year they paid "one sheep with its lamb" for herbage tax. They also paid other minor taxes, including wine for grazing rights. Arctardus also did plowing and sowing for the monastery and performed other unpaid labor. Aclebertus, his wife, and Teutfridus, "who has his mother with him," were tenants who shared a manse "having 4 *bunnaria* of arable land, one *aripennum* of vineyard, 4 *aripennos* of meadow," a total of about 7.5 acres. Their workload for the abbey was a lot more demanding than that of their free neighbors, and in addition they paid "3 *modios* of wine for grazing tax, one *sestarius* [a measure of capacity for wine or grain] of mustard, 50 osier bundles, 3 chickens, 15 eggs." They also did "handiwork services when and where they are imposed on them. And the unfreewoman has to make a cloth from wool of the demesne and doughs as many as she is ordered to."⁸

Even though this was essentially a barter economy, there was money in circulation. The basic coin was the *denarius*, a silver penny. Twelve denarii equaled a gold *solidus*. Twenty *solidii* equaled one *libra*, one pound, a very large sum of money. It is impossible to give an exact value of the *solidus* and *denarius* in our terms; the most that can be said is that one *solidus* would buy an average ox.

Interestingly, these households were almost unigenerational—that is, there are only 26 grandmothers (out of 3,404 women) and no grandfathers listed by Irminon. Herlihy comments. "The classical stem family was not present on the estates of Saint-Germain."[9] This may well reflect the composition of the agrarian population, with an average life span of thirty-five to forty for both sexes, as well as a relatively late age of marriage (the evidence indicates that men and women were in their midtwenties when they married), which lowers population growth. Families were bilinear, with male and female lines of descent of equal importance. This indicates "a spirit of family cohesiveness that may have worked to keep the members of the same descent group together on the same farm, even in adulthood."[10] It also indicates that women exercised some agency, which was reflected in the prevailing opinion that bride and groom should be of similar age at the time of marriage. People also tended to crowd together in closely settled villages, leaving the surrounding forests to pannage for pigs, which made sense especially after the Viking incursions began. The almost 8,000 people who lived on the abbey estates tended to pack into population islands. The peasants not only had to support themselves, but they also had to produce an excess to support their lords, either secular or religious.

☙

Historians generally talk about society in the medieval centuries in terms of feudalism and the role of peasants within it. This word was invented by seventeenth-century French lawyers and antiquarians to describe the tangle of legal and customary relationships that they discovered in medieval documents in local French repositories. To make sense of this mass of medieval documentation, they gradually constructed a theory they called "feudalism," which attempted to describe the variety of institutions that had developed willy-nilly in different places and times. Radicals in the eighteenth-century Enlightenment and the French Revolution used the idea of feudalism to cast the aristocracy as exploitative of the lower orders and blacken their reputation. Later Karl Marx's theory of history used feudalism as the convenient precursor of capitalism. So feudalism became established as both historical theory and fact, albeit with a bad name, especially from the perspective of the Left.

The most important modern historian of feudalism was Frenchman Marc Bloch. His book *Feudal Society* (1939) was influenced by the French *annales* tradition of history writing. This shifted the historiographic focus from an emphasis on aristocratic politics to the underpinning socioeconomic structures of society, specific places and localities, and the experiences of ordinary people. It used local documentary sources to broaden our view of the past and encouraged a more sociological approach to history. Using these comprehensive perspectives, Bloch argues that, while the vassal did military service for his lord, so the peasant worked for the lord in exchange for protection and that both were essential components of feudalism. The Belgian historian François-Louis Ganshof came to history with a legal background. He defines feudalism more narrowly and focuses on the relationship between a lord and his warrior-vassal. His book *Feudalism* (1944) sees this relationship arising from a ceremonial commitment between the two that was specific to the disintegration of the post-Carolingian world. Ganshof defines feudalism as "a body of institutions creating and regulating the obligations of obedience and service—mainly military service—on the part of a free man (the vassal) toward another free man (the lord) and the obligations of protection and maintenance on the part of the lord with regard to his vassal."[11]

But more recently there has been a radical reappraisal of feudalism. Susan Reynolds argues that the term is a meaningless, misleading construct invented to make sense out of the confused mass of medieval documentation we have inherited. In her view, the word has no basis in historical reality. She says unequivocally, "Fiefs and vassalage are post-medieval constructs. . . . Historians . . . tend to fit their findings into a framework of interpretation that was devised in the sixteenth century and elaborated in the seventeenth and eighteenth. . . . We cannot understand medieval society and its property relations if we see it through . . . [these] spectacles."[12]

Reynolds is right. Sure, we know that free peasants like Bodo, Arctardus, and Aclebertus and Teutfridus the serf owed labor to the abbey in exchange for protection, just as they would if they had been on secular land. But to turn this into a highly articulated system is to massively complicate something that was a simple protective arrangement. Ganshof rightly argues that protective arrangements were important. And Bloch is right that the key issue in the tenth century was security in an age of disorder. The reality is that tenth-century people didn't live in a tidy, consistent society governed by a "system" of feudal law. At best there were various forms of local customary law. Personal relationships and interconnectedness, rather than a clear legal code, governed life.

Peasants were freemen attached to the land who pledged themselves to give military service to their lords in return for protection. This commitment involved mutually binding obligations: service and loyalty from the peasants and protection and at least rough justice from the lord. These practices were part of the Germanic-Frankish tradition, and they reemerged in the chaos of the late ninth century. The only practical response to this disorder was the seizure of power by local magnates who had represented the king in local regions or by adventurers who seized the main chance. Weaker people had no option but to support the strongmen.

There was also an economic element at work. While there were currencies in circulation, the main source of wealth and economic power was landownership. It is estimated that in the tenth century probably less than 25 percent of European land was owned by the church and monastic orders and that kings and magnates controlled 40 percent or more. Ordinary people owned about 30 to 35 percent, but the constant insecurity and chaos meant that they were still subservient to the local strongman because they needed his protection. The more land a person owned, the more powerful he was. In West Francia by the end of the tenth century, there was a patchwork of sixty or more counties, duchies, and other divisions. Each was independently ruled by a strongman with pretensions to nobility. Theoretically, each was a fief of the crown—that is, land "granted" to the lord in exchange for military service to the king. But each strongman effectively ruled independently of the crown. In contrast, Germany was far less divided, with a much smaller number of powerful magnates ruling much larger regions.

Not that order was lacking. In subsistence agricultural systems regularity is essential. The rhythms of agricultural life are determined by the seasons. Even the months had been renamed by Charlemagne to reflect this fact. May became *Winnemonat*, the month the animals returned to the meadows; June was *Brachmonat*, the plowing month; July was *Hewimonat*, hay month; August was *Aranmonat*, harvest month; September began the preparation for winter with woodcutting month *Witumonat*; October was wine month, *Windumemonat*.

The only breaks in the endless round of work came on Sundays and in the cycle of religious seasons: Easter, Pentecost, Christmas, Epiphany, Ascension; feasts of Our Lady such the Purification (February 2), Assumption (August 15), her birthday (September 8); saints days including Saints Peter and Paul (June 29), Lawrence (August 10), the Archangels (September 29), All Saints (November 1), Martin of Tours (November 11), Nicholas (December 6), Sylvester (December 31); and the anniversary of the consecration of the local church. These rest days were enforced. In 827 Louis the Pious decreed

> that no servile works shall be done on Sundays, neither shall men perform their rustic labours, tending vines, ploughing fields, reaping corn and mow- ing hay, setting up hedges or fencing woods, cutting trees or working in quarries or building houses; nor shall they work in the garden, nor come to law courts, nor follow the chase. . . . Women shall not do their textile works, nor cut out clothes, nor stitch them together with the needle, not card wool, nor beat hemp, nor wash clothes in public, nor sheer sheep: so that there may be rest on the Lord's day.[13]

After everyone had been to Mass, people danced, sang, drank, and often engaged in outrageous buffoonery with overt pagan overtones, much to the annoyance of more puritan priests and bishops. Peasants' horizons were parochial, and their only communication with the outside world depended on the arrival of the odd traveler or on stories and rumors. These were often ex- aggerated, which could lead to panic. Strangers were suspect, as the innocent "sky travelers" rescued by Archbishop Agobard discovered.

Women were an essential part of the economy. As well as performing daily tasks in the house and farmyard, women cared for livestock and poultry, milked cows and goats, sheared sheep, made dairy products, and washed clothes. They also produced the clothes the family wore and oftentimes worked with other women to manufacture textiles, sew, and embroider. Peasant clothing was prac- tical and unadorned. Depending on the season, men wore a drab-colored rough woolen or linen knee-length tunic belted at the waist. They also wore knee- length woolen trousers or leggings. Women wore long woolen dresses and chemiselike underskirts, and men wore a kind of undershirt or shrift to protect the upper body from the rough wool tunics. Both sexes used a kind of cowl or hat to cover the head and shoulders. Men and women wore clogs or shoes made of leather or thick cloth. Woolen or sheepskin overgarments were worn in winter to keep out the cold. Outer garments were never washed. The predominant colors were a kind of russet, gray, or red.

What—if anything—did they wear underneath? This remains something of a mystery because we rarely see it, except occasionally in illuminated manuscripts when a monk is depicting scenes of everyday life. Men sometimes wore linen breeches held up by a drawstring around the waist. In hot summers they sometimes stripped down to this basic garment. At other times they wore something like a baby's diaper, which covered their crotch. Usually, they wore no underwear at all, as was true for women. Female modesty was maintained by the long dress, which would be simply pulled up to meet the needs of nature. During menstruation women wore a kind of layered cloth attached to a belt. Underwear was always thoroughly washed.

Men and women rose at dawn. After a breakfast of homemade bread and rough home-brewed ale, men headed for the fields no matter what the weather to work either for themselves or for the lord. Women did domestic chores, looked after the vegetable garden, tended domestic animals, and baked the next day's bread. They also cultivated vineyards and in the plowing season may have driven the oxen. However, gender roles were controlled, and heavy work was seen as inappropriate for women. Nobleman saint Gerard of Aurillac (855–909) was scandalized when he saw a woman plowing. She told him her husband was sick and could not work. He scolded her, gave her money, and instructed her to get a male peasant to do the work. He assured her that, as Saint Ambrose of Milan had said, what she was doing was against nature and that "God abhorred that."[14]

The tenth-century diet usually consisted of in-season vegetables, fresh bread, stew, porridge, some fruit, and occasional meat. After animals were slaughtered, usually at the beginning of winter, meat would be salted for preservation. If there were a nearby stream, fish would be available. Because water near human settlement was often polluted by sewerage, experience showed that it was safer to consume alcoholic drinks, so everyone, including small children, tended to drink home-brewed ale (the best was produced by monasteries), mead (an alcoholic drink prepared from fermented honey and water), and a homemade wine produced from wild fruit. Quality wine was a more upper-class pleasure and was more likely to be drunk in France, Italy, and Spain.

Houses were either two-roomed wattle-and-daub structures or wood or stone structures with thatched roofs. Furnishings were basic, and beds consisted of straw mattresses. Small glassless slits let in light and air. A basic kitchen stove heated the common room, and the smoke escaped through a hole in the roof. The result was that clothing was saturated with the smell of wood smoke. In winter domestic animals shared the common room with the family, which at least helped maintain warmth.

ↅ

Childbirth in all premodern societies could be dangerous. It was certainly painful, since there were no effective drugs or painkillers, although women would have had knowledge of plants that helped ease pain. While new children were welcomed, there was always an element of anxiety in the birth process. The rate of infant mortality was probably not as high as modern presuppositions about medieval society suggests, although evidence from Zürich cathedral cemetery shows that 19 percent of children were dead before the age of two and 27 percent before they were 18. Only 54 percent grew to become adults. Childbirth was the province of women; men were excluded, and male doctors were called only when surgery was needed. An experienced midwife supervised the birth; she would often have other women with her whom she was training. Women relatives and friends were also present.

Infanticide was not widespread, even though abortion and infanticide were sometimes used to control fertility, especially if the child could not be supported. The church tried to stop the practice. Infanticide was not considered murder until the child was baptized, but the practice had decreased markedly by the tenth century, although it still happened, as the penitential books showed, often in periods of famine or stress.

Baptism immediately after birth didn't become common in Europe until the eleventh century, although there was a brief form of baptism for babies in danger of death. This was carried out either by the father or the midwife. So it is hard to be precise about baptismal practices in the tenth century, with many infants probably having to wait until the following Easter for baptism. Sacramental historian Joseph Martos says that "beginning in the eleventh century some bishops and councils noted that infants were always in danger of dying unexpectedly and started encouraging parents not to wait for the annual baptism at Easter."[15] Baptism brought the infant into the church, thus placing the child in a community larger than the clan or the kinship group. At baptism children had up to three godparents, who were expected to step in if the parents died, which was a real possibility.

Infantia (infancy) lasted from birth to age seven and *pueritia* (childhood), from eight to fifteen. After that a person was an adult. While they played their role in helping with household tasks, young children were allowed to play and were loved and valued and not treated as "little adults," as historians like Philippe Aries have suggested. C. H. Talbot correctly says that tenth-century people were not ignorant of child psychology and "were quite aware of the differing needs in children as they grew in stature, strength, and intelligence."[16] With the advent of *pueritia*, the child was expected to assume more household responsibility: boys in the fields, girls in the house. Even among peasant families illiteracy was certainly not as widespread as is often thought. Peasant boys could and did go to the parish school and learn basic literacy. Upper-class children went to either a monastery school or a schoolmaster. Discipline was severe, and the rod was applied vigorously.

Everyone, especially peasants, was subject to the vagaries of nature and crop failure. The rural economy was fragile, and people lived with insecure and sometimes inadequate food supplies. It is difficult to be precise as to how much people ate. Evidence from Corbie Abbey, just east of Amiens, indicates that an average family received about 6,000 calories per day and that its daily diet comprised about 4.2 pounds of bread, 10.5 ounces of vegetables, 3.5 ounces of cheese and eggs, and about 2 pints of ale. This seems pretty minimal for a hard-working man, a wife, and two or three children. It may reflect a bad year in which food was short. Probably a typical male peasant in a good season may have had a monotonous but adequate food supply of 6,000 calories per day. Nevertheless, the early medieval food supply was unreliable, often inadequate, and usually nutritionally unbalanced. Kathy L. Pearson says, "The majority of early-medieval people likely suffered some degree of malnutrition resulting from the irregular availability of foods necessary for a balanced diet." She shows that infant death rates were high, that women lived shorter lives than men, and "that overall average life expectancy for either sex rarely exceeded 35–40 years." Even well-fed late-Carolingian royals had a life expectancy "of 36 years for women and 39–40 years for men."[17] However, once someone got beyond forty, that person tended to live until sixty or more.

Things began to improve during the MWP, and there is evidence that in the two hundred years between 850 and 1050 average male European heights

were about 5'7" (1.7 meters), which indicates reasonable nutrition. Archaeological work by the Museum of London shows that "Londoners in the Saxon
period . . . were similar in height to us today."[18] This may be explained by London being a busy port where ample food supplies were available. Height decreased with the advent of the LIA, and the shortest people of the millennium
lived in the eighteenth century. We know for sure that there was a population
increase in Europe as the MWP progressed from about 18 million in 650 to
about 38.5 million in 1000.[19] Probably several causes contributed: with a better climate the food supply was more reliable, people were married earlier and
lived longer, nutrition improved, and more children survived into adulthood.

But that didn't mean that people were completely safe from starvation. In
975 the *Anglo-Saxon Chronicle* records that there was "a great famine and very
many disturbances."[20] But there were also generous people like Geatfleda, a
wealthy woman in Durham. During the 975 famine, a group of people with
their children had sold themselves into slavery in order to survive. Geatfleda
bought them. When the famine passed, she granted them manumission. "Geatfleda has given freedom for the love of God and for the need of her soul:
namely [to] Ecceard the smith and Ælfstan and his wife and all their offspring,
born and unborn, and Arcil and Cole and Ecgferth [and] Ealdhun's daughter
and all those people whose heads she took for their food in the evil days (i.e.,
bought as slaves). . . . And she has also freed the men she begged from Cwaes-
patric."[21] Nine more names follow. Clearly, Geatfleda was a sincere and committed Christian who used her wealth to care for the poor.

The bulk of food was derived from grain. Wheat was used to make better-
quality white bread. However, it was more difficult to cultivate than barley,
rye, and oats. Rye made lower-quality, darker, and denser bread and was a staple food. However, it can be affected by the fungal disease *Claviceps purpurea*,
which can lead to ergotism, a form of bread poisoning that causes burning
pains in the limbs, diarrhea, vomiting, closure of the major arteries leading to
gangrene, psychosis (this is why it was called "holy fire" or "St. Anthony's fire"),
and a painful death. There were outbreaks in the Rhine valley in 857 in which
thousands died and another in 943 around Limoges that killed large numbers.
Barley bread was also eaten by peasants, and barley water (used as a curative for
fever), beer, and ale were derived from the grain. Oats provided animal fodder
and in times of need a coarse food for humans. Millet was also used as animal
food and in soups and porridges.

Legumes were also staples. Beans (garden peas, lentils, chickpeas, broad beans) became more common, especially among monks and peasants. While causing flatulence, they were a source of protein and cattle fodder and they renitrogenated the soil. Pea soup, peas, and bacon were common foods. Umberto Eco argues that beans, peas, and lentils "saved civilization." Because the poor didn't eat much meat, the cultivation of legumes "had a profound effect on Europe. Working people were able to eat more protein; as a result they became more robust, lived longer, created more children and repopulated a continent."[22] The tenth century became the "bean century." What Eco doesn't tell us is that all that protein intake led to an excess of particularly potent farting, which always caused fits of laughter in both high and low society! Vegetables, when available, also formed part of the staple diet. Root vegetables (beets, carrots, turnips, and parsnips), cabbage (for sauerkraut), kohlrabi, lettuce, leeks, chives, parsley, onions, shallots, garlic, cucumbers, celery, fennel, and radishes added to the variety. The most common fruits were apples, pears, plums, peaches, quinces, mulberries, figs, and cherries.

Fresh or cured meat was usually eaten by peasants only on feast days and holidays. It was preserved by salting, smoking, or storing the fat. Where fish were available, they were used as a secondary source of protein. Pigs were an important source of meat and fat. Usually slaughtered at the end of the year, they provided ham, bacon, and lard for the whole year; no part of the animal was wasted. Cows supplied milk to make butter and cheese and meat when slaughtered. Sheep, goats, chickens, rabbits, venison, ducks, and other birds were a subsidiary part of the diet. Eggs, cheese, and honey were staple foods for both upper and lower classes. However, animal sizes and plant yields were smaller than the genetically engineered and hybrid crops of today. "Chickens were generally smaller and produced smaller and fewer eggs. . . . Domestic livestock was overall 40–60% smaller than today's breeds."[23] Milking yields were also lower.

Although physical activity and strength were valued, people usually showed the effects of being out in the open at the mercy of the elements for most of their lives, working, hunting, and fighting. Across all classes the majority were weather-beaten and red-faced, with a leathery texture to their skin. This was why a soft, pale complexion and slender limbs were valued as beautiful and attractive in both men and women.

Perhaps if there is one word that sums up the peasant experience, it is "insecurity." Some of the people we know from Abbot Irminon's *Estate Book*, people like Bodo and Arctardus's sons and daughters, would have faced a succession of Viking invasions of the Paris region, and they and their children may well have been killed by the invaders. At the very least their farms would have been asset-stripped or destroyed. People from across the social spectrum, but especially those at the bottom of the pecking order, constantly faced the danger of having their homes destroyed, their crops stolen, and themselves robbed, raped, killed, or injured in a raid by some marauding thug from nearby or by Vikings, Magyars, or armies living off the land. This was the direct result of the breakdown of effective central authority. Perhaps the one advantage that tenth-century people had over us was life happened more slowly and they had time to prepare themselves or get out of the way. For whatever the threat, it could come only with the speed of the fastest horse.

By the tenth century 90 percent of people lived in rural settings and the old Roman cities had been either abandoned or become shadows of their former selves. Rome is a good illustration. As we saw, the population declined from close to 1 million in the first century to around 35,000 in 900. Nevertheless, Italy was one of the few regions where towns had to some extent survived. The urban tradition was much stronger there. Walled towns had a much better chance of protecting their citizens, and people living in an urban setting were much less likely to suffer from either strongmen, Vikings, or Magyars, although this didn't always work, as the Magyar siege and burning of Pavia in 924 showed. But the vast majority of the European population didn't enjoy this kind of security. They lived in the undefended rural landscape.

Another source of violence was the *lex talionis*, the duty of revenge, which became particularly widespread as central government collapsed. These blood feuds were very personal, could extend over several generations, and often created a kind of low-level warfare between clans and feudal lords. Where it existed, justice was often rough and ready and retribution, swift, bloodthirsty, and final. Emotions and feelings were often violently expressed and much more extreme than we experience today. Personal self-control was in short supply. People said what they felt and acted accordingly, often with what we would consider appalling brutality. For instance, gouging out of eyes, cutting out of tongues, cutting off of people's hands, and whipping were relatively common punishments. There were notable exceptions to this violence. The Saxon monarchy, for instance, was noted for its clemency and reconciliation with malefactors, even with those who had been disloyal to the royal house. They also built cooperative alliances and *amicitia*, friendship bonds, with rivals and even enemies. Henry the Fowler was a past master at these kinds of bonds, and as Gerd Althoff says, they "seem to have been fundamental to the consolidation of [his] rule."[24]

We usually suppose that early medieval society was hierarchical and that subordinate people had no choice but to obey those above them. But there was more flexibility than at first appears. We have seen that the Saxon kings spent a lot of time making sure that their subordinate magnates were kept loyal. This was not just confined to the Ottonians, but also extended right across society. According to Althoff, this was "a 'state' made up of groups of people rather than institutions."[25]

An interesting and, to us unusual, phenomenon was the personal, cooperative pacts (*compaternitas*) people made between each other. These were not strictly friendships in our sense, but often did involve social get-togethers for hunting and feasts. Sometimes they were based on familial or spiritual kinship, such as being a godparent at baptism. In fact, "bonds of kinship, friendship and co-operation often proved far more powerful than the [hierarchical] bond."[26] Althoff argues that early medieval society was not so much a state in the modern sense with an overarching system of government as a complex association of kin groups held together by an equally complex system of commitments that individuals and groups of people made to each other. In this kind of society the oral was as important as the written in the sense that people were only as good as their word.

Ritual actions had a significant place in tenth-century life. This is particularly hard for us to comprehend given that our egalitarian public life largely lacks any real sense of ritual. Early medieval politics was not government by abstract principle and transparent procedures but by behind-the-scenes, face-to-face negotiation and personal commitment. These agreements were then acted in public assemblies with maximum solemnity to let the plebs know what their betters had decided. We have already seen an example of this in the elaborate ceremony of submission enacted by Henry the Wrangler when he returned the kidnapped child Otto III to his mother and grandmother. This kind of government was inherently unstable because not everyone was trustworthy, so it made sense to build as many political alliances as possible.

രൗ

The upper classes are far easier to comprehend than the peasants, given that their lives were more frequently discussed in contemporary writings. Yet we do not know for sure how someone became a noble. This is a complex problem, and the answer must combine two viewpoints.

The "older" view, eloquently defended by Bloch, was that nobles were mainly "new" men, soldiers of fortune who seized the opportunity to better themselves and make the most of their opportunities. The "modern" view holds that they were the descendants of noble officials from the Carolingian period. Some of them, particularly in West Francia, began as counts. The count was the emperor's man at the county level. His obligations were legal, military, and financial. The count presided over the county judicial assembly, the *mallus*, which dealt with serious crime and major issues. *Placita generalis*, or local courts, were presided over by viscounts, who dealt with the bulk of ordinary crime and other business. Viscounts were lower-grade officials roughly equivalent in rank to bailiffs. Many "noblemen" also originated as viscounts.

The count defended the county from external attack, relying on support from his troops, other local lords, representatives from church lands, and the obligation of all freemen to bear arms in a crisis. The count also acted as collector of royal dues, including taxes from freemen not doing military service, court fines, and tolls on rivers, bridges, and highways. In times of danger he could levy an undefined tax for protection of the local region. "All these dues were in essence *regalia*—that is to say the count took them as the king's representative; but his own share of them grew steadily. . . . [He] must have been seen by those he governed as primarily a tax-collector; in the tenth century that often was his chief pre-occupation."[27]

Because counts were entrusted with real power, the opportunity for independence was great. They were chosen with care and under Charlemagne kept well under control. They were subject to the visitations of *missi dominici*, royal envoys or inspectors-general, whose function was to check on them and the performance of their duties. But by the death of Charles the Fat in 888, the whole system of central government had collapsed. Counts became increasingly independent because they had their own troops. Naturally, they handed on power to their sons, thus setting up hereditary succession.

A similar disintegration threatened in East Francia after the premature death of Emperor Arnulf (896–899) and the ascension of Louis the Child (900–911).

Archbishop Hatto of Mainz, as regent, was able to resist some of the centrifugal tendencies of the magnates. The big advantage East Francia had was that there were only a small number of dominant kin groups. These ruled what are sometimes called "stem duchies." Originally tribal units, they were Saxony, Bavaria, Franconia, and Swabia; sometimes Lotharingia, Carinthia, and Thuringia are added. Franconia and Swabia had two kin groups who fought each other until the duchy was dominated by the victorious clan. The genius of Henry the Fowler after his election as German king was that he was able to manage the magnates and preserve the unity of Germany.

But the magnates of East and West Francia were not the only opportunists. There were also the freebooters who were particularly active in Italy. Alberico I of Spoleto, Marozia's first husband, for instance, was originally an ambitious Frankish upstart. He first appears in the records as a page to Duke Guido III of Spoleto. He then seems to have become margrave of Camerino, and after he murdered Guido IV, he became duke of Spoleto. Alberico is typical of this class of men: they took the main chance and simply seized power. Robert the Strong, the forefather of the Capetian dynasty, is another example. Richer of Saint-Rémi says Robert was *ex equestri ordine*, "from the equestrian order," in other words an ordinary knight.[28] "He obtained his power," according to Constance Bouchard, "while fighting the barbarians for Charles the Bald, and his ancestry is a virtual blank in spite of many ingenious attempts . . . to discover his origins."[29] The reign of Charles the Bald was the key period when many of these transitions occurred.

We can see this kind of social climbing in the counts of Anjou, who were centered on the town of Angers near the confluence of the Loire and the Maine. Originally controlled by Robert the Strong, Angers eventually passed into the hands of a man named Ingelgarius, variously described as *habitator rusticanus* (a rustic hick), *cliens* of Charles the Bald (meaning someone socially inferior), and *miles optimus* (a most able soldier). He was probably all of these: a backwoodsman whom Charles raised above his station to become a soldier. Like many of these "new men," he married into an established family, to a niece of the archbishop of Tours and the bishop of Angers. He eventually became count of Anjou—some said because of his defense of the region against the Vikings, but more likely because of his wife's good connections. Dying in 898, he was succeeded by his son Fulk I "the Red" (898–941), who extended the county, fought the Vikings and the Bretons, and managed to arrange an upwardly mobile marriage. Fulk II "the Good" (941–958) was more of a scholar, but his son Geoffrey I "Greymantle" (958–987) consolidated the county and married Adele of Meaux, daughter of Robert of Vermandois, a direct descendant of Charlemagne. Thus, within four generations a family originating with a *habitator rusticanus* had managed to become counts of one of the most cohesive regions of medieval France, which eventually formed the nucleus of the Angevin empire that included England.

A new form of political arrangement was emerging as royal authority eroded and central government broke down. Over several generations real power in local regions devolved into the hands of territorial magnates and their clan groups. The collapse of central government seems to us to be a symptom of political decline, but for the people of the time it was more a change in political structure whereby power devolved from the center to local opportunists, many of whom were freebooters. As Bloch says, "The most striking feature of the history of the dominant families in . . . [the tenth century] is the shortness of their pedigrees."[30] This later led to many new noblemen arranging for an ancestry to be constructed, sometimes taking them all the way back to ancient Rome or even Troy.

So, for instance, where did someone like Fulk the Red live and how? He lived with an extended family in a well-defended manor house or motte; stone castles came in the early eleventh century. The house was essentially a wooden tower built on either a low hill or a high earth mound. In England the wooden tower was called a "motte," which could be 30 to 80 feet (9 to 25 meters) high, often surrounded by a wooden palisade. The motte was surrounded by an area of 1 to 3 acres (0.4 to 1.2 hectares) called a "bailey." Sometimes there were two or three baileys attached to the same motte. The bailey contained stables, other buildings, and open land for animals. It was surrounded by a moat about 10 feet (3 meters) deep and 30 feet (9 meters) across filled with water. On the inner side of the moat were a wooden palisade and a well-defended gate with a drawbridge. These defensive structures were basic, but they worked for several centuries until more sophisticated siege engines appeared in the twelfth century. Certainly, wooden structures were prone to fires, but besieging forces had to get close enough to set the heavy logs on fire. Stone castles first appeared in West Francia at the end of the tenth century, but motte and bailey structures were easy and quick to build. Usually each had a village attached with a couple of hundred inhabitants.

For someone like Fulk, the blood ties that created clan and family were central to being "noble." He lived in the motte with his wife, Roscille de Loches, and their immediate family. But there would have also been a large kinship group, or *familia* (what the Germans call *sippes*, or extended families) living in the bailey, including uncles, aunts, cousins, and a bevy of camp followers, poor relatives, and sundry hangers-on, who might or might not have a useful task but who expected to be fed well and treated generously. The priority was defending the land owned by the lord's family rather than personal property. Often the wife and her relatives brought more to this arrangement in terms of ancestry, wealth, land, and social position than the lord himself. This was especially so if she were of royal blood because such proximity to the king brought higher status. As the century progressed, many aristocrats began to recruit boys from the *familia* as professional, mainly mounted soldiers, who were later dubbed knights. Something similar happened in Germany, but here the groups from which the military were drawn were wider and included men of servile origin.

We saw earlier that peasant dress was basic and unadorned. Upper-class men were beginning to wear more "fitted" clothes, while women tended to wear looser and more voluminous clothing. Men were normally bareheaded; women, veiled. Noblemen wore a long-sleeved, knee-length tunic belted at the waist with a long cape, trousers, and high boots. Clothing was brightly colored. Noblewomen wore a floor-length underdress with an overgown with extremely wide sleeves. The outer tunic was often embroidered in a Byzantine style.

Given the primitive state of medicine at the time, the number of children born with serious health problems or defects or who developed them in their early years must have been very high. However, they were not abandoned. The extraordinary life of Hermann the Cripple demonstrates this. Born in July 1013 the son of Count Wolferat of Altshausen 30 miles (50 kilometers) north of Lake Constance, Hermann suffered from some form of spastic paralysis from infancy, making it difficult for him to move and speak. In 1020 he was taken to the monastic school at Reichenau, where he eventually became a monk. He turned out to be a genius in mathematics, astronomy, and music. He was one of the key figures, along with Gerbert of Aurillac, in introducing and spreading Arabic astronomical techniques into the Latin West, including the astrolabe, chilinder (a portable sundial to calculate altitude), quadrant, and abacus; he wrote treatises on these instruments. He was also a musical theorist who wrote a great hymn to the Blessed Virgin still sung today, *Alma redemptoris mater*, "Gracious Mother of the Redeemer." Hermann died in 1054.

ℰℛ

Although most tenth-century people's lives focused on the local and power was widely distributed with the breakdown of central government, the Roman imperial ideal of the *res publica*, the state, was not forgotten. Nor was the concept of order enshrined in Roman law and the vague but pervasive recollection that Europe had once been an empire spanning the known world. Thus, Rome was the mythical golden age to which people looked as a model of culture and civil order. Add to that a shared Catholic faith, and a powerful cohesive force held this society together. The idea of Charlemagne's Holy Roman Empire also persisted. In the ninth century there were many pretenders to the imperial crown, but it was not until Otto I that any were able to attain sufficient authority to restore an ordered state. In this fractious society, it took the cohesive force provided by the church to bind society together, as we shall see.

CHAPTER 15

Faith and Church in the Tenth Century

R ELIGION WAS CENTRAL to the tenth century. The entire population of Western Europe was Catholic. It was widely believed by both
clergy and rulers that pagans should be converted as soon as possible so that
they could share in the possibility of forgiveness of original sin and salvation
through baptism. To enter this religious sensibility, we have to infiltrate a world
that is very different from our own. Unlike our privatized religion today, tenth-
century faith was very public.

For us the natural world is ordered, self-sustaining, and explained by science; for them it was chaotic. For us God is detached from the world; for them
God constantly intervened as the proximate cause of all that happened. This
turned nature, social life, and ordinary interactions into a kind of incessant
"theophany," or manifestation of God. People felt that their lives were manipulated by irresistible forces, both good and malign, that needed to be propiti-
ated. People were terrified of the dark, of thunderstorms and lightning, of
eclipses of the moon or sun.

The monk Rodulfus Glaber says that in 989 a comet appeared that lit up
the sky, most probably Halley's Comet. "Whether this was a new star sent by
God," wonders Glaber, "or whether it was an existing star whose light He had
increased as an omen is known only to Him whose ineffable wisdom arranges
all things." Nevertheless, it "clearly portends some wondrous and awe-inspiring
event in the world shortly after." When the monastery and pilgrimage center
of Mont-Saint-Michel was burned down three years later, Glaber had his

"awe-inspiring event."[1] Burchard of Worms comments that fear of the dark was endemic: "If it is necessary to go out before first light many won't risk it, saying that they will put it off, and that before the cock crows it is not permitted to go out and that evil spirits have more power to harm people before dawn than afterwards."[2] Nevertheless, people were keen astronomical observers. The *Anglo-Saxon Chronicle*, for instance, records eleven observations of comets between 679 and 1114, as well as thirty-five eclipses of the sun or the moon, shooting stars, and appearances of aurora borealis.

Reality was seen as two-layered; everyone lived in dual worlds, both physical and spiritual. The physical world was experienced directly by the senses, but it drew its context and meaning from the much more extensive spiritual world. There was an intimate interaction between the two so that God, angels, the Blessed Virgin, and the saints, as well as Satan and the demons, intermingled intimately with everyday life. Heaven and hell were realities that impinged on life now, and the borders between the terrestrial and nonnatural worlds were permeable. Prayer and ritual were largely directed toward persuading powerful persons (God and Jesus to some extent, but especially the Blessed Virgin and the saints) who inhabited the spiritual realm to intervene directly in the physical world on behalf of petitioners and protect them from the forces of evil. Thus, people often interpreted anything unusual as miraculous or demonic.

Another set of permeable borders was that between the pagan Germanic world and Christian belief. For ordinary priests and rural people these realities inextricably interpenetrated. Existing parallel with the official ministry of the church was a vast world of what today we would call "popular religion," a realm of miracle-working saints, relics, angels, devils, charms, spells, and magic, a vast amalgam of Christianity and survivals from the still-lively remnant paganism of the peasants. The borders between life and death were also permeable. Danish king Cnut (1016–1035) of England, for instance, scoffed at the idea that Saint Edith, the bastard daughter of King Edgar (957–973) and the nun Wulfhilda, could possibly be a saint. The story goes that when he broke open Edith's tomb at Wilton, the corpse rose to a sitting position and slapped Cnut across the face. The king, a tough, experienced soldier, collapsed in terror and from then on exhibited great veneration for Saint Edith.

This is not to say that people completely discounted the natural causes of events. Indeed, there is evidence that people of this era appreciated the beauty of nature. However, they felt that nonnatural forces were also enormously important in manipulating nature—particularly the weather, crop success and failure, and health and illness. Subjected to the forces of nature in all its seemingly malign indifference, people were very aware of the difficulty and sheer hard work required to produce the basic necessities of life. This meant they had no romantic notions about the natural world. They needed all the supernatural help they could get to make the land and the animals productive so that they would not starve.

The Christian understanding of reality was accepted as basic, and notions of religious pluralism were inconceivable. Individuality in the modern sense of holding a personal, subjective view of belief was uncommon. Correctness in form and appearance was much more important than the kind of inner integrity we claim to value so much. Because Christianity explained all reality, and everyone was baptized and socialized into it, failure to accept it, at least externally, opened a person up to the possibility of both secular and ecclesiastical sanctions. The ultimate sanction was excommunication, which resulted in the loss of civil rights as well as exclusion from communion with the Catholic community. This carried over into the next life, and it was believed that excommunication meant banishment from heaven after death.

Religious mania and deviance were unusual, but as we will see in the final chapter, they were not unknown and much of such behavior was associated with the coming of the millennium. There were certainly strong personalities, both men and women, lay and clerical. So while unbelief was the ultimate form of social deviance, little was done about this as long as people kept their views to themselves. As we've seen, individuals like Gottschalk (ca. 804–869) showed unusual independence of mind, but the instinct to conform remained strong. Perhaps the key difference between our view of religion and theirs is that we see faith as an interior, spiritual commitment that demands specific standards of moral behavior, while for people living in the tenth century faith was external; it was about carrying out the right rituals, behaving in ways that society demanded. It was about conformity rather than commitment. Fear played an important role. Death and fear of damnation were embedded in people's psyches, which, in turn, led to pessimism about salvation. At the popular level this bred, as Jonathan Sumption says, "a fatalism in which the resort to rituals with the object of expiating sin becomes somewhat easier to understand."[3]

Two of the most important rituals were pilgrimages to sacred places and veneration of relics. While many people were firmly rooted in their places of birth, and their village and surrounding forests were the firm borders of their world, many also were great travelers because, in part, their hold on their land was actually quite tenuous. Jacques Le Goff says they "emigrated easily, because they barely had a homeland to leave." Property in our sense "was almost unknown"; everyone held land in trust from someone else.[4] But the major motivation for travel was faith.

Catholicism emphasized that life was a perpetual pilgrimage. As Jesus says, "There is no one who has left [all] . . . for my sake and the sake of the gospel who will not receive a hundredfold" (Mark 10:29). As followers of Jesus, "who had nowhere to lay his head," the early Irish monks left clan and homeland for exile, wandering across land and sea motivated by a driving desire to find God in the wilderness. They were driven "by a kind of restless energy and a spirit of penance . . . to seek God through the difficult life of a recluse or the lonely life of being a stranger in a foreign land . . . where you were utterly vulnerable and therefore dependent upon and open to God."[5] People went on pilgrimage for other reasons as well: to do penance, either self-imposed or as expiation for sin; to obtain a miraculous cure through the intercession of a saint at his or her shrine or out of devotion to a particular saint; to honor private vows that people had taken; to gain indulgences; or simply to satisfy curiosity about the world. Rome and Jerusalem were the ultimate destinations, and a reasonably safe overland route to Palestine opened up at the end of the tenth century. In Europe there were literally hundreds of pilgrimage places. Santiago de Compostela really took off near the end of the century with the decline of the caliphate, the death of Almanzor in 1002, and the long reign of Sancho the Great (970–1030) of Navarre. Hospices were built along the *Camino de Santiago*, with routes beginning at Paris, Vézelay, Le Puy, and Trier.

Needless to say, there was considerable competition among different sites. The opportunistic monks of Sainte-Foy (Saint Faith) at Conques in the hills of south-central France found themselves off the route to Santiago from Le Puy, which went through the old Roman town of Agen. Agen's abbey possessed a relic of third-century virgin-martyr Foy, who was killed as a Christian during persecution by Diocletian. Anxious to divert the pilgrimage traffic to their abbey, at the end of the ninth century the Conques monks hatched a plot and stole the relics. These they placed inside a golden reliquary, which was carried with clashing cymbals around the monastery lands whenever invaders threatened. Just as they hoped, the pilgrimage traffic (with the concomitant economic spin-offs) shifted from Agen to Conques.

Pilgrims were expected to be generous, and at Conques they were not backward in coming forward! "Come to my shrine at Conques and give me your gold bracelets," Sainte-Foy is said to have told the wife of Guillaume Taillefer, Count of Toulouse.[6] In another story a woman who refused to surrender her gold ring suffered fevers and nightmares as a result. Vézelay was another stopping place on the Santiago pilgrimage. A monastery was built there in 860, and soon afterwards the monks obtained the supposed relics of Jesus's friend Saint Mary Magdalene.

Many pilgrims expected that their saint would be surrounded by appropriate magnificence. They hoped to see a spectacular reliquary and impressive buildings. Sumption mentions a mid-ninth-century woman who was disappointed when she arrived at Prüm Abbey, which had just got some new relics: "A certain woman arrived [at Prüm] with a wagon full of food and drink and precious things which she proposed to offer to God and to the holy martyrs. But, seeing that the saints' tomb did not glitter with gold and silver, she uttered a contemptuous guffaw, as is the wont of foolish and ignorant minds. Then rushing back home, she bade her friends retrace their steps saying 'you won't find anything holy in that place.'"[7]

Those on long pilgrimages usually traveled light, since the roads generally were in poor condition. To a limited extent the old Roman roads still served, but they were not maintained and in some places had been torn up or used as quarries for other roads. Travelers were often forced to use narrow roads, often through dangerous wilderness areas and across mountain ranges such as the Alps. Bridges were few and far between, and even small rivers would be impossible to cross during floods. Usually travelers had to wade across at a ford, which might be in quite deep water. The best they could hope for were ropes stretching from bank to bank. The legend of Saint Christopher, which first became popular in Europe in the ninth century, probably originates in the idea of a strong man who carried pilgrims on his shoulders at a difficult river crossing.

Pilgrimage routes encouraged basic forms of road building. Diana Webb comments that "Shrines and roads existed in a complex symbiosis."[8] Roads ran along lower mountains to avoid river valleys, which were often waterlogged and malarial. Staging posts with food, water, and accommodation began to develop, normally at a day's journey distance from each other. An experienced merchant or traveler might be able to cover between 16 and 38 miles (25 and 60 kilometers) each day depending on conditions. Pilgrims would have been slower. Travel by sea was usually much faster but also more dangerous.

Closely associated with pilgrimage was the cult of relics, the devotion to the bodies of saints or to objects that had been in contact with them. Psychologically, cults arose from the natural instinct to respect the bodies of the dead. This began with the relics of Christians who were martyrs in the Roman persecutions. After the conversion of the Germanic people, there was increasing demand for martyrs' relics. This led to dismembering of bodies in the catacombs, even though this was contrary to Roman civil law. Always opportunists, the Romans began a trade in true and false relics, despite ecclesiastical legislation governing their sale and exchange. Many false relics, such as animal bones, were sold to naïve northerners. Rodulfus Glaber describes how one conman who used many aliases dug up graves, put the bones into coffers, "and sold them widely as the relics of holy confessors and martyrs." One of his most successful cons was when the supposed relics of Saint Justus were enclosed in the altar stone of the Abbey of S. Giusto in the Val di Susa below the Mont-Cénis Pass, an area that had been devastated by the Saracens. Glaber, who was present at the altar's consecration, claims he and "many men of sound judgment" were a wake-up to the trickster, but "the mass of the rustic population, corrupted by the pedlar . . . persisted for a long time in their error."[9]

Another extraordinary story concerns the relics of Saint Guinefort from the village of Sandrans, north of Lyons. Though a saint, Guinefort was not a person but a heroic pet greyhound! One day when his owner was absent, a large serpent approached the cradle of the owner's child. Guinefort attacked and killed the snake but was badly hurt himself. The child crawled away into another room. When the parents returned, they found both cradle and dog covered in blood. Assuming Guinefort had attacked the baby, they killed him but later found the baby safe and the snake torn to pieces. Local peasant women began to "visit the place and honor the dog as a martyr in quest of help for their sicknesses and other needs," particularly for the greyhound to cure sick babies.[10]

Underlying the cult of relics was the idea that contact with the relic released the power of God through the intercession of the saintly person. This was why relics were thought to work miracles or drive out demons. They became important on the basis of three theological emphases: first, the pervasive sense of sin and fear of damnation that dominated medieval religious psychology; second, a shift away from an emphasis on God's mercy toward a notion that focused on God's otherness and harsh judgment; and third, an overemphasis on the divinity of Christ and his distance from ordinary life. With a dominant notion of God/Christ as judge, people felt the need for intercessors, and so the cults of the Blessed Virgin and the saints came to the fore. People saw the saints as influential people in the heavenly court who could intercede with God on behalf of the petitioner. The saint was seen not as someone long dead but as a powerful personage who could make the link between heaven and earth and focus God's mercy and power on the petitioner's need.

Relics were so important to churches and monasteries that during Viking raids clerics and monks would take their relics with them when they fled. Daniel C. De Şelm says that "in addition to being material objects of devotion, [relics] provided a stable source of 'spiritual capital.' . . . Such capital could be leveraged by monks and clerics seeking to recoup losses sustained during Viking raids."[11] In a way the term "spiritual capital" sums up nicely how relics worked for those who owned them. They were usable commodities that put people in touch with the saint involved who in turn sought divine intervention in the life of the petitioners. The more saints people had on their side, the more spiritual capital they had to focus on their needs.

જી

If relics were important to tenth-century spirituality, clergy were even more so. They stood at the intermediary point between earthly reality and the sacred, between the everyday and the sacraments, which gave people access to the divine. The lowly and often ignorant local priest was thus regarded as the most important man in his village because he stood at the threshold of the spiritual. Nevertheless, his living standards would have been only slightly higher than those of the peasants to whom he ministered. He would have had little or no professional training. Few would have experienced a "vocation" in the modern sense. Some would have been ordained as the sons or nephews of priests, some appointed by the local magnate, and some dedicated to the service of the church by their parents. Most were poor men looking to better their social status and that of their family. Bishop Atto of Vercelli from 924–961 commented that men often came *nudi ad Ecclesiam*—that is, they came to the church with nothing in order to improve their lot through the priesthood.[12] In his *Capitulare* (Edict) Atto demands that priests be familiar with the sacred scriptures and church law and at least know the Apostles Creed and Nicene Creed by heart. They should be able to celebrate Mass and the sacraments in Latin, to bury parishioners freely, and to give them instruction in reading and writing. They were not to engage in business, lease property, or take interest on a loan.[13] In the Frankish lands priests were instructed to wear a stole around their neck as a symbol of office, especially when on a journey, somewhat like a dog collar today.

Interestingly, Atto was also convinced that there were ordained women priests and deacons in the early church. A priest named Ambrose had asked him why the ancient church canons used the words presbyter (*presbyterae*) and deacon (*diaconae*) in the feminine gender. Atto answered unequivocally that the words didn't refer to male priests and deacons' wives, but to the women who in the ancient church "were called *presbyterae* [women priests] who undertook the duty of preaching, ordering and instructing, just as deaconesses had assumed the duty of ministering and baptizing."[14] It was perhaps a logical position for someone opposed to clerical marriage, as Atto was.

Like Atto, Bishop Ratherius of Verona, whose own clerical career was rather checkered, took a dim view of the morals of his clergy. Addressing them at a synod during Lent 966, he complained that there are priests "who daily celebrate the Mass . . . [but who] frequently beget sons and daughters by adulterous intercourse"; others "belch yesterday's drunkenness and excess before the Lord's altar." Still others "are busy with continual law suits, who burn with greed, who waste away in hate and envy" or commit frauds.[15] Ratherius specifically attacked a priest named John, who "affianced [promised] his son [also a priest] to a girl [daughter of another priest] during Lent and . . . had them married on the Lord's night," that is, Easter Saturday, thus committing "double illegality": violation of the Lenten fast with the betrothal feast and supplanting of the celebration of Christ's resurrection with a clerical marriage. Ratherius claimed that "everyone knows . . . a priest or a deacon cannot have a lawful wife." So if the son "born from that . . . adultery the father makes a priest, and he likewise makes the son born to him a priest," then clerical adultery becomes endemic and the priestly office is passed on from father to son. It would be better, Ratherius says, for "your offspring to be laymen, and to marry your daughters to laymen, so that with your decease the adultery will be terminated."[16] Nevertheless, Ratherius reluctantly admits that "if I were to expel from the clergy those with many wives, whom would I leave in the church except boys?"[17]

Atto of Vercelli also complains that "the incontinent are many" and that some clergy "given over to lust allow obscene prostitutes to live in their houses, eat with them and are seen in public together."[18] Reformers like Atto and Ratherius constantly referred to priests' wives as "concubines," "prostitutes," or "adulteresses," claiming that priests could not enter a canonically lawful marriage and therefore the women living with them were really mistresses. Atto was a clerical misogynist who saw marriage as a distraction from seeking God: "It is good to live without women," he claims.[19]

By the end of the tenth century pressures were building to impose celibacy on all clergy. Three factors were especially important in the attempts to do so. The first was fear of the alienation of church property, a fear clearly illustrated by the Theophylacts and Alberico, who treated ecclesiastical property as their own. The second was something alien to us: a ritual taboo, originating in pagan custom and the Bible, against sexual pollution. The menses were seen as infected with demonic magic, and there was great fear of a priest celebrating Mass after intercourse with his menstruating wife. The third source was connected to the then-dominant Eucharistic theology: just as Christ had been born of a virgin, so the Eucharistic Christ should be born on the altars of chaste, uncontaminated, celibate priests.

Despite legislation by councils and synods demanding celibacy and denunciation by reforming bishops, clerical marriage was a fact of life. It was intimately linked to the *ecclesia propria*, the "personal church" owned by a local lay magnate, by a monastery like Saint-Germain-des-Prés, or by a priest himself. To understand this notion of *ecclesia propria*, we must realize that the structure of the tenth-century church was very different from that of today. The primary focus of the church then was the local priest. The bishop lived in town, and the pope was in faraway Rome, which had about as much reality to people then as Timbuktu does today. Most people wouldn't even have known the pope's name. Today all church property, including parishes, is owned by the diocese and administered by the bishop. (The exception is property owned by religious orders.) Then most church property, including parishes, was owned by laymen. This form of ownership is usually referred to as the "proprietary church," although this is a misleading term because we shouldn't think of it in modern terms of absolute ownership. Susan Wood defines the proprietary church as "a church that was some person or group's 'own' . . . a possession comprising not only the church building with its contents, but its land, buildings and stock, its tithes, dues and offerings, and the appointment of its priest."[20] However, there was much variation in methods of ownership and how people thought of things as "their" property.

Lay proprietorship of the church was a product of the shift from the predominantly urban world of the late Roman Empire, when most towns had a bishop and small group of presbyters (priests), to the Germanic rural world. In Roman law ecclesiastical property was held in the name of the bishop. After the fall of the Western Roman Empire, cities became rundown and the church began a several-centuries-long process of converting the Germanic tribes. By the middle of the sixth century, there were rural parishes throughout Europe, spreading initially from southern to northern Gaul and then to England and Germany. By the seventh century, local magnates were building churches on their own lands and employing priests, often a man from the village. From the death of Dagobert I in 639, the last effective Merovingian king, a wholesale secularization of church land began as powerful laity seized church possessions. The Germanic peoples conceived of society as arising from below rather than being controlled from above, so they found the traditional centralized diocesan structure foreign. Also, they were unable to comprehend the church as a public entity and to distinguish between the *ius publicum* and the *ius privatum*, ownership in public law and private ownership. So they simply treated the church as private property. There was no coherently organized parish "system" like today. The whole arrangement was ad hoc and piecemeal.

There was resistance to lay ownership by bishops, especially in Italy and Spain. Charlemagne and his successors tried to regulate church proprietors by stipulating that, while the land and building belonged to the landowner, the local priest was immediately subject to the bishop who supervised his training. The other thing bishops controlled was the priest's ordination. But the landowner employed, accommodated, and paid the priest. He was usually obliged to provide rent-free use of one hide of glebe (about 60 acres) and a garden. This is the origin of what is called a "benefice," a payment for the discharge of worship services.

The proprietor was like a franchisee of the church. He owned a lucrative asset that included the land on which the church stood, the church building, the priest's house, tithes (a one-tenth tax on agricultural production), stole fees and people's gifts, and the cemetery. These property rights could be sold, loaned, donated, mortgaged, exchanged, inherited, or split among several people. However, this arrangement was not a clear-cut, legally binding "system" that obtained right across Europe. Wood's massive study, *The Proprietary Church in the Early Medieval West*, shows that there was really no system and that the way proprietors understood their ownership was diverse, complex, and ambiguous. It was made even more confused by inheritance practices. Recent research in the rich archival stock of early medieval wills, charters, land deeds, and contracts shows a plethora of different arrangements. There is no consistency in the documentation on land and ownership arrangements, which were flexible and governed by customary law.

Priests too could be proprietors. Sometimes a priest built the church himself or inherited it, usually from a relative. According to Wood, often a priest simply took "his father's or uncle's place. Or he may have acquired the church by gift or purchase." The priest could nominate his successor (confusingly this was referred to in Medieval Latin as *ordinatio*) "or otherwise dispose of the church to a chosen heir; or . . . expect to be succeeded by a natural heir (a son or nephew)." Priests could own more than one church or have various sorts of interests in several churches, "perhaps as the sole priest in a group of kinsmen, or as one of a small consortium of priests."[21]

There are many examples of these practices. For instance, at Beaulieu-sur-Dordogne in 868 the priest, Adelbert, reported that his church with everything attached to it came to him from his grandfather Stardigius, who left it "to my father Ragamfred and my father to my brother the priest Landric, and Landric to me by the same *carta testamenti* [letter of testament or will]." Some priests bought, sold, or gave away churches, almost like land speculators today. Wood describes a deacon and priest in 958 giving "two-thirds of a church and its lands and cemetery" to the town of Béziers in Languedoc. In another case in 971 three priests "gave an alod [an estate held in absolute ownership] to Lézat [a village in the French Alps] including a church and its books, vestments, vessels, lands, vineyards and meadows for the souls of their kinsmen (two priests). . . . These same three priests bought a church from two lay couples."[22] While church property could not be alienated or used for another function, the whole business obviously left itself open to widespread abuse.

Because this approach was deeply embedded in the culture, it seemed natural that the church would be owned by the local lord and the priest would be one of his men. The overall result of lay ownership was that both the priest and the community were more attached to the local lord or magnate than to the bishop and diocese. It also enhanced the role of the priest at the expense of the bishop. Even more important was the lack of distinction between priests and laity. Ordination didn't create the clerical caste of today's Catholicism. Priests then shared the lives of their parishioners. Although priestly celibacy was the rule, it was much more honored in the breech than the observance, especially in rural areas. Few serious attempts were made to enforce celibacy until the eleventh century, and rural priests lived happily with their wives, or "concubines" as radical reformers called them. Essentially, priests were family men, just like the peasants.

We get a good idea of priests' actual lives and duties from guides for episcopal visitations of parishes. One example is Regino of Prüm's *Notebook of Ecclesiastical Discipline*, which sets out what an ideal priest is like; no doubt few actually measured up to Regino's high expectations.[23] The first set of questions in the *Notebook* concern church buildings and fittings. The bishop is to make sure the church is consecrated and to inspect the church structure, checking that the roof is intact and that birds, particularly pigeons, can't get in to nest, spreading bird shit and disturbing worship. The church must not be used as a granary. He should also check the quality and cleanliness of the altar cloths, chalice, and paten. He must make sure that the church's relics are secure and that either in the sacristy or beside the altar there is flowing water for the celebrants to wash their hands before and after the Eucharist. There must be a pyx containing preconsecrated communion hosts kept on the altar for viaticum (communion) for the dying. The church must also have a missal, lectionary, and antiphony. The bishop should check what other books are held in the church as well as the number and quality of priestly vestments, the lighting of the church, and the number of wax candles in stock. The atrium of the church was to be enclosed so that nothing *immuditia* (foul or lustful) could happen there.

The reference to vestments here is interesting because it was in the ninth and tenth centuries that Mass vestments took on their final form. Up until then they had been just a plain form of late Roman male dress. But at this period they began to become more ornate and elaborately decorated, and they increasingly symbolized the separation of clergy from laity. It was also this period that produced the bishop's miter, the strange triangular, shield-shaped hat that bishops still wear today at liturgical ceremonies. Its origin remains obscure.

Regino says that the bishop should then check on the private life of the priest. Does he have a woman living in the house? Is there a *mulier subintroducta*, a woman brought into the priest's house secretly? While there was much talk about celibacy, church authorities usually ignored married priests, and we know that many bishops were married, including several first-millennium popes such as Saint Peter himself. The last married pope was Hadrian II (867–872). More important were the priest's pastoral duties. Regino asks, does he visit the sick, reconcile and anoint them, and bring them communion personally? Does he emphasize the need for infant baptism, reconciliation of the sick, and burial of the dead? Does he say Mass in private homes—which was forbidden? Does he drink in taverns, or is he a drunkard? Is he litigious, addicted to hunting dogs or falcons, or seditious? There are then questions concerning the celebration of the Mass, with an emphasis on proclaiming the Word of God to the people in the vernacular.

Certainly, priests had many books of sermons on which they could model their own instructions. They were expected to rise early to celebrate Lauds, or Morning Prayer, followed by Mass. The priest sometimes had to fast until noon if there were pilgrims coming through the village when he celebrated Mass again. There was also a focus on social justice. Does the priest care for the poor, pilgrims, and orphans? Does he invite them to his own table for a meal?

ح

Another development of the early Middle Ages that had long-term consequences for Catholicism was the practice then called "tariff penance," later renamed "confession" or the "sacrament of penance." Nowadays it is called "reconciliation." In the early church only serious sins (apostasy, murder, adultery) were dealt with through the church's penitential discipline, which often involved long-term, humiliating, and onerous penances, publicly imposed. By the sixth century this discipline had fallen into disuse, and a new form of penitential discipline gradually took root in Irish monastic circles. It involved private confession to a priest, the imposition of a penance, followed by absolution. Alcuin was right up-to-date when he told the young monks of Tours that God had provided "a place for self-accusation of our sins before a priest of God."[24] Penitentials, or guides for rural priests for penances, were drawn up, containing penances "precisely determined for all offences whether grave or slight in character." This form of penance, generally known as tariff penance (i.e., the "price" paid for a particular sin), spread from Ireland to England and then Europe.[25]

The word *paenitere* means "to fast," and abstention from food and drink was often part of the penalty imposed by the penitentials. Fasts on bread and water, abstinence from meat and wine, were imposed. Renunciation of the use of weapons was imposed for attacking another person, and almsgiving was often a penance for the wealthy. "The duration of these penances [was] graded according to the gravity of the sins and varies in [different] penitential books."[26] For example, drunkenness got seven days' penance, whereas immoderate eating got one day. For repeated offenses each individual act was taken into account. The whole thing gradually became very mechanical. For instance, a long penance could be shortened by a more intense commitment over a shorter period: a year's penance, for instance, could be shortened to a three-day complete fast. Penances could also be "redeemed" by getting a proxy to perform the penance. This began when a person was hindered from doing a penance because of illness, but it degenerated into paying someone else to do the penance. In the penitential canons incorrectly ascribed to King Edgar, "a magnate could finish his seven-year penance in three days by means of an equivalent number of fasts by hired men."[27] While "confession was primarily a means . . . to enable the priest to determine the penance appropriate to . . . the sins," theologians argued that "satisfaction [via a penance] was still the real efficient cause of the forgiveness of sin."[28]

Bernhard Poschmann points out that the penitential books were written for a relatively primitive society and that, although the danger of a purely mechanical approach was ever-present, theologians emphasized the importance of sincere contrition and conversion. The priest was the key to the operation of the system. Guided by his penitential, he had to adapt the penance to the seriousness of the sin and the particular circumstances of the penitent. A focus on sexual sins began with the conviction that reproduction was not a purely private affair but rather affected family, inheritance, and, ultimately, the social order itself and was thus the concern of everyone, especially the church.

Burchard, Bishop of Worms's *Decretum*, which reflects late-tenth-century practice, gives us some idea of the kind of detail found in the penitential books.[29] The *Decretum* covers a wide range of human iniquity, including violence, murder, incest, incantations, spells, gluttony, fornication, perjury, oaths, stealing, and abduction. The *Decretum* is laconic, factual, and unemotional. The hierarchy of penances corresponds to the offenses, and "the severity of the punishment depends on whether or not the sin disturbs the public peace."[30] Purely subjective, private sins deserve a less severe penance. Also, Burchard believes that women need special guidance because they are a disruptive influence on men.[31] Like the promiscuous duke of Mantua in Verdi's *Rigoletto*, Burchard thought that *La Donna è Mobile*—"Woman is fickle." Burchard says they are weak, deceitful, and easily led astray, and they should be kept under the close control of their husbands. They are also lecherous, and he inquires into the intimacies of female sexuality, including masturbation, relationships between women, and relationship of women and children. A true clerical misogynist, he blames women for prostitution, abortion, and the death of their children, even if accidental.

Focusing specifically on sexual sins (a preoccupation of penitential books), Burchard says that the priest should question the penitent to get the precise species of sin while being careful not to reveal anything about other sexual possibilities and permutations. Book XIX of the *Decretum* is so detailed on sexual sins that it is a kind of early medieval Kinsey report! Male masturbation earned ten days' fast on bread and water, as did fornication with an unmarried woman or maidservant. Mutual masturbation earned thirty days. Female masturbation with a dildo incurred a year's penance. Intercourse in a nonmissionary position incurred ten days' fast, although only five days was required if the sinner was drunk. Oral sex was severely penalized. Sexual intercourse was prohibited when a wife was menstruating, pregnant, or nursing a child, as well as in Lent, Advent, Pentecost, Easter week, and on fast days and Sundays. Such actions brought forty days' fast.

For sins that upset the social order, such as abduction, adultery, bestiality, seizure of another's wife or a nun, or an offer of a wife to other men, the sinner incurred forty days' penance each year for seven years. Those who killed next of kin or blood relatives did seven to fourteen years of penance, and infanticide after baptism received ten years' penance. As Georges Duby says, "Abduction and adultery . . . destroyed marriage contracts, [by] committing a public crime that caused hatred between families, gave rise to reprisals . . . and divided the community."[32] Murderers received the same punishment. Burchard is lenient with the failures of young unmarried men and with male homosexuality, which, like Hincmar of Reims, he equates with fornication. John Boswell argues that judging from the penances assigned homosexual activity, with the exception of anal intercourse with a married man, they "were about as serious as challenging a friend to a drinking bout."[33]

Given that priests had to administer this penitential discipline, it is important to ascertain how they were trained. For the most part, they weren't. While a few may have obtained a reasonably good education in a monastery, these were the exception. For rural clergy training was at best ad hoc and usually came from the local priest. Priest-fathers would certainly have taught their son the basics: the Latin of the Mass and sacraments; the creeds, prayers, and rituals; and the social role of the priest in the village.

This lack of training is significant because so much depended on the local priest. The spiritual vitality of the community rose or fell depending on the quality of the priest. Certainly, the local lord wanted a competent priest since he had a vested interest in his own church property. But when push came to shove, spiritual and educational competence was not his highest priority. All he really wanted was a good caretaker.

എ

Beyond the local community were the diocese and the bishop. In the tenth century there were a little more than 350 dioceses in Europe and its mission territories, of which 170 were in Italy. While Rome was recognized as the diocese of the apostle Peter and as the center of the church's communion, bishops were dominant in their own dioceses, and the power of the fifty-seven metropolitan archbishops was considerable. Local bishops were usually nominated by local rulers or sometimes elected by the clergy. Approval and consecration by the metropolitan followed. Rome played little or no role in the appointment of bishops. Some bishops were not only local ecclesiastical leaders; they were also civil functionaries in royal administrations, or they governed one of the five small ecclesiastical enclaves like Reims in northern France.

Church and state were inseparable, and both operated within the context of the reality they called *Christianitas*, what we would call "Christendom." This was a departure from the caesaropapism of the late Roman and Byzantine world in which a theocratic state controlled the church; that is, the church was a function of the state. In the tenth century, church and state were seen as different aspects of the same reality, two sides of the same coin. Kingship was a sacred office, and the anointing of a monarch was sacramental in much the same sense as priestly and episcopal ordination. Because the king was a sacred personage, it was appropriate for bishops and clerics to be appointed by him and work as civil functionaries.

But this was dangerous for the church. If there was no effective distinction between sacred and secular, ambitious aristocrats could gain more and more control over church offices and land. The nobility treated its geographical domains and everybody and everything within them as personal property. As a result, the church was no longer a counterbalance to the aristocracy. The two were interlocked and interdependent. This included even pastoral office. This interdependence was reinforced by ritual. After a bishop was sacramentally ordained, he knelt before the appointing king or lord and was invested by him with ring and pastoral staff. This symbolized his entry into possession of the estates that went with his office. Thus, the idea gained ground that the local aristocrat or king really owned the office and its appurtenances and that he was bestowing it on the chosen cleric. This led to complete confusion between spiritual and temporal roles. Often the spiritual and ministerial duties of ecclesiastical office came to be disregarded, simony (buying and selling of ecclesiastical offices) became widespread, and totally unworthy characters, such as the younger sons of aristocrats, some of them (as we saw) mere children, were appointed to important ecclesiastical positions as bishops and abbots.

Hatto I, Archbishop of Mainz from 891 to 913, was a typical bishop of the time, a man who doubled as both an ecclesiastical and a political administrator. Historically, he has an undeserved bad reputation. There is a late-fifteenth-century depiction of him in full episcopal regalia with rats crawling all over him. This comes from the untrue legend, popularized in English by Robert Southey's 1799 poem *God's Judgment on Hatto*, that during a famine he lured the starving poor into a large barn promising them food, only to bar the door and set the building alight. But, says the legend, revenge was swift. Next day rats destroyed Hatto's own supplies, and he took refuge in the *Mäuseturm*, the mouse tower on a Rhine island near Bingen. Here he was attacked by rats. "They gnaw'd the flesh from every limb," and he died a terrible death. There are two problems with the legend. It first appears in the fourteenth century almost four hundred years after Hatto I, and it was his successor, Hatto II, who restored the *Mäuseturm* in 968. Nevertheless, what is clear is that Hatto I was divisive enough to attract bad publicity. Ambitious and ruthless, his name was blackened by Henry the Fowler, who had a vested interest in badmouthing him.

Born about 850 into the Swabian aristocracy near Lake Constance, Hatto was educated at Ellwagen abbey, became a monk at Fulda, and was elected abbot of Reichenau in 888. But all his political activity doesn't mean that Hatto stopped being a bishop. As well as administering his diocese and province (the archbishopric of Mainz was the metropolitan archdiocese for the East Frankish kingdom), he was committed to church affairs. His influence can be seen at the Council of Tribur (May 5, 895), where he presided together with the Metropolitan Archbishops Herimann of Cologne and Ratbod of Trier. This council gathered twenty-six bishops from East Francia. Its decrees covered a range of pastoral issues, including recommending baptism by triple immersion to remind Christians of the three days that Christ spent in the tomb; emerging from the water was seen as a symbol of the resurrection. The council further decreed that marriage was completed by the exchange of consent and the ritual blessing, that no layman could be buried in a church, that if bandits were captured or wounded, they could confess to a priest or deacon and shouldn't be denied communion. There was also the usual grab bag of decrees concerning the lives of priests.

The council dealt with an ongoing dispute between Archbishop Herimann of Cologne, the archbishop of Hamburg-Bremen, and the papacy. The dispute started in 845 when Hamburg was destroyed by the Vikings and the two dioceses of Hamburg and Bremen were combined. Pope Nicholas I confirmed this change in 864. It offended the metropolitan of Cologne because Bremen was a suffragan diocese of Cologne. Instructed by Pope Formosus to submit the case to Rome, the Council of Tribur refused to obey the papal edict, and the case remained unresolved until Sergius III confirmed the decisions of Nicholas I.

Bishops were not mere ciphers. Originally, they were chosen by *electio canonica* (canonical election) by the clergy and people of the local church. By the tenth century this process had been taken over by kings and magnates. However, the notion of election was maintained by the participation of cathedral canons, influential laymen, vassals of the diocese, and even local people. There was often conflict among these disparate interest groups, but their participation was considered by church law to be essential. Church historian Friedrich Kempf reports, "Since the business of the election was still regarded as a full, active process in which clergy and people participated, an unwanted chief pastor could not be forced upon diocesans. Regardless of the manner in which clergy and people assented, their assent had to be given somehow; otherwise the election was uncanonical, invalid."[34]

New bishops were sacramentally ordained by three other bishops, followed by installation by the king or local lord. This led to the notion that the ruler was bestowing a *beneficium* on the new bishop—that is, he bestowed the property and the fiscal goods belonging to the diocese. This later came to be called "investiture." Although not intended to have sacramental or even canonical/legal standing, investiture could easily confuse things.

However, not every bishop was a royal administrator like Hatto. Some northern Italian bishops, for example, tended to be more independently minded, perhaps because the urban structure of the church was still more intact there. One of these was Ratherius of Verona (887–974), a neurotic, eccentric, churlish man who fell out with almost everyone. Born in Liège, he was educated at the monastery of Lobbes on the French-Belgian border. Described by his contemporary Folcuin as a "most quick-witted scholar," he left Lobbes unable to stand monastic life any longer, went to Italy, and in 931 was elected bishop of Verona.[35] In 834 Ratherius fell foul of King Hugo, Marozia's husband; was expelled from the bishopric; and was imprisoned for two and a half years in one of Pavia's many towers. Liutprand of Cremona reports that "there he wrote a book describing in witty and elegant language the sorrows of his banishment."[36] His *Praeloquia* (Prefaces) was actually written as a preface to another work entitled *Agonistic* (Christ's Athlete), which was never written. Ratherius translator Peter Reid says that the *Praeloquia* is "a unique kind of work that covers the duties of human beings in their many capacities." It describes an extraordinary cross-section of Verona society as well as dealing with issues such as the relationship between church and king, between canon and civil law, in addition to criticizing corrupt practices and individual ecclesiastics. Without reference books he still cites quotations from scriptures, the early church fathers and theologians, and the classics, thereby testifying "to a mind of extraordinary capacity."[37] A decade of almost compulsive wandering followed his release from prison.

Then out of the blue, Ratherius was invited back to Verona by a desperate King Hugo, who was now struggling to maintain his position against Berengar II. But during his return to Italy, Ratherius was captured by Berengar. After devious maneuvers Ratherius regained his see in 946, but only for two years. The local count, Milo, turned everyone against him. "Day and night," Ratherius told Pope Agapitus II, "I was so wretched, so nervous, exhausted, weary of my life that I would gladly have been in that tower . . . at Pavia than in the cathedral at Verona."[38] He lost the diocese of Verona again in 948 when Hugo lost the war to Berengar. Once again Ratherius was on the road, wandering aimlessly from place to place. In 951 after a brief return to monastic life, he joined the court of Otto I, where he met Liutprand, and in September 953 he was made bishop of Liège. But again his neuroticism surfaced, the diocese rebelled, and he resigned in 955. Another period of wandering and writing followed; for a brief time he was abbot of a small monastery.

By 961 Otto was back in Italy, and he got Ratherius restored to Verona for the third time. Again the diocese revolted, this time led by the former bishop. In 963 Ratherius complained about the senior clergy of his diocese to Bishop Hubert of Parma in a long, obsessive letter. He accuses them of sexual incontinence, gambling, avariciousness, drunkenness, neglect of spiritual duties, gluttony, and a rebellious attitude toward him.[39] There is something deeply neurotic about his endless complaints, yet his honesty about himself is disarming. For instance, in late 964 he says that after lunch "I fell from the staircase fifteen feet below. . . . I broke my right arm, which has not so far mended. Confined I spent the time in constant despair that I had returned [to Verona], not for my resurrection, but to my own ruin."[40]

Constant petty struggles with his senior clergy over a whole range of issues eventually wore him down. Things came to a head in early July 968 when the clergy publicly accused him before the whole city of looting the episcopal palace, among other irregularities. He begged Ambrose, Otto I's Italian chancellor, to rescue him. "For God's sake help me, I beg, as I will soon perish unless speedily helped." But Ambrose ignored his petitions, and Ratherius complained, "The Emperor could not care less about my safety and survival. . . . Unless this . . . violence, provocation and conspiracy against me are put down by a letter from the Emperor it is all over with me."[41] The imperial letter never came, and Ratherius left Verona for the last time. He returned to Lotharingia demanding to be appointed abbot of Lobbes, which, needless to say, led to contention between himself and the then-incumbent Folcuin, who accused him of arriving with a large amount of gold and silver from Verona. Given his attacks on clerical avariciousness and simony, we can only conclude that as Reid says "he felt so depressed by how he had been treated in Verona that he determined to use whatever resources he could carry with him for material security in his late old age."[42] Ratherius got his way at Lobbes, but eventually he had to surrender the abbey and retire to a small monastery where he died in his late eighties in 974, an extraordinarily long life for a tenth-century man. His turbulent career and many misfortunes had been caused by his own self-righteousness, fractiousness, intolerance, and reforming zeal. Just the same, he was an extraordinary person, intelligent and very well read, and his "inner questioning, the repeated meditation on his own worth, gives us a glimpse of self-analysis rare before modern times."[43]

Most bishops fell somewhere in between the politics of Hatto I and the neuroticism of Ratherius. All of them were in one way or another embedded in the proprietary church system. In all of these debates the papacy played little role after the time of Nicholas I and Formosus. As Rosamond McKitterick says, "In all these contemporary discussions and decisions concerning the administration and organization of the church, little reference is made to the pope and his role vis à vis the churches, provinces and diocesan sees of Christendom."[44] The most that can be said is that many archbishops went to Rome to get their palliums. Except as a court of last resort, Rome was largely ignored by the rest of the church.

∾

The ninth and tenth centuries were also important for the liturgy. For centuries there had been a number of different ways of celebrating worship. There were various Gallican rites, Celtic rites, Old Spanish (Mozarabic) rites, and the Ambrosian rite in Milan. To assist in the unification of the Frankish kingdom, Pippin and Charlemagne attempted to impose the Roman rite throughout their realm. Alcuin played a key role in this process as Charlemagne's liturgical adviser. The imposition was not entirely successful largely because of the differences in temperament between the more restrained, sober Roman rite and the more dramatic Frankish rites.

But the tendency toward unification continued under the Ottonian rulers. As part of the unification process, a team of monks at the abbey of Sankt Alban in Mainz around 950 drew up a *Pontificale* (a worship book setting out bishops' ceremonies) that included Roman, Frankish, and German liturgical elements. This work, often called "Otto's Pontifical," was undertaken at Otto I's command and was supervised by Otto's brother Bruno, Archbishop of Cologne. The Mass had increasingly dramatic elements added to it, such as processions, incensations, a solemn gospel proclamation, more elaborate vestments and chants, and, most importantly, a kind of feeling of mysteriousness created by the increasing exclusion of the laity, who could no longer understand Latin as separate vernacular languages emerged. This distance was exacerbated by the actual movement of the altar to the back wall of the church, with the laity banished from the sanctuary. The Mass now became the business of the bishop and priest. This new genre, the Franco-Roman liturgy, slowly made its way back to Rome to become the universal worship of the Western Church until the reforms of the Second Vatican Council in the 1960s.

Walafrid Strabo was the first to reflect theologically on these new liturgical developments. We first met him as a friend of both Bodo and Gottschalk. The son of Swabian peasants, Walafrid came to Reichenau as a child oblate and was educated there and at Fulda. After his stint in Aachen as tutor to Louis the Pious's son Charles (Charles the Bald), he became abbot of Reichenau in 838. Although a highly intelligent and affectionate man, he didn't have an easy time as the independent Reichenau community justly felt that he had been imposed on them. He was tragically drowned in August 849 in the Loire while on a diplomatic mission for Charles the Bald. He was forty years old.

Walafrid was part of the first generation that profited from Charlemagne and Alcuin's educational reforms, and he had a broad education in the classics and theology. While Early German was his native tongue, he was an exceptional Latinist. Despite his active life, Walafrid wrote the first-ever historical study of liturgy in the early 840s, *Libellus de exordiis et incrementis quarundam in observationibus ecclesiasticis rerum*, "A Small Book About the Origins and Development of Some Aspects of the Liturgy." Written at the request of Reginbert, the longtime monk-librarian at Reichenau, *Libellus* was meant to instruct students and guide priests in dealing with contemporary issues in worship. The book ranges across church architecture, the Eucharist, and various liturgical issues. While Walafrid was an advocate of Roman usage, he was happy to recognize that there were other forms of liturgical expression that remained within the church's doctrinal tradition, and communicated with those who used them. As he says, "Within one faith the church's diversity of practice does no harm."[45]

What is striking about the book is that Walafrid writes, as Walafrid scholar Alice L. Harting-Correa says, "in the manner of a modern historian whose aim is to present historical facts based on accurately cited sources."[46] Because he was well educated in the classics, Walafrid also understands that history is a form of rhetoric "worthy of the most harmonious combination of style and matter." He recognizes that worship itself is "a kind of rhetoric in action."[47] In other words, the liturgical action (i.e., the words and movements of the celebrants), the building and architecture (the sacred space), the singing and music and engagement of the senses (hearing, sight, and smell from incense), and the common feeling that emerges from the worshipping community itself come together in a wholeness that draws the participants into a transcendent space in which genuine worship of God occurs.

As part of the unification of the liturgy, the Roman form of chant was imposed on the Frankish kingdoms. Roman chant was probably Byzantine in origin, and cantors were brought from Rome to train the locals. But the Franks already had their own tradition of chant, and what we today call "Gregorian chant" is probably a combination of the Roman and Frankish traditions. One thing we are sure about is that Pope Gregory I did *not* invent Gregorian chant. Like the Franco-Roman liturgy, Gregorian chant returned to Rome from the Frankish kingdoms from the tenth century onward.

The chant required a trained choir to sing it. This was usually composed of monks or clerics. The language of the chant was, of course, Latin. This further excluded the laity from active participation in worship even though the people's singing had traditionally been part of Eucharistic worship. But with the professionalization of the liturgy and its increasing inflexibility, the people were forced to fall back on nonliturgical hymns. These were sometimes allowed during Mass, for instance after the sermon, but they were gradually excluded from the Eucharist. As a result, people tended to sing vernacular hymns and songs during pilgrimages and other religious events.

But lay exclusion didn't mean that religion was in decline. For as the tenth century drew to a close, millennial expectation grew. Preachers and people were asking, would the millennium be the end of the world? Would judgment day arrive on January 1, 1000? Who would be saved, and who would be damned? As the year 1000 approached, these questions came increasingly to the fore, although we should not exaggerate their importance. As we shall see, millennial expectation actually became more of a problem for twentieth-century historians and commentators than it had been for tenth-century ones, many of whom weren't even sure of the actual date. From an apocalyptic perspective the year

1000 was almost as disappointing as the year 2000 when the Y2K millennium computer bug didn't appear.

Neither Gerbert of Aurillac, who was pope (as Sylvester II) in the year 1000, nor Otto III, who was emperor, was in any way particularly interested in the millennium. They were trying to realize a much larger and grander dream: the restoration of the Roman Empire and the achievement of a religious and secular union between the West and the Byzantine Empire. So before we consider millennial expectations, such as they were in the year 1000, we will tell the story of the greatest genius of the early Middle Ages and one of the greatest polymaths in Western European history, Gerbert of Aurillac, who was born a peasant and died a pope. As we shall see, he, perhaps more than any other individual, contributed most toward the birth of what we call the West for he was the one who made Western science and technology possible. Intimately associated with him is Theophano's only son, Otto III, the three-year-old who was kidnapped by Henry the Wrangler and who grew up to be an idealistic emperor whose life was tragically cut short by sickness. It is to these two truly significant figures that we will now turn.

PART FIVE

A MILLENNIAL VISION

CHAPTER 16

Gerbert, the Magician of the Millennium

AURILLAC TODAY IS a rather nondescript French town. Its population numbers 27,000, and its major industry is umbrella making. Aurillac lies on the Cantal uplands, a high plain 2,100 feet (640 meters) beside the Jordanne River southwest of the Massif Central, chains of inactive volcanoes now covered by forests and lakes and making up the largest extinct volcanic region in Europe. Close to the center of town on the northern bank of the Jordanne River is a 12-foot-high (3.7 meters) bronze statue of a pope. It represents Aurillac's most significant son, Gerbert—Pope Sylvester II (999–1003). Erected in 1851, the statue tells us more about mid-nineteenth-century French ultramontanism than it does about Sylvester II. Ultramontanism (from the Latin *ultra montes*, "beyond the mountains") refers to the tendency of many French Catholics in the nineteenth and first half of the twentieth century to look beyond the Alps to papal Rome as the sole source of power, discipline, and doctrine in Catholicism. Paradoxically, this papalist ideology is the antithesis of Sylvester's views. It's the statue's outfit that gives the ultramontane game away. Facing the rather tiny Place Gerbert with his back to an unremarkable car park, the statue is replete with triple tiara and attached twin lappets, baroque cope, and long lace surplice, and it looks much more like Pius IX (1846–1878) than a pope from a thousand years ago. In fact the real Gerbert would have been horrified.

Undoubtedly one of the greatest polymaths in European history, Gerbert was born about 945, most likely of free-peasant stock. His birthplace was somewhere near Aurillac, though no one knows the exact site. The monk Richer of Saint-Rémi, a former student, says in his *Histories* that Gerbert was *Aquitanus genere*, "born in Aquitaine," possibly a tiny village named Belliac.[1] There is some evidence that his father's name was Agilbertus.

Exactly how and when he entered the strictly observant monastery of Saint Gerald in Aurillac are uncertain. He may have taken up an offer to study at the monastery school, or he may have been offered by his parents as a boy oblate. In any event, young Gerbert was happy in the monastery, and he clearly saw Abbot Gérauld as the father of the family who nurtured and cared for him. Saint Gerald's abbey offered him formation as a monk and an education far beyond anything he could have imagined or obtained anywhere else. Here Gerbert learned the educational basics that would form the foundation of his extraordinary genius.

Founded about 904, the monastery of Saint Gerald later adopted the reform of Cluny. Aurillac was also a stopping-off point for the pilgrimage to Compostela, which meant that the community came in contact with a cosmopolitan clientele of pilgrims. Like Cluny, Saint Gerald's was directly subject to the papacy and independent of the count of Auvergne. (Sadly, nowadays there is virtually nothing left of the original monastery.)

Monastic life put Gerbert in contact with a wider world that opened his mind, stimulated his curiosity, and instilled a lifelong personal discipline. However, as Friedrich Kempf says, "the ritualistic excess [of the Cluniac reform] left the monks little time for study, and manual labor [had] all but disappeared."[2] Perhaps Gerbert's inquiring mind would have been constrained by the endless ritual, although it would have introduced him to spirituality, music, and beauty. Abbot Gérauld entrusted Gerbert's education to monk Raymond of Lavaur, who laid sound intellectual foundations. Gerbert's affection for these men is palpable in his letters. Of Gérauld he says, "I don't know whether the Divinity has granted anything better to [us] than friends. . . . The features of my friend remain fixed in my heart. I mean him who is my lord and father—Gérauld."[3]

Raymond would have taken Gerbert through the *Trivium*, the basic study of Latin grammar, dialectic, and rhetoric that was the primary educational process used from post-Roman times until the seventeenth century. Dialectic, or logic, was the art of thinking clearly and coherently and using the art of rational disputation to critically examine opinions; grammar, the ability to arrange and express thought in a consistent, comprehensible form; and rhetoric, the art of elegant persuasion, the facile adaptation of language to communication.

Later in life Gerbert also remembered Raymond with gratitude. As an adult, in a letter to Gérauld he says that he would like his "former master Raymond" to join him in Reims as a teacher in the cathedral school, repeating the invitation a year later. Later he speaks of Raymond as the one "to whom I owe everything." Gerbert kept up a semiregular correspondence with Raymond after he became abbot of Aurillac in succession to Gérauld.[4]

Raymond was liberal-minded enough to allow Gerbert to study the Latin classics; many other monastic "reformers" would not permit pagan works to be part of the curriculum. Gerbert quickly completed the *Trivium*, but faced a problem: no one in southern France could take the brilliant boy any further. The next course of study was to be the *Quadrivium*: arithmetic, geometry, music, and astronomy. Having completed both courses, a pupil was considered properly prepared to study philosophy and theology. But teachers of the *Quadrivium* were few and far between, and Raymond was not one of them; he was not interested in the exact sciences. Abbot Gérauld realized that Gerbert had outgrown Aurillac.

A solution appeared when Borrell II, Count of Barcelona visited Aurillac in 967 while preparing for his marriage to a local noblewoman, Ledgarda. The abbot asked Borrell "whether there were men in Spain who were completely proficient in the liberal arts." When Borrell said there were, "the abbot urged him to take one of his charges . . . to be educated in this subject matter" across the Pyrenees.[5] So Gerbert left Aurillac with Borrell on the journey south either across the Col d'Ares, a 4,900-foot (1,513-meter) pass over the Pyrenees that would have brought them straight to Barcelona, or along the coastal Via Domitia, the old Roman road into northern Spain. There had been close political links between southern France and Catalonia since late Roman times, so this would not have been entirely "foreign" territory for Gerbert. The church in northern Spain was experiencing a widespread reform movement associated with Cluny and was increasingly providing some sense of order in the region as government collapsed into chaos in southern France and Catalonia.

Richer dismisses Gerbert's stay in Spain from 967 to 971 in a sentence and a half. He says Gerbert "made great strides in the study of the mathematical arts" under Bishop Atto of Vic, a town 46 miles (75 kilometers) north of Barcelona.[6] This is clearly a reference to the *Quadrivium*. During Gerbert's Spanish sojourn, the caliphate of Córdoba was ruled by the cultured al-Hākim II (961–976). While in Spain Gerbert seems to have drifted increasingly from the disciplines of monastic life and to have embraced the life of a scholar. Richer speaks of "the young man's diligence and love of learning."[7] He was probably twenty-one or twenty-two and was already committed to becoming a teacher.

Richer's brevity about Gerbert's Spanish years gave medieval chroniclers an opening to spin wild yarns about him. More than a century after Gerbert's death, the English monk William of Malmesbury (1095–1143) has him "either disgusted at a monastic life or seized by lust for glory," escaping into the night "to learn astrology and other sciences . . . from the Saracens." William correctly says that Gerbert acquired the astrolabe; studied astronomy, astrology, arithmetic, music, and geometry; and brought the abacus to Europe. He also "learned what the singing and the flight of birds portended and acquired the art of calling up spirits from hell." William's story gets fantastic when Gerbert befriends an old Muslim magician who lets him copy all his books except a book of magic spells. So Gerbert seduces the man's daughter, and the two of them get him drunk, and the daughter steals the book from under her father's pillow. Gerbert immediately flees with the father in hot pursuit, no doubt a difficult maneuver for someone already intoxicated! Gerbert hides under a bridge and eventually escapes. William at least has the honesty to admit that "probably some may regard all this as a fiction."[8] But it reinforced the dark legend, popular in his own time and among earlier historians, that as pope Gerbert was a wizard or magician in league with the devil. How else, contemporaries asked, could he know so much? Fortunately, recent studies have decisively dispensed with this arrant nonsense.

Modern historians have, in fact, gone to the opposite extreme and minimized and even denied Gerbert's role in bringing Arabic knowledge of mathematics and science to Western Europe. They argue that it was only in the eleventh century that such knowledge appeared. They maintain that Gerbert could not have acquired the knowledge he was purported to have had because there was nowhere in Christian Spain where he could have got it. They ask, where were the libraries with Latin translations of Arabic scientific texts that Gerbert could have studied in Catalonia? Who could have taught him? These mainly French historians argue that if *they* don't know how Gerbert obtained his knowledge, then he can't have had it. Such argumentation betrays a curious logic now been shown to be factually wrong.

While Richer says little about Gerbert's time in Spain, he does unequivocally acknowledge that in 970 Gerbert impressed Pope John XIII with his knowledge of music, astronomy, and mathematics, so much so that the pope immediately informed Otto I. Richer also describes Gerbert's teaching of mathematics at Reims. While he mentions that Gerbert taught arithmetic, music, and geometry, he also gives detailed descriptions of the various instruments that Gerbert built to introduce his students to mathematics and to help them observe the position of the stars and constellations. Clearly, Gerbert knew a considerable amount about Arabic science, mathematics, and astronomy, even if some pedantic French historians don't know how he got it.

What we do know is that while in Spain, Gerbert attended Atto's cathedral school in Vic (where he mastered the *Quadrivium*, especially mathematics and astronomy) and also certainly visited the nearby monastery of Santa Maria de Ripoll, founded in 879 by Count Wifred "the Hairy." Ripoll had a large library, and the monastery served as a kind of bridge between Christian and Muslim culture. But the evidence is that the library's main growth period, including the addition of a number of translated scientific texts, came *after* Gerbert's time in Spain. We also know that the library at Vic had no books by classical authors or any that would have assisted study of the sciences. So how did Gerbert acquire this knowledge if there were no known translations of Arabic scientific sources available in Catalonian libraries in his time in Spain?

The answer lies not in libraries but in diplomatic, political, and cultural ties between al-Andalus and Catalonia and in the involvement of a Jewish scholar, scientist, administrator, and diplomat whom we have already met, Hasdāi ibn Shaprut. We know that Hasdāi was deeply interested in science, medicine, and mathematics; that he served Caliphs Abd al-Rahmān III and al-Hākim II as an administrator; and that he was very active in the negotiations between Córdoba and Catalonia that kept the peace during these two caliphates. Lasting peace allowed the formation of small groups of people who knew both cultures well and exchanged ideas. One such group gathered around Bishop Gotmar of Girona, a friend and patron of Bishop Atto, who had originally been a priest in Girona. Others in the group were the scholarly count and later bishop of Girona (971–984) Miró Bonfill, Borrell II himself, and, no doubt, Gerbert. Hasdāi was apparently a kind of corresponding member of the group. Gotmar had certainly visited Córdoba as an ambassador in the company of Hasdāi. As historian Marco Zuccato, who first highlighted these interconnections, comments, "Therefore if Gotmar had brought from Córdoba, or received from Hasdāi any scientific writings, then Gerbert, once in Catalonia, could have accessed it easily through his master, Atto of Vic, or his friend Miró", thus learning and benefiting from al-Andalus's scientific knowledge.[9]

Later in life Gerbert maintained contact with his old friends in Spain. In a letter to the archdeacon of Barcelona Lupitus, Gerbert asks him to send a copy of a book *Sententiae astrolabii*, which the archdeacon had translated from Arabic. Gerbert himself comments that this is "one of the earliest works known to have been translated from Arabic into Latin."[10] Earlier Gerbert had asked Abbot Gérauld to send him "a little book *De multiplicatione et divisione numerorum* written by Joseph the Spaniard" left at Aurillac by a mutual friend, the Spanish Abbot Guarin, also a friend of Miró. A later letter asks Miró for the same book by Joseph *Sapiens* (Joseph the Wise).[11] Who is this Joseph *Sapiens*? Recent research strongly suggests that he is none other than Hasdāi ibn Shaprut. It is clear that Hasdāi made manuscripts from al-Andalus available in Catalonia as well as Jewish works from the wider Islamic world. Zuccato points out the particularly striking parallels between the astronomical manuscript prepared for Hasdāi by North African Jewish scientist Dunāsh ibn Tamīm and the course later taught by Gerbert at Reims. Zuccato comments that Dunāsh's "pedagogical program passed entirely into the astronomical teachings [of Gerbert] as described by Richer."[12] What is particularly striking is Gerbert's use of the celestial sphere as suggested by Dunāsh, which he could have come to know only via his acquaintance with Joseph *Sapiens*, aka Hasdāi ibn Shaprut.

Did Gerbert actually visit al-Andalus or even Córdoba? Given his inquiring mind and adventurous spirit, it seems likely that he would have at least ventured over the border into Islamic territory, even if he didn't get as far south as Córdoba. If he had done so, he certainly wouldn't have drawn attention to the fact. As Oscar G. Darlington points out, "The political common sense of a man like Gerbert, who aspired to high ecclesiastical office, would dictate silence upon a subject [like visiting a Muslim region] that ran counter to the contemporary popular sentiment of Christendom."[13]

While in Spain Gerbert learned the distinctive West-Arabic variant of the Hindu-Arabic numerical system, the numbers 1 to 9; zero came later. The Arabs derived this system from Hindu India. The Christian West had previously been dependent on the Roman numerical system, which was awkward and complicated to use arithmetically. Even simple addition was difficult. Because of this advanced numerical system, the Arabs were much more sophisticated arithmetically; they had moved on to algebra and developed astronomy and the use of the abacus, which Gerbert adapted for calculation with the Hindu-Arabic numerals. Gerbert is attributed with introducing Arabic numerals to Europe. The astrolabe, which he also brought to Europe, helped with accurate timekeeping and "greatly increased the precision with which celestial events and bodies could be located in time and space."[14]

After his years in Catalonia, Gerbert accompanied Count Borrell and Bishop Atto to Rome in late 969 to meet Pope John XIII to discuss making Vic an archdiocese. Gerbert impressed John with his brilliance, particularly in mathematics, which transcended anything known in Europe at the time. The pope not only made Vic an archdiocese, at least briefly; he also kept Gerbert in Rome so that he could learn from him. To free Gerbert to teach and travel, the pope dispensed him from his monastic vows. He was later ordained a priest in Reims, probably in late 972. Pope John meanwhile introduced Gerbert to Otto I, who appointed him Latin tutor to the young Otto II. During this brief interlude with the Saxon monarchs, he had a chance to see the Germanic-Roman idea of a strong, semicentralized empire at work. Given his background in the political chaos of south-central France and Spain, Gerbert became an admirer of the order the Saxons were restoring through the reactivation of the Holy Roman Empire.

જૂ

Gerbert was certainly ambitious; the strong drive to better his position probably arose from his peasant origins. At a time when noble birth was the usual prerequisite for both ecclesiastical and secular preferment, he was one of the few who made it into the ranks of the powerful from social obscurity. He was fascinated by knowledge, and he increasingly felt that he had a vocation to be a teacher. His tutoring of young Otto finished when the young man married Theophano, and a new opportunity for Gerbert presented itself during their marriage celebrations in Rome in April 972. A chance meeting with outstanding logician Gerannus, Archdeacon of Reims persuaded Gerbert to leave the imperial service and join Reims cathedral school as *scholasticus* (master). Reims was a tiny independent ecclesiastical enclave wedged between the German kingdom to the northeast, France to the southwest, the kingdom of Burgundy to the southeast, and the duchy of Lorraine to the west. This made the town an accessible crossroads of commerce and scholarship in the Frank-ish heartlands.

What was the educational world like into which Gerbert next moved? The two key educational theorists of the late Roman world were Martianus Capella (early fifth century) and Cassiodorus Senator (ca. 490–ca. 593). They articu-lated the philosophy and division of subjects that dominated educational the-ory for the next thousand years. Neither was an original thinker. Capella's *De nuptiis Philologiae et Mercurii* (The Marriage of Philology and Mercury) is an odd, allegorical work made up of prose and verse that are sometimes funny and often bizarre. The Christian Cassiodorus had a public career in the late Roman world and then retired to a monastery on his estates in southern Italy. His writings are both wordy and "worthy." His *Historia tripartita* (History in Three Parts) is full of errors but was used as a history text for centuries. His ed-ucational text, *Institutiones divinarum et saecularium litterarum* (The Arrange-ment of Divine and Human Readings), is a better work. His aim was a synthesis of secular knowledge and the Bible, and his work followed the division of the liberal arts as proposed by Capella. Cassiodorus distinguishes dialectic, gram-mar, and rhetoric from the sciences of arithmetic, geometry, astronomy, and music. He was also interested in theology. Like Capella, he excludes medicine and architecture from the liberal arts.

But it was Boethius (ca. 475–ca. 526), a brilliant philosopher, politician, and translator of Aristotle, who exercised the strongest influence on medieval education. He was interested in the *Quadrivium*, and his translations of Aris-totle's logical and mathematical works and his own theological works were used for the next millennium. The final influence on medieval education was Bishop Isidore of Seville (ca. 560–636), who studied at the cathedral school of Seville in the Visigothic period a century before the Muslim invasion. Like Gerbert, he was fascinated by knowledge and compiled the *Etymologiae* (Etymologies, in the sense of the history of words), a condensation of universal knowledge that, unlike many other works in this period, included an emphasis on theology. He had studied Greek and Hebrew, and two centuries before their revival in al-Andalus, he promoted the study of Greek philosophy and Aristotle.

By the mid-sixth century Europe had descended into the pre-Carolingian "dark ages," but these late Roman educational ideas survived, largely in the monasteries and cathedral schools. Reims, for instance, had a cathedral school at least by the seventh century, probably earlier, which prepared boys for the clerical life and political administration. The monasteries educated boys for entry into the monastic life.

A real revival of education occurred under Charlemagne. His biographer Einhard says Charlemagne could speak Latin and understood Greek better than he could speak it. He also "spent much time and effort in studying rhetoric, dialectic and especially astrology. He applied himself to mathematics and traced the course of the stars with great attention and care." The emperor could read and was highly intelligent but, tragically, could not actually write. "He tried to learn to write. . . . He used to keep writing tablets and notebooks under the pillows on his bed. . . . But although he tried very hard, he had begun too late in life and made little progress."[15]

Deeply concerned with clerical ignorance and laxity, Charlemagne and Louis the Pious promoted education in cathedral and monastic schools in which sacred and secular learning were intimately interconnected. The result was an increase in the number of literate men, with the written word becoming, as Rosamond McKitterick says, "a fundamental element of Carolingian culture."[16] The Reims cathedral school had been prominent in the second half of the ninth century under Archbishop Hincmar, and it experienced another renaissance in the late tenth century focused on Gerbert. Intellectual networks began to emerge. The liberal arts curriculum became increasingly important for the training of clerics and laymen, many of whom went on to become the bureaucrats upon whose work Ottonian government was based. Bishops, abbots, priests, and monks were constantly called on to carry out secular functions, even leading armies into war.

Gerbert spent eight fruitful years at Reims devoted to study, teaching, building up a personal library, and developing his rare technical talent. Here his creativity was first shown to the world. Not that he held membership in a "university faculty." Cathedral schools comprised a cluster of students congregated around a particular master. So for the years that he was there, Gerbert effectively *was* the Reims cathedral school. Richer was one of his most enthusiastic students.

Gerbert's educational approach was very flexible; he attuned the *Trivium* to the needs of the students and his own interests following the general educational outline developed during the Carolingian period. He taught dialectics as a way of training students in intellectual subtlety and mental gymnastics. Much later he wrote a short treatise on the subject for Otto III, *De rationali et ratione uti* (On the Rational and the Use of Reason). According to Richer, Gerbert also taught logic and rhetoric, introducing students to "the poets with whom he thought they ought to be made acquainted, expounding and teaching the poets Virgil, Statius and Terence, the satirists Juvenal, Persius and Horace, and the historian Lucan. When the students had been familiarized with these authors and trained in the modes of expression, he promoted them to the study of rhetoric."[17]

Gerbert wrote a commentary on Aristotle and was very much influenced by Cicero, who linked rhetoric to integrity of character. Gerbert told Abbot Ebrard of Tours, "Since philosophy does not separate the science of morals from the science of speaking, I have always considered as equal the study of the good life and the study of good speaking. . . . When one is as we are entangled in public affairs, both are necessary."[18] Linking morality and communication has contemporary relevance in our era of "spin" and the twenty-four-hour news cycle when no one has time to check the truth or falsity of anything presented as news.

To improve the teaching of secular subjects in the *Quadrivium*, Gerbert revised and expanded the teaching curriculum using Boethius and Cassiodorus. Some of his priestly students resisted the *Quadrivium* because they didn't see the relevance of it to their ministry. In response, Gerbert provided students with practical applications of what they were learning. Richer says, Gerbert expended "much effort . . . on the mathematical arts."[19] He introduced students to Hindu-Arabic numerals, replacing the old-style Roman numerals. He devised a specially adapted flat-board twenty-seven-column abacus with "a thousand markers . . . made out of horn" for arithmetical calculations on which zero was represented by a space; his *Regula de abaco computi* (Rules for Computing on the Abacus) explained how to use the abacus to add, subtract, multiply, and divide.[20] Two examples of such abacus boards belonging to Gerbert's students were discovered in 2001 from the monastery of Echternach (Luxembourg). Gerbert could do arithmetical calculations in his head, probably the first person in Europe to achieve this. That he was influenced by Boethius's *De arithmatica* is clear from his correspondence with his friend Constantine of Fleury concerning superparticular numbers, the arithmetic relationship of two sequential numbers where the dividend equals the divisor plus one.[21] Gerbert's interest here was derived from music; such calculations are useful in understanding harmony.

He advanced from mathematics to astronomy. Gerbert didn't see the world as flat, but as an orb or spherical body. He insisted on the actual observation of the stars in astronomy, constructing a large hemisphere, a precursor of the telescope, for making astronomical observations. Zuccato comments that, while Gerbert had a thorough knowledge of traditional astronomy, his approach was characterized by a "strange unorthodoxy" that was revolutionary for its time. To help students, he invented visual aids through which "the orthodox method of absorbing classical sources was replaced by the practical use of actual spherical instruments," one of which "had no precedent in the Latin tradition."[22] He made four celestial spheres to help the students understand the movements of the heavens. A drawing of his planetary sphere has been found in the Vatican Library. Some of his instruments could have been used to tell time, and he may have had a *horologium*, a water clock, but he certainly didn't invent a mechanical clock as some have maintained.

In music he introduced the monochord, a musical instrument consisting of a soundboard with a single string and moveable bridge, for establishing correct pitch, especially in organ pipes. He matched the pipes mathematically so that a continuous sound and consistent harmonic pitch created a resonance better than anything ever heard in the West previously. There was speculation that Gerbert had constructed a water-driven organ, but that is now discounted. His theoretical interest in music led him to reflect on the relationships among the musical movement of the celestial spheres, the functions of the human body, and the sounds of voices and instruments.

Gerbert was as much a pedagogue as an inventor. Many of his students advanced to greater things: at least thirteen became bishops; six, abbots; one, a king (Robert II); and another, pope (Gregory VI). Many became prominent scholars, politicians, and administrators. Without doubt he was the greatest scholar of the tenth century and contributed immensely to the foundation of modern science.

೮⁄ට

When Gerbert arrived at his cathedral school, Archbishop Adalbero of Reims could not believe his luck. Gerbert was a double blessing: a teacher who would improve clerical education in Reims and the surrounding dioceses and a secretary-adviser who could assist Adalbero as senior hierarch of the French church.

A patron of libraries and scriptoria (there were at least five in the Reims region), Adalbero followed in the tradition of Hincmar, acting as a reforming churchman with widespread influence in church and state. Born into the

Lotharingian nobility, Adalbero had been a monk at the reformed monastery of Gorze and a canon of Metz cathedral. Elected archbishop in 969, he promoted monastic reform in Reims diocese, instituted a rule of life for cathedral canons (Gerbert became a canon), and supported the cathedral library.

Working with Adalbero introduced Gerbert to ecclesiastical politics, and in November 980 he put teaching aside to accompany Adalbero on a journey to Rome for a synod. On the way they were received by Otto II in Pavia, who took the opportunity to invite his former tutor and the archbishop to spend Christmas 980 with Theophano and himself in Ravenna. So they all sailed together down the Po to Ravenna, where Theophano would have felt perfectly at home among the splendid Byzantine mosaics and buildings. Otto didn't tell Gerbert that he intended to get him to engage in debate with Otric of Saxony, *scholasticus* at the palace school at Magdeburg. Richer says that the immature and impulsive Otto hoped that if Gerbert "was unexpectedly attacked, he would then pursue his opponent with more vigour in the disputation."[23] Otric was a self-important fellow who had already sent a monk-spy to Reims to dig out any weak points in Gerbert's teaching. The spy returned to Magdeburg with a half-cocked version of Gerbert's views.

A few days after Christmas Otto sprung the debate on Gerbert, having already invited a crowd of scholars and students to attend. It focused on the classification of knowledge. Otric incorrectly claimed that Gerbert treated physics as a subspecies of mathematics, whereas Richer says that Gerbert actually claimed "that mathematics, physics and theology are all coequal species of the same genus, in which they participate equally."[24] This may seem to us a complete irrelevance, but in the context of the time it was an argument about the interpretation of ancient authorities such as Boethius's *Arithmatica*. Gerbert's strength was that he clearly understood what Boethius was saying, whereas Otric was confused by his spy about Gerbert's position. The value of these debates was that they strengthened the ability of debaters and, more importantly, those students listening to the argument to analyze and develop clarity and precision of expression. Gerbert seems to have been declared the winner, and with an enhanced intellectual reputation, he traveled on to Rome with the emperor and Adalbero. In Rome they attended the important Lateran Synod (March 9–10, 981), which condemned simony and appeased Otto by rearranging the Saxon dioceses.

The debate had reminded the impulsive Otto II of Gerbert's talents. Sometime in 981 Otto appointed him abbot of Bobbio, which Pope Benedict VII

(974–983) confirmed. This was an ill-judged move that offered Gerbert a poisoned chalice. Unlike his father, Otto II's hold on Italy was tenuous. His policy was to place men loyal to him in powerful positions there. He wanted Gerbert to administer the important abbey and its vast holdings as count and abbot in the interests of the Saxon monarchy. Gerbert took up the office on his return from Rome—his time there would be difficult and unpleasant.

Founded by Irishman Saint Columbanus in 612, the monastery in the northern foothills of the Apennines became a center of learning with wide political influence across the Po region. There was a grand library of almost 670 manuscripts, which attracted Gerbert. But by the tenth century, as we have already discovered in the Patrimonium, monasteries were seen as easy pickings by magnates hungry for land. Long-term rented monastic land was alienated by ruthless tenants as freehold through legal loopholes. Abbots often didn't have the coercive power to prevent this happening, so they were forced to accept it. In this situation Gerbert was an innocent abroad, and as a foreigner he was even more deeply resented by the local land-grabbers who preyed on the monastery. He was also resented by the monks who wanted one of their own as abbot. So to protect himself and keep a record of what had happened, in early 982 he began recording copies of his letters. He told Otto in May–June 982 that "my monks [are] wasting away from hunger and suffering from nakedness" and that the monastery was being asset-stripped by "what they call 'little books.'" These were the contract-letters granting land to lessees in exchange for specific goods and services to the monastery. Gerbert complained that these conditions were not being fulfilled. He told Otto that "the money which was collected is nowhere to be found; the storehouses and granaries have been emptied; in the purses there is nothing." Gerbert confronted the serial thief, Boso of Nebiano: "Let us avoid superfluous words . . . and keep to facts. . . . Restore to Saint Columbanus the hay which your followers took [stole]" from the monastery.[25] Gerbert's predecessor, Abbot Peter, had personally alienated movable monastic property via a legal loophole, giving it to Prior Petroald, who came from a powerful local family. Gerbert was blunt even to the most powerful. He told Empress Adelheid that he couldn't grant monastic assets to her favorites: "If we give the whole away, what shall we [monks] keep?" He accused Peter Canepanova (later Pope John XIV), Bishop of Pavia and Otto's chancellor for Italy of "thefts from our church . . . [and] distributing our possessions to your knights as if they were your own."[26] Gerbert faced corruption on a grand scale.

Bobbio was 50 miles (80 kilometers) from the imperial palace at Pavia, and Gerbert was often obliged to attend to business there. Resentment over his attempted reforms meant he had many enemies, both covert and overt, which inevitably led to scuttlebutt spreading about him. It was said that he had a wife and children and that he was an *equum emissarium* (literally, horse drain), meaning something like a stud horse or a promiscuous ladies man. There is no evidence beyond rumor that Gerbert was sexually involved with anyone, although he liked women and trusted them. He somewhat innocently attributed these slurs to "the customs of this region" (i.e., northern Italy). But they affected him, and by September 983 he was in despair. "For what part of Italy does not contain my enemies[?] . . . When they are unable to strike me with the sword, they assail me with the darts of words. . . . Because I refuse to comply with the provisions of the 'book leases' . . . I am called faithless, cruel, tyrannical. The scoundrels compare Caesar himself [Otto II] . . . to an ass."[27]

Following Otto's death on December 7, 983, Gerbert was in physical danger from many locals and was also unpopular with the monks. Leaving the monastery in the hands of Prior Petroald, he fled to the imperial palace in Pavia, where he again encountered Theophano on her way north to deal with the kidnapping of the young Otto III by Henry the Quarreler. Probably looking for allies wherever she could find them, she seems to have recruited Gerbert as a lobbyist to persuade the important south German churchmen to support her as she tried to rescue her son. Looking for a secure base from which to help Theophano, he headed back over the Alps to Reims and remained there for the next fourteen years (until 998).

Gerbert nevertheless remained de facto Abbot of Bobbio until he was elected pope on April 2, 999. Prior Petroald ran the abbey in his name. Gerbert's subsequent interest in the monastery seems to have been intermittent. On March 18, 984, he reprimanded the rebellious monks who had cast the Benedictine rule aside "by deserting your pastor [Petroald]" and joining up with people Gerbert had excommunicated. A loyal monk, Rainard, then wrote to tell him that Petroald had been overthrown. What was he to do? "I urge and advise you," Gerbert responds, "to think and act as best you can according to your knowledge and ability." Soon afterward he called the loyal Bobbio monks and vassals his "true sons . . . for your constant fidelity towards me." He promised he would soon return, but this doesn't seem to have happened. Three years later he wrote again to Rainard and gave him permission to change monasteries.[28] After that his interest in Bobbio seems to have faded; he was far more caught up in the political currents of the time.

∽

Returning to Reims, Gerbert quickly became involved again with Archbishop Adalbero in both imperial and French affairs. The immediate issue was helping Theophano rescue Otto III from Henry the Quarreler. Gerbert's efforts are recorded in a series of letters from the year 984. He wrote to influential Bishop Notker of Liège, accusing him of "ignorance of the times" and warning him of the "ambitious plans of Henry" to make himself king, replacing Otto. Influenced by Gerbert, Notker eventually came over to the side of Theophano. His next letter was to his friend Lady Imiza (a nickname for Irmintrud), a niece of Adalbero and a member of Theophano's court. He asked her to inform Theophano "in my name" that "the kings of the French [the plural refers to both King Lothar and his son Louis V] are well disposed toward her son and that she should attempt nothing but the destruction of Henry [the Quarreler]'s tyrannical scheme for he desires to make himself king under the pretext of guardianship." In fact, Adalbero and Gerbert had hatched an ill-advised scheme for Lothar to become protector of Otto III. In the same letter he tells Imiza, "I consider myself fortunate in being accepted as a friend by such a remarkable woman [as you]."[29] Whether their friendship was anything more than platonic (as the Italian scuttlebutt maintained) remains completely unknown, but he clearly had real affection for her.

Gerbert's main task was to keep the Lotharingian and the south German bishops on Otto's side. Writing in Adalbero's name, Gerbert unsuccessfully urged Archbishop Egbert of Trier to abandon the notion that Otto was half-Greek (clearly Egbert's disquiet was with Theophano rather than Otto), and he challenged Egbert to remember "the benefits bestowed on you by the Ottos. . . . Bid your great intelligence return; reflect on their generosity, unless you wish to be an everlasting disgrace to your race." He wrote to Bishop Dietrich of Metz, a Saxon and former chancellor of Otto I, to "support the house of Israel [i.e., Otto III]." Archbishop Willigis of Mainz was also a hard nut to crack. Again writing in Adalbero's name, he warns Willigis, who was the primate of Germany, about the danger of supporting Henry. He asks, "Will he [Henry], who has attempted to kill two Ottos be willing that a third should survive?" Three months later he writes in his own name to Willigis in

a confidential tone telling him that, while he is distracted by his Italian enemies, he is still profoundly concerned about what has happened to Otto. It
was proper that "the lamb be entrusted to his mother, not to the wolf."[30]
Three days later (June 26, 984) the "wolf" Henry surrendered the "lamb"
Otto to Theophano.

Gerbert, having been a faithful servant, now felt he should be rewarded by
the empress-regent. He had committed himself to her not just because it was
expedient to do so but also because he was convinced that the church could
prosper only when intimately linked to the empire. In a slightly pathetic letter
in mid-July 984, Gerbert asks that "my lady Theophano [be] mindful of me."
He points out that he has succeeded in keeping Lotharingia on Otto's side and
that he "has aroused as many persons as possible to aid [Otto]." He then asks
what he should do: should he remain in Reims "as a reserve soldier" or join
Theophano at court "as it was decided in the palace at Pavia"? Six months later
Theophano summoned him, but he was unable to get to Saxony because of
the disturbed state of things around Reims in January 985.[31]

Meanwhile, Adalbero and Gerbert had become immersed in the internecine
complexities of French politics. In the late tenth century the contenders for the
French crown were Kings Lothar and his son Louis V, the last of the Carolingian line; and Hugh Capet, Count of Paris. Both archbishop and scholar favored Hugh, whom they were trying to persuade to ally himself with Otto III.
Gerbert undermined Lothar by suggesting that he governed France in name
only while Hugh was the real ruler, which was actually true. Things were complicated by Lothar's determination to seize Lotharingia from the Ottonians and
Adalbero's close family ties there, where his brother Godfrey was count of Verdun (which had been seized by Lothar) and a cousin and two nephews were
bishops. This placed Gerbert and the archbishop in the firing line in a complex
situation of conflicting loyalties. Gerbert's letters to the king's enemies show
that he acted to undermine Lothar, leading to some characterizing him as an
"intriguer."[32] Gerbert conveyed his real feelings when he told Theophano in
April 985 that the French kings "look upon us [Adalbero and himself] in an
unfavourable light because we do not agree with them about fidelity to you."
He asked her "if any road through the enemy [is] open" so that he could get to
see her. He says that Adalbero's life had been threatened and "the same is true
of myself, as if I was arousing him against the policies of the French," which, of
course, was precisely what he was doing.[33]

But it was almost two years before he heard from Theophano again; she was preoccupied with other problems. Meanwhile, Adalbero was charged with treason by Lothar at an assembly at Compiègne, but he was saved from trial when Lothar suddenly died on March 2, 986, from an illness whose symptoms were fever, vomiting, cramps, and bleeding, which led to talk of poisoning. Adalbero staged a splendid funeral for him at Reims.

Louis V succeeded him. A petulant youth of nineteen, popularly referred to as *Le Fainéant* (from *qui nihil fecit,* "who did nothing"), he was very much under his mother, Queen Emma's, tutelage. She was a daughter of Empress Adelheid by her first marriage and thus a half-sister to Otto II. Emma favored Adalbero and Gerbert, and Gerbert wrote on her behalf to Adelheid to counter the seemingly false rumor that she was having an affair with Adalbero's nephew the bishop of Laon. People "have fabricated the wickedest things against the bishop of Laon," she says, "to my disgrace and that of my whole family." She confesses that she looks on her own son Louis "as an enemy" because he had suddenly broken loose from her and attacked Reims.[34] Adalbero was again charged with treason. But before he came to trial, he was again saved by a death: Louis fell from his horse and died while hunting. Others claimed he was poisoned.

The man with the best claim to succeed Louis was his uncle, Duke Charles of Lower Lotharingia. But influenced by Adalbero and Gerbert, the French nobles opted for an elective kingship. Hugh Capet, who was the only real contender, was elected king on June 1, 987. A month later he was crowned and anointed in Reims by Adalbero. He poured the chrism on Hugh's head from a phial said to have been brought by a dove from heaven for Clovis's baptism, thus giving the king sacral authority. (Clovis was the first king of the Franks, who converted to Catholicism in 496.) Hugh also needed the support of the German court for his election, and he sent Gerbert, now his letter writer and adviser, as an ambassador to secure Theophano's backing for his coronation. Gerbert managed to catch the empress somewhere on the road near Frankfurt. The price of German support was the return of Verdun to the empire.

However, Hugh's kingship was more symbolic than real because beyond his power base in central-northern France between Paris and Orléans, the country remained divided among many feudal lords, with about twelve different languages and codes of law. Certainly, Duke Charles was not going to take Hugh's coronation lying down. He besieged Reims and in May 988 seized the well-defended town of Laon, nabbing Queen Emma and her reputed lover, Bishop Ascelin, in the process. By now Gerbert's political connections and astuteness were widely recognized, and Charles set out to win him over to his side, while Gerbert's main aim was to win the release of Emma and Ascelin. In mid-summer 988 Gerbert was suffering from exhaustion and "violent fevers," possibly the symptoms of dysentery. He was still sick in late August.[35] Then, complicating matters further, Archbishop Adalbero died on January 23, 989. Gerbert was so sure he would be the next archbishop that he turned down an offer of a position in Germany. He told a correspondent that Adalbero "with the assent of the whole clergy, of all the bishops and certain knights had designated me as his successor."[36]

So Gerbert was bitterly disappointed when King Hugh appointed his former student Arnoul, the twenty-four-year-old bastard son of King Lothar and a nephew of Duke Charles, as archbishop of Reims. Gerbert should have foreseen that a king's bastard would be preferred to a peasant's son no matter how well educated and experienced, and that from Hugh's perspective the *realpolitik* was right. Then, unexpectedly, Arnoul offered Gerbert the job of secretary; he accepted, hoping to influence the new archbishop. But he knew his position was tenuous and dangerous, so he continued to keep the lines of communication open with Theophano's court. In June 989 he asked Archbishop Willigis to "pray remind my Lady Theophano of the fidelity that I have always maintained towards herself and her son. Do not allow me to become the prize of her enemies whom I reduced to disgrace and scorn on her behalf whenever I was able."[37] Theophano's failure to reply showed a degree of gracelessness; she replied only when Gerbert was of use to her.

Archbishop Arnoul soon showed his true colors. One night in September 989 he secretly ordered a priest named Adalger to open the gates of Reims to Duke Charles's troops, who proceeded to sack the town. Arnoul pretended to be innocent of any conspiracy and got himself taken "prisoner" by Charles to Laon. Trapped in Reims and trying to keep the city administratively afloat, Gerbert showed amazing mental gymnastics when he wrote to Archbishop Egbert of Trier on Arnoul's behalf asking for advice as to which side Arnoul should support, Hugh or Charles? In May 990 Hugh summoned a synod of bishops to meet in Senlis to sort out the situation in Reims. Gerbert fled from Reims and joined the Senlis synod, which proceeded to excommunicate "the priest Adalger . . . and also those who were the originators of this betrayal. . . . To these villains we add the attackers of the bishop of Laon."[38] Now a wake-up call to

Arnoul, Hugh wrote to Pope John XV via Gerbert telling him that "the arch-bishop himself threw open the gates [of Reims] to enemies; and the clergy and people entrusted to his fidelity he allowed to be distributed as captives and booty," forcing people to perjure themselves and revolt against Hugh as king. The bishops at Senlis asked the pope to take action against Arnoul as "a noto-rious apostate . . . [and] second Judas."[39] John XV ignored the letter.

The impasse between Hugh and Charles was broken when the resourceful Bishop Ascelin tricked Duke Charles and Archbishop Arnoul and delivered them into the hands of King Hugh. Charles died in prison two years later, probably poisoned. What were they to do with Arnoul? Under pressure he re-signed at a council in the basilica of St.-Basle-de-Verzy in June 991. Gerbert was elected archbishop of Reims. This action was criticized by Abbot Abbo of Fleury (ca. 940–1004), who was a champion of papal primacy; Abbo denied the right of councils to depose bishops, claiming this was reserved to the pope alone. In fact, he was really trying to protect his independence from the local episcopal jurisdiction that papal exemption gave his monastery. This led to an antipapal speech (possibly written by Gerbert) by another Arnoul, this one the bishop of Orléans who was Gerbert's friend. The Orléans bishop correctly re-minded the other bishops of the corruption of the papacy: "Of old we received [from Rome] the illustrious Leos, the great Gregorys, . . . But what do we see there today?" Specifically referring to John XII, he asked, "To such wicked monsters, ignorant of all learning, human and divine, are countless good and learned priests to be subject[?] . . . In comparison with the Roman Pontiff, ig-norance in other bishops is to some extent tolerable; but of him who is to judge the faith, life and morals of other bishops, and of the whole Catholic church, it is quite intolerable."[40]

The news of the deposition of Arnoul of Reims was unwelcome in Rome, where the French bishops were perceived as too independent. This didn't augur well for Gerbert.

Now in his midforties, he seemed to be suffering from recurrent illnesses. In a letter of December 990 he says that he "contracted those illnesses whereby pestilential autumn almost wrested our life away." The medieval belief was that autumn was the most dangerous season for illness. Perhaps he had severe flu or pneumonia.[41]

ᥫᩬ

Gerbert was now accused of overweening ambition to become archbishop of
Reims. If that were true, it was an ambition misdirected, for his time as archbishop gave him nothing but grief. Doubtless he was telling the truth when he
wrote to John XV that that "God and those who know me are my witnesses
that it was not with the hope of usurping his [Arnoul's] office, as my rivals
say."[42] Remember, Arnoul was no mature churchman but a youthful, callow,
royal bastard appointed by King Hugh for purely political purposes, whereas
Gerbert was the greatest scholar of the age, a man with a long history as an ecclesiastical administrator and reformer, exactly the right person for the episcopate. Nevertheless, this energy-sapping conflict with the papacy over Reims
was to drag on for six more years.

Despite all this, Gerbert was a good bishop. He instilled discipline and charity into his clergy and worked for their ongoing education. The diocese was in
poor shape after three years of chaos. Gerbert and the bishops of the province
threatened the excommunication of feudal "encroachers, scoundrels and
tyrants . . . [because they] murder the clergy and do not cease their thefts from
clergy, monks and paupers."[43] He was a bishop in the tradition of Gregory the
Great's *Regula pastoralis* (Pastoral Rule), which laid down the lineaments of an
effective church leader. Besides caring for his clergy, Gregory stipulated that
the bishop should preach in Latin to clergy and in the vernacular to the people.
He should visit parishes, celebrate confirmation, and join the canons of the
cathedral in the regular chanting of the canonical hours. Above all, the bishop
was called to be a living example of a committed spiritual and moral life. In all
this Gerbert was a model bishop. His pastoral experience led him to advise,
"The salvation of souls must be handled with great moderation."[44]

But his pastoral care was stymied by constant battle with Rome over his appointment. Arnoul's partisans—mainly stubborn monks like Abbo protecting
their own interests —quickly got the ear of John XV, who refused to recognize
Gerbert and accused him of being an "invader" of Reims. Gerbert became increasingly fixated on defending himself, and since he could not fall back on a
noble family to support him, he had only his raw talent to help him in maintaining his position. In December 992 King Hugh invited the pope to come to
France, but John XV refused.

It is ironic that Gerbert, who was destined for the papacy himself, should
find himself in confrontation with a pope. What were his views on the role of
the papacy? As archbishop-metropolitan of Reims and the most senior bishop in

France, he understandably wanted to restrict the interference of the faraway pope in what he and most others saw as local ecclesiastical affairs. The reputation of the papacy was deservedly at rock bottom, and local churches asked why should they be subject to the decisions of scandalous and evil popes. Propapalist historians tend to see Gerbert as a proto-Gallican—that is, one who saw the French church as independent of the ecclesiastical authority of the papacy. This is misleading because Gerbert saw himself in the tradition of metropolitan archbishops like Hincmar who exercised authority over the provincial church and brooked no interference from faraway Rome. In a long, convoluted treatise riddled with embedded classical references written in December 995 and sent to Bishop Wilderode of Strasbourg, Gerbert justifies the sacking of Arnoul on the basis that the pope did nothing about the loutish young archbishop, so the French bishops were forced to act, basing their action on the laws and customs of the early church. Gerbert was neither a theologian nor an ecclesiologist (that is, a theorist concerning the nature of the church and its government). The ethos of the tenth century was practical and spiritual rather than theological and speculative, so Gerbert saw the question of the election or dismissal of an archbishop as a practical problem to be settled within the context of the *limits* of papal power and the rights of local bishops acting collegially.

Essentially, the whole struggle was between French interests (King Hugh and the French bishops) who supported Gerbert and French monks led by Abbo of Fleury who supported Arnoul. John XV supported Arnoul in order to protect his sole right to dismiss archbishops. The imperial court also supported Arnoul because Theophano had died in 991 and Adelheid, who disliked Gerbert intensely, had become regent. Richer reports, "The bishops of Germany had been sending a steady stream of letters to Pope John advising him to invalidate the elevation of Gerbert . . . and [to] express outrage at the illegal deposition of Arnoul."[45] Eventually, the pope summoned a synod at Mouzon, east of Reims, for June 2, 995. A legate, Abbot Leo of Sant' Alessio on the Aventine, was appointed by the pope to preside.

The strategic issue here was control of Lotharingia, which the German *Reich* was obviously unwilling to cede to the French. Richer suggests that the whole affair got caught up in a political plot devised by the bishop of Laon and the ambitious Odo I, Count of Chartres "to bring Otto into Gaul as king and to depose Hugh and Robert [his son] by stratagem and force of arms."[46] The aim was for the Germans to nab the French kings at Mouzon and depose them.

This, Richer claims, was why King Hugh forbade the French bishops to attend the synod. This left Gerbert completely exposed.

So under pressure from King Hugh, the French bishops, with the exception of Gerbert, refused to attend. However, four German bishops and "many abbots from different places" did.[47] Gerbert gave a dignified and powerful speech arguing that Adalbero had openly designated him as his successor, but that Arnoul had gained the see by "simony," by which he meant that Arnoul had bribed King Hugh to appoint him. He says that he gave Arnoul "loyal service . . . until I learned for myself that he had openly apostatized," by which he presumably meant that Arnoul had betrayed the archdiocese to Duke Charles. So Gerbert abandoned Arnoul "not as my rivals claim because I hoped to succeed to his office" but because he would not cooperate in evil. He then reminded the synod that it was only after "all the sanctions of the church had been exhausted" and Arnoul had been removed that he was called upon "by the brothers and the chief men of the realm" to "grudgingly" undertake the office of archbishop. "My conscience is clear in all I did," he says. As to consulting the pope, he says the French bishops waited "for [Rome's] decision for eighteen months" without receiving a reply. It was only then that they decided to act.[48]

Gerbert's powerful speech failed to impress the synod. Somewhere around this time he was excommunicated by John XV, although the French bishops and king refused to recognize the pope's decision. Further skirmishing occurred, but by January 996 it was clear that Gerbert's position in Reims was becoming unsustainable. The fanatical Abbot Abbo was in Rome in February 996, and Gerbert told a correspondent that "the power, importance and dignity of the bishops" were threatened.[49] By mid-996 he seems to have become exhausted, so he left Reims, never to return. But Gerbert's career was far from over.

CHAPTER 17

Otto III

A "New Rome"?

GREAT SCHOLAR THAT HE WAS, Gerbert could be oddly obtuse at times. Throughout his scholarly career in Reims, he found it almost impossible to comprehend that his personal welfare and career prospects were of little interest to Theophano as Otto III's regent. Nevertheless, he kept trying to draw attention to himself. Repeatedly ignored, he started asking friends at court to "suggest good words on [my] behalf" and "make my Lady Theophano mindful of me." He naïvely tells a correspondent in 986 that "the imperial court will summon me quickly," and he later informs his old teacher Raymond that Theophano has ordered him "to depart into Saxony with her" to prepare for war on the eastern frontier against the Slavs.[1] Above all, he wanted to be a bishop in the German lands, so great was his admiration for Ottonian government. On June 21, 988, writing in Archbishop Adalbero's name, he asked Theophano straight out for a diocese: "If any church at all on the border of the kingdoms be lacking a pastor, no other be established in it except one whom we [i.e., Adalbero] with impartial judgment have represented to you as suitable in all ways."[2] This was really yet another roundabout way of saying, "Please give Gerbert a diocese!" The irony is that, as we saw, the German bishops and Otto III's regent Adelheid ultimately destroyed his career as archbishop of Reims.

Theophano had bigger problems than getting a diocese for Gerbert. Her regency had begun with the kidnapping of the three-year-old Otto by his nearest male relative, and, as we've seen, the rest of her life was involved in the political task of maintaining Otto III's position. At the time of her death in June 991, Otto III was still only ten. Empress-Grandmother Adelheid assumed the regency and maintained the stability and policies established under Theophano. What is particularly striking about the minority of Otto III is the role played by the *dominae imperiales*, the "imperial ladies," who remained both physically and emotionally close to Otto. Besides Theophano and Adelheid, there were Otto's aunt and Theophano's friend Mathilda, Abbess of Quedlinburg, and his sisters Adelheid and Sophie, both of whom became abbesses. Because the family ties were so strong and intimate, it is hard to pinpoint a specific date when Otto III came of age, but by 995 he was certainly undertaking the royal itinerary on his own. But the influence of the kinswomen remained strong, and there was a gradual shift from regency to personal rule.

One of the first issues Otto dealt with as ruler was the Reims dispute, but his exact role is unclear. After the Mouzon synod failed to resolve the dispute and Gerbert's position became increasingly unsustainable, a German synod was held at Ingelheim on February 5, 996. In preparation for this, Gerbert wrote the long, self-justifying letter to Bishop Wilderode of Strasbourg dated December 31, 995, referred to in the previous chapter. Nothing seemed to have been resolved at Ingelheim, and Otto left Regensburg for Rome in February 996 at the request of the nepotistic and greedy John XV, who had been driven out of Rome by the local strongman Crescentius II Nomentanus. The news that Otto was heading south forced Crescentius to reconcile with John XV, who, however, died of a violent fever while Otto was still in Pavia. Perhaps as a sign of his immaturity (he was then only fifteen), Otto appointed his well-educated twenty-four-year-old second cousin, Bruno of Carinthia, as pope. He took the style Gregory V (996–999), the first pope from north of the Alps. Meanwhile, Gerbert had followed Otto to Rome. On the feast of the Ascension (April 996), Pope Gregory crowned Otto Holy Roman Emperor.

Otto clearly had a soft spot for Gerbert, whom he now took into his service as a notary and private secretary. Almost immediately Gerbert composed a letter for Otto informing his grandmother Adelheid he had been crowned emperor. By August Otto was in Pavia on his way back to Germany. But Otto's patronage didn't help Gerbert in Rome, so he returned to Reims. Gerbert's enemies, including the scheming Abbo of Fleury, who had now ingratiated himself with Gregory V, kept denouncing him to the new pope, but the pope put off making a decision until Arnoul had been heard.

Returning to Reims, Gerbert became seriously ill with a tertian fever, which he had clearly picked up in malaria-infested Rome. He told Empress Adelheid in February 997, "Old age threatens me with my last day. . . . This whole year has seen me lying ill in bed, I have suffered a relapse, and am seized with chills and fevers on alternate days."[3] There are several letters from the next few months in which Gerbert encouraged the archbishops of Tours and Sens to maintain their refusal to surrender to independently minded monks or to interfering popes. By April 997 his position in Reims was becoming untenable, primarily because King Hugh Capet had died in October 996 and Gerbert had refused to celebrate the marriage of Robert II, Hugh's son and successor, to his cousin Countess Bertha after he had repudiated his first wife.

The situation worsened in May 997 after Gregory V declared Gerbert an "intruder" in the archbishopric of Reims and Arnoul its lawful bishop. It was an outrageously stupid decision to give the diocese to an ill-educated youth, but there was nothing Gerbert could do. This was clearly a case where nobility of blood rather than nobility of character was paramount. Even his closest collaborators abandoned Gerbert; he speaks of "the undeserved persecution of my brothers."[4] So sick, betrayed, and exhausted, he fled to the royal court at Aachen, asking his friend Bishop Arnoul of Orléans to look after his interests in France. Now about fifty-two, he never set foot in France again.

By June Gerbert was in Magdeburg with Otto. On October 21, 997, Otto invited Gerbert to become his teacher and to free him from his Saxon *rusticitas* (ignorant simplicity) and replace it with Greek *subsilitas* (subtlety).[5] He now entered Otto's court permanently. Thietmar says that he built a horologe (a clock, timepiece, or even abacus) in Magdeburg, "positioning it correctly after he had observed through a tube the star that sailors use for guidance."[6]

The relationship with Otto had its ups and downs. For instance, Otto had given Gerbert an estate at Sasbach near Strasbourg that was part of the imperial fisc. But someone claiming to act for Otto while the emperor was fighting the Slavs on the eastern frontier reclaimed the estate. Offended, Gerbert reminded Otto that he had served both his father and grandfather, that he "exhibited the most incorruptible fidelity . . . [and] exposed my person, however small, to raging kings and frenzied people" to support the Ottonians. And so he asks, "By what contradiction [am I] said to have offended you and your followers so that my service is so suddenly displeasing[?]"[7] Ten days later Otto wrote to him asking him to become his tutor, but ignoring the Sasbach affair. Gerbert accepted the invitation and became a member of the court and remained close to Otto for the rest of their lives.

A year previously in October 996, Gerbert had joined Otto in Mainz, spending several weeks of discussion in the emperor's company. Adalbert, Bishop of Prague was also present in what was clearly an intimate exchange of views. The three men withdrew into something of a spiritual and philosophical retreat, and such discussions became regular occasions in Otto's life. He was sixteen at the time; youths of equivalent age and class would have been out hunting. While Chris Wickham unjustly calls Otto "irritatingly juvenile," Gerd Althoff has shown that he was very sensitive to the political and socioritual processes of his day.[8] He understood that he "embodied" the state in his person and had to operate according to an unwritten and complex set of rules and procedures. Otto's interlocutors, especially Gerbert, would have perfectly understood his mental world and the challenges facing him. Medieval kingship involved consultation and listening to wise advice, especially from elder churchmen, although Althoff wonders "how members of the ecclesiastical hierarchy, especially someone like Archbishop Willigis of Mainz, reacted when the young emperor withdrew for long conversations with such men, no matter how learned and exemplary."[9] Otto was lucky he ruled during a period of relative stability.

So what would it have been like dealing with this sixteen-year-old emperor? We must not project onto Otto any modern notions of adolescent psychology; this was a period when a shorter life span forced people to reach maturity earlier. Nevertheless, Otto's sometimes-erratic actions and passionate idealism tempt us to see both as conventional adolescent behavior. While avoiding the many pitfalls of historical psychoanalysis, modern developmental psychology tells us that high-intensity feelings and impulsiveness are characteristic of young people. These inspire them to pursue ideals of spirituality, beauty, music, art, and other great endeavors. But the problem is their neurobehavioral systems are immature and self-control is not easy to achieve. This can help us understand Otto's idealism and instability.

Otto grew up in an environment dominated by powerful women and older sisters. While this would have developed the gentler, feminine side of his personality, it would have also stimulated his need for strong male models in his life. Perhaps this goes some way to explaining his seeking the company of older men like Gerbert. Theophano made sure her intelligent child was well educated. His main tutors were Theophano's friend Greek-speaking Archbishop Johannes Philagathos, who schooled Otto in Greek language and culture; and from 987 to 993 Bernward, a highly educated priest, imperial chaplain, descendant of a noble Saxon family, and bishop of Hildesheim, whose advice Otto valued highly and to whom he was very close after Theophano's death in 990. Other *familiares* (intimate advisers) whose close company and advice he valued highly were Bishops Adalbert of Prague, saintly Greco-Italian hermit Nilus, and ascetical monk Romuald. Bishop Franco of Worms and Archbishop Heribert of Cologne were younger friends who were on very intimate terms with Otto. It was from these men that he imbibed a deep mystical spirituality, as well as an excellent education.

There were two other men with whom Otto was on even more intimate terms in relationships that were certainly unusual for a Saxon monarch. According to monk Pietro Damiani's *Vita Romualdi* (Life of Saint Romuald), Count Tammo, Otto's chaplain and brother of Bishop Bernward, was "so intimate and dear to the king that they wore each other's clothing and often used a single spoon when eating," and they joined hands together when they touched in the washing dish before eating.[10] The clothing exchange particularly drew attention to the intimacy between the two young men. Damiani cites a similar intimacy between Otto and Bruno of Querfurt, whom Otto called *anima mea* (my soul), conveying a sense of alter ego or soul mate. Thietmar's *Chronicon* says that Bruno "was admired by Otto III who took him into his service," but that he eventually left the court for the life of a hermit. He later became a missionary bishop near the border between Prussia and Russia (present-day Lithuania), where he was martyred in 1009.[11]

In our genitally obsessed, post-Freudian world, issues of homosexuality immediately arise concerning these relationships. But human sexuality is far more polymorphous than we imagine, and tenth-century notions of *amicitia* (friendship) were quite different from ours. We almost can't imagine close friendship without sexual expression, but then sexuality was a far less fraught issue than it is today. Otto and his friends were influenced by Plato and Cicero's writing on idealized friendship, and a generalized homoeroticism was broadly accepted. As we saw, it was later fanatics like Pietro Damiani who spread the moral panic about homosexuality.

To balance his inner life, Otto was also immersed at an early age in the military duties of a Saxon king. Having been presented with a camel and other gifts by Duke Mieszko of Poland at Easter 986 at Quedlinburg, he "assailed the Slavs with many harsh campaigns. He also conquered certain peoples in the East, who presumed to rise up against him."[12] Even as a boy he was present at a number of other campaigns, including the conquest of Brandenburg in September 991. Although he valued the interior life above all, Otto was far from a cloistered monarch. From the age of fourteen he acted as king and emperor and had a decisive influence on all the main issues of the day. It is to his active politico-military life that we will now turn.

❧

On reaching his majority, Otto inherited the problems of the always-restive eastern frontier. Here three new nations were rising. The first of these was Hungary, which emerged in the mid-Danube Carpathian Basin after the decisive 955 defeat by Otto I of the Magyars at the Battle of Lechfeld. Their leader, Duke Géza (972–997), under threat from Otto II, rejected missionaries from Constantinople and converted to Catholicism for "political survival," even though he still "sacrificed to pagan idols to honour the ancients."[13] The conversion of Hungary was consolidated by his son Stephen (997–1038). Hungary emerged as a non-Slav wedge between the West (or North) Slavs (today's Poles, Slovaks, and Czechs) and the South Slavs (today including Serbia, Croatia, Bulgaria, Romania, Bosnia, Slovenia, and Macedonia). With the exception of the duchy of Croatia, which was Catholic, the South Slavs largely fell under the ecclesiastical influence of the Eastern Orthodox Church from Bulgaria, an independent kingdom until 1014 when Byzantine emperor Basil II (976–1025) defeated the Bulgarians and brutally blinded 10,000 men.

The West Slavs had a different history. Bohemia and Poland had emerged by the middle of the tenth century, and both had interfered ineffectively in German affairs, attempting to support Henry the Wrangler after the death of Otto II. In 962 Bohemia under Duke Boleslav I (ca. 935–ca. 967)—he had gained the dukedom after murdering his brother "Good King Wenceslaus"—acknowledged the overlordship of Germany and this continued under Boleslav II (ca. 967–999). A diocese was established in Prague in 973; Otto III's friend Adalbert was appointed bishop there.

At first pagan Poland had opted to stay outside the *Reich*, but to keep the Germans at bay, Duke Mieszko I (ca. 960–992) converted to Catholicism in 966, although this didn't guarantee him freedom from attack on the volatile frontier. For instance, in June 972 Margrave Hodo I of the Saxon Ostmark (East March) impulsively attacked Mieszko. But the battle ended in a German defeat, leading to the death "of all the best warriors." This infuriated Otto I, who was then in Italy. According to Thietmar, he "ordered Hodo and Mieszko to leave off their fighting and preserve the peace . . . or risk losing his favour."[14] To forestall further difficulties, Mieszko established a Catholic diocese at Poznan, which he shrewdly placed directly under the authority of the pope, thus making sure its bishop was not a suffragan of a German metropolitan archbishop. A suffragan bishop had full authority in his own diocese, but his cooperation could be required by his metropolitan archbishop on provincial issues. By now Poland stretched from the Oder River in the west to Baltic Prussia in the north and eastward to Russia. To resist German pressure, Duke Mieszko in March 991 placed the whole country, a well-organized state, under the authority of the papacy, thereby making it part of the patrimony of Saint Peter. Although without much practical significance, this action symbolically placed Poland outside the authority of the *Reich*. Duke Mieszko was succeeded by his son Bolesław I Chobry "the Brave" in May 992. He cooperated with the Germans in their attempts to pacify and convert the Slavic tribes living northeast of the Elbe and further east in Pomerania.

One of the more extraordinary events of Otto III's reign was his trip to the shrine of his old friend martyred Bishop Adalbert at Gniezno. Adalbert had an extraordinary life. Born in Bohemia, his Czech name was Vojtech (Wojciech in Polish). He was educated at Magdeburg, where he took the name Adalbert after his teacher. Quickly appointed bishop of Prague in 982, he tried to deepen Christian faith among the half-converted Bohemians. He was exiled in 990, went to Rome, and became a monk. Boleslav II persuaded him to return to Prague and supported him, but trouble broke out again, and he returned to Rome in 995. As we saw, he became a friend of Otto III, advising him on Slavic issues. Always restless and now supported by the Polish Bolesław I, Adalbert returned to Eastern Europe in an attempt to convert the Prussi, a now-extinct Baltic tribe from eastern Pomerania near Danzig. On April 23, 997, he was killed while saying Mass in a sacred grove of trees, which local pagans understandably saw as a desecration. He was also probably perceived as a Polish spy. His body was repatriated to Poland by Duke Bolesław I and buried at Gniezno.

In February 999 Otto learned that his sister Abbess Mathilda of Quedlinburg had died; then in December 999 his grandmother Adelheid also died. So he decided he needed to return to Germany and make a pilgrimage to Adalbert's grave in Gniezno. Departing Rome at Christmas 999, Otto crossed the Brenner Pass in midwinter (January 1000), journeying through Bavaria and southeastern Germany, with crowds flocking to see him and bishops and magnates welcoming him. This was not an impulsive trip; it had a planned itinerary in which Otto was met on the border by Duke Bolesław I, who accompanied him to Gniezno. Thietmar recounts, "Seeing the desired city from afar, [Otto] humbly approached barefoot. . . . He was led into the church where, weeping profusely, he was moved to ask the grace of Christ for himself through the intercession of Christ's martyr."[15]

Bolesław accompanied Otto back to Germany and concluded a *foedus amicitiae*, a treaty of friendship, which was sealed by an exchange of gifts and a lavish feast. Thietmar, who despised Bolesław (he refers to him as "that deceitful man"), criticizes Otto "for making a *dominus* (lord) out of a *tributarius*" (a person who owed rent or tribute).[16] Otto also founded a new church province in Poland, with Gniezno as the metropolitan archdiocese. One present that Otto received in Poland that particularly pleased him was a gift of three hundred armored horsemen. Accompanied by Duke Bolesław I, Otto traveled to Magdeburg for Easter and then on to Aachen with Bolesław still in tow.

Otto III had now achieved what his father and grandfather had failed to complete: the stabilization and securing of the eastern frontier of the *Reich*. The Slavs were now friends rather than constant threats to the Saxon heartland. To be fair, things were easier for Otto III; the hard work of conversion of the West Slavs and Hungarians to Catholicism had already been carried out in the previous two reigns. The stabilization of the frontier meant that Germany was now a coherent cultural and national entity and its eastern neighbors were also well on the way to a similar status. Europe as we know it was starting to take shape, and the cultural world and civilization that we have inherited as Westerners had begun its journey to today.

ↄ໐

Back in the *Reich*, as we saw, Otto III spent an extended time in dialogue with Gerbert and Adalbert in October 996. The emperor then spent the next year in Germany, an absolute necessity for any Saxon monarch. Long absences in Italy and elsewhere were resented by the magnates, and the royal itinerary and presence were necessary to keep the powerful loyal. He was also tied up in two unsuccessful campaigns in the first half of 997 against the yet-to-be-converted-and-absorbed Elbe Slavs, or Wends, who lived wedged between the Saale and Elbe rivers west of Poland and east of Thuringia.

But trouble was also brewing in Rome. In late September 996 the Romans, led by Crescentius II (Crescentius of the Marble Horse), again revolted and drove Otto's pope, Gregory V, out of the city, first to Spoleto and then to Pavia. Gregory begged Otto to intervene, but the emperor took his time, and it wasn't until early December 997 that Otto again crossed the Brenner and headed to Pavia, where he celebrated Christmas with Gregory.

Ten months earlier the Romans had elected themselves a new pope, none other than Otto's godfather and former Greek tutor, Johannes Philagathos, previously chancellor for Italy, archbishop of Piacenza, and, according to the anti-Greek Pietro Damiani, the lover of Theophano. Most recently, Johannes had acted as special ambassador to Constantinople seeking a Byzantine bride for Otto III. But driven by what saintly hermit and abbot Nilus calls "*insatiabili aviditate*" (insatiable ambition) and under pressure from Crescentius, he accepted election as Johannes XVI in February 997.[17] Philagathos was influenced by the Byzantine bishop Leo of Synada in Phrygia (now central Turkey), who claimed to have manipulated the Romans to get him elected. Leo was in Rome for two years representing Emperor Basil II in the on-again, off-again marriage negotiations between Otto and Byzantium, and he wrote to a friend in the court in Constantinople in early 997, "I know that you're laughing at me but I suspect you'll roar when you hear that I appointed Philagathos pope—when I should have strangled him."[18] Leo, who had a real sense of humor, aimed to detach Rome from German allegiance and bring it into Constantinople's sphere of influence. It is also interesting that the Romans preferred a Greek pope (even if a southern Italian Greek) to a German one. Certainly, there were still many Greek clerics in and around Rome, and the connection to Constantinople was still strong among the Roman elite. Most contemporaries, however, seem to have had a very low opinion of Philagathos, including Bishop Leo, who says, "That Philagathos . . . whose mouth was full of cursing and bitterness, blasphemy, wickedness, and abuse . . . that murderous pope, that pompous and haughty creature."[19]

Johannes's action is hard to understand. Why he would abandon the Ottonians after the favors Theophano and Otto had bestowed on him and whose approbation he could reasonably continue to expect after his relatively successful marriage negotiations with the Byzantines to take up with a thug like Crescentius? No doubt the reason was ambition, but he probably justified it to himself by naïvely thinking he could bring peace between the Germans and the Byzantines. He was quickly excommunicated by the Western bishops and Gregory V. His survival at Rome now depended on Crescentius, and both were entirely reliant on the protection of the Byzantines, which was not forthcoming. Indeed, there is evidence in a letter to Gerbert (probably from Archbishop Willigis of Mainz) that Johannes XVI had written to Otto around August 997 offering to surrender and submit himself "to the rule of our Caesar."[20] This implies that Johannes was willing to perform a ritual act of submission to the emperor, thereby handing himself over to Otto's mercy.

Otto was in no hurry to push on to Rome. He visited Cremona and then traveled down the Po to Ravenna on a decorated ship provided by the doge of Venice. He marched on Rome in mid-February 998 and found the city undefended. Crescentius took refuge in the Castel Sant'Angelo with a small band of retainers, while Johannes XVI fled into hiding in a castle in the Campagna, perhaps hoping to escape to Byzantine territory after things cooled down. Meanwhile, the panicking Romans immediately reached a settlement with Otto, and he entered the city as an occupier. He was clearly cautious, however, like his grandfather Otto I, telling his sword-bearer Count Ansfrid, "Today, while I am praying at the threshold of the Apostles, you must continually hold the sword above my head for I am well aware that the Romans' loyalty to our predecessors was often suspect."[21]

Johannes Philagathos was quickly traced and captured by Count Berthold of Breisgau in late February 998. It was almost certainly Berthold who was responsible for Johannes's gruesome mutilation; he was later rewarded by Otto for his appalling violence to the antipope. The Byzantine bishop Leo describes what happened:

He [Johannes] was pronounced anathema to the Western Church; second, his eyes were put out, third, his nose and fourth, his lips were cut off; fifth, his overpowering tongue which constantly babbled unmentionable things. Sixth after this, he led a procession solemnly riding a shabby little donkey which he held by the tail, too. A shred of ancient goatskin with its head upright covered his own. Seventh, he went to trial, was condemned, was dressed in and stripped of his ecclesiastical garb, was dragged out backwards through the very nave, the narthex, the courtyard with the fountain and was thrown in the dungeon as a respite.[22]

Leo has conflated two distinct phases of Philagathos's punishment here. The awful mutilation, which even contemporaries considered appalling, occurred soon after his capture. It was after this that his compatriot Abbot Nilus, now almost ninety, outraged by what had happened, set out for Rome and unsuccessfully begged both emperor and pope to surrender Johannes to his care. Gregory V was clearly still dissatisfied and wanted Philagathos put on trial, which resulted in his condemnation and the stripping of ecclesiastical garb. Incarcerated in a Roman monastery, Philagathos died in August 1001, we hope in peace.

The situation regarding the capture of Crescentius II was more complex. He was safe while holed up in the Castel Sant'Angelo, which was pretty much impregnable. It was not until after Easter that Crescentius was captured, executed, his body degraded and his wife taken as a concubine by the emperor. One account holds that he was betrayed through a false promise of a safe conduct by Otto. Another, recounted by Rodulfus Glaber, was that Crescentius threw himself on Otto's mercy but was rejected. He returned to the Castel, which was soon penetrated by Otto's troops. Crescentius was severely wounded in the fighting and then captured. "Those found with him were all killed." When Otto was asked what to do with Crescentius, he replied, "'Cast him off the ramparts in the sight of the people, so that the Romans will not be able to say that you have stolen their prince.' So it was done and afterwards they bound him and dragged him behind oxen in the mud of the streets, and . . . left him to hang on a high gibbet in full view of the city."[23] According to Thietmar, he "was beheaded and hanged with a rope by his feet."[24] Glaber's version is probably as close to accurate as we'll get, for his source was most likely Abbot Odilo of Cluny, who was in Rome with Otto's party.

Pope Gregory V and Otto III were primarily responsible for this appalling cruelty. Although some sources say Otto repented his action, the treatment seems to have been part of a deliberate policy of terror tactics. The emperor's circle considered that the Romans had become a *sentina*, a rabble, a cesspool, the lowest of the low, and that both men were *perversi* and *apostata*, "perverts" and "apostates," who should be treated as such. Also, Crescentius had been shown imperial clemency previously, and such mildness was not repeated for a backslider. This would explain why in Glaber's version of the story Otto refuses to negotiate or exercise the kingly virtue of mercy. The treatment of Philagathos is harder to explain, although some sources suggest that he planned to hand over Rome and the papacy to the Byzantines. Clearly, the whole Ottonian camp, including Gerbert, was determined to make an example of the two "perverts." Thus, the brutality was not considered personal; nor was it a desire for revenge by emperor or pope. It was simply the rules of the game. Patience and mercy were not endless. Althoff says that "a person could only hope for *pietas* (mildness) once."[25] Nevertheless, there seems to have been at least some penitence on Otto's part. Soon after dealing with Philagathos and Crescentius, he made a barefoot pilgrimage of Saint Nilus's cell at the shrine of Saint Michael the Archangel at Monte Gargano near Foggia, a distance of about 210 miles (340 kilometers).

In the middle of all this nastiness, on April 28, 998, Otto persuaded Gregory V to make Gerbert archbishop of Ravenna after the death of the previous archbishop. The pope sent Gerbert the pallium and made him prince of Ravenna. Thus, the Reims problem was finally solved. But the principles that Gerbert had defended in the dispute—the traditional rights of metropolitans and the episcopate vis-à-vis the papacy and monastic orders—remain important issues in the contemporary Catholic Church. Gerbert based himself on traditional ecclesiastical laws, and he considered that any papal decision contrary to such laws was null and void. He was to modify this view somewhat as pope, but this position reflected his considered opinion. As archbishop, Gerbert began to institute reforms in Ravenna, and he also maintained some level of contact with his abbey at Bobbio. But the chaos and violence were far from over. Otto thought that his decisive actions had finally put an end to the Roman tendency to revolt; he couldn't have been more wrong.

ᘓᘔ

Nowadays there is a lovely public park in Rome on the Aventine Hill close to upper-class apartments, residences, and religious houses. It is called the Giardino

degli Aranci (Garden of Oranges) or the Parco Savello; it is full of pomegran-
ate trees and looks out over a splendid view across the Tiber and the city toward
Saint Peter's. It is just behind Rome's most beautiful ancient basilica, Santa
Sabina. It was here that Otto most probably lived in a former Theophylact
fortress-palazzo. Only one wall remains at the side of the garden. Perhaps this
site was chosen because it was one of the few places in the city considered to be
relatively free of malaria.

To the Romans it seemed as though Otto intended to reoccupy their city as
a kind of Roman emperor, and there was talk in court circles about a *renovatio
imperii Romanorum*, a "restoration of the Roman Empire." But that is all it
seems to have been—talk. There were dreams about Constantine's Christian
Roman Empire, about the possibility of a renewal of the Roman ideal of universal rule in which all Christian peoples, both Byzantine and European, would
come together in a confederation. Gerbert had certainly filled Otto's head with
grand ideas. "'Ours, ours,' he told him, 'is the Roman Empire! . . . Our august
emperor of the Romans art thou, Caesar, who sprung from the noblest blood
of the Greeks, surpass the Greeks in empire and govern the Romans by hereditary right, but both you surpass in genius and eloquence.'"[26]

This *renovatio* was never intended as a reimposition of the old Roman *imperium* (domination), but rather as a confederation that drew Christian people
together in a kind of transnational unity. Nor was this a "policy" in the modern sense. Ottonian monarchs didn't have policies; they had ideals for which, at
least in theory, their administrations strove. And they thought of themselves
in terms of these ideals.

Another manifestation of this idealized empire is the famous portrait of the
emperor in the *Gospel Book of Otto III*, produced by the scriptorium of Reichenau and now held in Munich's *Staatsbibliothek* (state library), in which Otto
is dressed in imperial garments surrounded by soldiers and learned clerics. He
is enthroned holding a scepter and a cross-inscribed orb representing universal
authority. Opposite the portrait are four female figures approaching him in an
attitude of obeisance. They symbolize the European "nations": *Roma* leads the
way, and she is followed by *Gallia* (the old Carolingian empire in the Low
Countries, France, and southwestern Germany), then *Germania* (the area between the Rhine and the Elbe) and finally *Slavia* (the Slavic nations). This kind
of portraiture indicates that Otto imagined himself as a kind of new Constantine and Charlemagne combined.

Clearly, Otto, Gerbert, and at least some of their advisers were beginning to think in terms of a kind of transnational polity, a union of Christians that transcended national boundaries and that recognized the Holy Roman Emperor as a symbol of this unity. It is significant that they hoped to include Byzantium in this *renovation*, but they had not thought out the *realpolitik* of precisely how the two emperors (Byzantine and German) were going to sort out their respective powers. While all this might have been something of a dream, the Ottonian court was confident enough in its own control of Germany and Italy to think in such speculative terms. Above all, Gerbert and Otto and their confidants were no longer people thinking in localized and parochial terms. In a couple of generations the Ottonians had risen far above the chaos resulting from the collapse of the Carolingian empire, and even if they saw Gerbert's notion of the restoration of the Roman Empire as nothing more than a dream, they felt that the possibility of the restoration of Charlemagne's empire was feasible. Otto III surely saw himself in terms of Charlemagne.

This self-image was reinforced when with a few companions Otto personally opened the tomb of Charlemagne in the palace church in Aachen on Pentecost Sunday 1000. He had just returned from the Gniezno pilgrimage. One of his companions was Count Otto of Lomello, whose eyewitness report was recorded in the *Chronicle of Novalesia*, a monastery near Susa in northwest Italy. According to Count Otto, Charlemagne's body was not lying down "but sat as if he were living." When they entered the tomb, "a strong smell struck us." The body was dressed as an emperor, and "the fingernails had penetrated through the gloves and stuck out." They rerobed the corpse "with white garments, [and] cut his nails." Otherwise, they found the body, buried 186 years previously, incorrupt: "Emperor Charles had not lost any of his members to decay, except only the tip of his nose. . . . Emperor Otto replaced this with gold, took a tooth from Charles' mouth, walled-up the entrance to the chamber and withdrew again."[27]

What are we to make of this somewhat macabre occurrence? Like Constantine before him, Charlemagne was seen as a saintly-priestly figure, and Otto probably wanted him formally declared a saint, suggesting that Otto viewed the body as a relic. Saints' tombs were often opened. Incorruptibility was a sure characteristic of sanctity, and the tooth was taken as a relic. John F. Moffitt shows that burying an important person enthroned was not all that unusual, and that incorruptibility was also common because corpses were sometimes preserved with wax. All inner organs were removed, and the corpse both inside and out was coated with a wax resin. In this way a body could be preserved for many years and the notion of incorruptibility promoted. Moffitt argues that this is likely what happened in Charlemagne's case.[28]

Not only was young Otto being cast as a second Charlemagne, but also some contemporary images were even casting him in an almost divine role. There is another image of him in the Aachen gospels, also from the Reichenau scriptorium, from around the year 996. Here Otto is depicted as Christ surrounded by the symbols of the four gospel writers and a scroll that represents the gospel text. Above his head is a mandorla, a symbol of divinity that is usually linked to Christ in glory. Something similar is reflected in the *Cambridge Songs*, a collection of Continental poems or songs held in the Cambridge University Library. Most of the poems praise particular German emperors. The *Modus Ottinc* (ca. 1000) focuses on Otto III:

> *Great Caesar Otto . . .*
> *Brave in war,*
> *Powerful in peace*
> *But mild in both . . .*
> *In war or peace*
> *He always thought of his poor*
> *And is therefore*
> *Called father of the poor.*[29]

After the Charlemagne incident in Aachen, Otto III returned to Italy in mid-1000 via Lake Constance, Chur, and probably the Septimer Pass and then on to Como and Pavia. Here he met a Venetian ambassador with whom he arranged an extraordinary secret meeting with Doge Pietro II Orseolo. (As this meeting actually occurred in April 1001, we'll discuss it later.) He arrived back in Rome in the last quarter of 1000.

Remarkably, Otto seems to have done very little governing, especially in the German lands. This was a period of stability, and there is a sense that public affairs worked reasonably smoothly on their own. The *Annals of Quedlinburg* says that Otto spent a week in the Saxon heartland in 1000, "reigning, letting people off and returning things to them, giving largesse and rewarding."[30] These were the key tasks of a Saxon monarch. Much of the work had been done by

Otto's aunt Mathilda, Abbess of Quedlinburg who acted as his "viceroy in Saxony." She forced the Slavs into submission "not through any instruments of war (although capable enough of this) but rather through prayers and vigils."[31] She was a real loss to the emperor when she died in 999.

But it was not all smooth sailing. Two ecclesiastical controversies troubled the ruling circles. The first centered on the diocese of Merseburg just west of Leipzig. Erected in 968, the diocese was suppressed in 981 by Benedict VII under instructions from Otto II when Bishop Giselher transferred from Merseburg to Magdeburg. Then suddenly in early 999 Gregory V ordered Giselher to appear in Rome to justify his abandonment of Merseburg and his "seizure" of Magdeburg. According to Thietmar's *Chronicon* (a biased source because Thietmar himself subsequently became bishop of Merseburg and was furious about the suppression of the diocese), Otto III wanted the diocese restored because of a nightmare Theophano had about the "eternal salvation" of Otto II. She dreamed that he had lost his soul because he had suppressed the diocese, "seduced by the words of a man [Giselher] whose guilt causes discord among a great multitude of Christ's elect."[32] The Merseburg question was a constant irritant during Otto III's rule. An opportunity to do something about it arose when Giselher was out of favor because of his military failures against the Slavs and the appointment in 996 of a crony of the emperor as bishop of Halberstadt. Halberstadt had received some of Merseburg's territory when it was suppressed and was now willing to surrender it. Merseburg was eventually restored in 1004.

The second ecclesiastical controversy centered on Otto III's elder sister Sophia and the royal convent at Gandersheim. The home convent of Hrosvitha, Gandersheim became almost as important as Quedlinburg, and Otto II and Theophano had placed their daughter Sophia (975–1039) there to be educated by Abbess Gerberga II. As we saw, the sisters were canonesses regular, ministerially active vowed women like the virgins and widows of the early church or the different sisters communities of today. Canoness status gave these women more flexibility and was thus more suitable for royal princesses like Sophia.

A problem arose on October 18, 987, when Sophia, aged about twelve, was ready to take the veil. Usually there was a special High Mass, an episcopal blessing of the veil and habit and a public commitment to the community. Sophia demanded that she be veiled by Archbishop Willigis of Mainz rather than by the somewhat rustic Bishop Osdag of Hildesheim, who claimed legal jurisdiction over the convent. Sophia was a determined young woman, and she wanted only the most senior prelate to celebrate her veiling. So Willigis barged in without so much as a by-your-leave from Osdag, claiming that Gandersheim was in the far northern corner of Mainz diocese. A standoff ensued and was eventually resolved so that Osdag would veil all the other sisters except Sophia, who was to be veiled by both Osdag and Willigis. But on the actual day, with Otto III, Theophano, princes, and bishops present, Osdag stole a march on Willigis by placing his episcopal throne right next to the altar, jumping the gun and demanding that those to be veiled recognize him as their bishop, and extracting a pledge of obedience to him and his successors. His temerity left everyone flabbergasted, and it is significant that a "hick" bishop could substantially get his way despite the presence of the most powerful people in the *Reich*, including the emperor, the regent, and the archbishop of Mainz.

Sophia and Gandersheim again became the center of controversy in the year 1000. Despite Abbess Gerberga's protests, Sophia was often at court between 995 and 997, acting as a kind of consort for Otto III. Although aging and infirm, Abbess Gerberga had a new church built for the convent. It was presumed that Osdag's successor and Otto's former tutor, Bishop Bernward, would consecrate the church. Now bedridden, Gerberga appointed Sophia as her deputy. Sophia immediately approached her friend Archbishop Willigis to celebrate the consecration. There were already rumors circulating that the relationship of the two was "more" than a platonic friendship. The date for the consecration was set for September 14, 1000, and both bishops agreed to come. Then at the last moment Willigis pulled out and changed the date to September 21. Bernward said that date was inconvenient for him and arrived on September 14. Nothing was prepared for the consecration. Nevertheless, he celebrated Mass and preached. Throughout the Mass there was loud whispering among the canonesses, and at the Offertory all hell broke loose. According to the *Vita Bernwaldi*, when the sisters approached Bernward with the bread and wine, they "threw down their offerings angrily and with incredible fury uttered savage curses against the bishop." Bernward, "in deep contrition of spirit," finished the Mass.[33] The sisters' action was symbolic. It was a way of showing their displeasure about what to them was an illegal invasion of their space. There was no doubt that Sophia was behind the scene.

When Willigis arrived the following week for the consecration, he found Bernward's friend Eggehard, the exiled bishop of Schleswig, present as his representative. Eggehard demanded that the ceremony by canceled until a council of bishops of the *Reich* could be convened to decide what to do. Meanwhile, Bernward had set out for Rome, where he got a good reception from Otto and Gerbert, now Pope Sylvester II. The emperor "could not wait because of his longing to see his old teacher. . . . [Otto] received [Bernward] with great love, embraced and kissed him like his best friend. . . . As long as he remained, the Emperor cared richly for all his needs."[34]

Going to Rome was a shrewd move on Bernward's part because nothing took the place of physical presence and conversation with powerful people. Needless to say, a Roman synod decided in Bernward's favor, while a synod in Gandersheim called by Willigis focused on the issue of diocesan boundaries. Sylvester sent the young and able Cardinal Friedrich von Sachsen as legate to Germany with full powers to preside over a council at Pöhlde in Lower Saxony to try to solve the dispute between the two bishops. All that was achieved was a riot, with Willigis storming out. He was suspended as archbishop by von Sachsen. Meanwhile, at Gandersheim the sisters made it clear that Bernward was unwelcome at their convent. Two more synods at Frankfurt and Fritzlar were unable to solve the problem. Bernward appealed again to Rome, and a synod at Todi (December 27, 1001) with pope and emperor present and the cardinal legate as witness put off any decision until a sufficient number of German bishops arrived. When Otto died on January 23, 1002, the resolution of the dispute was further delayed, and it dragged on for another forty years.

In a way this dispute vividly illustrates the limitations of royal power. At most Otto could exercise influence rather than make decisions in this kind of affair. Archbishop Willigis exercised power through his ability to preside over all synods in the *Reich*. Also, Otto was caught between two groups of relatives and friends: on one hand, his assertive sister, now Abbess Sophia, and his senior archbishop Willigis; on the other, his teacher and friend Bernward. It also indicates the limitations of papal authority at the time: powerful metropolitans like Willigis could simply ignore the pope and Roman synods. As Althoff correctly points out, "The course of the conflict makes clear how little the church in this period was hierarchically structured with Rome at its apex."[35]

☙

On February 18, 999, Gregory V, aged twenty-eight, died suddenly and unexpectedly, not from poison as was rumored at the time but from malaria. The papacy was in the gift of Otto III, who was visiting Saint Nilus at Gaeta at the time. Having taken the advice of Abbot Odilo of Cluny, Otto appointed Gerbert pope on April 2, 999. There does not seem to have been an election.

Now settled in Ravenna, Gerbert can't have lusted after the papacy. Although ambitious, he had already experienced disasters in Bobbio and Reims. And Gerbert, who had so strongly defended the rights of metropolitan archbishops against the claims of the papacy, was now pope. The papacy was hardly an attractive proposition for a non-Roman because Rome was a dangerous place for a non-Roman or non-Italian to live. While it had settled down somewhat since the execution of Crescentius, the situation for foreigners was always insecure not only because of the always-restive locals, but also because of the danger of malaria. Unlike the permanent residents, non-Romans had not built up immunity to the disease carried by mosquitoes from the swamps along the Tiber. Fear of malaria was one of the best defenses the Romans had against interfering outsiders; it was dangerous to stay too long.

Nevertheless, Gerbert was a deserving candidate and was undoubtedly the greatest genius ever made pope. Gerbert chose the style Sylvester II after Sylvester I (314–335), who had worked with Constantine to bring Christianity out of the catacombs into the mainstream of Roman society and culture.

After the execution of Crescentius, a descendant of Theophylact, Gregory of Tusculum, emerged as dominant local magnate, and even though he was denounced as a "tyrant" by Saint Nilus, he was favored by Otto and Sylvester. Gregory was also related by marriage to the Crescentii. However, when Otto returned from Aachen in July 1000 to Italy, he found much of non-Byzantine southern Italy in revolt, with widespread unrest across the Italian peninsula. At a meeting at Como Sylvester pressured Otto to return the lands of the Roman church that had been seized by the emperor, who was rightly deeply concerned about church lands falling into the hands of local magnates. Otto was convinced that the so-called Donation of Constantine, according to which the Papal States had been handed over to the popes by Emperor Constantine, was a forgery. He was right: it had been concocted in the papal court in the eighth century, although Otto thought it a more recent forgery. Despite his deep concerns about the alienation of church land by local magnates, in January 1001 he handed over the Pentapolis, the five cities making up the old Exarchate of

Ravenna, the northern section of the Papal States along the Adriatic coast, to Sylvester as pope, but he emphasized that as emperor he had the power to make the grant to the papacy.

Otto's policy toward the papacy was increasingly autocratic. His caesaropapist attitude (the idea that the church is an instrument of the state) was reflected in his rhetoric. He referred to himself as *servus Jesu Christi* (servant of Jesus Christ), and in an imperial charter from late January 1001 addressed to Sylvester, he called himself *servus apostolorum*, "servant of the apostles and, according to the will of God our Saviour, august emperor of the Romans." In this same document he also refers to himself as a most devoted and faithful *dilatator* (expander, from the verb to "propagate" or "extend") of the churches. Otto's charter sees Rome as *caput mundi*, the "head of the world," in the sense that it is the church of Peter and the apostles as well as the "mother of all the churches."[36] The document goes on to say that Otto wanted to give a gift of papal territory (specifically the Pentapolis) to Saint Peter precisely because it was his to give. In other words, just as a donor could freely give a gift to the church of a saint, so the emperor could give a free gift of land to Saint Peter. As Otto saw the matter, the Papal States, rather than being the donation of Constantine, were in fact the donation of Otto III to Saint Peter.

But Sylvester didn't allow this caesaropapism to cripple him. Immediately on becoming pope, he began a reform of the church, denouncing simony, nepotism, and clerical marriage. He called for regular diocesan synods; he held synods twice yearly for the Roman church. He encouraged monastic reform and granted several important monasteries immunity from local control by placing them directly under the papacy, thus preventing their being bought and sold. No doubt he recalled the alienation of monastic land at Bobbio. But by exempting monasteries from episcopal control, he weakened the authority of local bishops. At the royal convent at Quedlinburg he granted papal protection to Otto's sister Abbess Adelheid I, guaranteed the free election of future abbesses, and decreed that "no bishop at all shall presume to enter the said premises except only the Roman pontiff."[37]

He intervened in church affairs across Europe, working to reform the episcopate, which he saw as a basis for reform of the church. For example, in January 1002 he attempted to initiate reform of the Venetian clergy by requesting Doge Pietro II Orseolo and the patriarch of Grado (then senior bishop of the Venetian region) call a provincial synod to tackle clerical marriage and simony.

"Your bishops and priests openly secure wives and, like money-changers and money-lenders, pursue worldly wealth."[38] He defended the rights of the papacy to make binding decisions throughout the church and to discipline recalcitrant bishops and metropolitans. It was a big shift from the days when he denied that any pope could interfere in internal diocesan affairs, especially in a metropolitan diocese like Reims. He ordered recalcitrant bishops to attend synods, and he called the ecclesiastical politician par excellence, Bishop Adalbero of Laon, who had spent his life playing all sides, "a Judas," ordering him in December 999 to attend a Roman synod for judgment.[39] Sylvester's most generous letter is to Arnoul, Archbishop of Reims in December 999. In it he restores Arnoul's full episcopal authority, saying that Arnoul had been "deprived of . . . pontifical honour because of certain excesses," but that he was now restored "through the gift of Roman compassion."[40] Gerbert's letters reflect genuine pastoral concern; forgiveness for him is at the heart of Catholic faith. He instructs Arnoul not to deny the Eucharist to the dying. "We command that the dying not be prejudged and that the Eucharist be denied to no one who, at the point of death, professes repentance."[41]

Sylvester worked with Otto, who was always concerned about peace on the eastern frontier, to organize the church in Poland and Hungary. Thietmar says that "with the favour and urging of [Otto] . . . Vajk [i.e., King Stephen of Hungary (1001–1038)], brother-in-law of Duke Henry of the Bavarians, established bishoprics in his kingdom and received the crown and consecration."[42] Under Stephen's father, Géza, Hungary was semiconverted to Catholicism. But the short, highly intelligent Vajk (Stephen was his baptismal name) was thoroughly educated at home as a Christian. He married Gisela, sister of Bavarian duke Henry IV, who was to become Otto's successor as Emperor Henry II (1002–1024). Stephen, a humane man who, contemporaries claimed, never laughed, was determined to bring Hungary within the ambit of Western Catholicism. The Hungarians still had much of the old warrior Magyar spirit in them, but Stephen knew how to lead them into a committed Christian faith through his ability to identify with people of all social strata. When he succeeded as duke, Stephen sent Bishop Astrik to Rome to ask Sylvester for a blessed royal crown so that he could be made a king. The pope seems to have had the crown especially made, although there are conflicting stories as to its actual design and making. The upper part of the crown seems to be what Sylvester sent to Stephen. It was last used in 1916 at the coronation of Austro-Hungarian emperor Charles I (Charles IV in Hungary) and is now held in the parliament building in Budapest. The lower part of the crown is of Byzantine design and probably of a later date. Stephen didn't enjoy all plain sailing in the imposition of Christianity, but he made sure Hungary was firmly placed within the ambit of Western Christianity in alliance with the *Reich*.

Bohemia, meanwhile, remained under German influence, with Prague diocese ecclesiastically subject to the archbishop of Mainz. Poland was different. As we saw, Otto had already concluded a *foedus amicitiae* with Duke Bolesław I. On March 11, 1000, Otto unilaterally founded a new church province in Poland with Gniezno as the metropolitan diocese. Bolesław was determined not to become subject to Magdeburg and became increasingly independent, especially after Otto's death. This eventually led to war with Emperor Henry II. Sylvester also wrote to King Olaf Trygvversön, who forcefully converted the Norse to Christianity. Looking even farther afield, the pope approached Vladimir I, Prince of Novgorod and Kiev in December 999 and received a delegation from him some time in 1001. In this period there was no antagonism between the Russian and the Western Latin churches, and Prince Vladimir was friendly and supportive of Western missionary and Otto III's old friend Bruno of Querfurt, on his way to convert the Pechenegs, a Turkic tribe who lived to the south and east of the Kievian Russians.

After returning to northern Italy in June 1000, Otto eventually reached Rome in late summer. He did little for the rest of the year. Sylvester, meanwhile, had run into trouble the previous May while celebrating Mass in Orte, 43 miles (70 kilometers) northeast of Rome in the Sabine region, which was controlled by the Crescentii family. Sylvester told Otto that "a tumult and a riot" broke out during Mass while some people "were offering little Roman gifts" to him. "And so, within the holy of holies swords were drawn, and we withdrew from the city amidst the swords of frenzied enemies."[43] This indicates just how fragile peace was in the Patrimonium, and it was a signal of worse to come because things were changing in Italy. Urban and regional autonomy was always important in Italy, and as economic prosperity increased, towns were demanding more freedom, especially from foreign rulers. "In Rome itself the communal republican tradition was now far more deeply rooted than was any feeling for a foreign Emperor, even if he called himself 'Roman.'"[44]

Trouble soon broke out again, this time in Tivoli, a hill town to the east of Rome. In January 1001 Tivoli revolted against Otto's governor Mazelinus and

he was murdered, probably because he was interfering with the town's munic-
ipal liberties. In a good strategic position, Tivoli proved difficult to recapture.
Sylvester and Bishop Bernward of Hildesheim were with Otto at this time
(Bernward seemed to be constantly absent from his diocese), and according to
his *Vita*, he played a major role in getting the citizens to surrender. He and
Sylvester then persuaded Otto to show mercy to the inhabitants after they carried out a *deditio*, a ritual act of submission in which they threw themselves on
the emperor's mercy. Led by the pope and Bernward, important citizens approached Otto naked, offering him a sword and a rod. "Whomever he regarded
guilty he might execute with the sword, or if he preferred to show mercy, he
might order them to be beaten at the whipping post with the rod." Otto forgave
them all.[45]

Tivoli was symptomatic of trouble brewing. A couple of weeks later an
unexpected revolt occurred in Rome that seems to have been concocted by
Gregory of Tusculum, Otto's *praefectus navalis* (naval prefect or admiral), even
though he had no ships to command, and other nobles. The revolt seems to
have been a desultory affair, beginning with an attempt to ambush and kid-
nap Otto. Some of Otto's supporters were killed, and a half-hearted siege of
the imperial palazzo on the Aventine began. While most of his troops were
outside the city with Henry of Bavaria, Otto rallied those within, and a show
of force by the palace guard, followed by diplomatic negotiations, brought
things to a peaceful conclusion. "The Romans, however, were shamed by the
guilt of their now obvious crime and accused one another bitterly. They . . .
humbly requested the emperor's grace and peace. But Otto distrusted their
deceptive words."[46]

Instead, he gave the Romans a dressing-down. His speech has an element of
petulance and hurt pride in it: "I have adopted you [Romans] as sons, I have
preferred you to all others. . . . I have made myself loathed and hated by all . . .
and in return you have cast off your father and have cruelly murdered my
friends."[47] The Romans responded with tears and beat up two of the ringleaders. Again, their performance was a ritual action symbolizing their willingness
to settle the dispute peacefully.

But Otto was still furious with the Romans, and in April 1001 he went on
what seemed an impulsive escapade, but there was a reason for it. In Como
and Pavia the previous year he had received the Venetian ambassador and
arranged to visit the doge secretly. From Ravenna he was picked up at night

with a few companions by a Venetian ship at what is now Lido di Pomposa. Otto stayed three days in Venice, holding discreet discussions with Doge Pietro II Orseolo in which a *foedus amicitiae* was negotiated. The emperor also acted as godfather at the baptism of the doge's daughter. It was only after Otto had returned to Ravenna that both emperor and doge revealed that the secret meeting had taken place. The doge had recognized the emperor's seniority, but it is hard to see what Otto had achieved. Byzantine sensitivities about Venice and the possibility that the negotiations might collapse were probably the reasons for the secrecy.

Otto then visited famous hermit Romuald living in the fenland and swamps of the Po delta. The emperor's mystical tendencies were still strong, and he was attracted to ascetics like Romuald. Previously, he had spent time in a hermit's cell at the Roman church of San Clemente near the Coliseum and had made retreats at Saint Benedict's monastery at Subiaco. When he was with Romuald, Otto seemed depressed and confused.

However, he was determined to get the Roman situation under control, and he summoned army units from Germany. But before they assembled, Otto became sick. They marched south but got only as far as the castle of Paterno in Cività Castellana, 65 miles (100 kilometers) north of Rome. Here, just short of his twenty-second birthday and surrounded by his friends, he received the sacraments and died on January 22, 1002, from *morbus Italicus*, which might refer to malaria or perhaps to some form of epidemic illness. With as much secrecy as could be maintained, his troops retreated with his embalmed body, although they were attacked by ruffians from the Roman clans. Eventually, they got the body across the Alps to Cologne and on to Aachen, where they buried him on Easter Sunday 1002 in the choir of Charlemagne's magnificent palace church. Otto's death was a tragedy. He had never married and left no direct heirs. While he is dismissed by some as an adolescent dreamer, he was precisely the kind of visionary that his world needed. He had a genuine vision of what the German *Reich* could achieve.

Otto left behind three sisters, two of whom were abbesses. There was no direct heir, so the German magnates offered the throne to Henry, Duke of Bavaria, son of Henry the Quarreler, Otto's second cousin. Henry, who had been destined for the priesthood, was well educated, pious, and cautious. Nevertheless, German control of Italy swiftly collapsed. The upstart Margrave Arduin of Ivrea, a consistent opponent of German hegemony, seized the kingship of Italy. Rome fell back under the control of the Crescentii clan, now led by John III Crescentii.

We don't know if Sylvester was present at Otto's deathbed. But he was now politically powerless in Rome and the Patrimonium. However, he held a council in the Lateran on December 3, 1002, concerning a dispute between the bishop of Perugia and a local monastery that had claimed papal exemption. Little is recorded in the last five months of his life, and he died on May 12, 1003.

Gerbert was a remarkably attractive man with a vivid personality. His knowledge was so universal and his ideas so original that few of his contemporaries could grasp that he was a polymath and genius who was far ahead of his time. But he was also a great and successful pope. An extraordinary missionary expansion had occurred that by the time of the millennium had extended Catholicism from Iceland and Greenland to the Byzantine frontier. But Gerbert's boundaries were not geographical but intellectual. His vision of Christian faith in tandem with science and reason was to find fulfillment only later in the genius of Thomas Aquinas, and it remains a challenge for the Catholicism of today.

ও

Instability returned after Sylvester's death. Three popes were elected in the next nine years, all of them nominees of John Crescentius. The most long-lived of them was John XVIII (1003–1009). Thietmar says that his surname *Fasan* meant "the rooster" or "cock," and he followed Crescentius's policy of reconciliation with the Eastern Church. According to Thietmar, both John and his successor Sergius IV "greatly desired the king's [i.e., Henry II (1002–1024)] advent but various enemies long delayed it," the main enemy being John Crescentius, who was strongly pro-Byzantine.[48] In the last year of John's papacy, famine and plague struck and Saracens appeared again on the Italian coast between Pisa and Rome. Not long before he died, John XVIII resigned the papacy and retired to the monastery of Saint Pauls Outside the Walls, where he died in July 1009. He was succeeded by Sergius IV (1009–1012). Of lower-class Roman origins and nicknamed *bucca porci* (pig's snout), Sergius was the creature of John Crescentius. He was nevertheless in touch with Henry II and supported Henry's creation of a diocese at Bamberg on the upper Main River. Both Crescentius and Sergius died within a week of each other in early May 1012. A major political upheaval followed.

The Theophylacts, who had been out of power for a generation, descended from their stronghold at Tusculum led by Count Gregory, took Rome, and expelled the Crescentii clan, who retreated to their holdout in the Sabine hills. Count Gregory imposed his second son, Theophylact, on the papacy in mid-May 1012; he was most probably a layman before his election. He took the style Benedict VIII (1012–1024). The Crescentii clan's candidate, another Gregory, fled to Germany, where he appeared in "full papal regalia and sadly complained to everyone about his expulsion from the city."[49] Henry II gave him a cool reception.

Although his father was anti-imperial, Benedict continued the policy of conciliation with Henry II, confirming the rights of Henry's favorite diocese of Bamberg, giving the pallium of the archbishop of Mainz, and inviting Henry to Rome. Accompanied by his wife, Cunegunde, Henry took up this invitation in late 1013, crossing the Brenner and meeting Benedict in Ravenna. Arduin fled, and Henry and his powerful army proceeded to Rome, where he was given the usual over-the-top welcome, which disguised the fact that while the imperial party welcomed him, there were still many who utterly despised the Germans. Henry and Cunegunde received the imperial crowns in February 1014 from Benedict VIII in Saint Peter's. But in the best Roman tradition, a major fight broke out a few days later on the Ponte Sant'Angelo, probably started by Crescentii hooligans acting as partisans of King Arduin. Fortunately, Arduin died in 1015 after having retired to a monastery. Northern Italy was secure again.

After Henry returned to Germany, Benedict acted as a local baron and political administrator, using his own army to counter the power plays of the local magnates of the Papal States and Italy. His aim was to make Rome the center of Italy. The Saracens were again active in 1016 around Lombardy; "they occupied the whole region and abused the occupants' womenfolk."[50] Allied with Pisa and Genoa, Benedict assembled a Christian army and navy, which, after initial setbacks, defeated the Saracens. Sardinia was recaptured.

Resentment against the Byzantines was again building in southern Italy, and Benedict saw this as a chance to assert papal claims. He invited in Norman knights, the beginnings of the Norman kingdom of Sicily. But the Byzantines successfully counterattacked, and Benedict was forced to take up an invitation to go to Germany to seek Henry's help. Pope and emperor celebrated Easter 1020 together at Bamberg and the pope concluded his visit to Germany with a High Mass on May 1, 1020, at the abbey of Fulda. Henry followed up in

1021 with an invasion of southern Italy, which did little more than halt the advance of the Byzantines. The Germans seem to have been brought low by malaria, and they felt they had to get north to a colder climate as quickly as possible. Henry halted at Pavia.

Henry and Benedict now focused their attention to church reform. A reforming council was held at Pavia, probably in late 1022. It addressed clerical marriage and simony. The pope's main preoccupation was the alienation of church property as a result of clerical marriage. He claimed that the worst offenders were on-the-make serfs who, with no wealth of their own, had become priests and then married freewomen so that their children would be free. Getting their sons ordained as priests, they were able to pass church property on to them. To prevent this alienation, Benedict decreed that all clerics were forbidden to marry and that any children born of such clerical marriages would be reduced to serfdom. His exclusive concern was with church property, not with spirituality or effective ministry.

Benedict died on April 9, 1024, and was succeeded by his younger brother Romanus, another layman, who took the style John XIX (1024–1032). Glaber speaks of the "impudence of the Romans" and of how Romanus obtained "the papal throne by bribery," which is a bit rich after all the righteous talk about poor married priests alienating church property.[51] John XIX was sharply criticized by Abbot William of Saint-Bènigne in Dijon, who told him "if the river is stagnant close to its source there can be no doubt that lower down it stinks. Who buys the care of souls purchases his damnation! I want you, pontiffs and bishops alike, to be mindful of the judge who wields the axe and stands before the door!"[52]

John was politically astute and managed the clans, including the Crescentii, to his advantage. He also seems to have reached a basic agreement with the Byzantines regarding the respective Roman and Eastern spheres of influence in southeastern Europe. King Conrad II (1024–1039) of Germany, Henry II's successor, came to Rome in March 1027 and was crowned Holy Roman Emperor. Conrad, an able but arrogant man, treated John with considerable contempt, although the pope was held in high regard by King Cnut of England, who happened to be in Rome for the imperial coronation. John XIX was a patron of art and a lover of beauty, and he took care to celebrate the liturgy with sensitivity and diligence. He died in October 1032. His successor was to rival John XII as a papal blackguard.

Bribed by his father, Count Alberico III "Major," the electors chose Theophylact as pope; he took the style Benedict IX and had three stints as pope: 1032–1044; 1045; 1047–1048. "Elected" is, of course, a euphemism. What happened was that the ruling family nominated the pope, priests and local people gave "consent," and the name was sent to the emperor for approval. But real power was held by the ruling clan, and the election of another Theophylact indicated that the counts of Tusculum were in charge. It was just one hundred twenty years since the first Theophylact had come down to Rome from Tusculum and established the family power base; the process had gone full circle.

Benedict was a violent, immoral twenty-something of whom Pietro Damiani correctly says, "To the end of his life he was skilled in the filth of riotous living."[53] But as under other loathsome popes, the work of the chancery continued—new dioceses were established, privileges were issued, contact was kept with the wider church, and the policies of Benedict's predecessors were followed. We know little of his first three years as pope except that Glaber maintains that on Friday, June 29, 1033, the one thousandth year since Christ's crucifixion, during "a terrible event," actually an eclipse of the sun, an attempt was made on Benedict's life. The sun was obscured "from the sixth to the eighth hour. The sun itself took on the colour of sapphire and its upper part looked like the moon in its last quarter. Each saw his neighbour looking pale as though unto death, everything seemed to be bathed in a saffron vapour. The extreme terror gripped the hearts of men."

Some in Rome clearly took advantage of the eclipse to make an attempt on Benedict's life. "That very day . . . in the church of Saint Peter, some of the Roman princes conspired together and rebelled against the Roman pontiff. They sought to kill him." They were unsuccessful and "only succeeded in expelling him."[54]

Benedict must have made his way back to Rome because in 1037 another attempt was made by the Crescentii to expel him. They were successful, and it was this that persuaded Emperor Conrad II to intervene again in Italy. He crossed the Alps and summoned Benedict. They met in Cremona. Imperial support guaranteed Benedict's return to Rome. But there was also trouble in Capua and Naples, with the Normans playing an increasingly destabilizing role in southern Italy. After establishing order in northern Italy, Conrad marched south, but his army was hit with the plague and had to retreat via the Adriatic

Sea, eventually reaching Germany. Conrad died suddenly on June 4, 1039, and was immediately succeeded by his intelligent, strong, and politically able twenty-two-year-old son, Henry III (1039–1056).

We know little about what Benedict did between his return to Rome in 1039 and his next expulsion in September 1044. The cause, it was said, was his immoral life and violence, but the real reason was that the political alignments were shifting against the Tusculum clique; the Crescentii were plotting a return to power. In late January 1045 they proceeded to elect Sylvester III, who held the office for only two months. A counterattack by Benedict's partisans restored him to Rome, but within less than two months he abdicated in favor of his godfather, Giovanni Gratiano, Gregory VI (1045–1046). Benedict seems to have been motivated by a desire to marry his cousin and to pocket the considerable sum (between 1,000 and 2,000 pounds of gold) on offer from Gratiano for the papacy.

Gregory was a man of some integrity, and his purchase of the papacy seems to have been motivated by a desire to rescue it from the deplorable Benedict. In his twenty months as pope, Gregory tried to restore public order and rebuild papal finances. The entrenched corruption, however, beat Gregory, and both Benedict (possibly disappointed in love) and Sylvester returned to establish armed enclaves in the city. Many people had had enough. A group of clerics, bishops, cardinals, monks, laywomen, and laymen under the leadership of an archdeacon named Peter formed and contacted Henry III, asking him to come to Rome to deal with the whole mess. Henry was anxious to receive the imperial crown, but he was unwilling to receive it from a papal sleaze. In late 1046 he arrived in Italy with a large army and proceeded to hold a synod at Sutri (December 20, 1046), where both Sylvester and Gregory were deposed. Benedict, who had refused to attend, was deposed by a Roman synod on Christmas Eve 1046. Henry then immediately appointed the bishop of Bamberg as Clement II (1046–1047), who crowned him emperor on Christmas Day in Saint Peter's.

Clement, who retained his title as bishop of Bamberg, traveled widely with Henry and began the task of church reform. But he died suddenly on October 9, 1047, after Henry had returned to Germany. His body was taken to Bamberg, where it still lies in Bamberg Cathedral. His tomb was opened in 1731; he was found to be a tall, blond man well over six feet in height. Toxicological examination of his remains in the mid-twentieth century confirmed centuries-old rumors that he had been poisoned with lead sugar, a toxic compound with a sweet taste.

Benedict reappeared and bribed his way back into the papacy. But on Henry's orders he was expelled from Rome. He retreated to Tusculum and maintained that he was rightful pope until his death around 1055. His successor, Damasus II, lasted only three weeks in office (July–August 1048).

With his third choice for the papacy Henry was more successful. Leo IX (1048–1054) succeeded in transforming the papacy. The power of the clans was finally destroyed, and a thoroughgoing reform of the papacy was begun.

ഔ

We have now come full circle. We began with the parochialism of Rome and the Papal State. Now we have come to the beginning of the massive reform of the papacy that the German emperors from Otto I onward had called for and struggled to achieve for one hundred years. That reform was to make the papacy the greatest power in Europe after a gargantuan struggle with the very empire that had initially reformed it. What is important here is that by 1050 the chaos of the late ninth and early tenth centuries has been overcome and a new polity had emerged, the German *Reich*. Europe had been born, but it still needed a reformed church and papacy to make it complete. And the reform of the papacy led, in turn, to a struggle to define the politics of the West and still influences our ideas on the separation of church and state.

But that is a story that belongs to the eleventh and twelfth centuries.

CHAPTER 18

The Millennium

F OR MANY PEOPLE, mention of the millennium conjures up visions and madness. Indeed, there were apocalyptic ideas around as the millennium approached, most of them derived from the last book of the Bible, the Book of Revelation, and the Old Testament Book of Daniel. Both books have provided fodder for religious cranks over the centuries, including today. Both focus on ideas about a coming millennial kingdom, defeat of the devil, a final judgment, and a vision of a new heaven and a new earth. The vivid poetic imagery of both texts provides literalists and fundamentalists with rich ground for speculation about apocalyptic scenarios and the end of the world. So it was inevitable that as the first millennium approached, religious extremists and hellfire preachers would focus on both books.

The literary form of both the Book of Revelation and the Book of Daniel is couched in terms of Jewish apocalyptic literature, and the original actual context of both books is persecution. The author of Revelation, usually identified with the apostle John, is telling first-century persecuted Christians in a highly symbolic way that because God is the master of history, he will intervene to cast down the persecutors and save the faithful. Revelation is full of symbols that had relevance for the book's original readers, even if they are obscure to us now. It is, in essence, a call to hope and trust in God in a time of persecution. The Book of Daniel took its final form during the persecution of the Jews under Syrian domination in the second century BC. The problem is that the very obscurity of the symbols opens up Revelation and Daniel to interpretations totally at variance with the original intention, making them a rich mine

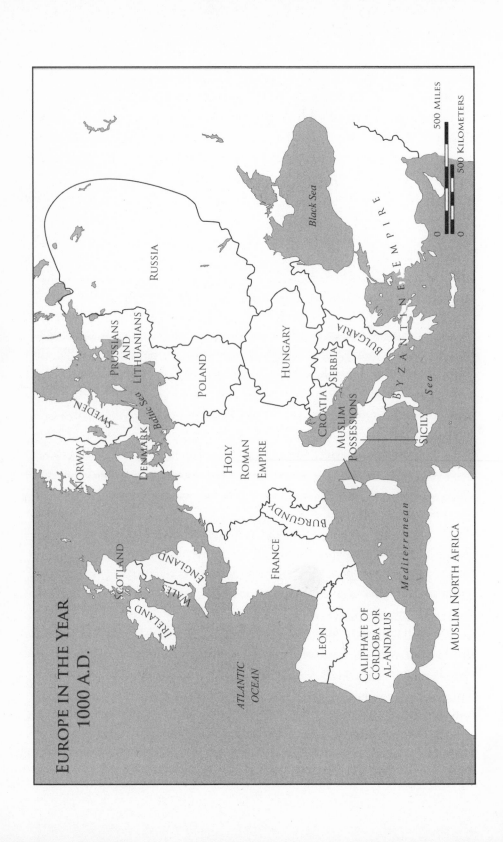

EUROPE IN THE YEAR
1000 A.D.

NORWAY

SWEDEN

PRUSSIANS
AND
LITHUANIANS

DENMARK

Baltic Sea

RUSSIA

POLAND

HUNGARY

Black Sea

CROATIA

SERBIA

BULGARIA

BYZANTINE EMPIRE

MUSLIM
POSSESSIONS

SICILY

Aegean Sea

HOLY
ROMAN
EMPIRE

BURGUNDY

FRANCE

ENGLAND

WALES

SCOTLAND

IRELAND

ATLANTIC
OCEAN

LEÓN

CALIPHATE OF
CÓRDOBA OR
AL-ANDALUS

Mediterranean

MUSLIM NORTH AFRICA

500 MILES

500 KILOMETERS

0

0

for religious cranks. That is how they were used by some as the first millennium approached. The particular text that provided the stimulus for much of the millennial speculation was the vision of Christ's thousand-year reign (Revelation 20:4–5) and the defeat of Satan, who has conquered the world. A day of judgment follows, leading to the establishment of the new heaven and the new earth, a time of prosperity and peace.

There were really two Christian millennia. The first, in the year 1000, commemorated the birth of Christ (the consensus now is that Christ was born around 5–6 BC), and the second was the year 1033, the thousandth anniversary of the crucifixion of Jesus.

But before we examine the way in which the first millennium played itself out, let us see how millennial expectation was played out in the years leading up to 1000. A good example is described by the monk-chronicler Rodulfus Glaber concerning the madness of a peasant, Leutard, "from the village of Vertus in the county of Châlons-sur-Marne in Gaul. . . . This is how his stubborn madness began." Sometime around the year 1000 Leutard "was working alone on an agricultural task in the field [when] he became tired and fell asleep and he dreamt that a great swarm of bees entered his body through nature's secret orifices. They came out of his mouth buzzing loudly and stinging him many times." The bees then ordered him "to do things impossible for humankind." After he awoke, he returned to his house and sent away his wife, justifying the separation by a confused reference to the text in Matthew's gospel (19:29) about leaving everything and following Christ. "Then . . . when he entered the church he seized and broke the cross and image of the Saviour. Everyone who saw this trembled with fear, believing him to be mad (as indeed he was), but he managed to persuade them that he was doing this as the result of a wonderful revelation from God. . . . He poured forth a great many empty and useless sermons and aspiring to be a great teacher, he caused men to forget the Master of all teaching." His worst crime was that he "claimed that it was completely unnecessary and mere folly to pay tithes." This was serious social deviance and linked to "his pretended reputation for faith . . . soon won over to him many of the common people." The local bishop, probably the experienced Gebuin I, was shrewd enough not to tackle him head-on but gradually revealed to people "how Leutard's madness had led to heresy."[1] Bishop Gebuin didn't rush to judgment but took his time to talk people around, leaving poor Leutard isolated. After his followers abandoned him, Leutard committed suicide by throwing himself into a well. This is one of the few known instances of suicide in the period.

Leutard had probably experienced a psychotic episode, which expressed itself in terms of religious and social dissidence. While we are not all that clear about his teachings, they seem to have resonances with the ideas of the Bogomils, a Balkan Manichaean sect characterized by a rejection of matter and the body as the work of Satan; only the soul is of God. These kinds of ideas were increasingly floating around France; Leutard probably picked them up from visiting merchants. His village of Vertus was in a region that was a center of the wool trade, and there would have been many visiting merchants around.

ↄ

Historiographic interest in the first Christian millennium escalated in the years leading up to 2000. As early as the 1830s French historian Jules Michelet was talking of "the terrors of the year 1000," and throughout the nineteenth century the accepted historiographic wisdom was that the years leading up to 1000 were characterized by widespread fear that the world would come to an end. However, from the year 1900 onwards a decidedly more secularist and skeptical approach dominated historiography, first represented by Ferdinand Lot. The new theory was that virtually no one in the tenth century was interested in, let alone terrified by the approaching millennium. It was simply business as usual. A note of caution to this denialist position was introduced by the influential historian Georges Duby in his book *L'An Mil* (1980).

In the last thirty years things have changed, and the denialist school has been vigorously challenged. Boston University historian Richard Landes argues that, while apocalyptic fear was widespread, the main emphasis was on hope for a better future, especially among the poor and dispossessed. He refers to Glaber's comment that "the good Creator brought forth for men miracles and signs and portents in the elements . . . [to engender] both fear and hope."[2] Landes says the key issue is that poor people hoped that the world could be a better place. The clerical and lay elites were opposed to such apocalyptic expectations because they had the most to lose.

The problem, of course, is that often these hopes speak to those oppressed, not the powerful; they thus seem to anticipate a now-unwelcome Marxist language of revolution. As a result these hopes rarely express the attitudes we find in the written sources which reflect the views of the *potentes* (powerful), the dominant aristocratic élite; and at the same time such hopes find their greatest audiences among the *paupers* (poor), those powerless masses who do not leave us documentary evidence of their thoughts and deeds.[3]

Landes also argues that people knew the correct date of the millennium and that in some cases there is even evidence of a "countdown" to the event. And then when the year 1000 passed without incident, people looked toward the millennium of the death of Jesus. That also passed without incident.

Landes's views have started an animated historical controversy. The reconciliation of these two positions lies in the kind of sensible middle position articulated by Timothy Reuter, who says that, even though many people at the turn of the millennium were not living in fear, "it is more likely that the intensification of religious experience around the millennium, perceptible in a number of ways, was, at least in part, a response to the millennium itself."[4]

So what evidence is there that people were afraid of the approaching millennium? There was certainly a general apprehension that this was the "last age" and that the end of the world was not far away. The operative text here was the Book of Daniel. The literary form of Daniel is hard to classify; it is probably best called an "apocalyptic novel." Written in an apocalyptic style, it is addressed to the Jews suffering under the oppressive occupation of Antiochus IV Epiphanes (175–63 BC), a Syrian-Greek ruler who attempted to impose paganism on the Jews. In Chapter 7 Daniel has a dream in which he sees four beasts, which represent four kingdoms usually identified with the Neo-Babylonian Empire and the empires of Cyrus the Great, Alexander the Great, and Rome. This is followed by a fifth, more righteous empire ruled by "the Ancient One," to whom "was given dominion and glory and kingship that all peoples, nations and languages should serve him" (Daniel 7:13–14). The Frankish kings and Saxon emperors of the period thought of themselves as the rulers of this final peaceful empire defending the world from Antichrist. The peaceful empire would be followed by the last days, the rule of Antichrist, and the second coming of Christ as judge. But how widespread were these beliefs?

The first place to look for evidence of apocalyptic expectation is in the most common form of religious communication at the time, sermons. Abbot Abbo of Fleury says in his 995 *Apologia to Kings Hugh and Robert* that he strongly opposed preaching about the end of the world. He says that as a young man "I heard a sermon to the people in the cathedral of Paris concerning the end of the world which claimed that as soon as a thousand years were completed, the Antichrist would come and soon after that universal judgment. I resisted this sermon as strongly as I could from the Gospels, and the Books of Revelation and Daniel. . . . A rumor had spread through almost the whole world that when the Feast of the Annunciation (March 25) coincided with Good Friday, without doubt the end of the world would occur."[5] This confirms that there was preaching about the forthcoming millennium, but Abbo makes clear that at least better-informed monks and clerics, including himself, opposed such preaching.

Another example is the Anglo-Saxon abbot Ælfric of Eynsham, just west of Oxford. In a book of forty-five sermons, only two directly address the question of the end-times. One discusses the text describing the final judgment in Matthew's gospel (25:31–46). This sermon is a model of restraint, and Ælfric simply allows the gospel text to speak for itself; there is no reference to the millennium or anything apocalyptic. In another more dramatic discourse he describes the visions of a Scottish priest named Furseus who experienced a series of "near-death" incidents. While some of Furseus's visions are dramatic, this is not the stuff of panic-educing fear of the end of the world.[6]

Around 950 Otto I's younger sister Queen Gerberga, wife of Louis IV of West Francia, asked Abbot Adso (d. 992) of Montier-en-Der, a Cluniac monastery near Troyes, a series of questions about Antichrist. Adso tells Queen Gerberga in detail about the origin and life span of Antichrist. But the key point he makes is Antichrist will come only after the demise of the Roman Empire and that this has not occurred because it continues in the rule of the Frankish kings. Also, Christians will not be left without warning of the end-time; the prophets Enoch and Elijah "will defend God's faithful . . . with divine arms and will instruct, comfort and prepare the elect for battle with three and a half years of teaching and preaching." But in the end God will triumph, and either Jesus or Archangel Michael will slay Antichrist. Then there will be a forty-day penitential period and a chance for repentance before the final judgment.[7] Gerberga's questions and Adso's interpretation point toward a consciousness of the end-times, and there is no doubt that the texts from both Daniel and Revelation were used in preaching, leading to a perceptible nervousness about the approaching millennium among both the nobility and the ordinary people.

Natural events were also interpreted in an apocalyptic sense. Halley's Comet was visible for a month after August 11, 989. It was actually not well reported in Europe, though the Chinese saw it. Among the Europeans who mention it is Glaber. "A star of the sort called a comet appeared in the western sky. . . . It shone with such brilliant light that it lit up the greater part of the sky." But Glaber didn't interpret it in an apocalyptic sense. "Whether this was a new star sent by God, or whether it was an existing star whose light he had increased as an omen, is known only to him."[8] Glaber also says that there were widespread fires in Italy and Rome in 991 in which Saint Peter's itself was under threat. He also mentions that in 1007 Mount Vesuvius near Naples "spewed forth, by more mouths than usual, sulphurous fire and a great many rocks, which were thrown distances of up to three miles." But he doesn't interpret any of these events in an apocalyptic sense. His translator, John France, says that Glaber "is pretty sceptical of any notion of the imminence of Antichrist."[9]

Glaber also reports a weeping crucifix and a wolf bell ringer in Orléans in 988. The crucifix was in a convent where "for a period of some days a river of tears flowed continuously from the eyes of the image." There were many witnesses who believed "it was a divine portent of some calamity which was about to overtake that city." Then the wolf with a penchant for bell ringing arrived in Orléans. One night before Matins "a wolf suddenly appeared; entering the [cathedral] it seized the bell-rope in its jaws and, pulling upon it, made the bell ring." The locals drove the wolf out, but according to Glaber these events were portents because in the following year "the whole city with all its houses and even its churches was burnt down" in a fire.[10] Fire was always a problem when almost all buildings were constructed of wood.

Another sign of the millennium was that pilgrimages to Jerusalem became the flavor of the month. Glaber tells us that "the first to go were petty people, then those of middling estate, and next the powerful, kings, counts, marquises, and bishops; finally, and this is something which had never happened before, numerous women, noble and poor, undertook the journey. Many wished to die there."[11]

Even with the overland route through Hungary open, people still faced the challenges of passing through Bulgarian and Byzantine territory and then the real dangers of penetrating Fatamid territory, the Muslim dynasty based in Egypt that controlled Palestine from 969 to 1161. Jerusalem would have been even more dangerous to pilgrims under the fanatical madman-caliph al-Hākim

(996–1021), who ordered the destruction of the Church of the Holy Sepulchre and many other churches and shrines in Egypt and Palestine. Such pilgrimages involved real risk.

Heresies and social deviance were also interpreted as apocalyptic signs. One of the earliest manifestations of this was by a young serf-girl, Flothilda (d. 942), who was connected with the convent of Avenay in Normandy. She had two sets of visions, which caused quite a stir. The first series focused around her escape from men on horses and harassment by demons, which reflects a vulnerable young woman's understandable anxiety about sexual violence. The second set focus on ecclesiastical politics at Reims, the dangers facing France, and the decline of the morals of the clergy. Flothilda died soon after her visions ceased.

More important is a Manichaean outbreak in a couple of places in France around 1018–1022. Manichaeism is a radically dualistic belief based on the supposed primeval conflict between light and darkness and the eternal conflict between God and Satan. To achieve release from darkness, Manichaeans practiced severe asceticism, celibacy, and vegetarianism. There were various levels in the sect, and initiation was gradual as adherents rose up the ladder of "enlightenment." Orléans was a veritable hotbed of this heresy.

There was a Manichaean group in Orléans with laity, nuns, and some senior priests involved. Adhémar of Chabannes says that they had been misled by an unnamed peasant "who claimed that he could give them great strength and who carried about with him dust from dead children which quickly made anyone who came in contact with it a Manichee." He claims that they denied the reality of the incarnation, the validity of the sacraments, and the authority of scripture and that, while they appeared ascetical, "among themselves they enjoyed every indulgence."[12] The accusation of sexual promiscuity among the Manichees, and heretics generally, is probably untrue. While it is impossible to pin down the source of this Manichaean outbreak, the origin may have again been the Bogomils.

According to the monk Paul of St. Père de Chartres, the Orléans Manichees were exposed when an out-of-town spy named Aréfast with "admirable native cunning" penetrated the group. He tricked them into thinking he was a convert and persuaded them to reveal their teaching. Both Paul and Adhémar accuse the Manichees of group sex. Paul says that after their liturgy "each of them grabbed whatever woman came to hand, and seized her to be put to ill use. . . . They regarded that intercourse as holy and religious work." Any children born of these unions were burned, and the ashes were kept "to be given as a last sacrament to the sick when they are about to depart this life."[13] Group sex and burning of children are the types of rumor that always surround dissident, secretive sects.

When King Robert II the Pious and Queen Constance arrived in Orléans in 1022, a council was gathered at the request of Aréfast to try ten members of the group. When they refused to retract their beliefs, Robert II stripped the priests of their orders and condemned them. One of them, Stephen, had been Queen Constance's confessor. She struck him in the eye "with the staff she carried." Outside the city walls they were confined in a house, and "a large fire was lit . . . and they were all burned . . . except for one clerk and a nun who had repented by the will of God."[14] This is the earliest known judicial burning for heresy in European history.

☙

But there is a broader context for "the fears." The tenth century was a time of considerable change as a new culture started to emerge from the ruins of the Carolingian empire, what I have called "the birth of the West." Cultural change is never an easy process, and major shifts in cultural values create a kind of unconscious fear and uncertainty. Simplistic people often take refuge in fundamentalism and apocalyptic expectation. Perhaps because these fears remain unconscious and unarticulated, they are more threatening. Those unable to cope with change can react in bizarre ways and interpret their experience in a supernatural context in which God intervenes to protect them. Something similar is happening with fundamentalists of all sorts today as we too experience a major cultural shift.

The millennium saw the beginning of long-term social change that would eventually become Western European civilization. After a century or more of the disintegration of central government and authority and the reality of almost constant low-level warfare, beginning from about the reign of Otto I and the defeat of the Magyars in 955 at the Battle of Lechfeld, people started to feel generally safer from external attack. The fear engendered by the Vikings, Magyars, and Saracens lessened and eventually disappeared altogether. The Magyars and Vikings had become Christian, and Saracen incursions were under control. A model of effective central government had emerged from Saxony, and the German *Reich* was now a working realm. The despair engendered by the collapse of central government in the last decades of the ninth century was now a thing of the past, at least in northern Europe, even if England, Ireland, and France had some distance to go before good order was restored. The Peace of God was beginning the process of confronting the feudal warlords of France with community action and church sanctions. Monastic reform was under way, and there was a revival of learning. Glaber says that "throughout the whole world, but most especially in Italy and Gaul," a church reconstruction process began in which "each Christian community . . . [aimed] to surpass all others in the splendour of construction." He then makes this interesting comment: "It was as if the whole world were shaking itself free, shrugging off the burden of the past, and cladding itself everywhere in a white mantle of churches."[15] While the "white mantle of churches" is often highlighted by historians (it essentially refers to the churches and monasteries built as a result of the Cluniac reform), the comment about the world "shaking itself free, shrugging off the burden of the past" seems to me to be a much more significant remark. It points to a new energy, a new spirit, a vision of a better world with new possibilities. The creativity of Gerbert of Aurillac sums up this new spirit.

But at an even deeper level change was occurring. The millennium saw the first stirrings of the emergence of "individuality." Modern individualism is usually said to have begun during the Renaissance. But more recent research has pushed "the discovery of the individual," as Colin Morris calls it, back to the mid-eleventh century. Individuality here refers to a sense of self-awareness, personal identity, and moral responsibility. It also involves spirituality. As Morris says, "A sense of individual identity and value is implicit in a belief in a God who has called each man by name."[16] He argues that Christianity provided the basis for the evolution of the Western concept of the self.

It is in spirituality that we see this notion of individuality most strongly. One of the finest artistic representations of this new spirit is the Gero cross in Cologne cathedral. It is the oldest surviving crucifix in northern Europe, carved before 976 in a style ahead of its time. Sadly, nowadays the cross is framed by a black baroque monstrosity, and it requires a closer look to see that Jesus is a young man who has suffered terribly but is calm in death. He is covered by a beautifully carved loincloth held in place by complex wrapping. The cross, named after Archbishop Gero of Cologne (969–976), who commissioned it for the cathedral, is 6 feet 2 inches tall (almost 2 meters) and carved from oak. Thietmar says that it was made by a "high artisan" and that originally it stood above the archbishop's grave.[17] Here Christ is not the triumphant pantocrator of Byzantine art, the sublime ruler of the universe even on the cross, but neither is he suffering in a grotesque way as represented by crucifixes in the later Middle Ages.

What the Gero cross signifies is the emergence of a more individual, human Christ who is not longer a triumphant, superhuman figure reigning supreme in heaven. The cross shows a truly human Christ who died a terrible death but is now at peace. This represents a shift in spiritual emphasis. The Byzantine pantocrator-Christ was magnificently beautiful, but far beyond the human condition and therefore difficult to relate to as a representation of human death. In contrast, the human Christ of the Gero cross is truly one of us, a man who has suffered terribly and died as a human individual, not a divine abstraction. People could relate to that.

We have already met strong individuals such as Gottschalk, Walafrid Strabo, Hrosvitha, Theophano, Liutprand, Gerbert, and John Scottus Erigena. These strong personalities formed their own views and went their own way. That they were educated enriched their ability to imagine new possibilities; it also opened up for them a kind of social fluidity, so that someone like Walafrid, the son of peasants, could become tutor to the children of Charles the Bald and abbot of Reichenau, and Gerbert from a similar background could become pope.

Individuality is the product of spirituality. The most original spiritual thinker of the whole period is without doubt John Scottus Erigena. He developed a profoundly mystical interpretation of the relationship of God and the world drawn from Neoplatonic sources and from his translation from Greek of the works of Pseudo-Dionysius. Historian of spirituality Bernard McGinn says that John held that God "is within the world as its deepest reality . . . but at the same time he is not in the world, being negatively *above and beyond* it."[18] John envisages a dialectic in which God is simultaneously and reciprocally both totally present and totally beyond. This frees the divine from our projections and constraints. But it also protects us from a manipulative God who is always interfering in nature and its processes, above all in human life. It is a movement toward conscientious responsibility for the self and an enhancement of individual self-consciousness and conscience. So while it protects God's separateness, it also assures our individuality. In John's understanding, while we will eventually return to God, we will retain our selfhood, which will not be lost or absorbed into some generic form of cosmic unconsciousness. In other words the tenth century sees the beginning of a new emphasis on the theology of the incarnation, the idea that God is to be found within the very "stuff" of the material world, the body, and the human condition.

At a less profound level monastic spirituality also encouraged self-discovery through its emphasis on silence, solitude, thoughtful reading, and meditation, which finds its fullest expression in prayer and contemplation. The energy driving the monastic lifestyle was an insatiable desire to transcend the self and reach out to God, which, paradoxically, led the individual back into a deeper consciousness of the self.

ↄ

What I have tried to outline in this book is the story of the birth of the Western culture that we all share as the inheritors of the European tradition. Our culture was born in the tenth century. The driving force of that birth was Western Christianity, more specifically Catholicism. The church was the cohesive driver that bound together the disparate elements that make up our cultural inheritance and was the energy that drove the process forward. Today we stand at a crossroads in Western culture, caught up as we are in a seemingly inexorable movement toward globalism, multiculturalism, and internationalism. There is a strong impetus today to deny our cultural roots altogether, or at least to pretend that we live in a kind of "post-Christian," purely secularist society. Perhaps my next book should be entitled "The Death of the West." However, I think such declarations are premature. We are still living on "the bedrock of feeling on which our civilization is based," as literary critic Peter Craven so correctly says, and that "bedrock" is Christianity.[19] Our problem is that we are caught up in a cultural amnesia, a forgetfulness of our origins. That is why it is so important to recall the birth of the West and to acknowledge the cultural components that have made our civilization what it is.

Our other difficulty with accepting our Catholic and Christian past and integrating its contributions to the present is that nowadays we are instinctively suspicious of "metanarratives," to use postmodern jargon. In other words, this is a "big" story that tries to interpret the particularities and details of the past in a broader, overall perspective. Postmodernism notwithstanding, I would argue that we need these kinds of "grand narratives" to help us gain perspective on where we are now. And even if we do want to move into a global, secularist, multicultural, post-Christian society (personally I don't), we will still need to recall, acknowledge, and integrate the past. If we forget where we came from, we will simply drift into the future with nothing to offer it. That is why we need to know and understand the birth of the West.

In a way there is something unsatisfactory about this ending. Probably it's because history doesn't ever end tidily. It is an ongoing, messy process. It is just like Europe at the end of the tenth century—all over the place! Different countries and groups of people had developed differently, and some were ahead of others. Clearly the German *Reich* led the way; that is why I said early in the book that the book's subtitle could have been "How the Germans Saved Civilization." By the end of the tenth century Germany was a coherent and working realm. France was to remain a basket case for several centuries to come. England had become a coherent state at the beginning of the tenth century under Alfred the Great and his successors, but by the end of the century it had collapsed again into chaos in the face of a renewed Viking aggression. It was not until the Norman invasion under William the Conqueror in 1066 that England was unified again. In Spain the *reconquista* was well under way, but the country would have to wait until the fifteenth century before it was reunited completely as Catholic Spain. By the time of Malcolm II Scotland had an effective kingship, but after the brief unity achieved by Brian Boru Ireland degenerated again into anarchy, setting itself up for conquest by the Normans in the late eleventh century. But by the end of the tenth century the Eastern European countries had emerged and the Vikings had been converted to Christianity. Italy remained a "geographical expression," an amalgam of principalities and independent cities with the whole of the center of the peninsula straddled by the Papal States. It was not to be finally unified until 1870.

But no matter how untidy the birth of the West was, by the time of the millennium the foundations had been laid. Something new had come into existence. The West had been born.

How it was to develop is another story entirely.

ACKNOWLEDGMENTS

What surprised me as I wrote *The Birth of the West* was that so much source material for the book was available either in major libraries or on the Internet. The reason is because nineteenth- and twentieth-century national projects in European countries had made available their *monumenta* (their chronicles and records) to the public beyond those specialists who could consult them in archives and read the original script. So I have been very much in the debt of those projects and the libraries that hold them, particularly the National Library of Australia and the J. B. Chifley Library of the Australian National University, both in Canberra, my hometown. I was able to consult much of this primary (and secondary) material without leaving home. I also never cease to be amazed at the generosity and helpfulness of librarians in these institutions; they are the unsung champions of our cultural heritage. There is also an amazing amount of archival material available on the Internet, particularly at the sites making available the massive collections of documents contained in the *Monumenta Germaniae Historica* (Bayerische Staatsbibliothek) and John Paul Migne's *Patrologiae cursus completa* (at the Web page *Documenta Catholica Omnia*). This book is also very dependent on the work of many other historians, and I have acknowledged them either in the footnotes or in the bibliography.

I especially want to thank Professor Constant Mews of Monash University, who read some of the early material in the book and made many valuable suggestions. Also special thanks to Jean and John Lombard of Chateau, France, who acted as guides to Cluny and its fascinating surrounds. Thanks also to Simon Bryden-Brooke (London), Peter McLaughlin (Winchester), Margret and John May (Dublin), and Judith Champ (Birmingham). My literary agent, Mary Cunnane, has been not only a great support but also a good friend for a decade or more. Thanks also to my New York agent, Kathleen Anderson, and to Claire Anderson-Wheeler. To Clive Priddle of PublicAffairs and to editor Brandon Proia, project editor Collin Tracy, copy editor Jan Kristiansson, and proofreader Lisa Zales, many thanks for all your help. It was a dream to work with you. Thanks to Patti Jacobs for preparing the maps. Needless to say, in a work of this size there will be mistakes. I am entirely responsible for them.

Canberra, Australia

May 2012

The Descendants of Charlemagne

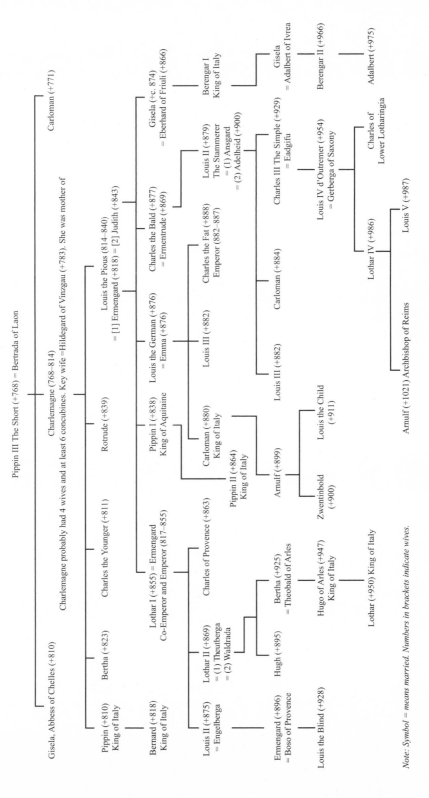

Note: Symbol = means married. Numbers in brackets indicate wives.

The Saxon Kings and Selected Relatives

Liudolf (c. 805–c. 866), founder of the Ottonian (Liudolfing) dynasty

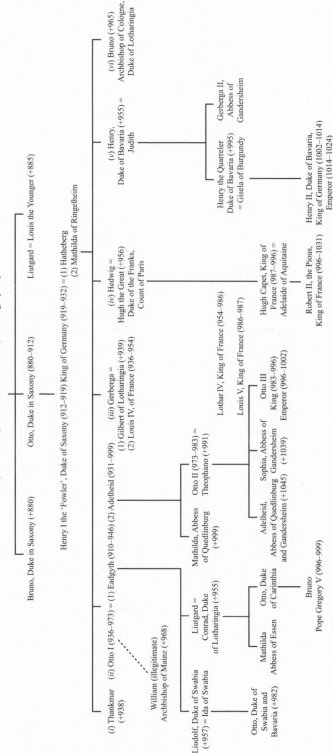

Bruno, Duke in Saxony (+880)

Otto, Duke in Saxony (880–912)

Liutgard = Louis the Younger (+885)

Henry I the 'Fowler', Duke of Saxony (912–919) King of Germany (919–932) = (1) Hatheberg
(2) Mathilda of Ringelheim

(i) Thankmar (+938)

(ii) Otto I (936–973) = (1) Eadgyth (910–946) (2) Adelheid (931–999)

William (illegitimate) Archbishop of Mainz (+968)

(iii) Gerberga = (1) Gilbert of Lotharingia (+939) (2) Louis IV, of France (936–954)

(iv) Hedwig = Hugh the Great (+956) Duke of the Franks, Count of Paris

(v) Henry, Duke of Bavaria (+955) = Judith

(vi) Bruno (+965) Archbishop of Cologne, Duke of Lotharingia

Liudolf, Duke of Swabia (+957) = Ida of Swabia

Liutgard = Conrad, Duke of Lotharingia (+955)

Mathilda, Abbess of Quedlinburg (+999)

Otto II (973–983) = Theophano (+991)

Lothar IV, King of France (954–986)

Louis V, King of France (986–987)

Hugh Capet, King of France (987–996) = Adelaide of Aquitaine

Henry the Quarreler Duke of Bavaria (+995) = Gisela of Burgundy

Gerberga II, Abbess of Gandersheim

Otto, Duke of Swabia and Bavaria (+982)

Mathilda Abbess of Essen

Otto, Duke of Carinthia

Adelheid, Abbess of Quedlinburg and Gandersheim (+1045)

Sophia, Abbess of Gandersheim (+1039)

Otto III King (983–996) Emperor (996–1002)

Robert II, the Pious, King of France (996–1031)

Henry II, Duke of Bavaria, King of Germany (1002–1014) Emperor (1014–1024)

Bruno Pope Gregory V (996–999)

Note: Symbol = means married. Numbers in brackets indicate wives. Italic numbers indicate the children of Henry the Fowler.

SOURCE ABBREVIATIONS

AB	*Annals of Saint-Bertin*
AHR	*American Historical Review*
ASC	*Anglo-Saxon Chronicle*
AU	*Annals of Ulster*
CMH III	*New Cambridge Medieval History* (Reuter)
DBI	*Dizionario Biografico degli Italiani* (Romanelli)
EHD	*English Historical Documents, c. 500–1042* (Douglas)
Fulda	*Annals of Fulda*
LP	*Liber pontificalis* (Duchesne, Davis)
MGH	*Monumenta Germaniae Historica*
MGH Conc	*Concilia* (councils)
MGH Dip	Diplomatic documents
MGH Epistolae	Letters
MGH LL	Laws
MGH SS	Writers
MGH SSRG	Writers in a separate series from 1871 onward
PBSR	*Papers of the British School at Rome*
PL	*Patrologiae cursus completa, series latina* (Migne)

NOTES

PROLOGUE

1. *Stiftsbibliothek*, St. Gallen, Cod. Sang. 904.

2. Robin Flower, *The Irish Tradition* (Oxford: Clarendon Press, 1947), 38.

3. *Anglo-Saxon Chronicle*, 869, in G. N. Garmonsway, ed., *Anglo-Saxon Chronicle* (London: J. M. Dent, Everyman's Library, 1953), 70.

4. Adam of Bremen, *History of the Archbishops of Hamburg-Bremen*, I, 39, in Francis J. Tschan, trans., *History of the Archbishops of Hamburg-Bremen* (New York: Columbia University Press, 2002), 37.

5. Abbo of Fleury, *The Martyrdom of St. Edmund*, in Paul Halsall, comp., *Medieval Sourcebook*, www.fordham.edu/halsall/source.

CHAPTER 1

1. Agobard of Lyons, "De grandine et tonituris," in L. van Acker, ed., *Agobardi Lugdinensis Omnia Opera* (Turnhout: Brepols, 1981), 52:3–15.

2. Ibid., 4, author trans.

3. Michael McCormack et al., "Volcanoes and Climate Forcing of Carolingian Europe, A.D. 750–950," *Speculum* 82 (2007): 874.

4. Adriaan Verhulst, *The Rise of Cities in North West Europe* (Cambridge: Cambridge University Press, 1999), 90.

5. Annals of Saint-Bertin, 839, in Janet L. Nelson, trans., *The Annals of Saint-Bertin: Ninth-Century Histories* (Manchester: Manchester University Press, 1991), 42.

6. Jacques Le Goff, *Medieval Civilization 400–1500* (Oxford: Basil Blackwell, 1988), 133.

7. Adriaan Verhulst, *The Carolingian Economy* (Cambridge: Cambridge University Press, 2002), 11.

8. Michael Williams, *Deforesting the Earth: From Pre-History to Global Crisis* (Chicago: University of Chicago Press, 2003), 103.

9. Chris Wickham, "European Forests in the Early Middle Ages," in *Land and Power: Studies in Italian and European History, 400–1200*, ed. Chris Wickham (London: British School at Rome, 1994), 190.

10. Ibid., 160.

11. *AB*, 864, in Nelson, 111–112, 134.

12. Wickham, "European Forests," 167.

13. Ibid., 184, 186.

14. Vito Fumagelli, *Landscapes of Fear: Perceptions of Nature and the City in the Middle Ages* (Cambridge: Polity Press, 1994), 127.

15. Ibid., 100, 104.

16. Colin McEvedy and Richard Jones, *Atlas of World Population History* (Harmondsworth: Penguin, 1978), 21; Josiah C. Russell, "Population in Europe," in *The Fontana Economic History of Europe: The Middle Ages*, ed. Carlo M. Cipolla (Glasgow: Collins, 1972), 1:36.

17. Fumagelli, *Landscapes*, 16.

18. Paul the Deacon, *History of the Longobards*, Book II, chap. IV, in William Dudley Foulke, trans., *History of the Lombards* (Philadelphia: University of Pennsylvania Press, 1974), 57–58.

19. *AB*, 856, in Nelson, 81.

20. *The Annals of Xanten*, 857, in MGH, SSRG, 12, author trans.

21. Flodoard of Reims, *Annals*, 924, 927, 934, 956, in Steven Fanning and Bernard S. Bachrach, eds., *The Annals of Flodoard of Reims 919–966* (Peterborough, ON: Broadview Press, 2004), 12.

22. Ibid., 61.

23. Burchard of Worms, *Decretorum Libri XX*, Book X, chap.10, in *PL*, 140, 834.

24. Benedict, *The Holy Rule of St. Benedict*, 54, in Boniface Verhayen, OSB, trans., *Rule of Saint Benedict* (Atchison, KS: Saint Benedict's Abbey, 1949).

25. Norbert Ohler, *The Medieval Traveller* (Woodbridge: Boydell Press, 1989), 85.

26. William Stubbs, ed., *Memorials of Saint Dunstan Archbishop of Canterbury, Rerum Britannicarum Medii Aevii Scriptores* (London: Longman, 1874), 63, cap. VII, 391–398.

27. J. E. Tyler, *The Alpine Passes in the Middle Ages (962–1250)* (Oxford: Basil Blackwell, 1930), 23–24.

28. Victoria Clark, *The Far-Farers: A Journey from Viking Iceland to Crusader Jerusalem* (New York: Walker and Company, 2003), 12.

CHAPTER 2

1. Rodolfo Amadeo Lanciani, *The Destruction of Ancient Rome: A Sketch of the History of the Monuments* (London: Macmillan, 1901), 159.

2. Robert Browning, *The Ring and the Book*, 10, lines 29–88, www.ebooks@adelaide .edu.au.

3. Ibid., lines 72–74.

4. Ibid., line 88.

5. Lanciani, *Destruction,* 159.

6. Richard Krautheimer, *Rome: Profile of a City, 312–1308* (Princeton, NJ: Princeton University Press, 1980), 143.

7. Robert Coates-Stephens, "Housing in Early Medieval Rome, 500–1000 AD," *PBSR* 64 (1996): 256.

8. Gary Macy, *The Hidden History of Women's Ordination: Female Clergy in the Medieval West* (New York: Oxford University Press, 2008), 75.

9. Thomas F. X. Noble, *The Republic of Saint Peter: The Birth of the Papal State 680–825* (Philadelphia: University of Pennsylvania Press, 1984), 231, 225.

10. *Liber pontificalis*, II, 44, in Raymond Davis, trans., *Lives of the Ninth-Century Popes: The Ancient Biographies of the Popes from A.D. 817–891* (Liverpool: Liverpool University Press, 1995), 93–94.

11. Ibid., 94.

12. Ibid., 92.

13. Ibid., 95–96.

14. Ibid., 96.

15. *AB*, 846, in Nelson, 63.

16. Ibid.

17. Lanciani, *Destruction*, 129.

18. *AB*, 847, in Nelson, 64–65.

19. A. W. Lawrence, "Early Medieval Fortifications Near Rome," *PBSR* 32 (1964): 90.

20. Quoted in Peter Partner, *The Lands of St Peter* (Berkeley and Los Angeles: University of California Press, 1972), 46.

21. Bronwen Neil, *Seventh-Century Popes and Martyrs: The Political Hagiography of Anastasius Bibliothecarius* (Turnhout: Brepols, 2006), 11.

22. *Annals of Fulda*, 883, in Timothy Reuter, trans., *The Annals of Fulda* (Manchester: Manchester University Press, 1992), 106–107.

23. Chris Wickham, *Early Medieval Italy: Central Power and Local Society 400–1000* (Ann Arbor: University of Michigan Press, 1987), 47–63.

24. *Fulda*, 896, in Reuter, 132.

25. Ibid., 132–133.

26. Liutprand, *Antapodosis*, I, 7, in F. A. Wright, trans., *The Works of Liutprand of Cremona* (London: George Routledge, 1930), 51–52.

27. *Fulda*, 896, in Reuter, 133.

28. Ibid., 134.

29. Peter Llewellyn, *Rome in the Dark Ages* (London: Constable, 1971), 299; Giorgio Falco, *The Holy Roman Republic: A Historic Profile of the Middle Ages* (London: George Allen and Unwin, 1964), 153.

30. Liutprand, *Antapodosis*, II, 48, author trans.

31. Eugenius Vulgarius, *Epistolae et carmina*, in Ernst Dümmler, *Auxilius und Vulgarius: Quellen und Forschungen zur Geschichte des Papstthums im Anfrage des Zehnten Jahrunderts* (Leipzig: Herzel, 1866), 146, author trans.

32. *LP*, in Louis Duchesne, ed., *Le Liber Pontificalis: Texte, introduction, et commentaire* (Paris: E. Thorin, 1892), 2:243.

33. Llewellyn, *Rome*, 300.

34. Flodoard, *Annals*, 933, in Fanning, 23.

35. Ambrogio M. Piazzoni, "Giovanni XI," in *Enciclopedia dei papi* (Rome: Instituto della Enciclopedia Italiana, 2000), 2:70, author trans.

36. Auxilius, *In defensionem*, in Dümmler, *Auxilius und Vulgarius*, 58–95. See also *PL*, 129, 1059–1102.

37. Dümmler, *Auxilius und Vulgarius*, 117–139.

38. *Invectiva*, in *PL*, 129, 828, 831–832, 830–831, author trans.

39. Louis Duchesne, *The Beginnings of the Temporal Sovereignty of the Popes, 754–1073* (New York: Burt Franklin, 1907), 209.

40. Liutprand, *Antapodosis*, II, 48, in Wright, 93.

41. John X to Archbishop Herman I of Cologne, 916, in Philippus Jaffé, *Regesta Pontificum Romanorum* (Leipzig: Veit, 1885), 1:450.

42. Chris Wickham, "Rome in Italy in the Late Ninth and Tenth Centuries," in *Early Medieval Rome and the Christian West: Essays in Honour of Donald A. Bullough*, ed. Julia M. H. Smith (Leiden: Brill, 2000), 160.

43. Liutprand, *Antapodosis*, III, 19, in Wright, 117.

44. Liutprand, *Antapodosis*, III, 43, in Wright, 132.

CHAPTER 3

1. Flodoard, *Annals*, 929, in Fanning, 19; Liutprand, *Antapodosis*, III, 43, in Wright, 132.

2. Quoted in Horace K. Mann, *The Lives of the Popes in the Early Middle Ages* (London: Kegan Paul, Trench, Trubner, 1925), 4:190.

3. Heinrich Fichtenau, *Living in the Tenth Century: Mentalities and Social Orders* (Chicago: University of Chicago Press, 1991), 70.

4. Benedict of San Andrea di Monte Soratte, *Chronicon*, in G. Zucchetti, ed., *Fonti per la storia d'Italia* (Rome: Instituto Storico Italiano, 1920), 55:161, author trans.

5. Ibid., 167, author trans.

6. Liutprand, *Antapodosis*, III, 44, in Wright, 134.

7. Ibid., 134–135.

8. Benedict, *Chronicon*, in Zucchetti, 166, author trans.

9. Ibid.

10. Liutprand, *Embassy*, LXII, in Wright, 273.

11. Flodoard, *De Triumphis Christi*, 12, 7, in *PL*, 135, 832, author trans.

12. Liutprand, *Antapodosis*, I, 37, in Wright, 57.

13. Ferdinand Gregorovius, *History of the City of Rome in the Middle Ages* (London: George Bell, 1895), 3:294.

14. *Fulda*, 900, in Reuter, 140–141.

15. Flodoard, *Annals*, 18, in Fanning, 28.

16. Benedict, *Chronicon*, in Zucchetti, 167, author trans.

17. Girolamo Arnaldi, "Alberico di Roma," in *DBI*, 1:651, author trans.

18. Benedict, *Chronicon*, in Zucchetti, 171, author trans.

19. Peter Partner, "Notes on the Lands of the Roman Church in the Early Middle Ages," *PBSR* 34 (1966): 70.

20. Llewellyn, *Rome*, 307.

21. Bernard Hamilton, *Monastic Reform, Catharism, and the Crusades (900–1300)* (London: Variorum Reprints, 1979), II, 2, 50.

22. Ibid., III, 265–310.

23. Liutprand, *Chronicle*, IV, in Wright, 217–218.

24. Partner, "Notes on the Lands," 87.

25. Liutprand, *Chronicle*, III, in Wright, 216.

26. Thietmar of Merseburg, *Chronicon*, IV, 32, in David A. Warner, trans., *Ottonian Germany: The Chronicon of Thietmar of Merseburg* (Manchester: Manchester University Press, 2001), 175.

27. *Liber pontificalis*, quoted in Mann, *Lives of the Popes*, 4:254.

28. Liutprand, *Chronicle*, V, in Wright, 218.

29. Liutprand, *Chronicle*, X, in Wright, 223.

30. Liutprand, *Chronicle*, XIV, in Wright, 226–227.

31. Liutprand, *Chronicle*, XV, XVI, in Wright, 228–229.

32. Liutprand, *Chronicle*, XIX, XX, in Wright, 230–231.

33. Liutprand, *Chronicle*, XIX, in Wright, 231.

34. Thietmar, *Chronicon*, II, 28, in Warner, 112.

35. Benedict, *Chronicon*, XXXIX, quoted in Mann, *Lives of the Popes*, 4:286.

36. Regino of Prüm, *Chronicon*, 888, in MGH SSRG, 50, 129, author trans.

CHAPTER 4

1. Abbo of Saint-Germain-des-Prés, *Bella parisiacae urbis*, in Nirmal Dass, trans., *Viking Attacks on Paris* (Leuven: Peeters, 2007), lines 37–60, 31.

2. Introduction, in ibid., 12.

3. Letter of Dedication, in ibid., 25.

4. *AB*, 841, in Nelson, 50.

5. David Hill et al., "Quentovic Defined," *Antiquity* 64 (1990): 51.

6. *AB*, 843, in Nelson, 55–56.

7. Adrevald of Fleury, *Ex miraculis S. Benedicti*, quoted in Nicholas Hooper and Matthew Bennett, *Cambridge Illustrated Atlas of Warfare: The Middle Ages, 768–1487* (Cambridge: Cambridge University Press, 1986), 20.

8. Ermentarius of Noirmoutier, *Ex miraculis S. Filiberti*, in MGH SS 15 (1), 298, 302, author trans.

9. *AB*, 845, in Nelson, 60–62.

10. Ibid.

11. *AB,* 856–857, in Nelson, 83–85.

12. Paschasius Radbertus, *Commentary on Jeremiah*, in *PL*, 120, 1220, author trans.

13. Quoted in Simon Coupland, "The Frankish Tribute Payments to the Vikings and Their Consequences," *Francia* 26 (1999): 46.

14. *AB*, 865, in Nelson, 122.

15. Ibid., 127.

16. Ibid., 128.

17. *AB*, 866, in Nelson, 130.

18. Abbo, *Bella*, I, lines 28–36, in Dass, 29–30.

19. Carroll Gillmor, "War on the Rivers: Viking Numbers and Mobility on the Seine and Loire, 841–886," *Viator* 19 (1988): 79–109.

20. Abbo, *Bella*, I, lines 63–64, 69, 109–110, in Dass, 31, 35.

21. Abbo, *Bella*, I, lines 79–80, in Dass, 33.

22. Abbo, *Bella*, I, lines 504–505, in Dass, 55.

23. *Annals of St. Vaast*, anno 886, quoted in James H. Robinson, *Readings in European History* (Boston: Ginn, 1904), 167.

24. Abbo, *Bella*, II, lines 321, 327, in Dass, 81.

25. Widukind of Corvey, *Res gestae saxonicae sive annalium libri tres*, III, 65, in MGH SSRG, 60, author trans.

26. Henri Pirenne, *Mohammed and Charlemagne* (New York: Norton, 1939).

27. Barbara M. Kreutz, *Before the Normans: Southern Italy in the Ninth and Tenth Centuries* (Philadelphia: University of Pennsylvania Press, 1991), 26.

28. Fred E. Engreen, "Pope John the Eighth and the Arabs," *Speculum* 20 (1945): 321.

29. Quoted in Partner, *The Lands of Saint Peter*, 67.

30. Liutprand, *Antapodosis*, I, 3, in Wright, 33–34.

31. Liutprand, *Antapodosis*, I, 4, in Wright, 34.

32. Flodoard, *Annals*, in Fanning, 5, 28, 32, 34, 56.

33. Tyler, *The Alpine Passes*, 53–54.

34. *AB*, 838, in Nelson, 38.

35. Romilly Jenkins, *Byzantium: The Imperial Centuries AD 610–1071* (Toronto: University of Toronto Press, 1987), 273.

36. Jacques Ellul, *The Subversion of Christianity* (Grand Rapids, MI: Eerdmans, 1986), 99.

37. Z. J. Kosztolnyik, *Hungary Under the Early Arpads, 890s to 1063* (Boulder, CO: East European Monographs, 2002), 5.

38. Leo VI the Wise, *Taktika*, 18, 40–73, in George T. Dennis, ed. and trans., *The Taktika of Leo VI* (Washington, DC: Dumbarton Oaks Research Library and Collection, 2010), 453–463.

39. Liutprand, *Antapodosis*, II, 30, in Wright, 85.

40. Thietmar, *Chronicon*, VIII, 4, in Warner, 364.

CHAPTER 5

1. Nithardus, *Historarum Libri* IV, Book II, 10, in Bernhard Walter Scholz, trans., *Carolingian Chronicles: Royal Frankish Annals and Nathard's Histories* (Ann Arbor: University of Michigan Press, 1970), 153–154.

2. *AB*, 841, in Nelson, 50.

3. Nithardus, *Historarum*, Book III, 1, in Scholz, 155.

4. Alain Mounier Kuhn, "Les Blessures de Guerre et L'Armement au Moyen Âge dans L'Occident Latin," *Médiévales* 39 (2000): 116.

5. Le Goff, *Medieval Civilization*, 45.

6. *Ordinatio Imperii*, quoted in Ernest F. Henderson, ed., *Select Historical Documents of the Middle Ages* (London: George Bell, 1896), 202.

7. *AB*, 838, in Nelson, 39.

8. *AB*, 840, in Nelson, 49.

9. Roger Collins, *Early Medieval Europe 300–1000* (Basingstoke: Macmillan, 1999), 347.

10. *AB*, 839, in Nelson, 42.

11. *AB*, 841, in Nelson, 50.

12. *AB*, 842, in Nelson, 53.

13. *AB*, 841, in Nelson, 50.

14. *AB*, 842, in Nelson, 53.

15. Nithardus, *Histories*, IV, 6, in Scholz, 172.

16. *AB*, 843, in Nelson, 56.

17. *Fulda*, 845, in Reuter, 23.

18. *AB*, 845, in Nelson, 61.

19. *AB*, 849, in Nelson, 67.

20. Nithardus, *Histories*, III, 6, in Scholz, 163.

21. *Fulda*, 858. Reuter trans., p 42.

22. *AB*, 855, in Nelson, 81.

23. Ibid.

24. *AB*, 858, in Nelson, 87.

25. Joseph Martos, *Doors to the Sacred: A Historical Introduction to Sacraments in the Catholic Church* (Liguori, MO: Liguori/Triumph, 2001), 368.

26. Stuart Airlie, "Private Bodies and the Body Politic in the Divorce Case of Lothar II," *Past and Present* 161 (1998): 15.

27. Martos, *Doors*, 369.

28. Hincmar of Reims, *De divortio Lotharii regis et Theutberga reginae*, in MGH Conc., 4, Supplementum I, 114, author trans.

29. Ibid., 182, author trans.

30. *Fulda*, 875, in Reuter, 77.

31. *AB*, 876, in Nelson, 197.

32. *AB*, 877, in Nelson, 201.

33. Ibid., 202.

34. Janet L. Nelson, *Charles the Bald* (London: Longman, 1992), 14.

35. Ibid., 16.

36. *AB*, 876, in Nelson, 190.

37. Eric Joseph Goldberg, *Struggle for Empire: Kingship and Conflict Under Louis the German 817–876* (Ithaca, NY: Cornell University Press, 2006), 339.

38. John VIII, Letter 261, in Jaffé, 412.

39. *Fulda*, 887, in Reuter, 113.

40. Simon MacLean, *Kingship and Politics in the Late Ninth Century: Charles the Fat and the End of the Carolingian Empire* (Cambridge: Cambridge University Press, 2003), 41.

41. *Fulda*, 887, in Reuter, 114.

42. *Fulda*, 888, in Reuter, 115.

43. Regino of Prüm, *Chronicon*, 888, in MGH SSRG, 50, 129, author trans.

44. Geoffrey Barraclough, *The Origins of Modern Germany* (Oxford: Basil Blackwell, 1946), 11.

CHAPTER 6

1. *Royal Frankish Annals*, 775, in Bernhard Walter Scholz. trans., *Carolingian Chronicles: Royal Frankish Annals and Nathard's Histories* (Ann Arbor: University of Michigan Press, 1970), 51.

2. *Royal Frankish Annals*, 785, in Scholz, 63.

3. Einhard, *The Life of Charlemagne*, II, 7, in Louis Thorpe, trans., *Two Lives of Charlemagne* (London: Penguin, 1969), 61–62.

4. Abbot Eigil, *The Life of St. Sturm*, in C. H. Talbot, trans., *The Anglo-Saxon Missionaries in Germany* (London: Sheed and Ward, 1954), 200.

5. *Capitulary for Saxony*, 4, 7, 8, in Halsall, *Medieval Sourcebook*.

6. Quoted in Eric J. Goldberg, "Popular Revolt, Dynastic Politics, and Aristocratic Factionalism in the Early Middle Ages: The Saxon Stellinga Reconsidered," *Speculum* 70 (1995): 478.

7. Nithardus, *Histories*, IV, 2 in Scholz, 167.

8. Goldberg, "Popular Revolt," 495.

9. *Annals of Xanten*, 841, in MGH SSRG, 12, 12, author trans.

10. *AB*, 842, in. Nelson, 54.

11. Nithardus, *Histories*, IV, 6, in Scholz, 173.

12. *Concilia aevi Karolini*, 843–859, in MGH Conc, 3, 165, author trans.

13. Timothy Reuter, *Germany in the Early Middle Age, 800–1056* (London: Longman, 1991), 77.

14. *Fulda*, 891, in Reuter, 121.

15. Reuter, *Germany*, 127.

16. Thietmar, *Chronicon*, I, 7, in Warner, 72.

17. Thietmar, *Chronicon*, I, 8, in Warner, 72.

18. Widukind of Corvey, I, 35, quoted in Reuter, *Germany*, 136–137.

19. Thietmar, *Chronicon*, I, 9, in Warner, 74.

20. Flodoard, *Annals*, 933, in Fanning, 23.

21. Widukind, *Res gestae*, II, 1, in MGH SSRG, 60, 65, author trans.

22. Fichtenau, *Living in the Tenth Century*, 164.

23. Widukind, *Res gestae*, II, 36, in MGH SSRG, 60, 95–97, author trans.

24. Flodoard, *Annals*, 936, in Fanning, 28.

25. Widukind, *Res gestae*, II, 20, in MGH SSRG, 60, 84–85, author trans.

26. Widukind, *Res gestae*, II, 11, in MGH SSRG, 60, 74–78, author trans.

27. Widukind, *Res gestae*, II, 24, in MGH SSRG, 60, 86–87, author trans.

28. Liutprand, *Antapodosis*, IV, 28, in Wright, 166–167.

29. Liutprand, *Antapodosis*, IV, 18, in Wright, 155; Widukind, *Res gestae*, II, 12, in MGH SSRG, 60, 78; Thietmar, *Chronicon*, I, 21, in Warner, 83.

30. Thietmar, *Chronicon*, II, 3–4, in Warner, 91–92.

31. Thietmar, *Chronicon*, II, 2, in Warner, 92; Widukind, *Res gestae*, II, 41, in MGH SSRG, 60, 99–100, author trans.

32. University of Bristol, "Bones Confirmed as Those of Saxon Princess Eadgyth," press release, June 17, 2010, http://bristol.ac.uk/news/2010/7073.html.

33. Flodoard, *Annals*, 946, in Fanning, 44.

34. Odilo of Cluny, *Epitaph of the August Lady, Adelheid*, in Thomas Head, ed., *Medieval Hagiography* (New York: Routledge, 2001), 262.

35. Thietmar, *Chronicon*, II, 6, in Warner, 95.

36. Widukind, *Res gestae*, III, 32, in MGH SSRG, 60, 93–94, author trans.

37. Widukind, *Res gestae*, III, 53, in Reuter, *Germany*, 162.

CHAPTER 7

1. Abbo, *Bella*, "Letter of Dedication," in Dass, 23.

2. Abbo, *Bella*, I, lines 96–104, 246, II, 23–30, in Dass, 33, 41, 65.

3. Regino of Prüm, *Chronicon*, 888, in *PL*, 132, 127–128, author trans.

4. Abbo, *Bella*, II, lines 203–209, in Dass, 75.

5. Abbo, *Bella*, II, lines 442–445, in Dass, 89.

6. *Fulda*, 867, in Reuter, 56.

7. *Fulda*, 888, in Reuter, 115.

8. Friedrich Kempf et al., *The Church in the Age of Feudalism* (New York: Herder and Herder, 1969), 3:286–287.

9. Quoted in Fichtenau, *Living in the Tenth Century*, 396.

10. Ibid., 26.

11. Flodoard, *Annals*, A 921, in Fanning, 5.

12. Flodoard, *Annals*, A 925, in Fanning, 14–15.

13. Flodoard, *Annals*, A 935, in Fanning, 26.

14. Flodoard, *Annals*, A 936, in Fanning, 28.

15. Pierre Riché, *The Carolingians: A Family Who Forged Europe* (Philadelphia: University of Pennsylvania Press, 1993), 256.

16. Flodoard, *Annals*, A 940, in Fanning, 33.

17. Flodoard, *Annals*, A 946, in Fanning, 44–45.

18. Flodoard, *Annals*, A 948, in Fanning, 49.

19. Synod of Ingelheim, canon I, in MGH LL 2, 25, author trans.

20. Flodoard, *Annals*, A 948, in Fanning, 51.

21. Jean Dunbabin, "West Francia: The Kingdom," in *CMH* III, 374.

22. Richer of Saint-Rémi, *Historiae libri quatuor*, I, 11, in Justin Lake, ed. and trans., *Richer of Saint-Rémi, Histories* (Cambridge, MA: Harvard University Press, 2011).

23. Richard Humble, *Warfare in the Middle Ages* (Lombard, IL: Mallard Press, 1989), 110.

24. Jean Dunbabin, *France in the Making 843–1180* (Oxford: Oxford University Press, 1985), 46.

25. *Chronicle of Saint Denis*, in Frederic Austin Ogg, *A Source Book of Medieval History* (Rpt., New York: Cooper Square Publishers, 1972), 171.

26. *AB*, 843, in Nelson, 55.

27. *The Chronicle of Nantes*, 29, in David C. Douglas, ed., *English Historical Documents, c. 500–1042*, 2nd ed. (London: Eyre Methuen, 1979), 1:317.

28. Flodoard, *Annals*, A 944, in Fanning, 40.

29. F. Donald Logan, *The Vikings in History* (New York: Routledge, 2005), 118.

30. Adamar, *Adamari historiarum libri III*, 3, in MGH SS 4, 123, author trans.

31. Flodoard, *Annals*, A 939, in Fanning, 31.

32. Archibald R. Lewis, *The Development of Southern French and Catalan Society, 718–1050* (Austin: University of Texas Press, 1965), 195.

33. Rodulfus Glaber, *Historiarum Libri Quinque*, III, 3, in John France, trans., *The Five Books of the Histories* (Oxford: Clarendon Press, 1989), 195.

34. Glaber, *Historiarum*, III, 8, in France, 111.

35. Glaber, *Historiarum*, IV, 16, in France, 197.

36. Ronald C. Musto, *The Catholic Peace Tradition* (Maryknoll, NY: Orbis, 1986), 72.

37. Flodoard, *Annals*, A 954, in Fanning, 60.

38. Riché, *The Carolingians*, 264.

39. Ibid., 265.

CHAPTER 8

1. *Mozarabic Chronicle of 754*, in *PL*, 96, 1271, author trans.

2. Ibid.

3. Ibid.

4. Einhard, *Life of Charlemagne*, 9, in Thorpe, 64–65.

5. Roger Collins, *Law, Culture, and Regionalism in Early Medieval Spain* (Ashgate: Variorum, 1992), 169.

6. Stephen O'Shea, *Sea of Faith: Islam and Christianity in the Medieval Mediterranean World* (New York: Walker and Company, 2006), 76.

7. Bernard F. Reilly, *The Medieval Spains* (Cambridge: Cambridge University Press, 1993), 79.

8. Ira M. Lapidus, "State and Religion in Islamic Societies," *Past and Present* 151 (1996): 9.

9. Ibid., 10.

10. Hugh Kennedy, "Sicily and al-Andalus Under Muslim Rule," in *CMH* III, 647.

11. Richard Fletcher, *Moorish Spain* (London: Weidenfeld and Nicholson, 1992), 48.

12. Russell, "Population in Europe," 36.

13. Fletcher, *Moorish Spain*, 37–38.

14. Eulogius of Toledo, *Memorialis Sanctorum* 2, 4, in *PL*, 115, 772, author trans.

15. Eulogius of Toledo, *De vita et passion SS. Virginum Florae et Mariae*, in *PL*, 115, 835–842.

16. Mark D. Jordan, *The Invention of Sodomy in Christian Theology* (Chicago: Chicago University Press, 1997), 28.

17. Fletcher, *Moorish Spain*, 53.

18. *The Life of John of Gorze*, quoted in Ann Christys, *Christians in Al-Andalus, 711–1000* (Richmond: Curzon, 2002), 110.

19. Michael Gerli, ed., *Encyclopaedia of Medieval Iberia* (New York: Routledge, 2003), 398.

20. Hugh Kennedy, "Sicily and al-Andalus," in *CMH* III, 652.

21. Fletcher, *Moorish Spain*, 75.

22. Hrosvitha, *Passio sancti Pelagii*, 188, in *PL*, 137, 1098, author trans.

23. Fletcher, *Moorish Spain*, 65.

24. Ibid.

25. Reilly, *Medieval Spains*, 69.

26. N. K. Singh et al., *Encyclopaedia of Islamic Science and Scientists* (New Delhi: Global Vision Publishing House, 2005), 1:373–374.

27. Reilly, *Medieval Spains*, 70.

28. Pendanius Dioscorides, *De materia medica*, sec. 3, http://www.ibidispress.scriptmania.com/custom.html.

29. David Levering Lewis, *God's Crucible: Islam and the Making of Europe, 570–1215* (New York: Norton, 2008), 335.

30. Ibid., 174, 173.

31. Fletcher, *Moorish Spain*, 173.

CHAPTER 9

1. *ASC*, 867, in Garmonsway, 68.

2. Ibid.

3. *ASC*, 871, in Garmonsway, 73.

4. *ASC*, 878, in Garmonsway, 75.

5. Asser of Sherborne, *The Life of King Alfred*, 56, in Simon Keynes and Michael Lapidge, trans., *Alfred the Great: Asser's Life of King Alfred and Other Contemporary Sources* (Harmondsworth: Penguin, 1983), 84–85.

6. Patrick Wormald, "The Ninth Century," in *The Anglo-Saxons*, ed. James Campbell (London: Book Club Associates, 1982), 135.

7. *ASC*, 896, in Garmonsway, 90.

8. *ASC*, 886, in Garmonsway, 80.

9. *ASC*, 894, in Garmonsway, 87.

10. *ASC*, 896, in Garmonsway, 89–90.

11. Richard Abels, "Alfred and His Biographers," in *Writing Medieval Biography 750–1250: Essays in Honor of Frank Barlow*, ed. David Bates, Julia Crick, and Sarah Hamilton (Melton: Boydell and Brewer, 2006), 63–64.

12. Asser, *Life*, 8, in Keynes, 69.

13. Asser, *Life*, 74, in Keynes, 88–90.

14. G. Craig, "Alfred the Great: A Diagnosis," *Journal of the Royal Society of Medicine* 84 (1991): 305.

15. *ASC*, 899, in Garmonsway, 91–92.

16. *ASC*, 901, in Garmonsway, 92.

17. *ASC*, 901, in Garmonsway, 93.

18. *ASC*, 904, in Garmonsway, 94.

19. Ibid.

20. Simon Keynes, "England, c. 900–1016," in *CMH* III, 466.

21. Sarah Foot, *Æthelstan: The First King of England* (New Haven, CT: Yale University Press, 2011).

22. *ASC*, 927, in Garmonsway, 107.

23. *ASC*, 937, in Garmonsway, 106–108.

24. Keynes, "England," 470.

25. *ASC*, 944, in Garmonsway, 111.

26. *Life of Saint Dunstan*, 20, in *EHD*, 1:900.

27. *Life of Saint Dunstan*, 21, in *EHD*, 1:901.

28. Keynes, "England," 477.

29. *ASC*, 959, in Garmonsway, 113.

30. *ASC*, 969, in Garmonsway, 119.

31. Jo Ann Kay McNamara, *Sisters in Arms: Catholic Nuns Through Two Millennia* (Cambridge, MA: Harvard University Press, 1996), 192.

32. *ASC*, 975, in Garmonsway, 121.

33. Anonymous, *Vita Sancti Oswaldi*, IV, in James Raine, ed., *The Historians of the Church of York and Its Archbishops* (London: Longmans, 1879), 449, author trans.

34. Frank Stenton, *Anglo-Saxon England*, 3rd ed. (Oxford: Oxford University Press, 1971), 372.

35. *ASC*, 975, in Garmonsway, 121.

36. Ibid.

37. *ASC*, 978, in Garmonsway, 123.

38. *ASC*, 980, in Garmonsway, 125.

39. Keynes, "England," 483.

40. Donald Scragg, ed., *The Battle of Maldon AD 991* (Oxford: Basil Blackwell, 1991), 31.

41. Logan, *The Vikings*, 155.

42. *ASC*, 999, in Garmonsway, 131–133.

43. *ASC*, 1002, in Garmonsway, 135.

44. *ASC*, 1011, in Garmonsway, 141.

45. *ASC*, 1016, in Garmonsway, 152.

CHAPTER 10

1. Thomas Cahill, *How the Irish Saved Civilization* (New York: Anchor, 1995).

2. Helen Waddell, *The Wandering Scholars* (London: Constable, 1942), 62.

3. Dáibhí Ó Cróinín, *Early Medieval Ireland 400–1200* (Harlow: Longman, 1995), 227.

4. Dáibhí Ó Cróinín, *Early Medieval Ireland*, 149ff.

5. Patrick J. Corish, *The Irish Catholic Experience: A Historical Survey* (Dublin: Gill and Macmillan, 1985), 21.

6. *Annals of Ulster*, 764, www.ucc.ie/celt/published.html.

7. *AU*, 774.

8. *AU*, 784, 788, 795.

9. *AU*, 841.

10. *AU*, 848.

11. *AU*, 851.

12. *AU*, 866.

13. *AU*, 902.

14. *The War of the Gaedhil with the Gaill*, in J. H. Todd, trans., *The War of the Gaedhil with the Gaill* (London: Longmans, Green, 1867), 41.

15. *AU*, 965.

16. *AU*, 980.

17. Michael Richter, *Medieval Ireland: The Enduring Tradition* (Dublin: Gill and Macmillan, 1988), 112.

18. Donnchadh Ó Corráin, *Ireland Before the Normans* (Dublin: Gill and Macmillan, 1972), 120.

19. Richter, *Medieval Ireland*, 113.

20. *The Book of Armagh*, 16, in John Gwynn, ed., *The Book of Armagh* (Dublin: Royal Irish Academy, 1913), 32.

21. *Wars of the Gaedhil*, 81–83, in Todd, 143–147.

22. *AU*, 1014.

23. Ó Corráin, *Ireland*, 130.

24. *AU*, 584.

25. *AU*, 806.

26. Alfred P. Smyth, *Warlords and Holy Men: Scotland AD 80–1000* (London: Edward Arnold, 1984), 176.

27. *AU*, 1054.

28. Smyth, *Warlords*, 238.

29. Asser, *Life*, 14, in Keynes, 71.

30. "*Juvencus Englynion,*" in Ifor Williams, *The Beginnings of Welsh Poetry* (Cardiff: University of Wales Press, 1972), 101.

CHAPTER 11

1. Liutprand, *Relatio*, II, in Wright, 236.

2. Ibid.

3. Liutprand, *Relatio*, I, in Wright, 235.

4. Ibid.

5. Liutprand, *Relatio*, I, in Wright, 235–236.

6. John Julius Norwich, *Byzantium: The Apogee* (London: Penguin, 1993), 169.

7. Paolo Squatriti, trans., *The Complete Works of Liutprand of Cremona* (Washington, DC: Catholic University of America Press, 2007), 9.

8. Liutprand, *Antapodosis*, III, 1, in Wright, 109–110.

9. Mann, *Lives of the Popes*, 4:255.

10. Squatriti, *Complete Works*, 7.

11. Jon N. Sutherland, *Liudprand of Cremona, Bishop, Diplomat, Historian: Studies of the Man and His Age* (Spoleto: Centro Italiano di Studi sull'alto Medioevo, 1988), xvi.

12. Ibid., 16–17.

13. Liutprand, *Antapodosis*, V, 13, and III, 7, in Wright, 152, 113.

14. Liutprand, *Antapodosis*, III, 1, in Wright, 109.

15. Giuseppe Sergi, "The Kingdom of Italy," in *CMH* III, 349.

16. Liutprand, *Antapodosis*, III, 3, in Wright, 110–111.

17. Flodoard, *Annals*, 6, in Fanning, 11.

18. Liutprand, *Antapodosis*, IV, 1, in Wright, 143.

19. Norwich, *Byzantium*, 169.

20. Liutprand, *Antapodosis*, V, 30, in Wright, 198.

21. Liutprand, *Antapodosis*, V, 8, in Wright, 147.

22. Liutprand, *Antapodosis*, VI, 3, in Wright, 206–207.

23. Liutprand, *Antapodosis*, VI, 5, Wright, 207–208.

24. James Trilling, "Daedalus and the Nightingale: Art and Technology in the Myth of the Byzantine Court," in *Byzantine Court Culture from 829 to 1204*, ed. Henry Maguire (Washington, DC: Dumbarton Oaks Research Library, 1997), 223.

25. Elizabeth Piltz, "Middle Byzantine Court Costume," in ibid., 40.

26. Liutprand, *Antapodosis*, VI, 5, in Wright, 207–208.

27. Liutprand, *Antapodosis*, VI, 6, in Wright, 208–209.

28. Liutprand, *Antapodosis*, VI, 7–9, in Wright, 209–211.

29. Liutprand, *Antapodosis*, VI, 7–10, in Wright, 209–212.

30. Liutprand, *Antapodosis*, V, 30, in Wright, 198.

31. Geoffrey Barraclough, *The Crucible of Europe: The Ninth and Tenth Centuries in European History* (London: Thames and Hudson, 1976), 103.

32. Liutprand, *Antapodosis*, V, 32, in Wright, 199–200.

33. Liutprand, *Liber*, II, in Wright, 216.

34. Squatriti, *Complete Works*, 9–10.

35. Liutprand, *Relatio*, I, in Wright, 236.

36. Karl Leyser, "The Tenth Century in Byzantine-Western Relationships," in *Relations Between East and West in the Middle Ages*, ed. Derek Baker (Edinburgh: Edinburgh University Press, 1973), 48.

37. Liutprand, *Relatio*, XLVI, in Wright, 262.

38. Liutprand, *Relatio*, LXV, XLIX, in Wright, 276, 264.

39. Jenkins, *Byzantium*, 274.

40. Norwich, *Byzantium*, 192.

41. Liutprand, *Relatio*, III, in Wright, 236–237.

42. Liutprand, *Relatio*, XL, in Wright, 258–259.

43. Liutprand, *Relatio*, VI, in Wright, 239.

44. Liutprand, *Relatio*, L, in Wright, 265.

45. Ibid.

46. Liutprand, *Relatio*, LVII, in Wright, 269–270.

47. Ibid., 270.

48. Liutprand, *Relatio*, LVII, in Wright, 270.

49. Sutherland, *Liudprand*, 98.

50. Claudio Leonardi, "Intellectual Life," in *CMH* III, 206.

51. Liutprand, *Homily*, 8, in Squatriti, 207.

52. Liutprand, *Homily*, 19, in Squatriti, 213.

53. Liutprand, *Homily*, 24, in Squatriti, 216.

54. Liutprand, *Homily*, 28, in Squatriti, 218.

CHAPTER 12

1. Kempf, *Age of Feudalism*, 206.

2. Thietmar, *Chronicon*, II, 14, in Warner, 102–103.

3. Kreutz, *Before the Normans*, 104.

4. Jenkins, *Byzantium*, 294, argues she was the daughter of Emperor Romanus II (959–963).

5. Widukind of Corvey, *Res gestae*, 74, in MGH SSRG, 60, 149.

6. Thietmar, *Chronicon*, II, 15, in Warner, 103.

7. Trier, *Stadtbibliothek*, MS, 7/9 8.

8. *Magdeburg Annals*, 982, in MGH SS 16, 152, author trans.

9. Thietmar, *Chronicon*, III, 1, in Warner, 126–127.

10. Thietmar, *Chronicon*, II, 15, in Warner, 103.

11. Karl Leyser, "Theophano *Divina Gratia Imperiatrix Augusta*: Western and Eastern Emperorship in the Later Tenth Century," in *The Empress Theophano: Byzantium and the West at the Turn of the First Millennium*, ed. Adelbert Davids (Cambridge: Cambridge University Press, 1995), 21.

12. James Viscount Bryce, *The Holy Roman Empire*, new ed. (London: Macmillan, 1925), 124–125.

13. Odilo, *Epitaph of the August Lady, Adelheid*, 7, in Head, 264.

14. Gerd Althoff quoted in Herwig Wolfram, "Bavaria in the Tenth and Early Eleventh Centuries," in *CMH* III, 305.

15. Reuter, *Germany*, 177.

16. Odilo, *Epitaph*, 5, in Head, 264.

17. Odilo, *Epitaph*, 6, in Head, 264.

18. Norwich, *Byzantium*, 230.

19. Thietmar, *Chronicon*, III, 25, in Warner, 147.

20. Thietmar, *Chronicon*, IV, 1, in Warner, 149.

21. Thietmar, *Chronicon*, III, 26, in Warner, 147.

22. Reuter, *Germany*, 188–189.

23. *Annals of Quedlinburg*, 984, in Gerd Althoff, *Otto III* (University Park: Pennsylvania State University Press, 2003), 36.

24. *Annals of Quedlinburg*, 985, in Althoff, *Otto III*, 37–38.

25. Althoff, *Otto III*, 40.

26. Ibid., 39.

27. Thietmar, *Chronicon* IV, 10, in Warner, 158.

28. Thietmar, *Chronicon*, IV, 9, in Warner, 156.

29. Althoff, *Otto III*, 48.

30. Krijnie Ciggaar, "Theophano: An Empress Reconsidered," in Davids, *The Empress Theophano*, 61.

31. *Annals of Quedlinburg*, 997, quoted in Warner, *Chronicon*, 173.

32. Pietro Damiani, *Letters*, 89, 20, in Owen J. Blum, trans., *The Fathers of the Church: The Letters of Peter Damian, 61–90* (Washington, DC: Catholic University of America Press, 1992), 334.

33. Althoff, *Otto III*, 51.

34. Odilo, *Epitaph of the August Lady, Adelheid*, 7, in Head, 264–265.

CHAPTER 13

1. John Boswell, *The Kindness of Strangers* (Chicago: University of Chicago Press, 1988); Mayke de Jong, *In Samuel's Image: Child Oblation in the Early Medieval West* (Leiden: Brill, 1996), 5.

2. De Jong, *Samuel's Image*, 286.

3. Hildemar of Corbie, *Expositio*, 59, in De Jong, *Samuel's Image*, 8.

4. De Jong, *Samuel's Image*, 214.

5. Rabanus Maurus, *De oblatione puerorum*, in *PL*, 107, 419, author trans.

6. John Boswell, *Christianity, Social Tolerance, and Homosexuality* (Chicago: University of Chicago Press, 1980), 189–190.

7. Gottschalk, *A Song in Exile*, in Philip Schuyler Allen, *The Romanesque Lyric: Studies in Its Background and Development* (Chapel Hill: University of North Carolina Press, 1928), 150–151.

8. Boswell, *Christianity*, 193.

9. Waddell, *Wandering Scholars*, 57.

10. Walafrid Strabo, *Ad amicum*, in ibid., 55.

11. Ibid.

12. Rabanus Maurus, *De oblatione puerorum*, in *PL*, 107, 431, author trans.

13. Victor Genke, "Gottschalk of Orbais and the Controversy over His Teaching on Twofold Predestination," 16, www.lectio-divina.org.

14. *AB*, 849, in Nelson, 67.

15. Ibid.

16. Kempf, *Age of Feudalism*, 163.

17. *Liber Vitae: Register and Martyrology of New Minster and Hyde Abbey, Winchester*, ed. Walter de Gray Birch (London: Simpkin, 1892), 241–242, author trans.

18. Pietro Damiani, *Epistolarum libri octo*, Liber V, esp. VIII, in *PL*, 144, 351, author trans.

19. Fichtenau, *Living in the Tenth Century*, 276.

20. Barraclough, *Crucible of Europe*, 154.

21. *Charter of Cluny*, in Ogg, *Source Book*, 247–249.

22. Jaffé, *Regesta Pontificum*, 452, 454, 494.

23. Michael E. Hoenicke Moore, "Demons and the Battle for Souls at Cluny," *Studies in Religion* 32 (2003): 490.

24. Friedrich Heer, *The Medieval World: Europe from 1100 to 1350* (London: Sphere Books, 1974), 50.

25. Kempf, *Age of Feudalism*, 335–336.

26. Marcel Pacaut, *L'Ordre de Cluny* (Paris: Fayard, 1986), 73.

27. Pietro Damiani, *Liber Gomorrhianus*, chaps. I, VI, in Pierre J. Payer, trans., *Book of Gomorrah: An Eleventh-Century Treatise Against Clerical Homosexual Practices* (Waterloo, ON: Wilfred Laurier University Press, 1982), 29, 42.

28. Anne Lyon Haight, *Hroswitha of Gandersheim: Her Life, Times, and Works* (New York: Hroswitha Club, 1965), 14.

29. McNamara, *Sisters*, 178–179.

30. Boswell, *Christianity*, 199.

31. Haight, *Hroswitha,* 21.

32. McNamara, *Sisters*, 195.

33. Macy, *Women's Ordination*, 86.

34. Jonathan Jarrett, "A Corner of Tenth Century Europe—Eat Like a Carolingian Nun," September 25, 2010, http://tenthmedieval.wordpress.com/tag/jean-verdon.

CHAPTER 14

1. *Polyptychum Irminonis abbatis sive Liber censualis antiques monasterii sancti Germani Pratensis,* http://www.kobobooks.com/ebook.

2. Eileen Power, *Medieval People* (London: Methuen, 1924), 23.

3. Robert Fossier, "Rural Economy and Country Life," in *CMH* III, 35, 37.

4. David Herlihy, *Medieval Households* (Cambridge, MA: Harvard University Press, 1985), 69.

5. Fossier, "Rural Economy," 38–39.

6. Irminon, *Polyptyque de l'Abbe Irminon*, 1, 2, in Roy C. Cave and Herbert H. Coulson, eds. and trans., *A Source Book for Medieval Economic History* (New York: Biblo and Tannen, 1965), 43; Ronald Edward Zupko, *French Weights and Measures Before the Revolution: A Dictionary of Provincial and Local Units* (Bloomington: Indiana University Press, 1978).

7. Ibid.

8. Irminon, *Polyptyque*, 3, 84, in Cave, 44.

9. Herlihy, *Medieval Households*, 71.

10. Ibid., 72.

11. François-Louis Ganshof, *Feudalism* (London: Longman, Green, 1952), xvi.

12. Susan Reynolds, *Fiefs and Vassals: The Medieval Experience Reinterpreted* (Oxford: Oxford University Press, 1994), 2–3.

13. Power, *Medieval People*, 30.

14. Odo of Cluny, *Vita Geraldi*, I, 21, in *PL*, 133, 656, author trans.

15. Martos, *Doors,* 162.

16. C. H. Talbot, "Children in the Middle Ages," *Children's Literature* 6 (1977): 17.

17. Kathy L. Pearson, "Nutrition and the Early Medieval Diet," *Speculum* 72 (1997): 28.

18. http://www.museumoflondon.org.uk/archive/exhibits/bodies/bodies.htm.

19. Cipolla, *Fontana Economic History*, 1:25–27.

20. *ASC*, 975, in Garmonsway, 121.

21. *EHD*, 1, 610.

22. Umberto Eco, "It Was the Bean That Set Pulses Racing," trans. William Weaver, http://www.themodernworld.com/eco/eco_bean.html.

23. Pearson, "Nutrition," 16.

24. Gerd Althoff, *Family, Friends, and Followers: Political and Social Bonds in Early Medieval Europe* (Cambridge: Cambridge University Press, 2004), 83.

25. Ibid., vii.

26. Ibid., 162.

27. Dunbabin, *France*, 7.

28. Richer, *Historiae*, I, 5, in MGH SS 38, 41.

29. Constance B. Bouchard, "The Origins of the French Nobility: A Reassessment," *AHR* 86 (1981): 512.

30. Marc Bloch, *Feudal Society* (Chicago: University of Chicago Press, 1961), 2:284.

CHAPTER 15

1. Glaber, *Historiarum*, III, 3, in France, 111.

2. Burchard, *Decretum*, XIX, in *PL*, 140, 971, author trans.

3. Jonathan Sumption, *Pilgrimage: An Image of Medieval Religion* (London: Faber and Faber, 1975), 21.

4. Le Goff, *Medieval Civilization*, 138.

5. Paul Collins, *Between the Rock and a Hard Place: Being Catholic Today* (Sydney: ABC Books, 2004), 54.

6. Sumption, *Pilgrimage*, 158–159.

7. Ibid., 153.

8. Diana Webb, *Medieval European Pilgrimage, c. 700–c. 1500* (Basingstoke: Palgrave Macmillan, 2002), 114.

9. Glaber, *Historiarum*, IV, 6–8, in France, 90–91.

10. Etienne de Bourbon, *De Supersticione*, in Halsall, *Medieval Sourcebook*.

11. Daniel C. De Selm, "Unwilling Pilgrimage: Vikings, Relics, and the Politics of Exile During the Carolingian Era (c. 830–940)" (PhD thesis, University of Michigan, 2009), vi–vii.

12. Atto of Vercelli, *Epistola* IX, in *PL*, 134, 116.

13. Atto, *Capitulare*, III, IV, VII, XVII–XX, in *PL*, 134, 27–52.

14. Atto, *Epistola*, VIII, in *PL*, 134, 113–114, author trans.

15. *Ratherii Synodica*, in Peter L. D. Reid, trans., *The Complete Works of Rather of Verona* (Binghamton, NY: Medieval and Renaissance Texts and Studies, 1991), 445.

16. *Ratherii Opusculum de nuptu cuiusdam illicito*, in Reid, 452, 454.

17. Ratherius, *Itinerarum*, December 966, in Reid, 472.

18. Atto, *Epistola*, IX, in *PL*, 34, 116–117, author trans.

19. Atto, *Epistola*, I, in *PL*, 34, 99, author trans.

20. Susan Wood, *The Proprietary Church in the Medieval West* (Oxford: Oxford University Press, 2006), 1.

21. Ibid., 659.

22. Ibid., 661.

23. Regino of Prüm, *Libellus de ecclesiasticis disciplinis*, in *PL*, 132, 187–456.

24. Alcuin, *Letter*, 131, in MGH *Epistolae Karolini aevi* II, 195, author trans.

25. Bernhard Poschmann, *Penance and the Anointing of the Sick* (London: Burns and Oates, 1964), 125.

26. Ibid., 126.

27. Ibid., 128.

28. Ibid., 141.

29. Burchard, *Decretum*, XIX, in *PL*, 140, 943ff.

30. Georges Duby, *The Knight, the Lady, and the Priest: The Making of Modern Marriage in Medieval France* (Harmondsworth: Penguin, 1984), 66.

31. Burchard, *Decretum,* IX, in *PL*, 140, 828, 819–830.

32. Duby, *Knight*, 68.

33. Boswell, *Christianity*, 206.

34. Kempf, *Age of Feudalism*, 275.

35. Folcuin, *Gesta abbatum Laubiensium*, in Eleanor Shipley Duckett, *Death and Life in the Tenth Century* (Ann Arbor: University of Michigan Press, 1971), 309.

36. Liutprand, *Antapodosis*, III, 52, in Wright, 138.

37. Reid, *Complete Works*, 5–6.

38. Ratherius, *Letter*, in Duckett, *Death and Life*, 310.

39. Ratherius, *Letter to Bishop Hubert*, in Reid, 353–380.

40. Ratherius, *Fragment*, in Reid, 412.

41. Ratherius, *Letter to Ambrose*, in Reid, 529, 530.

42. Reid, *Complete Works*, 11.

43. Ibid., 12.

44. Rosamond McKittrick, "The Church," in *CMH* III, 137.

45. Alice L. Harting-Correa, trans., *Walahfrid Strabo's* Libellus de exordiis et incrementis quarundam in observationibus ecclesiasticis rerum: *A Translation and Liturgical Commentary* (Leiden: Brill, 1996), 127.

46. Ibid., 21.

47. Ibid., 18.

CHAPTER 16

1. Richer, *Historiae*, III, 43, in Lake, 2:63.

2. Kempf, *Age of Feudalism*, 325.

3. Gerbert of Aurillac, *Letters*, 52, in Harriett Pratt Lattin, *The Letters of Gerbert with His Papal Privileges as Sylvester II* (New York: Columbia University Press, 1961), 92–93.

4. Gerbert, *Letters*, 23, 51, 105, 102, 171, 196, in Lattin, 51, 91, 140, 136, 200, 230.

5. Richer, *Historiae*, III, 43, in Lake, 2:71.

6. Ibid., 65.

7. Richer, *Historiae*, III, 44, in Lake, 2:65.

8. William of Malmesbury, *De rebus gestis regum Anglorum*, in Anna Marie Flusche, "*Organa doctorum*: Gerbert of Aurillac, Organbuilder?" (Doctor of Music thesis, Rice University, 1995), 93–94.

9. Marco Zuccato, "Gerbert of Aurillac and a Tenth-Century Jewish Channel for the Transmission of Arabic Science to the West," *Speculum* 80 (2005): 752.

10. Gerbert, *Letters*, 32, in Lattin, 69.

11. Gerbert, *Letters*, 25, 33, in Lattin, 63, 70.

12. Zuccato, "Gerbert," 757.

13. Oscar G. Darlington, "Gerbert, the Teacher," *AHR* 52 (1947): 463.

14. Katharine Park, "Observation in the Margins, 500–1500," in *Histories of Scientific Observation*, ed. Lorraine Daston (Chicago: University of Chicago Press, 2011), 24.

15. Einhard, *Charlemagne*, 25, in Thorpe, 79.

16. Rosamond McKitterick, *The Carolingians and the Written Word* (Cambridge: Cambridge University Press, 1989), 2.

17. Richer, *Historiae*, III, 47, in Lake, 2:71.

18. Gerbert, *Letters*, 50, in Darlington, "Gerbert," 465.

19. Richer, *Historiae*, III, 49, in Lake, 2:73.

20. Richer, *Historiae*, III, 54, in Lake, 2:83.

21. Gerbert, *Letters*, 3, 4, 5, 6, in Lattin, 39–45.

22. Zuccato, "Gerbert," 757–758.

23. Richer, *Historiae*, III, 57, in Lake, 2:89–91.

24. Richer, *Historiae*, III, 59, in Lake, 2:95.

25. Gerbert, *Letters*, 9, 10, 11, in Lattin, 49–51.

26. Gerbert, *Letters*, 12, 13, in Lattin, 51–52.

27. Gerbert, *Letters*, 18, 19, in Lattin, 56–58.

28. Gerbert, *Letters*, 26, 27, 89, 169, in Lattin, 65–66, 125–126, 198–199.

29. Gerbert, *Letters*, 30, in Lattin, 67.

30. Gerbert, *Letters*, 24, 34, 41, 35, 42, in Lattin, 62, 71, 82, 72, 82–84.

31. Gerbert, *Letters*, 45, 51, in Lattin, 86, 92.

32. Dunbabin, *France*, 129.

33. Gerbert, *Letters*, 59, in Lattin, 98–99.

34. Gerbert, *Letters*, 100, in Lattin, 135.

35. Gerbert, *Letters*, 132, 136, in Lattin, 163, 166–167.

36. Gerbert, *Letters*, 160, in Lattin, 188.

37. Gerbert, *Letters*, 166, in Lattin, 196.

38. Gerbert, *Letters*, 185, in Lattin, 215.

39. Gerbert, *Letters*, 188, 187, in Lattin, 218–219, 216–217.

40. Quoted in Mann, *Lives of the Popes*, 4:358–359.

41. Gerbert, *Letters*, 170, in Lattin, 199.

42. Gerbert, *Letters*, 199, in Lattin, 234.

43. Gerbert, *Letters*, 195, in Lattin, 229.

44. Gerbert, *Letters*, 212, in Lattin, 273.

45. Richer, *Historiae*, IV, 95, in Lake, 2:403.

46. Richer, *Historiae*, IV, 96, in Lake, 2:407.

47. Richer, *Historiae*, IV, 99, in Lake, 2:415.

48. Richer, *Historiae*, IV, 104, in Lake, 2:420–429.

49. Gerbert, *Letters*, 204, in Lattin, 265.

CHAPTER 17

1. Gerbert, *Letters*, 29, 45, 79, 102, in Lattin, 67, 86, 118, 136.

2. Gerbert, *Letters*, 125, in Lattin, 157.

3. Gerbert, *Letters*, 212, in Lattin, 272.

4. Gerbert, *Letters*, 220, in Lattin, 282.

5. Gerbert, *Letters*, 230, in Lattin, 294–295.

6. Thietmar, *Chronicon*, VI, 100, in Warner, 303.

7. Gerbert, *Letters*, 229, in Lattin, 294.

8. Chris Wickham, "Rethinking Otto III or Not," *History Today* 61 (2011), 72; Althoff, *Otto III*, 8–22.

9. Althoff, *Otto III*, 71.

10. Pietro Damiani, *Vita Romualdi*, 25, in Althoff, *Otto III*, 145.

11. Thietmar, *Chronicon*, VI, 94–95, in Warner, 300.

12. Thietmar, *Chronicon*, IV, 9, in Warner, 102–103.

13. Kosztolnyik, *Hungary*, 113.

14. Thietmar, *Chronicon*, II, 29, in Warner, 114.

15. Thietmar, *Chronicon*, IV, 45, in Warner, 183.

16. Thietmar, *Chronicon*, V, 10, in Warner, 212.

17. *Life of Saint Nilus*, 89, in MGH SS, 4, 616.

18. Leo of Synada, *Correspondence*, 6, in Martha Pollard Vinson, trans., *The Correspondence of Leo, Metropolitan of Synada and Syncellus* (Washington, DC: Dumbarton Oaks Research Library and Collection, 1985), 9.

19. Leo of Synada, *Correspondence*, 1, in Vinson, 3.

20. Gerbert, *Letters*, 225, in Lattin, 289.

21. Thietmar, *Chronicon*, IV, 32, in Warner, 175.

22. Leo of Synada, *Correspondence*, 1, in Vinson, 3.

23. Glaber, *Historiarum*, I, 12, in France, 27.

24. Thietmar, *Chronicon*, IV, 31, in Warner, 174.

25. Althoff, *Otto III*, 80.

26. Gerbert, *Letters*, 232, in Lattin, 298.

27. *Chronicon Novaliciense*, III, 32, in Althoff, *Otto III*, 105.

28. John F. Moffitt, *The Enthroned Corpse of Charlemagne: The Lord-in-Majesty Theme in Early Medieval Art and Life* (Jefferson, NC: McFarland, 2007), chap. 5.

29. MGH SSRG, 40, 33, 11, author trans.

30. *Annals of Quedlinburg*, 1000, in MGH SSRG, 72, 511, author trans.

31. *Annals of Quedlinburg*, 999, in MGH SSRG, 72, 501, Warner trans.

32. Thietmar, *Chronicon*, IV, 10, in Warner, 157.

33. Thangmar, *Vita Bernwaldi*, 17, in Althoff, *Otto III*, 114.

34. Thangmar, *Vita Bernwaldi*, 19, in Althoff, *Otto III*, 114–115.

35. Althoff, *Otto III*, 113.

36. MGH Dip, *Diplomatum regnum et Imperatorum Germaniae*, 2, 819–820, author trans.

37. Gerbert, *Letters*, 237, in Lattin, 314.

38. Gerbert, *Letters*, 256, 257, in Lattin, 350–352.

39. Gerbert, *Letters*, 253, in Lattin, 346.

40. Gerbert, *Letters*, 244, in Lattin, 327.

41. Gerbert, *Letters*, 263, in Lattin, 367.

42. Thietmar, *Chronicon*, IV, 59, in Warner, 193.

43. Gerbert, *Letters*, 246, in Lattin, 330.

44. J. B. Morrall, "Otto III: An Imperial Ideal," *History Today* 9 (1959): 820.

45. Thangmar, *Vita Bernwaldi*, 23, in Althoff, *Otto III*, 119.

46. Thietmar, *Chronicon*, IV, 48, in Warner, 186.

47. Thangmar, *Vita Bernwaldi*, 25, in Althoff, *Otto III*, 125.

48. Thietmar, *Chronicon*, VI, 100, in Warner, 303–304.

49. Thietmar, *Chronicon*, VI, 101, in Warner, 304.

50. Thietmar, *Chronicon*, VII, 45, in Warner, 338–339.

51. Glaber, *Historiarum*, IV, 4, in France, 177.

52. Glaber, *Life of St William*, X, in France, 283.
53. Pietro Damiani, *Opusculum decimum novum*, 3, in *PL*, 145, 429, author trans.
54. Glaber, *Historiarum*, IV, 24, in France, 211.

CHAPTER 18

1. Glaber, *Historiarum*, II, 22, in France, 90–91.
2. Glaber, *Historiarum*, I, 26, in France, 45.
3. Richard Landes, "Giants with Feet of Clay: On the Historiography of the Year 1000," http://www.mille.org/scholarship/10.
4. Reuter, "Introduction: Reading the Tenth Century," in *CMH* III, 21.
5. Abbo of Fleury, *Apologia to Kings Hugh and Robert*, in *PL*, 139, 471–472, author trans.
6. Ælfric of Eynsham, *Homilies*, in Benjamin Thorpe, ed., *The Homilies of the Anglo-Saxon Church* (London: Ælfric Society, 1846), 2:107–109, 343.
7. Adso of Montier-en-Der, *Letter on the Origin and Time of the Antichrist*, in Bernard McGinn, *Apocalyptic Spirituality* (Mahwah, NJ: Paulist Press, 1979), 89–95.
8. Glaber, *Historiarum*, III, 9, in France, 111.
9. John France, review of Richard Landes et al., *The Apocalyptic Year 1000*, *Medieval Review*, October 4, 2003, http://scholarworks.iu.edu/dspace/handle/2022/5729.
10. Glaber, *Historiarum*, II, 8, in France, 65–67.
11. Glaber, *Historiarum*, IV, 6, in France, 199–201.
12. Adhémar of Chabannes, *Chronicle*, in R. I. Moore, *The Birth of Popular Heresy* (London: Edward Arnold, 1975), 9–10.
13. Paul of St. Père de Chartres, *Gesta Synodi Aurelianensis*, in Moore, *Birth*, 12–13.
14. Ibid., 15.
15. Glaber, *Historiarum*, III, 4, in France, 115–117.
16. Colin Morris, *The Discovery of the Individual: 1050–1200* (London: SPCK, 1972), 10–11.
17. Thietmar, *Chronicon*, III, 2, in Warner, 128.
18. Bernard McGinn, *The Growth of Mysticism: Gregory the Great Through the 12th Century* (New York: Crossroad, 1996), 98.
19. Peter Craven, "Our Christian Cultural Bedrock," *The Age*, April 6, 2012.

BIBLIOGRAPHY

Primary Sources

Abbo of Fleury. *The Martyrdom of St Edmund*. In Paul Halsall, comp. *Medieval Sourcebook*. http://www.fordham.edu/halsall/source.

Abbo of Saint-Germain-des-Prés. *Bella parisiacae urbis*. In Nirmal Dass, trans. *Viking Attacks on Paris*. Leuven: Peeters, 2007.

Abbot Eigil. *The Life of St. Sturm*. In C. H. Talbot, trans. *The Anglo-Saxon Missionaries in Germany*. London: Sheed and Ward, 1954.

Adam of Bremen. *History of the Archbishops of Hamburg-Bremen*. In Francis J. Tschan, trans. New York: Columbia University Press, 2002.

Adamar. *Adamari historiarum libri III*. In MGH SS 4, 106–148.

Adso of Montier-en-Der. *Letter on the Origin and Time of the Antichrist*. In Bernard McGinn, ed. and trans. *Apocalyptic Spirituality*. Mahwah, NJ: Paulist Press, 1979.

Ælfric of Eynsham. *Homilies*. In Benjamin Thorpe, ed. *The Homilies of the Anglo-Saxon Church*. London: Ælfric Society, 1846, vol. 2.

Agobard of Lyons. "De grandine et tonituris." In L. Van Acker, ed. *Agobardi Lugdunensis Opera Omnia: Corpus Christianorum*. Turnhout: Brepols, 1981, 52:3–15.

Anglo-Saxon Chronicle. In G. N. Garmonsway, ed. *Anglo-Saxon Chronicle*. London: J. M. Dent, Everyman's Library, 1953.

Annals of Fulda. In Timothy Reuter, trans. *The Annals of Fulda*. Manchester: Manchester University Press, 1992.

Annals of Innisfallen. www.ucc.ie/celt/published.html.

Annals of Quedlinburg. In MGH SSRG, 72.

Annals of Saint-Bertin. In Janet L. Nelson, trans. *The Annals of St-Bertin: Ninth-Century Histories*. Manchester: Manchester University Press. 1991.

Annals of St. Vaast. In MGH SSRG 12, 40–82.

Annals of Ulster. www.ucc.ie/celt/published.html.

Annals of Xanten. In MGH SSRG, 12, 1–33.

Anonymous. *Invectiva* 29, 823–838. In *PL*, 129.

Anonymous. *Vita Sancti Oswaldi*. In James Raine, ed. *The Historians of the Church of York and Its Archbishops*. London: Longman, 1879.

Asser of Sherborne. *The Life of King Alfred*. In Simon Keynes and Michael Lapidge, trans. *Alfred the Great: Asser's Life of King Alfred and Other Contemporary Sources*. Harmondsworth: Penguin, 1983.

Atto of Vercelli. *Capitulare*. In *PL*, 134, 27–52.

———. *Epistolae*. In *PL*, 134, 95–124.

Auxilius. *In defensionem sacrae ordinationis papae Formosi.* In *PL,* 129, 1059–1102.

Benedict. *The Holy Rule of St. Benedict.* In Boniface Verhayen, OSB, trans. *Rule of Saint Benedict.* Atchison, KS: Saint Benedict's Abbey, 1949.

Benedict of San Andrea di Monte Soratte. *Chronicon.* In G. Zucchetti, ed. *Fonti per la storia d'Italia.* Rome: Instituto Storico Italiano, 1920, vol. 55.

Book of Armagh. In John Gwynn, ed. *The Book of Armagh.* Dublin: Royal Irish Academy, 1913.

Burchard of Worms. *Decretorum Libri XX.* In *PL,* 140, 537–1055.

Capitulary for Saxony and *Leges Saxorum.* In MGH LL, 5, 85–93.

Chronicle of Nantes. In *EHD.*

Davis, Raymond, trans. *Lives of the Ninth-Century Popes: The Ancient Biographies of the Popes from A.D. 817–891.* Liverpool: Liverpool University Press, 1995.

Douglas, David, ed. *English Historical Documents, c. 500–1042.* 2nd ed. London: Eyre Methuen, 1972, vol. 1.

Duchesne, Louis, ed. *Le Liber pontificalis: Texte, introduction, et commentaire.* Paris: E. Thorin, 1892.

Dunstan, Archbishop of Canterbury. In William Stubbs, ed. *Memorials of Saint Dunstan, Archbishop of Canterbury, Rerum Britannicarum Medii Aevii Scriptores.* London: Longman, 1874, vol. 63.

Einhard. *The Life of Charlemagne.* In Lewis Thorpe, trans. *Two Lives of Charlemagne.* London: Penguin, 1969.

Ementarius of Noirmouter. *Ex miraculous S. Filiberti.* In MGH SS, 15 (1), 298, 302.

Eugenius Vulgarius. *Epistolae et carmina.* In Ernst Dümmler. *Auxilius und Vulgarius: Quellen und Forschungen zur Geschichte des Papstthums im Anfrage des Zehnten Jahrunderts.* Leipzig: Herzel, 1866.

Eulogius of Toledo. *Memorialis Sanctorum.* In *PL,* 115, 731–818.

———. *De vita et passion SS. Virginum Florae et Mariae.* In *PL,* 115, 835–842.

Flodoard of Reims. *Annals.* In Steven Fanning and Bernard S. Bachrach, eds. and trans. *The Annals of Flodoard of Reims 919–966.* Peterborough, ON: Broadview Press, 2004.

———. *Historia Remensis Ecclesiae.* In MGH SS, 13, 405–698.

———. *De Triumphis Christi.* In *PL,* 135, 731–818.

Gerbert of Aurillac. *Letters.* In Harriett Pratt Lattin, trans. *The Letters of Gerbert with His Papal Privileges as Sylvester II.* New York: Columbia University Press, 1961.

Halsall, Paul, comp. *Medieval Sourcebook.* http://www.fordham.edu/halsall/source.

Head, Thomas, ed. *Medieval Hagiography: An Anthology.* New York: Routledge, 2001.

Hincmar of Reims. *De divortio Lotharii regis et Theutberga reginae.* In MGH Conc 4, Supplementum I.

Hrosvitha. *Passio sancti Pelagii.* In *PL,* 137, 1093–1102.

Jaffé, Philippus. *Regesta Pontificium Romanorum.* Leipzig: Veit, 1885.

"*Juvencus Englynion.*" In Ifor Williams. *The Beginnings of Welsh Poetry.* Cardiff: University of Wales Press, 1972.

Leo, Metropolitan of Synada and Syncellus. *Correspondence.* In Martha Pollard Vinson, trans. *The Correspondence of Leo, Metropolitan of Synada and Syncellus.* Washington, DC: Dumbarton Oaks Research Library and Collection, 1985.

Leo VI the Wise. *Taktika.* In George T. Dennis, ed. and trans. *The Taktika of Leo VI.* Washington, DC: Dumbarton Oaks Research Library and Collection, 2010.

Liber Vitae: Register and Martyrology of New Minster and Hyde Abbey, Winchester. Ed. Walter de Gray Birch. London: Simpkin, 1892.

Liutprand of Cremona. In F. A. Wright, trans. *The Works of Liutprand of Cremona.* London: George Routledge, 1930.

————. *Relatio de Legatione Constantinopolitana*. In Brian Scott, ed. and trans. *Relatio de Legatione Constantinopolitana*. Bristol: Bristol Classical Press, 1993.

Migne, Jean-Paul, ed. *Patrologiae cursus completa, series latina*. Paris: Imprimerie Catholique (later, Garnier), 1844–1855, 221 vols.

Mozarabic Chronicle of 754. In *PL*, 96, 1253–1280.

Nithardus. *Historarum Libri IV*. In Bernhard Walter Scholz, trans. *Carolingian Chronicles: Royal Frankish Annals and Nathard's Histories*. Ann Arbor: University of Michigan Press, 1970, 127–174.

Odilo of Cluny. *Epitaph of the August Lady, Adelheid*. In Thomas Head, ed. *Medieval Hagiography*. New York: Routledge, 2001.

Ordinatio Imperii. In Ernest F. Henderson, ed. *Select Historical Documents of the Middle Ages*. London: George Bell, 1896, 201–206.

Paschasius Radbertus. *Commentary on Jeremiah*. In *PL*, 120, col. 1220.

Paul the Deacon. *History of the Longobards*. In William Dudley Foulke, trans. *History of the Lombards*. Philadelphia: University of Pennsylvania Press, 1974.

Pendanius Dioscorides. *De material medica*. http://www.ibidispress.scriptmania.com/custom.html.

Pietro Damiani. *Letters*. In Owen J. Blum, trans. *The Fathers of the Church: The Letters of Peter Damian, 61–90*. Washington, DC: Catholic University of America Press, 1992.

————. *Liber Gomorrhianus*. In Pierre J. Payer, trans. *Book of Gomorrah: An Eleventh-Century Treatise Against Clerical Homosexual Practices*. Waterloo, ON: Wilfred Laurier University Press, 1982.

Polyptychum Irminonis abbatis sive Liber censualis antiques monasterii sancti Germani Pratensis. Ed. M. B. Guérard. Paris: L'Imprimerie Royal, 1844. Latin text available online at Kobo Books. http://www.kobobooks.com/ebook.

Rabanus Maurus. *De oblatione puerorum*. In *PL*, 107, 419ff.

Ratherius of Verona. In Peter L. D. Reid, ed. and trans. *The Complete Works of Rather of Verona*. Binghamton, NY: Medieval and Renaissance Texts and Studies, 1991.

Regino of Prüm. *Chronicon*. In MGH SSRG, 50.

————. *Libellus de ecclesiasticis disciplinis*. In *PL*, 132, 187–456.

Richer of Saint-Rémi. *Historiae libri quatuor*. In Justin Lake, ed. and trans. *Richer of Saint Rémi, Histories*. Cambridge, MA: Harvard University Press, 2011, vol. 2.

Rodulfus Glaber. *Historiarum Libri Quinque*. In John France, trans. *The Fives Books of the Histories*. Oxford: Clarendon Press, 1989.

Royal Frankish Annals. In Bernhard Walter Scholz, trans. *Carolingian Chronicles: Royal Frankish Annals and Nathard's Histories*. Ann Arbor: University of Michigan Press, 1970, 35–126.

Squatriti, Paolo, trans. *The Complete Works of Liutprand of Cremona*. Washington, DC: Catholic University of America Press, 2007.

Thietmar of Merseburg. *Chronicon*. In David A. Warner. trans. *Ottonian Germany: The Chronicon of Thietmar of Merseberg*. Manchester: Manchester University Press, 2001.

Van Acker, L., ed. *Corpus Christianorum: Continuatio Mediaevalis*. Turnhout: Brepols, 1981.

The War of the Gaedhil with the Gaill. In J. H Todd, trans. *The War of the Gaedhil with the Gaill*. London: Longman, Green, 1867.

Widukind of Corvey. *Res gestae saxonicae sive annalium libri tres*. In MGH SSRG, 60.

Wiegand, M. Gonsalva. *The Non-Dramatic Works of Hrosvitha*. St. Meinrad, IN: Abbey Press, 1936.

BIBLIOGRAPHY

Secondary Sources

Abels, Richard. "Alfred and His Biographers." In *Writing Medieval Biography 750–1250: Essays in Honor of Frank Barlow*, ed. David Bates, Julia Crick, and Sarah Hamilton. Melton: Boydell and Brewer, 2006.

Adamson, Melitta Weiss. *Food in Medieval Times*. Westport, CT: Greenwood Press, 2004.

Aguadé, Jorge. "Some Remarks About Sectarian Movements in al-Andalus." *Studia Islamica* 64 (1986): 53–77.

Airlie, Stuart. "Private Bodies and the Body Politic in the Divorce Case of Lothar II." *Past and Present* 161 (1998): 3–38.

Allen, Philip Schuyler. *The Romanesque Lyric: Studies in Its Background and Development*. Chapel Hill: University of North Carolina Press, 1928.

Allen, Valerie. *On Farting: Language and Laughter in the Middle Ages*. New York: Palgrave Macmillan, 2007.

Althoff, Gerd. *Family, Friends, and Followers: Political and Social Bonds in Early Medieval Europe*. Cambridge: Cambridge University Press, 2004.

———. *Otto III*. University Park: Pennsylvania State University Press, 2003.

Anderson, C. Colt. "When Magisterium Becomes Imperium: Peter Damian on the Accountability of Bishops." *Theological Studies*, 65 (2004): 741–766.

Aries, Philippe. *Centuries of Childhood*. New York: Vintage, 1962.

Arnaldi, G. "Alberico di Roma." In Raffaele Romanelli, ed. *Dizionario Biografico degli Italiani*. Rome: Trecanni, 1961, vol. I.

Bachrach, David. "Exercise of Royal Power in Early Medieval Europe: The Case of Otto the Great 936–973." *Early Medieval Europe* 17 (2009): 389–419.

Bachrach, David, and D. Bachrach. "Saxon Military Revolution, 912–973: Myth and Reality." *Early Medieval Europe* 15 (2007): 186–222.

Baker, Derek, ed. *Relations Between East and West in the Middle Ages*. Edinburgh: Edinburgh University Press, 1973.

Barraclough, Geoffrey. *The Crucible of Europe: The Ninth and Tenth Centuries in European History*. London: Thames and Hudson, 1976.

———. *The Origins of Modern Germany*. Oxford: Basil Blackwell, 1946.

Bates, David, Julia Crick, and Sarah Hamilton, eds. *Writing Medieval Biography 750–1250: Essays in Honor of Frank Barlow*. Melton: Boydell and Brewer, 2006.

Bernhardt, John W. *Itinerant Kingship and Royal Monasteries in Early Medieval Europe*. Cambridge: Cambridge University Press, 1993.

Bloch, Marc. *Feudal Society*. Chicago: University of Chicago Press, 1961, 2 vols.

Bober, Phyllis Pray. *Art, Culture, and Cuisine: Ancient and Medieval Gastronomy*. Chicago: University of Chicago Press, 1999.

Boswell, John. *Christianity, Social Tolerance, and Homosexuality*. Chicago: University of Chicago Press, 1980.

———. *The Kindness of Strangers*. Chicago: University of Chicago Press, 1988.

Bouchard, Constance B. "The Bosonids or Rising to Power in the Late Carolingian Age." *French Historical Studies* 15 (1988): 407–431.

———. "The Origins of the French Nobility: A Reassessment." *AHR* 86 (1981): 501–532.

Bowlus, Charles R. *The Battle of Lechfeld and Its Aftermath: The End of the Age of Migration in the Latin West*. Aldershot: Ashgate, 2006.

Bradley, Raymond S. et al. "Climate in Medieval Time." *Science*, October 17, 2003, 404–405.

Brøndsted, Johannes. *The Vikings*. London: Penguin, 1960.

Brown, Nancy Marie. *The Abacus and the Cross: The Story of the Pope Who Brought the Light of Science to the Dark Ages*. New York: Basic Books, 2010.

Bryce, James Viscount. *The Holy Roman Empire*, new ed. London: Macmillan, 1925.

Bullough, D. A. "Urban Change in Early Medieval Italy." *Papers of the British School at Rome* 36 (1966): 82–130.

Cahill, Thomas. *How the Irish Saved Civilization*. New York: Anchor, 1995.

Campbell, James, ed. *The Anglo-Saxons*. London: Book Club Associates, 1982.

Canning, Joseph. *A History of Medieval Political Thought 300–1450*. Abingdon: Routledge, 1996.

Cave, Roy C., and Herbert H. Coulson, eds. and trans. *A Source Book for Medieval Economic History*. New York: Biblo and Tannen, 1965.

Celli-Fraentzel, Anna. "Contemporary Reports on the Medieval Roman Climate." *Speculum* 7 (1932): 96–106.

Christys, Ann. *Christians in Al-Andalus, 711–1000*. Richmond: Curzon, 2002.

Cipola, Carlo M., ed. *The Fontana Economic History of Europe: The Middle Ages*. Glasgow: Collins, 1972, vol. I.

Clark, Victoria. *The Far-Farers: A Journey from Viking Iceland to Crusader Jerusalem*. New York: Walker and Company, 2003.

Coates-Stephens, Robert. "Housing in Early Medieval Rome, 500–1000 AD," *PBSR* 64 (1996): 239–259.

Collins, Paul. *Between the Rock and a Hard Place: Being Catholic Today*. Sydney: ABC Books, 2004.

———. *Papal Power*. London: Fount/HarperCollins, 1997.

———. *Upon This Rock: The Popes and Their Changing Role*. New York: Crossroad, 2000.

Collins, Roger. *Early Medieval Europe 300–1000*. Basingstoke: Macmillan, 1999.

———. *Law, Culture, and Regionalism in Early Medieval Spain*. Ashgate: Variorum, 1992.

Corish, Patrick J. *The Irish Catholic Experience: A Historical Survey*. Dublin: Gill and Macmillan, 1985.

Coupland, Simon. "The Frankish Tribute Payments to the Vikings and Their Consequences." *Francia* 26 (1999): 57–76.

Craig, G. "Alfred the Great: A Diagnosis." *Journal of the Royal Society of Medicine* 84 (1991): 303–305.

Craven, Peter. "Our Christian Cultural Bedrock." *The Age*, April 6, 2012.

Crompton, Louis. *Homosexuality and Civilization*. Cambridge, MA: Harvard University Press, 2003.

Curran, John. "The Bones of Saint Peter?" *Classics Ireland* 3 (1996): 18–46.

Darlington, Oscar G. "Gerbert, the Teacher." *AHR* 52 (1947): 456–476.

Daston, Lorraine, ed. *Histories of Scientific Observation*. Chicago: University of Chicago Press, 2011.

Davids, Adelbert. *The Empress Theophano: Byzantium and the West at the Turn of the First Millennium*. Cambridge: Cambridge University Press, 1995.

Davies, Wendy. *Wales in the Early Middle Ages*. Leicester: Leicester University Press, 1982.

Davis, Jennifer R., and Michael McCormick. *The Long Morning of Medieval Europe: New Directions in Medieval Studies*. Aldershot: Ashgate, 2008.

De Hamel, Christopher. *A History of Illustrated Manuscripts*. London: Phaidon, 1986.

De Jong, Mayke. *In Samuel's Image: Child Oblation in the Early Medieval West*. Leiden: Brill, 1996.

De Selm, Daniel C. "Unwilling Pilgrimage: Vikings, Relics, and the Politics of Exile During the Carolingian Era (c. 830–940)." PhD thesis, University of Michigan, 2009.

De Wald, Ernest T. "Notes on the Tuotilo Ivories in St. Gall." *Art Bulletin* 15 (1933): 202–209.

Dohrn–van Rossum, Gerhard. *History of the Hour*. Chicago: University of Chicago Press, 1996.

Doig, Allan. *Liturgy and Architecture from the Early Church to the Middle Ages*. Aldershot: Ashgate, 2008.

D'Onofrio, Giulio. *History of Theology: The Middle Ages*. Collegeville, MN: Liturgical Press, 2008.

Duby, Georges. *The Knight, the Lady, and the Priest: The Making of Modern Marriage in Medieval France*. Harmondsworth: Penguin, 1984.

———. *L'An Mil*. Paris: Éditions Gallimard, 1980.

Duchesne, Louis. *The Beginnings of the Temporal Sovereignty of the Popes, 754–1073*. New York: Burt Franklin, 1907.

Duckett, Eleanor Shipley. *Death and Life in the Tenth Century*. Ann Arbor: University of Michigan Press, 1971.

Dümmler, Ernst. *Auxilius und Vulgarius: Quellen und Forschungen zur Geschichte des Papstthums im Anfrage des Zehnten Jahrunderts*, Leipzig: Herzel, 1866.

Dunbabin, Jean. *France in the Making 843–1180*. Oxford: Oxford University Press, 1985.

Eco, Umberto. "It Was the Bean That Set Pulses Racing." Trans. William Weaver. http://www.themodernworld.com/eco/eco_bean.html.

Ellul, Jacques. *The Subversion of Christianity*. Grand Rapids, MI: Eerdmans, 1986.

Engreen, Fred E. "Pope John the Eighth and the Arabs." *Speculum* 20 (1945): 318–330.

Evans, Joan. *Monastic Life at Cluny 910–1157*. Rpt., New Haven, CT: Archon Books, 1968.

Falco, Giorgio. *The Holy Roman Republic: A Historic Profile of the Middle Ages*. London: George Allen and Unwin, 1964.

Fennell, John. *A History of the Russian Church to 1448*. London: Longman, 1995.

Fergusson, Robert. *The Hammer and the Cross: A New History of the Vikings*. London: Allen Lane, 2009.

Fichtenau, Heinrich. *Living in the Tenth Century: Mentalities and Social Orders*. Chicago: University of Chicago Press, 1991.

Fletcher, Richard. *Bloodfeud: Murder and Revenge in Anglo-Saxon England*. London: Allen Lane, 2002.

———. *The Conversion of Europe from Paganism to Christianity 371–1386 AD*. London: Fontana, 1997.

———. *Moorish Spain*. London: Weidenfeld and Nicholson, 1992.

Flower, Robin. *The Irish Tradition*. Oxford: Clarendon Press, 1947.

Flusche, Anna Marie. "*Organa doctorum*: Gerbert of Aurillac, Organbuilder?" Doctor of music thesis, Rice University, 1995.

Foot, Sarah. *Æthelstan: The First King of England*. New Haven, CT: Yale University Press, 2011.

France, John. Review of Richard Landes et al., *The Apocalyptic Year 1000. Medieval Review*, October 4, 2003. http://scholarworks.iu.edu/dspace/handle/2022/5729.

Fumagelli, Vito. *Landscapes of Fear: Perceptions of Nature and the City in the Middle Ages*. Cambridge: Polity Press, 1994.

Ganshof, François-Louis. *Feudalism*. London: Longman, Green, 1952.

Genke, Victor. "Gottschalk of Orbais and the Controversy over His Teaching on Twofold Predestination." www.lectio-divina.org.

Genke, Victor, and Francis X. Gumerlock. *Gottschalk and a Medieval Predestination Controversy: Texts Translated from the Latin*. Milwaukee, WI: Marquette University Press, 2009.

Gerli, Michael, ed. *Encyclopaedia of Medieval Iberia*. New York: Routledge, 2003.

Gillmor, Carroll. "War on the Rivers: Viking Numbers and Mobility on the Seine and Loire, 841–886." *Viator* 19 (1988): 79–109.

Goetz, Hans-Werner. *Life in the Middle Ages from the Seventh to the Thirteenth Century*. Notre Dame, IN: University of Notre Dame Press, 1993.

Goldberg, Eric Joseph. "Popular Revolt, Dynastic Politics, and Aristocratic Factionalism in the Early Middle Ages: The Saxon Stellinga Reconsidered." *Speculum* 70 (1995): 467–501.

———. *Struggle for Empire: Kingship and Conflict Under Louis the German 817–876*. Ithaca, NY: Cornell University Press, 2006.

Gregorovius, Ferdinand. *History of the City of Rome in the Middle Ages*. London: George Bell, 1895, vol. 3.

Gregory, Brad S. *Salvation at Stake: Christian Martyrdom in Early Modern Europe*. Cambridge, MA: Harvard University Press, 1999.

Guyotjeannin, Olivier. *Atlas de l'histoire de France IXe–XVe siècle: La France médiévale*. Paris: Editions Autrement, 2005.

Haight, Anne Lyon. *Hroswitha of Gandersheim: Her Life, Times, and Works*. New York: Hroswitha Club, 1965.

Hamilton, Bernard. *Monastic Reform, Catharism, and the Crusades (900–1300)*. London: Variorum Reprints, 1979.

Harting-Correa, Alice L., trans. *Walahfrid Strabo's Libellus de exordiis et incrementis quarundam in observationibus ecclesiasticis rerum: A Translation and Liturgical Commentary*. Leiden: Brill, 1996.

Head, Thomas, and Richard Landes. *The Peace of God: Social Violence and Religious Response in France Around 1000*. Ithaca, NY: Cornell University Press, 1995.

Heath, Ian, and Angus McBride. *Byzantine Armies 886–1118*. Oxford: Osprey, 1981.

Heer, Friedrich. *The Medieval World: Europe from 1100 to 1350*. London: Sphere Books, 1974.

Heidecker, Karl Josef. *The Divorce of Lothar II: Christian Marriage and Political Power in the Carolingian World*. Ithaca, NY: Cornell University Press, 2010.

Herlihy, David. *The Black Death and the Transformation of the West*. Cambridge, MA: Harvard University Press, 1997.

———. *Medieval Households*. Cambridge, MA: Harvard University Press, 1985.

Hibbert, Christopher. *Rome: The Biography of a City*. Harmondsworth: Viking, 1985.

Higounet, Charles. "Les forêts de L'Europe Occidentale du V au XI siècle." In *Settimane di Studio del Centro Italiano di Studi sull'alto Medioeve, XIII*. Spoleto: Presso La Sede del Centro, 1965.

Hill, David et al. "Quentovic Defined." *Antiquity* 64 (1990): 51–58.

Hooper, Nicholas, and Matthew Bennett. *Cambridge Illustrated Atlas of Warfare: The Middle Ages, 768–1487*. Cambridge: Cambridge University Press, 1986.

Horn, Walter et al. *The Forgotten Hermitage of Skellig Michael*. Berkeley and Los Angeles: University of California Press, 1990.

Humble, Richard. *Warfare in the Middle Ages*. Lombard, IL: Mallard Press, 1989.

Hylson-Smith, Kenneth. *Christianity in England from Roman Times to the Reformation*. London: SCM Press, 1999, vol. 1.

Jarrett, Jonathan. "A Corner of Tenth-Century Europe—Eat Like a Carolingian Nun," September 25, 2010. http://tenthmedieval.wordpress.com/tag/jean-verdon.

Jenkins, Romilly. *Byzantium: The Imperial Centuries AD 610–1071*. Toronto: University of Toronto Press, 1987.

Jordan, Mark D. *The Invention of Sodomy in Christian Theology*. Chicago: University of Chicago Press, 1997.

Kempf, Friedrich et al. *The Church in the Age of Feudalism*. New York: Herder and Herder, 1969, vol. 3.

Kessler, Ann. *Benedictine Men and Women of Courage*. Yankton, SD: Sacred Heart Monastery, 1996.

Kosztolnyik, Z. J. *Hungary Under the Early Arpads, 890s to 1063*. Boulder, CO: East European Monographs, 2002.

Krautheimer, Richard. *Rome: Profile of a City, 312–1308*. Princeton, NJ: Princeton University Press, 1980.

Kreutz, Barbara M. *Before the Normans: Southern Italy in the Ninth and Tenth Centuries*. Philadelphia: University of Pennsylvania Press, 1991.

Lanciani, Rodolfo Amadeo. *The Destruction of Ancient Rome: A Sketch of the History of the Monuments*. London: Macmillan, 1901.

Landes, Richard. "Giants with Feet of Clay: On the Historiography of the Year 1000." http://www.mille.org/scholarship/10.

Landes, Richard et al., eds. *The Apocalyptic Year 1000: Religious Expectation and Social Change 950–1050*. New York: Oxford University Press, 2003.

Lawrence, A. W. "Early Medieval Fortifications Near Rome." *PBSR* 32 (1964): 98–122.

Le Goff, Jacques. *Medieval Civilization 400–1500*. Oxford: Basil Blackwell, 1988.

Lewis, Archibald R. *The Development of Southern French and Catalan Society, 718–1050*. Austin: University of Texas Press, 1965.

Lewis, David Levering. *God's Crucible: Islam and the Making of Europe, 570–1215*. New York: Norton, 2008.

Leyser, Karl. *Communications and Power in Medieval Europe: The Carolingian and Ottonian Centuries*. London: Hambledon Press, 1994.

———. *Rule and Conflict in an Early Medieval Society: Ottonian Saxony*. London: Edward Arnold, 1979.

Llewellyn, Peter. *Rome in the Dark Ages*. London: Constable, 1971.

Logan, F. Donald. *The Vikings in History*, 3rd ed. New York: Routledge, 2005.

MacLean, Simon. *Kingship and Politics in the Late Ninth Century: Charles the Fat and the End of the Carolingian Empire*. Cambridge: Cambridge University Press, 2003.

MacShamhráin, Ailbhe. *The Vikings: An Illustrated History*. Dublin: Wolfhound Press, 2002.

Macy, Gary. *The Hidden History of Women's Ordination: Female Clergy in the Medieval West*. New York: Oxford University Press, 2008.

Maguire, Henry, ed. *Byzantine Court Culture from 829 to 1204*. Washington, DC: Dumbarton Oaks Research Library, 1997.

Man, John. *Atlas of the Year 1000*. London: Penguin, 1999.

Mann, Horace K. *The Lives of the Popes in the Early Middle Ages*. London: Kegan Paul, Trench, Trubner, 1906, 1925, vols. 3 and 4.

Martos, Joseph. *Doors to the Sacred: A Historical Introduction to Sacraments in the Catholic Church*. Liguori, MO: Liguori/Triumph, 2001.

McClendon, Charles B. *The Imperial Abbey of Farfa: Architectural Currents of the Early Middle Ages*. New Haven, CT: Yale University Press, 1987.

McCormack, Michael et al. "Volcanoes and Climate Forcing of Carolingian Europe, A.D. 750–950." *Speculum* 82 (2007): 865–895.

McEvedy, Colin, and Richard Jones. *Atlas of World Population History*. Harmondsworth: Penguin, 1978.

McGinn, Bernard. *The Growth of Mysticism: Gregory the Great Through the 12th Century*. New York: Crossroad, 1996.

McKitterick, Rosamond. *The Carolingians and the Written Word*. Cambridge: Cambridge University Press, 1989.

McNamara, Jo Ann Kay. *Sisters in Arms: Catholic Nuns Through Two Millennia*. Cambridge, MA: Harvard University Press, 1996.

Mitchell, Nathan. *Cult and Controversy: The Worship of the Eucharist Outside Mass*. Collegeville, MN: Liturgical Press, 1990.

Moffitt, John F. *The Enthroned Corpse of Charlemagne: The Lord-in-Majesty Theme in Early Medieval Art and Life*. Jefferson, NC: McFarland, 2007.

Moody, T. W., and F. X. Martin. *The Course of Irish History*. Cork: Mercier Press, 1967.

Moore, Michael E. Hoenicke. "Demons and the Battle for Souls at Cluny." *Studies in Religion* 32 (2003): 485–497.

Moore, R. I. *The Birth of Popular Heresy*. London: Edward Arnold, 1975.

Morrall, J. B. "Otto III: An Imperial Ideal." *History Today* 9 (1959): 820.

Morris, Colin. *The Discovery of the Individual: 1050–1200*. London: SPCK, 1972.

Mounier Kuhn, Alain. "Les Blessures de Guerre et L'Armement au Moyen Âge dans L'Occident Latin." *Médiévales* 39 (2000): 112–136.

Museum of London: http://www.museumoflondon.org.uk/archive/exhibits/bodies/bodies.htm.

Musto, Ronald G. *The Catholic Peace Tradition*. Maryknoll, NY: Orbis, 1986.

Neil, Bronwen. *Seventh-Century Popes and Martyrs: The Political Hagiography of Anastasius Bibliothecarius*. Turnhout: Brepols, 2006.

Nelson, Janet L. *Charles the Bald*. London: Longman, 1992.

Noble, Thomas F. X. *The Republic of Saint Peter: The Birth of the Papal State 680–825*. Philadelphia: University of Pennsylvania Press, 1984.

Norwich, John Julius. *Byzantium: The Apogee*. London: Penguin, 1993.

Nuttgens, Patricia, ed. *The History of York: Yorkshire from the Earliest Times to the Year 2000*. Pickering: Blackthorn Press, 2007.

O'Brien, Harriet. *Queen Emma and the Vikings*. London: Bloomsbury, 2005.

Ó Corráin, Donnchadh. *Ireland Before the Normans*. Dublin: Gill and Macmillan, 1972.

Ó Cróinín, Dáibhí. *Early Medieval Ireland 400–1200*. Harlow: Longman, 1995.

Ogg, Frederic Austin. *A Source Book of Medieval History*. Rpt., New York: Cooper Square Publishers, 1972.

Ohler, Norbert. *The Medieval Traveller*. Woodbridge: Boydell Press, 1989.

Osborne, Kenan B. *Priesthood: A History of the Ordained Ministry in the Roman Catholic Church*. New York: Paulist Press, 1988.

O'Shea, Stephen. *Sea of Faith: Islam and Christianity in the Medieval Mediterranean World*. New York: Walker and Company, 2006.

Pacaut, Marcel. *L'Ordre de Cluny*. Paris: Fayard, 1986.

Partner, Peter. *The Lands of St. Peter*. Berkeley and Los Angeles: University of California Press, 1972.

———. "Notes on the Lands of the Roman Church in the Early Middle Ages." *PBSR* 34 (1966): 68–78.

Payne, Blanche. *History of Costume*. New York: Harper and Row, 1965.

Pearson, Kathy L. "Nutrition and the Early Medieval Diet." *Speculum* 72 (1997): 1–32.

Phelan, Owen M. "Horizontal and Vertical Theologies: 'Sacraments' in the Works of Paschasius Radbertus and Ratramnus of Corbie." *Harvard Theological Review* 103 (2010): 271–290.

Piazzoni, Ambrogio M. "Giovanni XI." In *Enciclopedia dei papi*. Rome: Instituto della Enciclopedia Italiana, 2000, vol. 2.

Pirenne, Henri. *Mohammed and Charlemagne*. New York: Norton, 1939.

Poschmann, Bernhard. *Penance and the Anointing of the Sick*. London: Burns and Oates, 1964.

Power, Eileen. *Medieval People*. London: Methuen, 1924.

Rackham, Oliver. *Ancient Woodland: Its History, Vegetation, and Uses in England*. London: Edward Arnold, 1980.

Raymond S. Bradley et al. "Climate in Medieval Time." *Science*, October 17, 2003, 404–405.

Reilly, Bernard F. *The Medieval Spains*. Cambridge: Cambridge University Press, 1993.

Reiss, Frank. "From Aachen to Al-Andalus: The Journey of Deacon Bodo." *Early Medieval Europe* 13 (2005): 131–157.

Reston, James. *The Last Apocalypse: Europe in the Year 1000 AD*. New York: Doubleday, 1998.

Reuter, Timothy. *Germany in the Early Middle Ages, 800–1056*. London: Longman, 1991.

———, ed. *The New Cambridge Medieval History*. Cambridge: Cambridge University Press, 1999, vol. 3.

Reynolds, Susan. *Fiefs and Vassals: The Medieval Experience Reinterpreted*. Oxford: Oxford University Press, 1994.

Riché, Pierre. *The Carolingians: A Family Who Forged Europe*. Philadelphia: University of Pennsylvania Press, 1993.

Richter, Michael. *Medieval Ireland: The Enduring Tradition*. Dublin: Gill and Macmillan, 1988.

Roach, Mary. *Stiff: The Curious Lives of Human Cadavers*. London: Penguin, 2003.

Robinson, James H. *Readings in European History*. Boston: Ginn, 1904.

Romanelli, Raffaele, ed. *Dizionario Biografico degli Italiani*. Rome: Trecanni, 1925– , 76 vols.

Rouche, Michel. "La faim à l'epoque carolingienne: Essai sur quelques types de rations alimentaires." *Revue Historique* 508 (1973): 295–320.

Russell, Josiah C. "Population in Europe." In *The Fontana Economic History of Europe: The Middle Ages*, ed. Carlo M. Cipolla. Glasgow: Collins, 1972.

Santangeli Valenzani, Riccardo. "Residential Building in Early Medieval Rome." In *Early Medieval Rome and the Christian West: Essays in Honour of Donald A. Bullough*, ed. Julia M. H. Smith. Leiden: Brill, 2000.

Scragg, Donald, ed. *The Battle of Maldon AD 991*. Oxford: Basil Blackwell, 1991.

Shepherd, William R. *Historical Atlas*. 8th ed. Pikesville, MD: Colonial Offset, 1956.

Singh, N. K. et al. *Encyclopaedia of Islamic Science and Scientists*. New Delhi: Global Vision Publishing House, 2005, vol. 1.

Smith, Julia M. H., ed. *Early Medieval Rome and the Christian West: Essays in Honour of Donald A. Bullough*. Leiden: Brill, 2000.

———. *Province and Empire: Brittany and the Carolingians*. Cambridge: Cambridge University Press, 1992.

Smyth, Alfred P. *Warlords and Holy Men: Scotland AD 80–1000*. London: Edward Arnold, 1984.

Stafford, Pauline. *Queens, Concubines, and Dowagers*. Athens: University of Georgia Press, 1983.

Steckel, Richard H. "Remarkably Tall Stature of European Men During the Medieval Era." *Social Science History* 28 (2004): 211–229.

Stenton, Frank. *Anglo-Saxon England*, 3rd ed. Oxford: Oxford University Press, 1971.

Sumption, Jonathan. *Pilgrimage: An Image of Medieval Religion*. London: Faber and Faber, 1975.

Sutherland, Jon N. *Liudprand of Cremona, Bishop, Diplomat, Historian: Studies of the Man and His Age*. Spoleto: Centro Italiano di Studi sull'alto Medioevo, 1988.

Talbot, C. H. *The Anglo-Saxon Missionaries in Germany*. London: Sheed and Ward, 1954.

———. "Children in the Middle Ages." *Children's Literature* 6 (1977): 17–33.

Tellenbach, Gerd. *The Church in Western Europe from the Tenth to the Early Twelfth Century*. Cambridge: Cambridge University Press, 1993.

Treadgold, Warren T. *The Byzantine Revival, 780–842*. Stanford, CA: Stanford University Press, 1988.

Turnbull, Stephen and Peter Dennis. *The Walls of Constantinople AD 324–1453*. Oxford: Osprey, 2004.

Tyler, J. E. *The Alpine Passes in the Middle Ages (962–1250)*. Oxford: Basil Blackwell, 1930.

University of Bristol. "Bones Confirmed as Those of Saxon Princess Eadgyth." Press release, June 17, 2010. http://bristol.ac.uk/news/2010/7073.html.

Unwin, P. T. H. *Wine and the Vine: An Historical Geography of Viticulture and the Wine Trade*. London: Routledge, 1991.

Verhulst, Adriaan. *The Carolingian Economy*. Cambridge: Cambridge University Press, 2002.

———. *The Rise of Cities in North West Europe*. Cambridge: Cambridge University Press, 1999.

Veyne, Paul, ed. *A History of Private Life*. Cambridge, MA: Harvard University Press, 1987, vol. 1.

Waddell, Helen. *The Wandering Scholars*. London: Constable, 1927.

Webb, Diana. *Medieval European Pilgrimage, c. 700–c. 1500*. Basingstoke: Palgrave Macmillan, 2002.

Wemple, Suzanne Fonay. *Atto of Vercelli: Church, State, and Christian Society in Tenth-Century Italy*. Rome: Edizioni di Storia e Letteratura, 1979.

Wickham, Chris. *Early Medieval Italy. Central Power and Local Society 400–1000*. Ann Arbor: University of Michigan Press. 1981.

———, ed. *Land and Power: Studies in Italian and European History, 400–1200*. London: British School at Rome, 1994.

———. "Rethinking Otto III or Not." *History Today* 61 (2011): 71–73.

Wiegand, M. Gonsalva. "The Non-Dramatic Works of Hrosvitha." PhD thesis, St. Louis University, 1936.

Williams, Michael. *Deforesting the Earth: From Pre-History to Global Crisis*. Chicago: University of Chicago Press, 2003.

Wolf, Kenneth Baxter. "Christian Martyrs in Muslim Spain." Library of Iberian Resources Online. http://libro.uca.edu/martyrs/cm2.htm.

Wood, Susan. *The Proprietary Church in the Medieval West*. Oxford: Oxford University Press, 2006.

Woolf, Alex. *From Pictland to Alba: 789–1070*. Edinburgh: Edinburgh University Press, 2007.

Zuccato, Marco. "The Earliest Filtration of Arabic Science to the Latin World: Gerbert of Aurillac and the Case of Gotmar's Circle." PhD thesis, University of Melbourne, 2005.

———. "Gerbert of Aurillac and a Tenth-Century Jewish Channel for the Transmission of Arabic Science to the West." *Speculum* 80 (2005): 742–763.

Zupko, Ronald Edward. *French Weights and Measures Before the Revolution: A Dictionary of Provincial and Local Units*. Bloomington: Indiana University Press, 1978.

INDEX

Paul Collins is an historian, broadcaster, and writer. A Catholic priest for thirty-three years, he resigned from the active priestly ministry in 2001 due to a dispute with the Vatican over his book *Papal Power* (1997). He is the author of thirteen books. He is well known as a commentator on Catholicism and the papacy and he also has a strong interest in ethics, environmental, and population issues. He has a Master's degree in theology (ThM) from Harvard University, and a Doctorate of Philosophy (PhD) in history from the Australian National University. He lives in Canberra, Australia.